HANDBOOK OF PSYCHOLOGICAL ASSESSMENT

HANDBOOK OF PSYCHOLOGICAL ASSESSMENT

Gary Groth-Marnat

 VAN NOSTRAND REINHOLD COMPANY
——————————————— New York

Library of Congress Catalog Card Number: 83-21812
ISBN: 0-442-22927-5

Manufactured in the United States of America

Published by Van Nostrand Reinhold Company Inc.
135 West 50th Street
New York, New York 10020

Van Nostrand Reinhold Company Limited
Molly Millars Lane
Wokingham, Berkshire RG11 2PY, England

Van Nostrand Reinhold
480 Latrobe Street
Melbourne, Victoria 3000, Australia

Macmillan of Canada
Division of Gage Publishing Limited
164 Commander Boulevard
Agincourt, Ontario M1S 3C7, Canada

15 14 13 12 11 10 9 8 7 6 5 4 3 2

Library of Congress Cataloging in Publication Data

Groth-Marnat, Gary.
    Handbook of psychological assessment.

    Bibliography: p.
    Includes index.
    1. Psychological tests. I. Title. [DNLM:
1. Psychological tests – Handbooks. BF 176 G881h]
BF176.G76   1984   150'.28'7   83-21812
ISBN 0-442-22927-5

To the persons who taught me how to read and write — my parents, Barbara and Rudy

Preface

For many years I wondered why a composite book had never been written on interpreting the major psychological tests. This wondering began in graduate school with volumes of xeroxed manuals to accompany Anastasi and numerous expensive, often verbose texts on a single test. It became relatively easy to ignore the lack of such a book until I decided to teach a graduate course on assessment. There was simply no single book that I felt was adequate to address applied approaches to assessment. It was that dilemma which led to the writing of this book.

It is my hope that my colleagues and students will find the *Handbook of Psychological Assessment* to be a helpful, if not at times essential, aid in psychological assessments. In particular, I have tried to avoid the limitations of "cookbook" assessment procedures. Throughout the text, there has been continual reference to interrelations between scores, the importance of consulting outside sources, appropriate cautions relating to test data, defining the ideal role of the clinician, and the essential contribution that the client's personal history and observations of the client's behavior make towards the overall assessment procedure. It is hoped that this book will prove to be brief and succinct, but also that it will provide the tools necessary for developing a description of individuals that contains depth, accuracy, and clinical usefulness.

Since the book so often has seemed like a monster that just kept growing (and indeed is still hungry), I would like to make this preface brief and conclude with a tribute to those who were crucial, important, or helpful in my writing. The most important person is my original co-inspirer and co-conspirer, Dorothy Morena. Her initial help in editing and providing valuable ideas, rough drafts of the projective drawing chapter, and her overall integrity and warmth will always be remembered. Dayle Goldie also supplied much of the initial impetus, encouragement, and support. I would like to thank Mel Schwartz, Rick Thomas, Robert Zussman, George Sargent, and innumerable students for their reading of (and ideas regarding) different portions of the manuscript. Each of them, in his own way, served to correct my all-too-frequent nearsightedness and selective perception. I also greatly appreciate the two psychological evaluations contributed by George Sargent and Tom MacSpeiden. Finally, I would like to thank those persons who were directly involved in the preparation of the manuscript — especially Virginia Webster, who has aptly been described as "Wonder Woman" for her remarkable ability to mind read what to most people would appear to be unintelligible scribbles. More than just appreciation goes to Julie Fallscheer for her patience, tolerance of my mental absence, and preparation of the major portion of the reference section.

GARY GROTH-MARNAT

Contents

HANDBOOK OF PSYCHOLOGICAL ASSESSMENT

1
Introduction

The general purpose of the *Handbook of Psychological Assessment* is to provide a reference and instructional guide for professionals and students who are conducting psychological assessments. As a reference book, it can aid in the development of a large number and variety of interpretive hypotheses. It can also serve to point out obscure signs which are only infrequently encountered during evaluations but may still be crucial in developing a complete description of the client. As an instructional text, it provides the student with the basic tools relevant for interpreting the more frequently used psychological tests. Thus, it can relieve instructors of the need to cover a long discussion of interpretive hypotheses, thereby enabling them to devote more time to the evaluation and integration of test data. This book also provides a framework within which one can approach psychological test data in a coherent, problem-oriented manner. The goal is to aid the clinician and student in developing and integrating a wide variety of interpretive hypotheses within the context of a client's history, behavioral observations, and test data.

One significant and overriding emphasis in this book is its focus on assessing areas which are of practical use in evaluating individuals. It is applied in its orientation, and for the most part, theoretical discussions have been avoided. Many books written on psychological testing, as well as courses organized around these books, focus primarily on test theory and construction, and minimize actual interpretation of tests. In contrast, the intent of this book is to examine relevant features of test construction in such a way as to aid in evaluating psychological tests. Furthermore, the main approaches towards interpreting test data, both in a test battery and from individual tests, are outlined and elaborated upon.

However, the book was organized so as to provide a relatively brief discussion of approaches towards interpreting the main tests used in clinical practice. The danger of covering tests in such a relatively brief way is that clinicians, or especially students, may attempt to use the interpretive hypotheses in a "cookbook" fashion or treat the information from a "single sign" approach. For example, an examiner may read that large eyes on human figure drawings are a sign that the person is paranoid and may then not bother to integrate this finding with the other data. Thus, he may come to the possibly erroneous conclusion that the single sign of drawing large eyes equals paranoia. It is clearly stressed throughout the book that clinicians should consider single test findings merely as hypotheses in need of further verification and that any finding should always be understood within the context of other sources of data. In order to facilitate more valid and useful interpretations, therefore, cautions and guidelines are provided for evaluating clinical and psychometric data. This book should not be used merely to interpret test scores as much as to assess individual persons within their unique situations. Test scores, then, are one tool to be utilized in the overall assessment process.

A further area of emphasis is that students/clinicians should be well aware of the assets and, perhaps more important, the limitations of each of the tests. Within a larger context, they should likewise be aware of the assets and limitations of testing as a general strategy in understanding people. Many tests are misused and students of testing should be clearly aware of the ways in which they are most likely to misuse testing. In a later section in this chapter, some of the precautions which must be taken prior to, and during, test use are discussed. Furthermore, each chapter on psychological tests contains a section dealing with the assets and limitations of each test. It is only as a result of a thorough understanding of the limitations of each test that its specific strengths can be maximized.

ORGANIZATION OF THE HANDBOOK

The decision for the inclusion of various tests was based primarily on their being the most frequently used tools for assessment. For example, according to several studies (Crenshaw, Bohn, Hoffman, Matheus, and Offenbach, 1968; Sundberg, 1961; Wade and Baker, 1977), the six most commonly used tests are: the Wechsler scales, the Rorschach, projective drawings (Draw-A-Person, House-Tree-Person), the Bender Visual Motor Gestalt (Bender), the Thematic Apperception Test (TAT), and the Stanford-Binet. The Wechsler Adult Intelligence Scale — Revised (WAIS-R) and the Wechsler Intelligence Scale for Children — Revised (WISC-R) were chosen for inclusion instead of the Stanford-Binet, because the WAIS-R and WISC-R not only are useful in providing cognitive assessments but also are helpful in evaluating personality and providing useful clinical information. In addition, both the Minnesota Multiphasic Personality Inventory (MMPI) and the California Personality Inventory (CPI) were chosen for inclusion. The MMPI is the most frequently used personality inventory, and of all the tests, it has the highest number of studies that have been conducted on it or performed using it (Alker, 1978). Finally, the CPI was selected because of its excellent technical development (Anastasi, 1982), numerous research studies, and relatively high frequency of use.

The different chapters in this book follow the general steps clinicians take when conducting evaluations. Chapter 1 deals with the preliminary issues that clinicians must face prior to administering the tests. They must clarify their general role, evaluate the tests whose use they are considering, understand the setting in which they are working, and be aware of some of the major guidelines and cautions for using tests. It is also important for clinicians to have a general conceptual knowledge of the different phases of clinical assessment, beginning with a clarification of the problem and ending with the interpretation and integration of the data.

The middle part of the book (Chapters 2-8) provides a general working knowledge of the seven most frequently used tests. Each of these chapters begins with an introduction to the test in the form of a discussion of its history and development, current evaluation, and procedures for administration. The main portions of these chapters provide a guide towards interpretation which includes such areas as a discussion of the meaning of different scales, significant relations between scales, frequent trends which may be encountered, and the meaning of unusually high or low scores. When appropriate, additional subsections have been included. For example, the chapter on the Wechsler scales includes a discussion of the nature of intelligence because it is especially crucial for a clinician to understand the theoretical construct of "intelligence" prior to attempting an interpretation of I.Q. scores. Likewise, the chapter on the Thematic Apperception Test includes a summary of Murray's theory of personality because a knowledge of his concepts is also a necessary prerequisite for adequately understanding and interpreting the test.

The final step a clinician must take is the actual writing of the psychological report. Chapter 9 provides general guidelines for report writing, a report format, and four sample reports. The sample reports are representative of the four more common types of reports (psychiatric, legal, academic, personality) from the four most frequently encountered referral settings (medical setting, legal context, educational context, psychological clinic). It is hoped that the sequence will be a logical one for clinicians to follow and that the knowledge provided within the chapters will be useful, concise, and practical.

ROLE OF THE CLINICIAN

The central role of clinicians conducting assessments should be to answer specific questions and aid in making relevant decisions. This requires that clinicians be able to integrate a wide variety of data and bring into focus diverse areas of knowledge. Thus, they are not merely administering and scoring tests. A useful distinction which highlights this point is the contrast that Maloney and Ward (1976) have made between a clinician conducting psychological assessment and a psychometrist. Psychometrists tend more to use tests merely to obtain data, and their task is often perceived as emphasizing the clerical and technical aspects of testing. Their approach is primarily data oriented, and the end product is often a series of traits or ability descriptions. These descriptions are typically not related to the person's overall context and do not address unique problems the person may be facing. In contrast, psychological assessment attempts to evaluate an individual in a problem situation so that the information derived from the assessment can somehow help with the problem. Tests are only one method of gathering data, and the test data are not end products, but merely tools, in the overall process of assessment. Psychological assessment, then, places data in a wide perspective; with its main focus being problem solving and decision making.

The distinction between psychometric testing and psychological assessment can be better understood, and the ideal role of the clinician more clearly defined, by briefly elaborating on the historical and methodological reasons for the development of the psychometric approach. When psychological tests were originally developed, there was an early and noteworthy success of group measurements of intelligence. This was especially true in military and industrial settings where individual interviewing and case histories were too expensive and time consuming for general use. The data-oriented intelligence tests were considered to be advantageous because they appeared "objective" and thus seemed to reduce possible interviewer bias. More important, they were quite successful in producing a relatively high number of true positives when used for classification purposes. Their predictions were generally accurate and usable. However, this created the early expectation that all assessments could be performed using the same method and would provide a similar level of accuracy and usefulness. Later assessment strategies often tried to imitate the methods of earlier intelligence tests for such variables as personality and psychiatric diagnosis.

A further development consistent with the psychometric approach was the concept of the "test battery." It was reasoned that if a single test could produce accurate descriptions of an ability or trait, then a series of tests could be administered to create a "total picture" of the person. The goal then was to develop a global, yet quantitative, description of the person using purely objective methods. This encouraged the idea that the tool (psychological test) was the best process for achieving this goal, rather than being merely one technique in the overall assessment procedure. Behind this approach were the concepts of individual differences and "trait" psychology. These assume that one of the best ways of describing the differences among individuals is to measure their strengths and weaknesses with respect to various traits. Thus, the clearest approach to the study of personality involved developing a relevant taxonomy of traits and then creating tests to measure these traits. Again, there was an emphasis on the tools as primary, with a de-emphasis on the input of the clinician. The result of these trends was a bias towards administration and clerical skills. Within this context, the psychometrist requires little, if any, clinical expertise other than in administering, scoring, and interpreting tests. Thus, the most preferred tests would be those that are machine scored, true-false, or multiple choice, and which are constructed so that the normed scores — rather than the psychometrist — provide the interpretation.

The objective psychometric approach is most appropriately applicable to ability tests such as those measuring intelligence or mechanical skills. However, its usefulness decreases when attempting to assess personality traits such as dependence, authoritarianism, or anxiety. Personality variables are far more complex and therefore need to be validated within the context of history, behavioral observations, and interpersonal relationships. For example, a T score of 75 on the MMPI scale 9 (mania) takes on an entirely different meaning for a highly functioning physician than for an individual with a poor history of work and interpersonal relationships. When the purely objective psychometric approach is used for the evaluation of problems in living (neurosis, psychosis, etc.), its usefulness is questionable.

It is in the understanding and evaluation of personality and especially of problems in living that the approach which has been labeled *psychological assessment* is most useful. This is because these issues involve a particular problem situation having to do with a specific individual. The central role of the clinician performing psychological assessment is that of an expert in human behavior who must deal with complex processes and understand test scores within the context of a person's life. He must have knowledge concerning problem areas and, on the basis of this knowledge, be able to form a general idea regarding behaviors to observe and areas in which to collect relevant data. This involves an awareness and appreciation of multiple causation, interactional influences, and multiple relationships. As Woody (1980) has stated, "Clinical assessment is individually oriented, but it always considers social existence; the objective is usually to help the person solve problems."

In addition to an awareness of the role suggested by psychological assessment, there are also other specific areas of knowledge that clinicians should have. These include personality theory, abnormal psychology, and the psychology of adjustment, as well as a knowledge of test construction and of basic statistics. Furthermore, they should know the main interpretive hypotheses in psychological testing and be able to identify, sift through, and evaluate a series of hypotheses and decide on the most relevant ones. For each assessment device, it is also important that clinicians have a conception of what it is they are trying to test. Thus, rather than merely knowing the labels and definitions for various types of anxiety or thought disorders, they should also have in-depth operational criteria for them. For example, the concept of intelligence, as represented by the I.Q. score, can sometimes appear misleadingly straightforward. However, intelligence test scores can be complex, involving a variety of different cognitive abilities, the influence of cultural factors, varying performance under different conditions, and issues related to the nature of intelligence. Unless clinicians are familiar with these areas, they are not adequately prepared to handle I.Q. data.

A problem encountered in many training programs is that although students will frequently have a knowledge of abnormal psychology, personality theory, and test construction, they are usually not sufficiently trained in how to integrate these knowledge areas into the interpretation of test results. Instead, their training focuses on developing competency in administration and scoring, rather than on knowledge relating to what it is that they are testing.

The role stressed in this book is consistent with the approach of psychological assessment in that the clinician not only should be knowledgeable in regard to traditional content areas in psychology and the nature of what is being tested, but also should be able to integrate the test data into a relevant description of the person. This description, although focusing on the individual, should be able to take into account the complexity of his social environment, personal history, and behavioral observations. Yet, the end goal is not merely to describe the person, but rather to develop relevant answers to specific questions, aid in problem solving, and facilitate decision making.

EVALUATING PSYCHOLOGICAL TESTS

Prior to using a psychological test, a clinician should investigate and understand the theoretical orientation of the test, practical considerations, the appropriateness of the standardization sample, and the adequacy of its reliability and validity. Often, extremely helpful reviews which relate to these issues can be found in current and past editions of Buros's *Mental Measurement Yearbook*. Table 1-1 outlines the more important questions which have to be answered. The issues outlined in this table will be discussed further. The discussion is consistent with the practical orientation of this text in that it focuses on problems which clinicians using psychological tests are likely to confront. It is not intended to provide a comprehensive coverage of test theory and construction; if a more detailed treatment is required, the reader is referred to one of the many texts on psychological testing (e.g., Anastasi, 1982; Kaplan and Sacuzzo, 1982).

Theoretical Orientation

One of the foremost requirements prior to evaluating whether or not a test is appropriate is for examiners to understand the theoretical orientation of the test. They should research the construct that the test is supposed to measure and then examine the manner in which the test approaches this construct. This information can usually be found in the test manual. However, if for any reason the information in the manual is not sufficient, then further knowledge should be sought elsewhere. Clinicians can frequently obtain useful information regarding the trait by assessing the individual test items. Usually an individual analysis of the items, which can help the potential test user to evaluate whether or not these items appear relevant to the trait being measured, can be found in the manual.

Table 1-1. Issues to Address When Evaluating a Psychological Test.

Theoretical Orientation

1. Do you adequately understand the theoretical construct the test is supposed to be measuring?
2. Do the test items correspond to the theoretical description of the construct?

Practical Considerations

1. If reading is required by the examinee, does his ability match the level required by the test?
2. How appropriate is the length of the test?
3. Does the examiner require additional training? If so, how can this be acquired?

Standardization

1. Is the population to be tested similar to the population the test was standardized on?
2. Was the size of the standardization sample adequate?
3. Have specialized subgroup norms been developed?

Reliability

1. Are reliability estimates sufficiently high (generally .90 for clinical decision making and .70 for research purposes)?
2. What implications do the relative stability of the trait, the method of estimating reliability, and the test format have on reliability?

Validity

1. What were the criteria and procedures used to validate the test?
2. Has the test been constructed so as to produce accurate measurements?
3. Will the test produce accurate measurements within the context and purpose for which you would like to use it?

Practical Considerations

There are a number of practical issues which do not relate as much to the construction of the test as to the context and manner in which the test will be used. First of all, tests vary in terms of the degree of education which examinees must have in order to understand them adequately. This may be especially important in relation to any reading which is demanded of the examinee. The examinee must be able to read, comprehend, and respond appropriately to the test. Some tests are too long, which can lead to a loss of rapport with (or extensive frustration on the part of) the examinee. Sometimes this problem can be reduced by administering short forms of the test, provided these short forms have been properly developed and are treated with appropriate caution. Finally, clinicians have to assess the extent to which they will need training to administer and interpret the instrument. If further training is necessary, then a plan must be developed for acquiring this training.

Standardization

Yet, another central issue relates to the adequacy of norms. Each test has norms that reflect the distribution of scores by a specific standardization sample. The basis upon which individual test scores have meaning relates directly to the similarity between that individual and the standardization sample. If there is a similarity between the group or individual being tested and the standardization sample, then adequate comparisons can be made. For example, if the test was standardized on college students between the ages of 18 and 22, then, if one assumes that the test is otherwise sufficiently reliable and valid, useful comparisons can be made for college students within that age bracket. The more dissimilar the person is from this standardization group (e.g., over 70 years of age with low educational achievement), the less useful the test is in evaluating him. The examiner may need to consult the literature to see if research which followed the publication of the test manual has developed norms for different groups. This is particularly important for tests such as the MMPI and the Rorschach where norms for children and adolescents have recently been published.

There are three major questions relating to the adequacy of norms which must be answered. The first is whether or not the standardization group is representative of the population on which the examiner would like to use the test. The test manual should include sufficient information to determine the representativeness of the standardization sample. If this information is not sufficient or is in any way incomplete, then the degree of confidence with which the test can be used is greatly reduced. The ideal and current practice is to use stratified random sampling. However, this can be an extremely costly and time consuming procedure, and as a result, many tests are grossly deficient in this respect. The second question is whether the size of the standardization group is large enough. If the group is too small, then the results may not give stable estimates because there may be too much random fluctuation within the group. Finally, a good test will have specialized subgroup norms as well as broad national norms. Knowledge relating to subgroup norms will give examiners greater flexibility and confidence if they are using the test with similar subgroup populations. This is particularly important when subgroups produce significantly different sets of scores from the normal standardization group. These subgroups can be based on such factors as sex, geographic location, age, level of education, socioeconomic status, or urban versus rural environment. Knowledge of each of these subgroup norms allows for more appropriate and meaningful interpretations of scores.

Reliability

The reliability of a test refers to its degree of stability, consistency, and accuracy. In other words, it addresses the question of the extent to which scores obtained by a person will be the same if the person is reexamined by the same test on different occasions. Underlying the concept of reliability is the possible range of error or "error of measurement" of a single score. This is an estimate of the range of possible random fluctuation which can be expected in an individual's score. However, it should be stressed that there will always be a certain degree of error or "noise" in the system resulting from such factors as misreading of the items, poor administration procedures, or the changing mood of the client. If there is a large degree of random fluctuation, then the examiner cannot place a great deal of confidence in an individual's scores. It is the goal of the test constructor to reduce the degree of measurement error, or random fluctuation, as much as possible. If this is achieved, then the difference between one score and another is more likely to be due to some true difference in the characteristic being measured rather than some chance fluctuation.

There are two main issues relating to the degree of error in a test. The first is that there is an inevitable, natural variation in human performance. Usually the variability is less for measurements of ability than for those of personality. Whereas ability variables (intelligence, mechanical aptitude, etc.) show gradual changes resulting from growth and development, many personality traits are much more highly dependent on factors such as mood. This is particularly true in the case of a characteristic such as anxiety. The practical significance of this in evaluating a test is that certain factors outside the test itself can serve to reduce the reliability which the test can realistically be expected to achieve. Thus, an examiner should generally expect higher reliabilities for an intelligence test than for a test measuring a personality variable such as anxiety. This makes it the examiner's responsibility to know the nature of that which is being measured, especially with regard to the degree of variability that is to be expected in the trait being measured.

The second important issue relating to reliability is that psychological testing methods are necessarily imprecise. Within the fields of the "hard" sciences, a direct measurement can be made such as the concentration of a chemical solution, the relative weight of one organism compared to another, or the strength of radiation. In contrast to this are the constructs in psychology where measurements are often indirect. We cannot perceive something such as "intelligence" directly; rather, we infer its existence by measuring behavior we have defined as being intelligent. Whereas it is not possible to control for the natural variability in human performance, adequate test construction can attempt to reduce the degree of imprecision which is a function of the test. Both natural human variability and test imprecision make the task of measurement extremely difficult. Although some error in testing is inevitable, the goal of test construction is to keep it within reasonably accepted limits. A "high" correlation is generally .80 or more, but the variable being measured will also change the expected strength of the correlation. Likewise, the method of determining reliability will alter the relative strength of the correlation. Usually clinicians should look for correlations of .90 or higher in tests that will be used to make decisions about individuals, whereas a correlation of .70 or more is generally adequate for research purposes.

The purpose of reliability is to estimate the degree to which the test varies due to error. There are three primary methods of obtaining reliability. Reliability can refer to the extent to which the test produces consistent results upon retesting (test-retest), the relative accuracy of a test at a given time (alternate forms), and the internal consistency of the items (split half). Another way of summarizing this is that reliability can be time to time (test-retest), form to form (alternate forms), or item to item (split half). Whereas these are the main types of reliability, there is a fourth one — the Kuder-Richardson — which, like the split half, is a measurement of the internal consistency of the test items. However, this method is considered appropriate only for tests which are relatively pure measures of a single variable, and it will not be covered here.

Test-Retest Reliability. Test-retest reliability is determined by administering the test and then giving a repeat administration on a second occasion. The reliability coefficient is determined by correlating the scores obtained by the same person on the two different administrations. The degree of correlation between the two scores indicates to what extent the test can be generalized from one situation to the next. If the correlations are high, then the results are less likely to be due to random fluctuations in the condition of the examinee or the testing environment. Thus, the examiner can be relatively confident that differences in scores are the result of an actual change in the trait being measured.

There are a number of factors which must be considered in assessing the appropriateness of test-retest reliability. One is that the interval between administrations can affect reliability. Thus, a test manual should clearly specify the interval as well as any significant life changes that the examinees may have experienced such as counseling, career changes, or psychotherapy. For example, tests of preschool intelligence often give reasonably high correlations if the second administration is within several months of the first one. However, correlations with later childhood or adult I.Q.'s are generally useless because of the many intervening life experiences. One of the major difficulties with test-retest reliability is the effect that practice and memory may have on performance which can produce improvement between one administration and the next. This is a particular problem for speeded and memory tests such as those found on the Digit Symbol and Arithmetic subtests of the WAIS. Additional sources of error may be the result of random, short-term fluctuations in the examinee or variations in the testing conditions. In general, test-retest reliability is the preferred method only if the variable being measured is relatively stable. If the variable is a highly changeable one such as anxiety, then this method is usually not adequate.

Alternate Forms. The alternate forms method avoids many of the problems encountered with test-retest reliability. The logic behind alternate forms is that if the trait is measured several times on the same individual by using parallel forms of the test, then the different measurements should produce similar results. The degree of similarity between the scores represents the reliability coefficient of the test. As in the test-retest method, the interval between administrations should always be included in the manual as well as a description of significant intervening life experiences. If the second administration is given immediately after the first, then the resulting reliability is a measure of the correlation between forms and not across occasions. Correlations determined by tests given with a wide interval, such as two months or more, provide a measure of both the relation between forms and the degree of temporal stability.

The use of the alternate forms method has the advantage of eliminating many carry-over effects such as the recall of previous responses the examinee has made to specific items. However, there is still likely to be some carry-over effect in that the examinee can learn to adapt to the overall style of the test even when the specific item content between one test and another is unfamiliar. This is most likely to occur when the test involves some sort of ingenuity in which the same principle in solving one problem can be used to solve the next one. An examinee, for example, may learn to use mnemonic aids to increase his performance on an alternate form of the WAIS-R Digit Symbol. Perhaps the primary difficulty with alternate forms is determining whether or not the two forms are actually equivalent. For example, if one test is more difficult than its alternate form, then the difference in scores may represent differences in the tests rather than differences due to the unreliability of the measure. Since the test constructor is attempting to obtain a measure of the reliability of the test itself and not of the difference between the two tests, this could serve to confound and lower the reliability coefficient. A final difficulty is encountered primarily when there is a delay between one administration and the next because the examinee may perform differently due to short-term fluctuations such as mood, stress level, or the relative quality of his previous night's sleep. Thus, an examinee's abilities may vary somewhat from one examination to another, thereby affecting test results.

Despite these problems, alternate forms reliability has the advantage of, if not eliminating, at least reducing many of the carry-over effects found with the test-retest method. Yet a further advantage is that having alternate forms of the test can be useful for purposes other than determining reliability. This may include assessing the effects of a treatment program or monitoring a patient's changes over a period of time by administering the different forms on separate occasions.

Split Half Reliability. The best technique for determining reliability for a trait in which there is a high degree of fluctuation is the split half method. This is because the test is given only once, then the items are split in half and the two halves are correlated. Since there is only one administration, it is not possible for the effects of time to intervene as they might with the test-retest method. Thus, the split half method gives a measure of the internal consistency of the test items rather than the temporal stability of different administrations of the same test. To determine split half reliability, the test may be split on the basis of odd and even items. This method of splitting is usually adequate for most tests. Dividing the test into a first and second half can be effective in some cases, but this is often not appropriate because of the cumulative effects of warming up, practice fatigue, and boredom which can result in different levels of performance on the first half of the test compared to the second.

As with the other methods of obtaining reliability, there are also limitations to the split half method. When a test is split in half there are fewer items on each half, which results in wider variability because the individual responses cannot stabilize as easily around a mean. As a general principle, the longer a test is, the more reliable it will be because the larger the number of items, the easier it is for the scores to be stable and consistent. As with the alternate forms method, there may also be differences in content between one half and another.

The best form of reliability is in part dependent on the nature of the variable being measured and also on the purposes for which the test will be used. If the trait being measured is highly stable, the test-retest method is preferable, whereas split half is more appropriate for traits which are highly subject to fluctuations. When using a test to make predictions, then, the test-retest method is preferable since it gives an estimate of the dependability of the test from one administration to the next. This is particularly true if, when determining the reliability, there was an increased time interval between the two administrations. If, on the other hand, the examinee is concerned with the internal consistency and accuracy of a test for a single, one-time measure, then either the split half or the test-retest method on the same day would be best.

The acceptable range of reliability is a difficult question to answer and depends partially on the nature of the variable being measured. In general, unstable traits produce lower reliabilities than stable ones. Thus, in evaluating a test, the examiner should expect and look for higher reliabilities on stable traits than unstable ones. For example, a person's general fund of vocabulary words is highly stable and will therefore produce high reliabilities. In contrast is a person's level of anxiety — which is highly changeable — which means that examiners should not expect nearly as high reliabilities. A further consideration, which is also related to the relative stability of the trait, is the method of reliability that is used. Alternate forms are considered to give the lowest estimate of the actual reliability of a test and split half the highest. Yet another important way of estimating the adequacy of the reliability is by comparing the reliability derived on other similar tests. The examiner can then develop a sense of what the expected levels of reliability should be, thereby giving himself a baseline by which to make comparisons. In the example of anxiety, a clinician may not know what is an acceptable level of reliability. A general estimate can be made by comparing the reliability of the test under consideration with other tests measuring the same or a similar variable. The most important thing to keep in mind is that the lower the reliability, the less confidence the examiner can place in the interpretations and predictions based on the test data.

Another consideration in evaluating the acceptable range of reliability is the format of the test. Longer tests will usually have higher reliabilities than shorter ones. Also the format of the responses will affect reliability. For example, a true-false format is likely to have a lower reliability than multiple choice because the true-false items have a 50% possibility of the answer being correct due to chance. In contrast, a multiple choice format having five possible choices has only a 20% possibility of being correct due to chance. A final consideration is that tests with various subtests or subscales should report the reliability for the overall test as well as for each of the subtests. Generally, the overall test score will have a significantly higher reliability than its subtests. In estimating the confidence with which test scores can be interpreted, the examiner should take into account the lower reliabilities of the subtests. For example, a Full Scale I.Q. score on the WAIS-R can be interpreted with more confidence than the specific subscale scores.

Most test manuals include a statistical index of the amount of error that can be expected for test scores which is referred to as the standard error of measurement. The logic behind the standard error of measurement is that test scores consist of both "truth" and error. Thus, there will always be noise or error in the system, and the standard error of measurement gives a range of how extensive that error will be. The degree of error will depend on the test reliability so that the higher the reliability, the narrower the range of error. The standard error of measurement is a standard deviation score so that, for example, a standard error of measurement of 5 on an intelligence test would indicate that an individual's score has a 68% chance of being within ±5 I.Q. points from the estimated true score. Likewise there would be a 95% chance that the individual's score would fall within a range of ±10 points from the estimated true score. From a theoretical point of view, the standard error of measurement is a statistical index of how a person's repeated scores on a specific test would fall around a normal distribution. Thus, it is a statement of the relationship among a person's obtained score, his theoretically "true" score, and the test reliability. Since it is an empirical statement of the probable range of scores, the standard error of measurement has more practical usefulness than knowing the test reliability.

Validity

The most crucial issue in test construction is validity. Whereas reliability addresses the issues of accuracy and consistency, validity assesses what it is that the test is being accurate about. Although a test can be reliable without being valid, the opposite is not true. In other words, a necessary prerequisite for validity is that the test must first have achieved an adequate level of reliability. Thus, a valid test is one which accurately measures the variable it is intended to measure. For example, we might develop a test comprised of questions regarding a person's musical preference and erroneously state that it is a test of creativity. The test might be reliable in the sense that if it is given to the same person on different occasions, it will produce similar results each time. However, it would not be reliable in the sense that an investigation might indicate that it does not correlate with other more valid measurements of creativity.

Establishing the validity of a test can be extremely difficult. This difficulty arises primarily because psychological variables are usually abstract concepts such as intelligence, anxiety, and personality. They have no tangible reality and so their existence must be inferred through indirect means. In constructing a test, there are two necessary initial steps that a test designer must follow. First, the construct must be theoretically evaluated and elaborated; second, specific operations (test questions) must be developed to measure it. Even when these steps are closely and conscientiously followed, it is sometimes difficult to evaluate what the test really measures. For example, I.Q. tests are good predictors of academic success, but there are many questions as to whether they adequately measure the concept of intelligence as it is theoretically described. Another hypothetical test which, based on its item content, might seem to measure what is described as "musical aptitude" may in reality be highly correlated with verbal abilities. Thus, it may be more a measure of verbal abilities than of musical aptitude.

Content Validity.   During the initial construction phase of any test, the constructors must first be concerned with its content validity. This refers to the subject matter of the test items and is achieved by the appropriate selection of these items. During the initial selection of the items, the constructors must carefully consider the skills or knowledge area of the variable they would like to measure. Based on these criteria, they develop the items and submit them to a panel of experts who further judge the adequacy of the items. They may decide that the item content overrepresents, underrepresents, or excludes specific areas, and may recommend alterations accordingly. A good test will cover not just the subject matter of that which is being measured but also specific additional variables as well. For example, factual knowledge may be one criterion, but of additional importance are the application of that knowledge and the ability to analyze data. Thus, a test with high content validity must cover all major aspects of the content area and must do so in the correct proportion.

A concept somewhat related to content validity is face validity. However, these should not be considered synonymous because content validity pertains to the judgment by experts and face validity has to do with judgments by the test users. The central issue in face validity is test rapport. Thus, a group of potential mechanics who are being tested for basic skills in arithmetic should have word problems which relate to machines rather than to business transactions. Face validity then is present if the test "looks good" to the persons taking it, to policymakers who decide to include it in their programs, and to other untrained personnel.

One of the key factors in content validity is its heavy reliance on the personal judgment of the test designers. As an initial step, content issues are necessary, but as an end in itself, content validity is the least preferred method because of the subjectivity involved. In some cases, content validity can be adequate, such as in the development of achievement and occupational tests. This is because subject- or job-related criteria can be specified with a fairly high degree of accuracy. However, for aptitude and personality tests, content validity is usually inappropriate because the variables are both more complex and more abstract. These types of tests require more empirical verification through other validity procedures.

Criterion Validity.   A second major approach to determining validity is referred to as criterion validity, but it has also been called empirical or predictive validity. Criterion validity is determined by comparing the test scores with some sort of performance on an outside measure. The outside measure should have a theoretical relation to the variable that the test is supposed to measure. For example, an intelligence test might be correlated with grade point average, an aptitude test with independent job ratings, or general maladjustment scores with other tests measuring similar dimensions. The relation between the two measurements is usually expressed as a correlation coefficient.

Criterion-related validity is most frequently divided into either concurrent or predictive validity. Concurrent validity refers to measurements taken at the same, or approximately the same, time as the test. For example, an intelligence test might be administered at the same time as assessments of a group's level of academic achievement. Predictive validity is used to refer to outside measurements which were taken some time after the test scores were derived. Thus, predictive validity might be evaluated by correlating the intelligence test scores with measures of academic achievement a year after the time of initial testing.

Concurrent validation is often used as a substitute for predictive validation because it is simpler, less expensive, and not as time consuming. However, the main consideration in deciding whether concurrent or predictive validation is preferable depends on how the test will be used. Predictive validity is most appropriate for tests used for selection and classification of personnel. This may include hiring job applications, placing military personnel in specific occupational training programs, screening out individuals who are likely to develop emotional disorders, or identifying which category of psychiatric populations would be most likely to benefit from specific treatment approaches. These situations all require that the measurement device provide a prediction of some future outcome. Concurrent validation is preferable if an assessment of the client's current status is required, rather than a prediction of what might occur to the client at some future time. The distinction can be summarized by asking, "Is Mary Smith maladjusted?" rather than "Is Mary Smith likely to become maladjusted at some future time?"

An important consideration is the degree to which a specific test can be applied to a unique work-related environment. In other words, can the test under consideration provide accurate assessments and predictions for the specific environment in which the examinee is working? To answer this question adequately, the examiner must refer to the manual and assess the similarity between the criteria used to establish the test's validity and the situation to which he would like to apply the test. For example, can an aptitude test which has adequate criterion validity in the prediction of high school grade point average be used to predict academic achievement for a population of college students? If the examiner has questions regarding the relative applicability of the test, he may need to undertake a series of specific tasks. The first is to identify clearly the skills which are required for adequate performance in the situation involved. For example, the criteria for a successful teacher may include such attributes as verbal fluency, flexibility, and good public speaking skills. The examiner then must determine the degree to which each of these skills contributes to the quality of one's performance as a teacher. Next, the examiner has to assess the extent to which the test under consideration measures each of these skills. The final step is to evaluate the extent to which the attribute that the test measures is relevant to the skills the examiner needs to predict. Based on this, the examiner can estimate the confidence that he will place in the predictions developed from the test. This approach is sometimes referred to as synthetic validity since the examiner must integrate the criteria reported in the test manual with the variables he will be working with in his clinical or organizational setting.

The level or strength of criterion validity will depend in part on the type of variable being measured. Usually, intellectual or aptitude tests give relatively higher validity coefficients than personality tests because there are generally a greater number of variables influencing personality than intelligence. As the number of variables that influence the trait being measured increases, it becomes progressively more difficult to account for them. When there is a large number of variables which are not accounted for, the trait can be affected in unpredictable ways. This can create a much wider degree of fluctuation in the test scores, thereby lowering the validity coefficient. Thus, when evaluating a personality test, the examiner should not expect as high a validity coefficient as for intellectual or aptitude tests. A helpful guide is to look at the validities found in similar tests and compare them with the test being considered. For example, if an examiner wanted to estimate the range of validity to be expected for the extroversion scale on the Myers Briggs Type Indicator, he might compare it with the validities for similar scales found in the California Personality Inventory and Eysenck's Personality Questionnaire. The relative level of validity, then, will depend both on the quality of the construction of the test and on the variable being studied.

An important consideration is the extent to which the test accounts for the trait being measured or the behavior being predicted. Take, for example, the typical correlation found between intelligence tests and grade point average which usually ranges from .60 to .70. Since no one would say that grade point average is totally the result of intelligence, the relative extent to which intelligence determines grade point average has to be estimated. This can be calculated by squaring the correlation coefficient and changing it into a percentage. Thus, if the correlation of .70 was squared, it would come out to 49%. This would indicate that 49% of academic achievement can be accounted for by I.Q. as measured by the intelligence test. The remaining 51% may include such factors as motivation, quality of instruction, and past educational experience. The question facing the examiner is whether or not 49% of the variance is sufficiently useful for the purposes for which he would like to use the test. This ultimately depends on the personal judgment of the examiner.

The main problem confronting criterion validity is finding an agreed upon, definable, acceptable, and feasible outside criterion. Whereas for an intelligence test it may be acceptable to use grade point average as the criterion, it is far more difficult to specify adequate criteria for most personality tests. Even with so-called intelligence tests, many researchers argue that it is more appropriate to consider them tests of "scholastic aptitude" rather than of "intelligence." Yet another difficulty with criterion validity is the possibility of inadvertently biasing the criterion measure. This is referred to as "criterion contamination" and occurs when knowledge of the test results influences an individual's later performance. For example, a supervisor in an organization may act differently towards a worker who he knows has been tested and placed in a certain category. This may set up negative or positive expectations for the worker which could influence his level of performance. The result is likely to artificially increase the level of the validity coefficients. To work around these difficulties, especially in regard to personality tests, a third major method for determining validity must be used.

Construct Validity. The method of construct validity was developed because of the inadequacies and difficulties encountered with content and criterion approaches. Content validity relies too much on subjective judgment, while criterion validity is too restrictive in working with content areas and has a further difficulty in that there is often a lack of agreement in deciding upon adequate outside criteria. The basic approach of construct validity is to assess the extent to which the test measures a theoretical construct or trait. This involves three general steps. Initially the test constructor must make a careful analysis of the trait. This is followed by a consideration of how the trait should relate to other variables. Finally, the test designer needs to test whether or not these hypothesized relationships actually exist. For example, a test measuring dominance should have a high correlation with the individual accepting leadership roles and a low or negative correlation with measures of submissiveness. Likewise, a test measuring anxiety should have a high positive correlation with individuals who are measured while in an anxiety provoking situation such as an experiment involving some sort of physical pain. As these hypothesized relationships are verified by research studies, the degree of confidence which can be placed in a test increases.

There is not any one best approach to determining construct validity; rather, a variety of different possibilities exist. For example, if some abilities are expected to increase with age, then correlations can be made between a population's test scores and age. This may be appropriate for variables such as intelligence or motor coordination, but it would not be applicable for most personality measurements. Even in the measurement of intelligence or motor coordination, this approach may not be appropriate beyond the age of maturity. Yet another method of determining construct validity would be to measure the effects of experimental or treatment interventions. Thus, a post-test measurement may be taken following a period of instruction to see if the intervention affected the test scores in relation to a previous pre-test measure. For example, after a course in arithmetic, it would be predicted that scores on a test of arithmetical ability would increase. Often, correlations can be made with other tests which supposedly measure a similar variable. However, if the new test correlates too highly with already existing tests, then this may represent needless duplication unless the new test incorporates some additional advantage such as a shortened format, ease of administration, or superior predictive validity. Of particular relevance to construct validation is factor analysis, which is a statistical method originally developed to identify and assess the relative strengths of different psychological traits. Factor analysis can also be used in the design of a test to identify the primary factor or factors measured by a series of different tests. Thus, it can be used to simplify a test or tests by reducing the number of categories to a few common factors or traits. The "factorial" validity of a test is the relative "weight" or degree of importance that a specific factor has on a test. For example, if spatial organization has a weight of .72 on a picture arrangement type of test, then the factorial validity is .72.

Another method used in construct validity is to make estimates of the degree of internal consistency by correlating specific subtests with the test's total score. For example, if a subtest on an intelligence test does not correlate adequately with the overall or Full Scale I.Q., then it should be either eliminated or altered in such a way as to increase the correlation. A final method for obtaining construct validity is for a test to converge or correlate highly with variables which are theoretically similar to it. The test should not only show this "convergent validity" but also have "discriminate validity" in which it would demonstrate low or negative correlations with variables that are dissimilar to it. Thus, scores on reading comprehension should show high positive correlations with performance in a literature class and low correlations with performance in a class involving mathematical computation.

As indicated by the variety of approaches discussed, there is no quick, efficient method for determining construct validity. Almost any type of data can be used, including material from the content and criterion approaches. The greater the amount of supporting data, the greater is the confidence with which the test can be used. In many ways, construct validity represents the strongest and most sophisticated approach to test construction. It involves theoretical knowledge of the trait or ability being measured, knowledge of other related variables, hypothesis testing, and statements regarding the relationship of the test variable to a network of other variables that have been investigated. Thus, it is a never-ending process in which there are always new relationships that can be specified and investigated.

Conceptual Validity.   In addition to the three traditional methods of obtaining validity, Maloney and Ward (1976) have described a fourth method which they refer to as conceptual validity. The traditional methods are primarily concerned with evaluating the theoretical constructs within the test itself. In contrast, conceptual validity focuses on individuals with their unique histories and behaviors. It is a means of evaluating and integrating test data so that the clinician's conclusions make accurate statements about an examinee. There are similarities with construct validity in that construct validity also tries to test specific hypothesized relationships between constructs. Conceptual validity is likewise concerned with testing constructs, but they are constructs regarding the individual rather than constructs within the test.

The general approach for determining conceptual validity is that the examiner begins with individuals for whom no constructs have been developed. The next phase is to observe, collect data, and form a large number of hypotheses. If these hypotheses are confirmed through consistent trends in the test data, behavioral observations, history, and additional data sources, then the hypotheses can be considered to represent valid constructs regarding the person. The focus is on an individual in his specific situation, and the data are derived from a variety of sources. The conceptual validity of the constructs is based on the logicalness and internal consistency of the data. Unlike construct validity, which begins with previously developed constructs, conceptual validity produces constructs as its end product. Its aim is that these constructs provide valid sources of information which can be used to help solve the unique problems that an individual may be facing.

UNDERSTANDING THE REFERRAL SETTING

In addition to evaluating the nature and adequacy of the test(s) under considera-tion, clinicians should also clarify the referral question, and understand the unique problems and demands encountered in different referral settings. In fact, examiners who do not take these issues into consideration, but who may other-wise be skilled in administering and interpreting tests, may end up providing a large amount of useless information to their referral source. Furthermore, they may have undertaken a needless series of tests because, if they had investigated the underlying motive behind the referral, they might have discovered that evaluation through testing was not warranted.

One of the more frequent sources of error in test interpretation occurs because clinicians do not develop a clear comprehension of the referral question in its broadest context (Levine, 1981). However, requests for psychological testing are usually not made in a clear manner. For example, they may be worded as vaguely as "I would like a psychological evaluation on Mr. Smith" or "give this person a test battery." The request is usually posed neither as a question to be answered nor as a decision to be made when in fact this is almost always the position that the referral source is in. For example, a school admin-istrator may need testing to support a decision he has already made, a teacher may want to prove to parents that their child has a serious problem, or a psychi-atric resident may not be comfortable with the manner in which he is managing a patient. The surface motive for testing may even be as vague as that an organi-zation has someone tested as a matter of policy. Many of these situations need far more clarification for clinicians to be able to provide useful information in problem solving. Furthermore, many of these situations include issues other than those involved in the testing itself and are filled with hidden agendas which may not be adequately handled by conducting psychological testing.

It must be stressed that the responsibility for ferreting out and clarifying the true referral question lies with the clinician. This particularly involves helping the referring person organize the referral question in a new and more workable context, in which one can clearly perceive those issues that are relevant to, and those that are beyond the scope of, psychological assessment. Clinicians must understand what decisions the referral source is facing, as well as what alternatives are available and the relative usefulness of each of these alternatives. Clinicians must also specify the relevance of the psychological evaluation in regard to deciding on the different alternatives and the possible outcomes for each of these alternatives if adopted. They should make clear the advantages and usefulness of psychological testing, but they should also give the limitations of test data.

In helping to clarify the referral question, as well as in developing a relevant psychological evaluation, clinicians should become familiar with the types of environments in which they will be working. Levine (1981) has suggested that the most frequent environments in which examiners must work are the psychiatric setting, the general medical setting, the legal context, the educational context, and the psychological clinic. The following sections are a summary of the main points he makes relating to each of these environments.

The Psychiatric Setting

The role of the psychiatrist is usually that of an administrator, a psychotherapist, or a physician. In each of these roles, there are unique issues confronting him. The primary responsibility of clinicians is to develop a clear understanding of these roles so that their evaluations can directly address the problems with which the psychiatrist is likely to be faced.

One of the main roles a psychiatrist fills is that of a ward administrator. A position that frequently confronts ward administrators is having to make decisions related to such problems as suicide risk, admission/discharge, and the administration of a wide variety of medical procedures. In many situations, psychiatrists will use other persons to help with decisions even though they are still primarily responsible for these decisions. This represents a change from the typical role of psychiatrists 20 years ago. Originally, psychiatrists were mainly concerned with diagnosis and treatment, but currently issues revolving around custody, freedom of the patient, and the safety of society have taken over the primary focus. From the perspective of psychologists doing assessments, this means that giving a classical psychiatric diagnosis is not sufficient. For example, if a patient is labeled manic-depressive, this label does not, in and of itself, provide any information regarding his level of dangerousness to himself or others. Once patients have been admitted to a psychiatric setting, there are many practical questions which have to be answered, such as the type of ward in which to place them, the types of activities in which they should be involved, and the method of therapy which would be likely to benefit them the most.

The task confronting psychologists is to initially determine and clarify the questions they receive from the psychiatric administrator, particularly in regard to any decisions that must be made concerning the patient. Often psychologists in psychiatric settings are given the vague request for "a psychological" without further elaboration. Thus, a standard evaluation is developed based on the psychologist's preconception of what is involved in "a psychological." This may include a discussion of the patient's defense mechanisms, diagnosis, cognitive style, and psychosocial history. Often this is conducted without addressing the specific decisions that have to be made or perhaps only addressing two or three relevant issues and omitting others. In order to maximize the usefulness of an evaluation, examiners must both clarify and address these issues. This implies being aware of, and sensitive to, psychiatric administrators' legal and custodial responsibilities as given to them by society.

In contrast to ward administrators, the standard referral question from psychiatrists who are conducting psychotherapy is whether or not a particular patient they are considering working with is suitable for therapy. This situation is usually clear-cut and typically does not present any difficulties. Such an evaluation can elaborate on likely problems which may occur during the course of therapy, defenses, capacity for insight, cognitive style, level of affect, and diagnosis. However, if a referral is made during therapy, there may be a number of difficulties surrounding the referral which are not readily apparent from the referral question. An area for potential conflict arises when psychiatrists are attempting to fulfill the roles of both administrator (caretaker) and psychothera- pist, and yet have not attempted to clearly define these roles either for themselves or for their patients. The resulting ambiguity may cause defensiveness and resistance on the part of the patient so that the patient does not live up to the therapist's expectations. Thus, the resolution of this conflict cannot be found in the elaboration of a specific trait or need within the patient, but must rather occur in the interaction between therapist and patient. A standard psychological evaluation investigating the internal structure of the patient will not address this issue. A second possible problem area for client's referred in the midst of therapy can often be the result of personal anxiety and discomfort on the therapist's part. Thus, such issues as countertransference and possibly unreason- able expectations on the part of the therapist may be equally or even more important than looking at a patient's characteristics. The possibility of role ambiguity, countertransference, or unreasonable expectations needs to be investigated and if present, analyzed and communicated in a sensitive manner.

One of the main problems encountered when psychiatrists are acting in the role of physician is that they and the psychologist may have different conceptual models for describing the patient's disorder. Whereas psychiatrists function primarily from a disease or medical model, psychologists may speak in terms of difficulties in living with people and society. In effectively communicating the results of psychological evaluations, examiners must be able to deal with this conceptual difference. For example, a psychiatrist may ask whether or not a patient is schizophrenic, whereas a psychologist may not believe that the label schizophrenia is a useful or even a scientifically valid concept. However, the larger issue is that the psychiatrist is still faced with some practical decisions. In fact, the psychiatrist may even share some of the same concerns regarding the term "schizophrenia," but this conceptual issue may not be particularly important in dealing with the patient. For example, it might be required that the patient be given a traditional diagnosis because of legal requirements or hospital policies. The psychiatrist may also have to decide whether to give antipsychotic medication, electroconvulsive therapy, or psychotherapy. If a patient is diagnosed as schizophrenic rather than brain damaged or neurotic, then given a hospital's current economic and policy considerations, the psychiatrist may decide upon antipsychotic medication. An effective examiner should be able to see beyond possible conceptual differences and address practical considerations. A psychiatrist may refer a defensive patient who can't or won't verbalize his concerns and ask whether or not this person is schizophrenic. Beyond this are questions such as the quality of the patient's thought processes and whether the person is a danger to himself or others. Thus, the effective examiner must translate his findings into a conceptual model which is both understandable by a psychiatrist and useful from a task-oriented point of view.

The General Medical Setting

It has been estimated that more than two-thirds of the patients who are seen by physicians have significant emotional components to their illnesses. For example, emotional factors are often associated with lower back pain, headaches, and stomach upset. A complete approach to the patient, then, involves an awareness of the interaction between physical complaints and psychological correlates. Thus, the contributions that psychologists can make are potentially extremely important. In order to adequately work in this setting, psychologists must become familiar with medical descriptions, which often includes learning a complex and extensive vocabulary. Another important consideration is that even though physicians must often draw information from a variety of sources to aid in their decision making, they must take ultimate responsibility for whatever decisions are made.

The most frequent situations in which physicians might use the services of a psychologist involve possible emotional factors associated with medical complaints, screening for organicity, presurgical evaluations, and early detection and prediction regarding possible serious psychological disorders. Even though the physician has conducted a medical exam without finding any physical basis for the patient's complaints, he is still in the position of having to devise some form of treatment. It is within this situation that the psychologist can elaborate and specify how a patient can be treated for psychological difficulties. This involves somewhat of a role reversal since it is the psychologist who recommends the treatment plan and the physician who must perform the diagnosis, at least insofar as concluding that there is no physical basis for the patient's symptoms. Another major area for psychologists is providing neuropsychological assessments. Whereas physicians attempt to detect physical lesions in the nervous system, the neuropsychologist is more concerned with the psychological status of higher cortical functions. Another way of stating this is that physicians evaluate how the *brain* is functioning and neuropsychologists evaluate how the *person* is functioning as a result of possible brain abnormalities. Thus, they assess the presence of possible deterioration in higher intellectual processes such as memory, sequencing, abstract reasoning, and spatial organization. Based on these findings, physicians may decide to proceed with more intensive and possibly more hazardous medical diagnostic procedures such as exploratory surgery, angiography, or ventriculography. A physician is also sometimes interested in having a psychologist conduct a presurgical evaluation to assess the likelihood of a serious stress reaction to surgery. Finally, physicians, particularly pediatricians, are often concerned with detecting early signs of a serious psychological disorder which may have been brought to their attention by parents, other family members, or teachers. In such situations, the psychologist's evaluation should assess not only the patient's present psychological condition but also the contributing factors in his environment, and should provide a prediction of the patient's status during the next few months or years. When the patient's current condition, current environment, and future prospects have been evaluated, then the examiner can recommend the next phase in the intervention process. A psychologist may also help with the possible personal discomfort that a physician may feel in confronting a patient or the patient's family with the results of an evaluation. Such an approach has the significant advantage of going beyond merely confirming or disconfirming a physician's suspicions: it also provides specific guidelines for problem solving and decision making.

The Legal Context

During the past ten years, psychological testing has progressively become an important part of the legal system. However, in writing a useful report, the psychologist should be aware of the general approach to decision making in the legal system, as well as of the different stages in the legal proceedings at which he might be called in to help. Cowan (1963) has stated that the general emphasis in the training of a scientist (psychologist) is on creating generalizations. This contrasts with an attorney, who is trained to look at the unique and the individual. To an attorney then, no two cases are alike, and attorneys are most at home when deciding on a unique conflict situation in a unique way. The clinician must be able to bridge these two approaches and word an evaluation in such a way as to be relevant to the judicial system. Thus, the approach of conceptual validity as developed by Maloney and Ward (1976) and outlined earlier is particularly appropriate for the judicial system since it focuses on the uniqueness of an individual in his specific situation.

A psychological report can be perceived as including both test data and conclusions or inferences based on that data. The data describe what a person can and cannot do within the test context, but a clinician must still infer what he believes a person could and could not do in daily life. The bulk of a legal evaluation or court testimony covers test data and usually does not become problematic. However, attorneys, judges, and juries often object to inferences based on the data, and question the validity and meaning of these inferences. Thus, any inferences that are made should be both precise and clearly supported by the data. An inference which goes one step beyond the data is likely to be challenged and may later be used to descredit other inferences. For example, if a report concludes that a certain person has good parenting skills, then a description of what these skills are and how they relate to the data should be clearly but precisely made. Likewise, a clinician concluding that a brain injury is irreversible should clearly indicate why this inference has been made.

A psychologist can be called into the legal system at any stage in the decision making process. He may be used during the investigation stage to answer such questions as the reliability of a witness or to determine the category of crime which has been committed. A prosecuting attorney may request a psychologist to help determine the specifics of a crime; a defense attorney, to attempt an insanity plea. If a report is being written in an attempt to establish that the defendant is insane, then the clinician should have a detailed knowledge of the history and implications of the McNaughten rule, irresistible impulse, and the Durham rule. The psychologist may also be used to assist the judge in determining the sentence, the penal officer in determining the prison term, and the parole officer in planning for rehabilitation.

The Educational Context

As in the medical setting, a psychologist working in the educational context must be able to understand the educator's language and the manner in which alternatives are conceptualized. For example, a child referred for assessment with the vague description of having a "learning block" may be faced with the possibility of repeating a grade, transferring to a slower educational program, or advancing but with a recommendation for psychotherapy. A further consideration is that each school may have some programs that are of a high quality and others which, by comparison, are relatively weak. Typically the quality and effectiveness of special education programs have wide fluctuations from one school to another, and it is the responsibility of the clinician to assess both the general options available in most schools and the relative strengths and weaknesses present in any specific school.

Many schools base their treatment of students on the medical or "disease" model of disorders, and therefore attempt to develop an early diagnosis and focus primarily on the individual rather than on larger social variables. However, except for mental retardation and other neurologically based disorders, school difficulties usually do not involve disease. The main areas of difficulty typically involve factors related to poor family dynamics and interpersonal stress which prevent the student from developing a socially effective life-style. Whereas this psychosocial model is perhaps more true to reality, the examiner is often in the position of performing only individual testing. Traditionally, individual testing has been the accepted approach, but all too frequently it provides a relatively limited and narrow range of information. If it is combined with a family assessment, additional crucial data may be collected, but there is also likely to be significant resistance. This resistance may result from legal or ethical restrictions regarding the scope of the services that a school can provide or the demands that a psychologist can make on the student's parents. Often there is also an initial focus on, and a need to perceive, the student as a "problem child" or identified patient. This may have the effect of obscuring larger, more complex, and yet more significant issues such as marital conflict, a disturbed teacher, misunderstandings between teacher and parents, or a conflict between the school principal and the parents. All or some of these individuals may have an investment in perceiving the student as the identified patient rather than acknowledging that there may be a disordered school system or significant marital turmoil. An individually oriented assessment may be made with excellent interpretations, but unless all these possibilities are considered, understood, and addressed, the assessment may very well be ineffective in solving both the individual difficulties and the larger organizational or interpersonal problems.

Whereas one problem with the medical model is its overemphasis on the individual, another possible difficulty lies in the belief that early identification produces a higher "cure" rate. While this may be true in some cases, such an assumption is also filled with potential problems. First of all, early and therefore probably uncertain labeling may create negative expectations which could result in self-fulfilling prophecies. This is especially true with labels such as "juvenile delinquency." Furthermore, there is little evidence that early identification of children's difficulties actually results in more effective treatment (Levitt, 1957, 1963). This is partially due to the fact that one of the crucial factors involved in effective treatment is that the client must have a high level of motivation. Motivation is primarily the result of the client's experiencing a certain degree of psychological turmoil, and early on in the problem, this turmoil is not likely to be present. This means that the larger question for the clinician to assess is whether there is a sufficient degree of motivation so that intervention will be more likely to be successful. The clinician using a psychosocial model, then, should attempt to understand the problem in its overall context, as well as to assess whether or not there is a sufficient level of motivation for change. At the same time, he should be sensitive to the fact that school personnel may not be perceiving the problem using the same model and may therefore have different assumptions on how best to approach the situation.

The Psychological Clinic

In contrast to the medical, legal, and educational institution where the psychologist serves as a consultant to the decision maker, the psychologist working in a psychological clinic is often himself the decision maker. There are a number of typical referrals that come into the psychological clinic. Perhaps the most common ones are individuals who are self-referred and are seeking relief from psychological turmoil. For most of these individuals, psychological testing is not relevant and, in fact, may be contraindicated because the delay between the time of testing and the feedback of the results is usually time that could best be applied towards treatment. There may be certain groups of self-referred clients about whom the psychologist may have some question as to whether or not the treatment available in a psychological clinic is appropriate. This can include clients with extensive medical problems, individuals with legal complications that need additional clarification, and persons who may require inpatient treatment. With these cases, it might be necessary to obtain additional information through psychological testing. However, the main purpose of the testing would be to aid in decision making rather than to serve as a direct source of help for the client.

Two other situations in which psychological assessment may be warranted involve children who are referred by their parents for school or behavioral problems and referrals from other decision makers. Where referrals are made for poor school performance or behavioral problems involving legal complications, there are special precautions that must be taken prior to testing. Primarily the clinician must develop a complete understanding of the client's social network and the basis for the referral. This may include a history of previous attempts at treatment or the relationship among the parents, school, courts, and child. Usually a referral comes at the end of a long sequence of events, and it is important to obtain information regarding these events. Once the basis of the referral has been clarified, the clinician may decide to have a meeting with different individuals who have become involved in the case such as the school principal, previous therapists, probation officer, attorney, or teacher. This may uncover a myriad of issues that have to be decided on, such as family therapy, placement in a special education program, a change in custody agreements between divorced parents, individual therapy of other members of the family, and a change in schools. All of these may affect the relevance of, and approach to, testing, but these issues may not be apparent if the initial referral question is taken at face value. Sometimes psychologists are also confronted with referrals from other decision makers. For example, an attorney may want to know if an individual is competent to stand trial. Other referrals may involve a physician who wants to know whether a head-injured patient can readjust to his work environment or drive a car, or the physician may need to document changes in a patient's process of recovery.

The discussion on the different settings in which psychological testing is used has focused on the issue of when to test and attempted to clarify the manner in which tests can be most helpful in making decisions. There are several important summary points which must be stressed. First of all, it is unrealistic to believe that a referral source will be able to adequately formulate the referral question. It will usually be neither clear nor concise. This is further complicated by the fact that a psychologist is typically only used for consultation in the most difficult and complex cases. This means that it is the clinician's responsibility to look beyond the referral question and understand the basis for the referral in its widest scope. Thus, an understanding must be developed of the complexity of the client's social setting including interpersonal factors, family dynamics, and the sequence of events leading to the referral.

In addition to clarifying the referral question, a second major point is that the psychologist is responsible for developing knowledge about the setting for which he is writing his report. This includes learning the proper language, the roles of the individuals working in the setting, the choices facing the decision makers, and the philosophical and theoretical beliefs they adhere to. It is also important that clinicians understand the values underlying the setting and assess whether or not these values coincide with their own. For example, psychologists who do not believe in capital punishment, psychosurgery, or electroconvulsive therapy may come into conflict while working in certain settings. The issue behind this is that psychologists should be clear as to how the information they give their referral source will be used. It is essential for them to appreciate the fact that they have a great responsibility, since decisions that clients make, which are often based on the results of these assessments, can frequently be major changing points in their lives. If there exists the possibility that the information may be used in such a way as to conflict with the clinician's value system, then he should reconsider, clarify, or possibly change his relation to the referral setting.

A final point is that clinicians should not allow themselves to be trained into or adopt the role of a "testing technician" or psychometrist. This role ultimately does a disservice to the client, the practitioner, and the profession. In other words, clinicians should not merely administer, score, and interpret tests, but also understand the total referral context in its broadest sense. This also means that they engage in the role of an expert who can integrate data from a variety of sources. Tests in and of themselves are limited in that they are not flexible or sophisticated enough to address themselves to complex referral questions. In this sense, Levine (1981) writes that the formal research on test validity is

> ... not immediately relevant to the practical use of psychological tests. The question of the value of tests becomes not "Does this test correlate with a criterion?" or "Does the test accord with a nomological net?", but rather "Does the use of the test improve the success of the decision making process?"

hy making it either more efficient, less costly, more accurate, more rational, or more relevant. (p. 292)

All of these concerns are consistent with the emphasis on an examiner's fulfilling the role of an expert clinician performing psychological assessment rather than of a psychometrist acting as a technician.

GUIDELINES AND CAUTIONS FOR USING TESTS

During the past 15 years there has been increasing criticism of, and resistance to, the use of psychological tests. Such criticism has included the use of tests in inappropriate contexts, cultural bias, invasion of privacy, and the continued use of tests which are inadequately validated. This criticism has resulted in diverse changes such as restrictions on the use of certain tests, greater clarification within the profession regarding ethical standards, and increased skepticism from the public. As a result, many psychologists either have withdrawn from the practice of testing or have continued with testing but adopted a rigid adherence to fixed formulas, neither acknowledging the importance of test criticisms nor following the research which might help them to modify their approaches. The main damage done to the field of testing stems from two general sources. The first is an overreliance on, and excessive faith in, psychological tests by people such as psychiatrists, judges, physicians, social workers, educators, and business-men. Their uncritical faith and overoptimism can potentially result in the misuse of test data, and may also eventually result in disillusionment on their part when their expectations of test-based decisions do not adequately solve the problems confronting them. The second area of difficulty arises from the possible misuse of tests on the part of clinicians themselves. In order to conduct useful and accurate assessments, it is thus essential that clinicians be aware of the types of misuse which they could potentially make of their tools. The American Psychological Association (APA) has published guidelines for examiners in its *Standards for Educational and Psychological Tests* (1974) and in principles 5 and 8 of *Ethical Principles of Psychologists* (1981).

Cautions in Administration and Scoring

It has been well documented that the relationship between the examiner and the client can influence the outcome of the scores. Of significance is the fact that many of these influences can occur without the examiner's being aware of them. Thus, it is the examiner's responsibility to become aware of the possible influences he may exert on the client and to closely adhere to the standardized conditions specified in the manual. If these are not adhered to, the result is likely to be unreliable scores.

In analyzing the relationship between the examiner and the client, there are a number of variables to consider. One important variable is rapport, which has been found in many cases to significantly alter test performance. For example, enhanced rapport involving verbal reinforcement and friendly conversation has been shown to increase WISC I.Q. scores by an average of 13 points compared to an administration involving more neutral interactions (Feldman and Sullivan, 1971). It is significant that this is a difference of almost one full standard deviation. It has also been found that mildly disapproving comments such as "I thought you could do better than that" result in significantly lowered performances when compared with either neutral or approving ones (Witmer, Bornstein, and Dunham, 1971). Whereas there is little evidence (Lefkowitz and Frazier, 1980; Sattler, 1973a, 1973b; Sattler and Gwynne, 1982) to support the belief that black students have lower performances when tested by white examiners, it has been suggested that black students are more responsive to tangible reinforcers (money, candy) than white students, who generally respond better to verbal reinforcement (Schultz and Sherman, 1976). However, in a later study, Terrell, Taylor, and Terrell (1978) demonstrated that the main factor was the cultural relevance of the response. They found a remarkable 17.6 point increase in I.Q. scores when black students were encouraged with culturally relevant comments such as "nice job, blood" or "good work, little brother." Thus, the rapport and feedback, especially if that feedback is culturally relevant, can significantly alter test performance. As a result, the feedback and level of rapport should, as much as possible, be held constant from one test administration to the next.

A variable which has been extensively investigated by Rosenthal and his colleagues is that a researcher/examiner's expectations can influence another person's level of performance (Rosenthal, 1966). This has been demonstrated with humans as well as with laboratory rats. For example, when an experimenter was told to expect better performances from rats who were randomly selected as "maze bright" (compared with "maze dull"), the rats indeed tended to perform in such a way as to confirm the experimenter's expectations (Rosenthal and Fode, 1963). Despite criticisms which have been leveled at his studies (Barber and Silver, 1968; Elashoff and Snow, 1971; Thorndike, 1968), Rosenthal still maintains that an expectancy effect exists in some situations and suggests that the mechanisms of influence are through minute nonverbal behaviors (Cooper and Rosenthal, 1980). He states further that the typical effects on an individual's performances are usually small and subtle, and occur in some situations but not in others. The obvious implication for clinicians is that they should continually question themselves regarding their expectations of clients and check to see if they may in some way be communicating these expectations to them.

An additional factor which may affect the nature of the relationship between the client and the examiner is the client's relative emotional state. It is particularly important to assess the degree of the client's motivation and his overall level of anxiety. There may be times in which it would be advisable to discontinue testing because of situational emotional states which may significantly influence the results of the tests. At the very least, examiners should consider the possible effects of emotional factors and incorporate these into their interpretations. For example, it might be necessary to increase the estimate of a client's optimal intellectual level of functioning if the client was extremely anxious during the administration of an intelligence test.

A final consideration, which can potentially confound both the administration and — more commonly — the scoring of responses, is the degree to which the examiner likes the client and perceives him as warm and friendly. Several studies (Sattler, Hillix, and Neher, 1970; Sattler and Winget, 1970) have indicated that the more the examiner likes the client, the more likely he will be to score an ambiguous response in a direction favorable to the client. Higher scores can occur even on items in which the responses are not ambiguous (Donahue and Sattler, 1971; Egeland, 1969; Simon, 1969). Thus, "hard" scoring, as opposed to more lenient scoring, can occur at least in part due to the degree of subjective liking the examiner feels towards the client. Again, examiners should continually check themselves to assess whether or not their relationship with the client is decreasing the objectivity of the test administration and scoring.

Use with Minority Groups

One of the most controversial issues in psychological testing is the use of intelligence tests for the placement of cultural minorities. Critics believe that intelligence tests are heavily biased in favor, and reflect the values, of white, middle-class society. They argue that such tests cannot adequately assess intelligence or aptitude when applied to minority groups. Whereas the most controversy has arisen from the use of intelligence tests, the presence of cultural bias is also relevant in the use of personality testing. For example, blacks tend to score significantly higher on scale 8 (schizophrenia) on the MMPI (Miller, Knapp, and Daniels, 1968) than whites, but interpretations based on these elevations are often uncertain (Gynther, 1979). Thus, personality tests can also be prone to discriminatory bias.

The basic issue is whether or not tests are as valid for minority groups as for nonminorities. Clearly, differences exist between these two groups, but the meaning which can be attributed to these differences has been strongly debated. A further question is what the cause of these differences is. Some theorists believe that the differences are primarily the result of environmental factors (Kamin, 1974; Rosenthal and Jacobson, 1968), whereas others stress hereditary determinants (Jensen, 1969, 1972; Munsinger, 1975). Even though this debate is far from resolved, there have been guidelines established by the Equal Employment Opportunity Commission (EEOC; 1970) for the use of psychological tests with minority groups in educational and industrial settings. The basic premise is that a screening device (psychological test) can have an adverse impact if it screens out a proportionally larger number of minorities than nonminorities. Furthermore, it is the responsibility of the employer to demonstrate that the procedure produces valid inferences for the specific purposes for which the employer would like to use it. If an industrial or educational organization does not follow the guidelines as defined by the EEOC (1970), then the Office of Federal Contract Compliance has the direct power to cancel any government contract that the institution might have.

Of significance to the legal issues, research data, and guidelines for the individual clinician is the degree of validity contained within the tests. If investigated from the perspective of content validity, it appears on the surface that tests such as the Stanford-Binet are culturally biased. This is based on observations that children from inner-city regions usually do not have the opportunity to learn many of the test items (Kagan, Mass, and Siegel, 1963; Lesser, Fifer, and Clark, 1965). Thus, their lower scores may represent not a lack of intelligence but merely a lack of familiarity with the white, middle-class culture. Critics of the tests point out that it would clearly be unfair to assess a white person's intelligence based on whether he knows what the "funky chicken" is or what "blood" means, or for that matter, to ask him the meaning of British terms such as "shilling" or "lorry." Low scores would simply measure an individual's relative unfamiliarity with a specific culture rather than his specific mental strengths. A biased test, then, is one which does not reveal the test taker's strengths. If one uses this reasoning, many I.Q. and aptitude tests may appear to be culturally biased. However, studies in which researchers have, to the best of their ability, eliminated biased test items or items that statistically discriminate between minorities and nonminorities have not been successful in altering overall test scores. A representative study was one in which 27 items were removed from the Scholastic Aptitude Test (SAT) which consistently discriminated minorities from nonminorities. However, this did little to change either the test taker's individual scores or the differences between the two groups (Flaugher and Schrader, 1978). Thus, the popular belief, based on a superficial appraisal of many psychological tests, that biased items are responsible for test differences does not appear to be supported by research.

Another consideration is the adequacy of the predictive validity of various tests when used with minority groups. It has been demonstrated that blacks score a full standard deviation (15 points) lower in most I.Q. tests than whites and also score significantly lower on the SAT. Since one of the main purposes of these tests is to predict later performance, it is essential to evaluate the extent to which the scores in fact adequately predict areas such as a black person's performance in college. A representative group of studies indicates that the SAT predicts that minorities will perform better than they actually do in college

(Cleary, 1968; Kallingal, 1971; Pfeifer and Sedlacek, 1971; Tomp, 1971). Thus, the SAT in fact overpredicts the level of performance for blacks. Furthermore, both the WISC and the WISC-R are equally effective in predicting the academic achievement of blacks and whites (Reynolds and Hartlage, 1979). However, in actually working with minority groups, it is essential to become familiar with different subgroup norms and know the confidence with which predictions can be made based on their scores.

This discussion of content and predictive validity represents the traditional defenses of psychological tests. For many individuals, these defenses are still not sufficient (Garcia, 1981). The two main choices then are either to outlaw all psychological tests for minority groups or to develop psychological assessment approaches which will be more appropriate for minorities. A half-serious attempt towards a more appropriate measuring device is the Dove Counterbalance General Intelligence Test (Dove, 1968). It has since become referred to as the "Chitling Test" and includes items relevant for a black inner-city culture such as "a 'handkerchief head' is: (a) a cool cat, (b) a porter, (c) an Uncle Tom, (d) a haddi, (e) a preacher." A similar attempt was made by Williams (1974) in his development of the Black Intelligence Test of Cultural Homogeneity (BITCH). Although neither test has been standardized and validated, both contain vocabulary words and experiences with which most black children would be familiar but white children would be unfamiliar.

The rationale for the development of the BITCH is that the traditional I.Q. concept is still a form of racism under a scientific guise since the dominant culture continues to judge what is considered successful or "intelligent" behavior. Williams (1974) believes that a more appropriate and useful approach is what he refers to as a survival quotient (S.Q.), which would measure an individual's ability to cope in his particular environment. However, neither the "Chitling Test" nor the BITCH has been validated against any clearly defined criteria for "survivability." As such, they can be considered to test not intelligence or even survival ability, but rather the degree of familiarity an individual has with a particular environment (Cronbach, 1978).

The System of Multicultural Pluralistic Assessment (SOMPA) (Mercer, 1979) is an alternative and more complex method of evaluating minorities by using traditional assessment tools but correcting the bias involved with these tools. The assumption underlying this approach is that all cultural groups have the same average potential and any adequate assessment device should be able to accurately test this potential for a particular individual. One of its primary goals is to differentiate members of minorities who have been incorrectly labeled mentally retarded because of test bias from those who are in fact mentally retarded. The SOMPA method involves medical, social system, and pluralistic components. The "medical component" assesses whether or not students have any physical disorders which may be interfering with their level of performance. This includes tests of hearing, vision, and motor function. The rationale for the medically oriented assessment is that children from lower income groups are both more likely to have medical difficulties because of their harsher environment and less likely to obtain treatment for these difficulties because of financial constraints. The "social system" component uses traditional assessment tools such as the WISC-R to measure whether the student is functioning at a level consistent with social norms. The problem with this component is that it provides a narrow definition of successful functioning because the criteria are based on the dominant culture's definition of success (Reschly, 1981). Thus, the final "pluralistic" component attempts to correct for the narrow approach in the social system component by evaluating an individual's test scores against a culturally similar group, thereby — it is hoped — adjusting for such variables as socioeconomic status and cultural background. Thus, comparisons are made between performances within a specific subgroup, rather with the performance, values, and criteria of the dominant culture. The resulting adjusted scores are referred to as an individual's Estimated Learning Potentials.

There have been many critics of SOMPA (Johnson and Danley, 1981), most of whom argue that the criterion for judging it should be the adequacy with which it can predict school performance (Brown, 1979). Studies indicate that whereas WISC-R scores correlate at a level of .60 with grade point average, SOMPA scores have a correlation of only .40. Mercer refutes this criticism by pointing out that her intent was not so much to predict school performance as to identify students who had been falsely classified as mentally retarded. Its proponents have been persuasive enough so that SOMPA has been adopted by several states. The effect of SOMPA will hopefully be a more accurate labeling of mentally retarded students. However, students who are now labeled "normal" through the SOMPA approach, but were previously labeled "mentally retarded," might still require some additional form of special instruction. Even though the labeling process may be more accurate, it remains to be seen whether or not the individual needs of the student will be more accurately addressed.

What should be obvious from this discussion is that the problems are both complicated and far from being resolved. Several general solutions have been suggested; these include improving selection devices, developing different evaluation criteria, and changing the social environment. Improving the use of selection devices would involve paying continual attention to, and obtaining greater knowledge of, the meaning of different scores for different subgroups. This includes tailoring specific test scores to the types of decisions individuals may make in their lives. For example, blacks typically score equal to whites on the verbal portion of the SAT, but their average scores on math are lower. This suggests that black students have a greater development in their verbal skills than in their quantitative ones. This is further reflected by, and consistent with, the fact that blacks are more likely to chose verbally oriented majors in college. Based on this, it may be more accurate to predict the future college performance of blacks from their SAT verbal scores than from their math scores.

Another approach towards solving the problem of test bias is to develop different and more adequate criterion measures. For example, it has been found that WISC-R scores correlate highly with teacher classroom ratings for nonminorities but not for minorities (Goldman and Hartig, 1976). This indicates that using teacher classroom ratings as a criterion of academic achievement is not appropriate for minorities. In contrast, the WISC-R accurately predicts grade point average for both minorities and nonminorities, which suggests that grade point average is therefore a better criterion measure. Perhaps of greater relevance is the actual prediction of an individual's career performance. Current test predictors for graduate school (LSAT, MCAT) give generally satisfactory predictions for later academic performance, but they do not predict whether an individual will be a good attorney or physician. In fact, it has been shown that medical school grades themselves are not associated with later success as a physician (Loughmiller, Ellison, Taylor, and Price, 1970). This issue may become particularly pronounced in comparing the relative effectiveness of minorities and nonminorities when working in different cultural settings. For example, if a white and a Chicano attorney are both placed in settings in which they will be working with Chicanos, it is probable that the Chicano attorney would be more effective because of his increased rapport with, and familiarity with the language and values of, his clientele.

Another solution involves changing the social environment. Part of the rationale for emphasizing this approach is the belief held by many that the differences in test scores between minorities and nonminorities are not due to test bias but rather that the tests accurately reflect the effects of an unequal environment and unequal opportunities (Flaugher, 1978; Green, 1978). Even though different minority norms and additional predictive studies on minority populations are often necessary for effective interpretation of scores, the literature suggests that tests are not as biased as they have been accused of being. For example, removal of biased or discriminating SAT items still results in the same average scores, the WISC-R provides accurate predictions of grade point average for both minorities and nonminorities, and the SAT even overpredicts the college performance of black students. However, changing an individual's environment can increase his skills as measured by current tests of aptitude, I.Q., and achievement. Whereas improving selection devices and developing different criterion measures are important, future efforts should also stress more equal access to educational opportunities.

All of these solutions can give some direction to the profession in general, but it is the responsibility of individual clinicians to keep abreast of research relating to minority groups and to incorporate this knowledge into the interpretations they make of test scores. As Mercer (1979) has emphasized, test scores are neither valid nor invalid, but inferences by clinicians based on these scores are.

Examiner Qualifications

In order to administer and interpret psychological tests, an examiner must be properly trained. This generally includes an adequate amount of graduate course work combined with a long period of supervised experience. Intensive training is particularly important for individually administered I.Q. tests and the majority of personality tests. Students who are taking or administering tests as part of a class requirement are not adequately trained to administer and interpret tests. Thus, test results obtained by students have questionable validity, and they should clearly inform their subjects that the purpose of their testing is for training purposes only.

In addition to the general guidelines presented, there are specific skills which examiners should also acquire. These include the ability to evaluate the technical strengths and limitations of a test, the selection of appropriate tests, and a knowledge of issues relating to the test's reliability and validity. In addition to familiarity with the material in the test manual, examiners should also be aware of relevant research both on the variable the test is measuring and on the status of the test since its publication. This is particularly important with regard to newly developed subgroup norms and possible changes in the meaning of scales as a result of further research. Once examiners evaluate the test itself, they must also be able to evaluate whether the purpose and context for which they would like to use it are appropriate. Sometimes an otherwise valid test can be used for purposes that it was not intended for, resulting in either invalid or useless inferences based on the test data. Examiners must also be continually aware of, and sensitive to, conditions affecting the examinee's performance. These may include expectations on the part of the examiner, minor variations from the standardized instructions, degree of rapport, mood of the examinee, or timing of the test administration in relation to an examinee's life changes. In order to help develop accurate conclusions, examiners should have a general knowledge of human behavior. Areas which are particularly relevant are personality theory, abnormal psychology, and the psychology of adjustment. Furthermore, interpretations should only be made after evaluating other relevant information beyond the mere test scores. A final consideration is that if interns or technicians are administering the tests, then an adequately trained psychologist should be available as a consultant or supervisor.

Communicating Test Results

The knowledge areas just discussed refer primarily to the test or test situation itself. However, no matter how accurate the collection and interpretation of data are, they will be meaningless unless the results can be communicated effectively. This involves understanding the needs and vocabulary of the referral source, client, and other persons who may be affected by the test results such as parents or teachers. Initially, there should be a clear exploration of the rationale for testing and the nature of the tests being administered. This may include the general type of conclusions that will be drawn, the limitations of the test, and common misconceptions surrounding the test or test variable. If a child is being tested in an educational setting, then a meeting should be arranged with the school psychologist, parents, teacher, and other relevant persons. Such an approach is crucial for I.Q. tests, which are more likely to be misinterpreted than achievement tests. Feedback of test results should be given in terms that are clear and understandable to the receiver. Descriptions are generally most meaningful when performance levels are clearly indicated along with behavioral references. For example, in giving I.Q. results to parents, it will be only minimally relevant to say that their child has an I.Q. of 130 with relative strengths in spatial organization, even though this may be appropriate language for a formal psychological evaluation. A more effective description might be that their child is currently functioning in the top 2% when compared with his peers and is particularly good when organizing nonverbal material, for example, piecing together puzzles, putting together a bicycle, or building a playhouse. In providing effective feedback, the examiner should also consider the personal characteristics of the receiver, such as his or her general educational level, relative knowledge regarding psychological testing, and possible emotional response to the information. The emotional reaction is especially important when a client is learning about his personal strengths and shortcomings. Facilities should be available for additional counseling if needed. Since psychological assessment is often requested as an aid in making important life decisions, the potential impact of the information should not be underestimated. Clinicians are usually in positions of power, and with that power goes responsibility since the information that the clients receive and the decisions that they make based on this information will often be with them for many years.

Unwarranted Applications

One of the more frequent misuses of psychological tests occurs when an otherwise valid test is used for purposes for which it was not intended. Ordinarily such misuses are done in good faith and with good intentions. For example, an examiner might use a TAT or Rorschach as the sole means of inferring an individual's I.Q. Similarly, the MMPI, which was designed to assess the extent of psychopathology in an individual, is often inappropriately used to assess a normal person's level of functioning. Although some conclusions can be drawn from the MMPI relating to certain aspects of a normal person's functioning or I.Q. estimates based on projectives can be made, they should be extremely tentative since the tests were not designed for these purposes and, as a result, such inferences do not represent their strong points. A somewhat more serious misuse can occur when a test such as the MMPI is used to screen applicants for personnel selection. Results from MMPI type tests are likely to be irrelevant for assessing most job-related skills. Of equal importance is the fact that the type of information derived from the MMPI is typically of a highly personal nature and, if used in personnel selection, is likely to represent an inappropriate invasion of privacy.

Invasion of Privacy

One of the main difficulties which examinees can encounter in relation to psychological tests is that the examiner might discover facts which the client would rather keep secret. There is also concern that this information may be used in ways which are not in the best interests of the client. The Office of Science and Technology (1967), in a report entitled *Privacy and Behavioral Research,* has defined privacy as "the right of the individual to decide for himself how much he will share with others his thoughts, his feelings, and the facts of his personal life" (p. 2). This right is considered to be "essential to insure dignity and freedom of self determination" (p. 2). The issue of invasion of privacy usually becomes most controversial with personality tests since items relating to motivational, emotional, and attitudinal traits are sometimes disguised. Thus, persons may unknowingly reveal characteristics about themselves which they would rather keep private.

Public concern over this issue culminated in an investigation by the Senate Subcommittee on Constitutional Rights and the House Subcommittee on Invasion of Privacy. Neither of these investigations found evidence of deliberate or widespread misuse of psychological tests (Brayfield, 1965). Dahlstrom (1969) has argued that public concern over the invasion of privacy is based on two basic misconceptions relating to tests. The first is that tests have been oversold to the public, with a resulting exaggeration of their scope and accuracy. The public is usually not aware of the limitations of test data and may often feel that tests are more capable of discovering hidden information than they actually are. The second misconception is that obtaining information about persons which they either are unaware of themselves, or would rather keep private, is not necessarily wrong or evil. The more important issue is the use to which the information will be put. Furthermore, the person who controls where or how this information will be used is generally the client. The ethical code of the APA (1981) specifically states that information derived from any source by a psychologist can be released only with the permission of the client. Although there may be ethical dilemmas arising between minors and parents, or when clients are a danger to themselves or others, the ability to control the information is usually clearly defined as being held by the client. Thus, the public often underestimates the power they have as clients in determining how the test data will be used.

Despite ethical guidelines relating to testing, there are sometimes dilemmas which arise. For example, during personnel selection, applicants may feel pressured into revealing personal information on tests because they want a certain position. Also applicants may unknowingly reveal information because of subtle, nonobvious test questions, and perhaps more important, they have no control over the inferences which examiners will make in relation to the test data. Lovell (1967), in referring to the function of tests in personnel selection, argues that they are unacceptable based on ethical, scientific, and community service reasons. He states that ethically they often have no place in a free society, scientifically they do not have adequate validity for specific institutional settings, and in the long run, they do not serve the public's best interests. For routine personnel selection, these objections to testing may have some relevance. However, if a position requires careful screening and serious negative consequences may result from poor selection, then it is necessary to evaluate an individual as closely as possible. Thus, the use of testing for personnel in the police, delicate military positions, or important public duty overseas may be warranted. A complete discussion of the restrictions for tests used in personnel selection can be found in the "Guidelines on Employee Selection Procedures" established by the Equal Employment Opportunity Commission (1970).

Usually, in a clinical setting, obtaining personal information regarding clients does not present problems. The agreement that the information will be used to help clients develop new insights and change their behavior is generally clear and straightforward. However, should legal difficulties arise relating to areas such as child abuse, involuntary confinement, or situations in which clients may be a danger to themselves or others, then ethical dilemmas often arise. Usually there are general guidelines regarding the manner and extent to which information should be disclosed. These are included in the APA's *Ethical Principles of Psychologists* (1981), and test users are encouraged to familiarize themselves with these guidelines.

Adequate handling of the issue of an individual's right to privacy involves both a clear explanation of the relevance of the testing and obtaining informed consent. Examiners should always have a clear conception of the specific reasons why the tests are given. Thus, if personnel are being selected based on their mechanical abilities, then tests measuring such areas as general maladjustment should not be administered. Examiners must continually evaluate (1) whether or not a test or series of tests is valid for a particular purpose, and (2) whether each set of scores has been properly interpreted in relation to a particular context. Furthermore, the general rationale for test selection should be provided in clear, straightforward language that can be understood by the client. Informed consent involves communicating not only the rationale for testing but also the kinds of data obtained and the possible uses of these data. This does not mean showing the client the specific test subscales or items beforehand, but rather describing in a general way the nature and intent of the test. For example, if a client is told that a scale measures "sociability," this foreknowledge might alter the test's validity in that the client may answer the questions based on popular, but often erroneous, stereotypes. If the test format and intent are introduced in a simple, respectful, and forthright manner, the chance that the client will perceive the testing situation as an invasion of privacy will be significantly reduced. This explanation should include a clear statement of the relevance, intent, and nature of the testing, and should inform the client of his rights to confidentiality and to information regarding the test results.

Inviolacy

Whereas invasion of privacy refers to concerns related to discovering and misusing information which clients would rather keep secret, inviolacy involves the actual negative feelings created when clients are confronted with the test. Inviolacy is particularly relevant when clients are requested to discuss information which they would rather not think about. For example, the MMPI contains questions on many ordinarily taboo topics relating to sexual practices, toilet behavior, bodily functions, and personal beliefs about human nature. This may produce anxiety by making the examinees more aware of deviant thoughts or repressed, unpleasant memories. Many individuals obtain a certain degree of security and comfort by staying within familiar realms of thought. Even to be asked questions which may indicate that there are unusual alternatives can serve as an anxiety provoking challenge to their existing rules and norms. This problem is somewhat related to the issue of invasion of privacy; it too requires one-to-one sensitivity, as well as providing clear and accurate information about the assessment procedure.

Labeling and Restriction of Freedom

When individuals are given a medical diagnosis for physical ailments, there are rarely negative consequences attached to the label. In contrast to this are the potentially damaging consequences of many psychiatric diagnoses. One of the main dangers is the possibility of a self-fulfilling prophecy based on the expected role associated with a specific label. As Rosenthal (1966) has demonstrated, many of these expectations are communicated nonverbally and also beyond our immediate awareness. Other self-fulfilling prophecies may be less subtle, for example, the person who is labeled as a chronic schizophrenic; is not given treatment because chronic schizophrenics, by definition, do not improve; and therefore, does not improve perhaps mainly because he has not received treatment. Another negative consequence of labeling is the social stigma attached to different disorders. Thus, due largely to the public's misconceptions of such terms as schizophrenia, labeled individuals may be socially avoided.

Just as labels imposed by others can have negative consequences, self-acceptance of labels can likewise be detrimental. Thus, clients may use their label as a means of providing an excuse and denying responsibility for their behavior. This is congruent with the medical model which usually assumes that a "sick" person is the helpless victim of an invading disorder. Thus, in our society, "sick" persons are not considered to be responsible for their disorders. However, the acceptance of this model for behavioral problems may have the effect of perpetuating behavioral disorders because persons see themselves as being helpless, passive victims (Szasz, 1965). This sense of helplessness may serve to lower their ability to deal effectively with new stress. In contrast to this is the belief that what clients require in order to effectively change their behavior is an increased sense of responsibility for their lives and actions.

A final difficulty associated with labeling is that it may unnecessarily impose limits on either an individual or a system by restricting progress and creativity. For example, an organization may conduct a study to determine the type of person who has been successful at a particular type of job and may then develop future selection criteria based on this study. This can result in the future selection of a relatively homogeneous type of employee, which could prevent the organization from changing and progressing. There may be a narrowing of the "talent pool," in which people with new and different ideas are never given a chance. In other words, what has been labeled as adaptive in the past may not be adaptive in the future. One alternative to this predicament is to look at future trends and develop selection criteria based on these trends. Furthermore, diversity might be incorporated into an organization so that different but compatible types can be selected to work on similar projects. In approaching labels, then, clinicians should be sensitive to the potential negative impact resulting from labeling by outside sources or self-labeling, as well as to the possible limiting effects that labeling may have.

PHASES IN CLINICAL ASSESSMENT

An outline of the phases of clinical assessment can provide both a conceptual framework for approaching an evaluation and a summary of some of the points already discussed. Although the steps in assessment will be isolated for conceptual convenience, in actuality they often occur simultaneously and interact with one another. There is an emphasis throughout these phases on a clinician's fulfilling the role of an integrator of data and an expert on human behavior rather than merely an interpreter of test scores. This is consistent with the belief that a psychological assessment can be most useful when it addresses specific individual problems and provides guidelines for decision making regarding these problems.

Clarification of the Problem

Many of the practical limitations of psychological evaluations are due to an inadequate clarification of the problem. Since clinicians are aware of the assets and limitations of psychological tests and since they are responsible for providing useful information, it is their duty to clarify the nature of the requests which are made of them. Furthermore, it cannot be expected that initial requests for an evaluation will be adequately stated. Clinicians may have to ferret out hidden agendas, unspoken expectations, and complex interpersonal relationships, as well as to explain the specific limitations of psychological tests. One of the most important general requirements is that they have an understanding of the vocabulary, conceptual model, dynamics, and expectations of the referral setting in which they will be working.

Acquiring Knowledge Relating to the Content of the Problem

Before beginning the actual testing procedure, examiners should carefully consider the nature of the problem, the adequacy of the test they will be using, and the specific applicability of that test to an individual's unique situation. This may require referring both to the test manual and to additional outside sources. Clinicians should clearly be aware of operational definitions for such problems as anxiety disorders, psychoses, personality disorders, or organic impairment so that they can be continually alerted to their possible expression during the assessment procedure. Competence in merely administering and scoring the tests is not sufficient to conduct effective assessments. For example, being able to develop an I.Q. score does not necessarily indicate that an examiner is aware of differing cultural expressions of intelligence or of the limitations of the assessment device. It is essential that clinicians have in-depth knowledge regarding the variables they are measuring or else the results of the evaluations are likely to be extremely limited.

Related to this is the relative adequacy of the test in measuring the variable being considered. This includes evaluating certain practical considerations, the standardization sample, and reliability and validity as outlined in Table 1-1. It is important that the examiner also consider the nature of the problem in relation to the adequacy of the test and decide whether he can appropriately use a specific test or tests on an individual or group of individuals. This involves knowledge relating to such areas as the client's age, race, educational background, motivation for testing, anticipated level of resistance, social environment, and interpersonal relationships.

Data Collection

After the referral question has been clarified and knowledge relating to the problem has been obtained, then clinicians can proceed with the actual collecting of information. This may come from a wide variety of sources, the most frequent of which are test scores, personal history (case study), and interview data including noteworthy behavioral observations. Clinicians may also wish to obtain school records, previous psychological evaluations, or police reports, or to discuss the client with parents or teachers. It is important to realize that the tests themselves are merely one tool or one source for obtaining data. The case history is of equal importance since it serves to provide a context for understanding the client's current problems and, through this understanding, renders the test scores meaningful. In many cases, a client's history is of even more significance in making predictions and in assessing the seriousness of his current condition than his test scores. For example, a high score for depression on the MMPI is not as helpful in assessing suicidal risk as are historical factors like the number of previous attempts, age, sex, details regarding any previous attempts, and length of depression. Of equal importance is the fact that test scores in and of themselves will usually not be sufficient to answer the referral question. For specific problem solving and decision making, clinicians must rely on multiple sources and, using these sources, check to assess the consistency of the observations they make.

Interpreting the Data

The end product of assessment should be a description of the client's present level of functioning, considerations relating to etiology, prognosis, and treatment recommendations (Woody, 1969). Etiological descriptions should avoid simplistic formulas and focus on the influence exerted by several interacting factors. These factors can be divided into primary, predisposing, precipitating, and reinforcing causes (Coleman, 1980), and a complete description of etiology should take all of these into account. Further elaborations may also attempt to assess the person from a systems perspective in which patterns of interaction, mutual two-way influences, and the specifics of circular information feedback are evaluated. These considerations indicate that the description of a client should not be a mere labeling or classification but rather should provide a deeper and more accurate understanding of the person. This understanding should allow the examiner to perceive new facets of the person in terms of both his internal experience and his relationships with others.

In order to develop these descriptions, clinicians must make inferences from their test data. Although these data are objective and empirical, the process of developing hypotheses, obtaining support for these hypotheses, and integrating the conclusions is dependent on the experience and training of the clinician. This process generally follows a sequence of developing impressions, identifying relevant facts, making inferences, and supporting these inferences with relevant and consistent data. Maloney and Ward (1976) have developed a seven-phase approach (Figure 1-1) towards evaluating data. They note that in actual practice

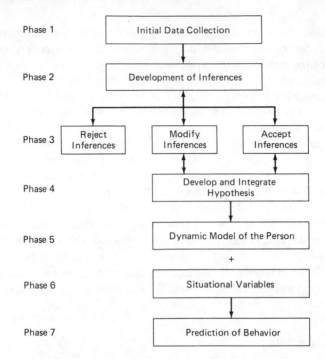

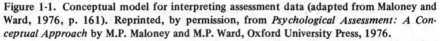

Figure 1-1. Conceptual model for interpreting assessment data (adapted from Maloney and Ward, 1976, p. 161). Reprinted, by permission, from *Psychological Assessment: A Conceptual Approach* by M.P. Maloney and M.P. Ward, Oxford University Press, 1976.

these phases are not as clearly defined as indicated in Figure 1-1. Oftentimes they may occur simultaneously. For example, when a clinician reads a referral question or initially observes a client, he is already developing hypotheses about that person and checking to assess the validity of these observations.

Phase 1.   The first phase involves collecting data about the client. It begins with the referral question and is followed by a review of the client's previous history and records. Already at this point the clinician is beginning to develop tentative hypotheses and to clarify questions he would like to investigate in more detail. The next step is actual client contact in which the clinician conducts an interview and administers a variety of psychological tests. The client's behavior during the interview, as well as the content or factual data, are noted. It is out of this data that the clinician begins to make his inferences.

Phase 2.   Phase 2 focuses on the development of a wide variety of inferences about the client. These inferences serve both a summary and an explanatory function. For example, an examiner may infer that a client is depressed which also serves the purpose of explaining his slow performance, distractibility, flattened affect, and withdrawn behavior. The examiner may then wish to evaluate whether this depression is a deeply engrained trait or more a reaction to a current situational difficulty. This may be determined by referring to test scores, interview data, or any additional sources of available information. The emphasis in the second phase is on developing multiple inferences which should initially be tentative. They serve the purpose of guiding future investigation so as to obtain additional information which is then used to confirm, modify, or negate later hypotheses.

Phase 3. Since the third phase is concerned with either accepting or rejecting the inferences developed in phase 2, there is a constant and active interaction between these phases. Often, in investigating the validity of an inference, a clinician will alter either the meaning or the emphasis of an inference, or will develop entirely new ones. It is rare that an inference will be entirely proved, but rather the validity of that inference can become progressively strengthened. This is achieved by evaluating the degree of consistency and the strength of data which support a particular inference. For example, the inference that a client is anxious may be supported in WAIS-R subscales, MMPI scores, and behavioral observations, or it may only be suggested by one of these sources. The amount of evidence to support an inference directly affects the amount of confidence which a clinician can place in this inference.

Phase 4. As a result of the inferences developed in the previous three phases, the clinician can move in phase 4 from specific inferences to general statements about the client. This involves an elaboration of each inference in order to describe trends or patterns of the client. For example, the inference that a client is depressed may be due to cognitive self-verbalizations in which the client continually criticizes and judges his behavior. This may also be expanded to give information regarding the ease or frequency with which a person might enter the depressive state. The central task in phase 4 is to develop and begin to elaborate on statements relating to the client.

Phases 5, 6, and 7. The fifth phase involves a further elaboration of a wide variety of the personality traits of the individual. It represents an integration and correlation of the client's characteristics. This may include describing and discussing such factors as need for achievement, dynamics involved in depression, level of anxiety, conflicting needs, intellectual potential, problem solving style, and relative level of social skills. Although phase 4 and 5 are similar, phase 5 provides a general and integrated description of the person which is more comprehensive than phase 4. Finally, phase 6 places this comprehensive description of the person into a situational context and phase 7 makes specific predictions regarding his behavior. Phase 7 is the most crucial element involved in decision making and requires that the clinician take into account the interaction between personal and situational variables.

Establishing the validity of these inferences presents a difficult challenge for clinicians since, unlike medical diagnoses, psychological inferences cannot be physically documented. Furthermore, clinicians are rarely confronted with feedback regarding the validity of their inferences. Despite these difficulties, psychological descriptions should strive to meet the following four basic criteria: reliability, adequate descriptive breadth, descriptive validity, and predictive validity (Blashfield and Draguns, 1976). Reliability of descriptions refers to whether or not the description or classification can be replicated by other clinicians (interdiagnostician agreement) as well as by the same clinician on different occasions (intradiagnostician agreement). The next criterion is the breadth of coverage encompassed in the classification. In other words, any classification should be broad enough to encompass a wide range of individuals and yet specific enough to provide useful information regarding the individual being evaluated. Descriptive validity involves the degree to which individuals who are classified are similar on variables external to the classification system. For example, are individuals who have similar MMPI profiles also similar on other relevant attributes such as family history, demographic variables, legal difficulties, or alcohol abuse? Finally, predictive validity refers to the confidence with which test inferences can be used to evaluate future outcomes. These may include academic achievement, job performance, or the outcome of treatment. This is one of the most crucial functions of testing. Unless inferences can be made which effectively enhance decision making, the scope and relevance of testing are significantly reduced. Although these criteria are difficult to achieve and to evaluate accurately, they represent an ideal standard for which assessments should strive.

RECOMMENDED READING

Kaplan, R.M. and Sacuzzo, D.P. *Psychological Testing: Principles, Applications, and Issues.* Belmont: Wadsworth, 1982.
Levine, D. Why and when to test: the social context of psychological testing. In Rabin, A.i. (Ed.) *Assessment with Projective Techniques.* New York: Springer Publishing Co., 1981.
Maloney, M.P. and Ward, M.P. *Psychological Assessment: A Conceptual Approach.* New York: Oxford University Press, 1976.

2
The Wechsler Intelligence
Scales

The Wechsler Adult Intelligence Scale — Revised (WAIS-R) and the Wechsler Intelligence Scale for Children — Revised (WISC-R) are individually administered, composite intelligence tests in a battery format. They assess different areas of intellectual abilities and offer a format in which personality functioning can be observed. Both the WAIS-R and the WISC-R provide three different I.Q. scores: an overall or Full Scale I.Q., a Verbal I.Q., and a Performance I.Q. The WAIS-R Verbal I.Q. and Performance I.Q. are derived from averaged scores on 11 subtests: 6 are verbal and primarily measure an intellectual, memory factor; 5 are performance and measure visual-spatial abilities. The WISC-R has essentially the same subtests as the WAIS-R except that the content of the items is designed for children and there is an optional performance subtest (Mazes), which brings the WISC-R subtests to a total of 12. Although the Wechsler intelligence scales have a number of limitations, they have become some of the most frequently used tests in the field of psychology and have proved to be reliable and useful tools.

THE NATURE OF INTELLIGENCE

Developing an accurate definition for the term "intelligence" is difficult. Intelligence is an abstract concept and has no actual basis in concrete, objective, and measurable reality. It is a general label for a group of processes which are inferred from more observable behaviors and responses. For example, it is possible to observe problem solving techniques and to measure the results of these techniques objectively, but the intelligence assumed to produce these techniques cannot be observed or measured directly. Thus, the concept of intelligence is somewhat like the term "force" in physics: we know it by its effects, yet its presence must be inferred. Both "intelligence" and "force," however, provide terms which allow us to approach, discuss, and generalize certain types of objective events.

One of the first attempts at defining intelligence was made by Binet (in Sattler, 1982) who stressed that it is the tendency to take and maintain a definite direction; the capacity to make adaptations for the purpose of attaining a desired end; and the power of autocriticism. (p. 37)

Some additional, representative definitions of intelligence are:

... the ability to undertake activities that are characterized by (1) difficulty, (2) complexity, (3) abstractness, (4) economy, (5) adaptiveness to a goal, (6) social value, (7) the emergence of originals, and to maintain such activities under conditions that demand a concentration of energy and a resistance to emotional forces. (Stoddard, 1943; as quoted in Sattler, 1982, p. 37)

... adjustment or adaptation of the individual to his total environment, or limited aspects thereof ... the capacity to reorganize one's behavior patterns so as to act more effectively and more appropriately in novel situations ... the ability to learn ... the extent to which a person is educable ... the ability to carry on abstract thinking ... the effective use of concepts and symbols in dealing with ... a problem to be solved. (Freeman, 1955; as quoted in Sattler, 1982, p. 37)

One of the most frequently used definitions of intelligence was developed by Wechsler in 1958. He considers intelligence to be a global concept which involves an individual's ability to act purposefully, think rationally, and deal effectively with the environment. He further emphasizes that "general intelligence cannot be equated with intellectual ability, however broadly defined, but must be regarded as a manifestation of the personality as a whole" (in Matarazzo, 1972, p. 79). Thus, for Wechsler, intelligence can be social, practical, or abstract, but it cannot be measured or even considered independently from certain nonintellectual aspects of functioning such as persistence, drive, interests, or need for achievement.

A review of these definitions reveals that they all imply, include, or elaborate on the following five areas:

1. Abstract thinking
2. Learning from experience
3. Solving problems through insight
4. Adjusting to new situations
5. Focusing and sustaining one's abilities in order to achieve a desired goal

The practical significance of specifying the different components involved in intelligence is that it allows clinicians to fully appreciate the complexity of what they are attempting to evaluate. Such an appreciation should allow them to estimate more adequately which aspects of a client's intelligence have been measured and which have not. It should also help them evaluate the assets and limitations involved in using a specific test by contrasting the test items with the theoretical nature of intelligence. For example, an "intelligence" test which emphasizes verbal abilities will be limited in that it will not give an assessment of areas such as nonverbal problem solving or adjusting to new situations.

Maloney and Ward (1976) have discussed four general approaches to understanding the nature of intelligence. These are: (1) learning theory, (2) neurological-biological approaches, (3) psychometric theories, and (4) developmental theories. Each of these approaches has a certain degree of overlap with the others, and they vary in terms of their relative importance. Whereas the first two are interesting from a theoretical perspective, the last two have had more impact on the field and have been more thoroughly researched.

Learning Theory

The basic core of learning theorists' approaches to intelligence is their emphasis on understanding the general laws by which individuals acquire new behaviors. Their concern is with observable behaviors rather than understanding any inner construct of intelligence. This can be contrasted with the usual view of intelligence in which it is conceptualized as being an internal structure or trait which a person somehow "possesses." Learning theory looks at an individual's response to specific situations and the laws underlying how that person adapts to these situations. For these theorists, then, "intelligent" behavior can be translated as behavior in which the learning process occurs at a high level of functioning and in response to specific external demands. This involves an interaction between the person and his environment in which intelligence is judged by the relative appropriateness of the behavior as compared to some outside criteria.

A representative example of a learning theory of intelligence has been developed by Staats (1970) who says that each person inherits a similar biological structure which will, under the proper circumstances, allow him to develop desirable behaviors according to the laws of learning. With the exception of neurological impairments, individuals have an equal amount of potential to learn at birth, and later individual differences in ability can be attributed to different learning experiences. Thus, each person is born with an equal amount of potential. Staats does concede that individuals may have some biological differences in such areas as speed of neural impulses and sensory acuity, but he downplays these in favor of the relative effects of learning and experience. This approach is primarily based on a stimulus-response model in which each person enters a situation differently according to his past conditioning. There is also an organismic variable which mediates between the stimulus and the response, and can be summarized as including a person's "basic behavioral repertoires." These behavioral repertoires are learned, but they also determine our approach to, and the extent to which we can learn from, new situations. The extent and the quality of these behaviors are roughly equivalent to a person's intelligence. It is important to stress that for most learning theorists, intelligence is not by any means a trait but rather the quality of a person's previous learning. The learning circumstances themselves determine the quality and extent of an individual's behavioral repertoires and, therefore, one's relative "intelligence."

Neurological-Biological Approaches

All four of the general approaches to understanding intelligence assume that there is an underlying neurological substrate on which intelligence is ultimately dependent. It is therefore important to somehow conceptualize and search for the neuroanatomical and neurophysiological processes underlying the behaviors which are referred to as intelligent. The general approach then is fairly straightforward. Researchers should look for the basic anatomical, electrochemical, or physiological correlates of intelligence. The most simplistic approach might be to study the relationship between brain size and measurements of intelligence, which have indicated that there is only a small positive correlation. This type of theorizing has been the general trend, but it has been conducted in a far more complex and theoretical manner.

Halstead (1961) for example, has proposed a theory of biological intelligence. He believes that there are a number of brain functions relating to intelligence which are relatively independent of cultural considerations. They are biologically based and pertain to the brain functions of all individuals. The four factors he delineates (in Bolls, 1981) are central integrative (C), abstraction (A), power (P), and directional (D). These are summarized as follows:

1. The *central integrative* (C) factor involves one's ability to organize experience. A person's background of familiar experiences and past learning works with and integrates new incoming experiences; its main purpose is adaptive.
2. The *abstraction* (A) factor is the ability to group things in different categories, and to perceive similarities and differences among objects, concepts, and events.
3. The *power* (P) factor refers to cerebral power — the undistorted strength of the brain. It involves the ability to suspend affect so that rationality and intellectual abilities can grow and develop.
4. The *directional* (D) factor provides direction or focus to a person's abilities; it specifies the manner in which intellect and behaviors will be expressed.

Two other contributors to biological approaches to intelligence are Cattell (1963) and Hebb (1972). Cattell's conceptualization of fluid (Gf) and crystallized (Cc) intelligence, and Hebb's A and B intelligence, are sufficiently similar so that they will be discussed together. Both Cattell and Hebb emphasize the existence of certain areas of intelligence that are directly tied to brain function. Hebb refers to this as intelligence A and stresses that it is innate and biological, requires an intact nervous system, relates to problem solving abilities, and cannot be measured by psychological tests. Cattell's fluid intelligence (Gf) is similar and enables a person to perceive relations, similarities, and parallels. It is dependent on the brain's efficiency and relative intactness, and is sensitive to the effects of brain damage. Furthermore, it is primarily nonverbal and culture free, and it can be measured by tests such as matrices (progressive matrices), figural analyses, and number/letter series. Fluid intelligence increases until around the age of 14, at which time it levels off until age 20 when it shows a gradual decline.

In addition to the more fluid, biologically based aspects of intelligence, Cattell and Hebb also refer to more environmentally determined, content-oriented dimensions. Hebb labels this "intelligence B," and indicates that it is based on experience and can be reflected in the extent of a person's accumulated knowledge. It is this dimension of intelligence which most intelligence tests measure. Cattell's term "crystallized" intelligence suggests that it is relatively permanent and generally less susceptible to the effects of brain damage. It is developed from the interaction between a person's innate fluid intelligence and such environmental factors as culture and education. Cattell states that it grows and develops until the age of 40, at which time it generally shows a slow decline. Representative tests that measure crystallized intelligence are those which relate to acquired skills and knowledge such as vocabulary and general information. However, Cattell differs from Hebb in that he believes both fluid and crystallized intelligence can be measured, whereas Hebb believes that psychometric tests cannot measure intelligence A.

Biological approaches to intelligence generally have serious methodological and theoretical difficulties. So far, no specific neurological substrates have been found which clearly relate to intelligence. Also, it is extremely difficult to actually separate the effects of learning and culture from a hypothesized underlying biological structure. However, other theories clearly depend on this underlying neurological structure. It is hoped that as the techniques of psychological measurement parallel the increases in our knowledge of neuroanatomy and neurophysiology, this approach will become more integrated and the actual links between intelligent brain-behavior relationships will become more adequately understood.

Psychometric Approaches

The psychometric approach assumes that intelligence is a construct or trait in which there are individual differences. However, the early psychometrists were concerned not so much with understanding the nature of intelligence as with the practical issues of correct classification and prediction. It was generally only after intelligence tests were constructed that theoreticians began to become curious as to exactly which constructs were being measured by these tests. Thus, it is important to understand that within the psychometric movement, there have characteristically been two directions: one practical, which was oriented towards solving problems, and another more conceptual and concerned with theory. The following summary focuses primarily on the development of theoretical concepts relating to the nature of intelligence. However, a pressing concern, which will be discussed later, is and has been whether or not I.Q. is a scientifically valid construct and whether intelligence tests actually measure intelligence as it is theoretically understood.

In 1904 Binet petitioned the French government for a grant for funds to develop a tool to differentiate students who were incapable of learning from those who had potential but were not achieving. His basic task was one of correct classification, and it was not necessary for him to develop a theoretical understanding of that which he sought to measure. His early scales (1905, 1908) were based on the premise that each individual possesses both a "chronological age" (C.A.) or actual age in years, and a "mental age" (M.A.), indicative of the average intellectual abilities present within a specific age group. After computing a student's mental age, a comparison could be made with his chronological age to determine his relative standing in relation to persons with similar chronological ages.

Binet was already an accomplished lawyer, playwright, psychologist, and hypnotist, and after creating his "intelligence" test, he became one of the world's first psychometrists. The development of his initial scales began with his selecting a large number of problems that, at face value, seemed to test a student's ability to benefit from instruction. Next, he tested these items with a random sample of students to determine which ones were "good" items and which ones were "poor." "Good" items were those for which, as the age of the student increased, the number of items answered correctly also increased. Thus, as the students within the sample became chronologically older, they were able to obtain progressively higher scores since they could answer more and more of the items correctly. "Poor" items, on the other hand, were comprised of questions which did not demonstrate a relationship between the number of correct answers and chronological age. For example, a poor item was a question which all the students, regardless of age, answered incorrectly or which, as the students grew older, fewer and fewer of them answered correctly. By compiling and organizing the good items, and discarding the poor ones, Binet was able to develop a test which ranked the questions by age so that the student's mental age could be determined. For example, at age 7 or 8, relatively few children can define the word "connection." At 10 years of age, 10% can, and at 13 years, 60% are able to do so correctly. Therefore, a student's ability to define "connection" indicates a mental ability comparable to that of the average 13 year old and would be one of several items reflecting a mental age of 13. The student's mental age can then be compared with his chronological age to determine the extent to which he is ahead of, equal to, or behind his age-related peers.

Binet's original scale, which was first used in 1905, has gone through numerous revisions — the most significant ones being at Stanford University in 1916, 1937, and 1960. One of the more important revisions was the reconceptualization of the intelligence quotient, or I.Q., by Terman in 1916. The problem with Binet's early I.Q. (the difference between M.A. and C.A.) was its differing meaning for various age groups. A one-year lag for a child of 3 has a totally different meaning from that for a child of 14. This is because the greatest absolute change in intelligence occurs in the early years, so that a one-year lag for a 3 year old is much more severe than a one-year lag for a 14 year old. This problem was countered to a certain extent by Terman's (1916) computation of I.Q. as being equal to $\frac{M.A.}{C.A.} \times 100$. If one uses this formula, a child of 3 with a one-year lag would have an I.Q. of 66, whereas a 14 year old with a one-year lag would have a relatively higher I.Q. of 93. Thus, Terman's revision more adequately reflects the severity of a lower M.A. than C.A. for different age groups. However, it was assumed that mental age reaches a peak around the age of 16. Difficulties would then occur when evaluating adult I.Q.'s since adults' chronological ages would be greater than their mental ages. Furthermore, decreases in mental age due to aging or adult brain damage could also not be estimated accurately. For this reason, the 1960 revision of the Stanford-Binet used Wechsler's concept of the deviation I.Q. This is simply a standard score with a mean of 100 and a standard deviation of 16. It assumes that differences in ability are normally distributed around a mean. Thus, a person's score on an ability test can be compared with the performances of others in his age group. The result is that meaningful comparisons can be made between persons of different ages.

Whereas Binet did not specifically develop a theory of intelligence, Spearman (1927) became concerned with what it was that intelligence tests were supposed to be measuring. He stated that there is a general factor, or "g factor," common to all types of intellectual activity in addition to specific factors, or "s factors," which are unique to particular problems. Spearman stressed that the different tests of intelligence were highly correlated and further observed that persons who dealt effectively in one area generally were effective in others as well. This led him to stress that there is a g factor operating which serves to integrate and enhance most, if not all, of a person's abilities. Although Spearman's work has often been referred to as a two-factor theory, he clearly emphasized the importance of a single global factor (g) and attempted to assess the relative importance of g within any single test of intelligence.

Thurstone (1938) developed a theory which was a radical departure from Spearman's in that he did not believe in the existence of a unifying g factor. Rather, he believed that intelligence was made up of specific and separate abilities. This theory was developed through the factor analysis of different tasks in which Thurstone attempted to conceptualize and isolate the different skills required for the performance of these tasks. His factor analytic studies suggested that intellect was comprised of the following components, which he referred to as Primary Mental Abilities:

Verbal Ability
Verbal Fluency
Numerical Ability
Spatial Ability
Perceptual Ability
Inductive Reasoning
Memory

There are some vivid examples which do suggest that a specific factor can exist without a corresponding general unifying (g) factor. Among so-called idiot savants, there is typically the extreme development of only one ability, whereas in other areas of their lives they may be relatively incompetent. Cases have been documented in which an idiot savant could correctly and almost immediately compute the day of the week on which a certain date occurred several years ago or could reproduce a long piece of music after hearing it one time. Such a specific differentiation of abilities gives some support to Thurstone's contention that, at least potentially, s factors can exist without a globally unifying g factor. However, in most research studies, Thurstone's seven factors have been found to be highly correlated. This suggests that Thurstone's factors are not completely independent and that there is also a g factor which is common throughout the seven primary abilities.

For many years, the main issue in conceptualizing intelligence was whether it could be best represented by Spearman's single, unitary, generalized factor or Thurstone's multiple-factor theory. Vernon (1950) took an intermediate position stating that intelligence is integrated and unitary but is also comprised of a number of both large and small specific abilities. His model (Figure 2-1) is basically hierarchical with the g factor at the top indicating that it unifies all the abilities occurring at lower levels. The next level is comprised of verbal-educational and spatial-mechanical abilities. Smaller subdivisions at lower levels refer to increasingly more specific and discrete abilities such as verbal fluency, numerical reasoning, and creativity.

Guilford (1967) used a highly sophisticated series of factor analytic techniques to develop a further conceptualization of intelligence which he refers to as the

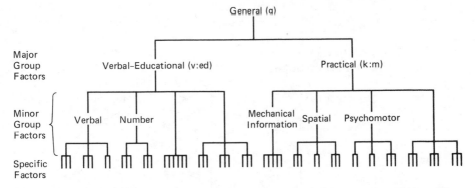

Figure 2-1. Vernon's hierarchical model of intelligence (adapted from Vernon, 1960, p. 22). Reprinted, by permission, from *The structure of Human Abilities* by P.E. Vernon, Methuen & Co., Ltd., 1960.

Structure of Intellect (SOI). He examined a far larger and more varied number of test items than previous researchers and broke down intelligence into 120 different factors. He reasoned that each intellectual skill involves a particular operation, on a particular type of content, to yield a particular product or outcome. Thus, Guilford believed that intelligent behavior involves an interaction of operations, contents, and products. Through his factor analytic techniques, he determined five operations or cognitive processes (Recognition, Memory, Divergent Production, Convergent Production, and Evaluation), four contexts (Figures, Symbols, Semantics, and Behaviors), and six outcomes or products (Units, Classes, Relations, Systems, Transformations, and Implications; see Figure 2-2). Each specific intellectual skill involves one of the operations performed on one of the types of contexts to produce one of the outcomes. The total (5 × 4 × 6) possible interactions yields Guilford's 120 specific intellectual skills, which he uses to define the structure of intellect.

Although Guilford's conceptualization of intelligence appears highly theoretical, it demonstrates a wide variety of intellectual skills and can potentially give insight into practical difficulties. For example, it can help us to see which skills are emphasized in our educational system and which are neglected. In general, our educational system trains students to deal with the physical world far more than the social world and to approach problems with logical thinking more than creative thinking. Using Guilford's terminology, students are usually far better trained to "converge" from a number of possible answers to one externally defined "correct" answer, rather than to "diverge" from one question to a number of possible answers.

Although Binet originally began the study of intelligence from a global and somewhat poorly defined concept, the understanding of cognitive functioning has become increasingly more specific and complex. This progression began with

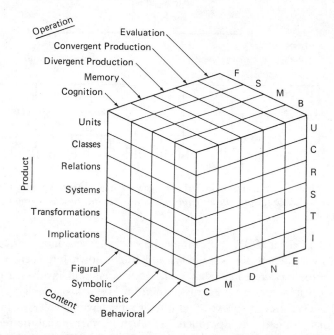

Figure 2-2. Three-dimensional model of the structure of intellect (from Guilford, 1967, p. 63). Reprinted, by permission, from *The Nature of Human Intelligence*, by J.P. Guilford, by McGraw-Hill Book Co., 1967.

Binet's (1908) implied global factor and proceeded to the contrasting views of Spearman's (1927) two-factor theory, with an emphasis on g, as opposed to Thurstone's (1938) multiple-factor theory. A resolution was attempted with Vernon's (1950) hierarchical model with g at the top and more specific abilities lower down on the hierarchy. The most current major theory is Guilford's (1967) classification of 120 separate abilities. From a practical standpoint, the views of intelligence presented here can help clinicians to understand and describe more precisely a client's intellectual abilities. However, a significant limitation of the psychometric approach is that even though theories relating to the nature of intelligence have been expounded, the tests of intelligence that have been developed may not actually measure these constructs. This discrepancy between theory and practicality should be taken into consideration when interpreting I.Q. test scores. Thus, I.Q. tests are generally highly effective when used to predict later academic performance, but they may not actually measure "intelligence." In a review of tests and theories of intelligence, Maloney and Ward (1976) state

In terms of scientific validity, the tests do seem to be inadequate. They bear little or no relationship to the theories we have examined and thus lack an adequate theoretical foundation or superstructure. Nevertheless, the items of intelligence tests have proven their practical value, such as the prediction of school achievement. Thus, while not conforming to any theoretical notions per se, the tests do relate to the types of performances that almost everyone agrees reflect the operation of intelligence, that is, school achievement. It is in terms of these practical effects that tests are designated "successful." (p. 224-225)

This is not to say that theories are useless but rather that they enable clinicians to perceive and discuss aspects of the client which were not accessible before they were conceptualized. Such theories increase our depth and breadth of vision. Likewise, I.Q. tests have relevance and usefulness in relation to specific types of predictions. The apparent discrepancy between theories of intelligence and tests of intelligence also suggests that this gap must be narrowed and indicates future directions for research and test construction.

Developmental Theory

One of the criticisms which has been directed at the psychometric approach is that test constructors have been more concerned with quantitative scores rather than with the quality of, or reasoning behind, an examinee's responses (Sigel, 1963). In contrast, Piaget began to develop his conceptions of intelligence by studying the incorrect responses of children to different questions or tasks. He was concerned not so much with whether the answers were right or wrong but rather with why they were right or wrong. Piaget soon noticed that there were certain patterns of responses which characterized different age groups. Further studies suggested to him that there were qualitative differences in the thinking of persons of certain ages. This led him to the following general conclusions regarding cognitive abilities:

1. Mental growth follows definite patterns and is nonrandom.
2. There are qualitative differences in the thinking of younger as opposed to older children.
3. As a person develops, there is a corresponding development in new cognitive structures and abilities.
4. Mental growth is complete somewhere during late adolescence.

Piaget (1950) views intelligence as a special form of biological adaptation between a person and his environment. It involves an interaction in which a person must somehow fit his personal needs into some workable relation with environmental demands. As a person grows and develops, he is in a continual process of reorganizing his psychological structures to deal more effectively with the environment. Piaget believes that this process occurs through both "assimilation" and "accommodation." Assimilation is primarily an inward process in which a person incorporates input from his environment into some sort of internal organized structure. It is a relatively active process beyond merely coping with the environment. Assimilation also has a certain degree of independence from the environment which allows for the growth and development of internal cognitive structures. For example, make-believe play with objects requires that a child act as if the objects are something else. This necessitates a certain degree of independence from the object, an active interaction with it, and the use and growth of new cognitive structures in relation to it. Whereas assimilation is more inward and active, accommodation looks outward in an effort to adapt and change cognitive structures in accordance with external demands. Thus, the changing or "accommodating" mental constructions must have a direct correspondence with the real world. Piaget stresses that both assimilation and accommodation occur simultaneously, independently of age, but also within all age groups. However, within these general processes there are specific age-related differences.

Piaget described four major stages of cognitive development:

I. Sensorimotor Period   Birth–2 years
   The child passes through six different stages. These begin with simple reflex actions and grow in complexity until simple mental schemata are developed to more effectively deal with the world. The stage ends with the first sign of internal or symbolic constructs.

II. Preoperational Period   2–7 years
   The child develops language and basic symbolic constructs. He can begin to think internally; is aware of the past present, and future; can engage in symbolic play; can search for hidden objects; and can engage in delayed imitation.

III. Concrete Operations Period   7–11 years
   At this stage, the child acquires conservation skills (in which independence from the stimulus properties of objects is developed, and the child is not fooled by mere perceptual transformations). He can add, subtract, classify, and serialize, and is less egocentric and more social. The child still has difficulty performing operations independently from his environment.

IV. Formal Operations Period   11 years and upward
   This stage marks the development of adult thinking in which the child can think abstractly, form and test out hypotheses, use deductive reasoning, and evaluate solutions.

The cognitive stages are action oriented in that a developing person actively operates on his environment and develops internal constructs based on these interactions. Piaget also emphasizes the qualitative changes which occur in a person's cognitive processes. He believes that it is more important to describe the nature and style of these changes than to quantitatively measure them. The different stages also occur within all cultures and cannot be varied. The later stages are dependent on earlier ones. However, even though the sequence cannot be changed, there is some variability as to when these stages occur between one individual and another, and from culture to culture. Thus, it may be important to consider what variables slow these stages down or accelerate them. In summary, Piaget's central theme is that intelligence is a developmental phenomenon of adaptation in which a person moves towards constructing reality in progressively more symbolic terms.

THE TESTING OF INTELLIGENCE: PRO AND CON

The testing of intelligence has had a consistent history of misuse, misunderstanding, and controversy. Criticisms have ranged all the way from moral indictments against labeling individuals, to cultural bias, and even to accusations of flagrant abuse of test scores. Although there are certainly valid criticisms against testing intelligence, there are also a number of advantages to continuing with such procedures.

One of the main assets of intelligence tests is their accuracy in predicting future behavior. Initially, Binet was able to achieve a certain degree of predictive success with his scales, and since that time, test procedures have become progressively more refined and accurate. A number of reviews on predictive studies of I.Q. have concluded that there are a greater number of correlates that are predictive of success in a wider variety of activities than for any other variable (Anderson and Messick, 1974; Kohlberg and Zigler, 1967). In particular, I.Q. tests are excellent predictors of academic achievement (Butcher, 1968). However, there are certain liabilities which are also associated with these successes. First of all, intelligence tests can be used to classify children into stereotyped categories which can result in limiting their freedom to choose fields of study (Kagan, 1971). Furthermore, I.Q. tests are extremely limited in predicting nontest or nonacademic activity (Masland, Sarason, and Gladwin, 1958), yet they are sometimes incorrectly used to make these inferences. It should also be stressed that intelligence tests are measures of a person's present level of functioning and, as such, can only provide short-term predictions. Long-term predictions, although attempted frequently, are less accurate because there are many uncontrolled, influencing variables. Similarly, even short-term academic placements that are made only on the basis of an I.Q. score have a high chance of failure since all the variables that may be crucial for success are not and cannot be measured by an intelligence test. It can sometimes be tempting for test users to extend the meaning of test scores beyond that for which they were originally intended, especially in relation to the predictions they can realistically be expected to make.

Another important asset of intelligence tests, particularly the WAIS-R and WISC-R, is that they give valuable information regarding a person's cognitive strengths and weaknesses. They are standardized procedures whereby a person's performance in various areas can be compared with that of his age-related peers as well as with his own relative strengths and weaknesses. In addition to supplying information for accurate educational interventions, the Wechsler and other individually administered tests provide the examiner with a structured interview within which a variety of tasks can be used to observe the unique and personal ways in which cognitive tasks are approached. Through a client's interactions with both the examiner and the test materials, an initial impression can be made of the individual's self-esteem, behavioral idiosyncrasies, anxiety, social skills, and motivation, while at the same time a specific picture of intellectual functioning is obtained.

Intelligence tests often provide clinicians, educators, and researchers with baseline measures which can be used to determine either the degree of change which has occurred in an individual over a period of time, or how an individual compares with other persons in a particular area or ability. This may have important implications for evaluating the effectiveness of an educational program or assessing the changing abilities of a specific student. In cases involving recovery from a head injury or readjustment following psychosurgery, it may be extremely helpful for clinicians to measure and follow the cognitive changes that occur within a patient. Furthermore, I.Q. assessments may be important in researching, and hopefully understanding more adequately, the effect of environmental variables, such as educational programs, family background, and nutrition, on cognitive functioning. Thus, they can provide useful information relating to cultural, biological, maturational, or treatment-related differences among individuals.

One of the criticisms that has been leveled at intelligence tests is that they almost all have an inherent bias towards emphasizing convergent, analytical, and scientific modes of thought. Thus, a person who emphasizes divergent, artistic, and imaginative modes of thought is at a distinct disadvantage. Guilford (1956) has specifically stated that the single I.Q. score does not do justice to the multidimensional nature of intelligence. Some critics (Kagan, 1971) have even stressed that the current approach to intelligence testing has become a social mechanism used by people with similar values to pass on educational advantages to children who resemble themselves. Not only do I.Q. tests tend to place creative individuals at a disadvantage (Sigel, 1963), but they are limited in assessing nonacademically oriented intellectual abilities. Thus, social acumen, success in dealing with people, the ability to handle the concrete realities of one's everyday world, social fluency, and specific tasks such as purchasing merchandise are not measured by any intelligence test. More succinctly, people are capable of many more cognitive abilities than can possible be measured on an intelligence test.

One frequent misunderstanding — and an area for potential misuse of intelligence tests — occurs when scores are treated as measures of innate capacity. I.Q. is not a measure of an innate fixed ability, nor is it representative of all problem solving situations. It is rather a specific and limited sample of abilities at a certain point in time which is subject to numerous alterations. It reflects, to a large extent, the richness of an individual's past experiences. Although interpretation guidelines are quite clear in pointing out the limited nature of a test score, there is a tendency to look at test results as absolute facts reflecting permanent characteristics within an individual. People often want a quick, easy, and reductionistic method to quantify, understand, and assess cognitive abilities, and the I.Q. score has become the most widely misused test score to fill this need.

One important limitation of intelligence tests is that, for the most part, they are not concerned with the underlying processes involved in problem solving. They focus on the final product or outcome rather than on the steps involved in reaching the outcome. In other words, they look at the "what" rather than the "how." Thus, if a person gives the correct response to the question How are a desk and couch similar? the examiner does not know if the response results from past learning, perceptual discrimination, syllogistic reasoning, or a combination of these (Sigel, 1963). The extreme example of this "end product" emphasis is the global I.Q. score. When the myriad assortment of intellectual abilities is looked at as a global ability, the complexity of cognitive functioning is simplified to the point of being almost useless. Labels can be applied quickly and easily, without examining specific strengths and weaknesses, thereby eliminating opportunities to make precise therapeutic interventions or to provide knowledgeable recommendations. This type of thinking contributes significantly to restricting the search for a wider, more precise, and more process-oriented understanding of mental abilities.

A further concern about intelligence tests involves their limited usefulness in assessing minority groups with divergent cultural backgrounds. It has been stated that intelligence test content is strongly biased in favor of white, middle-class values. Critics stress that minorities tend to be at a disadvantage when taking the tests because of deficiencies in motivation, lack of practice, and difficulties in establishing rapport. Numerous arguments against using intelligence tests for the assessment and placement of minorities have culminated in recent legal restrictions on the use of I.Q. scores. However, there are traditional defenses of I.Q. scores which suggest that they are not as biased as they have been accused of being. For example, the removal of biased items has done little to alter overall test scores, and I.Q.'s still provide mostly accurate predictions for many minorities. The issue has certainly not been resolved, and clinicians should continue to be aware of this dilemma, pay attention to subgroup norms, and interpret minority group I.Q. scores cautiously.

In summary, intelligence tests provide a number of useful and well-respected functions. They can adequately predict short-term scholastic performance, provide an assessment of an individual's relative strengths and weaknesses, reveal important personality variables, and permit the researcher, educator, or clinician to trace possible changes within an individual or population. However, these assets are only helpful if the limitations of intelligence tests are adequately understood and appropriately taken into consideration. They are limited in predicting occupational success and nonacademic skills such as creativity, motivational level, social acumen, and success in dealing with people. Furthermore, I.Q. scores are not measures of an innate, fixed ability, and they are often not appropriate or valid for use with minority groups. Finally, there has been an overemphasis on understanding the end products of cognitive functioning and a relative neglect of appreciating the underlying processes.

HISTORY AND DEVELOPMENT

During the 1930s, Wechsler began studying a number of standardized tests and selected 11 different subtests to form his initial battery. His search for subtests was in part guided by his conception that intelligence is global in nature and represents a part of the greater whole of personality. Several of his subtests were derived from portions of the 1937 revision of the Stanford-Binet (Comprehension, Arithmetic, Digit Span, Similarities, and Vocabulary). The remaining subtests came from the Army Group Examinations (Picture Arrangement), Koh's Block Design (Block Design), Army Alpha (Information, Comprehension), Army Beta (Digit Symbol, Coding), Healy Picture Completion (Picture Completion) and the Pinther-Paterson Test (Object Assembly). These subtests were combined and published in 1939 as the Wechsler-Bellevue Intelligence Scale. The Wechsler-Bellevue had a number of technical deficiencies primarily related to both the reliability of the subtests and the size and representativeness of the normative sample. Thus, it was revised to form the Wechsler Adult Intelligence Scale (WAIS) in 1955, and another revised edition (WAIS-R) was published in 1981.

The original Wechsler-Bellevue Scale was developed for adults, but in 1949 Wechsler developed the Wechsler Intelligence Scale for Children (WISC) so that children down to the age of 5 years 0 months could be assessed in a similar manner. Easier items, designed for children, were added to the original scales and standardized on 2200 white American boys and girls selected to be representative of the 1940 census. However, there is some evidence that Wechsler's sample may have been overrepresentative of children in the middle and upper socioeconomic levels. Thus, ethnic minorities and children from lower socioeconomic levels are penalized when compared to the normative group. The WISC was revised in 1974 and standardized on a new sample which is more accurately representative of children in the United States. It is currently published as the WISC-R. In 1967, the Wechsler Preschool and Primary Scale of Intelligence (WPPSI) was published for the assessment of children between the ages of 4 and 6 1/2. Just as the WISC is a downward extension of the WAIS, so the WPPSI is generally a downward extension of the WISC in which easier but similar items are used. Although most of the scales are similar in form and content to the WISC, a number of them are unique to the WPPSI.

RELIABILITY AND VALIDITY

In order to establish WAIS reliability, odd-even coefficients were computed for every subtest except Digit Span and Digit Symbol. To determine reliability for Digit Span, a correlation was made between Digits Forward and digits Backward. Since Digit Symbol is a highly speeded test, a split half technique could not be used and an alternate form was devised from the Wechsler-Bellevue subtest. The odd-even correlation was also computed for Full Scale I.Q., Verbal I.Q., and Performance I.Q.

The results demonstrated high correlations throughout the test. The Full Scale I.Q. yielded reliability coefficients of .97, and the Verbal and Performance I.Q.'s produced correlations of .96 and .94, respectively. Thus, all three I.Q.'s are very reliable in terms of internal (odd-even) consistency. The intersubtest correlations, although relatively high, produced somewhat lower correlations ranging from approximately .60 for Digit Span, Picture Arrangement, and Object Assembly to .96 for Vocabulary. Correlations for the WISC subtests tend to be slightly lower, though the same overall pattern of reliability is reported in the manual. Similar, although generally somewhat higher, reliabilities were reported for the 1974 and 1981 revisions of the WISC and WAIS. The average WISC-R reliability coefficient for 11 different age groups was .96 for the Full Scale I.Q., .94 for the Verbal I.Q., and .90 for the Performance I.Q. The subtest reliabilities are adequate and range from a low of .70 for Object Assembly to a high of .86 for Vocabulary. The WAIS-R reliabilities for the three I.Q.'s are likewise extremely high. The 1981 WAIS-R manual reports a Full Scale I.Q. reliability of .97, a Verbal I.Q. reliability of .97, and a Performance I.Q. reliability of .93. The reliabilities for the subtests are generally similar to the WAIS, with a low of .52 for Object Assembly at age group 16–17 and a high of .96 for Vocabulary for six of the nine age groups. All of these reliabilities are well within the acceptable level, and those for the three I.Q.'s in both the children and the adult tests are outstandingly high.

Although the WAIS manual itself does not contain any validity data, Wechsler emphasizes in a later book (Wechsler, 1958) and in the 1981 WAIS-R manual that the functions measured by his 11 chosen subtests not only fit the definition of intelligence, but have proved their accuracy in academic settings and clinical evaluations. furthermore, researchers have found intercorrelations among the subtests using factor analysis, which suggest that the scales measure three major components of intelligence. For example, Cohen (1957a, 1957b) has established WAIS factor loadings on *verbal comprehension* (Vocabulary, Information, Comprehension, Similarities), *perceptual organization* (Block Design, Object Assembly), and *memory* (Arithmetic, Digit Span). Kaufman (1975) and Silverstein (1980) have likewise found similar factor loadings on the WISC-R, but instead of Cohen's memory factor, Kaufman (1975, 1979) has emphasized *freedom from distractibility* as the primary factor for Arithmetic, Digit Span, and Coding. He also found *perceptual organization* to be important not only for Block Design and Object Assembly but also for Picture Completion, Picture Arrangement, and Mazes.

Content and construct validity studies have generally been sparse, with vague and nonspecific results. The primary focus of validity studies has been either on predicting behavior in a specific situation or on comparing the results of two tests or performances concurrently. The Wechsler scales have been correlated repeatedly with the Stanford-Binet (.85) and many other well-known intelligence tests with consistently high correlations (Guertin, Ladd, Frank, and Rabin, 1971; Matarazzo, 1972; Wechsler, 1958). Wechsler Verbal I.Q. scores tend to correlate somewhat higher with the Stanford-Binet than does either the Full Scale I.Q. or the Performance I.Q. However, the Performance I.Q. correlates highly with tests involving visual-spatial abilities and hand-eye coordination such as the Minnesota Paper Form Board Test (.72 for 16-year-old boys and girls; Janke and Havighurst, 1945) and Raven's Progressive Matrices (.70; Hall, 1957). Matarazzo (1972) has summarized a number of studies relating to academic achievement, and concludes that the correlation between WAIS scores and academic achievement is around .50. Similar studies have been performed on the WISC and WISC-R with comparable findings. For example, WISC-R Full Scale I.Q.'s correlate at levels of .82 with the Stanford-Binet (Wechsler, 1955) and .68 with the McCarthy Scales of Children's Abilities. The WISC-R correlates with various tests of scholastic achievement such as the Wide Range Achievement Test at approximately the .76 level (Reynolds, Gutkin, Dappen, and Wright, 1979) and there is a .39 correlation with school grades.

ADVANTAGES AND CAUTIONS IN
USING THE WECHSLER SCALES

Since their initial publication, the Wechsler scales have been evaluated in numerous research studies and have become widely used throughout the world. Thus, they have the advantage of being familiar to most researchers and practitioners, and have a long and extensive history of continued evaluation. Furthermore, the subtests are easy to administer, and the accompanying manual provides clear instructions, concise tables, and excellent norms.

Perhaps of even more practical importance to the clinician are the clear, precise data obtained about the person's cognitive functioning from the pattern of responses to the subtests. It is relatively easy for an examiner to determine a person's psychological strengths and weaknesses by comparing the results of each subtest. For example, relatively high scores on Block Design and Object Assembly suggest that the person is strong in perceptual organization, whereas an individual with relative peaks on Arithmetic and Digit Span is most likely strong on immediate memory and is not easily distracted. A clinician can become extremely sensitive to the different nuances and limitations of each of these subtests and the pattern of their results. In addition, a quick glance at a person's Verbal, Performance, and Full Scale I.Q.'s can point to areas of concern that may need further evaluation.

A final, but extremely important, asset of the Wechsler scales is their ability to aid in assessing personality variables. This can be done by directly observing the individual as he interacts with the examiner, studying the content of test item responses, or evaluating information inferred from the individual's pattern of subtest scores. For example, a person scoring low on Digit Span, Arithmetic, and Digit Symbol is likely to be experiencing anxiety, to have an attentional deficit, or a combination of both. On the other hand, another person who scores high in both Comprehension and Picture Arrangement is likely to have extremely good social judgment. Several researchers (Amolsch and Henrichs, 1975; Henrichs, Krauskopf, and Amolsch, 1982; Wechsler, 1958) have provided descriptions of how certain clinical groups characteristically perform. For example, adolescent sociopaths (delinquents) typically have Performance I.Q. scores significantly higher than Verbal I.Q., with Picture Arrangement and Object Assembly being relative peaks, and Information and Comprehension being relative weaknesses. When compared to other intelligence tests, the Wechsler scales are unique in the degree to which they can provide personality variables and clinical information.

Despite these strengths, there are also a number of weaknesses and limitations. The Wechsler scales do not adequately measure extreme ranges of intelligence (below 40 and above 160) when compared to tests such as the Stanford-Binet. There is a consistent tendency for the WISC-R to produce somewhat lower I.Q. scores for persons in the upper ranges of intelligence than the Stanford-Binet. It is not until the average and below-average ranges that the Wechsler scales and the Stanford-Binet begin to provide means that are comparable. Thus, the Stanford-Binet and WISC-R are closely correlated for the average or below-average child, but not for the child of superior intelligence. The WISC-R is likewise deficient when estimating the I.Q.'s of severely retarded children.

There are several additional limitations to the Wechsler scales. Some critics believe that norms may not be applicable for ethnic minorities or persons from lower socioeconomic backgrounds. Furthermore, there is a certain degree of subjectivity when scoring many of the items on Comprehension, Similarities, and Vocabulary. Thus, a "hard" scorer may come out with a somewhat lower score than an "easy" scorer. The Wechsler scales, like other tests of intelligence, are limited in the scope of what they can measure. They do not assess such important factors as need for achievement, motivation, success in dealing with people, or creativity. As a result, the scales tend to be relatively poor at predicting factors such as occupational success. Perhaps the most significant criticism leveled at the Wechsler scales has been the lack of a sufficient amount of data on their validity (Anastasi, 1982). Although they have been correlated with other measures, including the Stanford-Binet and academic achievement, for the most part there has been a notable lack of comparisons with behavior external to the scales themselves.

THE MEANING OF I.Q. SCORES

Since there is only a weak and vague relation between theories of intelligence and the tests themselves, it is important to understand the meaning of I.Q. scores. Furthermore, the concept of I.Q. has been and still is subject to many misinterpretations. The meaning of I.Q. scores can be partially clarified by briefly mentioning the more common misinterpretations and commenting on them. First of all, I.Q. is not a fixed, unchangeable, and innate factor. On the contrary, it is a current measurement which is subject to a wide variety of environmental influences. Secondly, I.Q. scores are not exact, precise measurements; rather, they are estimates in which there is an expected range of fluctuation between one performance and the next. Furthermore, tests such as the Wechsler scales measure only a limited range of abilities, and there are a large number of variables that are usually considered to be "intelligent" which are beyond the scope of most intelligence tests. No test or battery of tests can ever give a complete picture; rather they assess various areas of functioning. In summary, an I.Q. is an estimate of a person's current level of functioning as measured by the various tasks required in a test.

Another important aspect of I.Q. is the statistical meaning the different scores have. Binet originally conceptualized intelligence as the difference between a person's mental age and his chronological age. This was found to be inadequate and has been replaced by the use of the deviation I.Q. The assumption behind the deviation I.Q. is that intelligence falls around a normal distribution (see Figure 2-3). The interpretation of an I.Q. score, then, is straightforward in that it gives the relative position of a person compared with his age-related peers. The I.Q. can thus be expressed as deviation units away from the norm. Each of the three Wechsler I.Q.'s (Full Scale, Verbal, Performance) has a mean of 100 and a standard deviation of 15. Scores also have the advantage of being easily translated into percentile equivalents. For example, an I.Q. of 120 is 1 1/3

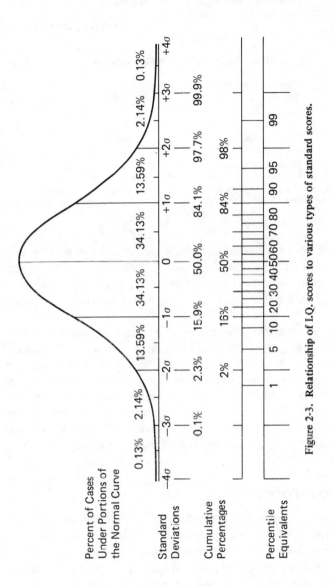

Figure 2-3. Relationship of I.Q. scores to various types of standard scores.

Table 2-1. Intelligence Classifications.

IQ	CLASSIFICATION	PERCENT INCLUDED THEORETICAL NORMAL CURVE	ACTUAL SAMPLE
130 and above	Very superior	2.2	2.6
120–129	Superior	6.7	6.9
110–119	High average	16.1	16.6
90–109	Average	50.0	49.1
80–89	Low average	16.1	16.1
70–79	Borderline	6.7	6.4
69 and below	Mentally retarded	2.2	2.3

NOTE: From Wechsler (1981, p. 28). Reproduced, by permission, from the *Wechsler Adult Intelligence Scale – Revised Manual.* Copyright © 1981 by The Psychological Corporation. All rights reserved.

standard deviations above the mean and places an individual in the 91st percentile. Thus, this person's performance is better than 91% of his age-related peers. The I.Q. cutoff for mental retardation is 70, which indicates that such individuals are functioning in the lower 2% when compared with their age-related peers.

A final consideration is the different classifications of intelligence. Table 2-1 lists commonly used diagnostic labels and compares them with I.Q. ranges and percentages. These terms are taken from the 1981 WAIS-R manual and the designations for high average, low average, and mentally retarded correspond to the earlier 1955 WAIS manual terms of bright normal, dull normal, and mental defective, respectively. Thus, an I.Q. can be expressed conceptually as an estimate of a person's current level of ability, statistically as a deviation score which can be transformed into percentile equivalents, and diagnostically using common terms for classification.

INTERPRETATION PROCEDURES

Sattler (1982) has recommended the following successive level approach to interpreting Wechsler scores. This approach provides the clinician with a sequential five-step format for working with and discussing a person's performance. Later in this chapter, a listing and brief discussion of the more frequently encountered interpretive hypotheses will be provided. This later section can serve as a summary and quick reference for clinicians, especially with regard to analyzing test profiles (levels II and III).

Level I — The Full Scale I.Q. An examinee's Full Scale I.Q. should be considered first since it provides the basis and overall context for evaluating other cognitive abilities. It is generally the single most reliable and valid score. The Full Scale I.Q. score gives the person's relative standing in comparison to his age-related peers and provides a global estimate of his overall mental abilities. It is often useful to transform the Full Scale I.Q. into a percentile rank or intelligence classification, especially when relating test results to untrained persons, because these designations are usually less subject to misinterpretation than I.Q. scores.

Level II — Verbal and Performance I.Q.'s. The second step is to consider the Verbal and Performance I.Q.'s, especially the relative difference between them. The Verbal I.Q. is an index of a person's verbal comprehensive abilities, while the Performance I.Q. provides an estimate of one's perceptual organizational abilities. If there is a wide discrepancy (more than 15 points) between these, then an explanation for the reason for these differences has to be developed. As with the Full Scale I.Q., it may also be helpful to convert the Verbal and Performance I.Q. scores into percentile rankings.

Level III — Intersubtest Scatter. The third step is to consider the degree to which the individual subtests deviate from the verbal or performance scale means and to make comparisons between the different subtests. The outcome should be a description of a person's relative cognitive strengths and weaknesses. A listing and discussion of the meaning of each subtest and the abilities it measures will be found in the next section of this chapter. Clinicians can refer to this section, as well as to the later section on common interpretive hypotheses, to develop their own interpretive hypotheses relating to important dimensions of intersubtest scatter. However, varying performance on the subtests can occur for many reasons, and the clinician must evaluate which of these reasons is most accurate. This can be accomplished not only by referring to the skills involved in each subtest but also by making careful behavioral observations and testing the limits of an examinee's abilities. For example, a clinician may speculate that a person scored low on Block Design because of poor spatial abilities. If this was the case, it would be expected that his arrangement of the blocks would be poor, perhaps characterized by rotations. On the other hand, if the clinician had tested the limits and observed that the individual could complete the task if given enough time, then the poor performance would be more the result of slow, spatial problem solving skills rather than an actual inability to perform.

Level IV — Intrasubtest Scatter. A further important area of analysis involves looking at the patterns of performance found within the items of each subtest. These items are arranged in sequences which become progressively more difficult. Thus, a normal and expected pattern would be for the examinee to pass the initial items and slowly but evenly begin to fail the more difficult ones. A more sporadic pattern, in which the examinee misses initial easier items but passes later more difficult ones, may suggest an attentional deficit or specific memory losses. If there is a highly sporadic performance, then the reason for this should be explored further. An analysis of the intrasubtest scatter can thus provide a different type of information from that obtained by merely looking at the quantitative scaled scores.

Level V — Qualitative Analysis. The final step is to look at the content of the responses on Information, Vocabulary, Comprehension, and Similarities. The presence of unique, highly personal, or unusual responses can often suggest some important dimensions of an individual's intellectual or personality functioning. For example, there may be responses which reflect aggressive tendencies, concrete thinking, or unusual associations.

THE WECHSLER SUBTESTS

In order to adequately interpret the Wechsler scales, it is essential to understand the various abilities that each of the subtests measures. In this section, the different abilities involved in each of the 12 subtests will be presented, followed by a discussion of their relevant features including the possible meaning associated with high or low scores. In keeping with the overall trend and approach of this book, any interpretations suggested in the discussion of the subtests should be considered tentative. They are merely beginning possibilities, which must be explored further and placed in a proper context. A further consideration is that no subtest is a pure measure of any one intellectual ability; rather, each represents a combination of skills. It is important o emphasize that a low or high score in a specific subtest can occur for a variety of reasons which the examiner must determine during his interpretation of the overall profile.

Verbal Scales

The Wechsler verbal scales assess an individual's proficiency in the following areas: (1) the ability to work with abstract symbols, (2) the amount and degree of benefit a person has received from his educational background, (3) verbal memory abilities, and (4) verbal fluency. The WAIS verbal scales are generally more subject to cultural influences, whereas the performance scales are considered to be somewhat more culture free. If an individual does significantly better (15 points or more) on the verbal scales compared to the performance subtests, it may indicate a number of interpretive possibilities including a relatively high level of education, a tendency towards overachieving, intact left cerebral hemisphere abilities, or possible psychopathology, particularly obsessive-compulsive conditions, schizophrenia, or severe depressive states.

Information:

Old learning or schooling
Intellectual curiosity or urge to collect knowledge
General fund of accumulated information
Alertness to everyday world
Remote memory

The Information subtest samples the type of knowledge average persons with average opportunities should be able to acquire (Matarazzo, 1972). This knowledge is usually based on habitual, overlearned material, particularly in the case of older children and adults. Both Information and Vocabulary are highly resistant to neurological deficit and psychological disturbance (Blatt and Allison, 1968), and are two of the most stable subtests on the WAIS. Because of this stability, Wechsler has referred to them as "hold" tests as opposed to "no hold" tests which are far more sensitive to deterioration and situational variables such as anxiety and fatigue (i.e., Arithmetic, Digit Symbol, Block Design). Furthermore, they are both good measures of general intelligence and are highly correlated with the WAIS Full Scale I.Q. (Cohen, 1957b, 1959). Although performance on the Information subtest involves remote memory and alertness to the environment, it is only influenced to a small extent by conscious effort and is believed to be only minimally affected by such factors as anxiety. In order to score well, the individual must have been exposed to a highly varied past environment, have an intact long-term memory, and possess a wide range of interests.

A high score on this subtest suggests that the examinee has good long-term memory, cultural interests, strong educational background, verbal ability, and possible intellectualization as his most frequently used defense mechanism. Low scorers may show superficiality of interests, lack of intellectual curiosity, and/or cultural deprivation.

Digit Span:

Short-term memory or immediate auditory memory
Concentration and attention
Ability to shift thought patterns (from Digits Forward to Digits Backwards)

Digit Span is considered to be a test of short-term memory and attention. The subject must recall and repeat auditory information in proper sequence. Bannatyne (1974) has described this as "auditory vocal sequencing memory." Correct responses require a two-step process. First the information must be correctly received, which requires attention and encoding. Persons who are easily distractible have difficulty in this phase. Second, the examinee must correctly recall, sequence, and vocalize the information. Persons who can perhaps receive the information correctly may have difficulty at this phase because they cannot hold the memory trace long enough. Sometimes the previous digit is forgotten as they are attempting to vocalize a present one. Whereas Digits Forward is a simpler more straightforward task requiring rote memory, Digits Backward is more complex. The examinee must usually hold the memory longer and also transform it prior to making a restatement. Thus, a good performance on Digits Backward is likely to reflect a person who is flexible, can concentrate, and is tolerant to stress.

Passive, anxiety-free individuals seem to do best on this test. It requires an effortless and relatively unhampered contact with reality which is characterized by open receptivity to incoming information. Performance is greatly hampered by increased anxiety or tension, and this is the subtest considered to be most susceptible to the effects of anxiety. In addition to Digit Span, the other two subtests which are sensitive to the effects of anxiety are Arithmetic and Digit Symbol, and they are sometimes referred to as the "anxiety triad."

Persons scoring high have good auditory short-term memory and excellent attention, and may be relatively unaffected by stress and anxiety. However, it should be stressed that just because a person has good short-term auditory memory for digits does not necessarily mean that his memory for more complicated information, such as music or verbally relevant information, will also be good. These more complex features of memory may have to be assessed by other means. Low scorers show a lack of ability to concentrate which may be the result of anxiety or unusual thought processes. A large discrepancy between Digits Forward and Digits Backwards can suggest the presence of an organic deficit, particularly if the overall backward Digit Span score is below "hold" tests such as Information and Vocabulary.

Vocabulary:

General verbal intelligence
Language usage and accumulated verbal learning ability
Rough measure of the subject's optimal intellectual efficiency
Educational background
Range of ideas, experiences, or interests which a subject has acquired

The Vocabulary subtest is a test of accumulated verbal learning, and represents an individual's ability to express a wide range of ideas with ease and flexibility. It may also involve one's richness of ideas, long-term memory, concept formation, and language development. Vocabulary is noteworthy in that it is the most reliable verbal subtest (test-retest = .86), and like Information, it is highly resistant to neurological deficit and psychological disturbance (Blatt and Allison, 1968). Although the Vocabulary subtest holds up with age, it has the tendency to fall off with those people for whom words are not necessary in order to adapt. It generally reflects the nature and level of sophistication of one's schooling and cultural learning. Vocabulary is primarily dependent on the wealth of early educational environment, but it is susceptible to improvement by later experience or schooling. It is the least variable of all the subtests, and subtest scores below the Vocabulary level often imply a drop of efficiency in that function. Vocabulary is the best single indicator of general intelligence. Because of its high degree of stability, it is often used as an indicator of a person's intellectual potential and is also used to make an approximate assessment of premorbid level of functioning.

The Vocabulary responses are similar to Comprehension and Similarities in that a qualitative analysis often provides a great deal of information relating to the examinee's thought processes, background, life experiences, and response to frustration. It is often important to explore incorrect responses to determine whether they were guesses, clang associations (i.e., "ponder" meaning "to pound"), concrete thinking, bizarre associations, or overinclusive reasoning. Even when a response is correct, a consideration of the style of approaching the word and specific content can be helpful.

High scores suggest high general intelligence, and indicate that the examinee can adequately recall past ideas and form concepts relating to them. Persons with high scores have a wide range of interests and a good fund of general information. Clinical populations who score high on Vocabulary may use compulsive or intellectualizing defense mechanisms. Low scorers usually have a limited educational background and can be naive and poorly motivated.

Arithmetic:

Numerical reasoning and speed of numerical manipulation
Concentration and attention
Reality contact and mental alertness; that is, active relationship to the outside world
School learning (earlier items)
Logical reasoning, abstraction, and analysis of numerical problems (later items)

The Arithmetic subtest requires not only a focused concentration but also basic mathematical skills and an ability to apply these skills. The skills required to complete this test are usually acquired by junior high school so that low scores are more likely to be the result of poor concentration. Arithmetic is likely to be more challenging and stressful than tests such as Information and Vocabulary both because the task itself is more demanding and because it is timed. Thus, persons who are susceptible to the disruptive effects of anxiety are likely to be adversely affected. However, examiners may want to establish whether the person simply lacked the necessary skills or rather had difficulty concentrating. This can be assessed by giving the person previously missed items a second time, but allowing him to use a paper and pencil without a time limit. Under these circumstances, persons with adequate mathematical knowledge who are distractible should be able to complete the items correctly.

Individuals from higher socioeconomic backgrounds, obedient teacher-oriented students, and persons with intellectualizing tendencies usually do well on this subtest. A helpful formula is that Information plus Arithmetic equals school achievement. Since numbers come from the outside environment, and create rule and direction, some individuals react rebelliously. This is particularly true for antisocial personalities. Histrionic personalities, who do not readily accept outside direction and generally refuse to take responsibility for their behaviors, will likewise do poorly. This is not to suggest that lowered arithmetic scores are diagnostic of these clinical groups, but rather that this lowering may at times be consistent with the way these individuals interact with their environment.

High scorers show alertness or even overalertness, capacity for concentration, and freedom from distractibility, and they may use intellectualizing defenses. Low scorers show poor mathematical reasoning, lack of capacity to concentrate, and distractibility. A poor educational background in which adequate mathematical skills have not been developed can also account for lowered performance.

Comprehension:

> Social judgment, common sense, or judgment in practical social situations
> Grasp of one's social milieu; for example, information and knowledge of moral codes, social rules, and regulations
> Ability to evaluate past experience; that is, proper selection, organization, and emphasis of facts and relationships
> Reality awareness, understanding, and alertness to the everyday world
> Abstract thinking (later items only)

Comprehension reflects the extent to which an examinee adheres to conventional standards, has benefited from past cultural opportunities, and has a well-developed conscience. It is also at least in part a test of information, which is supported by its high correlation (low to mid 70s depending on age) with the Information and Vocabulary subtests. Comprehension involves an adaptive response by the individual to a situation requiring him to select the most efficient way of dealing with a specific problem. The examinee not only must possess relevant information but must appropriately use this information for decision making. In this sense, the Comprehension subtest goes one step beyond the degree of complexity and synthesis required for the Information subtest. The examinee must not only have the necessary information, but must apply it in a coherent, problem-oriented manner. Thus, a Comprehension score significantly below the Information score suggests that an examinee is not effectively using his knowledge.

In assessing an examinee's responses, it can be important to distinguish between actually dealing with the material to develop an original response and merely repeating overlearned concepts. For example, parroting answers to "forest" or "bad company" does not indicate full comprehension and may simply be based on past experience rather than on accurate problem solving or good judgment. Thus, basic rule-of-thumb answers can significantly increase the total number of correct responses. However, in the later items, a correct response requires higher level problem solving, and these items, therefore, can still be a good measure of general intelligence instead of merely rote memorization.

Personality variables, especially those relating to judgment, are important areas to consider in this subtest. Thus, clinicians should note the pattern of responses, clichés, literalness, and any circumscribed responses. Good judgment involves the ability to engage in discriminative activity. Failure on the easy items indicates impairment of judgment, even though later, more difficult ones are passed. It is important to note emotional implications on this subtest since emotional responsiveness influences the way in which a person evaluates environmental events. For example, individuals who are highly analytical and use these analytical abilities to avoid emotions may have difficulty understanding the social components of situations as presented in Comprehension.

High scorers show reality awareness, capacity for social compliance, good judgment, and emotionally relevant use of information. Low scorers, especially if 4 points or more below Vocabulary, show poor judgment, impulsiveness, and hostility against their environment (Weiner, 1966). Mentally disturbed persons often do poorly on Comprehension, which may be the result of disturbed perceptions, idiosyncratic thinking, impulsiveness, or antisocial tendencies.

Similarities:

Verbal concept formation or conceptual thinking
Logical abstract reasoning
Associative ability combined with language facility

The Similarities subtest requires verbal concept formation and abstract reasoning ability. These are functions that mediate for the individual an awareness of the belonging-togetherness of objects and events of the everyday world. An essential aspect of adjusting to one's environment is using these abilities to clarify, reduce, and classify the style and manner to which they will respond. Inductive reasoning is required since the examinee must move from particular facts to a general rule or principle. Implicit in the test is the ability of individuals to utilize remote memory and apply elegant expressions in their responses. The more precise and abstract the expression, the higher the score, which indicates that verbal fluency is an important determinant. A particularly high level of abstraction is reached, however, when the items requesting the similarity between "praise-punishment" and "fly-tree" elicit correct responses. Individuals with a good ability for insight and introspection tend to perform highly on this subtest; thus it may be used as an indicator of favorable prognosis for psychotherapy. Scores decrease significantly in schizophrenics, rigid or inflexible thinkers, and patients with senile conditions. Examiners can therefore use this subtest to gain further information relating to the nature of an examinee's idiosyncratic or pathological form of concept formation.

High scorers show good verbal concept formation which, if unusually high, may reflect paranoid or intellectualizing tendencies. Low scorers show poor abstraction abilities, literalness, and inflexible thinking.

Performance Scales

In general, the performance scales reflect (1) the individual's degree of nonverbal contact with the environment, (2) the ability to integrate perceptual stimuli with relevant motor responses, and (3) the capacity to work in concrete situations. The performance subtests are generally less affected by educational background than the verbal scales. If an individual does significantly better (15 points or more) on the performance scales than on the verbal subtests, this may indicate a number of interpretive possibilities, including a tendency towards underachieving, a likelihood of acting out, delinquent behavior, a lowered likelihood of right cerebral hemisphere brain damage, individuals who could be described as doers rather than thinkers, or persons from lower socioeconomic backgrounds.

Picture Completion:

Visual acuity; awareness of environmental detail; reality contact
Perception of the whole in relation to its parts; visual conceptual ability
Ability to differentiate essential from nonessential details
Perceptual alertness and concentration combined with an ability to visually organize material

The Picture Completion subtest is a measure of visual concentration and is a nonverbal test of general information. It involves discovering consistency and inconsistency by paying close attention to the environment and accessing remote memory. It is dependent on, and also draws upon, an individual's experience with his culture. Thus, a person who is unfamiliar with common features of American society will often make errors due to a lack of experience rather than a lack of intelligence. A person will also make errors if he is unable to detach himself emotionally from the material, thereby making accurate discriminations difficult. For example, passive, dependent personalities often make errors because they notice the absence of people controlling the actions in the pictures. Typical responses might be that "there's nobody holding the pitcher," "there are no people rowing the boat," or "there's no flag pole." There are also characteristic responses which schizophrenic patients make, such as responding to number 4 (playing card) with "the other 48 cards are missing," or to number 12 (crab) with "there's no scales" (Weiner, 1966).

High scorers have the ability to recognize essential visual information, are alert, and demonstrate good visual acuity. Low scores indicate poor concentration and inadequate visual organization. Impulsiveness can often produce lowered performance since the examinee may make a quick response without carefully analyzing the whole picture.

Picture Arrangement:

    Accurately understanding interpersonal situations
    Ability to comprehend a total situation and evaluate its implications
    Visual organization and perception of essential visual cues
    Ability to anticipate consequences of initial acts and plan ahead in social relations
    Social-sexual adjustment [determined from projective stories requested for Nos. 2 (flirt), 8 (fish), and 10 (taxi)]

The Picture Arrangement test is primarily a test of the ability to plan, interpret, and accurately anticipate social events within a given cultural context. Thus, an individual's cultural background can affect his performance on the test, and often normal subjects with poor or different cultural backgrounds do poorly. Since many of the tests require subtle knowledge of American sociocultural values, the scores derived from persons of differing cultural backgrounds should be treated with caution. Wechsler (1958) has stated that the test requires an examinee to use general intelligence in nonverbal social situations. In fact, each of the items requires a person to respond to some practical interpersonal interaction. Both Picture Arrangement and Block Design are measures of nonverbal intelligence. However, Picture Arrangement is far more dependent on cultural variables than Block Design. Picture Arrangement is also a test which requires the person to grasp or size up the complete situation before proceeding to a correct response. In contrast, persons can achieve good scores on Block Design by approaching the task in small segments and then contrasting their performance on each segment with the whole design.

Within clinical populations, certain types of antisocial and histrionic personalities apparently can master the intrinsic planning ability required for the Picture Arrangement subtest. In particular, antisocial persons who are good "schemers" are able to do well. Social exhibitionists and extroverts are also good performers, whereas disturbed individuals and those somewhat distant from reality do poorly (Weiner, 1966). A high Picture Arrangement score for persons seeking therapy can be a favorable sign (Windle, 1952). An unusually low score in a protocol in which there is little difference between Verbal and Performance I.Q.'s implies an organic impairment consistent with a static lesion to the right anterior temporal lobe (Reitan, 1974). Right hemisphere lesions usually lower Picture Arrangements, Block Design, and Object Assembly scores (Russell, 1979).

There are two approaches towards obtaining additional qualitative information from Picture Arrangement. The first is to observe and record the manner in which the person attempts to solve the problem. Does he carefully consider the overall problem or rather impulsively begin altering the cards? Is he easily discouraged or does he demonstrate a high degree of persistence? Once the entire subtest has been completed, an examiner may also want to obtain projective stories relating to the pictures. This might be initiated by simply asking the examinee to "tell me what is happening in the pictures" or "make up a story about the cards." The cards that usually produce the richest information are Nos. 2, 8, and 10 on the WAIS-R. The following questions are especially important. Are the stories logical, fanciful, or bizarre? Are they original or rather stereotyped and conventional? Does the examinee reveal any emotional attitudes relating either to himself or to his interpersonal relationships? Were errors the result of incorrectly perceiving specific details or rather of neglect in even considering certain details? Did the examinee consider all the different relationships in the pictures, or were important aspects omitted?

Persons who score high in Picture Arrangement are usually sophisticated, have a high level of social intelligence, and demonstrate an ability to anticipate consequences of initial acts. Low scorers show paucity of ideas, lack of ability to plan ahead, difficulty in interpersonal relationships, and poor rapport.

Block Design:

Nonverbal concept formation
Visual-motor coordination and perceptual organization
Capacity for sustained effort; concentration
Visual-motor-spatial coordination; manipulative and perceptual speed

The Block Design subtest involves nonverbal problem solving skills because of its emphasis on analyzing a problem into its component parts and then reintegrating these parts into a cohesive whole. The examinee must apply logic and reasoning in such a way as to solve spatial relationship problems. As a test of nonverbal concept formation, Block Design demands skills in perceptual organization, spatial visualization, and abstract conceptualization. It is a sturdy and reliable test which correlates highly with general intelligence and is not likely to be lowered except by the effects of depression or organic impairment (Schorr, Bower, and Kiernan, 1982). In order to perform well, examinees must be able to demonstrate a degree of abstraction which is free from literal concreteness. They must also make a distinction between part and whole by the demonstration of analysis and synthesis. This test involves an ability to shift the frame of reference and maintain a high degree of flexibility. The examinee must be able to inhibit his impulsive tendencies and to persist in a designated task.

An important feature of Block Design is that it enables an examiner to actually observe the examinee's response. Some subjects are easily discouraged and give up, while others insist on completing the task even beyond the time limit. In approaching the task, one subject might impulsively place the blocks together in a nonrandom sequence, whereas another might demonstrate a meticulously sequential style. Potentially valuable information can be obtained by observing and recording these differences in problem solving.

Block Design is also a nonverbal, relatively culture-free test of intelligence. It is a reliable (.85) test which correlates highly with general intelligence (approximately 53% of its variance may be attributed to g) but has a relatively low correlation with education (.40–.46). Thus, it is a test which is only minimally biased by an examinee's cultural or educational background. Block Design scores can, therefore, be an important tool in assessing the intellectual potential of persons from divergent cultural and intellectual backgrounds.

An interesting and useful contrast is the difference between the performance of schizophrenics and the performance of brain-damaged patients. At least in part because Block Design is a structured, formal, impersonal task requiring little or no interaction with the examiner, schizophrenics usually have fairly good performances. The task is considerably more difficult for brain-damaged patients, particularly those with right hemisphere deficits. They have a difficult time analyzing and synthesizing nonverbal information to come up with new solutions. On other tests (i.e., Digit Symbol and Similarities), the two groups usually demonstrate similar patterns of deficits. The practical significance of this contrast is that it can aid in making a differential diagnosis between two disorders which often have similar behavioral expressions.

High scorers show a capacity for visual-motor-spatial perception,, a good ability to concentrate, and excellent nonverbal concept formation. Low scores suggest poor perceptual abilities, difficulties with visual integration, and problems maintaining a sustained effort. These can sometimes be the result of cerebral impairment, especially right hemisphere lesions.

Object Assembly:

Visual-motor organization
Synthesis; putting things together in a familiar configuration
Ability to differentiate familiar configurations
Manipulative and perceptual speed in perceiving the manner in which unknown
    objects relate to each other

Object Assembly is a good test of motor coordination and control, as are Digit Symbol (Coding) and Block Design. It measures the ability to differentiate familiar configurations, and also involves some anticipation and planning. However, scores are subject to a high degree of fluctuation primarily due to the accidental fitting together of parts. A further, but related, area which may create some confusion is that sometimes persons who are in the lower ranges of intelligence (60–75) do quite well, whereas persons with above-average I.Q.'s can do quite poorly. It is only a moderate measure of general intelligence (38% of its variance may be attributed to g) and is not highly correlated with Full Scale I.Q. scores (.56–.65). Furthermore, its correlation with other subtests is generally low (.30–.69) as is its reliability (.65–.71). Thus, it is one of the poorest subtests from a psychometric view, and scores should be treated with caution. The advantage of Object Assembly is that it tends to be a nonverbal "hold" test so that, along with Information and Vocabulary, it can be used to estimate a person's premorbid level of functioning. It is also similar to Block Design and Picture Arrangement in that an observant examiner can note a person's problem solving style and reactions to success or failure.

The test presents an "open" situation, and those who can work freely within this context usually do well. However, those with rigid visual organizations will stick with one clue without allowing themselves to change their frame of reference. This is often true of obsessive-compulsives. On the other hand, a flexible visual organization permits a rapid integration of new clues and an adaptation of these clues towards completing the task.

Persons scoring high on Object Assembly show good perceptual-motor coordination, have superior visual organization, and can maintain a flexible mental outlook. Low scorers show visual-motor disorganization, concreteness, and difficulties with visual concept formation.

Digit Symbol (Coding):

Visual-motor speed and coordination
Ability to learn an unfamiliar task; capacity for learning and responding to new visual material
Some degree of flexibility; ability to shift
Capacity for sustained effort, attention, concentration, and mental efficiency
Associative learning and ability to imitate newly learned visual material
Short-term memory

Visual-motor integration is implied by good performance on Digit Symbol. However, the most important function necessary for a high score is psychomotor speed. This test involves the appropriate combining of the newly learned memory of the digit with the symbol, as well as adequate spatial-motor orientation followed by executing the half-habituated activity of drawing the symbol. The subtest also requires the ability to learn an unfamiliar task, accuracy of eye-hand coordination, attentional skills, short-term memory, and the ability to work under pressure. This is a delicate and complex interaction which can be disturbed because of difficulties with any of the above skills. Whereas Vocabulary is a highly stable ("hold") subtest, Digit Symbol is extremely sensitive to the effects of either organic or functional impairment. In particular, depressed and brain-damaged patients have a difficult time with this subtest.

Since visual-motor coordination — particularly visual acuity and motor activity — is implied, it is not surprising to find that those individuals with high reading and writing experience are among the high scorers. The functions which are implicit in the task are rapid visual, spatial, and motor coordination, as well as the executive action of drawing the symbol. Since this task requires sustained attention and quick decision making, anxious hesitancy and obsessive doubt significantly lower scores. Furthermore, persons who are extremely competitive but also become highly anxious in competitive situations may be adversely affected. Not only can Digit Symbol scores be lowered by anxiety, but the psychomotor slowing found in depressive states or the confused orientation of schizophrenics likewise produces a decrease in performance. Thus, a rough index of the severity of a person's depression can be assessed by comparing the relative lowering of Digit Symbol with the other (especially "hold") subtest scores. Of particular significance are the facts that Digit Symbol is one of the subtests most sensitive to the effects of organic impairment (Fitzhugh and Fitzhugh, 1964; Hirschenfang, 1960a) and also that it tends to be one of the lower scores found in learning disabled individuals (Bannatyne, 1974).

High scorers show excellent visual-motor ability, mental efficiency, capacity for rote learning of new material, and quick psychomotor reactions. Lower scorers show reduced capacity for visual associative learning, impaired visual-motor functioning, and poor mental alertness.

Mazes (WISC-R):

Planning ability or foresight
Perceptual organization
Visual-motor coordination

The Mazes subtest is an optional portion of the WISC-R and is not extensively used. A disadvantage of Mazes is that its correlation with the Full Scale I.Q. is not especially high ($r = .44$), and it is also a poor measure of g (20% of its variance may be attributed to g). It does provide an additional and often useful test, particularly with nonverbally oriented children or when a further assessment of planning, sequencing, and perceptual organization is required. Its main advantage is that it is a relatively pure measure of perceptual planning ability.

Individuals with high scores have an efficient ability to plan ahead and maintain a flexible mental orientation, which further suggests an excellent ability to delay impulsive action (Glasser and Zimmerman, 1967; Ireland-Galman, Padilla, and Michael, 1980). Low scores reflect impulsivity and poor visual-motor coordination. Often unusually low scores may suggest poor reality orientation (Glasser and

Zimmerman, 1967) or organic cerebral impairment, particularly to the frontal areas (Waugh and Bush, 1971).

COMMON INTERPRETIVE HYPOTHESES

The following interpretive hypotheses are frequently used in interpreting WAIS-R and WISC-R profiles. Before approaching these hypotheses, there are several important cautions and considerations which clinicians should keep in mind. First of all, this list is by no means exhaustive and readers are encouraged to consult the references recommended at the end of this chapter (see Kaufman, 1979; Matarazzo, 1972; Sattler, 1982). Secondly, the research on the validity of subtest profile analysis is questionable and often conflicting. For example, there are an impressive number of studies which support the finding that Performance I.Q. is lowered by right hemisphere lesions and an equal number of studies challenging this. [A more complete discussion of this and related issues is beyond the scope of this book, and the reader is referred to discussions in other sources (see Golden, 1979; Kaufman, 1979).] The following items are therefore hypotheses and should be treated as such; they are tentative and need additional verification. They are possibilities which should serve to encourage further exploration. Finally, these hypotheses are organized as if they are equally applicable to children's (WISC-R) scores and to adults' (WAIS-R). Although for most hypotheses the principles are quite similar, examiners should be aware of possible differences. This is especially true for areas relating to possible organicity, since a young child's brain is not characterized by the same degree of specialization and localization as an adult's (hypotheses 1, 2, and 5). Furthermore, children do not have as well-defined sex roles as adults, so interpretations relating to these differences (hypothesis 6) will also have to be taken into consideration.

1. A Verbal I.Q. which is significantly above Performance I.Q. (15 points or more) can be indicative of:
    a) high level of academic and/or personal achievement (Imre, 1963);
    b) individuals from an urban environment (Wechsler, 1958);
    c) most "neuroses," particularly in anxiety and tension states, obsessive-compulsives, and depressives (Gilbert, 1969; Maley, 1970);
    d) learning problems based on perceptual difficulties (Rourke and Telegdy, 1971);
    e) patients with right hemisphere cerebral impairment (Blatt and Allison, 1968; Lansdell and Smith, 1972; Russell, 1972, 1979).
2. A Performance I.Q. which is significantly above Verbal I.Q. can be indicative of:
    a) underachievers, particularly if they have not made use of educational opportunities (Guertin, Ladd, Frank, Rabin, and Hiester, 1966; Heinicke, 1972);

b) a lower socioeconomic level (Kaufman, 1979);

c) sociopathic, delinquent individuals (Dean, 1977; Haynes and Bensch, 1981; Wechsler, 1958);

d) left hemisphere cerebral impairment with a static focal lesion (Goldstein and Shelley, 1975; Guertin, Ladd, Frank, and Rabin, 1966);

e) severe reading difficulties (Rugel, 1974).

3. Distractibility significantly lowers Digit Span scores as well as Arithmetic and Digit Symbol (Coding) (Kaufman, 1975). This distractibility is often directly related to anxiety, and Digit Span is generally considered to be the subtest most sensitive to the effects of anxiety (Allison, Blatt, and Zimet, 1968; Wechsler, 1958). Since all of these subtests, but primarily Digit Symbol and Digit Span, require sequencing, a general lowering may also represent a deficit in this area (Bannatyne, 1974; Smith, Coleman, Dokecki, and Davis, 1977); see hypothesis 8.

4. Psychotic individuals tend to have higher verbal than performance scores (Wechsler, 1958). Digit Span tends to be lowest, and usually Comprehension is also significantly lowered. Information, Block Design, and Vocabulary tend to be the highest scores for schizophrenics, whereas Picture Arrangement and Digit Symbol tend to be the lowest (Wechsler, 1958). However, these subtest scores can also be lowered by organic impairments; therefore, a differential diagnosis between disorders such as schizophrenia and organic brain syndrome should be made with appropriate caution and should never be based solely on the WAIS-R/WISC-R profiles.

5. Organically impaired individuals tire easily, and as a result, their timed test scores are generally lowered. Performance subtests are usually more difficult for these patients, particularly when the deficit is in the right hemisphere. The most sensitive test for brain damage is Digit Symbol (Coding), but Block Design, Digit Span, Arithmetic, and Picture Arrangement are also likely to be lowered. These represent Wechsler's "no hold" subtests, whereas Information and Vocabulary are considered to be "hold" subtests since, for adults, they are generally more resistant to the effects of organic or functional disorders (Gonen and Brown, 1968; Parsons, Vega, and Burn, 1969). When assessing children, however, the concept of "hold" versus "no hold" tests should be examined carefully since several researchers have found Vocabulary to be one of the subtests most sensitive to the effects of cerebral impairment, which is reflected by its being one of the lowest scores in such cases (Boll, 1974; Reitan, 1974a). A further caution is that "no hold" tests can also be lowered as a result of functional disorders such as schizophrenia. Evaluating the relative patterns of "no hold" tests for brain-damaged patients is, therefore, usually most appropriate for assessing the nature of their deficits only after a diagnosis of brain damage has been made.

6. Individuals filling stereotyped feminine roles score highest in overall Verbal I.Q. and are particularly high in Digit Span and Similarities. Con-

versely, strongly "masculine" subjects score highest in Arithmetic, Picture Completion, and Information (Wechsler, 1958). However, this pattern is more likely to be relevant for Caucasians and may not be appropriate for interpreting the results from persons of divergent cultural backgrounds.

7. Learning disabled individuals, particularly those with genetic dyslexia, often score highest on subtests requiring spatial abilities (Object Assembly, Block Design, and Picture Completion) in which little or no sequencing is required, (Bannatyne, 1974). Conceptual skills are intermediate (Comprehension, Similarities, and Vocabulary), and subtests requiring sequencing abilities (Digit Span, Digit Symbol, and Picture Arrangement) are lowest. Thus, their spatial ability is greater than their conceptual ability, which in turn is greater than their sequential ability (Bannatyne's Factors; Banatyne, 1974). A similar pattern was found by Naglieri (1980), in which Digit Span and Coding were the most frequent low points. Although these patterns often occur with learning disabilities, there are other patterns which do not necessarily fit this description (Sattler, 1980). This means that clinicians should be alert to many different expressions of learning disabilities other than those described by Bannatyne and Naglieri.

8. Delinquent, acting out persons usually score significantly higher on performance subtests than on verbal ones (Sacuzzo and Lewardowski, 1976; Wickham, 1978). In particular, scores on subtests reflecting academic achievement (Information, Vocabulary, and Arithmetic) are likely to be low, with difficulties in judgment often reflected by a lowered performance in Comprehension (Brandt, 1982). Although most verbal scales will tend to be lower, Similarities — which is a test of abstract thinking relatively independent of education — may still be relatively elevated. This pattern reflects the difficulty these individuals have in adapting and conforming to a structured academic environment, which results in a general lowering in those tests which depend on an adequate assimilation of traditional academic information.

ADMINISTERING SHORT FORMS

The administration of short forms is useful for screening purposes, but they have the main disadvantage of sacrificing useful clinical data. Each clinician must decide whether or not the amount of time saved is worth the loss of clinical data and lowered validity. The primary approach for giving a Wechsler short form is to give selected subtests which, either individually or as a group, have relatively high correlations with a full administration. A common short form composed of two verbal and two performance subtests consists of Arithmetic, Vocabulary, Block Design, and Picture Arrangement (Kaufman, 1976). These are then prorated to determine the person's overall I.Q. which has been found to have a

WAIS-R Profile Sheet

Name _____ Date _____ Birth Date _____ Age _____ Grade _____ School _____

School District _____ Examiner _____ VERBAL I.Q. _____ PERFORMANCE I.Q. _____ FULL SCALE I.Q. _____

Verbal Scale: Ability to work with abstract verbal symbols; perceptual skills included (auditory).

	5	6	7	8	9	10	11	12	13	14	15	16	17	18	19	SUBTEST MEANINGS
Information	·	·	·	·	·	·	·	·	·	·	·	·	·	·	·	Remote memory; experience and education; cultural background
Digit Span	·	·	·	·	·	·	·	·	·	·	·	·	·	·	·	Concentration; immediate auditory memory
Vocabulary	·	·	·	·	·	·	·	·	·	·	·	·	·	·	·	Educational background; general verbal intelligence; range of ideas
Arithmetic	·	·	·	·	·	·	·	·	·	·	·	·	·	·	·	Concentration; numerical reasoning; school learning
Comprehension	·	·	·	·	·	·	·	·	·	·	·	·	·	·	·	Practical knowledge and social judgment; common sense
Similarities	·	·	·	·	·	·	·	·	·	·	·	·	·	·	·	Verbal concept formation; logical and abstract reasoning

Performance Scale: Ability to work in concrete situation; perceptual skills included (visual).

	5	6	7	8	9	10	11	12	13	14	15	16	17	18	19	SUBTEST MEANINGS
Picture Completion	·	·	·	·	·	·	·	·	·	·	·	·	·	·	·	Visual concentration; ability to visually differentiate essential information
Picture Arrangement	·	·	·	·	·	·	·	·	·	·	·	·	·	·	·	Planning ability and foresight; ability to assess nonverbal social interactions
Block Design	·	·	·	·	·	·	·	·	·	·	·	·	·	·	·	Visual-motor coordination; spatial problem solving; concentration
Object Assembly	·	·	·	·	·	·	·	·	·	·	·	·	·	·	·	Visual-motor organization; seeing relationships of parts to wholes
Digit Symbol	·	·	·	·	·	·	·	·	·	·	·	·	·	·	·	Visual-motor speed; ability to learn rote tasks

Figure 2-4.

WISC-R Profile Sheet

Name _____ Date _____ Birth Date _____ Age _____ Grade _____ School _____

School District _____ Examiner _____

VERBAL I.Q. _____ PERFORMANCE I.Q. _____ FULL SCALE I.Q. _____

Verbal Scale: Ability to work with abstract verbal symbols; perceptual skills included (auditory).

	5	6	7	8	9	10	11	12	13	14	15	16	17	18	19	SUBTEST MEANINGS
Information	.	.	.	.	.	.	.	.	.	.	.	.	.	.	.	Remote memory; experience and education; cultural background
Similarities	.	.	.	.	.	.	.	.	.	.	.	.	.	.	.	Verbal concept formation; logical and abstract reasoning
Arithmetic	.	.	.	.	.	.	.	.	.	.	.	.	.	.	.	Concentration; numerical reasoning; school learning
Vocabulary	.	.	.	.	.	.	.	.	.	.	.	.	.	.	.	Educational background; general verbal intelligence; range of ideas
Comprehension	.	.	.	.	.	.	.	.	.	.	.	.	.	.	.	Practical knowledge and social judgment; common sense
Digit Span	.	.	.	.	.	.	.	.	.	.	.	.	.	.	.	Concentration; immediate auditory memory

Performance Scale: Ability to work in concrete situations; perceptual skills included (visual).

	5	6	7	8	9	10	11	12	13	14	15	16	17	18	19	SUBTEST MEANINGS
Picture Completion	.	.	.	.	.	.	.	.	.	.	.	.	.	.	.	Visual concentration; ability to visually differentiate essential information
Picture Arrangement	.	.	.	.	.	.	.	.	.	.	.	.	.	.	.	Planning ability and foresight; ability to assess nonverbal social interactions
Block Design	.	.	.	.	.	.	.	.	.	.	.	.	.	.	.	Visual-motor coordination; spatial problem solving; concentration
Object Assembly	.	.	.	.	.	.	.	.	.	.	.	.	.	.	.	Visual-motor organization; seeing relationships of parts to wholes
Coding	.	.	.	.	.	.	.	.	.	.	.	.	.	.	.	Visual-motor speed; ability to learn rote tasks
Mazes (optional)	.	.	.	.	.	.	.	.	.	.	.	.	.	.	.	Planning and foresight in following a visual pattern

Figure 2-5.

correlation in the range of .95 with a full administration (Dopplett, 1956; Kaufman, 1976). Other short forms include all the verbal subtests plus Block Design (.86), or Arithmetic, Block Design, and Vocabulary (.84). A very brief but popular two-subtest combination consists of Vocabulary and Block Design. Both these subtests correlate highly with g and with the Full Scale I.Q. (WISC-R = .78–.88; Ryan, 1981). Although this can be a good combination for screening purposes (Kilian and Hughes, 1978), it is not sufficiently valid for classification (King and Smith, 1972). Another approach is to administer all the subtests, yet give only every other or every third item within each subtest (Silverstein, 1967; Yudin, 1966).

PROFILE SHEETS

The forms in Figures 2-4 and 2-5 may be used to plot WAIS-R or WISC-R scores so that an individual's test results can be quickly and easily observed. The skills required for the 11 WAIS-R and the 12 WISC-R subtests are summarized on the far right side, and the scaled scores are plotted in the center. This provides persons reviewing the test results with a statement of the three I.Q.'s as well as a summary of their relative strengths and weaknesses. These forms can be especially helpful when explaining test results to persons who are not trained in psychological testing.

Table 2-2. Interpretive Rationales, Implications of High and Low Scores, and Instructional Implications for Wechsler Scales and Factor Scores.

ABILITY	BACKGROUND FACTORS	POSSIBLE IMPLICATIONS OF HIGH SCORES	POSSIBLE IMPLICATIONS OF LOW SCORES	INSTRUC- TIONAL RECOM- MENDATIONS
		Full Scale		
General intelligence	Natural endowment	Good general intelligence	Poor general intelligence	Focus on language development
Scholastic aptitude	Richness of early environment	Good scholastic aptitude	Poor scholastic aptitude	activities
Academic aptitude	Extent of schooling	Readiness to master a school curriculum	Not ready to master school curriculum	Focus on visual learning activities Develop concept formation skills
Readiness to master a school curriculum	Cultural opportunities Interests Rate of motor activity Persistence Visual-motor organization Alertness			Reinforce persistence

NOTE: Jerome Sattler, *Assessment of Children's Intelligence and Special Abilities*, Second Edition, pp. 597–598. Copyright © 1982 by Allyn and Bacon, Inc. Reprinted with permission.

Table 2-2. Interpretive Rationales, Implications of High and Low Scores, and Instructional Implications for Wechsler Scales and Factor Scores. (continued)

ABILITY	BACKGROUND FACTORS	POSSIBLE IMPLICATIONS OF HIGH SCORES	POSSIBLE IMPLICATIONS OF LOW SCORES	INSTRUC- TIONAL RECOM- MENDATIONS
		Verbal Scale		
Verbal compre- hension Application of verbal skills and information to the solution of new problems Verbal ability Ability to process verbal informa- tion Ability to think with words	Natural endow- ment Richness of early environment Extent of school- ing Cultural oppor- tunities Interests	Good verbal com- prehension Good scholastic aptitude Possession of knowledge of the cultural milieu Good concept formation Readiness to master school curriculum Achievement orientation	Poor verbal com- prehension Poor scholastic aptitude Inadequate under- standing of the cultural milieu Poor concept for- mation Bilingual back- ground Foreign back- ground Not ready to mas- ter school cur- riculum Poor achievement orientation	Stress language development activities Use of verbal enrichment exercises Focus on current events Use exercises in- volving concept formation
		Performance Scale		
Perceptual orga- nization Ability to think in terms of vi- sual images and manipulate them with fluency, flexi- bility, and relative speed Ability to inter- pret or orga- nize visually perceived material against a time limit Nonverbal ability Ability to form relatively ab- stract concepts and relation- ships without the use of words	Natural endow- ment Rate of motor activity Persistence Visual-motor organization Alertness	Good perceptual organization Good alertness to detail Good nonverbal reasoning ability Good persistence Good ability to work quickly and efficiently Good spatial ability	Poor perceptual organization Poor alertness to detail Poor nonverbal reasoning ability Limited persis- tence Poor ability to work quickly and efficiently Poor spatial ability	Focus on visual learning activities Focus on part- whole relation- ships Use spatial-visual tasks Encourage trial- and-error activities Reinforce persis- tence Focus on visual planning activi- ties Improve scanning techniques

NOTE: Jerome Sattler, *Assessment of Children's Intelligence and Special Abilities,* Second Edition, pp. 597–598. Copyright © 1982 by Allyn and Bacon, Inc. Reprinted with permission.

Table 2-3. Suggested Remediation Activities for
Combinations of Wechsler Subtests.

SUBJECTS	ABILITY	ACTIVITIES
Information, Vocabulary, and Comprehension	General knowledge and verbal fluency	(1) Review basic concepts, such as days of the week, months, time, distances, and directions; (2) have children report major current events by referring to pictures and articles from magazines and newspapers; (3) teach similarities and differences of designs, topography, transportation, etc.; (4) have children make a scrapbook of pictures of animals, buildings, etc.; (5) introduce words, dictionary work, abstract words; (6) have children repeat simple stories; (7) have children explain how story characters are feeling and thinking.
Similarities and Vocabulary	Verbal-conceptual	(1) Use show and tell games; (2) have children make a scrapbook of classifications, such as of animals, vehicles, and utensils; (3) have children match abstract concepts; (4) have children find commonality in dissimilar objects; (5) review basic concepts such as days of the week, month, time, directions, and distances.
Digit Span, Arithmetic, Picture Arrangement	Attention and concentration	(1) Have children arrange cards in a meaningful sequence; (2) have children learn telephone number, address, etc.; (3) use spelling word games; (4) use memory games; (5) have children learn days of week, months of year; (6) use mathematical word problems; (7) use dot-to-dot exercises; (8) have children describe details in pictures; (9) use tracing activities; (10) use tinker toys.
Block Design and Object Assembly	Spatial-visual	(1) Have children identify common objects and discuss details; (2) use guessing games involving description of a person, place, or thing; (3) have children match letters, shapes, numbers, etc.; (4) use jigsaw puzzles; (5) use block building activities.
Coding, Block Design, Object Assembly, Animal House, and Mazes	Visual-motor	(1) Use proper folding activities; (2) use finger painting activities; (3) use dot-to-dot exercises; (4) use scissor cutting exercises; (5) use skywriting exercises; (6) have children string beads in patterns; (7) use pegboard designs; (8) use puzzles (large jigsaw pieces); (9) have children solve a maze; (10) have children follow a moving object with coordinated eye movements; (11) use tracing exercises (e.g., trace hand, geometric forms, and letters); (12) have children make large circles and lines on chalkboard; (13) have children copy from patterns; (14) have children draw from memory.

NOTE: From Jerome Sattler, *Assessment of Children's Intelligence and Special Abilities*, Second Edition, p. 599. Copyright © 1982 by Allyn and Bacon, Inc. Reprinted with permission.

INSTRUCTIONAL RECOMMENDATIONS

Once a WAIS-R or WISC-R has been scored and interpreted, an examiner must still develop practical recommendations. Table 2-2 gives the interpretive rationales, implications of high and low scores, and possible instructional recommendations for persons scoring low on either the Full Scale, Verbal, or Performance I.Q. sections. Table 2-3 has a similar format but enables a clinician to develop instructional recommendations (activities) for commonly occurring groups of subtests. Although these tables were originally developed for the analysis of children's (WISC-R) scores, a clinician can also utilize the recommendations for adult (WAIS-R) scores by developing tasks which are similar but somewhat more difficult.

RECOMMENDED READING

Kaufman, A.S. *Intelligent testing with the WISC-R*. New York: John Wiley & Sons, 1979.

Matarazzo, J.D. *Wechsler's Measurement and Appraisal of Adult Intelligence*. Baltimore: Williams and Wilkins, 1972.

Sattler, J.M. *Assessment of Children's Intelligence and Special Abilities* (2nd ed.). Boston: Allyn and Bacon, 1982.

Wechsler, D. *Manual for the Wechsler Intelligence Scale for Children — Revised*. New York: Psychological Corporation, 1974.

Wechsler, D. *Manual for the Wechsler Adult Intelligence Scale — Revised*. New York: Psychological Corporation, 1981.

Zimmerman, I.L., Woo-Sam, J.M., and Glasser, A.J. *The Clinical Interpretation of the Wechsler Adult Intelligence Scale*. New York: Grune & Stratton, 1973.

3
The Bender Visual Motor Gestalt Test

The Bender Visual Motor Gestalt Test, usually referred to as the Bender Gestalt Test or the Bender, is widely used primarily in diagnosing brain damage. It consists of nine designs which are sequentially presented to the subject with the request that he or she reproduce them on a blank 8 1/2 X 11 inch sheet of paper. The subject's designs are then rated on their relative degree of accuracy and overall integration.

Although the Bender has most frequently been used as a screening device for brain damage, its research and clinical applications extend well beyond this area. Within child populations, it has been used to screen for school readiness, predict school achievement, diagnose reading and learning problems, evaluate emotional difficulties, and study mental retardation, and also as a nonverbal intelligence test (see reviews in Koppitz, 1975b). For adults and adolescents, the Bender has proved useful in the diagnosis of brain damage (e.g., see Hain, 1964; Hutt, 1969) and as a projective test for the assessment of various personality functions. Thus, the Bender, whose task appears simple at first glance, has given rise to a surprisingly diverse and flexible number of clinical and research uses. The diversity of the Bender and the amount of interest it has engendered have also resulted in a variety of administration procedures, scoring guidelines, and interpretation systems.

HISTORY AND DEVELOPMENT

The Bender Gestalt Test was originally assembled by Lauretta Bender in 1938 and discussed in her monograph *A Visual Motor Gestalt Test and Its Clinical Use*. The nine designs were adapted from a set of 30 configurations developed by Wertheimer (1923) which he used to demonstrate the Gestalt laws of perception. Wertheimer emphasized the normal individual's ability to respond to the designs in an integrated and coherent manner. Bender developed this theme further and demonstrated how an individual's level of performance could be impaired by delayed perceptual-motor maturation as well as by either a functional or an organically induced pathological state. Bender's primary use for her test was to provide an index of perceptual-motor maturation which could be inferred from the degree of integration reflected in the nine reproductions of the designs.

For many years after the publication of the test, the data derived from its administration were not reported in an objective and systematic manner, which made it initially difficult to evaluate the test's effectiveness. Many clinicians still use a subjective, intuitive approach, although several objective scoring methods have been developed. These more objective methods have made possible a more accurate and empirical assessment of the test's effectiveness. One of the earliest and most widely accepted scoring systems for adults was developed by Pascal and Suttell (1951). They view the approach which the individual takes towards the test as reflective of his overall approach towards his environment. The more adapted and adjusted individuals are, the more able they will be to respond to the designs in a coherent, integrated manner. Conversely, individuals who lack integrative capacities or who have poor emotional adjustment will do poorly. On the basis of matched samples of normals and abnormals, Pascal and Suttell were able to develop a scoring system with a mean of 50 and a standard deviation of 10. Test-retest reliabilities for normals over a 24-hour interval were around .70, and interscorer reliabilities for trained examiners were reported to be .90. Test cutoff scores were able to differentiate between normals, neurotics, and psychotics (scoring 50, 68.2, and 81.8, respectively), as well as to differentiate organics from both normals and psychotics (Tolor and Schulberg, 1963).

Although Pascal and Suttell recognized the effects of maturation on the test performance of young children, they used young children's test results merely as a means of comparison with adult records and did not develop separate norms or scoring procedures for children. In order to correct this limitation, Koppitz (1963, 1975b) developed a scoring system for children and carried out an extensive standardization of 1104 children from kindergarten through fourth grade. Interscorer reliabilities were excellent (.88 and .96), although test-retest reliability over a four-month interval was somewhat low (.58–.66). The correlations found between Koppitz's scoring method on the Bender and the WISC-R performance subtests ranged from –.51 (Block Design) to –.08 (Coding; Redfering and Collins, 1982). Relatively high validities are reported in assessing school readiness in first grade children (Koppitz, 1973) and predicting their subsequent level of educational achievement (Koppitz, 1962b; Wallbrown, Wallbrown, and Engin, 1977). Further significant correlations were found between the degree of mental retardation and the number of errors (Andert, Hustak, and Dining, 1978), as well as between first graders' Bender scores and their level of performance in reading and arithmetic (Ackerman, Peters, and Dykman, 1971; Koppitz, 1958a). Koppitz (1963, 1975b) reports significant differences between the scores of brain-damaged children and those of normals. However, she cautions that for a diagnosis of brain damage, the examiner should consider not only the child's scores but also additional observations such as the time required to complete the test, the amount of space utilized, behavioral observations, and an inquiry into the relative degree of awareness the child has regarding his errors. The Koppitz system is designed exclusively for children since, after the age of 10, the scores no longer correlate either with intelligence test results or with age because after age 10 almost all individuals obtain perfect scores. Her interpretive guidelines are summarized later in this chapter, and her manual for scoring children's protocols can be found in Appendix A of her book *The Bender Gestalt Test for Young Children* (1975b).

Hain (1964) developed a method of adult scoring which was somewhat different from the Pascal-Suttell system. Whereas Pascal and Suttell approached the designs card by card and identified 106 different potentially scorable characteristics, Hain approached the test performance as a whole. By a careful and systematic study of the Bender protocols of brain-damaged patients, he developed a 15-category scoring system. Any example of a scorable characteristic earns a ranked score for that category. For example, a rotation or reversal would earn 4 points, whereas an omission only scores 1 point. The Hain system has the advantage of being somewhat briefer and easier to learn; yet it still correctly distinguishes approximately 80% of brain-damaged patients from psychiatric and "non-brain-damaged" patients. For these reasons, Hain's procedures for scoring Bender protocols are included in Appendix C, and the discussion on adult Bender responses later in this chapter follows the general format of the Hain system.

Numerous additional scoring systems (Hutt, 1977; Jansky and de Hirsch, 1972; Keogh and Smith, 1961; Marley, 1982; Paulker, 1976; Plenk and Jones, 1967; Thweatt, Obrzut, and Taylor, 1972) have also been developed which have all met with varying degrees of success, popularity, and controversy (see Bender, 1970; Tolor and Brannigan, 1980). The ones most frequently quoted in the literature are those by Pascal and Suttell (1951) and Koppitz (1963, 1975b). However, all the scoring systems are similar in that they attempt to rearrange, tabulate, and assign different weights to the same commonly occurring responses such as lack of closure, perseveration, and rotations. Each one of these systems has various advantages and disadvantages, and none has yet become the dominant scoring method.

Despite some controversy and sometimes conflicting results, the Bender continues to generate continued research and is extensively used in clinical practice. In fact, 38 years after Bender's original 1938 monograph, Brown and McGuire (1976) published a survey of tests used in clinical practice and rated the Bender among the most widely used of all clinical tests. The extensive research and clinical interest in the Bender is reflected in the fact that over 1000 studies were listed in Buros's *Eighth Mental Measurements Yearbook* (1978).

RELIABILITY AND VALIDITY

Research studies using the more popular Bender scoring systems consistently confirm acceptable levels of reliability. Test-retest reliability using the Pascal and Suttell (1951) system on a sample population of normals over a 24-hour interval revealed a reliability of .70 (Pascal and Suttell, 1951), and interscorer reliabilities are reported at approximately .90 for trained scorers for both the Pascal and Suttell (1951) and the Koppitz developmental system (1975b).

Studies frequently confirm the validity of the Bender's usefulness in such areas as predicting school performance, assessing emotional problems, and differentiating brain-damaged patients from normals. For example, Hain (1964) indicated that scores on the Bender could correctly differentiate brain-damaged individuals from normals 81% of the time. Likewise, Koppitz (1975a) reported a fairly good ability to predict educational achievement of first graders. She also reports a significantly high correlation between Bender scores and performance in reading and arithmetic.

ASSETS AND LIMITATIONS

The Bender's relatively quick and easy administration has been one of the primary reasons for its popularity. It can usually be administered in 3–5 minutes and is an excellent way to initiate a testing session since it is typically perceived as being straightforward and nonthreatening. Furthermore, the test is flexible in that it can serve both as a projective test for studying personality and as a visuographic task for the assessment of organic impairment. In addition to these assets, most clinicians are familiar with the Bender, and it also provides a nonverbal developmental scale. It is sensitive in detecting malingering, can be used as an adjunctive technique in the assessment of brain damage, and has proved to be a useful research tool.

One primary advantage requiring further elaboration is that the Bender offers an excellent parallel between how the subject approaches general life situations and how he approaches reproducing the nine designs. This parallel has been demonstrated in both research and clinical settings. For example, schizophrenics might squeeze their drawings into one small section of the page and tend to rotate the figures in a haphazard manner (Nahas, 1976), or manic patients sometimes produce irregular sequences (Donnelly and Murphy, 1974), reflecting their difficulty with impulse control and their attentional deficits. Additional clinical information can be derived from observing anxious patients usually erasing and retracing their drawings, and compulsives often taking 3–5 minutes to complete each design and beginning by making extensive preliminary guidelines. Thus, the Bender is extremely useful in revealing the general style and manner of approach which the individual takes towards his world.

Although the Bender has a proven track record of achievements within the testing field, there are a number of cautions and limitations surrounding its use. The test has often been described as "assessing" brain damage, yet it is perhaps more accurate to say that it is a "screening device" for brain damage. It does not give in-depth information into the specific details and varieties of such damage. In fact, it is limited to relatively severe forms of brain damage especially in the right hemisphere, particularly the right parietal region (Filskov, 1978; Garron and Cheifetz, 1965; Hirschenfang, 1960). Thus, a patient may have significant left hemisphere lesions which could easily go undetected if a traditional scoring of the Bender was the sole method used to assess the presence of cerebral impairment. It is more correct to say, then, that the Bender is a screening device for generalized impairment and/or right parietal involvement.

There is often a certain degree of overlap between emotional and organic indicators on the Bender which adds to the risk of misdiagnosis. For example, one of the better indicators for organic impairment is the presence of rotations (Bender, 1938; Hain, 1964; Lacks and Newport, 1980; Symmes and Rapaport, 1972), yet moderate rotations, although less frequent, can also occur in the reproductions of psychotics or even neurotics (Billingslea, 1948; Fuller and Chagnon, 1962; Hutt and Gibby, 1970). Likewise, line tremors are often present in the drawings of chronic alcoholics particularly with Korsakoff's syndrome (Kaldegg, 1956; Pascal and Suttell, 1951), but they may also reflect nonorganic causes related to anxiety, tension, and the pent-up aggression which is often found in adolescent delinquent populations (Hutt, 1953; Pascal and Suttell, 1951; Zolik, 1958). The degree of overlap occurring in the scores of different populations has led some reviewers (Dana, Field, and Bolton, 1983) to seriously question the clinical usefulness of the Bender. From a clinical perspective, this means that an examiner must carefully consider and investigate all possibilities to determine why a subject produced certain types of responses on the test.

A further difficulty with the Bender is that there is no one commonly accepted and verified scoring and interpretation system. This has often resulted in research studies that have used different systems, which makes it somewhat difficult to compare their conclusions. Clinicians generally begin by learning a system of scoring and interpretation but end up with their own unique subjective approach based on clinical impressions. Although this may result in a highly workable, flexible approach, disagreements between "experts" can occur because of their differences in approaching the designs. Another difficulty in depending on clinical impressions is continued support for unsubstantiated and possibly incorrect clinical "lore."

When the Bender is used as a projective test, the same general criticisms which are true for any projective test are also true for Bender interpretations. These include a frequent, although often challenged, reliance on intuitive clinical guidelines; difficulty with objective scoring; inadequate validation studies; and test sensitivity to situational variables. Furthermore, projective approaches have often been subject to overinterpretation, because of clinician's using single signs as certainties rather than as hypotheses in need of further validation. Thus, to maximize its effectiveness, the Bender should be used in, and understood as, one test in an overall battery. Despite its limitations, the Bender remains an extremely prevalent, easily administered, reliable, and generally valid device for the clinician, particularly when an objective empirical method for scoring and interpretation is utilized.

ADMINISTRATION

When administering the Bender, the cards are presented one at a time and the person is asked to copy each design with a #2 pencil on a single sheet of blank 8 1/2 x 11 sheet of white paper which has been presented to them in a vertical position. The following verbal directions are recommended as a standard procedure:

> I have nine cards here with designs on them for you to copy. Here is the first one. Now go ahead and make one just like it.

When the person has completed the design, the next card is presented. No comments for additional instructions are to be given while the person is completing the drawings. If the person asks a specific question, he should be given a noncommital answer, for example: "Make it look as much like the picture on the card as you can." If the person begins to count the dots on figure 5, the examiner may say, "You do not have to count the dots, just make it look like the picture." If the person persists, this may show perfectionistic or compulsive tendencies, and this behavioral observation should be considered when evaluating the test results and formulating diagnostic impressions. Although examinees are allowed to pick up the cards, they are not allowed to turn them unless they are in the process of completing their drawing. If it looks as if they have turned the design and are beginning to copy it in the new position, the examiner should straighten the card and state that it should be copied from this angle. As many sheets of paper may be used as desired, although the client is presented with only one paper initially. There is no time limit, but it is important to note the length of time required to complete the test, since this information may be diagnostically significant.

In addition to the standard procedure for using the Bender Gestalt Test, a second, somewhat different administration of the designs is often diagnostically useful. Common procedures for this altered administration include: (1) asking the person to reproduce as many designs as possible from memory; (2) asking the person to draw the designs in any way he chooses — altering, combining, or elaborating at will; and (3) presenting the cards and asking the person what they remind him of. The last two techniques emphasize the projective possibilities of the Bender and provide information about the emotional adjustment of the person, much as a projective drawing or a free association test would do. The first variation provides an assessment of an individual's level of short-term visual-motor recall. Usually a normal subject with normal intelligence should be able to reproduce four or five designs. A further variation from the initial administration, which assesses a person's immediate visual memory, is to present him with a design for 5 seconds, remove it, and then have him reproduce it on his paper.

An important addition to Bender administration procedures for adolescents and adults is the Background Interference Procedure (BIP; Canter, 1963, 1966, 1976). This requires that the examiner complete the Bender designs on a specially designed paper with a confusing array of curved intersecting lines. It has been repeatedly demonstrated that brain-damaged patients show significant decrements in their BIP performance compared to their performances using a standard administration (Canter, 1966, 1971, 1976; Norton, 1978; Pardue, 1975). This is in contrast to functionally disordered patients and normals who typically do not show significant differences between the two administration procedures.

INTERPRETATION GUIDELINES: CHILDREN

As noted, a developmental scoring system was constructed by Koppitz (1963, 1975). This is in contrast to functionally disordered patients and normals scoring system to differentiate between distortions resulting from developmental delay or perceptual malfunctioning and those reflecting emotional factors and attitudes. The main purpose of her developmental scoring system is to provide a measure of a child's level of maturity in visual-motor perception In this section, we will summarize Koppitz's approach and provide general interpretive guidelines based on indicators for organicity, visual-motor perception difficulties, developmental maturation, and emotional indicators. The specific scoring criteria developed by Koppitz (1963, 1975b) for developmental level can be found in Appendix A of *The Bender Gestalt Test for Young Children* (Volume 2, 1975b). A different set of scoring criteria for emotional indicators has also been developed by Koppitz and is included in *The Bender Gestalt Test for Young Children* (1963). In order to obtain specific scores, clinicians should consult these criteria. Both texts by Koppitz (1963, 1975b) include important guidelines, cautions, and reviews of research, and clinicians are encouraged to consult these for further elaboration and discussion

Although some practitioners treat a protocol as either a test of visual-motor perception or a test of emotional adjustment and personality, it is often possible for both of these areas to be evaluated from a single protocol. By use of a multidimensional approach, the Bender designs can provide the examiner with valuable information regarding the individual's perceptual maturity, neurological impairment, and emotional adjustment.

Before one attempts to score the Bender protocol using Koppitz's specified guidelines, it is important to assess the quality of the drawings as a whole. As with any projective technique, the manner in which the task is completed and the behavioral observations made while the child is completing the task provide useful information when formulating a complete picture of emotional or perceptual adjustment. More specifically, the examiner should pay close attention to the line quality of the drawings, figure size, placement, the order and organization of the designs, erasures, distortions, omissions, reworking, time required to complete the test, comments made during the test, and any other unusual treatment of the drawings. When these general observations have been completed, the protocol can be evaluated for organicity, visual-motor perception, developmental maturation, and emotional difficulties.

Indicators for Organicity

When considering the possibility of organicity on a Bender protocol, it is important that the designs be evaluated as a whole group. Some of the indicators for brain damage are also indicators for emotional disturbance, and it is only when the protocol is evaluated as a complete unit, and all the unusual features are taken into consideration, that an appropriate diagnosis can be made. In many cases, however, the results of the Bender are not sufficient to make a differential diagnosis between brain damage and emotional disturbance, and additional information is needed to determine the nature of the individual's problems.

The categories of response listed below have been reported in the literature as being significant indicators of brain damage both for children and for adults. Although their presence may indicate impairment, it must be remembered that even if none of these factors is present, the person may still be suffering a neurological impairment. Conversely, a poor Bender performance may reflect a variety of factors, only one of which is neurological impairment. However, the following types of Bender responses have been selected because they are more likely to suggest organicity than other kinds of responses.

1. Rotation of all or part of a design (Billingslea, 1963; Diller, Ben-Yishay, Gertsman, Goodkin, Gordon, Weinberg, 1976; Smith and Martin, 1967)
2. Perseveration within one design or from one design to another (Hain, 1964; Lerner, 1972; Marley, 1982)
3. Distortions of figures (Beck, 1959; Lerner, 1972)
4. Fragmentation or omission of parts of a design (Gilbert, 1969; Hutt, 1977)

5. Substitution of lines for dots (Lerner, 1972; Small, 1973)
6. Closure problems, particularly on figures A and 4 (Pope and Scott, 1967)

There are also a number of important considerations when evaluating the performance of children. Some children mature more slowly than others, particularly in the area of visual-motor perception. For these children, Bender scores will improve dramatically within a few years. Some children may have a genetically determined weakness in visual-motor perception, whereas others may have lacked motivation, been temporarily upset, or been fatigued or ill during the test administration. A general guideline to follow is that if a Bender score is more than −1 standard deviation from the mean normative Bender score for a given age group (see Appendix A), the possibility of brain damage exists. However, a definite diagnosis of brain damage should never be made solely on the basis of a single test score. Furthermore, the possibility of brain damage cannot definitely be ruled out when a good Bender is obtained, since performance on this test will only be affected when specific areas of the brain are damaged. If other areas of the brain that are not needed for producing a good Bender are impaired, then a normal Bender is very likely. The guidelines summarized in Table 3-1 are useful in evaluating each Bender design for consideration of neurological impairment. However, Koppitz (1975b) has indicated that little is gained by using both the developmental scoring and the Bender indicators of brain injury since they do not complement or give additional information to one another. They are both equally effective in diagnosing the presence of brain injury, so an individual clinician may decide to use either approach.

If a clinician decides to use the neurological indicators outlined in Table 3-1, the basic approach is to consider the overall number of indicators that are present. A quick assessment can be made for children over 8 years of age by looking at the following eight characteristics, which are a composite of Koppitz's indicators. If four or more of these characteristics are present, then central nervous system impairment is a strong possibility.

1. Simplification of two or more figures to a level three or more years below the child's mental age
2. Collision of a figure with another figure or reproductions in which a figure runs off the edge of the paper
3. Fragmentation of one or more figures
4. Rotation of one or more figures 90° or more
5. Incorrect number of units in three or more figures
6. Perseveration from figure to figure of one type of unit
7. Tremulous line quality
8. Commas and/or dashes in two or more figures

Table 3-1. Bender Indicators of Brain Injury for Children 5–10 Years of Age.*

Extra or missing angles:

> Figure A — Significantly† more often in BI at all age levels.
> Figure 7 — Common in BI and NBI though more frequently in BI at all age levels; *no* BI drew correct angles before age 8.
> Figure 8 — Common in BI and NBI through age 6, significant† for BI thereafter.

Angles for curves:

> Figure 6 — Common in BI and NBI but significantly† more often in BI at all age levels; *all* BI drew angles up to age 7.

Straight line for curves:

> Figure 6 — Rare but highly significant‡ for BI when present.

Disproportion of parts:

> Figure A — Common in BI and NBI through age 6, significant† for BI thereafter.
> Figure 7 — Common in BI and NBI through age 7, significant† for BI thereafter.

Substitution of five circles for dots:

> Figure 1 — Present in BI and NBI but significantly† more often in BI at all ages.
> Figure 3 — Present in BI and NBI through age 6, significant† for BI thereafter.
> Figure 5 — Present in BI and NBI through age 8, significant† for BI thereafter.

Rotation of design by 45°:

> Figures 1, 4, and 8 — Highly significant‡ for BI at all age levels.
> Figures A and 5 — Significant† for BI at all age levels.
> Figure 7 — Present in BI and NBI through age 6, significant† for BI thereafter.
> Figure 3 — Present in BI and NBI through age 7, significant† for BI thereafter.
> Figure 2 — Present in BI and NBI through age 8, significant† for BI thereafter.

Failure to integrate parts:

> Figures A and 4 — Significant† for BI at all age levels.
> Figure 6 — Rare but significant† for BI when present at all age levels.
> Figure 7 — Common for BI and NBI through age 6, significant† for BI thereafter.

Omission or addition of row of circles:

> Figure 2 — Common in BI and NBI through age 6, highly significant‡ for BI thereafter.

Shape of design lost:

> Figure 3 — Present in BI and NBI through age 5, significant† for BI thereafter.
> Figure 5 — Rare and does *not* differentiate between BI and NBI at any age.

Line for series of dots:

> Figures 3 and 5 — Rare but highly significant‡ for BI at all age levels.

Perseveration:

> Figures 1, 2, and 6 — Common in BI and NBI through age 7, highly significant‡ for BI therafter.

NOTE: Reprinted, by permission, from E.M. Koppitz, *The Bender Gestalt Test for Young Children,* New York: Grune & Stratton, Inc., 1963.

† Significant = occurring more often, but not exclusively, in BI group.
‡ Highly significant = occurring almost exclusively in BI group.
*BI = brain injured; NBI = non-brain injured.

Visual Motor Perception Difficulties

In addition to assessing whether or not brain damage is present clinicians may also wish to evaluate how the damage affects visual-motor perception. Although damage to the cerebral tissue itself is permanent, the brain's overall functioning is often able to compensate and allow a child to overcome specific inadequacies. This is possible only if (1) the extent of the brain injury is not too extreme and the location is not too critical, (2) there is sufficient intellectual ability to learn alternative problem solving methods, and (3) there are no serious emotional handicaps which would interfere with adjustment.

Sometimes a child has learned to compensate for a visual-motor difficulty and his problem is not readily observable on his Bender protocol. However, by carefully observing the child's behavior while the Bender is being completed, such children can sometimes be recognized. Specific behaviors which may reflect that strategies to compensate for cerebral impairment have been learned include the following:

1. Excessive amount of time required to complete designs
2. "Anchoring" designs by placing a finger on each design as it is presented
3. Glancing briefly at a design card and then reproducing it from memory
4. Rotation of stimulus card and/or drawing paper in order to complete the designs properly
5. Checking and rechecking dots and circles several times, and being uncertain about the correct number
6. Impulsive, quickly executed figures which are erased and corrected with an unusual degree of effort
7. Expressed dissatisfaction with poorly executed drawings and repeated efforts to correct them.

Careful observation and evaluation of the Bender protocol can help to determine if a child's visual-motor perception problem is the result of a receptive disturbance (a problem in visual perception), an expressive disturbance (a difficulty in reproducing that which has been perceived), or both. When a child performs poorly because of a maturational lag, the receptive and expressive aspects of perception are both affected. Although these two functions may mature at slightly different rates in different children, when the difference between them is extreme, there is cause for concern. In young children, large discrepancies between receptive and expressive functions are to be expected, but as the child matures perceptually, these differences should decrease.

One of the easiest ways to determine if the child's receptive functioning is adequate is to ask him whether his drawing looks like the stimulus drawing. Often children with receptive problems do not perceive any differences between the two drawings, although the discrepancies may be quite obvious. When disturbance is in the expressive mode, the child can often describe how the drawing should look but be unable to reproduce it correctly on the paper. These children require a great deal of time to complete their designs but usually show little distortion in the figures. For these children, physical coordination is evident, but the ability to position the designs accurately is impaired.

Developmental Maturation

As is true with all areas of development, visual-motor perception skills increase with the growth of the child. Although children mature at different rates, the following guidelines as developed by Bender (1938) and outlined by Clawson (1962) can be used to understand the typical pattern of visual-motor development.

Two year old: scribbles, makes dots and dashes, keeps pencil on paper, has not developed the skills necessary to reproduce designs accurately.

Three year old: draws circles, loops, arcs, and lines.

Four year old: arranges loops or circles in a horizontal left-to-right direction.

Five year old: usually gives a square appearance to figures, crosses horizontal and vertical lines, creates many different designs.

Six year old: visual perception has developed and is integrated with kinesthetic-tactual perception to allow a fairly accurate reproduction of the Bender designs particularly figures A, 1, 4, and 5.

Seven year old: makes oblique lines fairly well, orders figures in sequence, and joins subparts in figures A and 8 more accurately than a six year old. Beyond the age of seven, there are no major additions to the child's drawing ability, but refinement in techniques continues with an increasing number of successful reproductions and combinations of basic forms.

Eight year old: is more accurate in making dots and joining subparts, and has better contours on curved figures; figure 6 is accurate except for obliqueness of vertical support; figure 3 appears as columns of arcs rather than angles; figure 2 is made of vertical rather than oblique columns.

Nine year old: verticalization tendencies disappear; rotations are less frequent; there is subtle improvement in detail of designs.

Ten year old: draws oblique columns in figure 2 and successful hexagons in figure 7 with accurate joining of subparts.

Eleven year old: provides accurate reproduction of all designs with good sequence, organization, and size.

Appendix B provides visual examples of these maturational guidelines. The percentages in each refer to the proportion of children in each age group who are able to reproduce the designs in the manner demonstrated. As can be observed, at age 11 years, all the designs should be reproduced accurately. By referring to these maturational norms, the clinician can quickly assess a child's protocol to determine the general level of development. A more specific rating of developmental level can be determined by scoring along the criteria developed by Koppitz (1975b). If there is a significant lag between the child's chronological age and the level at which he is reproducing the Bender designs, the possible causes should be explored with a more complete evaluation of the protocol as well as a review of other relevant data.

Emotional Indicators

Although the primary use of the Bender has been to evaluate neurological impairment and visual-motor perception, it has also been shown to be a useful projective technique for identifying emotional problems (Clawson, 1959; Hutt, 1977; Koppitz, 1963, 1975b). Research results support the hypothesis that children with poor visual-motor perception also show a higher incidence of emotional indicators than children without perceptual problems. However, there is a significant number of cases in which no perceptual problems are evident, yet the number of emotional indicators on the Bender is still high. Therefore, the Bender developmental score measures a different aspect of functioning from the emotional indicators, and it is important to consider both. As Koppitz summarizes (1975b), "Not all youngsters with poor Developmental Bender test scores necessarily have emotional problems, nor do all children with Emotional Indicators on their Bender test records inevitably show malfunctioning or immaturity in the visual-motor area" (p. 83).

The scoring manual for emotional indicators, developed by Koppitz and included in her 1963 text on the Bender, can be used to assess a Bender protocol for the possible presence of emotional disturbance. However, a single indicator is not necessarily a sign of emotional difficulties but may represent a trend or tendency of the particular examinee. If three indicators are present, this more strongly suggests emotional difficulties and the child should be evaluated more carefully. As the number of indicators increases, the likelihood of emotional problems also increases. Thus, any child with five or more indicators most likely has serious emotional maladjustment and should be given a full evaluation. Koppitz (1975b) urges that each emotional indicator be evaluated separately as an aid in understanding the possible meaning it may have for the examinee. Furthermore, the total number of emotional indicators is of value in alerting a clinician to the possible presence of emotional problems, but since they do not have internal consistency, the indicators are of little value beyond this. Specifically, the number and type of indicators cannot be used to differentiate neurotic, psychotic, and brain-damaged patients.

The following list contains the ten original indicators (1–10; Koppitz, 1963) plus two additional ones (11 and 12; Koppitz, 1975b), along with the interpretive hypothesis associated with them.

1. Confused order: poor planning, difficulty organizing information, and possible mental confusion (Koppitz, 1963); associated with learning disabled children if 8–10 years of age (Ackerman, Peters, and Dykman, 1971) and with acting out behavior (Naches, 1967).
2. Wavy line: lack of stability in motor coordination, expression, or both (Koppitz, 1963); emotional instability may cause poor motor coordination, or poor coordination can cause or exacerbate emotional instability.
3. Dashes substituted for dots: impulsiveness (Brown, 1965), aggressiveness (Handler and McIntosh, 1971), or in young children, a lack of interest or attention; suggests a preoccupation with personal difficulties to the extent that children attempt to avoid tasks which are presented to them (Koppitz, 1963).
4. Increasing size: poor ability to tolerate frustration, possible explosiveness (Koppitz, 1963), and acting out tendencies (Naches, 1967).
5. Large size: tendency towards acting out (Koppitz, 1963, 1975b; Naches, 1967).
6. Small size: constriction, withdrawal, anxiety, and/or timidity (Koppitz, 1963, 1975b).
7. Fine line: shyness, timidity, withdrawal (Koppitz, 1963, 1975b).
8. Careless overwork or heavily reinforced lines: impulsive, aggressive behavior consistent with children who act out (Handler and McIntosh, 1971; Koppitz, 1963, 1975b); overt hostility (Brown, 1965); however, careful reworking and erasures suggest high intelligence and good achievement (Bravo, 1972; Keogh, 1968).
9. Second attempt at drawing figures: aggressiveness (Handler and McIntosh, 1971), impulsiveness, anxiety (Koppitz, 1963, 1975b); indicates awareness that the first attempt is incorrect, yet individuals do not have sufficient inner control to correct the original.
10. Expansion: impulsive, acting out behavior (Brown, 1965; Naches, 1967) especially for older children who also have neurological impairment (Koppitz, 1963).
11. Box around design: impulsive tendencies, with weak inner control in which external limits are needed to control behavior (Koppitz, 1975b).
12. Spontaneous elaboration or additions to designs: intense fears, anxieties, preoccupation with inner thoughts (Koppitz, 1975b).

INTERPRETATION GUIDELINES: ADULTS

Many of the general interpretive considerations for adults are similar to those for children. Of particular importance is the fact that clinicians can approach adult protocols from a multidimensional perspective, in which both quantitative scorings of pathological indicators and projective considerations relating to personality can be made. This section will provide general guidelines for organic as well as emotional indicators. Quantitative scoring of organic indicators can be obtained by using the "Scoring System for the Bender Gestalt Test" developed by Hain (1964) and included in Appendix C. The results can be summarized and tabulated on the "Bender Adult Scoring Sheet" (Appendix D).

The projective interpretation of the Bender follows the same general approach as for other projective drawings (Draw-A-Person, Kinetic Family Drawing, etc.). The style and manner of drawing, including behavioral observations, should be noted during administration. Such observations are at least as important as the drawings themselves and provide a context in which to understand the examinee's approach to the task. Next, the examiner can evaluate general features of the drawing such as line quality, organization, size, and number of erasures. The meaning of these responses can then be interpreted within the context of results from the quantitative scoring, history, and other relevant test data. For example, a person with no indications of organicity who takes a greater than average length of time (5 minutes or more), demonstrates a high number of erasures, and has a sketchy line quality is most likely expressing a general trait of hesitancy and self-doubt. Another person with documented brain damage who also takes a greater than average time but insists on counting each dot precisely may be attempting to compensate for his impairment by developing obsessive behaviors.

The quantitative method of scoring adult Benders (Appendix C) is a relatively brief and straightforward procedure. Once this has been accomplished, a clinician can then check to see if the examinee's score falls within the brain-damaged range. Hain (1964) gives the normal range as falling between 0 and 5; borderline, from 6 to 12; and critical scores indicative of brain damage, 13 or greater (see Table 3-2). An analysis of Table 3-2 shows that a high score (13 or greater) is indicative of brain damage. Persons falling within this range can be diagnosed with a fairly high degree of accuracy. The chart also indicates that the best single cutoff score is 8. It is important to note that a low score does not necessarily indicate that the person does not have brain damage. Thus, the system has the advantage that there are few false positives but the disadvantage that there are likely to be a high number of false negatives. Other studies have indicated that although the system is effective in differentiating normals from either psychotics or organics, it has been criticized in that groups of organics and psychotics sometimes perform similarly (Verma, Wig, and Shah, 1972). This difficulty can be significantly reduced and the number of correct classifications of psychotics and organics can be increased through the use of Canter's Background Interference Procedure, since schizophrenics perform significantly better than organics when this procedure is used.

Table 3-2. Distributions of Bender Gestalt Scores in Original Validation Groups.

	SCORES	BRAIN DAMAGED	PSYCHIATRIC	CONTROL	PSYCHIATRIC AND CONTROL
Normal area	0	1	5	5	10
	1		4	5	9
	2		11	6	17
	3		5	3	8
	4	1	7	2	9
	5	2 (20%)*	2 (89%)	2 (92%)	4 (90%)
Borderline area	6	3	2	1	3
	7				
	8		1		1
	— — — — — — — — — — — —Best single cutoff — — — — — — — — — — — —				
	9	1			
	10	1			
	11	1	1		1
	12	2 (40%)	(11%)	(4%)	(8%)
Critical area	13	2			
	14			1	1
	15	2			
	16				
	17	2			
	18				
	19				
	20				
	21	1			
	22	1 (40%)	(0%)	(4%)	(2%)
Total		20 (100%)	38 (100%)	25 (100%)	63 (100%)

NOTE: From Hain, J.D. The Bender Gestalt Test: a scoring method for identifying brain damage. *Journal of Consulting Psychology,* 1964, *28,* 34–40 (p. 37). Copyright 1964 by the American Psychological Association. Reprinted by permission of the publisher and author.

*Number in parenthesis is the percentage of the distribution falling within the area marked off by the solid horizontal lines.

Indicators of Organicity

There are a number of indicators commonly associated with organic impairment. However, clinicians should be continually aware of the fact that poor performances on Bender protocols can also be made by emotionally disturbed persons such as schizophrenics. Furthermore, there are qualitative differences in the performances of persons with lesions in different areas of the brain. Whereas right hemisphere patients are more likely to make errors related to visuospatial abilities (e.g., asymmetry, rotations, unrecognizable drawings, unjoined lines), persons with left hemisphere lesions often make drawings that are shaky (line tremors) and smaller in size, with rounded corners and missing parts (oversimplification; Filskov, 1978). The problems with visuospatial abilities (right hemisphere) are those that are usually scored in most scoring systems. The following 15 indicators were selected by Hain (1964) because they successfully discriminated between brain-damaged groups and controls. The definitions and scoring criteria for each of them are included in Appendix C. Before each class of indicators, there is a number which gives a relative weight for the degree to which that sign is pathognomonic of organic impairment. For example, a rotation with a score of 4 is a stronger indicator of organicity than a separation which only has a score of 1.

4 points:
    Perseveration
    Rotations and reversals
    Concretism
3 points:
    Added angles
    Separation of lines
    Overlap
    Distortion
2 points:
    Embellishments
    Partial rotation
1 point:
    Omission
    Abbreviation (No. 1 or 2)
    Separation
    Absence of erasures
    Closure
    Point of contact on figure A

Since the first three indicators are so highly characteristic of the responses from organically impaired persons, they warrant further elaboration. Although it has been established (see review in Tolor and Brannigan, 1980) that perseveration occurs in both schizophrenic and organic populations, it is more strongly associated with organicity (Hain, 1964; Lerner, 1972; Pope and Scott, 1967). It can be defined as the continuation of a response beyond the required number that is expected based on the stimulus presented to the person. For example, a person is perseverating if he produces 14 or more dots on design 1 which only requires him to reproduce 12 dots. Perseverations are most common on designs 1, 2, and 3, but they can also occur on any design if the person draws the same design one or more times, does not ask if he can repeat his design, and fails to erase previous attempts. Marley (1982) divides perseverations into three different types. While each type is considered an indicator of organic impairment, she also associates different areas of mental functioning with each one. Type A occurs when numbers, letters, or other shapes are substituted for those elements found in the original Bender design. This suggests a loosening of associations, impaired planning, diminished attention, poor concentration, and a difficulty with immediate and delayed memory. It is characteristic of organic dementia and is associated with frontal, frontotemporal, or bilateral involvement. Type B perseveration occurs when additional elements are drawn into designs 1, 2, 3, and 5 or when additional curves are included in design 6. Possible areas of mental functioning are an inability to shift-set, dissociation from the task, diminished attention, poor concentration, concrete thinking, and perseverating behavior outside the testing situation. This is characteristic of dominant hemisphere temporal involvement. The final form of scorable perseveration (type C) occurs when the examinee redraws his designs without any effort to erase or cross out previous ones. This can be the result of impaired concentration, intermittent confused ideation, difficulty with planning, and impaired visual-motor functions. Type C perseveration is characteristic of cortical impairment in the parieto-occipital areas of the dominant hemisphere. These findings represent possibilities for the nature of the cognitive impairments and the location of lesions which may either support other data or point out directions for further exploration.

There has been ample research on rotations which emphasizes the importance of continued interest in this category of Bender response. A rotation is defined as a duplication of a design which is rotated 45° or more from its axis. Reversals, in which the figure is turned from 90° to 270°, are considered to be special cases of rotations and thus are still scored under the same category as rotations. They occur most frequently on designs 3 (28%) and A (17%), and least frequently on designs 6 (2%), 2 (5%), and 1 (6%) (Freed, 1966). Rotations occur both for organics and nonorganic psychiatric patients such as hospitalized mental retardates (Silverstein and Mohan, 1962) and for psychotics (Hutt and Gibby, 1970). However, it has been noted that organics produce more spontaneous rotations but they also have more difficulty in creating a rotation when specifically requested to do so (Royer and Holland, 1975). This suggests that one area which may have relevance for differential diagnosis is in assessing the relative difficulty a person experiences in making a deliberate rotation. Marley (1982) has noted that the primary mental functions associated with rotations are impaired attention and a limited capacity for new learning. As with other visuographic disabilities, the most likely area of the brain to be affected is the parietal lobe (Garron and Cheifetz, 1965). Although Bender rotations can occur with either right or left hemisphere lesions, the incidence is about twice as frequent for right hemisphere patients as for left (Billingslea, 1963; Diller, Ben-Yishay, Gertsman, Goodkin, Gordon, Weinberg, 1976).

Although concretism has not been the subject of the same amount of research as perseveration and rotations, Hain (1964) found it occurring almost exclusively in the records of organic patients. Concretism is scored when a patient reinterprets a Bender design so that it resembles another object. More specific criteria are provided in Appendix C, but two examples might be drawing design 3 to look like a tree or design 6 to resemble a snake. Patients creating such concrete responses appear to need a specific stimulus object to make the more abstract Bender design meaningful. Such responses can also suggest serious regression (Halpern, 1951) consistent with some schizophrenics (Kahn and Giffen, 1960), but as Hain (1964) emphasizes, concretism is usually associated with organic conditions.

Emotional Indicators

The more serious indicators outlined by Hain (1964) (perseveration, rotations, concretism) are characteristic of brain-damaged populations, but the indicators with lower weightings (1, 2, or 3 points) can also occur in the protocols of emotionally disturbed persons. However, distinguishing between the two categories of disorders based on Bender responses can often be difficult. This is further complicated by the fact that organically impaired persons will almost always have an emotional reaction to their deficits. It is often difficult, if not impossible, to differentiate accurately the extent to which their current problems are organic as opposed to functional. Related to this is the fact that schizophrenics may have a far greater number of abnormal neurologic signs than was previously believed (Reitan, 1980), which again makes a precise division into organic versus nonorganic difficult if not sometimes inappropriate. A consideration of the Bender cards themselves reveals that the same card may have different meanings for different persons. Thus, two persons may make the same response to a card but for different reasons. For example, a rotation may result from a neurological processing deficit in one person, but for another it may be the result of rebellious, oppositional tendencies. With the background of these cautions, the following discussion will approach Bender responses from two perspectives. The first is a summary of possible interpretations associated with specific Bender responses, and the second is a discussion of the general types of responses associated with anxiety and depression, acting out behavior, and schizophrenia.

The following interpretive hypotheses begin with a listing and discussion of Hain's scoring categories (1–6). The categories which were omitted either have not been researched with regard to emotional difficulties or were covered under previous categories. The later listings and descriptions (7–16) are important because they are frequently encountered in clinical practice and have also been discussed in the literature, yet they were not included in Hain's system.

1. Perseveration: rigid, cognitive set (Hutt, 1969; Marley, 1982) such as might be found in compulsive personalities (Hutt and Briskin, 1960); poor ego control and impaired reality testing (Hutt, 1977); difficulty with planning and poor concentration (Marley, 1982).
2. Rotations: a severe degree of dysfunction, possibly psychosis (Hutt and Gibby, 1970), oppositional tendencies (Hutt, 1968), poor attention with a limited capacity for new learning (Marley, 1982).
3. Concretism: regressive states (Halpern, 1951); difficulty with abstract thinking (Hain, 1964).
4. Added angles: poor visual-motor coordination (Hain, 1964; Marley, 1982); insecurity and hesitancy (Halpern, 1951). Further difficulties with angles include an increase in width, suggesting problems with controlling affect, and a decrease in width (more acute), suggesting a constricted, decreased affective responsiveness (Halpern, 1951; Hutt, 1969).
5. Overlap: insecurity and compulsive self-doubt (Hutt, 1977; Hutt and Gibby, 1970); potential for aggressive acting out (Brown, 1965; Hutt and Gibby, 1970).
6. Distortion: impaired ability to abstract and form categories; reflects a serious level of disturbance (Hutt, 1977).
7. Embellishments: extreme preoccupation with inner needs (Halpern, 1951); intense anxiety and difficulty concentrating (Hutt and Briskin, 1960).
8. Omission: difficulty synthesizing and integrating, disturbance in coordinated motor acts (Marley, 1982), disrupted ego functions to the extent that the person cannot work with the more complex aspects of the design (Hutt, 1969).
9. Abbreviations of No. 1 or 2: possibly negativism and/or low tolerance to frustration (Hutt and Briskin, 1960).
10. Lack of closure: anxiety, hesitancy, and self-doubt, with difficulty completing tasks (Hutt, 1977); relationships are usually seen as difficult and provoke anxiety (Hutt and Gibby, 1970); aggressive acting out behavior (Brown, 1965).
11. Sketching: anxiety, tension, and hesitancy (Halpern, 1951).
12. Expansion: insufficient emotional control, impulsivity (Mundy, 1972; Brown, 1965); aggressive acting out, perhaps consistent with an antisocial personality (Halpern, 1951); grandiose expansiveness to compensate for underlying feelings of self-doubt and inadequacy (Hutt and Briskin, 1960). A progressive and sequential expansion in the size of the figures suggests low tolerance for frustration, explosive acting out due to poor emotional controls, and/or social introversion (Hutt and Briskin, 1960).
13. Reduction in size: feelings of inadequacy, insecurity, tendency to withdraw, and emotional constriction (Hutt and Briskin, 1960; Mundy,

1972). A progressive and sequential reduction in size suggests acting out behavior, a low tolerance for frustration, and/or a person who is introverted and depressed (Hutt and Briskin, 1960).

14. Rigid, methodical arrangement: rigidity and meticulousness (Hutt, 1968) possibly in an attempt to create a sense of security due to underlying feelings of vulnerability and inadequacy (Halpern, 1951).

15. Confused, chaotic arrangement: strong feelings of anxiety (Hutt, 1968); disorientation, poor comprehension, and impaired judgment (Marley, 1982). Arrangements which are scattered and expansive suggest aggressive and rebellious acting out tendencies (Hutt and Briskin, 1960) or expansiveness consistent with a manic state (Murray and Roberts, 1956).

16. Constricted, compressed arrangement: depression (White and McGraw, 1975), with insecurity and feelings of inferiority (Johnson, 1973; Murray and Roberts, 1956).

Although knowledge regarding the possible meanings of specific Bender responses can be helpful, a further approach is to understand categories of responses associated with different emotional states. The following three emotional states are not intended to be all inclusive, but they are commonly encountered in clinical practice and have also been well researched in relation to Bender responses.

Anxiety and Depression

Anxiety and depression can be characterized as a person's withdrawing from and narrowing his contact with the world in an attempt to create security. Bender responses from either anxious or depressed persons likewise reflect a constriction of the designs (Gavales and Millon, 1960; Johnson, 1973; White and McGraw, 1975). Bender constriction is technically defined as the placing of all Bender designs in less than one-half of the sheet of paper. In addition to constricted placement, depressed or anxious persons also decrease the overall size of their reproductions (Gavales and Millon, 1960) and make their lines in a sketchy, hesitant manner (Clawson, 1962; Hutt and Briskin, 1960). The possibility of suicidal behavior is raised if, in addition to constricted, hesitantly drawn designs, the examinee also encounters difficulty maintaining design 2 in a horizontal position (Leonard, 1973) and draws design 6 penetrating into the open semicircular area of design 5 (Sternberg and Levine, 1965).

Acting Out

Persons who frequently engage in acting out behavior have a low tolerance for restraint or inhibition, find difficulty in completing an exacting task, and are likely to comply with requests in a superficial manner. If the Bender task is conceptualized as an exacting task requiring some degree of self-discipline, then acting out persons would also be expected to express their impulsiveness within this context. Brown (1965) has found that the following Bender responses have been associated with acting out potential:

Heavy line pressure
Substitution of circles for dots
Collision
Spikes and curves
Dot distortion
Dashes
Compression-expansion in placement
Crossing difficulty
Integration difficulty
Splitting and reduplication
Boundary violation

Schizophrenia

Both acting out and anxiety or depression are usually less severe than a psychotic disorder such as schizophrenia. This is reflected in the fact that the Bender responses for anxiety and depression are less highly weighted in the Hain (1964) system or may not even be included in his scoring criteria (i.e., sketching). As the severity of a functional disorder increases, the Bender responses will be more likely to resemble the responses of organically impaired persons. For example, the presence of hallucinations for schizophrenics also causes greater disruption in the selective perception required to adequately draw the Bender designs. Thus, schizophrenics reporting hallucinations will have significantly greater deficits on their Bender responses than nonhallucinating schizophrenics (Rockland and Pollin, 1965). The following specific indicators have been found to be associated with schizophrenia:

Concreteness (Halpern, 1951)
Fragmentation (Hutt, 1977)
Overlapping and crossing difficulty (Hutt and Gibby, 1970)
Perseveration (Gilbert, 1969; Hutt and Gibby, 1970)
Spontaneous elaborations, embellishments, and doodling (Gilbert, 1969; Hutt and Gibby, 1970)
Expansion in size (Kahn and Giffen, 1960)

In order to differentiate organic impairment from psychosis, the best approach is to use information from both the patient's history and his test scores. There are also several distinguishing signs related directly to the Bender. First of all, schizophrenics are more adept than organics at creating deliberate distortions. Secondly, schizophrenics are less likely to have the more serious indicators of organicity (4 points on the Hain system) and will probably have fewer of them. Finally, clinicians can use Canter's Background Interference Procedure (1966) which tends to decrease the performance of organics but not of psychotics (Canter, 1976).

RECOMMENDED READING

Clawson, A. *The Bender Visual Motor Gestalt Test for Children: A Manual.* Los Angeles: Western Psychological Corporation, 1962.

Hutt, M.L. *The Hutt Adaptation of the Bender Gestalt Test* (3rd ed.). New York: Grune & Stratton, 1977.

Koppitz, E.M. *The Bender Gestalt Test for Young Children,* Vols. 1 and 2. New York: Grune & Stratton, 1963 and 1975.

Marley, M.L. *Organic Brain Pathology and the Bender Gestalt Test: A Differential Diagnostic Scoring System.* New York: Grune & Stratton, 1982.

Ogdon, D.P. *Psychodiagnostics and Personality Assessment: A Handbook.* (2nd ed.) Los Angeles: Western Psychological Corporation, 1975.

Tolor, A. and Brannigan, G.C. *Research and Clinical Applications of the Bender Gestalt Test.* Springfield, Ill. Charles C. Thomas, 1980.

4
Interpretation of
Projective Drawings

Artists have understood for centuries the creative urge to express personal ideas, reactions, and interpretations of unstructured stimuli through symbolic media. However, it is only recently that this process has been studied in a systematic manner to gain insight and understanding about the artist himself. As the science of psychology has developed, and people have become more concerned with how man thinks and feels, it has become apparent that individuals who express themselves in artistic forms are actually sharing their perceptions and reactions to the world around them. Their art is not necessarily a realistic portrayal of the world but rather the expression of their subjective response to, and personal interaction with, their perceived reality. To put this in psychological terms, the person "actively and spontaneously structures unstructured material, and in so doing reveals . . . the principles of his psychological structure" (Rapaport, Gill, and Schafer, 1968, p. 225).

Drawings, though they have only recently been classified and understood as projective techniques, are more accurately expressive methods for revealing individual feelings and personality structures. As such, they have become a valuable tool for understanding and assessing the personality characteristics of an individual, and have gained popularity among clinicians because of their unique ability to allow the nonverbal expression of an individual's feelings and attitudes.

In order to appreciate the complexity and symbolic messages communicated through drawings, it is necessary to look at the theoretical assumptions that form the basis of projective drawing interpretation. In general, without a belief in the unconscious, the whole discussion of projective testing and interpretation is meaningless. Given the existence of an unconscious, there follows the assumption that this unconscious can reveal itself in symbolic form to the individual's conscious mind. Because man tends to view the world in an anthropomorphic manner, he can project his unconscious feelings, conflicts, attitudes, and reactions onto anything outside himself. Projection is most likely to occur when an individual feels threatened or insecure with certain personal feelings because it is less anxiety provoking to attribute problem areas to the outside world than to himself. Drawings, then, are just one technique of bringing into awareness uncon-scious feelings, attitudes, and reactions through the use of symbolic representation.

Given this set of hypotheses, the evaluation of a person's drawings provides useful information for clarifying areas of conflict and assessing the strengths and weaknesses available to handle these conflicts. In order to do this, both the style of the drawing and the specific content depicted in the drawing must be looked at. The style of the drawing, or the manner in which the person has represented the specific content of his drawing, may vary tremendously from person to person and from drawing to drawing. Some drawings are very bold, others quite sketchy; some small, others large; different perspectives may be used, as well as varying amounts of shading, erasures, and organization. The way a person elects to perform his drawing reflects the way he approaches his personal life situation. Evaluation of one's style of representation is useful in determining the person's strengths and abilities, and gives the interpreter a better understanding of how the person interacts psychologically with specific aspects of his life. The content of the drawings, that is, what the person has chosen to draw within the given set of directions, helps the clinician to assess specific areas of conflict within an individual. Since these areas are often not readily accessible to a person's consciousness, their recognition and clarification may also help the individual to understand his current situation and his reaction to it. Within the conscious areas of conflict, there are often underlying unconscious dynamics that are influencing a situation. As these areas of the unconscious become known and clarified for the individual, the conflicts often resolve themselves.

Of course, drawings must be interpreted with caution and treated with the same carefulness as any other type of psychological test data. One drawing may reflect a specific aspect of an individual, but the significance of that drawing in terms of how a person is functioning psychologically can only be determined when other drawings or data from other psychological tests have been evaluated and understood in the context of the person's present life situation. It is impor-tant then, when making clinical judgments, to consider how a person appears through the interpretations derived from a number of different psychological tests. What is most significant psychologically will appear consistently through-out the test data and will also be visible in the person's current life situation. When this kind of consistency is noted in the test results and interpretations, the examiner can be reassured that the conclusions are an accurate reflection of that person's level of psychological functioning.

HISTORY AND DEVELOPMENT

Psychological testing as a field of study was inconsequential until the turn of the century, and most of the early tests at that time focused primarily on obtaining measures of intelligence and scholastic achievement. There were a few early attempts to assess personality, but in the United States these were mostly standardized self-rating scales, and it was not until the mid-1930s that qualitative procedures allowing more freedom of interpretation were introduced. Thus, drawings were not originally intended as measures of personality, but rather were first introduced as techniques to assess an individual's intellectual level. Following the trend to create objective and standardized tests, rigid scoring methods were devised to obtain I.Q.'s based on a person's human figure drawing. However, as the use of drawings increased and the study of personality intensified, it became obvious that there were many other variables affecting the content and execution of an individual's drawings, and that these variables were quite independent of a person's intellectual level. In other words, the qualitative aspects of an individual's personality adjustment were revealed in his drawings just as obviously as the quantitative aspects of mental ability.

The *Draw-A-Person Test* (D-A-P), designed by Florence Goodenough in 1926, was the first published drawing test to assess children's intelligence. The child was told simply to "draw a person" and was given a pencil and a sheet of blank paper on which to execute the task. The method for determining a child's mental age, and subsequently his I.Q., was based in the number of details included in the drawing, and followed the assumption that accuracy and the inclusion of specific details in a drawing were direct results of a child's intellectual level of functioning. Following the same basic belief about the nature of drawings, Harris published a new version of Goodenough's test in 1963. In this revised test (Goodenough-Harris D-A-P Test), the subject was requested to make three drawings: one of a man, one of a woman, and one of "yourself." Separate point scales for evaluating the drawings of male and female figures were developed, and separate norms for boys and girls were provided. Goodenough and Harris both maintain that children's figure drawings are largely an intellectual task, and cannot be used as projective techniques to infer personality characteristics or underlying conflicts.

In 1949, Karen Machover became dissatisfied with using the D-A-P as only a tool for intellectual assessment, and on the basis of clinical observations she expanded Goodenough's rigorous scoring methods to include guidelines for evaluating personality variables. In the *Machover Draw-A-Person Test,* the person is initially asked to "draw a person." When this drawing is completed, a clean sheet of paper is provided and the person is asked to draw a figure of the opposite sex. This drawing may be followed by an inquiry, in which the individual may be asked either to make up a story to go with the picture or to answer some specific questions about the figures such as age, schooling, occupation, ambitions, personality characteristics, and family attitudes towards life. Koppitz (1968) further developed approaches to children's human figure drawings through a developmental scoring system and a listing of different indicators for emotional difficulties.

At the same time Machover was studying the D-A-P Test, J.N. Buck (1948) published the *House-Tree-Person Test* (H-T-P), which was one of the first drawing procedures designed specifically to assess personality adjustment. The technique was later expanded by Jolles (1952, 1971) to include three separate administration procedures involving an achromatic pencil drawing, interrogation phase, and chromatic crayon drawings. Although it was originally intended for use with children, the technique has been used extensively with individuals of all ages. The original procedure for test administration was to provide the individual with a clean sheet of paper in a horizontal position and give the instruction "draw me a picture of a house." When this is completed, another paper is presented in a vertical position with instructions to "draw me a picture of a tree"; finally, a third request is made with a clean sheet of paper in a vertical position to "draw me a picture of a person." A variation of this procedure which has become quite popular involves providing just one sheet of paper in a horizontal position, with the request that the individual "draw a picture that has in it a house, a tree, and a person." Interpretations are made based on the type of figures drawn, and with the composite drawing, the relation of the figures to each other is also studied. An optional inquiry may also be used to give the person an opportunity to verbalize feelings and attitudes towards the drawing.

The *Draw-A-Family Test* (D-A-F) is a relatively new procedure that was first discussed in the literature by Hulse in 1956. In this test, a person is asked to draw a picture of his family. Interpretations are made based on how the drawing is executed, who is included in the picture, and how the individuals are placed on the paper. A variation of this technique, the *Kinetic Family Drawing* (K-F-D), was first described as a projective test by Burns and Kaufman in 1970 and later expanded by Burns (1982). Although the method is similar to the Draw-A-Family Test, it differs in that the individual is asked to draw his family "doing something." The addition of movement to the picture places emphasis on the perceived relationships among the family members and how the individual feels towards his family. A more complete discussion and study of the usefulness of these drawings and their interpretations will be given later in this chapter.

Although *spontaneous drawings* do not fall into the strict definition of a psychological "test," their value as a projective technique has been known among clinicians for many years. In addition to allowing a therapeutic emotional release for the individual, the content and manner in which the picture is executed can provide valuable insight into the nature and functioning of the personality. For example, attempts have been made, especially in recent years, to understand the internal dynamics of individuals who primarily use spontaneous, nonverbal methods to express themselves (young children, artists, painters, photographers) by analyzing and evaluating their creations from a psychological standpoint. Just as the written or spoken word reveals the inner nature of an individual, so do nonverbal, symbolic expressions of art provide information about how an individual perceives and feels towards his world.

RELIABILITY AND VALIDITY

The nature of, and assumptions relating to, projective drawings make the task of establishing acceptable levels of reliability and validity a formidable one. From a strictly psychometric perspective, such drawings do not even begin to adequately fulfill the criteria for psychological tests. Whether or not they can ever be expected to fulfill these criteria is questionable. The attempts that have been made to do so have produced questionable and often inconsistent results.

There are several factors which make assessing the reliability of projective drawings difficult. First of all, there is generally a lack of objectivity in scoring procedures. This stems from the fact that the drawings themselves are highly rich and complex sources of information. Thus, they are difficult to place into specific quantitative categories and lend themselves more to global, qualitative interpretation. Finally, there is considerable variation between one drawing and the next. Because of this wide variability, retest reliability is all but impossible to determine.

There have been some attempts to establish the extent of interscorer reliability. For example, Cassel, Johnson, and Burns (1958) tested the degree of agreement of trained experts in "scoring" D-A-P protocols. The reliability for diagnostic category was only .33. Even after discussion and agreement among the clinicians on which scoring criteria to use, the reliability increased to only a moderate .71. These modest correlations can be attributed primarily to the necessarily vague and unclear definitions of the signs used for scoring.

The usual method of interpreting projective drawings is by means of signs. For example, a figure which is drawn with arms folded and body turned away is often believed to indicate guardedness and psychological inaccessibility. Likewise, a small and shrunken figure suggests a "shrunken" ego. Thus, there is usually extensive use of analogy and assumed isomorphy. Generally, assumptions about these "sign" interpretations are made with little concern for their actual validity. In fact, a review by Roback (1968) indicates that there are few data to support such sign approaches. There is even some evidence that persons will continue to interpret projective drawings based on assumed isomorphy and "folklore," despite their having been presented with data contrary to these beliefs (Chapman and Chapman, 1967).

Rather than emphasizing a sign approach, many clinicians have stressed the utility of an approach which is more global and integrates the various aspects of each drawing. Using such an approach, trained clinicians seem to have some ability to differentiate between clinical groups (Swenson, 1968). This is especially true in diagnosing cases with severe psychopathology or organicity. Even in these cases, however, the differentiations are still of a somewhat low order.

ASSETS AND LIMITATIONS

As has been implied, there is a great deal of controversy over the use of projective techniques in general, and this controversy extends pointedly into the area of drawing interpretation. Aside from problems which involve accepting the theoretical basis of the projective hypothesis, there are particular concerns about using drawings as psychological "tests" or assessment instruments. Many people do not even consider projective drawings to be psychological tests since they do not follow the formalized procedure for test construction and standardization. Criticisms focus on the facts that administration and scoring instructions are vague and inconsistent, norms for interpretation are unclear and nonsystematic, statistical data to support clinical observation are sparse, and objectivity in scoring is minimal. Reliability and validity information is generally lacking, and often the examiner must use sparsely tested experimental hypotheses, combined with clinical experience or testing "lore," as his primary guideline for interpretation. Frequently, interpretations are based on assumed isomorphy between signs found in drawings and "commonsense" signs. For example, talon-like hands indicate aggression and a small shrunken figure represents a shrunken ego. Furthermore, test interpreters run the risk of "projecting" their own personalities into their interpretations as much as the examinees do into their drawings. Thus, many people feel that the current literature should be viewed as containing only general guidelines for understanding and analyzing drawings, and that the interpretations of drawing "tests" should be viewed with caution.

In spite of these limitations, clinicians continue to use these procedures as a means of assessing and an aid in treating individuals. Drawings provide minimal external structure for the individual and thus allow an opportunity for the person to express himself with the least amount of influence from the task presented. Drawings are simple, easy to administer, and fairly nonthreatening to the individual; as a result, they are often a good "icebreaker" for the testing session. It is difficult for the examinees to understand exactly how the drawing will be used to determine psychological characteristics, so faking or attempting to bias the drawing in a particular direction is quite difficult and unconscious material is allowed to surface without activation of the usual defense mechanisms. For individuals who have a difficult time expressing themselves verbally, and particularly for children, this expressive technique can be invaluable in determining the critical variables underlying a particular personality dynamic. Many clinicians will also use these techniques in the process of therapy as a method of self-expression, understanding, and personal growth. However, for personality assessment, they are most appropriate when used as an accessory to other devices rather than as the primary diagnostic tool.

APPROACHING THE DRAWING

Because drawings are such unique and creative expressions of an individual, it is a grave injustice to interpret them with a rigid and dogmatic structure. When this is attempted, the rich variety of information and the depth of understanding that can be gained about a person are lost, and the personal characteristics that contribute to the expressions and symbols within the drawing are often discarded. On the other hand, some guidelines and training are necessary for the clinician to sharpen his interpretive skills and benefit from the experience of others who have attempted the same tasks. It is important for the evaluator to become familiar with the guidelines and use the standard interpretations as a springboard or baseline from which to branch out and explore the intricacies and unique characteristics of the particular drawing being studied.

The primary tool used by the skilled clinician to integrate the seemingly contradictory details within the drawing, and to understand the message conveyed through the symbols represented, is himself. No book or set of rules will contain the unique combination of characteristics that the evaluator is called upon to examine, and as a result, he must rely on his personal skill and expertise to determine the meaning of the drawing. Responsibility rests on the examiner, then, to continue developing himself and familiarizing himself with a variety of stimuli which will contribute to his skill as a clinician. Exposure to various avenues of understanding people — the arts, literature, psychological studies, and self-exploration — can greatly enhance the examiner's skill. The key to evaluating drawings is for the examiner to open himself up to any and all possibilities of interpretation, and the extent of exposure and interaction he had had with different worlds and people will enhance this process. When all possibilities have been considered, conflicting though they may appear to be at first, the subtler messages of the individual can be heard, and the true nature and expression of the drawing can be understood. When strict, formalized procedures are followed, these more elusive qualities are missed, and the full impact and meaning of the picture are lost. For the evaluation then, it is important (1) to be familiar with standard guidelines for drawing interpretation, (2) to be aware of all the possibilities contained within the drawings, (3) to be open and confront inconsistencies when evaluating a drawing, and (4) to integrate the observations with all the other information known about a person to crystallize one's understanding of the present drawing.

In addition to these areas of knowledge which the evaluator needs to develop, the following general guidelines should be utilized when attempting to interpret a drawing.

1. Once the drawing has been obtained, it is important to consider it in its totality. Rather than focusing attention on specific details, it is valuable to look initially at the whole picture and notice what mood or message is conveyed. This is

a very intuitive process, and involves stepping "into" the picture to see how it "feels" and what overall impression is portrayed. From these first impressions of the drawing, it is often possible to see how the individual relates in his world how receptive he is to outside influences, how he handles emotions, and how he feels about himself. It is valuable at this point to jot down initial impressions and reactions without any attempt to analyze, integrate, or understand the observations.

2. After this intuitive, impression gathering stage, the examiner should go back to the drawing and analyze the specific details in a more logical or rational manner, using published guidelines and previous clinical experience. Some interpreters conduct this process in a routine and systematic manner, often using a checklist to categorize the different components. Other examiners begin with the details that draw their attention and proceed from there to further observations. The details within a drawing that initially catch one's attention are usually quite obvious and can take numerous forms, such as the unusual treatment of a particular figure, a large inconsistency in how the drawing was executed, intense erasures or scratching over, or unusual figure placement on the page. They serve the function of focusing the evaluator's attention onto the drawing and often convey the primary message of the drawing quite clearly. Both of these approaches are valuable, and the preference of the examiner determines which is the more effective style to utilize.

3. The final step in interpreting a drawing is to evaluate the information obtained from steps 1 and 2, and integrate it with any other test results or background data known about the person. Things that are true and significant for an individual are usually repeated in numerous forms, and it is important for the evaluator to recognize this and obtain confirmation of his clinical conclusions from other information known about the person. In other words, drawings can only be understood in the context of other test data and the individual's personal life, and these must be considered when making final conclusions about a drawing's possible meaning.

Depending on the theoretical framework from which the examiner is operating, interpretations of a specific drawing may vary greatly. For example, a person with an analytic bias may see a particular drawing as representing conflicts from early childhood while a family therapist may emphasize current attitudes and feelings towards family members in the interpretation. Both interpretations may correctly portray different aspects of the individual, and both may be useful in terms of understanding the unconscious dynamics operating in a person's life. Some drawing tasks are more conducive to a particular theoretical framework than others, and it is up to the clinician to select the drawing tests that best meet his needs. A Kinetic Family Drawing or a House-Tree-Person Test, for example, may be ideal for revealing attitudes and feelings towards family members, while a Draw-A-Person Test may be more adept at uncovering sexual attitudes and feelings towards the self.

Once the clinician has found the drawing test that works well for his theoretical framework, he must become aware of the subtleties of interpretation. There are as many variations of the same drawing as there are persons doing the drawing. To complicate matters even further, a person's drawing can change considerably each time it is executed. Within this wide range of variation, however, there are some common characteristics which the trained eye can quickly assess to determine the emotional stability and psychological orientation of the individual.

The more exposure a person has had to interpreting drawings, the more accurate will his interpretive skills become. Also, the more open the interpreter can be to all the possibilities contained within a drawing the more he can trust his trained intuitions about the meaning of that particular drawing. There is a delicate balance in this process, combining the use of personal intuitive skills with concrete knowledge based on research and experience. When the balance is maintained between these two methods of observation, the interpretation and understanding of particular drawings is likely to be both accurate and meaningful.

THE HEALTHY DRAWING

There is a tendency in the field of psychology to focus on pathology, sometimes to the exclusion of the more stable and healthier aspects of personality. Rather than attempt the difficult task of defining emotional health with all its unique and individual variations, psychologists tend to focus on what is not healthy and to assume that the remaining attitudes, feelings, and behaviors fall within the broad spectrum of normalcy. In the field of psychological testing, this approach has predominated, with interpretations being based on what is "wrong" with the person rather than on what is "right." As would be expected then, in most drawing interpretation guidelines there is little mention of what constitutes a healthy drawing; rather there is subtle encouragement to study the drawing in extreme detail until the internal pathological dynamics of the unconscious are revealed.

When approaching drawing interpretation, the clinician needs to have a clear definition of his personal concepts of both psychological health and pathology. He should then be aware of how these concepts bias his orientation, as well as how they help clarify his drawing interpretations.

Although the theoretical framework and value system of each examiner may vary tremendously, there are certain characteristics of psychological health common to most orientations which should be considered when evaluating drawings. People whose lives appear to be working well for them are individuals who are able to identify and meet their psychological needs accurately and adequately. They feel positive about themselves, and are not afraid to express their ideas and feelings to others. In addition, these people are accurate in their self-perceptions, and feel they have power and control in their lives to effect change when necessary. In other words, they have the tools to handle their life problems and conflicts successfully. As would be expected, these traits are visible in the drawings of psychologically healthy individuals and are demonstrated clearly in the following guidelines.

Self-esteem. When the drawing contains a person, the figure is integrated and contains all the essential details (facial features, torso, hands, feet, legs, arms; Buck, 1948; Urban, 1963). It is drawn in proportion to the rest of the picture (Urban, 1963), and for males, the drawing is neither extremely large nor extremely small (Delatte and Hendrickson, 1982). Line quality is firm and definite, and the appearance of the figure is strong, solid, and open in position (Levy, 1958).

Security and Self-confidence. The figures in the drawing are grounded and represented as touching the earth or floor. They occupy the central area of the paper and do not cling to the edge of the sheet (Lakin, 1956). Line quality is firm and strong (Urban, 1963). Figures are often shown moving in the picture or having the potential to move; they possess arms, feet, and legs that are free and adequate for mobility in the environment.

Personal Relationships. The figures in the drawing are fairly close to each other and show some type of dynamic interaction or relationship. The figures themselves contain the essential tools for communication, that is, open arms with hands, ears, mouth, and eyes (Burns, 1982).

Openness. The figures in the drawing are standing in open posture or interacting with their environment in a positive manner. Buildings are drawn with windows and doors that are unencumbered and accessible to the environment (Barnouw, 1969; Jolles, 1971).

Stability and Orderliness. The drawing forms a complete picture, with the parts integrated and relating in a complementary manner. Each figure in the drawing contains its essential elements and relates with the other figures to form a unified and orderly picture (Jolles, 1971; Urban, 1963).

Sexual Identification. Figures of people are drawn as obviously male or female, and the first figure drawn is the same sex as the person doing the drawing (Gravitz, 1968). All figures (male and female) contain the details essential in a human figure drawing, are of comparable size, and are in proportion to the complete picture (Buck, 1966).

AGE CONSIDERATIONS

When interpreting drawings of young children, it is important to take into consideration their respective capabilities at various stages of development. A 2 year old will usually scribble when presented with paper and pencil. His muscle movements are uncoordinated and random, although he can make dots and dashes. He can move about the page, filling the unused portions and usually managing to stay on the paper.

The 3 year old can execute circles, loops, arcs, and lines. These earliest attempts to create identifiable objects often result in unrecognizable forms which the child may call "Daddy" or "Mommy."

At 4 years of age, a child can arrange loops and circles in a horizontal fashion, and is able to add lines to the circles to represent people's legs and arms. Although a 4 year old can orient himself on the paper from left to right, any other differentiation or order in the drawing is unusual.

The 5 year old is able to use combinations of circles, arcs, lines, and dots to create familiar objects. Most children at this age are able to cross vertical with horizontal lines.

By 6 years of age, the child is capable of integrating his drawing and has the fine motor control needed to represent his visual world more accurately. He can orient a square obliquely, produce vertical series, and successfully make dots which are not circles.

It is not until the child is about 7 or 8 that he is able to foresee sequences and therefore represent movement in his drawings. Until this age, the child's images are static and the figures often unrelated to each other. After the age of 7, the child is able to produce an integrated picture. He has the mental and fine motor skills necessary to represent the picture he has in his mind accurately on the paper.

GENERAL INTERPRETIVE GUIDELINES

There are general guidelines that should be taken into consideration when evaluating any projective drawing. Regardless of which drawing is being completed, the manner in which the task is approached and the way the drawing is presented are of equal importance to the content itself. The first step in analyzing the drawing, then, is to look at the overall picture and evaluate it in the following areas.

Line Quality. Variable pressure in an otherwise normal drawing suggests a flexible and adaptable personality (Urban, 1963). Unusually heavy pressure (indentations noted on the reverse of the paper) is a sign of tension (Jolles, 1971), high energy level (Hetherington, 1952), forcefulness, and possible acting out tendencies (Hammer, 1965, 1968, 1969b). Light, sketchy pressure often reflects a hesitant, indecisive, timid, and insecure individual (DiLeo, 1970, 1973; Machover, 1949). Most likely, this person is experiencing a lack of self-confidence and problems with self-assertion. In children, light pressure may suggest a restrained or inhibited personality with a low level of energy (Hammer, 1968). The use of shading and shaded strokes suggests anxiety when present in the drawings of adults (DiLeo, 1970, 1973; Jolles, 1971) but is frequently found in the drawings of normal children (Koppitz, 1968).

Size. The size of the drawing must be considered in relation to the size of the paper. Unusually large drawings suggest either aggressive, expansive, or grandiose tendencies (Koppitz, 1968) or acting out potential (Gilbert, 1969; Machover, 1949). People with feelings of inferiority or inadequacy may produce large drawings as a compensatory defense mechanism (Delatte and Hendrickson, 1982). When this dynamic is present, there are usually other signs in the drawing of conflict and insecurity. *Small drawings* directly reveal feelings of inferiority, timidness, insecurity, and ineffectiveness (Buck, 1969; Jolles, 1971; Machover, 1951; Prytola Phelps, Morissey, and Davis, 1978). People who draw small figures usually are hesitant to reveal their feelings, and tend to be restrained and inhibited in their interactions with others. Small figures may also be an indication of depressive and constricted behavior under stress (Handler and Reyher, 1964).

Placement. *Central placement* on the page suggests a normal, reasonably secure person especially if, when there is more than one figure in the drawing, the figures are balanced and in proportion to one another (Urban, 1963). Placement on the *right side* of the page indicates intellectualizing tendencies, sometimes to the point of inhibiting expression of feelings (Hammer, 1969b; Jolles, 1971). Right side placement may also show that the person's behavior is governed by the "reality principle" or that he candidly looks at the here and now (Hammer, 1969b; Marzoff and Kirchner, 1972). In addition, right side placement (especially in the lower right side) indicates that the material is approaching consciousness, and thus represents potential areas of development and integration. Placement on the *left side* suggests probable impulsive behavior with a drive towards immediate emotional satisfaction of needs (Hammer, 1958, 1969b). Orientations towards the past, that which is unknown, or the ending of some phase of life are also represented by drawings on the left side (Jolles, 1971; Urban, 1963).

Placement high on the page suggests a high level of aspiration (Machover, 1949), an active fantasy life (Buck, 1969; Jolles, 1971), or extreme optimism that is frequently unjustified (Machover, 1949; Urban, 1963). In children, high placement reflects high standards of achievement and high drive (Jolles, 1971). Placement low on the page reveals feelings of insecurity, low levels of self-esteem, possible depressive tendencies, and/or defeatist attitudes (Jolles, 1971). Using the lower edge of the paper as the base for the drawing may indicate a need for support associated with feelings of insecurity or a lack of self-confidence (Schildkrout, Shenker, and Sonnenblick, 1972).

Order and Organization. Most drawings will show some orderliness in their representations. People who are functioning well psychologically place the figures of the drawing evenly on the paper, and show a sense of proportion and interaction to create a complete picture (Lakin, 1956; Urban, 1963). People who are depressed or of a low intellectual level, however, may have a number of different figures or objects in their drawings, but the interaction among them is minimal or negligent. People with severe psychological disturbances such as schizophrenia may present their drawing in a very bizarre or disordered fashion, with the figures relating to each other in an unconventional or confusing manner (Hammer, 1954; McElhaney, 1969).

Sometimes, in an effort to maintain order in their drawings, individuals will box off or number the elements represented (Gilbert, 1969; Lerner, 1972). This is particularly true in drawing tasks where a person is asked to draw a number of different figures within one drawing (Bender Gestalt, Draw-A-Family tests). People who use this method to create order often have a difficult time controlling their lives, and rely heavily on external structures and guidelines. Without the external limits, they become quite anxious and unable to achieve their potential. Usually these persons tend to be rigid and meticulous in their dealings with the world, and lack the internal controls necessary to interact with their environment in a satisfactory manner. When only one element of a drawing is encapsulated, it may represent a desire on the part of the individual to remove this area of conflict from his/her life by putting a wall around it and preventing further interaction with it.

Symmetry. Extreme bilateral symmetry creates a stiff and rigid drawing which indicates that spontaneous impulses or emotions are repressed with obsessive-compulsive or excessive intellectualizing defenses (Hammer, 1958; Machover, 1949). Such people are often characterized as cold, distant, hypertense, and perfectionistic. Marked disturbance in symmetry suggests feelings of insecurity, "unbalanced" self-concept, or poor impulse control with overactivity and excessive spontaneity (Machover, 1949; Urban, 1963).

Erasures. Excessive erasures suggest uncertainty, indecisiveness, and restlessness (Machover, 1949; Schildkrout, Shenker, and Sonnenblick, 1972; Urban, 1963). Often these individuals are dissatisfied with themselves and are experiencing a great deal of anxiety (Hammer, 1958, 1968). When this condition is extreme, it may reflect an obsessive-compulsive personality (Machover, 1949). Frequent erasures are rarely seen in the drawings of children, schizophrenics, or organics. As would be expected, erasures focus attention on a particular area of the drawing and suggest conflict or concern about what that area represents to the individual. A few erasures in a person's drawing, however, are not unusual and perhaps are to be expected, since within the wide range of normal functioning, anxiety and concern over a particular area are common and possibly even desirable. If an erasure is made to improve the drawing, the person may be expressing a degree of flexibility which is consistent with a satisfactory adjustment (Jolles, 1971; Roback, 1968) and a striving for achievement (Wysocki and Wysocki, 1973).

Detail. Lack of detail in the drawing suggests either psychosomatic hypertensive conditions (Modell and Potter, 1949) or depressive and withdrawing tendencies (Hammer, 1954; Schildkrout, Skenker, and Sonnenblick, 1972). Excessive detail indicates obsessive-compulsive tendencies, rigidity, and/or anxiety (Hammer, 1958, 1965, 1969). People who are highly emotional and creative also tend to use a great deal of detail in their drawings. Bizarre details can be indicative of psychosis (McElhaney, 1969; Mursell, 1969).

Transparencies. When the body is represented as transparent and internal organs are depicted, there is a likelihood of somatic delusions and/or a schizophrenic or manic condition (Machover, 1949; Wolman, 1970). Transparent clothing drawn by an adult suggests voyeuristic or exhibitionistic tendencies and possible problems with sexual identity, depending on the nature of the drawing (Machover, 1949). Transparencies in children's drawings, however, are not unusual (Urban, 1963).

Distortions and Omissions. When a drawing is quite distorted or bizarre, the person's awareness of reality is often confused and disturbed, which may indicate a psychotic or schizophrenic condition (McElhaney, 1969; Urban, 1963). Omission of essential details may occur as a part of this distortion, or it may occur in an otherwise integrated drawing. In the latter case, omission of an important part suggests a strong area of conflict with the use of denial as the primary defense mechanism (Urban, 1963).

Perspective. A drawing that is represented as seen *from below* shows feelings of rejection, unhappiness, or inferiority (Jolles, 1971). Withdrawal tendencies and a desire for only limited interpersonal contact are typical. Drawings that are represented as seen *from above,* reflect a sense of superiority, possibly as a compensation for underlying feelings of inadequacy or other conflictual states existing within the person (Hammer, 1958; Landisberg, 1969). Drawings that are very distant and far away show feelings of inaccessibility and a desire to withdraw (Jolles, 1971). It may be that a particular situation is judged as being beyond the person's ability to handle effectively, or perhaps the individual has rejected this area of his life. A close appearance, on the other hand, suggests feelings of interpersonal warmth and psychological accessibility (Jolles, 1971).

Shading. In general, shading responses are indicative of anxiety (DiLeo, 1970, 1973; Machover, 1951, 1958). Often the area of the picture that is shaded will indicate the particular aspect of the person's life that is causing anxiety or conflict. When shading pervades the entire picture, anxiety may be more "free floating" and not attached to any particular area of disturbance. However, a moderate amount of shading is frequently found in the drawings of normals, and Deabler (1969) has even found a complete lack of shading to be associated with character disorders.

Line on the Bottom. The use of a line at the bottom of the drawing is typical of people who feel unstable and are trying to maintain a sense of security by creating a solid foundation (Jolles, 1971). As the width and the intensity of the shading on the lines increase, there is a corresponding increase in the severity of the disturbance. Lines are most frequently found under trees on the H-T-P and least frequently under person drawings.

Behavioral Observations. The manner in which the person approaches the drawing and how he interacts with the examiner while doing the drawing can often provide valuable information for assessment and evaluation. After the instructions have been given, people will often feel uncertain about how to proceed and can handle their anxiety in numerous ways. Sometimes people will ask if they should include anything else or if they should draw a specific type of house, tree, or person. At other times people will object that they can't draw. This is especially true of adults who feel they are not artistic. Sometimes gentle encouragement is appropriate, while one remains firm about the instructions for the task. It is important for the examiner to note the reactions of the person when the task is presented. People who have strong needs for approval or difficulty with unstructured tasks will often ask a number of questions, while individuals who are insecure and lack self-confidence will begin to apologize for their inability to do a good job. Most people will spend about 5 minutes completing the task, but when a person finishes the drawing in less than a minute or wants to spend longer than 10 minutes, some explanation must be incorporated into the personality evaluation. For example, a drawing performed in less than a minute may suggest resistance, defensiveness, or poor impulse control, while a drawing which takes an excessive length of time may reflect an obsessive-compulsive concern for detail or strong needs for approval.

While the person is completing the drawing, it is important to note the order in which the figures are drawn. Depending on the primary defense mechanisms employed by the individual, key figures generating the most anxiety will be drawn either first or last. Often a considerable amount of attention is given to a problem figure, with additional signs of anxiety relating to this figure appearing in other areas of the drawing.

Emphasis. Often attention is drawn to one figure or a part of a figure in a person's drawing because of the stronger or weaker line quality, excessive erasure, use of color, or bizarre or unusual treatment. This kind of selective emphasis within one drawing occurs when there is psychological conflict or anxiety associated with the particular area represented, or when there is a physical problem or illness affecting the specific body region (Jolles, 1971; Machover, 1949; Wolman, 1970).

Color. Many of the drawing procedures used in clinical practice do not encourage the use of colored crayons or pens. However a great deal of research [see, for example, Jolles (1971) or Luscher (1970)] has taken place regarding the possible psychological significance of certain colors for an individual. In particular, the interpretive approach to color becomes important when evaluating a person's spontaneous drawings. It is important to remember, though, that unless a full range of colors was made available to the individual when he was executing his drawing, an accurate interpretation of color use cannot be made.

   Colors may symbolize certain feelings, moods, or relationships in a person's life, and they may also represent a variety of different reactions or areas of conflict. Because of the ambiguity in interpreting color use, a great deal of caution must be used when evaluating a particular drawing. Furthermore, the conventional use of color is far less likely to have significance for the person than its unusual or bizarre use. For example, the use of red for a brick chimney or barn does not have the same meaning or significance as red used on the trunk of a tree. Recognizing the importance of color choice may enhance or influence an interpretation that would be quite ambiguous without the additional information derived from the use of color. However, if there is no other evidence in the drawing supporting a particular interpretation based on color, most likely that interpretation was too narrow and the full understanding of the color choice was not evident. It should be emphasized, though, that colors do not provide the sole basis for interpreting drawings; rather, they serve to amplify or emphasize the symbolic content of the objects and relationships within the picture. In general, when looking at the colors used in a drawing, the following tentative guidelines can be followed.

RED   An issue of vital significance (Zeeuw, 1957), a "burning" problem or danger, intense anger or violent reaction, strong emotional response (Piotrowski, 1957), sensuousness, or need for warmth and affection (Jolles, 1971).

ORANGE   Extroversion, externalization of affect (Schaie and Hess, 1964), emotional responsiveness to outer world, suspenseful situation, or life-death struggle; frequently implies ambivalence (Jolles, 1971).

YELLOW   Cheerfulness (Lowenfeld, 1954), intellectualizing tendencies, uninhibited expansiveness (Luscher, 1970), anxiety (Khan, 1960).

GREEN   Regulation (not repression) of affective tendencies (Zeeuw, 1957), homeostatic aspects of personality (Luscher, 1970), healthy ego, growth or newness of life, peacefulness, security (Jolles, 1971).

BLUE   Quiet, calm, well-controlled emotions (Jolles, 1971; Schaie and Hess, 1964); "cold"; pale blue indicates distance, fading away, or withdrawing.

PURPLE/   Personal identification with the figure colored purple (Luscher,
VIOLET   1970); inner emotional and affective stimulation (Zeeuw, 1957); internalization of affect, anxiety, tension (Schaie and Hess, 1964); "bold exterior"; need to control or possess (Jolles, 1971; Khan, 1960).

BROWN   Sensuousness, security (Luscher, 1970), fixation, rigidity (Zeeuw, 1957), guilt (Piotrowski, 1957), in touch with nature, struggle to overcome destructive forces and return to a healthy state (Schaie and Hess, 1964).

WHITE   Passivity, emptiness, depersonalization (Lowenfeld, 1954), loosening of reality contact (Schaie and Hess, 1964), expulsion of feelings (Zeeuw, 1957).

GRAY   Noninvolvement (Luscher, 1970), repression, denial (Schaie and Hess, 1964), emotional neutralization (Zeeuw, 1957).

BLACK   Depression (Jolles, 1971; Lowenfeld, 1954), suppression, cumulation of feelings (Luscher, 1970), inhibition, blocking, inadequacy (Schaie and Hess, 1964), self-depreciation (Khan, 1960), symbol of the unknown; if used as shading, black can be seen as a projection of dark thoughts and fears.

INTERPRETATION GUIDELINES

Human Figure

The human figure drawing is the most obvious and conscious representation of the self. With this drawing, the person reveals how he perceives himself and how he wants to present himself to others. The most common technique used to elicit a human figure drawing is to ask the individual to "draw a person." When this drawing is completed, a clean piece of paper is presented with instructions to draw a figure of the opposite sex. Sometimes a third drawing is requested of the self. Drawings depicting the same sex as the subject represent the attitudes and feelings of the subject towards himself (Schaefer, 1975; Van Dyne and Corskadon, 1978). Drawings of opposite-sex figures or drawings of family members represent how the subject perceives those individuals he/she has drawn. The following interpretive guidelines may be used for any drawing which contains a human figure.

Head. The head is considered the site of intellectual activities and aspirations, and often reflects a person's need for rational control of impulses and/or fantasies. The facial features and detail demonstrate the individual's social needs, abilities, and level of responsiveness. The head is almost always the first part drawn by children and is the primary part of the body with which a person identifies. In analytic terms, the head is associated with the ego. Most people give more attention and emphasis to the head than to other parts of their person drawings, although with maladjusted individuals this is often not true.

A disproportionately *large head* suggests grandiose tendencies, an inflated ego (Machover, 1949; Urban, 1963), intellectual aspirations (Buck, 1966), and/or fantasy preoccupations (Jolles, 1971). If a person is overly concerned with intellectual level or performance, as with retarded or gifted children, the head will often be drawn exceptionally large (Machover, 1949). Large heads are also drawn when the person is experiencing physical pain in this area of the body (Kahn and Giffen, 1960). *Oddly shaped heads* are common in organic or psychotic patients whose brain function is unusual and distorted (Burgemeister, 1962). It is important to remember, when looking at the size of the head, that children normally draw proportionately larger heads than adults, especially below the age of 7 years (Koppitz, 1968; Machover, 1949, 1960).

An unusually *small head* reveals a person who is feeling inadequate and inferior intellectually, socially, and/or sexually (Machover, 1949). When the head is cut off at the neck it may suggest fear of punishment (Hammer, 1968); when it is drawn last, it usually indicates a severe, although nonspecific, psychological disturbance (Levy, 1950, 1958; Machover, 1949).

Hair. Emphasis on hair suggests virility strivings, sexual preoccupation (Jolles, 1971), or compensation for feelings of sexual inadequacy or impotency (Buck, 1950; Levy, 1958). Elaborate or glamorous hairdos with unusual cosmetic emphasis may indicate psychosomatic conditions or excessive narcissism (Machover, 1949; McElhaney, 1969).

Facial Features. The omission of facial features reveals a person who is evasive and superficial in interpersonal relationships, or who is hostile and demonstrating extreme caution (Machover, 1949; Urban, 1963). This is a poor prognosis for therapy, since social skills and responsiveness are minimal (Fiedler and Siegal, 1949). Dimly drawn features show timidity and self-consciousness in interpersonal relationships (Levy, 1958), and strongly drawn features may suggest feelings of inadequacy and weakness which are being compensated for by aggressive and socially dominant behavior (Machover, 1949).

Eyes. Usually large eyes are drawn by people who need to be visually alert to their interpersonal and physical environment (Machover, 1949; Schildkrout, Shenker, and Sonnenblick, 1972). This includes not only individuals who are suspicious and anxious, with exaggerated needs to protect themselves (Gilbert, 1969), but also individuals who are excited about seeing into other peoples' lives with a voyeuristic curiosity (Jolles, 1971). The eyes may reflect wariness, uncertainty, or fear. When the eyes are omitted, there tends to be a general level of ineffectiveness and a pervasive desire to avoid perceiving the world (Gurvitz, 1951). Jolles (1971) has associated an absence of eyes with the presence of visual hallucinations. Large orbits of the eye with a tiny eye or pupil suggest strong visual curiosity and guilt feelings, probably regarding voyeuristic conflicts (Jolles, 1971). Small circles for eyes suggest regressive tendencies and self-absorption (Hammer, 1958, 1968), although in children's drawings they frequently occur. Emphasis on the outline of the eyes indicates paranoid conditions (Reznikoff and Nicholas, 1958).

Ears. Although ears are frequently omitted by well-adjusted persons, unusual treatment or representation of them in an individual's drawing suggests the presence of some level of psychopathology. When a particular part of the body is emphasized in a person's drawing, there is usually a problem in this area, either physical or psychological. In this respect, unusual representation of the ears may indicate a physical handicap, a paranoid need for auditory acuity, sensitivity to social criticism (Jolles, 1971), or auditory hallucinations (Buck, 1966; DiLeo, 1973).

Nose. The nose can be seen as a sexual symbol; consequently, unusual treatment usually indicates sexual difficulties, fears, inferiority feelings, or impotency (Jolles, 1971; Machover, 1949).

Mouth. Emphasis on the mouth suggests oral conflicts such as eating problems (Urban, 1963), speech difficulties, alcoholism, or verbal outbursts (Jolles, 1971). When the mouth is omitted, it may reflect guilt related to areas of oral conflict (Machover, 1949) or a reluctance to communicate verbally with others (Hammer, 1968). The presence of *teeth,* particularly in adult drawings, suggests infantile aggressive tendencies, anger, and hostility. A single line mouth indicates tension and possible hypercritical or aggressive tendencies (Buck, 1966; McElhaney,

1969). A wide grin or upturned mouth is normal in a child's drawing, but may suggest a forced congeniality or inappropriate affect in an adult (Machover, 1949; Urban, 1963).

Neck. The neck is the connecting link between the head and the body, and represents the integration of the intellectual and emotional aspects of an individual. In analytic terms, this could be seen as the link between the ego control and the id impulse. In general, the more the neck is emphasized, the greater is the person's need to control his threatening impulses. A short, thick neck suggests tendencies to be gruff, stubborn or "bullheaded" (Machover, 1949; Urban, 1963). A long neck may represent a socially stiff or rigid individual who invests a good deal of effort in rigidly controlling basic drives (Buck, 1969; Mursell, 1969). When the neck is omitted, the person often is immature and has trouble handling impulses rationally (Jolles, 1971; Machover, 1949; Mundy, 1972).

Arms. It is with the arms that a person reaches out to his physical and interpersonal environment. Therefore, the arms are seen as representing a person's feelings of personal power and contact with the world around him. Relaxed and flexible arms are frequently found in the drawings of normals, whereas rigid, compulsive, inhibited persons often draw arms stiff and close to the body (Buck, 1948; Jolles, 1971; Machover, 1949). Individuals who are feeling inadequate, powerless, or ineffective in their world often represent the arms in a limp, flimsy, or stunted fashion (DiLeo, 1973; Machover, 1949). Reinforced arms, especially with emphasis on the musculature, suggest power strivings and — when associated with broad shoulders — demonstrate aggressive, assaultive tendencies with a strong need for increased physical power (Burns, 1982; Hammer, 1969b; Jolles, 1971). Folded arms indicate denial, feelings of rejection, and a suspicious, hostile attitude (Buck, 1966; Hammer, 1954; Jolles, 1971). Omission of the arms may indicate guilt feelings, or an extreme depression or withdrawal from the environment (Buck, 1966; Kahn and Giffen, 1960; Machover, 1949; Mursell, 1969).

Hands. Hands can be viewed as extensions of the arms, and provide further emphasis and elaboration of the manner in which the arms are drawn. Vague or sketchy hands suggest a lack of confidence or productivity (Machover, 1949), and heavy shading of the hands shows anxiety or guilt feelings often associated with aggressive or masturbatory activity (Levy, 1958; Machover, 1949).

Legs. Drawings that show unusual treatment of the legs and feet are related to feelings of insecurity, lack of self-confidence, and inadequacy. A sketchy, feathery line quality emphasizes these feelings of inadequacy (Jolles, 1971; Machover, 1949), while reinforced or strong line quality may suggest aggressive or assaultive tendencies (Shneidman, 1958). It is also important to consider the stance of the figure, that is, how the legs are positioned in the drawing. A wide stance indicates aggressive defiance, especially when the figure is in the middle of the page (Buck, 1950; Jolles, 1971; Machover, 1949). Often this aggressive stance is a cover for underlying feelings of insecurity which may be revealed in another part of the drawing (Machover, 1949). When the legs float in space or do not touch the ground solidly, the individual is usually feeling insecure and unsure of himself (DiLeo, 1973; Machover, 1949). He is not "grounded" and thus is unable to move effectively in his world.

Feet. Just as the hands can be seen as extensions of the arms, so the feet can be seen as extensions of the legs and, likewise, refer to a person's feeling of mobility. It is important to look not only at how the feet are drawn, but also at the manner in which they come in contact with the ground (see discussion of leg stance). Often the feet in the drawings of normals are the most poorly drawn body part so interpretations should be made only with additional and complementary supporting evidence. Emphasis on the feet often indicates sexual problems or guilt feelings (Hammer, 1958; Machover, 1951, 1958). Small, tiny feet have been associated with insecurity, dependence, withdrawal, and depression (Brown, 1958; Buck, 1966, 1969; Jolles, 1971), whereas omission of the feet reveals lack of independence, helplessness, and possible psychosomatic conditions (Buck, 1966; Kokonis, 1972; Mursell, 1969).

Trunk. Most of the time the trunk is drawn in a simple, oval-like shape that may resemble the person's somatotype. The body has been associated with basic drives and thus reflects the individual's attitude towards these drives. Omission of the trunk is quite rare except in young children's drawings and, if this occurs in the drawings of older children or adults, indicates a severe degree of deterioration characteristic of organics, involutionals, hypochondriacs (Kahn and Giffen, 1960; Mundy, 1972), and poorly adjusted children (Koppitz, 1968). Often a person will draw the trunk with an emphasis at the waist in the form of a belt with shading or an exaggerated waistline. Usually this indicates sexual conflict or tension concerning bodily impulses (Buck, 1966; Jolles, 1971; Machover, 1949). This may be accompanied by a marked difference in the line quality of the drawing between the top and the bottom half of the figure. Genitalia are rarely drawn, but when present, they suggest primitive behavioral tendencies or schizophrenia (Deabler, 1969; Kahn and Giffen, 1960; Machover, 1949). Emphasis on the breasts is most often made by emotionally infantile males who are attached to their mothers and early adolescent girls who are concerned with their breast development (Jolles, 1971; Machover, 1949).

Clothing. The importance of clothing in a person's drawing is very similar to its importance on a live person. It is used to present a "socially acceptable" figure, to cover up the nakedness of the individual, and to present a facade to the "civilized" world. It is unusual for a person to draw a nude figure unless there is evidence of sexual maladjustment, egocentricity, body narcissism (Jolles, 1971; Levy, 1958), and/or a lack of sexual satisfaction (Hammer, 1968). Nudes drawn by artists or art students are not unusual, though, and reflect their training and occupation rather than psychological conflicts (Machover, 1949). Overclothed figures suggest sexual maladjustment, with a need to repress sexual impulses (Gurvitz, 1951) and to present a superficially sociable front to others (Buck, 1950; Machover, 1949). This is usually associated with a strong need for approval (Machover, 1949). An excessive degree of adornment in drawings by females suggests both seductiveness and the presence of strong needs to protect themselves from physical threat (Miller, Wagner, and Edwards, 1982).

Symmetry. In general, extreme emphasis on bilateral symmetry indicates a person with obsessive-compulsive defense mechanisms for controlling emotions (Hammer, 1958; Machover, 1949). Repression and overintellectualization are common in this type of person. Such individuals often appear rigid, mechanical, and emotionally distant, with high needs to present a "perfect picture" to the world.

Stick Figures. A person who draws stick figures may be revealing evasive tendencies, insecurity, and problems with interpersonal relationships (Hammer, 1969a; Jolles, 1971). However, many adults who feel awkward with their drawing abilities will produce a picture with stick figures rather than attempt the more difficult task of drawing a full person.

Caricatures. Some people will draw a person who resembles a cartoon figure, or a person dressed in some costume or heroic-figure garb. Usually these individuals are quite defensive about revealing themselves, and they often are immature and hostile towards others (Jolles, 1971; Levy, 1950). Depending on the type of figure drawn, these people may be using humor as a way to protect or hide themselves from others (Urban, 1963).

Male and Female Figures. One's feelings towards males and females are often pointedly visible when a person's drawings of the two figures are seen together. Levy (1958) found that 87% of normals, regardless of age, sex, or marital status, will draw a figure of their own sex first, and when this is not the case, there is often a severe problem with sexual identification (Green, Fuller, and Rutley, 1972; Jolles, 1971; Kurtzberg, Cavior, and Lipton, 1966). When the sexual characteristics of the figures are confused and inconsistent, sexual problems and maladjustment are indicated. With children, it is normal for the female drawing to be somewhat larger (Weider and Noller, 1953). However, with adult males, a larger female drawing suggests passivity and feelings of inadequacy (Levy, 1958), and with females, a larger female drawing suggests masculine strivings and feelings of hostility directed towards men (Levy, 1958; McElhaney, 1969). In general, when a person draws a figure in profile, there is evidence of evasiveness and guardedness (Machover, 1949). This is particularly emphasized when the figure of one sex is in profile and the other is in front view. For example, if a man draws his male figure in profile and his female in front view, there is the suggestion that he has a need to protect himself and, at the same time, expose women (Machover, 1949; Urban, 1963).

Aggression and Hostility. The following list represents a compilation of the different signs that indicate hostility and aggression (Saarni and Azara, 1977). The level of a person's hostility can be assessed by noting both the number of these signs and the relative intensity of each in any one record.

Scars
Gross asymmetry of limbs
Crossed eyes (in or out)
Oversize figures
Teeth
Transparencies
Disproportionately long arms
Disproportionately large hands
Omission of arms
Genitals

Anxiety. Saarni and Azara (1977) also compiled the following list of indicators for insecurity-lability. As for aggression and hostility, there is no exact cutoff score, but the clinician should note both the quantity, and the relative intensity of each sign.

Slanting figure more than 15°
Undifferentiated shading of face and neck
Disproportionately short arms
Arms clinging to sides of body
Three or more figures drawn
No hands and fingers
No eyes
No mouth
No legs
No feet (shoes)
No neck
Tiny figures (less than 3 inches)

Baseline or "grass" under figure
Excessive midline detailing
Faint scribbly-scratchy lines (not artistic)

House

House drawings are most often seen in the House-Tree-Person Test. Rarely is an individual requested to draw only a house, although this could at times be a possibility during an evaluation. Most drawings of houses contain a door, windows, a roof, and walls. If any of these essential features are missing, intellectual deterioration or severe emotional disturbance is indicated (Buck, 1955; Beck, 1948; Jolles, 1971). In general, the house is viewed as a reflection of the person, even though in reality it may be drawn to represent the individual's personal or childhood home. With children, as sometimes with adults, the house can also be seen as a reflection of their feelings towards their mothers. It is important to remember that characteristics inferred about the mother from the house drawing may not be objectively accurate since they only represent how the mother is seen through the eyes of the person doing the drawing.

In general, the evaluator can look at the person's house drawing and detect an overall mood from the way in which the house is represented. Some houses appear quite detailed and complex, sometimes with multiple doorways or wings. Other houses may be very simple and straightforward, and still others may look sparse or empty. Often these initial intuitive responses to the picture can result in surprisingly accurate interpretations. When the characteristics are evaluated in a more systematic manner, the first impressions and reactions are frequently substantiated.

Size. Very small houses indicate withdrawal tendencies, feelings of inadequacy, and rejection of the home and home life (Buck, 1948; Hammer, 1968). Large drawings, on the other hand, may indicate frustration because of a restricting environment, hostility, aggressive tendencies, or overcompensatory defenses (Buck, 1948, 1966).

Chimney. The presence of a chimney usually indicates psychological warmth and availability (Buck, 1966). When the chimney is missing, the person often feels a certain distance or coldness about his parents' home (Jolles, 1971; Mursell, 1969), unless this omission can be explained by some external reason such as an absence of fireplaces in the particular region in which the individual grew up or currently lives. Although a thin trail of smoke coming from the chimney is not unusual, when there is a great deal of smoke this may indicate considerable inner tension with a need to release pent-up pressure (Buck, 1966; Hammer, 1958; Marzoff and Kirchner, 1972).

Door. Most houses are drawn with a door; when it is missing, psychological inaccessibility is suggested (Buck, 1948; Hammer, 1954; Jolles, 1971). Doors that are very small also emphasize reluctant accessibility, and doors that are locked or heavily hinged reveal defensiveness, hostility, and suspiciousness (Buck, 1966; Hammer, 1958; Jolles, 1971). Very large doors may show the need to impress others with one's social availability or may reflect an overdependence on others (Hammer, 1958; Jolles, 1971).

Windows. Like doors, windows show the availability of a person to make contact with others and reveal himself. When windows are missing, the individual is usually feeling withdrawn, guarded, suspicious, and often hostile towards others (Buck, 1966; Jolles, 1971). When the windows are curtained, barred, or shuttered, there is evidence of guardedness and social withdrawal which corresponds with the degree to which the windows are covered (Buck, 1966; Hammer, 1958). Large, open windows, on the other hand, suggest possible exhibitionistic tendencies or an open readiness for environmental contact (Buck, 1966). The presence of curtains or window trim is normal in most drawings (Hammer, 1954), and it is only when the windows are heavily blocked that there is reason to attach significance to this feature. For example, Blain, Bergner, Lewis, and Goodstein, (1981) found an absence of windows, an enlarged head, geometrically drawn figures, and an absence of feet to be associated with children who had been abused. However, a moderate degree of guardedness and caution in a new situation such as testing is normal.

Walkways. Well-proportioned paths and walkways leading up to a door indicate accessibility and openness to others (Hammer, 1958; Jolles, 1971; Marzoff and Kirchner, 1972). Paths that surround a house without leading up to the door may be seen as a barrier or protection, while the absence of a walkway may reveal difficulty in interpersonal relationships with a tendency to be relatively unavailable to others (Jolles, 1952, 1971).

Trees

Like house drawings, tree drawings are usually seen in spontaneous drawings or as one of the essential components of the House-Tree-Person Test. Although some people believe that the tree drawing reveals aspects of the individual's personality or his impression of himself in relation to his environment, others maintain that the tree reflects the person's deeper and more unconscious feelings about himself. When drawing a person, the individual is more conscious of the parallels between the drawing and himself, where as with the tree drawing, inner feelings are allowed to surface with only a minimum of censoring. A tree drawing is also frequently seen as reflecting the person's attitudes towards, and relationship with, his father, particularly when it is considered within the context of the House-Tree-Person Test.

Interpretation of the tree drawings can be made in phases, much like the house drawings. The first step is to view the tree in its totality and note its size, shape, and position on the page. Based on the initial impression, the evaluator forms an opinion about the person's feeling responses, his receptivity to influences, and his attitudes towards others. In general, a tree drawing should contain a trunk and at least one branch. If these critical elements are missing, intellectual deterioration must be considered (Buck, 1948; Jolles, 1971). The second step is to systematically analyze the details of the drawing by using the following guidelines.

Placement. When the tree is more or less centered on the page, the individual is usually well balanced, receptive to both masculine and feminine influences, and able to relate to both men and women (Bolander, 1977). When the tree is shifted to the left side of the paper, there is often an emotional imbalance (Hammer, 1965) characteristic of a person who has grown up under the influence of a dominant mother (Bolander, 1977). Resentment of the mother's influence is common with left side placement in drawings done by both males and females (Bolander, 1977). In contrast, trees on the right side of the paper are typically drawn by individuals who have a strong identification with their father and male peers (Bolander, 1977). Trees placed at the top of the page indicate a person who is not well grounded in reality, may be using fantasy as an escape, and may have an unrealistically high need for achievement (Bolander, 1977; Jolles, 1971; Machover, 1949). Trees drawn at the bottom of the page suggest feelings of inadequacy, with an almost deliberate inhibition of fantasy and the presence of depression (Bolander, 1977; Mursell, 1969).

Types. Many people will draw a *foliated tree* which does not represent any particular generic type. When this sort of tree is drawn with fruit (or a *fruit tree* particularly) there is usually a sense of fulfillment or confidence in the individual's creative abilities (Bolander, 1977) and/or a desire for children (Jolles, 1971). However, with children, apples suggest strong dependency needs or, if the apples have fallen, feelings of rejection (Buck, 1966; Hammer, 1954; Jolles, 1971). In an open, leafy tree where the crown is built up of branches covered by leaves, the individual is most likely precise and meticulous (Bolander, 1977). People who do these types of drawings are careful, slow, and reflective, often believing that they control their interactions with the environment through their own choices. Only when the *delineation of the leaves* is extremely detailed are obsessive-compulsive patterns or overcompensatory perfectionistic traits considered (Levine and Sapolsky, 1969). *Winter trees* without leaves reveal persons who feel exposed and easily influenced by others (Bolander, 1977), but whether or not this is a problem for the individual depends on how the tree is drawn and how the branches are represented. *Dead trees* are drawn by people who feel victimized by external forces and powerless to exert any influence on their environment (Bolander, 1977; Hammer, 1958). They feel hopeless, defenseless, and depressed about their internal abilities to improve the situation, and they may be suicidal (Barnouw, 1969; Jolles, 1971). People who draw *palm trees* see themselves as adventurous, yet when confronted with new situations often become defensive (Bolander, 1977). This approach-avoidance conflict appears in numerous forms throughout their lives. They do not accept rational arguments but are influenced primarily by emotional and sexual appeals. Persons who draw *pine-like trees* are likely to be goal oriented with high achievement needs. They do not like to express their feelings openly or reveal their vulnerability to emotions (Bolander, 1977). *Abstract trees* resemble realistic trees but they are relatively sparse and simplified. In general, it can be assumed that individuals who draw these types of trees tend to seek a certain amount of emotional distance from the problems they may be facing and tend to avoid a direct confrontation or "look at reality" (Bolander, 1977). People who draw *fantasy-like* trees often use their "flights into unreality" to avoid clearly perceiving their world and may cope with their environment with the use of humor or satire (Bolander, 1977; Meyers, 1953; Muhle, 1967).

Leaves and Branches.   The upper part of the tree, or the crown, is representative of the spirit, intellect, imagination, self-development, and conscious awareness of the individual. The branches depict personality organization and an ability to derive satisfaction from the environment. In general, the characteristics of the branches represent the way in which the individual relates to his environment (Arnoff, 1972; Buck, 1966; Jolles, 1971). For example, when the branches are blunt and bleak, the person often feels his life is colorless and unhappy (Hammer, 1960, 1968). When the branches are broken, there are feelings of trauma, castration, and impotency (Bolander, 1977; Buck, 1966; Jolles, 1971); when they are turned inward, egocentric and introversive tendencies are suggested (Buck, 1950; Hammer, 1958). Tiny branches reveal an inability to derive satisfaction from the environment, and very faint branches indicate anxiety and indecision (Buck, 1948, 1969; Jacks, 1969). Excessive branches, on the other hand, suggest an overemphasis on environmental satisfaction seeking (Bolander, 1977; Buck, 1966; Jolles, 1971), and tall, narrow branches show an emphasis on fantasy satisfaction (Hammer, 1958).

The most common type of disturbance seen in the drawing of leaves is the obsessive-compulsive person's need to spend a great amount of time on the detail (Buck, 1966; Jolles, 1971). Leaves which are sharply pointed reflect aggressive and acting out tendencies (Buck, 1966; Jolles, 1971). It has been suggested that an absence of leaves is an indication of inner barrenness and a dissatisfaction with life (Levine and Sapolsky, 1969). However, this interpretation should be made with caution since leafless trees are frequently encountered in the trees of normal, well-adjusted persons (Bolander, 1977) and occur more often in winter (Judson and McCasland, 1960).

Trunks and Roots. Tree trunks in general represent the ego and reveal feelings of basic power and feelings about oneself, particularly one's level of self-esteem (Bolander, 1977). As is true with all the drawings, lightly drawn or small areas suggest feelings of inadequacy, and when this type of trunk is drawn in combination with a large branch structure, it suggests a high need for achievement (Bolander, 1977). Truncated trunks with many small, sprouting branches suggest stunted psychological and emotional growth with recent renewed growth (Bolander, 1977). Scars on trunks represent traumatic experiences (Jolles, 1971), and knotholes reveal feelings of inadequacy associated with a traumatic experience (Bolander, 1977). Frequently the placement of knotholes corresponds directly to the occurrence of a traumatic event in the person's life. The higher the knothole is on the tree trunk, the more recent the traumatic event.

Emphasis on the roots reveals a "deep" person who may also be overly concerned with his hold on reality or with his own security needs (Jolles, 1971). Often such people hide themselves from others, allowing only the superficial aspects of themselves to be seen above ground (Bolander, 1977).

HOUSE-TREE-PERSON TEST

Administration of the House-Tree-Person Test (H-T-P) is quite simple. Present the person with a blank sheet of paper (8 1/2 X 11 inches) in a horizontal position and a sharpened pencil with an eraser. Instruct the individual to "draw me a picture that has in it a house, a tree, and a person." No further instructions or elaborations are given. If the individual has any question, they are usually answered with "just draw me a picture that has in it a house, a tree, and a person."

Interpretations of the house, tree, and person drawings, regardless of the administrative procedures, can be made using the separate guidelines already presented for houses, trees, and human figures. When the composite drawing is considered though, the relationship of the three elements and the addition of any other features become important. In general, the House-Tree-Person Test can be interpreted as reflecting either attitudes and feelings towards significant people in an individual's life or feelings directed towards the self. For some people, the house reflects their relationship to their mother, the tree reflects feelings towards their father, and the person reflects feelings about themselves. For others, the house, tree, and person all reveal different aspects of how the individual is feeling about himself. In reality, both interpretations can be considered simultaneously, since the projections we make onto other people (including our parent) are actually outward expressions of self-perceptions and feelings.

In addition to the general interpretive guidelines for the House-Tree-Person Test, Buck (1948, 1966) has developed the following specific interpretive possibilities. First of all, it is important to note the relative position of each of the main features. When the house and tree are seen as parental representations, the placement of the person will often indicate whether the individual feels closer to, or identifies more with, his mother or father. Sometimes a person will be placed directly between the parental images, which may indicate a need for protection or an attempt to keep the two parents together. When there is more than one mother or father image, this may be represented by either additional houses or trees in the picture, or a single house or tree composed of two (or more) different styles. How the individual views the relationship of his parents is demonstrated in the way the house and tree relate to each other on the paper. When one parent is viewed as more powerful or overwhelming, the corresponding symbol is drawn proportionately larger; when parents are viewed as antagonistic or emotionally distant from each other, the symbols in the drawing are often separated by a great deal of space. When one parent has been away, very often the symbol is drawn much smaller or in the distance.

Just as the size of a drawing relative to the paper size is important, so is the size of the drawn features relative to each other. When the person is drawn extremely large in comparison to the house and tree, very often one's emotional energy is directed inward. This inward directedness could be the result of a number of different dynamics. These individuals may feel quite inadequate and insecure, and attempt to compensate for these feelings by projecting an image of strength to the world. They may also be working on expressing themselves more completely and understanding themselves more fully, so that their energy is turned inward, or they may be somewhat self-centered and exhibitionistic, thus approaching life in a forceful and attention seeking manner. Although it is important to pay close attention to the details in a drawing, the interpretations which are based on these observations may vary considerably and can be made accurately only with supporting evidence from other test results and interview data.

When a person is completing the House-Tree-Person Test, very often he will add further details to form a more complete picture. This is particularly true with individuals who are in the upper range of intellectual functioning and have a need to structure and control their lives. Very often these people see the variety and emotionalism in life, and want to express this in their drawing. Some drawings will contain so much detail that they portray an almost fantasy-like quality. People who do this frequently are hiding their true feelings from others with their "gingerbread"-like attitude. They are optimistic and cheerful most of the time, and have difficulty admitting to, or even seeing, the harsher realities of life. However, in making an accurate assessment, it is important to develop an understanding of the person on a deeper level rather than merely responding to the immediate and often more superficial presentation.

A normal House-Tree-Person Test shows each of the elements in proper relation to each other and balanced appropriately on the page. Often the person is demonstrating some form of movement, although this is not always necessary. The house usually shows the expected signs of openness, accessibility, and warmth (chimney, windows, door, walkway), and the tree is healthy, grounded, and balanced. The three elements show a positive relationship to each other and are presented in such a manner as to portray a complete picture. Additional details may be included, although this is not a critical element in determining the relative health of the individual.

After the individual has completed the drawing for the House-Tree-Person Test, the questionnaire in Appendix E may be administered completely or in part to provide further information and clues for interpreting the picture. The questionnaire actually becomes an additional projective technique, with its starting point in the drawing just completed by the individual.

FAMILY DRAWING TESTS

Draw-A-Family Test

The Draw-A-Family Test (D-A-F) was developed in 1956 by Hulse and is one of the first family drawing tests mentioned in the literature. In this procedure, the individual is presented with a blank piece of 8 1/2 X 11 inch paper and a sharpened pencil with an eraser, and is given the instruction, "Draw me a picture of your family." No further elaboration is made, and only if the person is hesitant or confused is gentle encouragement given. The value of this procedure is that the individual's feelings and reactions towards his family members can be revealed in a symbolic and, therefore, less threatening manner. For example, the person may be experiencing a great deal of anger towards his mother, but on a conscious level, he is afraid to express this for fear of losing her protection and love which are essential to his survival. However, the drawing allows the angry feelings to be expressed in symbolic form, thus bypassing the conscious defense mechanisms. Although the drawing of the family members includes drawings of persons, it is important to remember that the D-A-F Test emphasizes the individual's feelings towards the family, not his style and content for drawing individual persons. Some people attempt to use the persons in the family drawing to gauge the intellectual level of the individual, as can be done with the Draw-A-Person Test. However, this should be avoided since the dynamics involved in the two procedures are quite different.

As with the other drawing tests, it is important to note how the figures are represented, where the figures are placed, and in what order the figures are drawn.

The family member who is most impressive to the person is usually drawn first, although the feelings associated with the person may be either strongly positive or negative. From the placement of the figures on the page, it is possible to see how the person perceives relationships among family members, and where he or she fits into the family picture. Sometimes the individual may feel so inconsequential or powerless within the family that he will "forget" to include himself. In some instances, family pets may be deliberately drawn in positions of prominence, while siblings or the individual himself may be left out or made to appear much less important. If the drawing is done in pencil, feelings of ambivalence or anxiety towards specific family members may be expressed with variations in line quality or increased erasures on that particular figure. If colored crayons are used, the color chosen for each family member may emphasize or exaggerate specific feelings towards family members.

The Kinetic Family Drawing Test

In 1972, Burns and Kaufman described a variation of the Draw-A-Family Test that has received considerable attention. With their Kinetic Family Drawing technique, the person is presented with a blank paper and pencil, and asked to draw a picture of his family doing something. When the drawing is completed, the person may be asked to describe his drawing so that the examiner can accurately perceive the figures and correctly interpret the representations. With this procedure, it is possible to see how the individual views family relationships, in addition to gaining information about how he feels towards each family member. The emphasis here is on the dynamics within the family, that is, how the individual sees the family members interacting (or not interacting) with one another. Again, it is important to notice the order of the figures drawn, their placement with respect to one another, and the manner in which each figure is produced, along with the content of the picture itself. Burns and Kaufman have formulated detailed and extensive guidelines for interpreting Kinetic Family Drawings, including an Analysis Grid for quick and methodical scoring. The guidelines discussed here are adapted and condensed from the book *Actions, Styles and Symbols in Kinetic Family Drawings (K-F-D)* by Burns and Kaufman (1972).

Frequently, individuals draw their parents engaged in the stereotypic role activities they see most often around the house. For example, fathers may be pictured doing such things as mowing the lawn, reading, or watching TV; mothers are shown cooking, cleaning, or ironing; and the self is portrayed as playing, eating, or helping. Sometimes an individual figure will be placed in a *precarious position,* which is usually a reflection of tension associated with that person. If it is the individual himself who is in the precarious position, this may be reflecting their insecurity as a unit. Along the same lines, if a family member is reproduced on the *back of the paper,* it is often because of some tension or unresolved conflicts associated with that person; when it is the person himself, it may reflect insecurities concerning feelings of belonging to the family. Sometimes these feelings are so strong that a person is omitted from the drawing altogether. When this is the individual himself, it reflects his feeling of separateness from the family, and when someone else is omitted, it may show his desire to exclude that person for a variety of reasons. *Elevated figures* are used to express feelings of dominance or power in the family, and *extended arms* on figures represent an attempt to control the environment. Sometimes one of the family members will be drawn in a manner obviously different from the other figure. This *different* representation often reflects some characteristic or involvement of that person that is "different" from the rest of the family. For example, in a family where the father constantly demands excessive attention, the child may picture him rotated on the paper.

Very often in Kinetic Family Drawings, feelings between two people, or the "energy" or force between individuals, is, represented symbolically. For example, the figures may be looking at each other, thus representing love and emotional closeness, or they may be drawn with a *wall or other physical barrier* between them to show that the emotional energy between the two is blocked for some reason. Sometimes one or two figures in the picture may be *encapsulated* or boxed off to demonstrate difficulties in relating to those persons, and at other times each person may be *compartmentalized* in separate squares to show how feelings are cut off between individuals. Drawings like this show the beginning of social isolation and withdrawal that can lead to serious problems if left untreated. *Balls* are sometimes drawn as a concrete symbol of the interaction between two people and often depict how the individual handles competitive feelings. Frequently, when the individual has strong competitive feelings but is in a situation in which these feelings are prevented from being expressed, the ball is drawn bouncing up and down, not directed towards anyone else. *Fire, light,* and *representations of warmth* are also viewed as concrete representations of feelings or "energy" between two people. For example, fire often reveals a person's desire for love and affection, but it suggests that these feelings are also accompanied by anger stemming from a sense of not having these needs for affection adequately met. A symbol of light often represents the person's need for love without the accompanying feelings of anger.

When a person is feeling unstable in his world, he will often attempt to create some stability by *underlining* the entire drawing or the individuals with whom his relationships seem unstable. When figures are drawn close to the edge of the paper, it is often a reflection of the same feelings and needs for security and stability. Lines at the top of the page or *heavy clouds* are drawn when the world seems scary and full of darkness and worry.

Family Participation Drawing

One other variation of the family drawing tests that has been valuable as a therapeutic technique is having the entire family participate in creating a family drawing. With this procedure, a large piece of butcher paper is taped to a wall, and an assortment of crayons and drawing implements are provided. The family is instructed to draw a picture together. It is interesting in this task to be aware not only of the drawing content but also of the manner in which the family proceeds with the drawing. The interaction of the family members, while they are deciding what the drawing will be and how it will be executed, is a good "bird's-eye view" of how the family functions in general when presented with a problem situation. Sometimes, there will be very little discussion, with each member doing a separate drawing on the same piece of paper, while at other times one person takes over and directs the other members in a very dogmatic fashion. There are numerous variations to how a family may proceed, and an aware observer will be able to quickly identify the key dynamics within the family unit by using this procedure. In addition to being extremely valuable for the therapist in assessing the family dynamics, the drawing process is light and fun for the family, thus creating an atmosphere of playfulness and enjoyment in which they can, at the same time, learn to look at interaction patterns and areas for personal growth. Once the drawing is complete, the guidelines for interpreting the drawing may be followed to help the family understand and interpret the drawing and the feelings portrayed therein.

SPONTANEOUS DRAWINGS

Although spontaneous drawings do not necessarily come under the heading of a "projective technique," they can be used to reveal the personality characteristics and unique projections of the individual. Interpretation of an individual's spontaneous drawings may be useful in deepening the present understanding of that person, in addition to providing a means for following changes which are occurring at a nonverbal level. Spontaneous drawings are particularly useful with children whose verbal skills are limited. They are also valuable as a therapeutic technique for releasing feelings and gaining a new perspective on a particular situation. A person may be asked to draw a picture of how he is feeling, how he conceptualizes a specific situation, or how he reacts to someone or something. Based on the content of the picture, new insights or awareness may surface. The use of color, the choice of content, and the process by which the drawing is executed are all important in understanding what the individual is communicating. When the drawing is used as a therapeutic technique and not just as a diagnostic aid, further insights may be gained by asking the person to describe the picture, give it a title, and explain what the symbols mean. Very often, when given the opportunity and guidance, it is possible for the persons themselves to interpret their drawings quite accurately, thus discovering a method of understanding their own personal symbols and gaining a tool for bringing unconscious material into consciousness. Techniques for proceeding with this vary, depending on the theoretical bias of the therapist. For example, a Jungian might choose to use active imagination as a method of uncovering the unconscious material in the drawing; a Gestalt therapist might have the individual interact or "talk to" the various elements in the drawing; and a psychoanalyst might use free association in order to develop an understanding of the dynamics that influenced the person's reactions during childhood. All of these methods can be useful for working with the drawing and using it to further the assessment procedure itself as well as the client's personal growth and development.

RECOMMENDED READING

Bolander, K. *Assessing Personality through Tree Drawings.* New York: Basic Books, 1977.

Burns, R.C. and Kaufman, S.H. *Actions, Styles, and Symbols in Kinetic Family Drawings (K-F-D).* New York: Brunner/Mazel, 1972.

DiLeo, J.H. *Children's Drawings as Diagnostic Aids.* New York: Brunner/Mazel, 1970.

Ogdon, D.P. *Psychodiagnostics and Personality Assessment.* Los Angeles: Western Psychological Services, 1975.

Semeonoff, B. *Projective Techniques.* New York: John Wiley & Sons, 1976.

5
The Thematic
Apperception Test

The Thematic Apperception Test (TAT) is a projective test consisting of a series of pictures, in which the examinee is requested to create a story about what he believes is occurring. The test was originally developed by Henry Murray and his colleagues at the Harvard Psychological Clinic in 1938. Murray (1943) describes the TAT as "a method of revealing to the trained interpreter some of the dominant drives, emotions, sentiments, complexes, and conflicts of personality. Special value resides in its power to expose underlying inhibited tendencies which the subject is not willing to admit, or cannot admit because he is unconscious of them" (p. 1). It is different from the Rorschach and other "inkblot" projective tests in that the TAT cards present more structured stimuli, and require organized and complex verbal responses. In addition, the TAT relies on more qualitative methods of interpretation and assesses the "here-and-now" features of an individual's life situation rather than the basic underlying structure of personality. Since its origin, the TAT has become one of the more extensively used psychological tests in clinical practice and has also served as a model for the development of similar tests.

The TAT materials consist of 20 cards with ambiguous pictures on them. The examinee is instructed to make up a story which includes what is occurring in the picture, the thoughts and feelings of the characters, what events led up to this situation, and the outcome of the story. The examiner can interpret the responses either quantitatively (using rating scales to measure the intensity, duration, and frequency of needs) or qualitatively (evaluating the story themes intuitively). The final results can be an important adjunct and supplement to other psychological tests since the TAT produces not only highly rich, varied, and complex types of information but also personal data which bypass a subject's conscious resistances.

Since the original development of the TAT in 1938, there have been a number of significant innovations (Bellak, 1975; Wolk and Wolk, 1971) and a variety of different approaches towards scoring (Arnold, 1962; Bellak, 1975; Henry, 1956; Rapaport, Gill, and Shafer, 1968; Wyatt, 1947). The most frequently used derivative of the TAT is the Children's Apperception Test (CAT) which has the noteworthy feature of substituting animal figures for human ones. It was developed by Bellak in 1954 with the intent of designing pictures with which children could more readily identify. Other similar tests are the Pickford Projective Pictures (Pickford, 1963) and the Rosenzweig Picture Frustration Study (Rosenzweig, 1976, 1977, 1978). Ritzler, Sharkey, and Chudy (1980) have criticized the TAT for eliciting low energy, negatively toned stories. They constructed an alternative set of pictures derived from the *Family of Man* (Steichen, 1955) photo essay collection, which they found produced a balance of negatively and positively toned stories, as well as a variety of action and energy levels for the main character.

In addition to the TAT's derivatives, a number of different approaches to scoring and interpreting the TAT itself have been developed. The original approach by Murray involves assessing which character in the story is the "hero," or focal figure, and then quantifying the relative intensity of each expressed need on a five-point scale. Murray also includes measuring the forces of the hero's environment (press), types of outcomes, basic themes (themas), and interests and sentiments of the hero. In addition to Murray's system, there have been other variations developed by Arnold (1962), Bellak (1975), Dana (1955), Eron (1950), McClelland (1971), and Wyatt (1949). Although there are a variety of interpretive approaches from which to choose, this chapter will focus primarily on that developed by Murray since it is both the original and the most frequently used scoring system (Vane, 1981).

MURRAY'S THEORY OF PERSONALITY

The TAT is so integrally involved with Murray's concepts of personality that a survey of his basic theoretical components is important. In constructing his theory, Murray emphasizes the biological basis as well as the social and environmental determinants of behavior. He also is consistently aware of how individuals interact with their environment. This interaction includes how people are affected by external forces and how their unique set of needs, attitudes, and values influences their reaction to the world around them.

Perhaps more than any other theorist, Murray has analyzed and clarified the concept of needs. This has been the focus of his conceptual efforts, and the development of the TAT grew from his attempt to evaluate and assess the relative strength of the individual's specific psychological needs. Murray (1938) defined a need as

. . . a construct which stands for a force . . . which organizes perception, apperception, intellectualization, connotation and action in such a way as to transform in a certain direction an existing, unsatisfying situation. Thus, it manifests itself by leading the organism to search for, or to avoid encountering, or when encountered, to attend and respond to certain kinds of press (environmental forces). . . . Each need is characteristically accompanied by a particular feeling or emotion and tends to use certain modes . . . to further its ends. (pp. 123–124)

A need either can be provoked by internal processes or, more frequently, can be the result of specific environmental events, as shown in Table 5-1.

Although Murray makes a variety of distinctions among different types of needs, the most important is between primary or viscerogenic needs and secondary or psychogenic ones. Primary needs are linked to characteristic physiological events and are innate to each individual. They typically refer to physical satisfactions and can be illustrated by the needs for air, water, food, sex, and urination.

Table 5-1. Murray's List of Needs.

A. Needs Motivated by Desire for Power, Property, Prestige, Knowledge, or Creative Achievement
1. n Achievement
2. n Acquisition
3. n Aggression
4. n Construction
5. n Counteraction
6. n Dominance
7. n Exposition
8. n Recognition
9. n Understanding

B. Needs Motivated by Affection, Admiration, Sympathy, Love, and Dependence
1. n Affiliation
2. n Deference
3. n Nurturance
4. n Sex
5. n Succorance

C. Needs Motivated by Desire for Freedom, Change, Excitement, and Play
1. n Autonomy
2. n Change, Travel, Adventure
3. n Excitance
4. n Playmirth

D. Miscellaneous Needs
1. n Abasement
2. n Blame Avoidance
3. n Cognizance
4. n Harm Avoidance
5. n Passivity
6. n Rejection
7. n Retention
8. n Sentience

NOTE: Adapted from Murray (1938, pp. 152–226).

Sooondary needs are originally derived from primary needs and are acquired during the process of psychological development. They generally lack a strong connection to biological processes and are psychological in nature. Examples are needs for affiliation, achievement, recognition, dominance, autonomy, and acquisition.

Although it simplifies understanding to consider needs separately, in reality they do not function in isolation from one another. Rather they interact with one another to create areas of mutual influence and effect. For example, needs may be in *conflict* with one another, as when a need for power is antagonistic to a need for affiliation or a need for achievement is opposed to a need for pleasure. There may also be a *fusion* of needs in which separate needs such as power and achievement produce the same behaviors. Finally, there may be *subsidiation* of needs in which one need is subsidized by, or works for, another. For example, an individual may express a high degree of aggressiveness which is actually working to support an underlying need for acquisition.

When Murray uses the term "need," he refers to the significant determinants of behavior which reside in an individual. In contrast, "press" refers to the environmental determinants which elicit specific behaviors from an individual or constellate specific needs within him (see Table 5-2). "The press of an object is what it can do to the subject or for the subject — the power that it has to affect the well-being of the subject in one way or another" (Murray, 1938, p. 121). Murray conceptualizes press as either alpha or beta. Beta press refers to the individual's perceptions and interpretations of a specific aspect of the environment, and alpha press refers to the objective or real aspects of that environment. Most behaviors are a direct result of beta press, but it is important to be aware of the wide discrepancies between an individual's subjective interpretation of the world and the world as it actually is. A striking example of such a discrepancy is the delusional systems of paranoid patients who consistently distort external reality as a result of their inner psychological processes.

In order to conceptualize units of behavior which result from the interaction between needs and press, Murray developed the term *thema*. A thema is a small unit of behavior which can combine with other thema to form *serial thema*. An individual's *unity thema* is the pattern of related needs and press which gives meaning to the largest portion of his behavior. For example, a core and overriding feature of an individual might be rebelliousness or martyrdom. This may be sufficiently well organized and powerful enough to override even primary needs, as amply demonstrated in the case of a martyr who is willing to die for his beliefs. A unity thema is derived from early infantile experiences and, once developed, repeats itself in many forms during an individual's later life. It operates largely as an unconscious force, and Murray (1938) described it as ". . . a compound of interrelated — collaborating or conflicting — dominant needs that are linked to press to which the individual was exposed on one or

Table 5-2. Murray's List of Press.

A. Press of Deprivation
   1. p Acquisition
   2. p Retention

B. Press Descriptive of an Empty, Alien, or Rejecting Environment
   1. p Lack
   2. p Loss
   3. p Rejection
   4. p Uncongenial Environment

C. Press of Coercion and Restraint
   1. p Dominance
   2. p Imposed Task, Duty, Training

D. Press Descriptive of a Hostile, Aggressive Environment
   1. p Aggression

E. Press of Danger, Injury, and Death
   1. p Affliction
   2. p Death of Hero
   3. p Physical Danger
   4. p Physical Injury

F. Press of Friendliness, Sympathy, Respect, Dependence, and Love
   1. p Affiliation
   2. p Deference
   3. p Nurturance
   4. p Sex
   5. p Succorance

G. Miscellaneous Press
   1. p Birth of Offspring
   2. p Claustrum
   3. p Cognizance
   4. p Example
   5. p Exposition
   6. p Luck

NOTE: Adapted from Murray (1983, pp. 152–226).

more particular occasions, gratifying or traumatic, in early childhood" (pp. 604–605). The TAT was designed to assess both the small units of thema and the larger, core aspects of an individual's unity themas.

Figure 5-1 is a summary of the basic elements of Murray's theory. These elements are relatively simple and straightforward, but the specific details are complicated and comprehensive. The details include not only extensively enumerating a wide variety of needs and press, but also taking into account the complexities of their interactions.

In summary, Murray's theory is not a comprehensive understanding of personality, but rather a listing and description of various psychological needs.

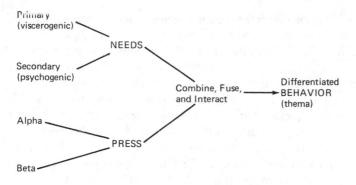

Figure 5-1. Outline of Murray's theory of personality.

He also focuses on motivational aspects of the person, with tension reduction being the central theme to explain the individual's external behavior. Although these contributions are significant, the main achievement of Murray has been the development of the TAT, which is a direct result of his theories and a support for his original formulations.

RELIABILITY AND VALIDITY

The responses which a subject makes to the TAT involve complex, meaningful verbal material. Because of the complexity of this material, exact quantitative analysis is difficult, and interpretations are based more on a qualitative analysis of story content. This makes most methods of determining reliability problematic. Some success in achieving adequate interscorer reliability has resulted from the development of quantitative scoring strategies and rating scales. This is especially true for the work of McClelland (1961) and Atkinson and Feather (1966) who developed complex scoring schemes for achievement, affiliation, and power. However, even though scorers can agree on the quantitative values assigned to different variables, these still do not constitute conclusions but are, rather, raw data. In other words, it remains questionable whether clinicians will make the same inferences based on the quantitative scores. Whereas good interscorer reliability relating to such areas as the weighting of different needs has been achieved, agreement between the conclusions based on these scores has not been adequately demonstrated. This is further complicated by the fact that in actual practice, clinicians rely primarily on subjective clinical judgment.

Another difficulty in determining reliability lies in the wide variability among different stories. If test evaluators wish to determine the internal consistency of the TAT, they are confronted with the fact that the various cards are not comparable. They were designed to measure separate areas of a person's functioning. Thus, a strategy such as split half reliability is inappropriate. Not only are comparisons of different stories in the same administration problematic but so are comparisons between two different administrations. When subjects were requested to tell different stories on different administrations, the quantitative scores for various needs did not produce significant retest correlations (Lindzey and Herman, 1955). Thus, important aspects of reliability either have not been achieved or, in some cases, are not even appropriate to attempt.

The task of achieving test validity is likewise difficult. One major problem lies in establishing agreed upon external criteria. If overt behavior is used as the criterion, there is often little correspondence with test scores. For example, high aggression in TAT stories does not reflect the degree to which a person actually expresses aggressive behavior. However, it may still be valuable to understand a person's internal processes even though these are not outwardly expressed. When measures of needs on the TAT are compared with needs measured on tests such as the Edwards Personal Preference Schedule and the Adjective Check List, there is little correspondence (Megargee and Parker, 1968). Furthermore, there is usually little agreement among different projective techniques when they are used to assess the same person. All of this makes it extremely difficult to develop useful generalizations based on TAT protocols.

One argument against subjecting the TAT to strict psychometric scrutiny is that rigid objective studies do not represent the way in which the TAT is actually used in clinical practice. When experienced clinicians were requested to provide individual descriptions of persons based on TAT stories, the descriptions did tend to match independent descriptions based on case histories. However, even though the descriptions by individual clinicians were fairly accurate, there was usually little agreement among different clinicians evaluating the same person. It might be argued that because of the complexity and richness of the material, each clinician is tapping into different aspects of the same person. Thus, studies that attempt to establish the validity of the TAT have produced meager, and sometimes negative, results.

ASSETS AND LIMITATIONS

Since the development of the TAT over 40 years ago, there have been serious questions raised regarding its validity and reliability. Despite such questions, the status of the TAT has remained essentially unchanged. In fact one reviewer has summarized this by stating that "there are still enthusiastic clinicians and doubting statisticians" (Adcock, 1965). However, before using the TAT, or any projective test, the examiner should fully understand its assets and limitations.

Like all projective techniques, the TAT is a valuable tool for the following reasons:

1. It offers access to the covert and deeper structures of an individual's personality.

2. There is less susceptibility to faking. The purpose of projective techniques is usually disguised, and the subject often slackens his conscious defenses while releasing unconscious material.
3. The focus is on the global nature of personality, rather than on the objective measurement of specific traits or attitudes. These include not only emotional, motivational, and interpersonal characteristics, but also general intellectual level, originality, and problem solving styles.
4. There is ease of rapport. Most projective tests are regarded as intrinsically interesting and nonthreatening to the person's prestige since there are no "wrong" answers. However, some individuals feel quite anxious and insecure with the lack of structure of projective techniques.

The following general criticisms have been leveled at projective techniques and therefore must be considered when using the TAT:

1. Inadequate standardization in respect to scoring and administration
2. Inadequate normative data and a resulting reliance on general clinical experience to interpret test performance
3. Difficulty developing accurate scorer reliability as well as retest reliability
4. Inadequate validation studies
5. Test sensitivity to situational variables such as stress, sleep deprivation, etc., which can significantly alter test performance, thereby reducing the likelihood that "core" aspects of personality are actually being measured

Although these general considerations must be understood when using projective techniques, there are also a number of characteristics specific to the TAT that should be kept in mind. One important aspect of the TAT, which helps to explain its widespread continued use, is that its manifest material (verbal stories) is not mysterious in appearance. Even a relatively untrained person can appreciate the differing themes, moods, and perspectives portrayed in the stories. The experienced tester also profits from this inherent familiarity or approachability of the test data.

A further asset of the TAT is its origin within an academic-humanistic environment. It is not closely aligned within any particular school of thought and therefore can be approached from, and interpreted by, a number of different theoretical orientations. Furthermore, the TAT was developed by the study of normal individuals, rather than by case studies or normative comparisons of pathological populations. This orientation has evolved directly out of Murray's belief that the proper beginning point for understanding personality is the intensive and detailed study of normal subjects.

The TAT potentially provides a comprehensive evaluation of personality, which has sometimes been referred to as a "wide-band" approach (Rabin, 1968). For example, among the comprehensive dimensions which the TAT can assess are a person's cognitive style, imaginative process, family dynamics, inner adjustment, emotional reactivity, general intelligence, and sexual adjustment (Henry, 1956). The TAT can also evaluate such areas as creativity, level of affect, problem solving skill, and verbal fluency. Thus, although the TAT primarily is oriented towards providing insight into a subject's fundamental conceptions and patterns of interpersonal interaction, it can also give important information about a far wider range of areas.

Although the TAT is extremely versatile, it is not self-sufficient, and a number of authors have emphasized that the TAT yields optimum results only when included in a battery of tests (Anastasi, 1982). Therefore, the hypotheses and interpretations derived from the TAT should be compared and contrasted with additional sources of information, such as objective personality tests, cognitive evaluations, historical data, and other projective techniques, to verify central themes and conclusions.

It has been assumed by most projective test originators, including Murray, that fantasy productions can be used to predict covert motivational dispositions. However, it is questionable whether or not high fantasy production actually does reflect overt behavior (Klinger, 1966; McClelland, 1966; Skolnick, 1966). In fact, fantasies may even serve to compensate for a lack of a particular group of behaviors. For example, in a 20-year longitudinal study by McClelland (1966), adolescents who obtained high achievement need scores on the TAT were often not among those who subsequently showed upward social mobility, but individuals who had shown upward social mobility typically obtained higher scores on the need for achievement as adults. The practical interpretive significance of this is that it might be better to see fantasy productions as samples of thoughts which may or may not accurately reflect overt behavior.

A further liability, which is particularly relevant for the TAT, is the subjectivity involved in both scoring and interpretation procedures. Although the various scoring methods have attempted to reduce the degree of subjectivity, intuitive judgment necessarily plays a significant role. This results in part from a lack in the development of adequate norms, and the norms that have been created are only rough approximations to common story themes. What frequently happens in clinical practice is that each person develops his own individual intuitive norms based on past experience. Thus, the clinician may have a general intuitive conception of what constitutes a "schizophrenic" or "psychoneurotic" story and will use this subjective image during diagnostic or interpretive procedures. This reliance on clinical experience becomes indirectly encouraged both by the lack of precise normative data and, more important, by the belief that norms tend to decrease the richness and comprehensiveness of the material being studied. However, because clinicians work predominantly with pathology, they are likely to focus on the pathological aspects of story content. Their firsthand experience of the characteristic reactions of normal people is limited; thus, they tend to distort their TAT interpretations in the direction of overemphasizing pathology.

ADMINISTRATION

General Considerations

The TAT was intended to be an interpersonal situation in which the subject verbally responds to pictures presented to him. However, when the examiner is absent, responses may be taped or written out by the individual himself. The disadvantage of these latter procedures is that the subject's responses are often more contrived and clichéd, since more time is available to censor fantasy material.

The TAT materials consist of 20 cards with ambiguous pictures on them. The cards are numbered so that a total of 20 cards can be presented to four different population groups: males, females, boys, and girls. Thus, the back of each card is coded with a number and/or letters to designate which sex and/or age group the card is intended for. A number without a letter indicates the card is to be administered to all subjects regardless of age or sex. A number with "M" or "F" designates that the card is intended for males or females, and "B" or "G" designates boys or girls, respectively. There may also be a number and either BM or GF indicating the card is to be given to boys/males or girls/females. In actual practice, however, clinicians usually select cards they feel will be most useful for eliciting certain types of information from the subject rather than strictly adhering to Murray's designations.

There is some controversy as to whether all 20 cards should be administered or a shorter version of selected cards. In actual practice, it is far more frequent to administer between eight and ten cards. The selection of cards may be idiosyncratic to the patient's presenting problem or based on previous information derived from relevant history or other test data. For example, if depression and suicide are significant issues for the client, the examiner might administer cards 3BM, 13B, and 14 in an attempt to gather specific information regarding the dynamics of the client's condition. Specific cards may also be selected because they typically produce rich responses. Bellak (1954, 1975) has found that cards 1, 2, 3BM, 4, and 13MF for adults, and 3GF, 7GF, 8GF, and 18GF for children, have the least number of refusals and the richest content. On the other hand, cards which are considered more difficult to identify with and therefore least useful are 11, 12BG, 18BM, and 19, (Bellak, 1975). If all 20 cards are used, they should be administered on two separate days to decrease the occurrence of fatigue. It is relatively rare that an individual can continue for more than an hour without losing interest.

The subject should be seated beside the examiner, with his chair turned away so that he cannot see expressions on the examiner's face. Ideally, this creates a situation in which the subject is comfortable and relaxed so that his imagination can freely respond to the cards. However, some individuals do not feel comfortable when turned away from the examiner, in which case they should be allowed to sit in a position which is more relaxing for them. Of primary importance are that adequate rapport is established and that the subject is comfortable and relaxed.

Instructions

Murray's original instructions from the TAT Manual (1943) are as follows:

> This is a test of imagination, one form of intelligence. I am going to show you some pictures, one at a time; and your task will be to make up as dramatic a story as you can for each. Tell what has led up to the event shown in the picture, describe what is happening at the moment, what the characters are feeling and thinking; and then give the outcome. Speak your thoughts as they come to your mind. Do you understand? Since you have fifty minutes for ten pictures, you can devote about five minutes to each story. Here is the first picture. (p. 3)

This set of instructions is suitable for adolescents and adults of average intelligence and sophistication. However, the instructions should be modified for children, adults with minimal education or intelligence, and psychotics. For these types of individuals, Murray (1943) suggests that the examiner state,

> This is a story-telling test. I have some pictures here that I am going to show you, and for each picture I want you to make up a story. Tell what is happening before and what is happening now. Say what the people are feeling and thinking and how it will come out. You can make up any story you please. Do you understand? Well, then, here is the first picture. You have five minutes to make up a story. See how well you can do. (pp. 3-4)

Such instructions may, of course, be modified, elaborated, or repeated to meet the individual needs of each subject. Any instructions can be used, provided they inform the subject that it is imagination, not a mere description of the picture, which is requested. Variations on the instructions should also emphasize the four requirements of the story structure:

1. Current situation
2. Thoughts and feelings of the characters
3. Preceding events
4. Outcome

The instructions, either in whole or in part, may be repeated at any time, particularly if the subject has given a story which is too short or too long, or if he/she has left out one or more of the four requirements.

Procedure

Time. The time measured should begin when the picture is first presented and end when the subject begins his/her story. It is particularly important to notice any long pauses or hesitations since these may reflect a struggle with conflictual or anxiety-laden material.

Recording. The subject's complete responses should be recorded, as well as any noteworthy behavioral observations. These may include exclamations, stuttering, pauses, blushing, degree of involvement, and changes in voice inflection. Thus, the general purpose of recording is not only to develop a reproduction of the verbatim story content, but to assess how the person interacts with the picture. As mentioned previously, ongoing verbal involvement with the cards is the preferable form of administration, since having the subject write out his own stories allows time for critically evaluating and censoring his responses. There is no objection to the use of a tape recorder, although under such conditions it is also helpful to have the examiner record noteworthy behavioral observations.

Questioning and Inquiry. If a subject omits certain aspects of the story such as the outcome or preceding events, the examiner should ask for additional information. This may take the form of questions such as What led up to it? or How does it end? However, these requests for clarification or amplification should not be stated in such a way as to bias the stories or reveal the examiner's personal reaction.
   A more detailed inquiry may be undertaken either after the entire administration of the cards or directly after each story, although Murray recommends that the inquiry should occur only after the administration of all the cards. Sample inquiry questions may include, What made you think of this story? or Do people you have mentioned in the story remind you of friends or acquaintances? As with questioning, the inquiry should not be too forceful since this may produce defensiveness and withdrawal. The overall purpose of both the questioning and the inquiry is to produce an unhampered and free flow of the subject's fantasy material.

Order of Presentation. Usually, the cards should be administered according to their sequential numbering system. However, at times, the examiner may be consciously interested in a specific problem and will therefore alter the sequence to more effectively obtain information concerning that problem area. For example, if the examiner is particularly interested in problems relating to family constellation in a male subject, he might include some of the feminine series involving sisters, sweethearts, or wives. It is often helpful to include a sprinkling of "neutral" cards with those selected to indicate the presence of a specific conflict. This serves to ease the tension that may otherwise result from a constant confrontation with potentially conflictual stimuli.

Use of the TAT (or CAT) with Children. Instructions for children should, of course, be modified in accordance with their age and vocabulary. It is usually helpful to describe the test as an opportunity to tell stories or as an interesting game. In general, cards from the TAT should be based on the likelihood and ease with which children may identify with the characters. As has been mentioned, cards having the highest number of interpretable responses and the lowest number of refusals, enumeration, or description are, in order of usefulness, cards 7GF, 18GF, 3GF, and 8GF (Bellak, 1975). In contrast, the least helpful are cards 19, 18BM, 11, and 12BG (Bellak, 1975).

It should be kept in mind that the stories of children are relatively easily influenced by recent events such as television, comic books, and movies. Children also tend to project their problems and conflicts into a story in a more direct and straightforward manner than adults, with little hidden meaning or masking of the relationships involved.

TYPICAL THEMES ELICITED

At the present time, there have been no formal normative standards developed for the TAT. However, a knowledge of the typical stories elicted by each of the cards and possible significant variations from the more frequent plots can serve to alert the examiner to unique, and therefore more easily interpretable, types of stories. Deviations from clichéd or stereotyped responses can be significant in that they can represent important areas of conflict, creative thinking, or important features of the subject's overall personality. Thus, if the examiner is equipped with expectations regarding typical versus unusual responses, it will enable him (1) to observe more easily specific attitudes towards the central problem; (2) to easily notice gaps where the inquiry can begin; (3) to assess which type of information the subject shows resistance to, as indicated by the use of noncommittal clichés; and (4) to notice any deviation from the expected information which may contain significant and interpretable responses.

Both Murray's TAT cards and Bellak's original version of the CAT will be described and discussed here. The descriptions of each TAT card, which follow, are divided into three sections: Murray's original description, plots frequently encountered, and a general discussion of the significance and overall usefulness of the card. The descriptions of the TAT cards are from Murray's *Thematic*

Apperception Test Manual (1943, pp. 18–20),* while the CAT descriptions are from Bellak's (1975) discussion of his test (pp. 186-187). The discussion of each picture is a summary of the work of Bellak (1975), Murray (1943), and Stein (1981).

Thematic Apperception Test (TAT)

PICTURE 1

I. Murray's Description.   A young boy is contemplating a violin which rests on a table in front of him.

II. Frequent Plots.   Typical stories emerging from this card revolve around a rebellious boy being forced by his parents, or some other significant authority figure, to play the violin, or around a self-motivated boy who is daydreaming about becoming an outstanding violinist.

III. General Discussion.   This is often considered to be the most useful picture in the entire TAT (Bellak, 1975). It usually elicits stories describing how the subject deals with the general issue of impulse versus control or, in a wider sense, the conflict between personal demands and external controlling agents. It also aids in providing information about the client's relationship with his parents, by making it relatively easy to see whether he views his parents as domineering, controlling, indifferent, helpful, understanding, or protecting (Bellak, 1975). This card frequently gives specific information regarding the need for achievement, and it is important to consider how any expressed achievement is accomplished.

Any variations from the frequent plots described should be taken into consideration as they are likely to provide important reflections of the subject's characteristic modes of functioning. For example, the attitude towards, and relationship with, any introduced figures, whether they are parents or peers, should be given special attention. Also of importance are the way in which the issue of impulse versus control is handled, any themes of aggression which may emerge, and particularly the specific outcome of the story.

PICTURE 2

I. Murray's Description.   This is a country scene: in the foreground is a young woman with books in her hand; in the background, a man is working in the fields and an older woman is looking on.

---

*Reprinted by permission of the publishers from Henry A. Murray, *Thematic Apperception Test,* Cambridge, Mass.: Harvard University Press. Copyright © 1943 by the President and Fellows of Harvard College, ©1971 by Henry A. Murray.

II. Frequent Plots. Frequently encountered stories for this card involve a young girl who is leaving the farm to increase her education or to seek opportunities which her present home environment cannot provide. Usually the family is seen as working hard to gain a living from the soil, with an overall emphasis on maintaining the status quo.

III. General Discussion. This picture usually provides an excellent description of family relations. As with card 1, there are varying themes relating to autonomy from the family versus compliance with the status quo. It is the only card in the series that presents the subject with a group scene and thus gives information relating to how the individual deals with the challenge of people living together. The card itself deals with a younger woman and an older male and female. Thus, it elicits stories dealing with parent-child and heterosexual relationships. There are usually the added dimensions of contrasting the new and the old, and demonstrating attitudes towards personal mobility and ambition. This card can also elicit stories relating to competition by the younger daughter for the attention of both or one of the parents, in which her rivals are either her siblings or the other parent, particularly the older female. The extent to which separations or alliances occur among the three figures represented is also quite revealing. For example, the two women may be united against the male who is "merely a hired hand," or the older male and female may be united against the younger female. Within either of these possible formations, it is important to note the attributes of each person, and the patterns and styles of interaction with one another. Since this card is relatively complex and has a large number of details, compulsive patients often spend an inordinate amount of time commenting and elaborating on the many small details.

PICTURE 3BM

I. Murray's Description. On the floor against a couch is the huddled form of a boy with his head bowed in his right arm. Beside him on the floor is a revolver.

II. Frequent Plots. The stories usually revolve around an individual who has been emotionally involved with another person or who is feeling guilty over some past behavior he has committed.

III. General Discussion. This has been identified as one of the most useful pictures (Bellak, 1975) since it concerns itself with themes of guilt, depression, aggression, and impulse control. The manner in which the object on the left is seen and described often gives a good deal of information regarding problems concerning aggression. For example, is the object, which is officially described as a gun, used for intra-aggression (e.g., the subject is going to use it to do damage to himself) or for extra-aggression (the subject has used it, or is going to use it, to harm another person)? If it is used for externally directed aggression, then what are the consequences, if any, for the focal figure as portrayed in the outcome? This picture is particularly important for depressed patients, regardless of whether they are male or female, since it can give important dynamics regarding the manner in which the depression developed and how it is currently being maintained. For example, denial of aggressive conflicts may be represented by completely overlooking the gun or rendering it harmless by depicting it as a toy pistol or a set of keys. On the other hand, excessive hesitation and detailed consideration of what the object might be could represent a compulsive defense surrounding conflictual aggressive feelings. Since this picture contains a lone figure, attitudes towards the isolated self are often aroused.

PICTURE 3GF

I. Murray's Description. A young woman is standing with downcast head, her face covered with her right hand. Her left arm is stretched forward against a wooden door.

II. Frequent Plots. As with 3BM, the stories usually revolve around themes of interpersonal loss and contemplated harm directed internally due to guilt over past behavior.

III. General Discussion. The same general trends which hold for 3BM are also true for 3GF in that they both tend to bring out depressive feelings. Frequently, however, it is more useful to use 3BM which brings out somewhat richer stories, and allows both males and females to identify easily with the central figure.

PICTURE 4

I. Murray's Description. A woman is clutching the shoulders of a man whose face and body are averted as if he were trying to pull away from her.

II. Frequent Plots. The primary task is to form some sort of conceptualization as to why the woman is restraining the man. Often the woman is seen as the advice giving moral agent who is struggling with the more impulsive and irrational man. In approximately half the stories, the vague picture of a woman in the background is brought into the story plot.

III. General Discussion. This picture typically elicits a good deal of information relating to the feelings and attitudes surrounding male-female relationships. Frequently, themes of infidelity and betrayal emerge, and details regarding the male attitude towards the role of women may be discussed. For example, the woman may be seen as a protector who attempts to prevent the man from becoming involved in self-destructive behavior or as a siren who tries to detain and control him for evil purposes. Likewise, a woman's attitude toward past male aggressiveness and impulsiveness may be revealed.

Yet a further area of interest is the vague picture of a seminude woman in the background. This often invokes themes of triangular jealousy in which one or more characters have been betrayed. When this picture is described, it is important to note whether the woman is depicted as a sexually threatening object or is seen as a more benign figure.

It is also important to notice who has the balance of influence, the man or the woman, and how the balance of influence is achieved and maintained. Does the man use intimidation, or the woman seductiveness, or are there eventually rational negotiations between the two? Thus, special attention should be paid to the manner in which the drama is resolved and whether the original outwardly directed plans of the man are actually carried out or abandoned.

PICTURE 5

I. Murray's Description. A middle-aged woman is standing on the threshold of a half-opened door looking into a room.

II. Frequent Plots. The most frequent plot is of a mother who either has caught her child misbehaving or is surprised by an intruder entering her house.

III. General Discussion. This picture often reveals information surrounding attitudes about the subject's mother in her role of observing and possibly judging behavior. It is important to note how the woman is perceived and how the situation is resolved. Is she understanding and sympathetic, does she attempt to invoke guilt, or is she seen as severely restricting the child's autonomy? Often voyeuristic themes are discussed which may include feelings related to the act of observing others misbehave. The examiner should note whether these feelings include guilt, anger, indifference, or fear, and the manner in which these feelings are resolved. Often this card elicits paranoid fears of attack or intrusion from an outsider that may be represented by stories in which the woman is surprised by a burglar.

PICTURE 6BM

I. Murray's Description. A short elderly woman stands with her back turned to a tall young man. The latter is looking downward with a perplexed expression.

II. Frequent Plots. This picture typically elicits stories of a son who is either presenting sad news to his mother or attempting to prepare her for his departure to some distant location.

III. General Discussion. Card 6BM is an extremely important one to include when testing males. It usually produces a rich source of information regarding attitudes and feelings towards mother or maternal figures in general. Since the stories usually revolve around a young man striving for independence, the specific manner in which the subject depicts this struggle is important. Does the struggle include an exaggerated amount of guilt, is there unexpressed or even overt anger towards the older woman, or does the young man succumb to the woman's wishes? Of equal importance is the mother's reaction to her son's behavior. To what extent does she control him, and how? It is also of interest to note whether the subject accepts the traditional mother-son version, or whether he/she chooses to avoid discussing this relationship directly. If such an avoidance is evident, then how are mother-son type themes depicted in other cards which may have elicited discussions of this area (i.e., cards 1 or 5)?

PICTURE 6GF

I. Murray's Description. A young woman sitting on the edge of a sofa looks back over her shoulder at an older man with a pipe in his mouth who seems to be addressing her.

II. Frequent Plots. The man is usually seen as proposing some sort of an activity to the woman and the plot often includes her reaction to this suggestion.

III. General Discussion. This card was originally intended to be the female counterpart to 6BM, and thus often elicits attitudes and feelings towards paternal figures. However, since the two figures are often seen as being somewhat equal in age, the card frequently does not accomplish this purpose. When clear father-daughter plots are not discussed, then the picture reflects the subject's style and approach to unstructured heterosexual relationships. For example, the subject may describe the woman as being startled or embarrassed or, on the other hand, may have her respond in a spontaneous and comfortable manner. It is important to note the manner in which the man is perceived by the woman. Is he seen as a seducer, does he offer her helpful advice, is he intrusive, or is he perceived as a welcome addition? A person who mistrusts interpersonal relationships will typically create a story in which the man is intrusive and the woman's reaction is one of defensiveness and surprise. Subjects who are more trusting and comfortable usually develop themes in which the woman responds in a more accepting and flexible manner.

PICTURE 7BM

I. Murray's Description. A gray-haired man is looking at a younger man who is sullenly staring into space.

II. Frequent Plots. Stories usually describe either a father-son relationship or a boss-employee situation. Regardless of which one of these variations is created, the older man is most frequently in the position of advising or instructing the younger one.

III. General Discussion. This card is extremely useful in obtaining information about authority figures and, more specifically, the subject's own father. The picture deals with hierarchical personal relationships and usually takes the form of an older, more experienced man interacting with a younger, less experienced one. Thus, this card can clearly show how the subject deals with external demands and his attitudes towards authority.

It is important to note whether the younger man reacts with an extreme amount of rebelliousness or aggression, to the extent that criminal or other antisocial reactions are involved, or whether he accepts the advice of the older man without resentment.

PICTURE 7GF

I. Murray's Description. An older woman is sitting on a sofa close beside a girl, and is speaking or reading to her. The girl, who holds a doll in her lap, is looking away.

II. Frequent Plots. This picture is usually perceived as a mother and her daughter, with the mother advising, consoling, scolding, or instructing the child. Less frequently, there are themes in which the mother is reading to the child for pleasure or entertainment.

III. General Discussion. The intention of 7GF is to bring out the style and manner of mother-child interaction. With older women, it often elicits feelings and attitudes towards children. Since both figures are looking away, this is sometimes perceived as rejection by either figure of the other. Thus, the card often elicits negative feelings and interactions, and it is important to note how these feelings are resolved, expressed, or avoided. Sometimes the older woman is described as reading a fairy story to the younger girl, at which time the most instructive data often come from the fairy story itself.

PICTURE 8BM

I. Murray's Description. An adolescent boy looks straight out of the picture. The barrel of a rifle is visible at one side, and in the background is the dim scene of a surgical operation, like an image in a reverie.

II. Frequent Plots. Stories revolve around either ambition, in that the young man may have aspirations towards becoming a doctor, or aggression. Frequently the aggressive stories relate to fears of becoming harmed or mutilated while in a passive state. Another somewhat less frequent theme centers on a scene in which someone was shot and is now being operated on.

III. General Discussion. The picture can be seen as a thinly veiled depiction of a young man's oedipal conflicts, with the concomitant feelings of castration anxiety and hostility. Thus, it is important to note what feelings the boy or other characters in the story have towards the older man performing the surgery. If the story depicts a need for achievement expressed by the younger man, it is also likely that he will identify with the older one and perhaps use him as an example. If this is the case, the details of how the identification takes place and specific feelings regarding this identification may be helpful.

PICTURE 8GF

I. Murray's Description. A young woman sits with her chin in her hand looking off into space.

II. Frequent Plots. Since this picture is vague and nonspecific, extremely diverse plots are developed and there are no frequently encountered themes.

III. General Discussion. This picture is difficult to generalize about and typically produces somewhat shallow stories of a contemplative nature.

PICTURE 9BM

I. Murray's Description. Four men in overalls are lying on the grass.

II. Frequent Plots. Stories typically provide some sort of explanation of why the men are there and frequently describe them either as hoboes or as working men who are taking a much-needed rest.

III. General Discussion. This picture is particularly helpful in providing information about relations with members of the same sex. Are the men comfortable with one another? Is there any competitiveness? Is the central person in the story merely observing the four men, or is he one of the four men in the picture itself? Sometimes homosexual tendencies or fears regarding such tendencies become evident in the story plot. Oftentimes social prejudice surrounding attitudes towards "lazy," lower class, or unemployed persons becomes apparent, particularly when the men in the picture are seen as hoboes.

PICTURE 9GF

I. Murray's Description. A young woman with a magazine and a purse in her hand looks from behind a tree at another young woman in a party dress running along a beach.

II. Frequent Plots. Usually the two women are seen as being in some sort of conflict, often over a man. Frequently, either in addition to this theme or in a separate story, the woman hiding behind the tree has done something wrong. It is very unusual to have a story in which cooperation between the women is the central plot.

III. General Discussion. This card basically deals with female peer relations and is important in elaborating on such issues as conflict resolution, jealousy, sibling rivalry, and competitiveness. Since the figure standing behind the tree is carefully observing the woman on the beach, stories may provide details surrounding paranoid ideation. At the very least, the dynamics of suspiciousness and distrust are usually discussed. Frequently, a man is introduced into the story who is often placed in the role of either a long lost lover, whom one or both of the girls are running to meet, or a sexual attacker, from whom the girl on the beach is attempting to escape.

PICTURE 10

I. Murray's Description. A young woman's head rests against a man's shoulder.

II. Frequent Plots. Stories usually center around some interaction between the male and the female, and may involve either a greeting between the two or a departure.

III. General Discussion. This card often gives useful information regarding how the subject perceives male-female relationships, particularly those involving some degree of closeness and intimacy. It might be helpful to notice the relative degree of comfort or discomfort which is evoked by emotional closeness. If the story is one of departure or even termination of the relationship, this may be reflective of either overt or denied hostility on the part of the subject. Sometimes males will interpret the embrace as involving two males, which may suggest the possibility of a repressed or overt homosexual orientation.

PICTURE 11

I. Murray's Description. A road skirts a deep chasm between high cliffs. On the road in the distance are obscure figures. Protruding from the rocky wall on one side is the long head and neck of a dragon.

II. Frequent Plot. Typically stories of attack and escape are elicited in which the subject takes into account the dragon, the path, and the obscure figures in the distance.

III. General Discussion. Since the form of this picture is quite vague and ambiguous, it is a good test of the subject's imaginative abilities and his skill in integrating irregular and poorly defined stimuli. The picture also represents unknown and threatening forces, and reflects the manner in which the subject deals with fear of attack. Thus, the examiner should take note of whether or not the characters in the story escape or become victims of their attackers. If they do escape, then how effective and coherent was the plan they devised to avoid danger, or on the other hand, were they saved by chance or "the forces of fate"? A subject's story can often suggest the degree to which he experiences a sense of control over his environment and over the course of his life.

The dragon may be seen as representing aggressive forces in the environment or the need for protection. In this respect, the dragon may be seen either as coming out of the cliff and attacking people or as a protecting creature whom the characters are using for refuge and safety. Such themes can suggest aspects of the subject's internal framework and mood. For example, when subjects report stories of "everything being dead," this is a strong indication of a depressive and extremely impoverished inner state.

PICTURE 12M

I. Murray's Description. A young man is lying on a couch with his eyes closed. Leaning over him is the gaunt form of an elderly man, his hand stretched out above the face of the reclining figure.

II. Frequent Plots. Stories center on illness and/or the older man using hypnosis or some form of religious rite on the younger, reclining figure.

III. General Discussion. The picture often elicits themes regarding the relationship between an older, usually more authoritative man and a younger one. This can have particular significance in predicting or assessing the current or future relationship between the therapist and the client. The manner in which the older man is perceived is particularly important. Is he sympathetic and giving aid, or is he an evil character who "sleeps upside down in a closet with his wings around his face"?

Thus the picture can represent specifics of the transference relationship and, as such, can be an aid in interpreting and providing feedback to the client regarding this relationship. It can also be used to predict a client's attitude towards, and response to, hypnotic procedures (White, 1941).

Stories of this picture may also represent whether passivity is compatible with the subject's personality or whether it is regarded as ego dystonic. In particular, subjects frequently reveal attitudes towards some external controlling force.

PICTURE 12F

I. Murray's Description. This is the portrait of a young woman. A weird old woman with a shawl over her head is grimacing in the background.

II. Frequent Plots. Stories center on the relationship or specific communications between the two figures.

III. General Discussion. This picture elicits descriptions and conceptions of mother figures. The background figure is frequently seen as a mother-in-law with a variety of evil qualities. Often these negative qualities are feelings that the subject has towards his/her own mother but can indirectly, and therefore more safely, project onto the figure of a mother-in-law.

PICTURE 12BG

I. Murray's Description. A rowboat is drawn up on the bank of a woodland stream. There are no human figures in the picture.

II. Frequent Plots. Stories frequently center on themes of loneliness, peace, or the enjoyment of nature.

III. General Discussion. With suicidal or depressed subjects, there may be the elaboration of feelings of abandonment and isolation, for example, the case of someone being lost or having fallen from the boat. More stable, adjusted subjects are likely to discuss the peace of being alone in the woods and perhaps fishing or having gone fishing further down the stream.

PICTURE 13MF

I. Murray's Description. A young man is standing with downcast head buried in his arm. Behind him is the figure of a woman lying in bed.

II. Frequent Plots. The most frequent plot centers on guilt induced by illicit sexual activity. Themes involving the death of the woman on the bed and the resulting grief of the man, who is often depicted as her husband, are somewhat less frequent.

III. General Discussion. This picture is excellent for revealing sexual conflicts in either men or women. In a general way, it provides information on the subject's attitudes and feelings towards his/her sex partner, particularly attitudes just prior to and immediately following sexual intercourse. Stories in which there are overt expressions of aggression or revulsion are significant variations and should be noted as relatively unusual features. In particular, the relation between a subject's aggressive and sexual feelings is frequently portrayed.

Since this picture has a relatively large number of details, obsessive-compulsive personalities frequently spend an excessive amount of time describing and explaining these details. This may be particularly evident because the picture often has a shock effect and may therefore create anxiety which brings out the obsessive-compulsive's style of handling anxiety by externally focusing on detail.

PICTURE 13B

I. Murray's Description.   A little boy is sitting on the doorstep of a log cabin.

II. Frequent Plots.   Themes of loneliness and stories of childhood are often elicited. However, since the stimulus is somewhat vague, the content and the nature of these stories tend to be extremely varied.

III. General Discussion.   This picture may be helpful with both adults and children in revealing attitudes towards introspection or loneliness. In adults, it frequently elicits reveries of childhood memories.

PICTURE 13G

I. Murray's Description.   A little girl is climbing a winding flight of stairs.

II. Frequent Plots.   The plots are similar to 13B in that they usually involve themes of loneliness and sometimes distant childhood memories.

III. General Discussion.   This picture lacks the specificity and impact found in other TAT cards. It usually produces stories which are highly varied but lacking in richness and detail. Like 13B, 13G can sometimes be useful in depicting a subject's attitude towards loneliness and introspection.

PICTURE 14

I. Murray's Description.   There is the silhouette of a man (or woman) against a bright window. The rest of the picture is totally black.

II. Frequent Plots.   This card produces themes of contemplation, wish fulfillment, depression, or feelings related to burglary.

III. General Discussion.   If a subject's presenting problem is depression, especially if there is evidence of suicidal ideation, this card along with 3BM is essential. In these cases, subjects often describe the figure in the picture and, more important, discuss the events, feelings, and attitudes which led up to the current self-destructive behavior. It becomes important during the inquiry phase of examination to investigate the particular methods and styles of problem solving which the story character has attempted or is attempting. Also significant are the character's internal dialogues and personal reactions as he relates to different life stresses.

This picture may also reveal the subject's aesthetic interests and personal philosophical beliefs or wish fulfillments. If a story involving burglary is depicted, it can be useful to consider the character's level of impulse control, guilt, or the consequences of his behavior. For example, is the character apprehended and punished for his behavior, or is he allowed to go free and enjoy the profits of his misdeeds?

PICTURE 15

I. Murray's Description. A gaunt man with clenched hands is standing among gravestones.

II. Frequent Plots. Themes usually revolve around beliefs or events surrounding death and a hereafter.

III. General Discussion. Stories from picture 15 reflect the subject's particular beliefs about, and attitudes towards, death and the dying process. For example, death may be viewed as a passive, quiet process, or in contrast, it can be experienced as a violent, aggressive situation. If the subject is having an extremely difficult time coping with the death of a friend or relative, the themes on picture 15 can provide useful information as to why this difficulty is being experienced. For example, the story may reveal a method of adjustment based on excessive denial with a seeming inability to engage in grieving and a resulting lack of resolution. The story might also indicate unexpressed and problematic anger directed towards the dead person due to a sense of abandonment.

Oftentimes depressive tendencies or even paranoid ideation may become particularly evident. For example, paranoid delusions may be expressed by stories in which the figure is casting a spell on someone else or making attempts to control his mind or capture his soul.

PICTURE 16

I. Murray's Description. This is a blank card.

II. Frequent Plots. Stories from this card are highly varied, although it frequently elicits stories related to current life dilemmas or outdoor settings.

III. General Discussion. Instructions for this card are to imagine a picture and then tell a story about it. From subjects with vivid and active imaginations, this card often produces extremely rich and useful stories. In these cases, the card does little to shape or influence the subject's fantasy material and can thus be seen as a relatively pure product from his/her unconscious. However, for anxious, resistant, or noncreative subjects, this card is often of little or no value since the stories are usually brief and lack depth or richness. In considering the story, it is helpful to note whether the story depicts a scene which is vital and optimistic, or desolate and flat.

PICTURE 17BM

I. Murray's Description.   A naked man is clinging to a rope. He is in the act of climbing up or down.

II. Frequent Plots.   Stories usually involve someone escaping from a dangerous situation or an athletic event of a competitive nature.

III. General Discussion.   Since the card depicts a naked man, attitudes regarding the subject's personal body image are often revealed. Possible homosexual feelings or anxiety related to homosexuality also becomes evident in the stories of some subjects. The particular direction in which the climber is going can have implications for either an optimistic, positive outlook indicated by his climbing up or a pessimistic, negative one as reflected by a downward movement.

PICTURE 17GF

I. Murray's Description.   On a bridge over water, a female figure leans over the railing. In the background are tall buildings and small figures of men.

II. Frequent Plots.   A great variety of stories are elicited, although themes surrounding departure and social or emotional distance do occur with some frequency.

III. General Discussion.   Attitudes towards a recent separation or the impending arrival of a loved one are sometimes described. This card can be particularly useful in cases of suicidal depression in which the figure on the bridge is perceived as contemplating jumping off as a last attempt to resolve her difficulties. As with cards 3BM and 14, an inquiry into the specific difficulties the story character has encountered and the manner in which she has attempted to resolve these difficulties can often reflect the subject's manner and style of coping with her own difficulties. Personal reactions to, and internal dialogue involving, life stresses can also be extremely informative. However, some of this material is available only through a more detailed inquiry after the initial story has been given.

PICTURE 18BM

I. Murray's Description.   A man is clutched from behind by three hands. The figures of his assailants are invisible.

II. Frequent Plots.   Typical themes involve either drunkenness on the part of the figure who is being supported by the three hands or stories in which he is being attacked from behind.

III. General Discussion. This picture, more than any of the others, is likely to produce anxiety due to the suggestive depiction of invisible forces attacking the figure. Thus, it is important to note how the subject handles his own anxiety as well as how the story character deals with his situation. Does he see himself as the victim of circumstance in which he is completely helpless? If so, how does he eventually resolve these feelings of helplessness? Is the helplessness a momentary phenomenon, or is it an ongoing personality trait? If the character is seen as the recipient of hard luck, then specifically what situations does the subject perceive as comprising hard luck? Exaggerated aggressiveness or attitudes towards addiction are also sometimes expressed with this picture.

PICTURE 18GF

I. Murray's Description. A woman has her hands squeezed around the throat of another woman whom she appears to be pushing backwards across the banister of a stairway.

II. Frequent Plots. Aggressive mother-daughter interactions or sibling relationships are often disclosed in response to this picture.

III. General Discussion. The manner in which the subject handles aggressive, hostile relationships with other women is the primary type of information this picture elicits. Particular note should be given to what types of events trigger this aggressiveness and the manner in which the conflict is or is not resolved. Does the character submit passively, withdraw from the relationship, plot revenge, or negotiate change? Feelings of inferiority, jealousy, and response to being dominated are also often described. Although the representation of aggressiveness in the picture is quite explicit, subjects will occasionally attempt to deny or avoid this aggressiveness by creating a story in which one figure is attempting to help the other one up the stairs. This may point to general denial and repression of hostility on the part of the subject.

PICTURE 19

I. Murray's Description. This card contains a weird picture of cloud formations overhanging a snow-covered cabin in the country.

II. Frequent Plots. Stories are highly varied due to the unstructured and ambiguous nature of the stimuli.

III. General Discussion. Since the picture is one of the more unstructured cards, the subject's ability to integrate disparate visual stimuli is tested. For certain subjects, the ambiguous nature of the picture can create anxiety and insecurity which provide the examiner with a means of observing how the subject handles his anxiety within the context of the story.

PICTURE 20

I. Murray's Description.   The dimly illuminated figure of a man (or woman) is depicted leaning against a lamppost in the dead of night.

II. Frequent Plots.   Stories range from the benign theme of a late evening date to a more sinister one, perhaps involving a gangster who is in imminent danger.

III. General Discussion.   The picture often elicits information regarding a subject's attitudes towards loneliness, darkness, and uncertainty. Fears may be made explicit through gangster stories, and as with 18BM, the method of handling these fears and the examinee's response to physical danger should be noted.

Children's Apperception Test (CAT)

The following descriptions of, and typical responses to, pictures on the CAT are adapted from Bellak (1975, pp. 185–186).*

PICTURE 1

I. Bellak's Description.   Chicks are seated around a table on which is a large bowl of food. Off to one side is a large chicken, dimly outlined.

II. Discussion.   Stories typically revolve around concerns relating to eating or sibling rivalry. The sibling rivalry may center on who is the best behaved, what the consequences of this behavior are, and which one gets more to eat. In order to obtain useful information on this card, it is particularly important to decide which character the subject identifies with. Food may be seen as reward for "good" behavior, or conversely, it can be used as punishment for "bad" behavior by being withheld.

PICTURE 2

I. Bellak's Description.   One bear is pulling a rope on one side, while another bear and a baby bear pull on the other side.

II. Discussion.   Of particular importance in interpreting this picture is whether the bear who is helping the baby bear is seen as a male (father figure) or a female (mother figure). The struggle which is depicted can either be seen as a playful game of tug-of-war or a struggle involving a high degree of seriousness and aggression. For example, the loser(s) may end up falling off the edge of the rock and into a pool of dangerous animals. In the most recent revision of the CAT,

*Descriptions of the CAT cards are reprinted from *The TAT, CAT, and SAT in Clinical Use*, New York: Grune & Stratton, 1975, by permission of the author Leopold Bellak, M.D.

the large bears were made equal in size to avoid having the largest bear (previously depicted on the right) identified as the father.

PICTURE 3

I. Bellak's Description. A lion, with pipe and cane, sits in a chair; in the lower right corner, a little mouse appears in a hole.

II. Discussion. Since the lion is pictured with the characteristic symbols of authority (pipe and cane), this picture elicits attitudes and feelings towards father figures. It is important to note whether this figure is seen as benevolent and protecting, or dangerous and threatening. Sometimes the subject will defensively attempt to minimize the threat of the lion by reducing him to a helpless cripple who needs a cane just to move around.

Most children notice the mouse in the hole and blend it into their stories. Since the mouse and the lion are frequently seen in adversary roles, it is important to note how the threatening presence of the lion is handled. Is the mouse completely under the control of the lion, and does it adapt by being submissive and placating? On the other hand, the mouse may be described as clever and manipulating in order to trick and outsmart the lion. Some subjects will switch their identification back and forth between the lion and the mouse suggesting some role confusion. This may be particularly true of enmeshed families or families in which the father is unable to set limits effectively.

PICTURE 4

I. Bellak's Description. A kangaroo, with a bonnet on her head, is carrying a basket with a milk bottle. In her pouch is a baby kangaroo with a balloon; on a bicycle, there is a larger kangaroo child.

II. Discussion. As in picture 1, this card elicits themes of sibling rivalry and occasionally themes revolving around a wish for regression, as demonstrated when the subject identifies with the baby kangaroo in the pouch. A regressive theme is particularly strong when a subject, who is in reality the oldest or middle child, identifies with the kangaroo in the pouch. On the other hand, a child who is actually the youngest may identify with the oldest kangaroo, thereby suggesting a strong need for autonomy and independence. On occasion, a theme of flight from danger may be introduced.

PICTURE 5

I. Bellak's Description. A darkened room contains a large bed in the background and a crib in the foreground in which there are two baby bears.

II. Discussion. Stories relating to attitudes and feelings about what occurs when parents are in bed are frequent responses to this card. They may involve such aspects as curiosity, conjecture, confusion, rejection, anger, and envy on the part of the children. Descriptions of the two children in the foreground may also center on themes of sexual manipulation and mutual exploration.

PICTURE 6

I. Bellak's Description. A darkened cave shows two dimly outlined bear figures in the background and a baby bear lying in the foreground.

II. Discussion. This is similar to picture 5 in that they both elicit stories of parental bedtime activity. However, this picture tends to enlarge upon and extend themes which have only begun to develop in picture 5. Stories may also revolve around feelings of jealousy of the perceived intimacy between parents or may reflect possible feelings about masturbation on the part of the baby bear in the foreground.

PICTURE 7

I. Bellak's Description. A tiger with bared fangs and claws leaps at a monkey that is also leaping through the air.

II. Discussion. The subject will often discuss his fears of aggression and his characteristic manner of dealing with it. At times, the anxiety produced by this picture may result in an unwillingness to respond to it at all. On the other hand, the subject's defenses may be either effective enough, or perhaps unrealistic enough, for him to transform the picture into a harmless story.

PICTURE 8

I. Bellak's Description. Two adult monkeys are sitting on a sofa drinking from tea cups. One adult monkey in the foreground is sitting on a hassock talking to a baby monkey.

II. Discussion. The subject often discusses his relative position and characteristic roles within the family. His description of the dominant monkey in the foreground as either a mother or a father figure should be noted as a possible indication of who has more control in the family. It is also significant to note how the dominant monkey is described. Is he threatening and controlling, or helpful and supportive?

PICTURE 9

I. Bellak's Description. A darkened room is seen through an open door from a lighted room. In the darkened one, there is a child's bed in which a rabbit sits up looking through the door.

II. Discussion. Typically, responses revolve around a subject's fears of darkness, possible desertion by parents, and curiosity as to what is occurring in the next room.

PICTURE 10

I. Bellak's Description. A baby dog is lying across the knees of an adult dog; both figures have a minimum of expressive features. The figures are set in the foreground of a bathroom.

II. Discussion. A child's attitudes and feelings about misbehavior and its resulting punishments are usually discussed in response to this card. In particular, his conceptions of right and wrong are often revealed. This picture is a good indicator of the child's degree of impulse control and his attitude towards authority figures when their role involves setting limits.

SCORING PROCEDURE

Since the original publication of the TAT Manual in 1943, there have been a number of alternate methods of interpretation developed by such individuals as Rapaport, Gill, and Schafer (1946); Wyatt (1947); Bellak (1954); Henry (1956); and Arnold (1962). Whenever there are a large number of different theories to explain a particular phenomenon, it is usually a strong indication that none of them is fully adequate and that they all have significant shortcomings. This is true of the many alternate interpretation methods for the TAT. Difficulty arises primarily due to the type of information which is under investigation. Fantasy productions involve extremely rich and diverse information which is difficult to place into exact and specific categories. Even the selection of which categories to use is open to question. For example, Murray prefers a listing and weighting of the primary needs and press expressed in the stories, whereas Arnold emphasizes a restatement of the essential theme of the story on an interpretive level so as to highlight the basic meaning or moral of the story. Once the examiner has decided which method to use and evaluated the stories according to this method, the examiner is able to infer qualities of the subject's personality according to the categorization based on the specific method selected. Whether or not this final inference is valid and accurate is open to question and depends on a number of variables including the skill and experience of the examiner, comparison with themes derived from other test data, and whether or not the state of the subject at the time of examination is representative of his usual orientation to the world.

For the purposes of this book, Murray's method of interpretation will be described because of its relatively concise and clear approach, as well as its more extensive history and familiarity within the field. However, all of the different approaches deserve consideration since each has its own unique advantages, and an examiner may find an approach other than Murray's to be more helpful in providing interpretive information.

Although Murray's approach involves a certain degree of quantification, it is basically a qualitative method focusing on specific story content. The goal is not so much to achieve a diagnosis of the subject, but to obtain a description of how the subject confronts and deals with basic universal life situations. In order to accomplish this, Murray suggests five categories of analysis:

1. The hero
2. Motives, trends, and feelings of the hero (needs)
3. Forces of the hero's environment (press)
4. Themes and outcomes
5. Interests and sentiments

These steps in scoring will be described in more detail. Although scoring and interpretation are discussed separately here, in actual practice it is difficult to distinguish between the two. Scoring, in its widest sense is also interpretation. The section designated "Interpretation" serves primarily as a summary for arranging the data as well as providing suggestions for making generalizations relating to the subject's personality. This system can be used equally well with the TAT or with such derivatives as Bellak's Children's Apperception Test. Summary sheets (Tables 5-3 and 5-4) are provided at the end of the descriptions as aids in totaling and comparing the different needs and press.

The Hero

The initial task of the examiner is to determine which story character is the focal figure. Presumably the subject has identified with this figure and is therefore likely to project personal needs, attitudes, and feelings onto him. The hero can be described as the central character around which the story events revolve.

However, the subject might identify with more than one character. This may become evident from continual references or attribution of needs to a secondary figure. In this case the weighting of the hero's needs should only be half those of the primary hero. If, on the other hand, there is no clear identification but rather an objective description of each character in turn, the needs and press of each character should be given equal weighting.

Motives, Trends, and Feelings of the Hero (Needs)

The recognition and quantification of the hero's needs is the next category to be considered. However, Murray gives some latitude as to which set of variables the examiner may find appropriate, and the selection of these variables depends on what the examiner wants to know about the subject. Although Murray clearly emphasizes his concept of needs, the examiner may wish to approach a description of the hero from additional conceptual frameworks.

Murray suggests a five-point scale with 1 representing the "slightest suggestion" of a need and 5 indicating "the intense form" or "a repeated occurrence of a milder form." For example, a response to card 1 (a boy playing a violin) may include a description of the boy "practicing relentlessly in the hopes of someday living up to his expectations of being a famous concert violinist." This would clearly receive a rating of 5 for need for achievement. In contrast to this, an achievement rating of 1 might occur in a story in which "he hoped someday he would be able to enjoy playing the violin, but he was presently preoccupied with finding out how he could go out and play with his friends."

Another consideration, other than intensity, in rating the needs within a story is the relative importance or centrality of the need to the story. In the example in which the boy is primarily concerned with associating with his friends, the low score in need for achievement is given not only because of its low intensity but also because the story, at least the segment which is given, concerns itself more with the expression of the need for affiliation which might have a score of 4 or 5 in this case. Another story might involve a man who extensively criticizes himself but compensates by working hard and trying to control other people. In this case, the most central need would be the need for abasement (5) with secondary needs being the need for achievement and the need for dominance (3 or 4). Even though the subject may choose to spend more time elaborating or discussing these latter needs, the underlying and central need would still be for abasement.

In some cases, more than one story is told for a particular card, or there might be a story within a story, for example, when a character elaborates on a dream he had. In this situation, some of the ratings may total more than 5, in which case the examiner should scale down the overall totals to keep them within the five-point range.

To summarize, the examiner should consider the number of times a need is mentioned, and of equal importance, he should look at its relative intensity and the degree to which it is central to the story. The same procedure should be used when scoring press (forces of the hero's environment).

When all the stories are rated on the five-point scale, the overall strengths of the subject's needs (and press) for all the stories can be totaled. Their total values can then be compared with one another and rank ordered to determine their relative strength for the subject. The examiner can also determine their average strength at each occurrence by dividing the total values (ratings) by the number of times each need occurs. The different needs and inner states are given in Table 5-3. In a similar manner, press is summarized in Table 5-4.

Table 5-3. TAT Summary Sheet for Needs and Inner States.

										CARD NUMBER											
	1	2	3	4	5	6	7	8	9	10	11	12	13	14	15	16	17	18	19	20	TOTAL
n Achievement																					
n Acquisition																					
n Aggression																					
n Construction																					
n Counteraction																					
n Dominance																					
n Exposition																					
n Recognition																					
n Understanding																					
n Affiliation																					
n Deference																					
n Nurturance																					
n Sex																					
n Succorance																					
n Autonomy																					
n Change, Travel, Adventure																					
n Excitance, Dissipation																					
n Playmirth																					
n Abasement																					
n Blame Avoidance																					
n Cognizance																					
n Harm Avoidance																					
n Passivity																					
n Rejection																					
n Retention																					
n Sentience																					
Conflict																					
Emotional Change																					
Elation																					
Dejection																					
Distrust																					
Jealousy																					
Irreality																					
Ego Ideal, Pride																					
Superego																					
Miscellaneous																					

The following material includes descriptions of each of Murray's needs which can be used for reference when deciding which story fragments represent specific needs. Inner states, which should be scored in the same manner as needs, are also discussed. Needs are designated by a small n before the specific name of each need. The definitions of needs and inner states have been adapted from Sanford's (1939) manual which appears in Stein's (1981) book on the Thematic Apperception Test.* The following list can be used as an aid in identifying which needs and inner states are illustrated in a subject's stories.

A. *Needs motivated by desire for Power, Property, Prestige, Knowledge, or Creative Achievement*

1. *n Achievement.* To work towards a goal with energy, persistence, and singleness of purpose. To set high standards for oneself and work independently towards realizing these standards. To overcome obstacles or master and manipulate objects, situations, or people. To accomplish or work persistently at a difficult task. To be ambitious, competitive, aspiring.

   After practicing every day for weeks, he finally feels that he is sufficiently skilled to play his first concert performance. His performance is a tremendous success and is the beginning of a brilliant career.

2. *n Acquisition*

   a) *Social.* To work for money, material possessions, or valuable objects. A desire for economic mobility. To bargain or gamble. Greed or acquisitiveness.

   She worked hard over a period of many years so she could eventually purchase a vacation home on the beach.

   b) *Asocial.* To steal, cheat, rob, forage, or swindle. Greed, which, in order to accomplish its goal, causes harm to others or involves breaking some ethical principle or law. The desired goal may be money, an object, or even a person (e.g., during a kidnapping).

   As a young man, he would break into the neighbors' homes to steal guns, money, or any other valuables he could find.

3. *n Aggression*

   a) *Emotional, Verbal.* To have a verbal fight or argument with another person. To become angry at, ridicule, blame, criticize, or curse. This may be expressed publicly by a speech or in writing.

---

*Definitions of the needs from pp. 50–59 of *The Thematic Apperception Test: An Introductory Manual for Its Clinical Use with Adults* (Second Edition, Second Printing, 1981, Springfield, Ill.: Charles C. Thomas) by Morris I. Stein. Copyright © 1981 by Morris I. Stein. By permission of the author and Nevitt Sanford.

In the middle of the conversation, he jumped up angrily and shouted his defiance at his political opponent.

b) *Physical, Social.* To kill or defend oneself in self-defense. To avenge an attack which was unwarranted and unprovoked. To defend one's country, for example, during war or become physically aggressive while upholding the law. Activity which is revolutionary may be on the threshold between (b) social and (c) asocial.

After the thief had stolen the little old lady's purse, a bystander jumped on the offender and held him down until the police came.

c) *Physical, Asocial.* Aggression against some legal or moral standard, or expressed without being provoked such as in criminal activity. To fight legal authorities or authority figures (parents, police, employer, school principal). To initiate a brawl, turn traitor, or express sadistic behavior.

Once his victim was chained to the floor, he began his relentless program of torture and unnatural acts.

d) *Destruction.* To attack or maim. To destroy, smash, vandalize, or burn.

When the police were at a safe distance,, the young hooligans approached their object of destruction only after having built up an incredible amount of ramming speed.

4. *n Construction.* To organize, build, create, or place something in a new order.

She eventually returns to the farm and repairs the fences and barn, and organizes the machinery in preparation for next year's planting.

5. *n Counteraction.* To make up for a previous failure or disappointment. To overcompensate for a weakness or to have a determination to overcome. n Counteraction depends on a response to a previous failure or humiliation. To repress fear or keep one's self-respect. To be resolute, determined, indomitable, dauntless, dogged, or adventurous as a reaction to an earlier difficult situation.

His stuttering had embarrassed him so strongly that he began practicing every day to speak clearly, with strength and dignity.

6. *n Dominance.* To control, influence, or direct one's human environment. This may involve being forceful, persuasive, assertive, masterful, decisive, or authoritative. To prevail upon, sway, lead, judge, set standards, induce, restrain, prohibit, manage, or govern.

The hypnotic induction proceeded until the subject was completely under his influence.

7. *n Exposition.* To relate information in an instructive or informative manner. To explain, lecture, interpret, instruct, teach. Merely telling

something to another person in a casual or everyday manner is not sufficient to score n Exposition. It is commonly fused with n Dominance, n Recognition, or n Achievement.

His elaboration on the intricacies of the space program kept his students writing page after page of notes.

8. *n Recognition.* To seek praise, prestige, appreciation, or attention. Making oneself conspicuous; dramatizing or performing. To boast or brag. The examiner should ask himself whether the hero's main motive is getting something done, in which case it would be scored as n Achievement, or actually being noticed.

After singing a few more songs and throwing down two or more shots of whiskey, he began dancing on tables as the audience stared in disbelief.

9. *n Understanding.* Striving for knowledge and wisdom. To attempt to understand the relation between one object or event and another. Discussion and argumentation with the goal directed towards increasing knowledge. Attempting to make thought correspond to fact. To analyze events and generalize.

The boy was carefully considering everything his music instructor had told him in an attempt to conceptualize how his violin worked.

B. *Needs Motivated by Affection, Admiration, Sympathy, Love and Dependence*

1. *n Affiliation*

a) *Associative.* To establish friendly relations. This may be focal, in which case the need is directed towards affectionate feelings for specific people. It may also be diffuse, in which case the feeling is directed towards all sorts of people such as groups or organizations.

As they saw more of one another, their friendship grew progressively stronger. After the church services, he usually felt a stronger bond with all members of his community.

b) *Emotional.* Feelings of strong attachment, closeness, affection, or respect towards another person. This may include getting married, remaining faithful, or falling in love.

Although the strength of their marriage was tested once again, the difficulty only brought them closer together than they had ever been before.

2. *n Deference*

a) *Compliance.* Quick to agree or cooperate. To obey the wishes or suggestions of another person. A willingness to please or follow another's leadership. It may be necessary at times to distinguish n Deference from n Abasement, in which there is compliance but it is unwilling.

Since he had been requested sincerely to help, Jim agreed to help with the work until it was completed.

b) *Respect.* To give praise to or express admiration towards. Hero worship or the acknowledgement of merit or talent. Dedication to a cause.

Awe for his virtuosity was continually supported each time the master gave another performance.

3. *n Nurturance.* To give sympathy to or gratify the needs of another. To help, feed, support, console, protect, or comfort those who are in need. Kindness, consideration, protection. To encourage and further the welfare of those who are helpless. This may include being liberal with time, energy, or money as a means of helping others. Giving freedom, condoning, or being lenient.

The man helped the lost child to find his parents and provided him with food until they came.

4. *n Sex.* To have or attempt to have a sexual relationship. To make sexual advances towards or seduce. Enjoying the company of members of the opposite sex, being fond of mixed parties and dancing. To fall in love. This may commonly be fused with n Affiliation (emotional) or, if not fused, should be distinguished from n Affiliation (emotional).

After cleverly slipping him an aphrodisiac while he was in the presence of a small amount of kryptonite, Lois Lane was able to steal his virginity.

5. *n Succorance.* A tendency to cry, plead, ask for help, aid, protection, or love. Being dependent, helpless, and perhaps capitalizing on one's mishaps. To crave affection or tenderness and accept favors without hesitation. To have a close and devoted protector or supporter. Seeking to be nursed, supported, sustained, advised, guided, indulged, forgiven, or consoled. Someone with n Nurturance satisfies the hero's succorance, although intranurturance may also be evident in an individual who derives some enjoyment as a result of his/her grief or seeks consolation through drugs, alcohol, or food.

All the other kittens in the litter had been eaten by a Doberman pinscher so the girl took home the one survivor and slowly nursed it back to health.

C. *Needs Motivated by a Desire for Freedom, Change, Excitement, and Play*
1. *n Autonomy*
a) *Freedom.* To escape, shake off restraint, or become independent. To be unattached or unrestrained. To avoid all encumbering alliances or terminate a confining relationship. To wander, drop out, leave school, break off a relationship. To fight or argue for liberty in a positive way. Determination to remain independent.

Finally, after arguments and much confusion, he decided that he needed more time to be alone and so he ended the relationship.

b) *Resistance.* To refuse to comply with the demands of another. Negativism and defiance. Resistance towards coercion. To be "stubborn as a mule," to be obstinate, to disobey one's parents, or to present revolutionary ideas. Typically a revolutionary will be scored on n Autonomy (a–c).

All the prisoners went on a hunger strike to protest the living conditions.

c) *Asocial.* To express behavior which is not allowed and is punishable. Behavior that is disorderly, unruly, and counter to moral or social standards. Lying, cheating, whoring, stealing, drinking. Crimes other than stealing since stealing would be classified under n Acquisition.

Then, as soon as the substitute teacher turned her back, the entire class assailed her with spitballs.

2. *n Change, Travel, Adventure.* To feel a sense of restlessness and a need to experience new lands or novel situations. To dream of exploring and having novel adventures. This need is commonly fused with n Autonomy.

After returning from his travels and settling down for a short while, he again caught the wanderlust, his feet began itching, and he began planning a trip to the South Seas.

3. *n Excitance, Dissipation.* To act in such a way as to create emotional excitement. This may involve travel (n Change), gambling (n Acquisition), involvement with drugs or alcohol (n Nurturance), or recklessly meeting danger. What distinguishes n Excitance, Dissipation from such needs as n Change or n Acquisition, is its emphasis on emotional excitement although these needs are frequently fused.

While in the police department, she volunteered to work on the "wrong side of the tracks" hoping that there would be more action.

4. *n Play.* To act for "fun" and without a purpose other than amusement. To laugh, make jokes, play games, be jolly, merry, and easygoing. This may include sports, dancing, drinking, clowning, or make-believe activity. Meeting situations in a lighthearted and jovial manner. However, in those cases in which the game is taken seriously, such as in athletic competition, then a score is given for n Achievement rather than n Play.

These girls are playing hide-and-seek and soon the one behind the tree is going out to look for her sister who is looking for a hiding place.

D. *Miscellaneous Needs*

1. *n Abasement.* To submit passively to an external force. To accept injury, blame, criticism, punishment, or to feel guilt or inferiority. To adopt an attitude that is passive, humble, meek, servile. Resignation or shame. To endure ordeals without attempting to counteract. Common fusions are with n Succorance, n Deference, or n Sex as in the case of masochism.

   After they were caught red-handed in the act, they were sent to a reform school where they willingly submitted to numerous restrictions.

2. *n Blame Avoidance.* To act in such a way as to avoid blame or rejection. To have fear of reproach; to inhibit one's asocial impulses. To avoid blame or punishment by refraining from misbehavior. To confess, apologize, atone, or repent in order to avoid more blame. This may involve being conventional, remorseful, apologetic, dutiful, or conscientious.

   After lashing out in anger, he begged her forgiveness and explained that it would never happen again.

3. *n Cognizance.* To express curiosity, search, investigate, explore, or act as a detective. To watch or gaze intently. Voyeurism. To ask questions, satisfy one's curiosity, look, listen, inspect. To read and seek knowledge. Common fusions occur with n Understanding, n Change (travel, etc.) or n Achievement.

   After opening the door and carefully observing every action they performed, she took another step forward so as to get an even better look.

4. *n Harm Avoidance.* To avoid physical pain, withdraw, flee, or conceal oneself from persons or objects who are attempting to inflict injury. This includes "startle" and "fear" reactions to such things as loud noises, loss of support, or the sudden appearance of strangers. To escape from a dangerous situation. To take precautionary measures. To be fearful, anxious, timid, cautious, wary, prudent, vigilant. To run away when chased by a dangerous animal or enemy. However, if the hero purposefully places himself in a situation of danger, even if he takes precautionary measures to avoid being killed or injured, this should not be scored as n Harm Avoidance but rather as n Excitance, Dissipation.

   The settlers immediately began to build a fort in order to protect themselves from roving bands of savages.

5. *n Passivity.* To seek or enjoy quiet, rest, tranquility, peacefulness. To feel tired, apathetic, lazy. To need quiet contemplation, meditation, or reflection.

After traveling to foreign lands, the monk longed for the quiet and solitude of his monastery.

6. *n Rejection.* To snub, ignore, or exclude others. To remain aloof and indifferent, or be discriminating in accepting others. To exclude, abandon, expel, or criticize. To demand a high standard of ability, intelligence, wit, or imagination. To reject a suitor, break with a friend, or withhold love. This is commonly fused with n Passivity or n Aggression. nRejection may also become directed inward, thus becoming fused with n Abasement, and perhaps resulting in feelings of depression or suicidal ideation.

The head of the committee scorned every attempt that Tim made to become a member of the club, and as a result, his application had already been turned down three times.

7. *n Retention.* To hold on to something, refuse to lend; to be possessive, miserly, and unwilling to give time, energy, and affection to others. To hoard or collect objects, or another person, with possessive love.

This dragon up at the top has a huge treasure he's protecting, and if any travelers pass by, he takes their money and spends the rest of the time devising how he will arrange it inside his cave.

8. *n Sentience.* To seek and enjoy sensuous impressions. To have delicate, sensitive perceptions. To perceive and comment upon the sensuous quality of objects. To remark upon the atmosphere, temperature, colors in the room, pictures, various sounds, tastes, or odors. A genuine delight in one or more of the arts. May be fused with n Sex (erotic sentience), n Construction (enjoying composition or creativity), or n Recognition (performing in public).

As soon as the feast was laid out on the table, the guests sat down to indulge in the culinary delights.

The following list describes the most frequently encountered inner states which can be scored in the same way as needs:

1. *Conflict.* A state in which two inner forces are pulling against one another; uncertainty, indecision. This may also include the conflict created by two opposing needs.
2. *Emotional Change.* To show an alteration in mood or attitude towards something or someone. To be labile, inconsistent, moody, or unstable.
3. *Elation.* Happiness, joyful enthusiasm, optimism, excitement, a positive outlook.
4. *Dejection.* Disappointment, discouragement, sadness, depression, melancholy, or despair.
5. *Distrust.* To have no confidence in; to be suspicious of; to be skeptical of. Refusing to accept other people's ideas, suggestions, or advice because of distrust. This may often be associated with n Rejection or n Autonomy.

6. *Jealousy.* To be afraid that a loved person will prefer or love another person. Envy. Requiring complete loyalty or faithfulness. Jealousy towards more favored or successful rivals.

7. *Irreality.* Visions or hallucinations. Reveries about the future or daydreams about the past. Entering into a hypnotic or dream state. An altered state of consciousness. However, this would not include mythological creatures (dragon, sorceress, unicorn, etc.) when the story takes place in a mythological setting, unless there was also an accompanying altered state existing within the hero.

8. *Ego Ideal, Pride.* Having a high opinion of one's own self-worth. To keep one's self-respect or to dream of a great future in which one will accomplish all one's goals. This may involve n Counteraction, n Achievement, n Autonomy (defiance), or n Aggression.

9. *Superego.* To be controlled by a conscience which demands a high moral standard. The hero, for example, might be extremely honest, dependable, and courageous, and express a high degree of integrity. This could be combined with n Achievement (working for a socially approved ideal), n Blame Avoidance (not succumbing to temptation), or n Abasement (confessing one's sins or experiencing guilt feelings).

10. *Miscellaneous.* The first nine items represent some of the more common inner states but cannot describe all the possibilities. Additional inner states can be identified and listed separately.

Forces of the Hero's Environment (Press)

The examiner, in addition to noting the needs occurring within the hero, should also observe the type of environment in which the hero lives and functions. The recommended rating for these environmental forces, or press, is on a five-point scale. As with the rating for the hero's needs, the scale for press uses a 5 to designate the highest possible mark for any press on a story and a 1 to indicate the slightest reference to that press. The criteria for the relative strength of a press are based on intensity, duration, frequency, and general significance in the plot. After each story is rated on the basis of the occurrence and strength of its press, the scores can be totaled and compared so as to gain an overall picture of how the subject sees his/her world. The following definitions of press are derived from Sanford's (1939) manual and appear in print in Stein's (1981) book on the Thematic Apperception Test.* A summary sheet (Table 5-4) is provided as an aid in totaling and comparing the different press.

By taking note of the subject's press, basic trends and themes can be isolated. For example, are people seen as friendly or unfriendly? What attributes are given

---

*Definitions of the press from pp. 45–49 of *The Thematic Apperception Test: An Introductory Manual for Its Clinical Use with Adults* (Second Edition, Second Printing, 1981, Springfield, Ill.: Charles C. Thomas) by Morris I. Stein. Copyright ©1981 by Morris I. Stein. By permission of the author and Nevitt Sanford.

Table 5-4. TAT Summary Sheet for Press.

	CARD NUMBER																				
	1	2	3	4	5	6	7	8	9	10	11	12	13	14	15	16	17	18	19	20	TOTAL
p Aquisition																					
p Retention																					
p Lack																					
p Loss																					
p Rejection																					
p Uncongenial Environment																					
p Dominance																					
p Imposed Task, Duty, Training																					
p Aggression																					
p Affliction																					
p Death of Hero																					
p Physical Danger																					
p Physical Injury																					
p Affiliation																					
p Deference																					
p Nurturance																					
p Sex																					
p Succorance																					
p Birth of Offspring																					
p Claustrum																					
p Cognizance																					
p Example																					
p Exposition																					
p Luck																					

to older men as opposed to younger ones, or older women versus younger ones? Are members of the same age and sex seen as basically threatening or primarily helpful and cooperative? Is the world one in which there is a marked absence of required beneficial press, or are personal needs provided for?

Although the following list of press and the scores that can be achieved by using them provide a certain amount of useful information, the examiner is encouraged to consider the unique and specific significance these have for the subject. For example, if a subject's highest press rating is for p Dominance, how does he characteristically cope with this press? Is it through rebellion, submission, impulsive acting out, or withdrawal and fantasy? In particular, does the subject see himself as being helplessly controlled by the forces of fate, or does he effectively control his environment and significantly affect the outcome of the stories? Thus, although the totals of the press scores are useful figures in and of themselves, it is also up to the examiner to broaden the significance of these totals by integrating their meaning into the overall story content and context. The following list can be used as an aid in identifying which press are present in a subject's stories.

A. *Press of Deprivation*
   1. *p Acquisition.* A person wants to dispossess the hero of money or property, to rob or swindle him. For example, a competitor in business threatens the hero's financial security.
      After developing false evidence against him, they hoped that his property would be turned over to themselves.
   2. *p Retention.* A person retains something the hero wants; refuses to lend or give something to the hero; is stingy, miserly, or possessive.
      He had been asking to borrow his father's tools, but his father said firmly that since he had not returned them in a timely manner before, he could not use them again.
B. *Press Descriptive of an Empty, Alien, or Rejecting Environment*
   1. *p Lack*
      a) *Things, Opportunities, Friends.* There are few desirable objects in the environment, few opportunities for enjoyment or advancement, or no jobs. The hero is poor and the family destitute, or the hero lacks status, influence, and/or friends.
         Even though the government was clearly in the wrong, every attempt he made was frustrated by the bureaucrats' keeping a closed mind.
      b) *Human Support.* The hero is miserable, solitary, helpless, and in need of assistance and support, encouragement, protection, food, medical care, or parental love and guidance. The hero has no father or no mother. The situation is insecure and perilous, or the hero is homesick. There are few nurturant people in the hero's environment. Commonly, fusions occur with p Loss, p Rejection, and n Succorance.
         He's sitting on the outside of his cabin and it's the first day of summer camp. He misses his mother and father, and realizes that no one in the camp really wants to make friends with him.
   2. *p Loss.* This is the same as for p Lack, except in this case the hero actually loses something or someone such as money, job, friend, or opportunity. This may include the loss of a loved one by departure, misfortune, or death. Another example is the loss of property through

bankruptcy, misfortune, swindling, or robbery. If the hero loses something and also experiences a sense of loss over an extended period of time, then a score on p Lack should also be given.

With one pronouncement of the judge, the family's entire holdings were turned over to the government.

3. *p Rejection.* A person rejects, scorns, loses respect for, repudiates, turns away from, or leaves the hero.

The older man has fallen in love with this woman, and she's explaining that she does not feel attracted to him in the least.

4. *p Uncongenial Environment*
   a) *Alien Objects.* The people in the hero's environment are not to his liking; there is no mutual sympathy or understanding. He finds no one in accord with his interests. There are people around him, but they dislike, reject, distrust, accuse, or disapprove of him. This refers to the hero's general human environment and not to one or two specific people within his environment. For example, this may be used to describe an overall feeling within an organization or community which rejects or is out of sympathy with the hero.

   Even though he had stood up for his beliefs, wherever he went within the village people gave him suspicious looks and avoided talking to him.

   b) *Physical Surroundings.* The hero is dissatisfied with his physical environment. He hates the farm, the city, the sea, or the island on which he is marooned. The environment is distrustful, ugly, sordid, dreary, barren (p Lack), noisy, or dangerous.

   He has worked in the graveyard for two years now, and he still hasn't gotten used to the sight of the cold, bleak gravestones.

   c) *Monotony.* The hero must submit to a dull routine; work is drudgery. There is a great "sameness" in his life. He is bored.

   Every day he worked steadily in the oppressive sameness of the coal mine and still he could not clearly see a way to end the routine work.

C. *Press of Coercion and Restraint*
   1. *p Dominance*
      a) *Coercion.* Someone tries to force the hero to do something. He is exposed to commands, orders, or strong arguments from a parent or authority.

      This guy has given him an offer he can't refuse, if you know what I mean, and so he has no other choice.

      b) *Restraint.* Someone tries to prevent the hero from doing something. He is exposed to checks, prohibitions, or restraints.

He tried many times to cross the border, but each time the border patrol apprehended him and sent him back to his own country.

c) *Inducement.* Someone tries to get the hero to do something, or not to do something, by pleading or by gentle persuasion, encouragement, clever strategy, or seduction. In this category, no threats of force are used.

When he heared what had happened, she begged him to stay, appealing to his sense of peace until finally he agreed to stay.

2. *p Imposed Task, Duty, Training.* The hero is given something to do: he must practice on the violin, study for an examination, accomplish something to keep his job, or win a reward. If the agent who imposes the task is named, then a score is also given to p Dominance (coercion).

When he received his draft papers, he knew that he would have to go defend his country.

D. *Press Descriptive of a Hostile Aggressive Environment*
   1. *p Aggression*
      a) *Emotional, Verbal.* Someone gets angry at the hero or hates him. He is cursed, criticized, belittled, reproved, reprimanded, or ridiculed. Someone slanders the hero behind his back.

      They're having a big argument now, and he's yelling and calling her some pretty bad names that I would hate to even admit are in my vocabulary.

      b) *Physical, Social.* The hero is in the wrong and is an aggressor or a criminal. Another person defends himself, retaliates, pursues, imprisons, or perhaps kills the hero. The state, the police, a parent, or some other legitimate authority punishes the hero for misconduct.

      Finally they have enough clues to track him down, and then in the dead of night, the police surround his house and prepare to take him into custody.

      c) *Physical, Asocial.* A criminal or a gang assaults, injures, or kills the hero. Another person starts a fight and the hero defends himself.

      Then, they took him out back to have him try on a pair of cement shoes before giving him a swimming lesson.

      d) *Destruction.* Something belonging to the hero is damaged or destroyed.

      After stealing her car, they drove it off a cliff where it was smashed to smithereens.

E. *Press of Danger, Injury, Death*
   1. *p Affliction*
      a) *Physical.* The hero has a physical handicap such as a hunchback or a chronic ailment. He is taken ill during the course of the story.

The cough started as a short, infrequent hacking and later developed into a serious case of pneumonia.

b) *Method.* The hero suffers from neurotic or psychotic symptoms. He is subject to hallucinations or obsessions. He experiences premonitions of insanity, or he is justifiably considered very strange.

Every day he would manicure his front lawn with scissors, and finally he completely went to pieces when a dog "dirtied" his garden.

2. *p Death of Hero.* This is weighted according to the stress placed on the event. The hero may die from physical or mental illness (p Affliction), from physical injury, from p Aggression, or he may commit suicide [n Abasement (intra-aggression)].

He eventually died a grisly death on the guillotine.

3. *p Physical Danger*

a) *Active.* The hero is exposed to physical danger from nonhuman forms. He is attacked by animals, caught in a storm at sea, hit by a train, or struck by lightning. He is exposed to a tremendous bombardment. The danger may be as small as a threat, or it may actually injure or kill the hero.

The meteor shower assaulted them from all sides so that the captain and his party just barely escaped with their lives.

b) *Insupport.* The hero is exposed to the danger of falling or drowning. His car overturns, his ship is wrecked, he is caught on the narrow ledge of a steep mountain, the ground is insecure.

As he was climbing, step by step, across the suspension bridge, all of a sudden two of the boards directly under him broke free.

4. *p Physical Injury.* The hero is hurt by a human aggressor (p Aggression); by a cave-in, collision, or fall (p Physical Danger); or by a wild animal. The hero is mutilated or disfigured.

The assassin opened fire and wounded him in the arm.

F. *Press of Friendliness, Sympathy, Respect, Dependence, and Love*

1. *p. Affiliation*

a) *Associative.* The hero has one or more friends or sociable companions; he is a member of a congenial group.

The men lay next to one another letting the warmth of the day and the comfort of their friendship settle into their thoughts.

b) *Emotional.* A person such as a parent, sibling, relative, or erotic object is devoted to the hero. The hero has a love affair which is reciprocated, or the hero gets married.

The story ends where they fall in love again and end up getting married.

2. *p Deference*
   a) *Compliance.* An individual or a group willingly follows the leadership or requests of the hero. A person is anxious to please him, to cooperate, or to obey. The obedience may be passive.

   At his command the entire battalion began to prepare for the next leg of their journey.

   b) *Respect.* The hero is admired by an individual or a group. His talents or merits are appreciated; he is rewarded or publicly applauded.

   With each deft stroke of his violin, the audience became driven into a fervor of awe.

3. *p Nurturance.* Someone nourishes, encourages, protects, or cares for the hero. He receives sympathy, consolation, pity.

   Finally, somebody found him in a corner of the store, gave him something to eat, and helped find his parents.

4. *p Sex.* Another person is in love with the hero, or his/her affections are engaged by a seductress/seducer. The hero gets married.

   She moved softly under the candle light and became a virtual Aphrodite to him.

5. *p Succorance.* Someone seeks aid, protection, or sympathy from the hero. There is a helpless, miserable, pitiful object to whom the hero reacts. Someone is rescued by the hero.

   The pathetic and whimpering puppy soon got Rick to take it home with him and nurse it back to health.

G. *Miscellaneous Press*
   1. *p Birth of Offspring.* A child is born to the hero, or a woman is going to have a baby. The amount of weight given to this press depends on the relative importance of the birth to the overall story.

   All the relatives and neighbors came to see the new baby.

   2. *p Claustrum.* The hero finds himself in a confining space such as a solitary hideout, house, deep valley, or cave. He might be locked in his room, imprisoned, trapped in a cave-in, or confined in a space such as a house, vault, or tunnel. The hero seeks to enter, tries to break out of, or is forcibly expelled from, such a place.

   Just when he thought he was going to drown, he was swallowed by a whale and became safely protected by its insides.

   3. *p Cognizance.* Someone is curious about the hero and his doings; he is watched. Someone peers or probes into his affairs, asks questions.

I don't know exactly why anyone would be so interested, but every time this guy walked into the room, there was an eye peering at him through this knothole.

4. *p Example*

a) *Good Influence.* A person, group, or cause (social ideal, philosophical) influences the hero in a constructive way. A talented man serves as an example.

Every time he heard his instructor play in a concert, he was inspired to practice even harder.

b) *Bad Influence.* The hero is led into crime by his associates; the level of the hero's conduct or his ideals are lowered by following the suggestions or inducements of an untrustworthy or irresponsible person.

When Mel showed him how much money he could make by selling drugs, he soon developed his own connections and networks for distribution.

5. *p Exposition.* Someone tells, explains, interprets, or teaches the hero something.

After three more classes, the theories of Marx, which had previously been so clouded in mystery, were clearly explained and seemed to make sense.

6. *p Luck*

a) *Good, Gratuity.* The hero is unusually privileged; he has everything he wants (status, wealth, friends). The hero is suddenly benefited by some unusual or unpredicted chance occurrence, or by some extraordinary opportunity which does not result from his own efforts. Although he may be deserving of the good fortune, he did not work directly for it. A benefactor is attracted by the hero's promise, and his ambitions are aided by another person, which would also involve p Nurturance.

Then, while walking down this dusty country road, he found a 50-year-old two-dollar bill.

b) *Bad.* Fortune is against the hero. He is underprivileged from the start, he must endure an extraordinary series of misfortunes, or he is suddenly confronted by a chance occurrence which serves to hinder or frustrate his efforts. However, the coercion from such sources as parents or enemies is not considered bad luck. In evaluating whether or not to score this press, the examiner should question to what extent fate, chance, or destiny played a part in the character's life.

It seemed as if wherever he drilled a well, Don never discovered oil despite his expertise.

Themes and Outcomes

Once the examiner has determined who the hero of the story is and what needs and press occur within the protocol, the next step is to put these together in a meaningful way. It is certainly helpful to know that, for example, a subject's heroes exhibit anxiety and passivity. It is also helpful to know that the environment may be seen as threatening and surrounded by domineering forces. However, this distinction is somewhat artificial since a hero and his environment are continually interacting to form certain outcomes as a result of these dynamics. Murray (1943) states that "the interaction of a hero's need (or fusion of needs) and an environmental press (or fusion of press) together with the outcome (success or failure of the hero) constitutes a simple thema" (p. 13). A complex thema is composed of "combinations of simple thema, interlocked or forming a sequence" (p. 13).

In considering outcomes or thema, Murray gives relatively vague instructions on how to score, categorize, or interpret. The following thematic concerns, adapted and expanded from Arnold (1962), can serve as a broader guideline for eliciting the basic themes which concern the subject.

Achievement Success or Failure, Happiness/Unhappiness, or Active Effort as Opposed to Lack of It. In assessing the first area of thematic concern, the examiner might ask himself the following questions: Is the hero successful in his attempts or does he fail? If he does fail, under what circumstances does he fail? Is the hero's path to success difficult or easy? What obstacles does he confront? Does the subject end up being happy or dissatisfied and sad? Of particular importance is to what degree the hero influences the outcome of the story or to what extent he is the passive recipient of fate. Is he generally active or passive?

Right and Wrong. The category dealing with right and wrong considers stories in which the ethical significance of an action and the resulting consequences to the hero are the primary focus of the story. Does the hero demonstrate adequate impulse control? If he acts out, is he punished for his behavior or does he avoid getting caught? Does he feel guilty about his behavior, and is this guilt realistic or the result of an overly oppressive conscience? Are his moral values based on simple fear of getting caught, or does he have a higher, internal set of ethical beliefs? Does he confess, atone, or reform? How much does the hero criticize himself?

Human Relationships. Human relationships include actions or attitudes towards others or others' attitudes towards the central character. What issues or preoccupations are the heroes concerned with? What types of activities do they spend the most time engaged in? How do they see other people: as domineering, threatening, affectionate, helpful, pushovers, boring, etc.? What major assets or deficits do the heroes have, especially in their ability to deal effectively with interpersonal difficulties?

Reaction to Adversity. The manner in which the hero deals with life stresses and problems is indicative of his reaction to adversity. What are the major dilemmas and conflicts with which the hero deals? Do these conflicts center around rivalry, love, deprivation, coercion, punishment, war, etc.? Is his approach characterized by withdrawal, manipulation, acting out, helplessness, or assertion?

Interests and Sentiments. The final category to be considered involves noting the characteristic interests which the subject attributes to the hero. These may include such areas as artistic appreciation, travel, athletic activities, creativity, or academic endeavors. Of particular importance are positive or negative feelings towards older women (mother figures), older men (father figures), and same-sex or opposite-sex persons of the hero's age.

INTERPRETATION

There are several introductory points which need to be made in regards to Murray''s scoring and interpretation system. Perhaps the most important is that scoring and interpretation cannot actually be differentiated from one another. The procedures considered here are a guide for arranging and summarizing previously obtained information rather than amassing additional data. Also, any of the numerous scoring and interpretation methods can be used, each of which will provide somewhat different perspectives and information on the TAT stories. Murray's approach, although it requires some quantification on the five-point scale for needs and press, is primarily qualitative. It is also oriented more towards content than towards the formal or stylistic attributes of the stories. Thus, Murray's approach, with its emphasis on content and qualitative aspects, is merely one method and is not intended to be all inclusive.

Once the stories have been analyzed and scored for needs and press, they can be tabulated on the summary sheets which have been provided in Tables 5-3 and 5-4. From these sheets a list of unusually high and unusually low needs and press can be determined. These can then be compared with a list of the prevalent themes, outcomes, and interests which have been analyzed according to Murray's procedure. Additional data may include historical facts about the subject and numerous behavioral observations.

Such information can be addressed from the perspective of two assumptions about the TAT. The first is that the attributes of the hero (needs, emotional states, and sentiments) represent characteristics of the subject's own personality. These may represent things the subject has done, things he has wanted or perhaps has felt tempted to do, core attributes of his personality of which he may be unconscious, feelings and wishes he is experiencing at the time of the test administration, or anticipations of his future behavior (Murray, 1943).

The second basic assumption is that the press which have been described in the stories represent a combination of the subject's actual environment and, more important, the manner in which he interprets that environment. These may include situations that he has actually encountered, ones that he dreams or fantasizes encountering out of hope or fear, momentary situations during the time of examination, or situations he expects to encounter (Murray, 1943). In other words, the press encountered in the TAT represent the subject's world view.

The variables of needs, inner states, and press should then be combined with the type of outcomes, themas, and interests to make generalizations about, and descriptions of, the subject. These conclusions, according to Murray (1943, p. 14), are to be regarded as good "leads" or working hypotheses, to be verified by other methods, rather than as proven facts.

Murray offers a number of additional considerations regarding the conclusions to be reached by the TAT. He states that approximately 30% of the stories are likely to be impersonal renditions or cliches of previously heard information and, because of their impersonal nature, cannot be used to infer the underlying determinants of personality. Yet another consideration is that even though for the most part high, moderate, or low scores on the stories correspond to high, moderate, and low characteristics within the subject, this is not always the case. For example, Murray found that there was a negative correlation (−.33 to −.74) between n Sex on the TAT and n Sex expressed in overt behavior. Of final and particular note are the subject's current life situation and his emotional state at the time of examination. One of the more important variables which can affect the emotional state of the subject, and therefore the test results, is the particular interaction between the subject and the examiner. A sensitive and accurate interpretation can be obtained only if the examiner takes into account the existence and possible influence of all these variables.

RECOMMENDED READING

Arnold, M.B. *Story Sequence Analysis: A New Method of Measuring and Predicting Achievement.* New York: Columbia University Press, 1962.

Bellak, L. *The TAT, CAT and SAT in Clinical Use* (3rd ed.). New York: Grune & Stratton, 1975.

Henry, W.E. *The Analysis of Fantasy: The Thematic Apperception Test in the Study of Personality.* New York: John Wiley & Sons, 1956.

Murray, H.A. *Explorations in Personality.* New York: Oxford University Press, 1938.

Murstein, B.I. *Theory and Research in Projective Techniques (Emphasizing the TAT).* New York: John Wiley & Sons, 1963.

Semeonoff, B. *Projective Techniques.* New York: John Wiley & Sons, 1976.

Stein, M. *The Thematic Apperception Test: An Introductory Manual for Its Clinical Use with Adults* (2nd ed.). Springfield, Ill.: Charles C. Thomas, 1981.

6
The Rorschach

The Rorschach is a projective test consisting of a set of ten bilaterally symmetrical inkblots, in which subjects are requested to tell the examiner what these inkblots remind them of. The overall goal of the technique is to obtain assessments of a client's structure of personality, with particular emphasis on understanding the unconscious manner in which he responds and organizes his environment. Despite attacks both from within the field of psychology and from outside, the Rorschach remains one of the most extensively used (Howes, 1981) and well-respected assessment devices.

The central assumption of the Rorschach is that stimuli from the environment are organized by a person's specific needs, motives, conflicts, and certain perceptual "sets." This need for organization becomes more exaggerated, extensive, and conspicuous when people are confronted with ambiguous stimuli such as inkblots. Thus, they must draw on their personal internal images, ideas, and relationships in order to create a response. This process requires that persons organize these perceptions as well as associate them with past experiences and impressions. Once the responses have been made and recorded, they are scored according to three general categories: the "location," or the area of the inkblot on which they focus; "determinants," or specific properties of the blot (color, shape, etc.); and the "content," or general class of objects to which the response belongs (human, architecture, anatomy, etc.). The interpretation of the overall protocol is based on the relative number of responses that fall into each of the above categories.

Although these scoring categories may appear straightforward, the specifics of scoring and interpreting the Rorschach are extremely complex. Furthermore, attempts to develop an exact and universally accepted coding system have not been entirely successful, which makes approaching the Rorschach technique itself somewhat confusing and ambiguous. Although the primary scoring systems have some agreed upon similarities, there are also significant differences in the elements of these systems. This in turn reflects the complexity and ambiguity in the nature of the responses that are made to the cards. Thus, effective use of the Rorschach depends on the thorough knowledge of a scoring system, clinical experience, and adequate knowledge of personality and psychopathology.

The general purpose of this chapter is to provide a general overview of the administration, scoring, and interpretation of the Rorschach according to John

Exner's "Comprehensive System." Exner's system was selected because it is the most ambitious and psychometrically sound Rorschach system to date. Furthermore, the most frequently used scorings and interpretations from the other systems have been included and integrated into Exner's approach. Thus, data derived from other systems can, with appropriate caution, be used with the interpretive hypotheses included later in this chapter. There has been some minor editing of Exner's system based on certain features being either insufficiently researched and/or idiosyncratic to his system. For the most part, however, there is a close parallel between the approach of this chapter and Exner's "Comprehensive System." In the Appendix, there are several tables which clinicians can use to compare the scores derived from their client's protocols with means developed from adults and children. Mean scores and standard deviations are provided for normals (nonpatients) as well as for various clinical subgroups. In order for clinicians to develop exact scoring tables and criteria, as well as a more extensive elaboration on interpretation, they are encouraged to consult Exner's original works (Exner, 1974, 1978; Exner and Weiner, 1982).

HISTORY AND DEVELOPMENT

The inkblot technique was first described by Hermann Rorschach in 1921. He died in 1922 at the age of 38, and his friend and colleague Emil Oberholzer published and elaborated on his work. In 1932, S.J. Beck completed his doctoral dissertation on the Rorschach, and in the following year he studied in Europe with Oberholzer. Beck is credited both with having brought the Rorschach to the United States and with developing one of the earliest formal scoring systems (1945). At the same time as Beck was studying with Oberholzer, Klopfer was likewise receiving formal training in Europe, and he also developed an early scoring system (1943).

Early studies of the Rorschach were conducted by administering the test to different psychiatric groups and noting the characteristic types of responses for each of these groups. Thus, initial norms were developed which were intended to help differentiate between various clinical populations. These early norms were developed for mental retardates, normals, artists, scholars, and other specific subgroups with known characteristics. By 1956, Klopfer, Ainsworth, Klopfer, and Holt listed almost 2700 publications pertaining directly to the Rorschach. In 1969, Exner estimated the number to be near 4000 and believed that there were more publications dealing with the Rorschach than with all other projective tests combined. It was also found to be the most popular (Exner, 1969) personality test, and when compared with all other psychological tests, only the Wechsler intelligence scales were used more frequently.

More recently, Exner (1974, 1978) has developed a comprehensive scoring system which combines features from both Beck and Klopfer. In addition, a computerized method for scoring and interpretation by use of the Piotrowski system became available in 1974. The computer-processed interpretation statements refer to different areas of functioning such as interpersonal skills, intellectual efficiency, initiative and autonomy, problem solving skills, and personality problems.

RELIABILITY AND VALIDITY

In general, researchers have frequently questioned the validity of the Rorschach, and studies have often come up with conflicting, negative, or confusing results. The somewhat inconclusive results of Rorschach studies can in part be explained by the wide differences in administration and scoring among various examiners. For example, one examiner might be relatively neutral when the subject gives his responses, whereas a different one might give encouragement by nodding his head or saying "good" after each response. The resulting test protocol could easily vary in the total number of responses from one examiner to another, thus altering the total number of responses and potentially altering the interpretation. There is also often a wide degree of variability in how different responses are scored. For example, one scorer might be quite liberal in scoring color (C) or human movement (M) responses, yet another one might be quite conservative. Again, the different scores would potentially alter the overall interpretation of the test protocol. Also test results may depend upon a large number of other variables, especially examiner-client interactions such as rapport (Allen, 1953), the sex of the examiner (Alden and Benton, 1951; Rabin, Nelson, and Clark, 1954), and the personality of the examiner (Sanders and Cleveland, 1965). Harris (1960) has listed over 30 factors which can potentially influence Rorschach performances. These complexities make achieving an adequate level of reliability on the Rorschach extremely difficult.

The original scoring and interpretation of the Rorschach was directed towards being able to differentiate between various clinical populations. This was based on past observations of a particular group's responses to the Rorschach, the development of norms based on these responses, and comparison of an individual's Rorschach responses with these norms. For example, a schizophrenic might have a relatively high number of poor quality form responses (F-) or a depressed patient might have very few human movement responses (M). To a certain extent this goal has been successful in that clinicians have been relatively accurate in predicting patient's characteristics. In particular, studies using the judgments of individual clinical psychologists who have had extensive training and experience with the Rorschach have frequently found it to be a valid tool (Karon, 1978). However, these findings do not represent formal validation but may indicate more that a specific clinician is intuitive and that somewhere in the Rorschach responses is the potential for valuable information.

Of significance is the fact that many of the more basic assumptions relating to the validity of the Rorschach have been challenged. Anastasi (1982) has reviewed criticisms of the Rorschach and listed the following four major challenges:

1. *Color itself has no effect on responses* (Baughman, 1958). Traditionally, the style in which a person responds to the colored inkblots has been believed to parallel the manner in which the person handles his emotions. However, in Baughman's study, a set of chromatic (standard) plates was given as well as an experimental set of achromatic ones. The results indicated that there was little or no difference in the two overall sets of responses.
2. *Scores are influenced by a subject's verbal aptitude* (Lotsoff, 1953; Sachman, 1952). Inferences are typically made about an individual based on his overall number of responses as well as the number of human movement *(M)* responses. However, Sachman (1952) found that the number of responses and especially the number of human movement *(M)* responses correlated positively with verbal aptitude. Thus, rather than a high number of responses and movements reflecting traditional Rorschach interpretive hypotheses, they may merely reflect a correspondingly high level of verbal aptitude.
3. *Response productivity is closely tied to age, intellectual level, and amount of education* (Fiske and Baughman, 1953). Many of the scoring data are based on ratios which are dependent in part on the overall number of responses. For example, a small number of responses will be likely to increase the overall percentage of whole as compared to detail responses, which has important implications for interpretation. Fiske and Baughman's study suggests that instead of actual personality variables affecting the percentage of whole responses, this may be altered more by a subject's age, intellectual level, and amount of education.
4. *Earlier validity studies were based on inadequately developed norms.* Even though the Rorschach is usually considered to be a tool for all ages from preschool to adult, its normative data were originally derived from adults and were not adequately developed for children, adolescents, and persons over 70. Despite this deficiency, many earlier validity studies were conducted using these inadequate norms. The possibly erroneous conclusions from these studies are still likely to be prevalent both in clinical practice and in the literature. However, norms for children, adolescents, and persons over 70 have been developed more recently by Ames, Metraux, and Walker (1971); Ames, Metraux, Rodell, and Walker (1974); Exner (1978); and Exner and Weiner (1982) so that future studies should be more solidly based on these norms.

It is hoped that these challenges will serve to stimulate further research and to sensitize clinicians to the limitations of specific protocols and of the interpretations derived from these protocols.

During recent years, test-retest reliability has been adequately demonstrated in several studies for Exner's "Comprehensive System." For example, Exner, Armbruster, and Viglione (1978) found that the basic objective indices on the Rorschach were quite stable (.90–.66) even for protocols administered three or more years after the first administration. Interrater reliability for each of the different scoring categories has been demonstrated at least at the level of .85 (Exner, 1974, 1978). Wagner and Daubney (1976) tested brain-damaged patients and likewise found fair test-retest reliability. However, adequate reliability does not necessarily indicate adequate validity; rather, it is an initial prerequisite for validity.

Of significance, especially for this chapter, are Exner's (1974, 1978; Exner and Weiner, 1982) relatively recent attempts to give the Rorschach a sound psychometric standing. His "Comprehensive System" combines the most frequently used features from earlier systems and also contains a number of unique features. The emphasis is on quantitative and structural variables rather than on those that are more qualitative and content oriented. Exner also avoids single scores and rather stresses ratios, indices, and the total configuration of results. Furthermore, his approach is not tied to any one personality theory but focuses on interpretations which are closely tied to data. He has collected much of the data himself, and his system gives extensive child, adult, patient, and nonpatient norms, as well as studies on test-retest reliability. The uniformity of his approach and its emphasis on empirical data allow for the possibility of comparisons with other research findings.

Despite past controversy over test validity, there are several major arguments for the Rorschach's continued use. First of all, there are few better methods for obtaining information regarding what is usually referred to as a subject's unconscious processes. Second, most validity studies do not consider the manner in which the test is actually used in clinical practice. Specifically, the Rorschach is almost always used in the context of other test materials in an overall battery so that each source of information provides checks and balances against other sources. Thus, one test might verify, elaborate, modify, or negate the findings from another. The results, then, ideally become clinically cross-validated in specific testing cases, thereby creating more dependable overall information. Finally, the extensive work of Exner offers renewed hope in the Rorschach as an effective clinical and psychometric tool.

ASSETS AND LIMITATIONS

As with other projective tests, it is essential that a clinician understand the strong points as well as the potential weaknesses of the technique. This is particularly true for the Rorschach since it is perhaps the most complex psychological test in use. Because of its complexity, there are numerous errors a clinician can make during the administration, scoring, and interpretation sequence. One temptation in particular is the tendency to reduce the complexity of the data by using a single sign approach rather than viewing each sign in the context of the overall configuration. Since Rorschach "elevations" are often subject to a large number of possible interpretive hypotheses, a single sign approach is particularly subject to error. Thus, interpretations must be continually checked and rechecked against both the overall Rorschach configuration and additional sources of data, specifically other test data and the patient's history.

Yet a further limitation of the Rorschach is its questionable validity. Whereas some categories of Rorschach responses have fairly high agreement regarding interpretations for the subject, other categories have been criticized for producing contradictory findings. As discussed earlier, many of the Rorschach hypotheses for children, adolescents, and persons over 70 were based on inadequately developed norms. Furthermore, some of the basic assumptions relating to the validity of the Rorschach have been challenged. General criticisms regarding validity have been generated both from within the profession and from outside. Thus, clinicians should be well grounded in the controversies surrounding validity and should learn to approach any interpretations based solely on Rorschach data with caution. They should also be aware of recent research and use up-to-date normative data for their comparisons.

A final limitation of the Rorschach is the extensive training required for its effective use. Clinicians must be familiar with the complexities of scoring as well as possess an in-depth knowledge of personality theory and psychopathology. Perhaps most important, they must be able to skillfully integrate complex test data in order to develop accurate interpretive hypotheses. With the increasing demand for psychology graduate students to develop a wide diversity of specific skills beyond the realm of testing, it has become increasingly more difficult for students to find the time necessary to develop an adequate knowledge of the Rorschach.

In addition to these limitations, there are also a number of significant assets. Perhaps the most important is that the Rorschach provides one of the better instruments for bypassing a subject's conscious resistance and obtaining information about his unconscious processes. The intention behind the Rorschach test is usually opaque and mysterious to the subject, and it is difficult for him to decipher exactly how his responses will be interpreted. As a result, the Rorschach is an extremely difficult test to fake (Seamons, Howell, and Roe, 1981). This is in contrast to the TAT or even to projective drawings in which the content material is somewhat more familiar and, therefore, could potentially be more easily edited or embellished according to what image the subject would like to portray.

A further asset of the Rorschach is its focus on elaborating the underlying structure of personality. Thus, it gives information on such areas as a person's inner images, conflicts, relation between emotion and form, cognitive style, and perceptual organization. Whereas the Rorschach is often seen as providing information about a person's underlying structure, the TAT elaborates more on the content which is expressed from that structure. Thus, the two tests can potentially complement one another.

Finally, the Rorschach is a relatively simple device to handle and administer. This partial simplicity is often obscured by the different detailed scoring methods and numerous refinements which create a certain degree of complexity. At its most basic and central level, the Rorschach inkblots are a set of stimuli which provide a model for how an individual approaches his world and colors it with his unique, personal, internal images.

ADMINISTRATION

Examiners should attempt to standardize their administration procedures as much as possible. This is particularly important since research has consistently indicated that it is relatively easy to influence a subject's responses. For example, just saying the word "good" after each response can increase the overall number of responses on the Rorschach by as much as 50% (Hersen and Greaves, 1971). However, if the fluctuations in administration style are minor, it is unlikely that they will significantly influence a subject's responses (Phares, Stewart, and Foster, 1960; Williams, 1954). In general, examiners should attempt to minimize the variations in their administration procedures as much as possible and the following sequence of steps is recommended.

Step 1: Introducing the Respondent to the Technique

One of the most important tasks at which examiners must initially work is allowing the examinee to feel relatively comfortable with the testing procedure. This is complicated by the fact that tests in our culture have usually been associated with anxiety. Although in some cases an increase in anxiety may provide some information that cannot be obtained when the subject is relaxed, anxiety is usually regarded as a hindrance. Typically, anxiety interferes with a person's perceptions and the free flow of fantasy, both of which are essential for adequate Rorschach responses. Thus, subjects should be as relaxed as possible. Their relaxation can be enhanced by giving a clear introduction to the testing procedure, obtaining personal history, answering questions they might have, and generally avoiding any behavior that might increase the subjects' anxiety. In describing the test, examiners should emphasize relatively neutral words such as "inkblot," "interests," or "imagination" rather than more potentially anxiety provoking words like "intelligence" or "ambiguous."

For the most part, any specific information regarding what subjects should do or say ought to be avoided. The test situation is designed to be ambiguous, and examiners should avoid any statements that might influence the responses. If subjects push for more detailed information about what they should do or what their responses may mean, they should be told that additional questions can be answered after the test is completed.

Step 2: Giving the Testing Instructions

Although some Rorschach systematizers recommend that the subject tell the examiner "everything you see" (Beck, 1961), the "Comprehensive System" attempts to keep the task as ambiguous as possible. Thus, Exner (1974) recommends that the examiner hand the subject the first card and ask, "What might this be?"

Commentary on, or discussion of, the cards by the examiner should be avoided as much as possible. At times, it might be acceptable to briefly describe how the designs were made or, if questioned regarding what one is supposed to see, the examiner might state that "people see all sorts of things in the blots." Comments from the examiner which indicate the quantity or type of response and whether or not the subject can turn the cards should be strictly avoided. If the subject asks specific questions, such as the type of responses he is supposed to give or whether or not he can turn the cards, the examiner might reply that it is up to him to decide.

The main objective is that the subject be left as free as possible to respond to the stimuli however he chooses. To enhance this, it is preferable that the subject and the examiner not be seated face-to-face, but rather side-by-side so as to decrease the possible influence that the examiner's nonverbal behavior might have (Exner, 1974). The overall instructions and testing situation should be designed both to keep the task as ambiguous as possible and to keep examiner influence at a minimum.

Step 3: Free Association during the Testing

Throughout the testing procedure, the basic conditions of step 2 should be adhered to as closely as possible. However, there are often specific situations which arise as subjects are free associating to the Rorschach designs. If a subject requests specifics on how to respond or asks the examiner for encouragement or approval, examiners should consistently reply that one can respond however one likes. The idea that there are no right or wrong answers might sometimes be mentioned.

The examiner should time the interval between when subjects first see the card and when they make their initial response, as well as the total time they spend with each card. These measurements can be helpful in revealing their general approach to the card and possible difficulties in coming up with responses. It should be noted that Cards II, III, and V are generally considered relatively easy to respond to and usually have shorter reaction times than Cards VI, IX, and X which typically produce the longest reaction times (Meer, 1955). Since overt timing of subjects' responses is likely to produce anxiety, any recording should be done as inconspicuously as possible. It is recommended that rather than using a stopwatch, the examiner should glance at a watch or clock and record the minute and second positions for the initial presentation, the first response, and the point at which the subject hands the card back to the examiner.

In recording subjects' responses, it is best to write down everything verbatim. In order to simplify this process, most clinicians develop a series of abbreviations. One set of abbreviations used throughout all the Rorschach systems consists of the symbols ($\wedge$, $<$, $\vee$, $>$) in which the peak indicates the angle of the card (Loosli-Usteri, 1929). It is also important to note any odd or unusual responses to the cards such as an apparent increase in anxiety, wandering of attention, or acting out on any of the percepts.

Step 4: Inquiry

The inquiry should begin after all ten cards have been administered, and its purpose is to collect additional information required for an accurate scoring of the responses. The inquiry should not end until this goal has been accomplished. Levitt (1980) recommends that the instructions for the inquiry should closely approximate the following:

> That's fine. Now you have identified these different objects. I would like to give you the cards again so that you can tell me something more about the objects you have identified. It is not that I want you to see any more objects, but only to describe something more about the ones that you did see. Now, for example, here on Card I you said that it looks like. . . . (p. 13)

The inquiry should closely follow the general theme of the overall administration in not influencing the subject's responses. Thus, any questions should be as nondirective as possible. One should begin by merely repeating what the subject has said and waiting. Usually he will begin to clarify his response. If this information is insufficient to clarify how to score the response, the examiner might become slightly more directive by asking, "What about it made it look like a [percept] ?" The examiner should not ask, "Is it mainly the shape?" or "How important was the color?" These questions are far too directive and are worded in such a way as to exert an influence on the subject's descriptions of his responses. The examiner should consistently avoid leading the subject or indicating how he should respond.

The outcome of a well-conducted inquiry is the collection of a sufficient amount of information to decide on scoring for location and determinants. If, on the location, the examiner does not have enough information based on the subject's verbal response, he should have him point to the percept. An additional feature of the inquiry is to test the subject's awareness of his response. For example, does a strange percept represent coherent creativity, or does it reflect a lack of contact with the environment in which the subject may have no awareness of the strangeness of his responses? The overall approach of the inquiry is to word questions in such a way as to be flexible without being too directive.

RORSCHACH FACTORS

The next step following administration is the quantitative scoring of the different categories. There is general agreement throughout the different Rorschach systems that these categories include location, determinants, content, and popularity. After these have been scored, a series of quantitative summaries is created based on reorganizations of, and comparisons among, the scores on the different categories.

This section summarizes Exner's categories of scoring. However, certain areas have been selected whereas others have been deleted. The criteria for selecting specific subcategories were (1) that they were the ones most frequently used in other systems and (2) that they were most thoroughly researched. Conversely, exclusions were made on the basis of areas which were generally less well researched and were found primarily in the Exner system only. Thus, omitted from determinants were dimensionality *(FD)*, pairs and reflections, and organizational activity. Several formulas were deleted including Blends/R, a/p (active/passive), M^a/M^p, and $H + A/Hd + Ad$. These deletions are further reflected in the sections on interpretation and in the Appendix. However, the vast majority of the scoring categories used by Exner are included.

It should be stressed that this is merely an attempt to list and outline the scoring categories and quantitative summaries. In order to achieve accurate scoring, it would be necessary to consult Exner's scoring guides (see recommended readings) which include specific scoring criteria, tables, charts, and diagrams. The inclusion of specific scoring criteria is beyond the scope of this chapter because of the length and details involved. The focus is rather on providing a key to interpretation which is concise, accountable, and familiar. The following definitions and tables serve as to outline and briefly define the primary Rorschach factors.

Location

The location of the responses refers to the area of the inkblot which is used (Table 6-1). This can vary from the use of the entire blot (whole response) to

Table 6-1. Categories of Location Responses.

Symbol	Definition	Criterion
W	Whole response	Where the blot is interpreted as a whole. All portions of the blot must be used.
D	Common detail response	A frequently identified area of the blot.
Dd	Unusual detail response	An infrequently identified area of the blot.
S	Space response	A white space area is used in the response (scored *only* with another location scoring).
DW or DdW	Confabulated whole response	The blot is interpreted as a whole secondarily, the primary answer being based on a detail feature of the blot.
DdD	Confabulated detail response	A commonly perceived detail area is interpreted secondarily, the primary answer being based on an unusual detail area.

NOTE: From Exner, J.E. *The Rorschach: A Comprehensive System,* 1974, p. 54. Reprinted by permission of John Wiley & Sons, Inc.

Table 6-2. Symbols and Criteria Used for the Differentiation of Location Response.

Symbol	Definition	Criteria
+	Synthesized response	Unitary or discrete portions of the blot are perceptually articulated and integrated or combined into a single percept.
o	Ordinary response	A discrete area of the blot is selected and articulated so as to emphasize the gross outline and obvious structural features of the area selected.
v	Vague response	A diffuse or general impression is offered to the blot or blot area in a manner which avoids the necessity of articulation of specific outlines or structural features.
–	Arbitrary response	Articulation of the blot or blot area is inconsistent with the structural limitations of the blot.

NOTE: From Exner, J.E. *The Rorschach: A Comprehensive System,* 1974, p. 63. Reprinted by permission of John Wiley & Sons, Inc.

the use of an unusual detail. Exner also outlines a further breakdown of the different location responses based on how well organized and integrated they are as opposed to how fragmented and disorganized (Table 6-2). Once the location of the responses has been determined, usually with the aid of diagrams with specific location designations, they are then scored for the degree of differentiation or organization of these responses in accordance with Table 6-2. Thus, each location response is given both a designation of the specific area of the blot and a symbol to indicate the degree of organization of that response.

Determinants

Determinants refer to the style or characteristic of the blot to which the examinee responds, such as its shape, color, or texture (Table 6-3). The determinants

Table 6-3. Symbols and Criteria for Scoring Response Determinants.

Category	Symbol	Criteria
Form	F	*Form answers.* To be used separately for responses based exclusively on the form features of the blot, or in combination with other determinant scoring symbols (except *M* and *m*) when the form features have contributed to the formulation of a percept.
Movement	M	*Human movement response.* To be used for responses clearly involving a kinesthetic perception, the content of which involves behavior restricted to humans or, in animals, is humanlike.
	FM	*Animal movement response.* To be used for responses involving a kinesthetically marked movement involving animals. The movement perceived must be congruent to the species identified in the content. Animals perceived in movement *not* congruent to their species should be scored *M*.
	m	*Inanimate movement response.* To be used for responses involving the movement of an inanimate, inorganic, or insensate object.
Color (chromatic)	C	*Pure color response.* To be used for responses based exclusively on the chromatic color features of the blot. No form is involved.
	CF	*Color-form response.* To be used for responses which are formulated because of the color features of the blot or blot area and in which the form involved is of secondary importance.

NOTE: Adapted from Exner, J.E. *The Rorschach: A Comprehensive System,* 1974, pp. 71-72. Reprinted by permission of John Wiley & Sons, Inc.

Table 6-3. Symbols and Criteria for Scoring Response Determinants. (continued)

Category	Symbol	Criteria
	FC	*Form-color response.* To be used for responses which are formulated because of the form of the blot area, and in which color is used secondarily for purposes of clarification and/or elaboration.
	Cn	*Color naming response.* To be used when the colors of the blot or blot area are identified by name with no form involved and with the intention of presenting a response.
Color (achromatic)	*C'*	*Pure achromatic color response.* To be used when the response is based exclusively on the gray-black-white features of the blot or blot area, as they are identified as color. No form is involved.
	C'F	*Achromatic color–form response.* To be used when the response is based primarily on the gray-black-white features of the blot or blot area, as they are identified as color, and where form has been involved secondarily.
	FC'	*Form–achromatic color response.* To be used when the response is based primarily on form, and the achromatic coloring of the blot or blot area is used for purposes of elaboration and/or clarification.
Texture (shading)	*T*	*Pure texture response.* To be used for responses where the shading components of the blot are interpreted as representing a textural phenomenon with no involvement of the form of the blot.
	TF	*Texture-form response.* To be used for responses where the shading features of the blot or blot area are interpreted as texture, and form is used secondarily for purposes of elaboration and/or clarification.
	FT	*Form-texture response.* To be used for responses in which form is a primary determinant, and the shading is interpreted as textural for purposes of clarification and/or elaboration.
Dimensionality (shading)	*V*	*Pure vista response.* To be used when the shading features of the blot or blot area are interpreted as depth or dimensionality with no form involvement.
	VF	*Vista-form response.* To be used for responses in which the shading components of the blot or blot area are interpreted as depth or dimensionality, and the form features are used for purposes of clarification and/or elaboration.

NOTE: Adapted from Exner, J.E. *The Rorschach: A Comprehensive System,* 1974, pp. 71–72. Reprinted by permission of John Wiley & Sons, Inc.

Table 6 3. Symbols and Criteria for Scoring Response Determinants. (continued)

Category	Symbol	Criteria
Dimensionality (shading)	FV	*Form-vista response.* To be used for responses in which form is the primary determinant, and the shading features are included secondarily to represent depth or dimensionality.
Shading (general-diffuse)	Y	*Pure shading response.* To be used for responses based exclusively on the light-dark features of the blot which are completely formless and do not involve reference to either texture or vista.
	YF	*Shading-form response.* To be used for responses which are based primarily on the light-dark features of the blot or blot area, and in which the form features are used for purposes of clarification and/or elaboration.
	FY	*Form-shading response.* To be used for responses which are based primarily on the form of the blot or blot area, and in which the shading features are used for purposes of elaboration and/or clarification.

NOTE: Adapted from Exner, J.E. *The Rorschach: A Comprehensive System*, 1974, pp. 71–72. Reprinted by permission of John Wiley & Sons, Inc.

Table 6-4. Symbols and Criteria for Scoring Form Quality.

Symbol	Definition	Criterion
+	Superior	The unusually well-developed and articulated use of form in a manner that enriches the quality of the percept without sacrificing the appropriateness of form involved. The + answer need not involve an "original" percept, rather it should be unique by the manner in which the form is used and specified.
o	Ordinary	The obvious, easily developed use of form, wherein the content and blot areas are congruent. The answer is generally commonplace and easy to see, with no enrichment of the quality of the answer by the manner in which the form is used and specified.
w	Weak	The unconvincing, ill-conceived use of form manifesting a shift away from a congruence between the blot area and the content. Form fit is not grossly distorted yet fails to meet the criterion of being easily perceived.
−	Minus	The distorted, arbitrary, unrealistic use of form as related to the content offered, where an answer is imposed on the blot area with total, or near total, disregard for the structure of the area.

NOTE: From Exner, J.E. *The Rorschach: A Comprehensive System*, 1974, p. 120. Reprinted by permission of John Wiley & Sons, Inc.

also receive a scoring for their level of form quality (Table 6-4). The form quality scoring refers to how accurately the percept relates to the form of the inkblot. For example, an angel on Card I is considered to be an "ordinary" form quality response, which is empirically reflected in the fact that nonpsychiatric populations perceive it far more frequently than psychiatric patients (see Appendix F). Initially examiners should give a percept its appropriate classification regarding its determinant. This should then be followed by scoring the determinant for its relative form quality as described in Table 6-4.

Content

The scoring of content is based on the type and quantity of specific subjects which examinees perceive in their responses. Each Rorschach system uses different lists of content categories although they all agree on such basic contents as human, human detail, and animal. Table 6-5 provides a listing of Exner's content categories with the symbols and descriptions for each one.

Table 6-5. Symbols and Criteria to Be Used in Scoring for Content.

Category	Symbol	Criterion
Whole human	H	Involving or implying the percept of a whole human form.
Whole human (fictional or mythological)	(H)	Involving or implying the percept of a whole human form of a fictional or mythological basis, i.e., gnomes, fairies, giants, witches, King Midas, Alice in Wonderland, monsters (human like), ghosts, dwarfs, devils, and angels.
Human detail	Hd	Involving the percept of an incomplete human form, i.e., a person but the head is missing, an arm, fingers, two big feet, and the lower part of a woman.
Human detail (fictional or mythological)	(Hd)	Involving the percept of an incomplete human form of a fictional or mythological basis, i.e., the hand of God, the head of the devil, the foot of a monster, the head of a witch, and the eyes of an angel.
Whole animal	A	Involing or implying the percept of a whole animal form.
Whole animal (fictional or mythological)	(A)	Involving or implying the percept of a whole animal form of a fictional or mythological basis, i.e., unicorn, flying red horse, Black Beauty, Jonathan Livingston Seagull, the horse of Napoleon, and a magic frog.

NOTE: From Exner, J.E. *The Rorschach: A comprehensive System,* 1974, pp. 128–130. Reprinted by permission of John Wiley & Sons, Inc.

Table 6-5. Symbols and Criteria to Be Used in Scoring for Content. (continued)

Category	Symbol	Criterion
Animal detail	*Ad*	Involving the percept of an incomplete animal form, i.e., the hoof of a horse, the claw of a lobster, the head of a fish, the head of a rabbit.
Animal detail (fictional or mythological)	*(Ad)*	Involving the percept of an incomplete animal form of a fictional or mythological basis, i.e., the wing of the bird of prey, Peter Rabbit's head, the head of Pooh Bear, the head of Bambi, and the wings of Pegasus.
Abstraction	*Ab*	Involving the percept which is clearly an abstract concept; i.e., fear, depression, elation, and anger. Abstract paintings *are not* included in this scoring.
Alphabet	*Al*	Involving percepts of Arabic numerals, i.e., 2, 4, and 7, or the letters of the alphabet, i.e., A, M, and X.
Anatomy	*An*	Involving the percept of anatomy (internal organs) of either human or animal content, i.e., a heart, lungs, stomach, a bleached skull of a cow, a brain of a dog, and the insides of a person's stomach.
Anthropology	*Ay*	Involving percepts which have a specific cultural relationship, i.e., a totem pole and a helmet like those used by Romans.
Art	*Art*	Involving percepts of paintings, either definitive or abstract, plus other art objects, i.e., a family crest, the seal of the president, and a sculpture of a bird.
Blood	*Bl*	Involving the percept of blood, either human or animal.
Botany	*Bt*	Involving the percept of any plant life, i.e., flowers, trees, bushes, and seaweed.
Clothing	*Cg*	Involving the percept of any clothing ordinarily associated with the human, i.e., hat, boots, jacket, trousers, and tie. Articles of clothing associated with fictional or mythological characters, i.e., the seven-league boots, a witch's hat, should be scored as *(Cg)*.
Clouds	*Cl*	Involving the percept of clouds. Variations of this category, such as fog, mist, and so on, should be scored either as *Na* (nature) or written out in full.
Explosion	*Ex*	Involving percepts of an actual explosion, occurring most commonly to Card IX, as an atomic explosion or blast. The scoring determinant for inanimate movement *(m)* should always accompany this scoring. Percepts of an explosion "aftermath," such as "a blast has just occurred and things are lying all over the place," should be scored for other content or written out in complete form.

NOTE: From Exner, J.E. *The Rorschach: A Comprehensive System*, 1974, pp. 128–130. Reprinted by permission of John Wiley & Sons, Inc.

Table 6-5. Symbols and Criteria to Be Used in Scoring for Content. (continued)

Category	Symbol	Criterion
Fire	*Fi*	Involving percepts of actual fire, smoke associated with fire, burning candles, flame given off from a torch, and such. These percepts will ordinarily involve the determinant scoring of *m* to denote the inanimate movement of the "fire" association, but unlike the "explosion" content score, this will not always be the case. In other words, fire might be perceived as fire without movement being involved. The most common example of this occurs to the upper red areas (*D*2) of Card II, seen as "fire," with neither movement nor form reported.
Food	*Fd*	Involving the percept of any edible such as ice cream, fried shrimp, chicken legs, a piece of steak. The intent or meaning of the association must be clearly associated with "everyday" consumer produce, as in the instance of lettuce, cabbage, carrots, fried foods, etc., or must be presented in such a manner as to suggest that the object perceived is identified as a food substance, i.e., "Looks like a chicken like we used to have for Sunday dinner."
Geography	*Ge*	Involving percepts of any maps, specified or unspecified, i.e., a map of Sicily or a map of an island, peninsula, and continent. The percepts of *Ge do not* include the actual percept of definite or indefinite land masses which are "real" rather than representations. These type of percepts are scored as *Ls* (Landscape) or written out in rare instances.
Household	*Hh*	Involving percepts of interior household items, i.e., chairs, beds, bedposts, plates, silverware, and rugs. The scorer should be cautioned not to score "highly idiographic" percepts *Hh*, as for instance "a butcher knife," but rather to write out the full content so as to manifest the idiographic meaningfulness in the scoring.
Landscape	*Ls*	Involving percepts of landscapes or seascapes, neither of which would be scored as *Bt* or *Ge*. A tree or a bush might legitimately be scored as *Bt*, whereas "trees" or "a bunch of shrubs" are more ordinarily scored *Ls*. This category includes some underwater scenes where specific animals are not identified, or in some instances is a secondary score, as in Card X where a few specific animals may be cited but the bulk of the percept is left vague.

NOTE: From Exner, J.E. *The Rorschach: A Comprehensive System,* 1974, pp. 128–130. Reprinted by permission of John Wiley & Sons, Inc.

Table 6-5. Symbols and Criteria to Be Used in Scoring for Content. (continued)

Category	Symbol	Criterion
Nature	*Na*	Involving percepts of a wider natural scope than are included in *Bt, Ge,* or *Ls,* usually including sky, snow, water, raging sea, a storm, night, ice, rainbow, and such. In some responses, the idiographic representation of the content is intense or peculiar, as in "a tornado sweeping everything up in its path." The content score here is legitimately *Na;* however, a written out content scoring of "tornado" may be more appropriate.
Sex	*Sx*	Involving percepts of sex organs or activities related to sex function, i.e., intercourse, erect penis, menstruation, vagina, testes, and breasts.
X-ray	*Xy*	Involving percepts of x-ray, most of which pertain to bone structure, i.e., the x-ray of a pelvis, the x-ray of some bones, but may also involve x-rays of organs or organ-like structures, i.e., an x-ray of the stomach and an x-ray of the intestines. *Shading is always* involved in these percepts.
Vocational (supplementary)	*(Vo)*	Involving percepts which *may* be interpreted as related to the occupation of the subject. This scoring is *never* used as the primary or main content score but may be included as secondary or additional so as to alert the interpreter to a vocational or occupational percept.

NOTE: From Exner, J.E. *The Rorschach: A Comprehensive System,* 1974, pp. 132–133. Reprinted by permission of John Wiley & Sons, Inc.

Table 6-6. Popular Responses.

Card	Location	Criterion	% Nonpsy- chiatric Reporting	% Schizo- phrenic Reporting
I	W	Bat or butterfly. The response always involves the whole blot, and alterations in location or content have not been found to be popular.	86	32

NOTE: From Exner, J.E., *The Rorschach: A Comprehensive System,* 1974, pp. 132–133. Reprinted by permission of John Wiley & Sons, Inc.

Table 6-6. Popular Responses. (continued)

Card	Location	Criterion	% Nonpsy-chiatric Reporting	% Schizo-phrenic Reporting
I	D4	Human figure, ordinarily reported as female. The figure is described as a whole human or headless human. No other variations are P, nor is the lower half of this area (D3) described as a part of a human found to be P. Where the percept to D4 is of a male figure, the scoring of (P)* may be most appropriate.	48	13
II	D1	Animal forms, usually the heads of dogs or bears, however the frequency of the whole animal to this area is sufficient to warrant the scoring of P. If the content does not specify a dog or bear, the (P) score may be more appropriate. Note: the percept of whole humans or whole animals using the entire blot does not meet the P criterion but does approach that level (26%) and may be scored as (P).	39	9
III	D1 or D9	Two human figures, or representations thereof, such as dolls and caricatures. The scoring of P is also applicable to the percept of a single human figure to area D9. Human movement, as a determinant, is frequently associated with, but not necessary for, the scoring of P.	82	50
III	D3	Butterfly, designated by reason of form but sometimes involving color as a determinant.	44	12
IV	W or (W − D1)	Animal skin, or human figure dressed in animal skin or an appropriate variation therof, such as "in a fur coat." This category of popular response also includes the large "furry" animal. The proof of the P rests with the designation of the "furry" pelt or pelt-like covering.	38	16
IV	D6	Shoe or boot, seen separately or in association with an animal or human figure. The designation of the shoe or boot in the D2 area has not been discovered to be P.	44	12

NOTE: From Exner, J.E. *The Rorschach: A Comprehensive System*, 1974, pp. 128–130. Reprinted by permission of John Wiley & Sons, Inc.

*(P) is a refinement used for percepts which are similar to, but not identical with, those listed as P.

Table 6-6. Popular Responses. (continued)

Card	Location	Criterion	% Nonpsy- chiatric Reporting	% Schizo- phrenic Reporting
V	W	Bat or butterfly, the apex of the card upright or inverted. Variations of the content, such as moth, vulture, and eagle, are probably best scored as *(P)*.	91	28
VI	W or D1	Animal skin, hide, rug, or pelt.	68	24
VII	D1	Human heads or faces, ordinarily perceived as women or children. A *W* response involving the human percept typically notes the lower *D*4 portion of the blot as a content separate from the *Hd,* such as a rock, pedestal, and bush. Where the *D*4 is reported as part of the human figure, the scoring might better be *(P)*.	54	9
VIII	D1	Whole animal figure. This is the most frequently perceived common answer, the content varying considerably, e.g., bear, dog, rodent, fox, wolf, and coyote. All are scored as *P.* The *P* is also scored when the animal figure is reported as part of a *W* percept as in a family crest, seal, and emblem.	95	37
IX	D4	A human face or head, usually reported as male and frequently identified as T. Roosevelt or perceived as an infant. This percept occurs with the least frequency of all popular answers.	34	6
X	D1	Crab, lobster, or spider. In some instances, the object has greater specificity as in sand crab, daddy longlegs, and crawfish. Other variations of multilegged animals are not *P.*	57	26

NOTE: From Exner, J.E. *The Rorschach: A Comprehensive System,* 1974, pp. 132–133. Reprinted by permission of John Wiley & Sons, Inc.

Popular Responses

Rorschach popular or P scoring refers to the presence of frequently perceived responses. Although different systems have somewhat varying lists of populars, Exner (1974) has used the occurrence of at least once in every three protocols from nonpsychiatric populations as the cutoff for inclusion as a popular. Exner's list and description of popular responses are given in Table 6-6.

Quantitative Formulas

After the examinee's responses have been scored according to the locations, determinants, contents, and populars, they are then rearranged into quantitative formulas. These formulas reflect the proportions of, and comparisons between, various Rorschach factors. It is on the quantitative formulas that the primary interpretations are based. The following material illustrates the method for deriving the most frequently used formulas.

EB (Experience Balance or Erlebnistypus):

$$\frac{\text{Sum of Human Movement}}{\text{Sum of Weighted Color}} \quad \text{or} \quad \frac{\text{Sum } M}{\text{Sum Weighted } C}$$

The different weighting for C responses is based on $FC = 0.5$, $CF = 1.0$, and C or $Cn = 1.5$. All human movement responses are included in the formula whether or not they are the major determinant of the response.

EA (Experience Actual):

$$\text{Sum of Human Movement} + \text{Sum of Weighted Color}$$
$$\text{or}$$
$$\text{Sum } M + \text{Sum Weighted } C$$

eb (Experience Base):

$$\frac{\text{Sum of All Nonhuman Movement}}{\text{Sum Shading or Achromatic Features}} \quad \text{or} \quad \frac{\text{Sum } FM + m}{\text{Sum } Y + T + V + C'}$$

ep (Experience Potential):

$$\text{Sum of All Nonhuman Movement} + \text{Sum of All Shading or Achromatic Features}$$
$$\text{or}$$
$$\text{Sum } (FM + m) + \text{Sum } (Y + T + V + C')$$

FC/(CF I C). The ratio *FC/(CF + C)* indicates the total number of form dominated chromatic color responses as compared with the absolute number of color dominant chromatic responses. To calculate this formula, each of the chromatic color determinants is weighted equally as a 1, which is in contrast to the different weightings of sum *C* used in the *EB* and *EA*. *Cn* determinants are included in this formula since they are responses which are color dominant.

W:M. The ratio of *W* to *M* represents a comparison between the total number of whole responses and the total number of human movement responses.

W:D. The ratio *W:D* compares the total number of whole responses with the total number of common details.

L (Lambda)

$$\frac{\text{Pure Form Responses}}{\text{Non-pure Form Responses}} \quad \text{or} \quad \frac{\text{Sum Pure } F R\text{'s}}{\text{Sum Non-pure } F R\text{'s}}$$

In calculating Lambda, only responses involving form are used (*F, M, CF*, etc.) and not determinants without form (*C, C', T*, etc.).

$$\frac{\text{Sum of Form Plus and Form Ordinary Responses}}{\text{Sum of Pure Form Responses}} \quad \text{or} \quad \frac{\text{Sum } (F+\%) + (Fo)}{\text{Sum } F}$$

This formula refers only to pure form responses and is an indication of what proportion of good quality form responses (superior or ordinary) is present compared to all pure *F* responses.

X+%

$$\frac{\text{Sum of All Good } F \text{ Dominant Responses (+ and } o)}{\text{Total Number of Responses}}$$
$$\text{or}$$
$$\frac{\text{Sum } F \, (+ \text{ or } o)}{\text{Total } R}$$

X+% is an extension of *F+%* in that it is a measure of the degree to which good form is used in any response involving form (*FY, M, CF*, etc.). To calculate *X+%* the sum of all + and *o* responses involving form is divided by the total number of *R*. The total number of *R* is used as the denominator because where form is absent from a response (pure *C', Y*, etc.), it shows a disregard for form which can be seen as a poor use of the stimulus similar to a *F –* response.

A%

$$\frac{\text{Animal} + \text{Animal Detail}}{\text{Total Number of Responses}} \quad \text{or} \quad \frac{A + Ad}{R}$$

Afr **(Affective Ratio)**

$$\frac{\text{Sum of Responses to Last 3 Cards}}{\text{Sum of Responses to First 7 Cards}} \quad \text{or} \quad \frac{\text{Sum } R(\text{VIII} + \text{IX} + \text{X})}{\text{Sum } R(\text{I–VII})}$$

$(H + Hd)/(A + Ad)$

$$\frac{\text{Human} + \text{Human Detail}}{\text{Animal} + \text{Animal Detail}}$$

XRT **Achromatic**

$$\frac{\text{Sum of Reaction Times I, IV, V, VI, VII}}{5}$$

This formula refers to the average reaction time for the first response to the achromatic cards (Cards I, IV, V, VI, VII).

XRT **Chromatic**

$$\frac{\text{Sum of Reaction Times II, III, VIII, IX, X}}{5}$$

This formula refers to the average time for the first response to the chromatic cards (Cards II, III, VIII, IX, X).

INTERPRETATION

The following description of interpretive information is meant to serve as a quick reference guide to alert Rorschach interpreters to a potentially wide range of possible interpretive hypotheses. Even though the format is as concise as possible, interpreters should still be aware of the tremendous richness inherent in most Rorschach data. Effective interpreters should also have this richness reflected in the wide variety of possible interpretive hypotheses they generate. A mere labeling or simplistic "sign" approach should be avoided. Rather, clinicians must begin and end by continually being aware of the total overall configuration of the data. For example, the same number of *C* responses in two protocols can easily have entirely different meanings depending on the implications from, and interactions with, other aspects of the Rorschach data.

The typical sequence for Rorschach interpretation should follow the general conceptual model for testing developed by Maloney and Ward (1976) and discussed in Chapter 1. This requires that clinicians initially take a propositional stance towards the protocol (phase 2). The purpose of this stage is to develop as many tentative hypotheses as possible based on the quantitative data, verbalizations, and client history. The number and accuracy of these hypotheses will depend on the individual richness of the data as well as on the individual skill and creativity of the clinician. The final stage is the integration of the hypotheses into a meaningful and accurate description of the person (phase 4). This involves rejecting, modifying, or confirming previously developed hypotheses (phase 3). Once this is accomplished clinicians can then integrate the Rorschach interpretations into the overall report itself (phases 5, 6, and 7).

During the description of different interpretive hypotheses, there will be continual reference to "high" and "low" scores. These relative weightings are based on extensive normative data which have been accumulated on the Rorschach. For comparisons of scores on individual protocols with normative ratings, the clinician should refer to Appendix G and H.

Number of Responses

In using Exner's set of instructions, the mean for the total number of responses for nonpatients is 21.75 with a standard deviation of 5.1. However, different methods of administration can influence this number to a certain extent. For example, Ames, Metraux, Rodell, and Walker (1973) report an overall adult average of 26; Beck (1961) gives 32 for his adult mean; and both use instructions somewhat different from Exner's. Deviations from the normal range present the following possible interpretive hypotheses.

Low R (Less than 17). A low number of *R* suggests defensiveness, constriction, organicity, depression, or attempted malingering (Exner, 1974). A clinician cannot confirm any of these hypotheses based solely on the occurrence of a low number of *R*, but they are raised as possibilities. In order to confirm these hypotheses, factors from both within and outside the test must be used. A further caution is that percentages derived from a low *R* protocol can often be inaccurate or misleading and therefore have limited usefulness.

High R (Greater than 33). A significantly higher than average number of responses suggests several possibilities including an introversive character (Murstein, 1960; Wagner, 1971), above-average intelligence with a relatively high level of academic achievement (Beck, 1945; Goldfried, Stricker, and Weiner, 1971), and a high degree of creativity (Adams, Cooper, and Carrera, 1963; Dana and Cocking, 1968; Raychaudhuri, 1971). It can also suggest a high level of personal insight (Kagan, 1960) and good ego functioning including the ability to plan ahead, adequate impulse control, and the ability to tolerate stress (Goldfried et al., 1971; Klopfer and Davidson, 1962). Among persons with psychopathology, high *R* is found among manics and obsessive-compulsives (Alcock, 1963; Beck, 1945, 1951; Pope and Scott, 1967).

A high number of *R* is likely to alter the meaning of, or render useless, specific formulas. There is likely to be a higher proportion of *D* and *Dd* responses since the number of *W* responses is usually exhausted sooner. Pure *F* responses will also tend to increase in frequency, and there are usually relatively more *R* for Cards VIII and X, thus elevating the Affective Ratio *(Afr)*. Thus, interpretations based on the quantitative formulas derived from a high number of *R* should be treated with appropriate caution.

Location

In general, the area of the inkblot to which the examinees choose to respond is a reflection of the overall style in which they approach their world. This is especially true for the manner in which they confront uncertainties and ambiguities in their lives. For example, one person might perceive only the most obvious concrete aspects of a situation, whereas another might avoid important aspects of a stimulus by focusing on small details and neglecting dangerous, more significant issues. An analysis of Rorschach locations does not provide information regarding why people approach their world in a certain manner but rather is limited to a description of what their particular style is.

Rorschach locations can be divided into usual and unusual features depending on the area of the inkblot that is used. Frequently used locations, if they are within the normal number and of good quality, usually reflect good ties with reality, intelligence, ambition, good reasoning, and an ability to generalize. Unusual locations involving rarely used areas of the blot are associated with neurotic symptomatology such as fears, anxiety, and obsessive or compulsive tendencies. If there is an extreme use of unusual features, this may reflect more serious psychopathology.

Whole Response (*W*). Whereas whole responses occur with the greatest frequency in children from 3 to 4 years of age (Ames et al., 1971), there is a gradual decline in later childhood and adolescence until 25–30% of normal adult responses are wholes. The average adult ratio of whole:detail is approximately 1:2.

High W. Rorschach (1921) originally believed that a high number of *W* responses reflected a person's ability to organize and integrate his environment. However, subsequent research has modified this in that W responses do reflect intellectual activity but this activity can only be understood by looking at the quality of W responses (relative number of W+; Friedman, 1952) and the relative complexity of responses (Exner, 1974). In considering the complexity of responses, it should be noted that W occurs with greatest frequency for Cards V, I, IV, and VI, and lowest for Cards X, IX, III, and VIII (Beck, 1945). Thus, W responses for the latter cards require significantly greater organizational activity. If there are present both good quality responses and a high degree of organizing activity, then a high number of W responses would reflect good synthesizing and abstracting abilities (Smith, 1981), ambition (Schachtel, 1966), good ties with reality (Abrams, 1955; Levitt and Truuma, 1972), and excellent problem solving abilities (Beck, 1961; Rossi and Neuman, 1961).

Low W. Low W responses can reflect depression (Beck, 1960; Rapaport, Gill, and Shafer, 1968) or anxiety (Eichler, 1951). If the frequency, quality, and complexity are low, then more serious levels of maladjustment (Exner, 1974) are indicated, such as intellectual deterioration possibly related to brain damage (Goldfried et al., 1971) or mental retardation (Allison and Blatt, 1964).

Common Detail (D). The D response is generally an indication of the degree to which a person reacts to and perceives the obvious aspects of a situation (Rorschach, 1921). This is supported by normative data in which nonpsychiatric groups and outpatients gave 62 and 67% of their responses as D, whereas inpatient nonschizophrenics and inpatient schizophrenics gave 46 and 47% D responses, respectively (Exner, 1974). D tends to be most frequent for Card X (Exner, 1974).

High D. D is often high in persons who overemphasize the concrete and obvious aspects of situations (Beck, 1961; Klopfer, 1954). Such an emphasis may further suggest that they sacrifice the full use of their intellectual potential by merely focusing on the safe and obvious rather than probing into the more novel and unusual. This is sometimes reflected in the remitted schizophrenic who focuses on a relatively safe, conservative, and socially desirable response which is suggested by pre- and post-treatment D% changes from 40 to 73%, respectively (Murillo and Exner, 1973).

Where D+ is high, there is the likelihood of an excellent level of developmental functioning (Goldfried et al., 1971). On the other hand, if D is high but the quality of responses is low (v and –), a severe level of maladjustment is indicated (Exner, 1974).

Low D. Persons under stress show a decrease in D and a corresponding increase in Dd (Exner, 1974). Furthermore, low D can reflect inadequate perceptual habits (Klopfer, Ainsworth, Klopfer, and Holt, 1954) which may suggest brain damage (Reitan, 1955). The proportion of *D* is lowest in young children and gradually increases with age (Ames, Metraux, and Walker, 1974).

Unusual Detail *(Dd)*. The *Dd* response is considered to represent a pulling back from a person's environment by focusing on details rather than either perceiving the whole situation or noticing the more obvious elements of the environment. A clinician would expect the number of *Dd* responses to comprise approximately 5% of the total *R* for a normal person. However, for schizophrenics or severely impaired compulsives, this proportion can increase to 25% or more (Exner, 1974). When *Dd* is in good proportion to *W* and *D*, it reflects a healthy adjustment in which a person combines initiative with an appropriate ability to withdraw.

High Dd. Persons with high *Dd* scores reflect a need to pull back from the ambiguities which may be contained in a whole response. When this occurs in schizophrenics, it suggests an attempt to narrow their perceptions of their environment in order to make them more congruent with their inner world (Exner, 1974). If *Dd* perceptions are combined with movement, this gives further support to the hypothesis that the person's thought processes are impairing his perceptions (Exner, 1974).

Compulsives use *Dd* to focus on the details of a situation in an attempt to reduce their anxiety and exert more control over their perceptions. Their thought processes are not flexible enough to take in a sufficient number of whole responses. This rigidity becomes more exaggerated as the overall number of *Dd* responses increases and the size of each perception decreases.

Space *(S)*. A high number of *S* responses is associated with negativism and oppositional tendencies (Beck, 1961; Rapaport et al., 1968). If *S* responses also occur with poor form quality and/or poor primitive movements, a clinician should consider the presence of anger, hostility, and potential acting out (Exner, 1974). A moderate number of *S* responses, especially if combined with good form quality, may suggest a constructive expression of self-assertion (Klopfer et al., 1954; Piotrowski, 1957).

Confabulated Whole or Confabulated Detail *(DW, DdW, DdD)*. Confabulations occur when there is confusion and lack of definition associated with the boundary of a percept. The current research on confabulated responses is insufficient and tentative. However, Beck (1961) suggests that confabulations indicate illogical thinking and autistic associations. Exner (1974) further emphasizes that a high number of confabulations is a "unique and serious sign" and reflects gross intellectual dysfunction.

Determinants

Since the majority of research has been done on the determinants, they are frequently seen as the core of the Rorschach data. An analysis of the person's determinant scores shows the psychological activity that he engaged in while the response was being created. It examines his unique style of perception and thinking, and how these interact with one another. In general, research has isolated specific details of the determinants which could possibly lure the clinician into a rigid and potentially inaccurate "single sign" approach. Again, a Rorschach interpreter should focus on the interaction among a wide number of variables in order to modify, confirm, or reject tentative hypotheses derived from any single determinant score.

Form *(F).* The amount of pure F in a protocol has generally been used to indicate to what extent the person can remove affect from a situation. The presence of form in a response represents a certain degree of respect for the standards of one's environment and reflects intact reasoning abilities. It is seen both as related to attention and concentration and as an index of affective control or delay. The presence of a pure F response does not necessarily mean that no conflict is present, but rather that the person is able to suspend temporarily the affect associated with a conflict. Conversely, people in emotional turmoil are likely to produce a significantly lower number of pure form responses, reflecting their inability to remove their affect from their experience. (See Appendix F.)

High Pure F. Persons with a high pure F score either are highly defensive and constricted (Leavitt and Garron, 1982) or merely demonstrate a good ability to deliberately suspend or control their affect (Beck, 1945; Klopfer et al., 1954). When a person is in a more defensive position, the number of pure F responses increases. For example, pure F increases in populations of recovering schizophrenics (Goldman, 1960a), which may be the result of their attempting to cautiously give a socially acceptable answer in which they have to limit their affect. Also, pure F is higher among paranoid schizophrenics than other types of schizophrenics (Rapaport et al., 1968), reflecting their greater degree of organization and caution. Pure F increases for persons who have been given some prior knowledge of the purpose of the test (Henry and Rotter, 1956) or who are requested to respond as quickly as possible (Hafner, 1958).

After ECT, pure F is usually higher (Kelly, Margulies, and Barrera, 1941), which corresponds to patients' subjective reports of decreased affect. Also, alcoholics give more pure F responses than do psychopaths (Buhler and LeFever, 1947), and Leavitt and Garron (1982) have found an increase in $F\%$ in the protocols of patients having both psychological disturbances and lower back pain.

Low Pure F. If pure *F* is low, there is the likelihood that a person's level of turmoil is sufficiently high so that he cannot screen out his affective response to a situation. For example, acute schizophrenics who have difficulty reducing their level of affect also have a low number of pure *F* responses (Exner and Murillo, 1973). Likewise, certain characterological disorders (Buhler and LeFever, 1947) and organic disorders, in which there is difficulty controlling impulses, both have a low number of pure *F* responses (Exner, 1974).

Human Movement *(M).* Probably more research has been done on the *M* response than any other Rorschach variable. Most of this research is consistent in viewing *M* as reflecting inner fantasies which are connected to the outside world. More specifically, *M* represents the bridging of inner resources with reality or what might be described as "internalization of action" (Exner, 1974). *M* is also an inhibitor of outward behavior even though that inhibition may only be temporary. It has been associated with creativity (Dudek, 1968; Hersh, 1962; Richter and Winter, 1966) and introverted thinking (Kunce and Tamkin, 1981), and there is a close relationship between *M* and daydreaming (Dana, 1968; Page, 1957). Schulman (1953) has shown *M*'s relation to abstract thinking which involves both an active inner process and a delay in expressing behavior. Thus, *M* can be generally understood as involving deliberate inner experience. In its positive sense, *M* can indicate good ego functioning, ability to plan, impulse control, and ability to withstand frustration. In a more negative vein, it can suggest an overly developed fantasy life.

While interpreting *M,* it is important to look carefully at the different components of the response. For example, does the movement involve conflict or rather cooperation? The clinician should also consider other data both from within the test and external to it. Further elaboration regarding *M,* especially as it relates to the person's degree of control of impulses, can be derived by referring to the *EB* and *EA* ratios.

High M. High *M* responses, especially if *M*+, are associated with high I.Q. level (Abrams, 1955; Goldfried et al., 1971) and increased creativity (Dudek, 1968; Hersh, 1962; Richter and Winter, 1966). Dana (1968) has proposed that high *M* can represent any or all of several different psychological processes including fantasy, an accurate sense of time, intellect, creativity, delay, and certain aspects of interpersonal relations. Further studies include abstract thinking as an important correlate to *M* (Schulman, 1953) and an introverted thinking orientation (Kunce and Tamkin, 1981).

A relatively high number of *M* responses suggests that the individual is overly invested in his fantasy life, which might be similar to a "Walter Mitty syndrome." With a high number of *M*– responses, the person is likely to be deficient in social skills and to have poorly developed interpersonal relationships (Molish, 1967;

Weiner, 1966) or even psychotic symptoms (Phillips and Smith, 1953). Schmidt and Fonda (1954), for example, have found a high number of *M* responses in manic patients.

Low M. In many respects a low *M* response indicates the opposite of what is suggested by a high *M*. Persons, especially depressives, who have a difficult time using their inner resources, usually have low *M* scores (Ames, 1959; Beck, 1945). It is also associated with inflexible persons who have difficulty accepting and adjusting to change (Alcock, 1963; Goldfried et al., 1971; Rapaport et al., 1968). This inflexibility can at least in part be explained by a low level of empathy and a lack of imagination (Klopfer et al., 1954; Piotrowski, 1960, 1969). Since successful psychotherapy involves both flexibility and a relatively active inner life, low *M* is indicative of a poor prognosis (Goldfried et al., 1971; Klopfer et al., 1954).

Animal Movement *(FM).* Whereas human movement responses serve as a mediation between the inner and outer environment, animal movement reflects more unrestrained emotional impulses in which there is less ego control. The impulses are more urgent and more conscious, and are seeking to be gratified. This is reflected in the higher number of *FM*'s in children (Ames et al., 1971) and the aged (Klopfer et al., 1956), and it correlates positively with MMPI scales which measure irresponsibility, aggressiveness, and distractibility (Thompson, 1948). Whereas human movement responses involve delay, animal movements do not.

High FM. A high number of *FM* responses suggests persons who are governed by their needs and urges. They generally have a difficult time delaying gratification and therefore rarely plan towards long-term goals (Exner, 1974). Typically, they will be highly defensive, using intellectualization, rationalization, regression, and substitution as their primary means of reducing anxiety (Haan, 1964). If the *FM* responses are aggressive, it is more likely that they will be assaultive (Sommer and Sommer, 1958). The general overall theme of high *FM* responses is the unrestrained expression of emotional impulses.

Low FM. Low *FM* reflects persons who are overly inhibited in expressing their emotions and may deny their basic needs (Klopfer and Davidson, 1962). For example, Ames, Metraux, Rodell, and Walker (1974) have associated low *FM* with a decreased energy level in children.

Inanimate Movement *(m).* The number of inanimate movement responses provides an index of the extent to which persons are experiencing drives or life events which are beyond their ability to control. The drives reflected by *m* are ones which threaten peoples' adjustment in that they are helpless to effectively deal with them (Klopfer et al., 1954). This helplessness is usually related to interpersonal activities (Hertz, 1976; Klopfer et al, 1954; Piotrowski, 1957, 1960). For example, Exner (1974) has found one or more m responses in the records of both in- and outpatient schizophrenics, and Piotrowski and Schreiber (1952) found no m scores in the records of successfully treated patients. The number of m responses is also more frequent with juvenile delinquents, to the extent that by 16 years of age an average of 1 per record is perceived (Majumber and Roy, 1962). The view that m represents threat from the external world is supported by the observation that sailors at sea create significantly more m during severe storms than during normal conditions (Shalit, 1965).

High m. The presence of m should serve as a warning sign to indicate that there is the marked presence of conflict and tension. Subjects probably see themselves as surrounded by threatening persons and are unable to reconcile themselves with their environment. In order to gain a more complete understanding of the individual meaning of m, clinicians should investigate the possible resources and the characteristic means of resolving conflict by looking at M, sum C, frequency of D and S, and the accuracy of their perceptions as reflected in $F+\%$ and $X+\%$.

Color — Chromatic *(C, CF, FC, Cn)*. The manner in which color is handled reflects the style in which people deal with emotions. If color dominates *(C, CF, Cn)*, then their affect is likely to be poorly controlled and disorganized. In such cases, affect is disruptive, and the persons would usually be emotional, labile, and overreactive. If the responses are more dominated by form *(FC)*, affect will be more delayed, controlled, and organized. For example, Gill (1966) demonstrated that subjects who could effectively delay their responses in a problem solving task had a higher number of *FC*'s in their protocols whereas those who had difficulty delaying their responses had more *CF* and *C* responses. It has also been shown that there is a positive correlation between individuals having color dominated responses and independent measurements of impulsiveness (Gardner, 1951). Furthermore, the chromatic cards produce a greater frequency of aggressive, passive, and undesirable contents than do the achromatic cards (Crumpton, 1956).
have between a 3:1 and a 4:1 ratio of form dominated color to color dominated responses $[FC/(CF + C)]$. This is contrasted with an average outpatient ratio of 1:1.5, nonschizophrenic patients of 1:1, and schizophrenics of 1:2 (Exner, 1974). Pure C responses are predominant in the protocols of very young children as is color naming (Ames et al., 1974; Rabin and Beck, 1950).

High C and Cn. Individuals with a high proportion of color dominated responses typically have little regard for the adaptiveness of their expressions and discharge their emotions in an impulsive manner (Gardner, 1951). This suggests that a person's higher cognitive abilities have been suspended or possibly overwhelmed by affective impulses. Storment and Finney (1953) were able to differentiate between assaultive and nonassaultive patients based on the assaultive patients having a higher number of poor quality color responses. Likewise, Townsend (1967) found a higher level of aggressiveness in adolescents who produced a greater than average number of *CF* responses combined with an absence of human movement. In general, a high number of color dominant responses suggests that the person is more labile, suggestible (Brennan and Reichard, 1943; Linton, 1954; Steisel, 1952), sensitive, and irritable (Allen, 1954; Shapiro, 1960).

Color naming suggests that the person is giving a concrete response to the stimuli, which is primitive and poorly conceptualized. Although research is inconclusive, Piotrowski (1937) considered it to be a sign of organic involvement, which is supported somewhat by the finding that many brain-damaged subjects show an increased interest in color and seem to be more "stimulus bound" in their perception of it (Goldstein and Sheerer, 1941; Schilder, 1953).

Low C and CF.   An absence of *C* and *CF* occurs more frequently with depressed persons (Fisher, 1951; Kobler and Steil, 1953) and those with a low level of spontaneity who consistently dampen and overcontrol their emotional expression (Costello, 1958). If other suicidal indicators are present, a low color dominant protocol may give additional support to the presence of suicidal tendencies (Goldfried et al., 1971). Low *C* and *CF* responses from schizophrenics can be a good sign for successful treatment (Stotsky, 1952).

High FC.   A moderately high number of *FC*'s can indicate a good level of integration between controlling emotions and appropriately expressing them (Beck, 1945; Klopfer et al., 1954; Pope and Scott, 1967). Typically, this level of *FC*'s indicates that individuals have the ability to develop good rapport with others (Allison et al., 1968; Schafer, 1954) and can learn under stress (Phillips and Smith, 1953). The prognosis for therapy is good (Goldfried et al., 1971) because they can experience emotions, yet also conceptualize and give form to the expression of these emotions. Beck (1945) has stated that a moderately high number of *FC*'s indicates that schizophrenia is unlikely. In children, it may reflect the effects of overtraining with a corresponding decrease in natural spontaneity (Klopfer et al., 1954; Shapiro, 1960). Within adult populations, it may also reflect overcompliance and a dependent personality (Schafer, 1954).

Low FC.   Low *FC* suggests poor emotional control (Klopfer et al., 1954) which is likely to negatively affect interpersonal relationships (Piotrowski, 1957; Schafer, 1948). This can also indicate anxiety states (Rapaport et al., 1968) and gives support to a hypothesis of schizophrenia (Beck, 1945; Thiesen, 1952) if other indicators of schizophrenia such as poor quality responses are present.

Color — Achromatic (C, C'F, FC'). Achromatic color responses constitute one of the least researched areas of the Rorschach. However, it has been theorized that C' responses reflect constrained, internal, and painful affects (Klopfer, 1938). In other words, there is a dampened emotional expressiveness in which the person is cautious and defensive. Exner has referred to C' as the "psychological equivalent of biting your tongue." Most Rorschach systematizers have consistently used C' as an index of depression (Klopfer, 1938; Piotrowski, 1957; Rapaport et al., 1968). In considering the meaning of achromatic color responses, a clinician should look at the relative influence of form. If form is dominant (FC'), then there is likely to be definition and organization to the affect with a stronger ability to delay the behavior. On the other hand, dominant C' responses suggest the immediate presence of painful emotions.

The average number of achromatic color responses for normals is 0.6. In contrast to this are outpatients who have an average of 1.3 per record and schizophrenics with an average of 1.2 (Exner, 1974).

High C'. C' occurs most frequently among those patients who constrain their emotions such as psychosomatics, obsessive-compulsives, and depressives (Exner, 1974). The pain and constraint associated with these emotions may adversely affect the person's overall level of adjustment. An absence of shading responses combined with a large proportion of C' responses has been suggested as predictive of suicidal acts (Exner, 1974).

Texture (Shading; T, TF, FT). Texture responses represent painful emotional experiences combined with needs for supportive interpersonal relationships (Beck, 1945, 1968, Klopfer et al., 1954). Persons with a high number of texture responses reach out although they do so in a guarded and cautious manner (Hertz, 1976). If form plays a relatively insignificant role and texture is predominant, subjects tend to feel overwhelmed with painful experiences which would probably be sufficiently intense to disrupt their ability to adapt. Conversely, if form dominates (FT), not only is the pain likely to be more controlled but also the need for supportive contact from others would be of primary concern (Beck, 1968; Klopfer et al., 1954). Coan (1956) has suggested that a combination of movement and texture responses relates to inner sensitivity and empathy. If chromatic color and texture occur together, the subjects' behaviors would not only be less mature in seeking affection, but would also be more direct and unconstrained (Exner, 1974).

Responses in which texture dominates show an increase through childhood, reaching a maximum by 15 years of age and gradually subsiding over the next few years until a form dominated texture response is most characteristic in late adolescence and adulthood (Ames, et al., 1971). Kallstedt (1952) hypothesizes that this is due to the greater personal and sexual vulnerability of mid-adolescence. Nonpsychiatric populations average 1.4 texture responses per record whereas psychiatric populations average 2 or more per record (Exner, 1961). They usually appear ten times more frequently on Cards IV and VI than the other cards (Exner, 1961).

High T or TF. High scorers for *T* or *TF* are characterized as having intense needs for affection and dependency. This might result in their being overly sensitive in personal relationships to the extent that they may have a difficult time in reconciling the intensity of these needs with what they can realistically expect from their relationships.

Low T. The absence of any *T* responses may suggest an emotional "impoverishment" in which the person has ceased to look for meaningful emotional relationships (Exner, 1974). For example, inpatient depressives have the lowest average number of texture responses but the highest number of diffuse shading responses (*Y;* Exner, 1974). Likewise, psychosomatic patients give fewer *T*'s than other types of patients (Brown, 1953) which would correspond with their constrained expression of affect. In general, *T, Y,* and *C'* all represent an "irritating emotional experience" such as anxiety, tension, apprehension, and internal discomfort (Exner, 1978).

Dimensionality (Shading; *V, VF, FV*). Rorschach systematizers have generally considered dimensionality, especially pure *V,* to represent a painful process of self-examination in which the person creates a sense of distance from himself in order to introspect (Klopfer and Davidson, 1962). This introspection usually involves depression and a sense of inferiority. However, if the *V* responses are dominated by form, introspection is still suggested, but the process is unlikely to be emotionally painful. This is in contrast to the negative type of self-examination associated with pure *V.* Even a single pure *V* response in a Rorschach protocol can be an important indicator.

Within normal populations, *V* responses occur on the average of 0.36 per record. On the other hand, inpatient nonschizophrenics (mostly depressives) average 1.89, while inpatient schizophrenics and nonpsychotic outpatients score 0.64 and 1.13, respectively (Exner, 1974). Phillips and Smith (1953) have found *V* to be rare in the protocols of children and the aged.

High V. If pure *V* responses are created by depressed patients, this indicates a deep level of self-critical introspection (Klopfer and Kelly, 1942). Stutterers also produce more pure *V* responses (Light and Amick, 1956), as do alcoholics

(Buhler and LeFever, 1947), which reflects the painful self-criticism that usually occurs in these patient groups. V responses have also been suggested as an index of suicidal risk (Exner, 1974), although for adolescent females this response suggests a favorable prognosis for psychotherapy (Bradway, Lion, and Corrigan, 1946). With high $FM + m$, $C + CF$ greater than FC, or a high number of $F-$ responses, the introspection is of a self-destructive nature, and the chance that the individual will act on it also increases (Exner, 1974).

Low V. A low V is usually a positive sign, and the presence of a single form dominated V merely represents the ability to introspect (Exner, 1974). Although there may be a certain degree of pain involved with the introspection, the more important fact is that the resulting information can be integrated and eventually used productively.

Shading (General-Diffuse; Y, YF, FY). Klopfer et al. (1954) and Beck (1945) have described Y as representing a sense of helplessness and withdrawal which is frequently accompanied by anxiety and is often a response to ambiguity. Beck (1945) further elaborates that subjects are experiencing psychological pain and have also resigned themselves to their situation. The same general rule for looking at the influences of form with dimensionality (V), texture (T), and color (C, C') also applies for shading. When F is dominant, subjects are more able to delay their behavior, and their experience is more controlled, organized, and integrated. This ability to delay behavior also gives them time to mobilize their resources. When Y is dominant, there is a much greater sense of being over-whelmed. Although these individuals are characteristically withdrawn, any expression of pain and helplessness is direct. Since there is little ability to delay their impulses, they do not have enough time to mobilize their resources.

Within the general population, 86% of people give at least 1 Y (Y, YF, or FY) response. Schizophrenics give more Y's than nonpatients and outpatients, and nonschizophrenic patients give twice the number of Y's that normals do (Exner, 1974). In order to accurately understand the meaning of Y responses, the clinician should look for other indicators of coping. In particular, these might include the number and manner in which pure form is used, the quality of organization, and the number of human movement responses. If there is a high number of Y and these "coping indicators" are absent, the person is likely to be overwhelmed and will probably be unable to adapt or respond effectively (Exner, 1974).

High Y. A high number of Y is associated with anxiety (Beck, 1961; Klopfer and Davidson, 1962) and a constrained expression of emotions, even though the experience of these emotions may be direct (Salmon, Arnold, and Collyer, 1972). It is more frequent in the protocols of depressed patients and outpatients

(Exner, 1978). High Y is also associated with a sense of resignation to life events and an attempt to create distance between oneself and the environment (Elstein, 1965). Y is higher in alcoholics (Buhler and LeFever, 1947) and increases during experimentally induced stress (Cox and Sarason, 1954; Eichler, 1951).

Low Y. Since ambiguity is purposefully built into the test situation, it is expected that some Y, usually *FY,* will occur in any protocol. The absence of Y suggests an extremely indifferent attitude towards ambiguity (Exner, 1974).

Content

The different content categories have generally been regarded as information relating to a person's needs, interests, preoccupations, and social interactions. Several researchers have found positive correlations between a large variety of contents and intelligence (Paulker, 1963). They have also shown that whereas a high variety in content is associated with intellectual flexibility, a low variety suggests intellectual constriction and rigidity. Persons' occupational interests are often represented in a higher number of contents relating to their specific career choice. For example, biologists and medical personnel usually give a higher number of anatomy responses than the general population (Exner, 1974). This may merely indicate that the person has an interest in his career, or it could also suggest that a person is overconcerned with his career to the extent that he neglects other areas of his life, perhaps even impairing his overall level of adjustment. For example, physicists who see only nature contents may be using a preoccupation with their careers as a means of withdrawing from interpersonal relationships (Exner, 1974).

While interpreting Rorschach content, it is important to look at the variety of contents, the number of each content, and their overall configuration, as well as the implications other Rorschach factors may have for the meaning of the content scorings. It is usually essential to consider the age of the subject and to use age-appropriate norms. For example, children usually have significantly fewer human and human detail responses than adults, and the variety of their contents is also lower (Ames et al., 1974). Another important consideration is to study contents relating to aggressiveness (fire, explosions, etc.), facial features, and orality. Although the focus of this chapter is on a quantitative approach to the Rorschach, such considerations can also be extremely important in conducting a more qualitative analysis.

Human and Human Detail (*H* and *Hd*). Human responses constitute one of the most thoroughly researched contents. Beck (1961), in general agreement with other researchers, has found that *H* and *Hd* gradually increase with age until the median for 10-year-old children is from 16 to 18%. This remains unchanged through adolescence until the overall adult proportion of 17%. Exner (1974) found that whereas adult nonpatient $H + Hd$ responses were 19%, adult outpatients and schizophrenics only scored 13%. He also demonstrated that the ratio of human to human detail ($H:Hd$) for nonpatients was 3:1. In contrast to this were schizophrenics whose average ratio was approximately 1:1 and outpatients whose ratio was 2:1. Molish (1967) suggests that when there is an increase in Hd compared to H, the subject is prone to use constricted defenses. Others have theorized that it suggests intellectualization, compulsiveness, and a preoccupation with the self that restricts the degree of contact with others (Klopfer and Davidson, 1962). Beck (1945) associates high Hd with anxiety, depression, and a low intellectual level.

High H. A high number of human contents occurs with individuals who have a wide interest in people (Beck, 1968), are more likely to have high self-esteem (Fisher, 1962), and possess greater intelligence (Beck, 1968; Rawls and Slack, 1968). A higher H content has been consistently found to be associated with a greater likelihood of successful psychotherapeutic treatment (Goldfried et al., 1971; Goldman, 1960; Halpern, 1940). As might be expected, human responses are more frequent in the records of psychologists and anthropologists (Roe, 1952).

Low H. An unusually low number of H contents suggests a low level of empathy and a withdrawal from interpersonal relationships (Allison et al., 1968; Kahn and Giffen, 1960). The overall $H\%$ has been found to be lower for schizophrenics than for normals (Duran, Pechoux, Escafit, and Davidow, 1949; Sherman, 1952). The prognosis for successful psychotherapy with low H scorers is poor (Piotrowski and Bricklin, 1961), and if this is accompanied by a low number of M responses, their termination from therapy is likely to be abrupt probably due to a high level of anxiety combined with a low intellectual level (Affleck and Mednick, 1959; Rapaport et al., 1968).

Animal and Animal Detail (A and Ad). Most of the literature indicates that animal content is associated with the obvious aspects of adaptiveness and the most concrete features of reality testing (Draguns, Haley, and Phillips, 1967). Since animal contents are the easiest to perceive, their presence suggests that examinees are using routine and predictable ways of responding. Conversely, a low number of animal responses suggests highly individualistic persons who see their world in their own personal and unique ways.

Animal responses occur more frequently than any other content category and comprise 38–48% of the normal adult record (Beck, Rabin, Thieson, Molish, and Thetford, 1950; Cass and McReynolds, 1951; Wedemeyer, 1954), with a slightly higher amount for children (Beck, 1961). Schizophrenics and outpatients average 31 and 41%, respectively, whereas depressives score much higher with an average of 41% per protocol (Exner, 1974). Other studies have found that $A\%$ is low for manics (Kuhn, 1963; Schmidt and Fonda, 1954) and high for alcoholics (Buhler and LeFever, 1947).

High A.   A high A suggests a predictable, stereotyped manner of approaching the world (Klopfer and Davidson, 1962; Levitt and Truumaa, 1972) often associated with depression and the use of constrictive and conforming defenses (Beck, 1945, 1960). There has been some evidence to suggest that high A responses are a sign of brain damage (Goldfried et al., 1971), but variables from without as well as within the test should be carefully considered before making this diagnosis.

Low A.   Persons who are spontaneous, nonconforming, unpredictable, and of higher intelligence often have a low number of A responses (Allen, 1954; Kahn and Giffen, 1960).

Anatomy (An).   The significance of anatomy responses has also been well researched, and along with human and animal contents, anatomy is one of the most frequently occurring responses. Beck (1961), for example, found that it occurs on an average of 1.5 responses per normal protocol. Anatomy content has an obvious connection with concern for the body, and the literature supports this connection in that it occurs more frequently for psychosomatic patients than for neurotics (Shatin, 1952). Anatomy responses also occur with greater frequency with the onset of psychological difficulties related to pregnancy (Zolliker, 1943). As might be expected, they occur more often in the protocols of biologists and persons with medical training (Dorken, 1954; Roe, 1952; Schactel, 1966). A review of the literature by Draguns et al. (1967) reveals that anatomy content can serve as an index of the degree of involvement persons have in their inner fantasy life or may reflect physical changes such as illness, puberty, or pregnancy. It has also been suggested that anatomy content is associated with withdrawal from the environment and obsessive defenses (Exner, 1974).

It is important to take into consideration the relative proportion of anatomy to x-ray responses. Although anatomy responses are generally low for both psychiatric and nonpsychiatric groups, a combined anatomy and x-ray score allows for a more clear differentiation between the two. Whereas, the combined *An* and x-ray responses for a nonpsychiatric group give an average of only 0.6 response, outpatients give 1.5, schizophrenics 1.4, and nonschizophrenic patients give 1.8 responses which, for the last group, accounts for 9% of their total number of responses (Exner, 1974). Anatomy responses occur most frequently for Cards VIII and IX, and x-ray responses are most frequent for Card I. Exner (1974) suggests that x-ray responses reflect a concern with the self which is painful but that subjects are attempting to deal with this pain by distancing themselves from it or at least disguising their responses to it. On the other hand, anatomy responses reflect a process in which the person focuses more directly on the stress and there is more of a direct emotional release.

High An.   High *An* responses are associated with hypochondriasis (Carnes and Bates, 1971; Wagner, 1973) and psychosomatic conditions (Shatin, 1952). In congruence with these disorders, there are likely to be intellectualizing defenses (Allison et al., 1968), anxiety (Wagner, 1961), obsessive traits, and withdrawal (Exner, 1974). High *An* may also reflect a concern with physical functioning due to aging (Ames et al., 1973) or career choice (Dorken, 1954), and it can reflect a greater than average level of narcissism in patients going through a physical rehabilitation program (Levi, 1951). Schizophrenic patients sometimes give an unusually high number (8 or more) of anatomy responses (Brar, 1970; Goldfried et al., 1971).

Botany, Geography, and Nature.   Either the specific combination of botany, geography, and nature or a high content score of any one of these has been associated with passivity or immaturity unless it can be more appropriately explained by occupational choice (Draguns et al., 1967). Nature and landscape responses can suggest superior intelligence in normal people (Piotrowski, 1957) and, in psychiatric populations, feelings of ineffectiveness and inferiority (Phillips and Smith, 1953).

Food and Water.   Although the research on the significance of food and water is inconclusive and somewhat contradictory, there is some evidence that a high number of food responses occurs in persons who are "emotionally starved" (Griffith, 1961). Water landscapes occur more frequently in the records of alcoholics (Griffith, 1961; Piotrowski, 1957) and in dependent persons with feelings of insecurity and helplessness (Phillips and Smith, 1953).

Sex and Blood.   The combination of sex and blood is more frequently found among persons whose ability to control their impulses is impaired by a psychotic condition (Draguns et al., 1967). A higher number of sexual answers occurs in those who have a newly acquired sense of independence (Draguns et al., 1967), persons in psychoanalysis (Klopfer and Davidson, 1962), and artists (Rawls and Slack, 1968).

Popular Responses

The number of popular responses reflects the subjects' degree of similarity to most people, the extent to which they conform to social standards, and the relative ease with which they can be influenced in interpersonal relationships. Persons who reject conventional modes of thinking give a significantly lower number of populars than those who are conforming and relatively conventional. With Exner's (1974) scoring system (see Table 6-6), the average number of P responses for nonpsychiatric subjects is 6.45. Outpatients and nonschizophrenic patients, likewise, give approximately 7 per record, whereas inpatient schizophrenics give 3 or less, characterological disorders give an average of 5.3, but depressives have a mean score of 7.0 (Exner, 1974).

High P. High P suggests that the subject is experiencing anxiety related to a fear of making mistakes and, therefore, clings to common perceptions as a means of achieving approval. These individuals can be described as conventional, overconforming, guarded, and frequently, depressed (Exner, 1974; Levitt and Truumaa, 1972; Weiner, 1961).

Low P. The lowest number of P responses is given by inpatient schizophrenics, which is consistent with their poor contact with reality. They can be described as poorly adjusted, detached, aloof from their environment, and unable to see the world as others see it. Molish (1967) has suggested that if neurotic subjects, especially obsessive-compulsives, have low P, then the possibility of latent schizophrenia should be investigated. Patients diagnosed as having character disorders also have low P which reflects their rejection of conventionality and their lack of conformity.

Since populars are extremely common in Cards I, III, V, and VIII, the absence of them from these cards is significant in that it more strongly suggests the trends just discussed. However, the assumption that low P responses alone confirm maladjustment should be approached with caution. For subjects who have good form quality ($F+\%$ and $X+\%$) and whose organizational activity is also good, it is more likely that they are creative individuals who are avoiding common, ordinary perceptions and want to extend their imagination. If organization and form quality are poor, then there is a high likelihood that the psychopathological dimensions are more predominant.

Quantitative Formulas

The quantitative formulas give the relationships between the determinants, locations, contents, and populars. Thus, the formulas provide a more extensive elaboration beyond these variables, and it is from them that some of the most important elements of interpretation are derived.

Experience Balance or Erlebnistypus [*EB*; (*M:C*)]. The Experience Balance formula or Erlebnistypus was originally devised by Rorschach and is the ratio between the sum of all M responses compared with the sum of all weighted color responses ($FC = 0.5$, $CF = 1.0$, pure C and $Cn = 1.5$). Rorschach systematizers and researchers have come to view the Experience Balance ratio as the extent to which a person is internally oriented as opposed to being more externally directed and behaviorally responsive to outside stimuli. Although the EB ratio is usually relatively stable, it can temporarily change during times of stress or become more permanently altered during the course of successful psychotherapy (Exner, 1974). In an extensive literature review, Singer (1960) described the two sides of the ratio as representing dimensions of "constitutional temperament." These dimensions are introversives (higher M scores) who have a preference for internal experience as opposed to extratensives (higher C scores) who are more prone to activity and external expression. The introversive can more effectively delay his behavior, whereas the extratensive is more emotional and is likely to discharge his affect into some form of external behavior. Both types respond differently to stress and to problem solving tasks (Molish, 1967). It should be emphasized that in their moderate forms, neither one is any more or any less effective than the other nor is either one more prone to psychopathology (Molish, 1967).

Higher M (Introversives). Rorschach stated that persons with a relatively higher number of M responses were more oriented towards using their inner fantasy life. Thus, they are directed inward and use their inner experience to satisfy most of their basic needs. This is not so much an absolute necessity as, rather, a preference. In fact, these individuals may, on a more superficial level, even appear to be extroverted. Researchers have found them to be cautious, deliberate, submissive (Kurz, 1963; Rosenthal, 1962), and less physically active than persons scoring relatively higher on the C side of the ratio (Mukerji, 1969).

Higher C (Extratensives). Persons who have relatively lower M responses and higher C's (extratensives) tend to use external interactions as the most important means of satisfying their needs. They characteristically direct their energy towards the outside world. Extratensives are usually spontaneous and assertive, but also have difficulty delaying their responses (Alcock, 1963; Palmer, 1970; Piotrowski, 1957, 1960). In children, higher C scores may represent a lack of self-assurance (Palmer, 1970).

M and C Equal (Ambitents). If M and C are equal, the persons are more likely to be flexible during interpersonal relationships, but they are also less sure of themselves during problem solving and tend to vacillate (Exner, 1978). They usually need to verify every sequence in the solution of a problem at hand and do not profit as much from mistakes as either the introversive or the extratensive (Exner, 1978). Whereas the latter types are more sure of which response style to take in approaching an ambiguous situation, they have a liability when flexibility is required (Exner, 1978). Thus, the ambitent is more able to adjust in situations that require flexibility. Unusually high scores on both M and C suggest a manic condition (Beck, 1960; Singer, 1960).

Experience Actual [EA; (M + C)]. Whereas the Experience Balance ratio emphasizes the assessment of a person's type, the Experience Actual indicates the "volume of organized activity" (Beck, 1960). The M side of the formula shows the extent to which persons are able to organize their inner lives, and the C side indicates the extent to which emotions are available. The emphasis here is that both the M and C represent organized activity, which is contrasted with the disorganization associated with nonhuman movement (FM, m) and responses related to the gray-black features of the blot (T, V, Y).

For the most part, the ratio between M and C is remarkably stable, yet the sum of M and C can sometimes fluctuate on a daily basis which parallels the effects of changes in mood (Erginel, 1972). It has been further noted that after successful treatment, M and C typically both increase (Beck, 1960; Piotrowski and Shreiber, 1952), indicating that there is a greater increase in the degree of organization of the person's inner life and that more emotions have also become available. In fact, Exner (1974) found that EA increases significantly more for patients who improved in therapy than for those who showed little or no improvement. Furthermore, persons who underwent an insight-oriented treatment showed much more of an increase in EA than those in a treatment that emphasized a combination of support and environmental manipulation (Exner, 1974). This is consistent with the goal of insight therapy which focuses on helping patients to understand and organize their internal resources.

Experience Base [eb; (FM + m)/(Y + T + V + C')]. The Experience Base ratio was originally suggested by Klopfer et al. (1954) and later developed in its present form by Exner (1974). The nonhuman movement side of the ratio reflects tendencies to respond in ways that are not completely acceptable to the ego. These tendencies appear out of control, impinge on the individual, and are disorganized (Klopfer and Davidson, 1962). The opposite side of the ratio, which is a sum of the responses relating to the gray-black features of the blot, is a reflection of the pain and disharmony the person is feeling as a result of unresolved stress. The eb ratio indicates which of these two areas of functioning is more predominant. If the eb is small on both sides, it suggests that the person is not experiencing very much pain and that his needs are well organized.

Experience Potential [ep; (FM + m) + (T + V + C')]. Experience Potential is the sum of the nonhuman movement responses and all responses relating to the gray-black features of the inkblot. These are all responses reflecting that the person's functioning is disorganized and that there are forces acting on the person which he feels are beyond his control. Thus, the *ep* sum is an index of a person's degree of disorganization and helplessness. Persons scoring high on *ep* have a low frustration tolerance, and it is difficult for them to be persistent, even in meaningful tasks (Exner, 1978).

Important information can be obtained by comparing the amount of organization the person has as represented by *EA* with how much chaos and helplessness he experiences as represented by *ep*. Normal populations usually have a higher *EA* than *ep*, whereas psychiatric populations have a higher *ep* than *EA* (Exner, 1974). Exner (1978) has suggested that the ratio between *EA* and *ep* can provide an index of the degree to which a person can tolerate frustration. This difficulty dealing with frustration would be primarily due to high-scoring *ep* persons having a limited ability to process and mediate cognitive information (Wiener-Levy and Exner, 1981). As would be expected, a correlate of successful psychotherapy is that there is a decrease in *ep* and a corresponding increase in *EA*, which suggests that at least some of the patient's activity has become more organized (Exner, 1974). Exner (1974) found that subjects who were rated as unimproved after therapy also showed little change in their Rorschach responses in that their *ep* still remained high in relation to *EA*. In another study, Exner (1974) demonstrated that most persons in successful insight therapy had an increase in *EA* compared to *ep*, which was significantly greater than that in therapy emphasizing support or environmental manipulation. In fact, the latter forms of therapy showed no or little change in the *ep:EA* ratio. This suggests that patients in successful insight therapy were able to either neutralize or reorganize the forces which were "acting on" them.

Whole: Movement (*W:M*). The *W:M* ratio is a rough formula which, at the present time, is somewhat lacking in research. It can be generally understood by reconsidering that the *W* response is an indicator of the degree to which subjects can effectively organize and conceptualize their environments. It is an effort to encompass and include a number of different details in one coherent response. Although *M* represents the degree of investment subjects have in their fantasy lives, it also suggests how effectively they can bridge their inner resources with external reality and perform abstract thinking. Thus, the *W:M* ratio gives a rough comparison between a person's aspiration level as represented by *W* and his actual capability as represented by *M* (Exner, 1974). Nonpatients usually score between 2:1 and 3:1. If a person has a *W:M* ratio of 3:1 or more, his need to achieve would be expected to be greater than his actual ability. On the other hand, a ratio of less than 2:1 suggests that the individual is performing below his actual ability level (Klopfer et al., 1954) but that he may have good creative potential (Klopfer and Davidson, 1962).

FC/(CF + C). The ratio of form dominated color responses to color dominant responses provides a measure of the degree of control a person has over his impulses. If form is predominant (3:1 or greater), it strongly suggested that the person has good control over his impulses and satisfying interpersonal relationships (Exner, 1969, 1974; Klopfer and Davidson, 1962). Exner (1978), for example, has found that schizophrenics who have *FC* responses greater than *CF* + *C* have a better response to psychotherapy with less likelihood of a relapse. The high form suggests that they can put an accurate, reality-oriented interpretation on their perceptions. However, if there are no color dominant responses (no *CF* + *C*), the person will be overly constricted and have little contact with his emotions (Exner, 1978). If the *CF* + *C* side of the ratio is high (2:1 or less), it suggests a weak control over one's impulses in which there may be aggressive acting out, perhaps consistent with a narcissistic personality (Exner, 1969; Klopfer and Davidson, 1962). The perception of both internal and external events will typically be distorted and inaccurate, as will the responses to these events (Exner, 1974). The number of pure *C* responses increases with pathological groups, as indicated by only 26% of nonpatients giving pure *C*'s in contrast to 53% of depressives, 55% of outpatients, 71% of schizophrenics, and 79% of character-disordered patients (Exner, 1978).

Whole:Detail (*W:D*). The *W:D* ratio compares the extent to which an individual attempts to create a more challenging response requiring a high degree of organization *(W)* rather than choosing a less demanding and easily perceived area *(D)*. Normals and outpatients usually have a ratio of 1:2 (Exner, 1974). If the person includes a relatively large number of *D*'s, it suggests that he takes the least challenging and possibly least productive way out of a conflict situation. It could be assumed that his characteristic way of dealing with ambiguity is to withdraw from it and focus on the obvious. If *W* is predominant, the person is perhaps overdriven in his attempts to organize his perceptions. If, with a high *W*, both the *W* and the *D*'s are of poor quality, this suggests that a person is withdrawn and unrealistically striving for perfection (Exner, 1974). However, when *W*'s and *D*'s are both of good quality, it is more likely to represent the successful intellectual efforts of a creative person (Exner, 1974).

Lambda [*L;* (Pure *F:*Non–pure *F*)]. The lambda index was developed by Beck (1950) as an improvement on the *F%* which had been used by other Rorschach systematizers. The earlier *F%* used the total number of *R* as the denominator, whereas the Lambda uses the total number of non–pure *F*. The Lambda ratio is used as an overall index of the degree of responsiveness versus lack of responsiveness to stimuli (Exner, 1978). Thus, persons can range from being highly constricted and withdrawn to being completely emotionally flooded by their responses to stimuli. The Lambda for normals is between .52 and 1.12, with a mean of .82. In contrast to this are outpatients, .05-85; inpatient nonschizophrenics, .20-.58; and inpatient schizophrenics, .23-63 (Exner, 1978). Although these statistics characterize psychiatric groups as having a generally lower Lambda ratio, this can be somewhat misleading. The more important factor is that psychiatric groups have a much wider range than normals, even though they tend overall to have lower scores. Thus, a maladjusted person may have a Lambda either greater than 1.2 or less than .50. What is significant is that Lambda gives specifics regarding the form this maladjustment takes. It is also important to look at other information within the test such as form quality and Experience Balance to obtain a more complete conceptualization of the meaning of L.

High L (L > 1.1). Since pure F is a withdrawal from experiencing a situation fully and an avoidance of perceiving all the possibilities which may be present, the high L person is likely to be conservative, insecure, and fearful of involvement (Exner, 1974). Such individuals have also been described as defensive, constricted (Klopfer et al., 1954; Piotrowski, 1957), unimaginative (Alcock, 1963; Levi, 1976), and anxious (Riessman and Miller, 1958; Singer, 1960). Levitt and Truumaa (1972) have demonstrated the association of high L with depression, guilt, and an increased potential for suicide. Lambdas of 1.20 or greater are found in persons who have an excessive degree of affective detachment, often screening out relevant information (Exner, 1978). Thus, they avoid the complexities of a stimulus and often develop "tunnel vision" relating to certain ideas or perceptions. However, with adolescents, an interpretation which focuses on maladjustment should be made with caution since Ames (1959) and others (Ames et al., 1971) have found that they usually have a higher proportion of pure F responses.

Low L (L < .50). A low Lambda generally indicates that the person becomes overly involved with stimuli to the extent that his affects disrupt his cognitive functioning (Exner, 1974). It should be noted that the only group of people with a total absence of pure form responses consisted of inpatients (Exner, 1974). Low L scorers have also been described as having inadequate control over their emotions, which results in difficulty maintaining satisfactory interpersonal relationships because of frequent, impulsive acting out (Allison et al., 1968; Exner, 1978; Klopfer and Davidson, 1972). Such people often have an impaired ability to attend to their environment (Alcock, 1963), and Beck (1945, 1951) has even associated low L with manic excitement.

Form Quality $[(F+\% \text{ and } X+\%); \dfrac{(F+) + (Fo)}{\textbf{Pure } F} \text{ and } \dfrac{(F+) + (Fo)}{R}]$. The number of form quality responses measures the degree to which a person perceives things realistically and conventionally. It also reflects a person's formal reasoning ability, respect for reality, and "regard for the standards of the environment" Rapaport et al., 1968). (See Appendix F)

Rorschach originally conceptualized the use of $F+\%$, and Rapaport (1946) recommended an extended version ($X+\%$) of it with the total number of responses as the denominator. His rationale was that responses in which there is an absence of form (i.e., pure C, T, Y, etc.) indicate a disregard for form which should be categorized as if they were $F-$ responses. Thus, the $F+\%$ and $X+\%$ serve to check one another to make sure they produce similar results. For normals, the frequency of $F+\%$ or $X+\%$ should be around 75, with 70 being the lower limit (Exner, 1974). It would also be unusual for a person to have 100% $F+$ responses.

High F+% and/or X+%: A moderately high percentage indicates an excellent ability to deal with stress (Lerner and Shannon, 1972), above-average intelligence, and perceptual clarity (Kahn and Giffen, 1960; Klopfer et al., 1954). Furthermore, the ability to form concepts is likely to be above average (Holzberg and Belmont, 1952), and this response is a contraindication of brain damage (Gottlieb and Parsons, 1960).

An extremely high number of $F+$ responses suggests an excessive concern with reality, convention, and conformity (Exner, 1974). The person is likely to be hypernormal, inflexible, rigid, and lacking individuality in his perceptions of the world (Exner, 1974). Thus, a certain amount of perceptually altering the card stimuli is to be expected, but an exact "echoing" of the card stimuli indicates excessive rigidity and overadaptiveness.

Low F+% and/or X+%. An $F+\%$ or $X+\%$ of 70 or below suggests limited intellectual endowment (Beck, 1944, 1961), retardation (Klopfer and Kelly, 1942), or schizophrenia (Beck, 1944, 1945, 1968; Kahn and Giffen, 1960). If a schizophrenic's $F+\%$ is below 60 and the form quality is low, it suggests a poor prognosis with a history consistent with process schizophrenia (Hertz and Paolino, 1960). Low scorers are likely to have poor ties with reality, inadequate abstracting ability (Holzberg and Belmont, 1952), a high level of anxiety (Arnaud, 1959), and low ego strength (Beck, 1945; Meyer and Caruth, 1970). A low $F+\%$ or $X+\%$ can also suggest organic impairment (Reitan, 1955) which may be caused by a number of factors including senility (Ames et al., 1973; Beck, 1968).

Affective Ratio *(Afr;* $\dfrac{R \text{ for Cards VIII, IX, X}}{R \text{ for Cards I–VII}}$*).* Since the last three cards are color cards and the first seven are primarily achromatic, the Affective Ratio indicates the extent to which color makes an impact on the person. Normals usually show an *Afr* between .63 and .75, with a mean of .69.

High Afr *(Greater than .75)*. A high Afr indicates an overinvolvement with affect (Exner, 1974), reflecting that the person is more receptive to emotional inputs and more likely to respond immediately rather than to delay behavior (Exner, 1978). *Afr* is correlated with *EB* in that introversives will usually have a low *Afr* (mean of .62) and extratensives a high one (mean of .79; Exner, 1978). It is also important to evaluate the $FC/(CF + C)$ proportion to assess the degree of control the person has over his emotions. In other words, the *Afr* measures the responsiveness and degree of affect, whereas the $FC/(CF + C)$ indicates the ability to control what affect is present.

Low Afr (Less than .55).   Persons with low *Afr* scores tend to withdraw from their emotions and, if they have an unusually low *Afr*, may attempt to exert an extreme amount of control over their affective responses (Exner, 1974).

Animal Percentage [A%; (A + Ad)/R)].   Animal responses are among the most common and most basic perceptions on the Rorschach. They are usually concrete, simple, and obvious contents to observe. Thus, persons scoring a relatively high percentage of animal responses would tend to be more predictable and conforming in their behavior, whereas a low *A%* suggests that persons have unique and more personal perceptions of the world. The *A%* range for normals is from 31 to 47.

High A%.   A relatively high *A%* suggests stereotyped and conventional thinking (Klopfer and Davidson, 1962; Levitt and Truumaa, 1972) in which the person has an extremely narrow range of interests. It may also indicate depression, constriction, immaturity, and low intelligence (Ames and Gillespie, 1973; Beck, 1945, 1960; Klopfer and Davidson, 1962). Goldfried et al. (1971) have found that it can be associated with brain damage.

Low A%.   Individuals who are spontaneous, nonconforming, and of higher intelligence often have low *A%* (Allen, 1954; Kahn and Giffen, 1960). However, manic patients also score low on *A%* (Kuhn, 1963; Schmidt and Fonda, 1954), so it is important to look at the *F+%*, the degree of organizational activity, and the meaning derived from the type and variety of the other content categories in order to best understand its implications for each individual examinee.

Human to Animal Contents [(H + Hd)/(A + Ad)].   The relative proportion of human to animal responses provides an index of the amount of interest an individual has in others (Exner, 1974). An extremely high loading on the human side of the ratio indicates an extremely high concern with others, perhaps to the point of being overly preoccupied with them. However, if the responses are primarily mythical, there is an interest in others along with a simultaneous avoidance and defensiveness towards them. Thus, the attempts that are made to establish contact are shielded through the use of fantasy and the perception of one's own inner world, thereby making interpersonal contact difficult (Exner, 1974). A high number of human details can also indicate avoidance and defensiveness. A high loading on the animal side of the ratio suggests an indifference and avoidance of others. The human to animal ratio for normals is between 1:2 and 1:2.5. The clinician should also refer to descriptions of the significance of *A%*, *H* content, *A* content, and especially *Ad* and *Hd* for a more complete understanding of the human to animal ratio.

XRT **Achromatic** $\left(\dfrac{RT \text{ Cards I, IV, V, VI, VII}}{5}\right)$ and

XRT **Chromatic** $\left(\dfrac{RT \text{ Cards II, III, VIII, IX, X}}{5}\right)$. Rorschach (1921) originally began studying reaction times but mainly concerned himself with evaluating the average length it took to create a response. He noted that long reaction times suggested a difficulty in formulating a response because of constriction related to a relatively high degree of threat associated with the stimulus. Other systematizers have noticed that although there is a wide variability within groups, the largest reaction times occur in depressives, compulsives, and certain types of brain-damaged patients, whereas the shortest times are for children, manics, and impulsive persons. In general, there has been an insufficient amount of research done on reaction time, and some of the basic assumptions have been challanged. Meer (1955) has criticized some of the research by pointing out that actually the main variable affecting length of reaction time is the complexity, and therefore the difficulty, of the stimuli. Thus, reaction times for Cards VIII, IX, and X are longest, due not so much to color but rather to their difficulty. For these reasons, conclusions based on reaction times should be tentative, and the clinician should look for support from other variables within the test.

Beck (1961) and Klopfer et al. (1954) believed that it was more helpful to determine the average reaction time for the achromatic cards compared to the chromatic ones. They reasoned that this would give a measure of the degree of "shock" or threat which affective stimuli (chromatic) produced in contrast with nonaffectively charged stimuli (achromatic). Thus, a significantly longer reaction time to the chromatic cards (8–10 seconds or more) suggests that subjects are attempting to carefully control their affective responses. For example, schizophrenics give significantly shorter reaction times to the chromatic cards than do nonschizophrenics (Exner, 1974).

It can also be important to evaluate the implications of unusual reaction times to specific cards. If subjects give quick responses to chromatic cards, this may suggest that they have been overwhelmed or compelled to respond by the stimuli. If the responses are dominated by color (i.e., *C, CF*), this would give further support to the hypothesis that they were unable to control their reactions. On the other hand, by studying responses in which there are unusually long delays, clinicians can develop clues as to how subjects organize and cope with stressful situations.

RECOMMENDED READING

Exner, J.E., Jr. *The Rorschach: A Comprehensive System,* Vol. 1. New York: John Wiley & Sons, 1974.

Exner, J.E., Jr. *The Rorschach: A Comprehensive System,* Vol. 2: Current Research and Advanced Interpretations. New York: Wiley-Interscience, 1978.

Exner, J.E., Jr. and Weiner, I.B. *The Rorschach: A Comprehensive System,* Vol. 3: Assessment of Children and Adolescents. New York: John Wiley & Sons, 1982.

Wiener-Levy, D. and Exner, J.E., Jr. The Rorschach Comprehensive System: an overview. In McReynolds, P. (Ed.) *Advances in Psychological Assessment,* Vol. 5. San Francisco: Jossey-Bass, 1981.

7
Minnesota Multiphasic
Personality Inventory*

The Minnesota Multiphasic Personality Inventory (MMPI) is a standardized questionnaire which elicits a wide range of self-descriptions that are scored to give a quantitative measurement of an individual's level of emotional adjustment and attitude to test taking. Since its development by Hathaway and McKinley in 1940, not only has it become the most widely used clinical personality inventory, but it has over 6000 published research references (Alker, 1978). Thus, in addition to its clinical usefulness, it has also stimulated a vast amount of literature and has frequently been used as a measurement device in research studies.

The test format consists of 566 affirmative statements which can be answered "true" or "false." The different categories of responses can be either hand or machine scored and summarized on a profile sheet. An individual's score as represented on the graph can then be compared with the scores derived from the normative sample on which the test was originally standardized.

Presently, the MMPI has a total of 13 scales of which 3 relate to validity and 10 to clinical or personality indices (see Table 7-1). These scales are known both by their scale numbers and by scale abbreviations. In addition, there are a large number of experimental scales which have been created for research purposes, and new scales are constantly being reported in the literature. Examples of such scales include ego strength (ES), dependency (Dy), dominance (Do), prejudice (Pr), and social status (St).

The majority of MMPI questions are relatively obvious with respect to content and deal largely with psychiatric, psychological, neurological, or physical symptoms. However, some of the questions are psychologically obscure in that it is not intuitively obvious what underlying psychological process they are assessing. For example, the item "I sometimes tease animals" is empirically answered "false" more frequently by depressed subjects than normals. Thus, it was included under scale 2 (depression) even though it does not, on the surface,

---

*Items from the MMPI are reproduced, by permission, from Hathaway, Starke R. and McKinley, J. Charnley, *The Minnesota Multiphasic Personality Inventory,* University of Minnesota Press, Minneapolis, Minn. Copyright © 1943 by the University of Minnesota.

Table 7-1. Basic Minnesota Multiphasic Personality
Inventory (MMPI) Scales.

Scale Name	Abbreviation	Code No.	No. of Items
Validity Scales			
Cannot say	?		
Lie	L		15
Infrequency	F		64
Correction	K		30
Clinical Scales			
Hypochondriasis	Hs	1	33
Depression	D	2	60
Hysteria	Hy	3	60
Psychopathic deviate	Pd	4	50
Masculinity-femininity	Mf	5	60
Paranoia	Pa	6	40
Psychasthenia	Pt	7	48
Schizophrenia	Sc	8	78
Hypomania	Ma	9	46
Social introversion	Si	0	70

NOTE: Reprinted, by permission, from *An MMPI Handbook, Volume I: Clinical Interpretation* by W. Grant Dahlstrom, George Schlager Welsh, and Leona E. Dahlstrom. University of Minnesota Press, Minneapolis. Copyright © 1972 by the University of Minnesota.

appear to directly assess an individual's degree of depression. For the most part, however, the statements are more direct and self-evident, such as "I wish I could be as happy as others seem to be" (true) or "I cry easily" (true), both of which also reflect an examinee's level of depression. The overall item content is extremely varied and relates to such areas as general health, occupational interests, preoccupations, morale, phobias, and educational problems (see Table 7-2).

Once a test profile has been tabulated, the scores are frequently arranged or coded in such a way as to summarize and highlight the significant peaks and valleys. However, it is extremely important to take into consideration all the scale scores of the profile. In many instances, the same scaled score on one test profile can mean something different on another profile when the elevations or lowerings of other scales are also considered. For example, an elevated scale 3 (hysteria) may indicate an individual who denies conflict, demands support from others, expresses optimism, and is somewhat interpersonally naive. However, if this elevation is also accompanied by a high 4 (psychopathic deviate), there is likely to be a strong undercurrent of repressed anger. This anger is usually expressed indirectly, and any negative effects on others are likely to be strongly denied. Thus, it is important that the clinician not utilize purely quantitative or mechanical formulas for interpreting the profile but rather examine the scores

Table 7-2. Content Classification of the MMPI
with Illustrative Items.

Category	Representative Items	No. of Items
Attitudes		
Religious	I believe in a life hereafter.	19
Sexual	I am worried about sex matters.	16
Social	I am a good mixer.	72
Test taking	It is always a good thing to be frank.	15
Education	I liked school.	12
General health	I have diarrhea once a month or more.	81
Masculinity-femininity	If I were an artist I would like to draw flowers.	55
Mood	I usually feel that life is worthwhile.	56
Morale	I am certainly lacking in self-confidence.	33
Occupation	I think I would like the work of a librarian.	18
Phobias	I am afraid to be alone in the dark.	29
Preoccupations	Evil spirits possess me at times.	46
Miscellaneous	I dream frequently.	98

NOTE: Items reproduced, by permission, from Hathaway, Starke R. and McKinley, J. Charnley, *The Minnesota Multiphasic Personality Inventory*, University of Minnesota Press, Minneapolis, Minn. Copyright © 1943 by the University of Minnesota. Content categories adapted from Marks, Seeman, and Haller (1974).

within the overall context of the other scale evaluations and valleys. Not only should a patricular scale be examined within the context of the overall test configuration, but additional sources such as behavioral observations, other psychometric devices, and relevant history can be extremely helpful in increasing the accuracy, richness, and sensitivity of personality descriptions.

A further important general interpretive consideration is that the scales represent measures of personality traits rather than simply diagnostic categories. Although the scales were originally designed to differentiate normal from abnormal behavior, it is generally regarded as far more useful to consider the scales as indicating clusters of personality variables. For example, scale 2 (depression) may suggest such characteristics as mental apathy, self-depreciation, and a tendency to worry over even relatively small matters. This approach has characterized the extensive research performed on the meanings of the two highest scales (two-point code types) which are summarized in the later portions of this chapter. Rather than merely labeling a person, this descriptive approach creates a richer, more in-depth, and wider assessment of the individual being tested.

HISTORY AND DEVELOPMENT

The original development of the MMPI was begun in 1939 at the University of Minnesota by Starke R. Hathaway and J. Charnley McKinley. They wanted an instrument which could serve as an aid in assessing adult patients during routine psychiatric case workups and which could accurately determine the severity of their disturbances. Furthermore, they were interested in developing an objective estimate of the change produced by psychotherapy or other variables in a patient's life.

The basic approach during construction of the MMPI was empirical criterion keying. This refers to the development, selection, and scoring of items within the scales based on some external criterion of reference. Thus, if a clinical population was given a series of questions to answer, the individuals developing the test would select questions for inclusion or exclusion based on whether or not this clinical population answered differently from a comparison group. Even though a theoretical approach might be used initially for the development of test questions, the final inclusion of the questions would not be based on this theoretical criterion. Instead, test questions would be selected based on whether or not they were answered in a different direction from a contrasted group. For example, a test constructor may believe that an item such as "sometimes I find it almost impossible to get up in the morning" is a theoretically good statement to use in assessing depression. However, if a sample population of depressed patients did not respond to that question differently from a normative group, then the item would not be included. Thus, if a person with hysterical traits answers "true" to the statement "I have stomach pains," it is not so important whether he actually does or does not have stomach pains, rather it is more important from a test construction point of view that he says he does. In other words, the final criterion for inclusion of items within an inventory is based on whether or not these items are responded to in a significantly different manner by a specified population sample.

Using this method, Hathaway and McKinley began with an original item pool of over 1000 statements derived from a variety of different sources. These sources included previously developed scales of personal and social attitudes, clinical reports, case histories, psychiatric interviewing manuals, and personal clinical experience. The original 1000 statements were reduced and changed until there were 504 statements which were considered to be clear, readable, not duplicated, and balanced between positive and negative wording. The statements themselves were extremely varied and were purposely designed to tap as wide a number of areas as possible in an individual's life (see Table 7-2). The next step was to select different groups of normal and psychiatric patients to whom the 504 questions could be administered. The normals were primarily friends and relatives of patients at the University of Minnesota hospitals who were willing to complete the inventory. They consisted of 226 males and 315 females who were screened with several background questions including age, education, marital status, occupation, residence, and current medical status. If they were under the care of a physician at the time of the screening interview, they were excluded from the study. This group was further augmented by the inclusion of other normal subjects such as recent high school graduates, Work Progress Administration workers, and medical patients at the University of Minnesota hospitals. This composite sample of 724 individuals was closely representative in terms of age, sex, and marital status of a typical group of individuals from the Minnesota population as reflected in the 1930 census. The clinical group was comprised of patients representing the major psychiatric categories who were being treated at the University of Minnesota hospitals. These patients were divided into clear subgroups of 50 in each category of diagnosis. If there was any question regarding a patient's diagnosis or if a person had a multiple diagnosis, then he was excluded from the study. The resulting subgroups were hypochondriasis, depression, hysteria, psychopathic deviate, paranoia, psychasthenia, schizophrenia, and hypomania.

Once the normals and psychiatric patients had been administered the 504-item scale, Hathaway and McKinley could then compare their responses. If a specific item was able to correctly differentiate between these two groups, then it was included in the resulting clinical scale. For example, the item "Much of the time my head seems to hurt all over" was answered "true" by 12% of the sample of hypochondriacs and only 4% of the normals. It was thus included in the clinical scale for hypochondriasis. The comparisons, then, were between each clinical group and the group of normals rather than among the different clinical groups themselves. By use of this selection procedure, tentative clinical scales were developed.

This was still not the final step in the scale constructions. Just because the items were endorsed differently by the group of 724 Minnesota normals than by the patients from various clinical populations did not necessarily indicate that the items could then actually be used for clinical screening purposes. The next step was to attempt to cross-validate the scales. This was accomplished by selecting a new group of normals and comparing their responses with a different group of clinical patients. The items which still provided significant differences between these groups were selected for the final version of the scales. It was reasoned, then, that these items and the scales comprised of these items would thereby be valid for differential diagnosis in actual clinical settings.

Whereas this procedure describes how the original clinical scales were developed, two additional scales were also developed using slightly different approaches. The scale of masculinity-femininity (Mf) was originally intended to be able to differentiate male homosexuals from males with a more exclusively heterosexual orientation. However, there were found to be few items which could effectively perform this function. The scale was then expanded to distinguish items which were characteristically endorsed in a certain direction by the majority of males from those which were characteristically endorsed in a certain direction by females. This was accomplished in part by the inclusion of items from the

Terman and Miles I Scale (1936). The second additional scale was social introversion (Si) which was developed by Drake in 1946. It was initially developed using empirical criterion keying in an attempt to differentiate female college students who participated extensively in social and extracurricular activities from those who rarely participated. It was later generalized to reflect the relative degree of introversion for both males and females.

It soon became apparent to the test constructors that persons could alter the impression they made on the test by various test taking attitudes. Hathaway and McKinley thus began to develop several scales that could detect the types and magnitude of the different test taking attitudes which were most likely to invalidate the other clinical scales. The four scales that were developed were the cannot say (?), the lie (L), the infrequency (F), and the correction (K) scales. The cannot say scale (?) is simply the total number of unanswered questions. If a high number of these are present, it would obviously serve to reduce the validity of the overall profile. The lie scale represents a naive and unsophisticated effort on the part of the examinee to create an overly favorable impression. The items selected for this scale were those which indicated a reluctance to admit to even minor personal shortcomings. The F scale is comprised of those items that were endorsed by less than 10% of normals. A high number of scorable items on the F scale, then, reflects that the examinee is endorsing a high number of unusually deviant responses.

Perhaps the most sophisticated of the validity scales is K which reflects an examinee's degree of psychological defensiveness. The items for this scale were selected by comparing the responses of known psychiatric patients who still produced normal MMPI's (clinically defensive) with "true" normals who also produced normal MMPI's. Those items which differentiated between these two groups were used for the K scale. Somewhat later, the relative number of items endorsed on the K scale was used as a "correction" factor. The reasoning behind this is that if some of the scales were lowered because of a defensive test taking attitude, then a measure of the degree of defensiveness could be added back into the scale to compensate for this. The result would be a more accurate appraisal of the person's clinical behavior. The scales which are not given a K correction are those whose raw score still produced an accurate description of the person's actual behavior.

The MMPI was originally copyrighted and published by the University of Minnesota Press in 1943. It was later published and distributed by the Psychological Corporation (1943) along with newly developed standard manuals, forms and scoring materials. Recently (1983), it has again been published and distributed by the University of Minnesota Press and is distributed by Interpretive Scoring Systems. Over the past 40 years it has been translated into numerous languages, and it is available in many nations throughout the world.

RELIABILITY AND VALIDITY

Reliability studies performed on the MMPI have not been overly encouraging. For example, test-retest reliabilities for psychiatric patients, in which retesting was performed less than a year after the initial measure, range from a low of 50 to highs in the range of .90, with median scores in the .80s. Proponents of the MMPI have pointed out that fluctuations in test scores are to be expected. This is especially true for psychiatric populations since the effects of treatment or stabilization in a temporary crisis situation are likely to be reflected in a patient's test performance. Bergin (1971) has demonstrated that scale 2 (depression) is particularly likely to be lowered after successful treatment. Thus, test-retest reliability may actually be an inappropriate method of evaluating this scale for certain types of populations. This defense of the test's reliability is somewhat undermined by the observation that test-retest reliability is actually more stable for psychiatric populations than for normals. Whereas the median range for psychiatric patients is around .80, median reliabilities for normals are around .70. Split half reliabilities are likewise low, having an extremely wide range from .05 to .96, with median correlations in the .70s. Reliability, then, has not proved to be one of the MMPI's strong points.

Further difficulties relate to the construction of the scales themselves. One significant problem is that intercorrelations between many of the scales are quite high probably because of the extensive degree of item overlap. Sometimes the same item will be simultaneously used for the scoring of several different scales, and most of the scales have a relatively high proportion of items common to other scales. For example, scales 7 (psychasthenia) and 8 (schizophrenia) have fairly high item overlap which is reflected in correlations ranging between .64 and .87 depending on the population sampled (Dahlstrom and Welsh, 1960). Scale 8, which has the highest number of items (78), has only 16 items that are unique to it (Dahlstrom, Welsh, and Dahlstrom, 1972). Because of the high inter-correlations between scales, several factor analytic studies have been conducted which have consistently found that two major variables could account for most of the variance (Block, 1965; Dahlstrom and Welsh, 1960; Dahlstrom et al., 1972, 1975; Welsh, 1956). All of this strongly suggests that there is a high degree of redundancy regarding what the scales measure.

The fact that the different scales correlate so highly can, in part, be understood by considering that the original selection of the items for inclusion in each scale was based on a comparison of normals with different clinical groups. The items, then, were selected based on their differentiation of normals from various psychiatric populations, rather than their differentiation of one psychiatric population from another. Even though the psychiatric groups varied from the normals on several traits, this manner of scale construction did not serve to develop accurate measurements of these different traits. Rather, the scales are filled with many heterogeneous items and measure multidimensional, often poorly defined attributes. This approach has also resulted in many items being shared with other scales. In contrast, an approach in which specific psychiatric groups had been compared with one another would more likely have resulted in scales with less item overlap that could also measure more unidimensional traits.

A final difficulty relating to scale construction is the imbalance in the number of "true" as opposed to "false" items. In the L scale, all the items are scorable if answered in the "false" direction; on the K scale, 29 of 30 items are scored if answered "false"; and scales 7, 8, and 9 have a ratio of approximately 3 to 1 of "true" as compared to "false" items. The danger of this imbalance is that persons having response styles of either acquiescing ("yea saying") or disagreeing ("nay saying") will answer according to their response style rather than to the content of the items. A theoretically sound approach to item construction would have an even balance between the number of "true" and "false" answers. Some authors (Edwards, 1957, 1964; Messick and Jackson, 1961) have even suggested that test results do not reflect psychological traits as much as generalized test taking attitudes. Thus, a controversy has arisen over "content variance," in which an examinee is responding to the content of the items in such a way as to reflect psychological traits, as opposed to "response style variance," in which responses reflect more the examinee's tendency in a certain biased direction. In a review of the literature, Koss (1979) concluded that although response sets can and do exist, the examinee's tendency to respond accurately to the item content is far stronger.

These difficulties with reliability and scale construction would suggest that the MMPI's validity is questionable. Rodgers (1972) has even referred to the MMPI as a "psychometric nightmare." However, even though the strict psychometric properties are not satisfactory, this has been somewhat compensated by extensive validity studies. More specifically, the meanings of two- and three-point profile code types have been extensively researched, as have the contributions which the MMPI can make towards assessing and predicting specific problem areas. Dahlstrom et al. (1975), in Volume 2 of their revised MMPI handbook, cite 6000 studies investigating profile patterns. This number is continually increasing (see, for example, Bennet and Schubert, 1981; Conley, 1981), and past studies provide extensive evidence of the MMPI's construct validity. For example, violence in women has been associated with elevations in scales 4 (masculinity-femininity) and 5 (psychopathic deviate), and these individuals can be described as defensive, lacking contact with their impulsiveness, nonconforming, and being at variance with the stereotyped definition of femininity (Huesmann, Lefkowitz, and Eron, 1978; McCreary, 1976). A further example is that the development of alcoholism has been found to occur more frequently in persons having elevations on scales F, 4, and 9, which suggests that they are gregarious, impulsive, and less socially conforming (Hoffman, Loper, and Kammeier, 1974). Individual clinicians can consult research on code types to obtain specific personality descriptions and learn of potential problems to which a client may be susceptible. It is primarily because of these extensive validity studies that the MMPI continues to be used.

ASSETS AND LIMITATIONS

In the discussion of reliability and validity, several limitations associated with the MMPI were highlighted. These included marginally adequate reliability and problems related to the construction of the scales, such as item overlap, high intercorrelations between scales, multidimensional poorly defined scales, and imbalances between the relative proportion of "true" as opposed to "false" items. Added to these difficulties are criticisms that the test is too long and that many of the items are considered to be offensive, especially those related to sex and religion.

A significant caution related to the construction of the MMPI is that it is generally inadequate for the assessment of normal populations. The items were selected on the basis of their ability to differentiate — in a bimodal population — normals from psychiatric patients. Thus, extreme scores can be interpreted with a fairly high degree of confidence, but moderate elevations must be interpreted with appropriate caution. An elevation in the range of 1 standard deviation above the mean is more likely to represent an insignificant fluctuation of a normal population than would be the case if a normally distributed group had been used for the scale construction. This is in contrast to a test like the California Personality Inventory (CPI) which used a more evenly distributed sample (as opposed to a bimodal one) and, as a result, can make meaningful interpretations based on moderate elevations. Evaluation of normals is further complicated by the observation that many normal persons achieve high scores. Thus, neither the items themselves nor the scales were designed for the assessment of normals.

Another difficulty with the MMPI is that its organization can be misleading since the scales labels use traditional diagnostic categories. A person might read a scale such as "schizophrenia" and infer that a person with a peak on that scale therefore fits that particular diagnosis. Although it was originally hoped that the MMPI could be used to make differential psychiatric diagnoses, it was soon found that it could not adequately perform this function. Thus, even though schizophrenics may score high on scale 8, so do other psychotic groups. Also, moderate elevations can occur for normal persons. With the publication of the most recent *Diagnostic and Statistical Manual of Mental Disorders* [DSM III; American Psychiatric Association (1980)], the traditional labels upon which the scale names were based became somewhat outdated. This causes further confusion related to diagnosis since the scales reflect older categories. For example, scales 1, 2, and 3 are called the "neurotic triad," and scale 4 is labeled psychopathic deviate; yet clinicians are often faced with translating scale elevations into DSM III terminology.

In order to compensate for the difficulties related to scale labels, clinicians should become aware of the current meanings of the scales based on research rather than the meanings implied by the often misleading scale titles. This can be helped in part by the use of scale numbers rather than titles. For example, scale 8 suggests such attributes as apathy, feelings of alienation, philosophical interests, poor family relations, and unusual thought processes rather than "schizophrenia." It is the clinician's responsibility to determine which of these attributes are most characteristic of the person being evaluated. Clinicians should also be aware of the relations between scales as represented by the extensive research performed on two- and three-point code types. Usually the patterns or profiles of the scales are more useful and valid than merely considering individual scale elevations. It is this body of research which is far more significant than the work done on the original normative sample. In fact, the size (724) and representativeness (Minneapolis adults) of the normative sample have frequently been questioned. Anastasi (1982) (p.506) suggests that it is more appropriate to view this sample as a "non-normative fixed reference group" which can be used to compare and define the different scale scores. The subsequent research performed on empirical code profiles is far more useful than the original normative scale comparisons. It is the extensiveness of research in this area which represents what is probably the strongest asset of the MMPI.

A further significant asset is the MMPI's immense popularity and familiarity within the field. Extensive research has been performed in a variety of areas, and new developments have included abbreviated forms, new scales, the use of critical items, and computerized interpretation systems. The MMPI has been translated into all the major world languages and is available in numerous countries. Normative and validity studies have been conducted on several different cultural groups (Butcher and Pancheri, 1976), which makes possible the comparison of data collected from varying cultures. In contexts where no norms have been developed, at least the test format lends itself to developing more appropriate norms which can then be used in these contexts.

Although the MMPI has been used in the assessment of persons from different cultural contexts, such assessments should be made with extreme caution. There are likely to be even larger cultural differences for a personality test such as the MMPI than for ability tests. Cultural differences would be especially pronounced if a clinician used the original Minnesota norms rather than ones developed for the particular group he was evaluating (Butcher and Pancheri, 1976). When interpreting the profiles of culturally divergent groups, clinicians should have a knowledge of the beliefs and values of that culture and should consult appropriate norms when available. There are a wide variety of possibilities as to why persons from different cultural groups score in a certain direction. Although scores may be due to the accurate measurement of different personality traits, they may also be the result of cultural tendencies to acquiesce by giving socially desirable responses, differing beliefs relating to modesty, role conflicts, or varying interpretations of the meaning of items. Profiles may also reflect the results of racial discrimination in that scales associated with anger, impulsiveness, and frustration may be elevated.

Related to the cultural issues is the importance of taking into consideration a variety of demographic variables. It has been demonstrated that age, sex, race, place of residence, intelligence, education, and socioeconomic status are all related to the MMPI scales. Often the same relative elevation of profiles can have quite different meanings when corrections are made for demographic variables. Some of the more important and well researched of these will be discussed here and should be taken into account when interpreting test profiles.

Age. Typically, elevations occur on scales 1 (hypochondriasis) and 3 (hysteria) for older normal populations (Leon, Gillum, Gillum, and Gouze, 1980). On the other hand, scales 4 (psychopathic deviate), 7 (psychasthenia), and 8 (schizophrenia) are commonly elevated for younger populations (Marks, Seeman, and Haller, 1974). As the population which is sampled becomes older, the deviations of the latter group of scales tend to decrease. A further finding has been that scale 9 (mania) is more commonly elevated in younger persons but decreases with age until it becomes the most frequent low point in older populations (Gynther and Shimkuras, 1966). As a general rule, the left side of the profile (scales 1, 2, and 3) increases with age, which parallels the trend in older persons towards greater concern with health (scales 1 and 3) and depression (scale 2). Conversely, the right side of the profile decreases with age, which parallels decreased assertiveness (scale 4), increased introversion (scales 2 and 0), and a decrease in energy level (scale 9). However, in specific cases there may also be a complex interaction with gender, health, socioeconomic status, and ethnicity. In addition to considering scale elevations related to aging, it may be helpful to evaluate individual item content. Swenson, Pearson, and Osborne (1973) provide a list of 30 items which are likely to be affected by aging such as No. 9: "I am about as able to work as I ever was" (false) and No. 261: "If I were an artist I would like to draw flowers" (true). An analysis of these items indicates that older persons generally express a decrease in hostility (No. 39, 80, 109, 282, and 438), have more "feminine" interests (No. 132 and 261), and are more dutiful, placid, and cautious (Gynther, 1979a).

A significant feature found within adolescent populations is a general elevation in many of the MMPI scales. This has led to the development of a separate set of adolescents norms (Marks et al., 1974) which should be used when interpreting an adolescent profile.

Race and Culture. In general, test results obtained from black psychiatric patients need to be interpreted with a good deal of caution. This would involve correlating as many additional sources of information as possible, including other test findings, psychosocial history, and interview data. A consistent finding within black populations is a tendency to score higher on both scales 8 (schizophrenia) and 1 (hypochondriasis). What is significant is that elevations on scale 1 may not actually reflect somatic concerns (Miller et al., 1968), and the "psychotic" profiles (scales 8 and F) of blacks could result in inaccurate interpretive descriptions of their behavior (Gynther, 1979b; Smith and Graham, 1981). Other scale elevations occurring frequently in blacks are on L, F, and 9 (mania; Gynther, 1972, 1978a; Miller et al., 1968). In a review of the literature, Gynther (1972, 1978) stressed that the most consistent finding was that normal blacks scored higher on scales F, 8 (schizophrenia), and 9 (mania). This was true regardless of age, gender, or urban versus rural environment. The MMPI scores themselves reflect higher levels of nonconformity, alienation, and impulsivity. However, these trends may be due merely to different values and perceptions rather than higher levels of maladjustment. At this point, the issue of MMPI bias against blacks has not been resolved, and further studies relating to actual behavioral predictions are needed (Pritchard and Rosenblatt, 1980).

If one assumes that blacks' scores on the MMPI are biased, there are two approaches towards diminishing the difficulties associated with scale differences between blacks' and whites' scores. One is to decrease the importance of scales F, 8, and 9 when interpreting a black person's profile. A second strategy is the use of the R scale which is comprised of 27 items to which blacks and whites respond differently (White, 1975). By means of this scale, adjustments can be made on scales F, 4, and 8 which theoretically compensate for the effects of differing cultural background.

Although black versus white scale differences are more frequently encountered in the literature, similar research has been conducted, and norms developed, for a number of other groups. This includes work on populations from Israel (Merbaum and Hefetz, 1976), Pakistan (Mirza, 1977), South Africa (Lison and Van der Spuy, 1977), Chile (Rissetti, Butcher, Agostini, Elgueta, Gaete, Marguilies, Morlans, and Ruiz, 1979), Mexico (Nunez, 1968, 1980), and Japan (Tsushima and Onorato, 1982), as well as on Mexican-Americans (Padilla and Ruiz, 1975; Quiroga and Bessner; Reilly and Knight, 1970). Whenever clinicians work with different cultural groups, they should consult the specific norms that have been developed for use with these groups, as well as become familiar with any research that may have been carried out with the MMPI on these groups. Useful sources are Butcher and Pancheri's (1976) handbook for cross-national MMPI research and a review of current cross-cultural research by Butcher and Clark (1979).

Intellectual Level. Individuals with higher intelligence and education frequently score higher on "feminine" interests (scale 5). Furthermore, scales L and F decrease as intellectual level increases (Gynther and Shimkuras, 1966). As a result, either low scores on scale 5 (masculinity-femininity) or higher elevations on the L or F scale take on increased significance with more educated populations. Thus, a man with a university education who has an average or moderate elevation (T = 50–65) on scale 5 (masculinity-femininity) may actually be more representative of men who place a strong emphasis on traditional expressions of masculinity. Likewise highly educated persons scoring moderate elevations on L or F may be more characteristic of other persons who score somewhat higher.

The advantages and cautions for using the MMPI clearly indicate that a considerable degree of psychological sophistication is necessary. Both its assets and its limitations must be understood and taken into account. The limitations are numerous and include marginally adequate reliability, problems related to scale construction, excessive length, offensive items, limited usefulness for normal populations, misleading labels for the scales, inadequacy of the original normative sample, and the necessity of considering demographic variables. However, these limitations are balanced by a number of significant assets especially the extensive research relating to the meanings of the different scales and the relations between scales. Further assets are the MMPI's familiarity in the field, the development of new norms, and extensive research relating to specific problem areas. Of central importance is the fact that the MMPI has repeatedly proved itself to be of practical value to clinicians, especially because the variables that the scales attempt to measure are meaningful and even essential areas of clinical information. Butcher (1979) has poignantly summarized the current status of the MMPI by calling it "an outmoded but as yet unsurpassed psychopathology inventory" (p. 34).

NEW DEVELOPMENTS

In addition to the standard approaches to the MMPI, a number of significant developments have served to enhance the usefulness and information which can be derived from this test. Most of these developments are also attempts to compensate for the test's deficiencies which have already been discussed. They include abbreviated forms, new scales, critical items, and computerized interpretations.

Criticism regarding the extreme length of the MMPI has led to the development of several abbreviated forms. The one which has achieved the most popularity, but also the most severe criticism (Newmark, 1981), has been Kincannon's (1968) Mini-Mult. The form consists of 71 items and was developed by omitting items which had the greatest degree of scale overlap. Scales Mf and Si were also excluded. The overall scale configurations correspond fairly closely with the standard long form of the MMPI, with correlations ranging from .60 to .89. Two major criticisms of the Mini-Mult are that scales L, F, and Ma have low correlations with corresponding long-form scales and that it underestimates extreme scores. In order to correct the first of these criticisms, Dean (1972) revised the Mini-Mult scales L, F, and Ma until they correlated at a level of .80 with their corresponding long-form scales. The resulting 86-item MMPI abbreviation has been referred to as the Midi-Mult. Another short form was developed by Spera and Robertson (1974) who attempted to correct the second criticism by including Grayson's (1951) critical items which are significant items relating to pathology. These items can be analyzed according to their individual content but also serve to make the clinical scales more sensitive to extreme dimensions of pathology. The resulting 104-item form has been called the Maxi-Mult. Whereas, both the Mini- and Midi-Mults have been found to be insensitive to extreme levels of pathology, the Maxi-Multi is good for assessing these populations (Fauschingbauer and Newmark, 1978). However, it is inadequate for mildly pathological outpatients and normal college samples, and these inadequacies have been found to be particularly pronounced in the assessment of females (Newmark, Owen, Newmark, and Fauschingbauer, 1975; Newmark and Thibodeau, 1979).

Two additional short forms have been found to be more versatile than these variations of Kincannon's Mini-Mult. The FAM (Fauschingbauer, 1974) was developed using similar methods to the Mini-Mult. However, the inclusion of significantly more items (166) and the somewhat different organization of these items have resulted in correlations of .85 or greater with the standard long form. Another short form is the MMPI-168 (Overall and Gomez-Mont, 1974) which uses only the first 168 items of the standard MMPI. The rationale for this is that most of the reliable variance in the standard MMPI can be accounted for in these initial 168 items (Overall and Gomez-Mont, 1974). Both these short forms have been found to be extremely useful with psychiatric inpatients and normal college populations, but they are somewhat deficient in the assessment of mildly pathological outpatients (Newmark and Thibodeau, 1979). Thus, the selection of which abbreviated short form to use should depend primarily on its relative appropriateness for specific populations. Whenever possible, clinicians should validate a short form they are using within their population of interest (Greene, 1983).

Since the initial publication of the MMPI, over 300 new scales have been developed. Their purpose has been to assist in evaluating the different content responses a client makes. Some of these scales have been developed for normals and are unrelated to pathology, such as dominance (Do) and social status (St). Others relate more directly to pathological dimensions, and often use the original data from Hathaway and McKinley's standardization sample. It is beyond the scope of this chapter to discuss all of the major new scales, but several of the most frequently used ones will be outlined.

One of the most popular developments has been the reorganization by Harris and Lingoes (1955, 1968) of the standard scales into more homogeneous content categories. These subscales were constructed by intuitively grouping together items which seemed to reflect a single trait or attitude. The Harris and Lingoes subscales represent a specific breakdown of the already existing scales 2, 3, 4, 6, 8, and 9, and are presented here:*

---

*From *Subscales for the Minnesota Multiphasic Personality Inventory: An Aid to Profile Interpretation* by Robert E. Harris and James C. Lingoes (1968). Reprinted by permission of James C. Lingoes, Department of Psychology, University of Michigan.

Scale 2 (Depression)
D1 Subjective Depression
D2 Psychomotor Retardation
D3 Physical Malfunctioning
D4 Mental Dullness
D5 Brooding

Scale 3 (Hysteria)
Hy1 Denial of Social Anxiety
Hy2 Need for Affection
Hy3 Lassitude–Malaise
Hy4 Somatic Complaints
Hy5 Inhibition of Aggression

Scale 4 (Psychopathic Deviate)
Pd1 Familial Discord
Pd2 Authority Conflict
Pd3 Social Imperturbability
Pd4A Social Alienation
Pd4B Self Alienation
Pd4 Alienation (a summation of 4A and 4B)

Scale 6 (Paranoia)
Pa1 Persecutory Ideas
Pa2 Poignancy
Pa3 Moral Virtue

Scale 8 (Schizophrenia)
Sc1A Social Alienation
Sc1B Emotional Alienation
Sc1 Object Loss (a summation of Sc1A and Sc1B)
Sc2A Lack of Ego Mastery, Cognitive
Sc2B Lack of Ego Mastery, Conative
Sc2C Lack of Ego Mastery, Defective Inhibition, and Control
Sc2 Lack of Ego Mastery (a summation of Sc2A, Sc2B, and Sc2C)
Sc3 Sensorimotor Dissociation

Scale 9 (Hypomania)
Ma1 Amorality
Ma2 Psychomotor Acceleration
Ma3 Imperturbability
Ma4 Ego Inflation

Serkownele (1975) has used a similar approach to develop subscales for scales 5 and 0. They can be used as an extension of the Harris and Lingoes scales:

Scale 5   (Masculinity-Femininity)
  Mf1   Narcissism-Sensitivity
  Mf2   Stereotypic Feminine Interests
  Mf3   Denial of Stereotypic Masculine Interests
  Mf4   Heterosexual Discomfort–Passivity
  Mf5   Introspective-Critical
  Mf6   Socially Retiring

Scale 0   (Social Introversion)
  Si1   Inferiority–Personal Discomfort
  Si2   Discomfort with Others
  Si3   Staid–Personal Rigidity
  Si4   Hypersensitivity
  Si5   Distrust
  Si6   Physical Somatic Concerns

Scoring directions for the earlier Harris and Lingoes subscales can be found in Dahlstrom et al. (1975), and scoring directions for both sets of subscales can be found in Graham (1977). Although the Harris and Lingoes subscales show high intercorrelations with the parent scales (Harris and Lingoes, (1968), the internal consistency of these scales is somewhat low (.04–.85; Gocka, 1965). Several initial validity studies are available (Boerger, 1975; Calvin, 1975; Gordon and Swart, 1973) which demonstrate their potential clinical usefulness. Validity and reliability studies are not yet available for Serkownek's (1975) subscales. The practical importance of both subscales is that they provide a useful supplement for interpreting the original scales. For example, a clinician can assess whether a person scoring high on scale 4 (psychopathic deviate) achieved that elevation primarily because of family discord (Pd 1) or authority problems (Pd 2) and social imperturbability (Pd 3). Based on this knowledge, more accurate evaluations can be made of such areas as acting out potential or response to psychotherapy.

In contrast to the attempt of Harris and Lingoes to develop subscales for already existing MMPI scales, Wiggins (1966) developed scales based on an overall analysis of the contents of the MMPI items. He began with item clusters which were based on such areas as authority conflicts and social maladjustment. These clusters were revised and refined using factor analysis and evaluations of internal consistency. The results are the following 13 scales:

SOC   Social Maladjustment
DEP   Depression
FEM   Feminine Interests
MOR   Poor Morale
REL   Religious Fundamentalism
AUT   Authority Conflict

PSY   Psychoticism
ORG   Organic Symptoms
FAM   Family Problems
HOS   Manifest Hostility
PHO   Phobias
HY   Hypomania
HEA   Poor Health

The Wiggins scales have acceptable levels of reliability, and validity studies have so far been promising (Boerger, 1975; Lachar and Alexander, 1978; Payne and Wiggins, 1972; Peteroy et al., 1982). Norms and directions for scoring are available in Graham (1977), as well as in Fowler and Coyle (1969) and Wiggins (1971). Like the Harris and Lingoes subscales, the Wiggins categories can provide additional useful information in the interpretation of the standard MMPI scales.

Two other frequently used scales are the MacAndrews (1965) scale (AMac) for alcoholism and Barron's (1953) ego strength scale (Es). Both scales were constructed using empirical methods in which items were selected based on response frequencies of a criterion group as compared to the frequencies of a suitable comparison group. The MacAndrews (1965) scale (also AMac, MAC, Mac scale) consists of 49 items which significantly differentiate between outpatient alcoholics and nonalcoholic psychiatric outpatients. Persons scoring high on this scale are characterized as uninhibited, sociable and they use repression and religion as means of attempting to control rebellious, delinquent impulses (Finney, Smith, Skeeters, and Auvenshine, 1971). The scale has been found to effectively differentiate alcoholic from other psychiatric patients (Clopton, 1978b; Clopton, Weiner, and Davis, 1980; Svanum, Levitt, and McAdoo, 1982) and to identify persons who are at a high risk of later developing alcohol-related problems (Williams, McCourt, and Schneider, 1971). However, the scale has difficulty differentiating alcohol abusers from other substance abusers (Burke and Marcus, 1977), and appropriate caution should be taken in assessing males as opposed to females since female alcoholics have consistently higher scores than males with similar difficulties (Butcher and Owen, 1978). Barron's (1953) ego strength (Es) scale consists of 68 items and was designed to assess the degree to which patients benefited from psychotherapy. However, validity studies have produced somewhat mixed results. Graham (1978) summarizes these studies by suggesting that Es is successful in predicting the response of neurotic patients to insight-oriented therapy, but is not useful for other types of patients or other kinds of treatments. In a correlational study with other tests, Harmon (1980) found that Es relates to the degree to which a person has an underlying belief in self-adequacy, along with tolerant, balanced attitudes.

An alternative method of constructing new scales is the interpretation of single items. Several attempts have been made to isolate those items which are considered critical to the presence of psychopathology. Answering in a significant direction on these items could represent serious pathology regardless of how the person responded on the remainder of the inventory. These items have been referred to as "pathognomonic items," "stop items," or more frequently, "critical items." It has been assumed that the direction in which a person responds represents a sample of the person's behavior and acts as a short scale which indicates his general level of functioning. Two of the most frequently used lists of critical items are Grayson's (1951) list of 38 items and Caldwell's (1969) more comprehensive list of 69 items (see Appendix I). Both of these were intuitively derived and are useful in differentiating patients undergoing crises from those who are not in crises (Koss, Butcher, and Hoffman, 1976). Furthermore, the Caldwell items were helpful in differentiating which category of crisis a particular patient was in (acute anxiety, depressed-suicidal, mental confusion, etc.). In contrast, the Grayson items could indicate that the person was in crisis, but they were limited primarily to being able to specify the presence of psychotic complaints (mental confusion, persecutory ideas). Attempts to establish an efficient cutoff score for differentiating normals from psychiatric patients have met with only minimal success due to the extensive response overlap between the two groups (Koss et al., 1976). It is most advantageous, then, to look at the individual content of the items in relation to what specific types of information they reveal rather than to look at the overall number of items answered.

A recent list of critical items was developed by Lachar and Wrobel (1979) for use with computerized MMPI reports. It attempts to provide a wide range in content, to possess face validity, and to result in valid samples of behavior. The list, which comprises 98 items, was developed through both empirical and intuitive procedures.

A final important development in approaches to the MMPI is the use of computerized interpretation systems. The number of such services has grown considerably since 1965 when the first system was developed by the Mayo Clinic. Major providers are the Roche Psychiatric Service Institute (RPSI), Clinical Psychological Services, Inc. (using the Caldwell Report), the Institute for Clinical Analysis (ICA), and Behaviordyne Psychodiagnostic Laboratory Service. A description and evaluation of these services is included in Buros's *Eighth Mental Measurements Yearbook* (Nos. 617–624, 1978). Each of the computerized systems has a somewhat different approach. Some provide screening, descriptive summaries, and cautions relating to treatment, whereas others are highly interpretive or may provide optional interpretive printouts for the clients themselves. The rationale behind computerized systems is that they can accumulate and integrate large amounts of information derived from the vast literature on the MMPI which even experienced clinicians cannot be expected to recall. However, serious questions have been raised regarding an increase in the possibility of misuse by untrained personnel. Computerized services are limited to standard interpretations and are not capable of integrating the unique variables that are usually encountered in dealing with clinical cases. This is a significant factor which untrained personnel may be more likely to either overlook or inadequately evaluate. In response to these issues, the American Psychological Association (APA) developed a set of guidelines to ensure the proper use of computerized interpretations (1966). It should be stressed that although computerized systems can offer information from a wide variety of accumulated data, their interpretations are still not end products. Like all test data, they need to be placed in the context of the client's overall background and current situation, and integrated within the framework of additional test data.

INTERPRETATION PROCEDURE

Seven steps in interpreting an MMPI have been recommended by Webb, McNamara, and Rodgers (1981). They should be followed with a knowledge and awareness of the implications of demographic variables such as age, culture, intellectual level, education, social class, and occupation. A summary of the relation between MMPI profiles and some of the main demographic variables including age, culture, and intellectual level has already been provided. While looking at the overall configuration of the test (step 5), clinicians can elaborate on the meanings of the different scales and the relations between scales by consulting the interpretive hypotheses associated with them. (These can be found in the sections on "Validity Scales," "Clinical Scales," and "Two-point Codes.") The discussion of the various scales and codes represents an attempt to integrate and summarize the work of a number of different clinical and research sources, the most important of whom have been Dahlstrom et al. (1972); Gilberstadt and Duker (1965); Grahahm (1977); Lachar (1974); Marks et al. (1974); and Webb et al. (1981). The seven steps in interpretation follow:

1. The examiner should initially note the length of time required to complete the test. For a mildly disturbed person with an average I.Q. and 14 years or more of education, the time for completion should be between 60 and 75 minutes. If two or more hours are required, the following interpretive possibilities must be considered: (a) major psychological disturbance, particularly a severe depression or functional psychosis; (b) below-average I.Q. or poor reading ability resulting from an inadequate educational background; or (c) cerebral impairment. If, on the other hand, an examinee finishes in less than an hour, one should suspect an invalid profile, an impulsive personality, or both. For individuals with reading difficulties, particularly certain aphasic conditions, a tape-recorded method of administration might be considered.

2. Note any erasures or pencil points on the answer sheet. The presence of a few of these signs may indicate that the person took the test seriously and

reduces the likelihood of random marking; a great number of erasures may reflect obsessive-compulsive tendencies.

3. Complete the scoring and plot the profile. Specific directions for tabulating the raw scores and converting them into profiles are provided in Appendix J. Compile additional information including I.Q. scores, relevant history, demographic variables, and observations from steps 1 and 2.

4. Arrange the test scores in the following manner:

    a) Arrange the ten clinical scales in order of descending elevation and place the three validity scales last.

    b) Using the following Welsh code symbols, indicate the relative elevation of each scale:

Range	Elevation Symbol
Over 99 T	**
90–99 T	*
80–89 T	"
70–79 T	'
60–69 T	–
50–59 T	/
40–49 T	:
30–39 T	#
Under 30 T	No symbol

In other words, all T scores above 99 have two asterisks (**) after them, all T scores between 90 and 99 have one asterisk after them. The following is an example of how to Welsh code a set of T scores:

Before Welch coding (step 4a):

No.	1	2	3	4	5	6	7	8	9	0			
Scale	Hs	D	Hy	Pd	Mf	Pa	Pt	Sc	Ma	Si	L	F	K
T score	75	60	66	65	43	80	85	92	83	50	56	63	44

After Welsh coding:

$$8*796''1'432-0/5:L/F-K:$$

This coding not only allows for a shorthand method of recording the results but also is used in many MMPI handbooks to look up profile interpretations. For example, the test profile given can be summarized as an 87, and a personality description could be looked up under that abbreviation in books such as Dahlstrom, Welsh, and Dahlstrom (1972, 1975) or in the section on two-point codes in this chapter. Mild elevations in a person's profile (T = 60–65) represent tendencies or trends in the individual's personality, although interpretations should be treated cautiously. Elevations above 70 are more strongly characteristic of the individual and are increasingly likely to represent core features of one's personality dynamics.

An equally acceptable alternative is to simply note the highest and lowest clinical scales as well as relative scores on the validity scales. Code types can be determined by looking at the two or three highest elevations. If the scores need to be summarized, they can be arranged in descending order of elevation with the validity scales presented in their original order (L, F, K) at the end. A clinician might also wish to place them in the order in which they occur on the profile sheet (L, F, K; 1, 2, 3, etc.). However, any summary of scores should always include and be described in terms of T scores.

5. Examine the overall pattern or configuration of the test and note the relative peaks and valleys. Typical configurations, for example, might include the "conversion V" typical of hysterical disorders or elevated scales 4 and 9 which reflect a high likelihood of acting out behavior. The overall configuration can then be used to amplify or modify the interpretations derived from step 4. Note especially any scales greater than 70 or less than 40 as being particularly important for the overall interpretation. The meaning of two-point code configurations can be determined by consulting the section in this chapter which discusses them. In approaching diagnosis, the discussions of both the scales and the code types attempt to use DSM III categories when possible, but sometimes traditional DSM II categories such as neurosis are also used. The tester may also wish to consult one of the MMPI handbooks listed in the recommended readings for a more complete understanding and interpretation of the profile which has been obtained.

6. Score the critical items (see Appendix I) and make note of which ones indicate important trends. It is often helpful to go over these items with the client and obtain elaborations, or to establish whether or not the person understood what the item was asking.

7. Examine the answer sheet and note which questions were omitted. A discussion with the client of why he chose not to respond might shed additional light on how he is functioning psychologically and what areas are creating conflict for him.

THE VALIDITY SCALES

The ? Scale

The ? scale is usually not considered to be a scale as such since it does not directly measure any specific personality trait. It is simply a total of the number of items which have been left unanswered throughout the entire test questionnaire. If there are less than 30 items that have been left unanswered (T = 50), the test results are considered to be valid only if the other validity scales are within normal limits. Moderate elevations, in which from 30 to 60 questions have been omitted (T = 50–70) may indicate either a reading difficulty or obsessional indecision. Additional possibilities to explain this degree of indecisiveness are the presence of extreme intellectualization, unusual interpretations of the items, or legalistic overcautiousness perhaps due to a paranoid condition. As the number of unanswered items increases above 60, the likelihood of a valid profile becomes increasingly more remote. Any questionnaire having 100 or more unanswered questions represents an invalid profile, and clinical conclusions based on the profile cannot be accurately made.

The L Scale

The L scale includes 15 items selected on the basis of face validity which indicate whether or not an individual is presenting, either consciously or unconsciously, a naively perfectionistic view of himself. The items all represent attitudes and values which, although rated highly in our culture, are rarely found in all but the most conscientious of individuals. For example, responding "false" to the statement "I do not like everyone I know" suggests an unrealistically positive self-perception. The scale was designed to identify a deliberately evasive response, although it also indicates individuals who are relatively defensive, naive, or unsophisticated. L is determined by counting the total number of "false" responses in items number 15, 45, 75, 105, 135, 165, 195, 225, 255, 285, 30, 60, 90, 120, and 150.

T = 56–63. Moderate elevations suggest a strong need to appear in a favorable light and may indicate psychological rigidity or conscious deception. These traits may be associated with limited intelligence or educational background unless they can be explained on the basis of occupation (e.g., clergy). The individual who scores in this range is likely to present himself as overly conforming and conventional, and will usually give socially approved answers concerning self-control and moral values.

T = 64–69. Individuals scoring in this range have a naive, unrealistic view of the world and utilize denial, repression, and perhaps conscious deception. They exaggerate their moral qualities and positive scruples but do so in a rigid, self-centered, and uncompromising manner. Underneath they tend to be insecure, self-critical, and frustrated, and they expend a lot of effort glossing over any flaws they see in themselves. They have little insight into their own behavior and usually make poor candidates for psychotherapy.

T = 70 or More. These scores are extremely rare and represent an intensification of the trends already mentioned. Such people are usually highly introspective and ruminative, and have difficulty establishing interpersonal relationships. This may occur in paranoid individuals (check scale 6) or during conscious deception by sociopaths.

The F Scale

The F scale consists of 64 items on which 90% of the normal population agrees. In other words, each item would be endorsed by only one out of ten normals. Representative statements are "I can easily make other people afraid of me, and sometimes do for the fun of it" (true) and "I have nightmares every few nights" (true). Thus, an elevation on the F scale represents a significant variation from the norm suggestive of nonconventional thinking in which the individual is likely to exaggerate or at least be unusually open concerning his psychological difficulties. Furthermore, the scale does not measure any one specific trait but rather a diversity of unusual responses. Increasing elevations on F are usually accompanied by heightened elevations on most of the other clinical scales.

High scores suggest the following possibilities: (1) endorsing deviant items in an attempt to intentionally look pathological, (2) a lack of cooperation, (3) random responding, (4) incorrect understanding of the items, and (5) a cry for help. Occasionally, individuals who are intensely anxious may get extremely high F scores and yet still have a generally valid overall profile. If K is correspondingly low, this pattern is sometimes referred to as "a cry for help" because of the overt and explicit admission of distress combined with the assumption on the part of the examiner that the individual is attempting to call attention to his need for treatment.

T = 55 or Less. Usually such individuals are free from stress and can be described as honest, dependable, calm, and conventional. They also tend to have narrow interests, engage in conventional thinking, and sometimes attempt to deny or minimize problems. They may even be attempting to "fake good," particularly if K is elevated.

T = 55–65. An F scale score within this range suggests independent and mildly nonconformist thinking, as well as some negativity and pessimism. If scores are in the upper part of this range, it may also reflect some degree of restlessness, instability, moodiness, and dissatisfaction.

T = 65–80. This elevation indicates markedly unconventional, unusual thinking and is typical of rebellious, antisocial, schizoid, or "bohemian" personalities. Within adult populations, a T score from 70 to 80 can reflect ego disorientation and feelings similar to psychotic or severely neurotic patients. Other possibilities which should be considered are that the individual is "faking bad," clerical errors in scoring, malingering, or a borderline state. Adolescents who are relatively normal but are struggling with identity problems and exhibiting nonconformist behavior may score within this range. This emphasizes the importance of using a different set of norms for adolescents, particularly for this scale.

T = 80 or More. The overall profile should be approached with caution, is probably invalid, and may reflect clerical errors in scoring, lack of cooperation, distortion due to confused and delusional thinking, or an overt attempt to falsely claim mental symptoms.

The K Scale

The K scale was devised to measure guardedness or defensiveness in test taking attitudes as well as a tendency to describe oneself in an overly positive manner. Individuals who score high on K are relatively without insight into their interpersonal relationships, and have a great desire to obtain the approval and confidence of others. Representative items are responding "false" to "I frequently find myself worrying about something" and "I find it hard to make talk when I meet new people." Persons scoring high may have significant underlying conflicts but are unwilling to discuss these difficulties and spend a considerable amount of effort in defensively concealing their true thoughts and feelings. This scale is in many ways similar to the L scale but differs primarily in that it is more subtle and effective. Whereas only naive, moralistic, and unsophisticated individuals would score high on L, more intelligent and psychologically sophisticated persons might have high K scores and yet be unlikely to have any significant elevation on L.

T = 45 or Less. This indicates a lack of normal defensiveness which is often associated with a poor self-concept, acute pathology, malingering, or "a cry for help." Usually the person's defenses are not functioning adequately, and he has a poor degree of emotional and behavioral controls. It is important to note, however, that persons of lower social class frequently obtain low K scores without necessarily reflecting these other characteristics. Likewise, adolescents often score low on the K scale, which indicates openness and a certain degree of self-criticism centered around a search for identity and a close examination of their personal values.

T = 50–60. Moderate elevations suggest adequately functioning defense mechanisms, self-acceptance, and good ego strength. There is usually a balance between self-disclosure and appropriate self-protection. Although such individuals are willing to admit to socially acceptable limitations, they may tend to minimize other conflicts.

T = 61–72. With increasing elevations, there occur corresponding increases in individuals' defensiveness and stronger tendencies to overlook faults in themselves, their families, and their life situation. There are also corresponding lack of insight and general resistance to psychological evaluation. Not only are these people intolerant of personal flaws and insecurities, but they also are unaccepting of unconventional or nonconformist behavior in others. Although extremely concerned that they present a positive image to others, nonetheless they are not accurately aware of many of the impressions that others have of them. They view the psychological problems of others as weaknesses and are reluctant to be placed in a patient role.

Moderate elevation on K is a positive sign for successful psychotherapy, but individuals with scores above T = 65 have difficulty benefiting from therapeutic intervention. Generally speaking, the prognosis tends to be poor with either extremely high or extremely low scores. A moderate elevation on an adolescent's profile is a contraindication of acting out.

T = 72 or More. Higher elevations show continued intensification and rigidification of the characteristics discussed under T = 61–72.

The F – K Index

The ratio between F and K can be used as an indication of "faking good" or "faking bad" and is computed by subtracting the raw score of K from that of F.

When F – K = +11 or More. This is a "fake bad" pattern and suggests a conscious attempt to look bad, for example, in malingering. It could also be a "cry for help" as a response to an acute life crisis, or it may reflect an overdramatization by a narcissistic, histrionic, self-indulging, and unstable person ("psychochondriac") who is attempting to manipulate pity and attention from others. A further possibility may be that the individual is acutely psychotic and has a distorted perception of his self as compared to the way in which others perceive him.

F – K = –11 or Less. This strongly suggests that the person is defensively minimizing any conflicts he might have in an attempt to look good. Interpretations of the clinical scales (1–0) should be evaluated keeping this in mind.

F – K = –20 or Less. This represents doubtful validity of test results because of an exaggerated need to cover up any areas of conflict. This may be the result of overt conscious deception, extreme rigidity, or a clear negativism and refusal to cooperate.

THE CLINICAL SCALES

Scale 1: Hypochondriasis (Hs)

Scale 1 attempts to assess the degree to which an individual has an undue concern with physical health. Elevations typically reflect exaggerated expressions of vague and nonspecific disorders in which subjects are covertly seeking to control and manipulate others. They will often be pessimistic, whiny, sour, and passive-aggressive, frequently making others around them miserable. Furthermore, they are egocentric, immature, and lacking in insight concerning the emotional component of their bodily complaints. Thus, not only do they focus their psychological and emotional complaints into physical channels, they also lack insight into this process. Since their degree of psychological sophistication is minimal, they have a difficult time with self-reflection, and psychotherapy with these individuals tends to be slow and difficult. Typically, they have demonstrated a high degree of skill in frustrating physicians as they demand care and attention, yet criticize and reject the help which is offered to them. The long, involved, and almost ritualistic listing of their complaints has sometimes been referred to as an "organ recital."

Scale 1 is often somewhat elevated along with scales 2, 3, and 7; this may reflect depressive conditions, anxiety states, and somatoform or dissociative disorders. A "conversion V" occurs when there are elevations on scales 1 and 3 with a significantly lower (10 points or more) scale 2. In these individuals, psychological conflicts are masked by a histrionic personality in which there is usually the presence of "somatized" complaints (see 13/31 code type). Although there tends to be a low to moderate increase in scale 1 during the presence of actual physical disease, the higher elevations are restricted to hypochondriacal traits.

Moderately Low Scale 1 (T = 40–50). These persons can be described as showing good judgment and being generally alert, capable, and responsible. Interpersonally, they may appear to others as conscientious, perhaps to the point of being moralistic. However, most interpretations of a low score on scale 1 should be made cautiously, since this primarily indicates merely a lack of physical complaints.

High Scorers (T = 65 or More). These persons are pessimistic, narcissistically egocentric, and stubborn; they manipulate others with their complaints and generally make others around them miserable as a result. Typically they have been to a large number of physicians and have rejected and criticized the "help" which has been offered to them. The symptoms are usually not reactions to immediate stress, but rather are long-standing problems. The anxiety level of such people is also usually low (check scale 7), but if it is somewhat elevated or can be increased, this improves the prognosis in psychotherapy. As scores increase above 70, there is an intensification of all these trends.

Scale 2: Depression (D)

Scale 2 includes 60 items which measure the extent to which an individual expresses worry, discouragement, and low self-esteem. The questions are centered around the five major features of depression which include brooding, physical slowness, subjective feelings of depression, mental apathy, and physical malfunctioning. An elevation on scale 2 is the most frequent peak seen with psychiatric patients when admitted to hospitals, and scale 2 provides the best single index of a person's current level of satisfaction, comfort, and security. High scorers on scale 2 tend to be seen by others as aloof and withdrawn as well as silent, retiring, and self-critical.

Although an elevation on scale 2 generally indicates the level of pessimism/ optimism, the meaning of that trend varies according to the relative elevations of other scales. In establishing a differential diagnosis within the different types of "neurotic" disorders, it is particularly important to look at possible elevations on 1, 2, 3, and 7. For this reason, scales 1, 2, and 3 are often referred to as the "neurotic triad," and elevations in one of them will frequently be accompanied by elevations in the other two. It is also common to have an accompanying elevation on scale 7, which reflects that the self-devaluation and intropunitiveness of the depression also include tension and nervousness. However, moderate elevations on scales 2 and 7 are desirable for a favorable prognosis in psychotherapy since they reflect an introspective orientation as well as some awareness of personal problems. Of equal importance is that scales 2 and 7 measure the degree of psychological discomfort, pain, and anxiety the person is undergoing which can also be important motivators for change. Thus, they are often referred to as the "distress scales" (see code type 27/72). Another important configuration is an elevation on scales 2 and 8 which indicates that the depression also includes a sense of isolation, alienation, disaffiliation, and unusual thoughts (see code type 28/82).

The possibility of suicide increases when scale 2 is elevated, particularly if that elevation is accompanied by elevations in 4, 7, 8, and/or 9. However, there is no completely valid and useful "suicidal profile" as such. Certainly elevations on scales 2, 4, 7, 8, and 0 are reflective of conditions which excite or release suicidal behavior, but rigid interpretive and predictive formulas should be avoided. If there is *any* suspicion of suicidal potential raised by either test scores or any other means, additional assessment should be made as comprehensively as possible. Furthermore, specific indications of suicidal tendencies may be observed in the person's responses to the critical items that refer to guilt and suicide (see Appendix I).

Low 2 (T = 28–44). Individuals scoring low on scale 2 are likely to be active, alert, cheerful, and outgoing. They are seen by others as enthusiastic, self-seeking, and perhaps given to self-display. In certain cases, a low 2 may represent a denial of depressive feelings, particularly in a cyclothymic, labile person.

Moderate Elevations (T = 60–69). If 2 is the only elevated scale, this is usually indicative of a reactive depression resulting from a current life crisis. If the elevation typifies a more permanent component of their personality, such people tend to be pessimistic, have a narrow range of interests, and be particularly adept at convincing themselves of their own helplessness and hopelessness. Furthermore, they may feel unable to work, have poor morale, and be dejected and discouraged. Others are likely to see them as aloof, timid, and inhibited.

High Elevations (T = 70–85). Often psychiatric patients with a clinically significant level of depression score in this range. Individuals with high scores tend to worry over relatively insignificant problems, and will typically feel helpless and hopeless with regard to interpersonal problem solving. Social withdrawal, indecision, worry, and pessimism are often characteristic features. At extremely high elevations (T = 80 or more), there will typically be a loss of appetite, sleep disturbances, extreme apathy, and self-deprecation with some delusional thinking. If 2 is the only high point on the profile, this probably represents a depressive response to a situational crisis. Scale 2 usually shows a significant decrease following successful therapy.

Scale 3: Hysteria (Hy)

Scale 3 is comprised of 60 items centered around assessing (1) the presence of specific physical complaints and (2) defensive denial of emotional or interpersonal difficulties. What is significant in persons with conversion disorders is that these themes occur simultaneously. In other words, such people establish a certain degree of adjustment by maintaining an exaggerated degree of optimism and channeling any personal conflicts into the body where these conflicts are indirectly expressed through physical complaints. Furthermore, they constantly demand affection and support from others, but they do so in indirect and manipulative ways. Frequently, they will have traits consistent with a histrionic personality in that they are socially uninhibited and highly visible, yet their contact with others is superficial, self-centered, and extremely naive. They often act out sexually and aggressively, with a convenient lack of insight into either their underlying motives or the impact of their behavior on others.

If there is an elevation in scale 3, the individual is unlikely to be psychotic despite accompanying elevations on scales 6 or 8. Although it is certainly possible that such a profile may in some cases still reflect a psychotic condition, this interpretation should be approached with caution. The "neurotic triad" and the "conversion V" have been mentioned in discussing scales 1 and 2 (see code types 12/21, 13/31, and 23/32). A further frequent and noteworthy profile occurs when scale 3 is accompanied by an elevation on K, particularly if scales F and 8 are lowered. Such individuals are likely to be affiliative, inhibited, and overconventional, and have an exaggerated need to be liked, and approved of, by others (see code 38/83).

Low 3 (T = 24–44). Low scorers on scale 3 are usually conventional, constricted, and controlled. They are sometimes described as socially nonparticipating, conforming, and having narrow interests.

Moderate Elevations (T = 60–69). Individuals scoring moderate elevations are likely to be well-functioning persons with some histrionic personality traits. They are often described as naive, self-centered, and having strong needs to see themselves in a favorable light. Typically, they lack insight into their interpersonal relations, and tend to be indirect and manipulative in their attempts to have their social needs satisfied by others. If scale 1 is significantly higher than 3, there will most likely be a tendency to redirect their emotional conflicts into physical complaints during times of stress.

High Elevations (T = 70–80). Higher elevations on scale 3 reflect persons who are conforming, immature, naive, childishly self-centered, and impulsive. They are demanding of affection and support, and yet seek these in covert and manipulative ways. Interpersonal communications are often used to obtain an emotional effect on others rather than to accurately convey information, and their relationships are superficial and immature. There is a lack of insight into the motivations for their behavior, which is maintained by perceiving events globally rather than attending to the specific and often relevant details of a situation. Their main defenses are denial and repression which often result in a displacement or conversion of psychological conflicts into the physical realm. Since one of their central needs is to be liked, they often respond to therapy in an enthusiastic and overly optimistic manner. However, when their defenses are challenged, they will become intolerant and attempt to manipulate the therapist into a nonconfrontive and overly supportive role. This frequently culminates in the expression of impossible demands which are made on the therapist. Their resistance to treatment tends to be whiny, and is interspersed with complaints of mistreatment by the therapist and the implication that they are being misunderstood. At times, high 3 scorers can be verbally aggressive with their core conflicts revolving around issues of dependence versus independence.

Scale 4: Psychopathic Deviate (Pd)

The 50 items in scale 4 are designed to measure general social maladjustment. More specifically, the questions deal with the individual's degree of alienation from his family, the extension of difficulties to school and to authority figures in general, social imperviousness, and alienation both from self and from society. This scale also measures the degree of impulse control, and elevations on this scale are nearly always associated with acting out behaviors. Furthermore, people with elevations on scale 4 have difficulty learning from the consequences of their behavior and spend a good deal of time trying to beat the system. A significant rationale for the development of this scale is that quite frequently, high scale 4 personality types make an excellent initial impression. As a result, they may go undetected by acquaintances and even friends until they are confronted with a situation which demands a sense of responsibility, consideration, and the expression of loyalties. This scale, then, can potentially assess such persons even though, at the time of testing, they may not be engaged in, or may not for some time have been involved with, impulsive acting out behavior.

If there is a corresponding elevation on scale 9, there will almost always be a history of consistent impulsive behavior. Not only do such individuals have a certain degree of anger and impulsiveness, they also have the energy to act on these impulses. Often their behavior occurs in such a way as to damage their families' reputation, and criminal antisocial acts are not uncommon. If elevations are, for example, between 55 and 65, and these are the relative high points, such trends would still be present, but they may be channeled in less extreme and more socially accepted manners, possibly resulting in adequate or even excellent levels of adjustment (see code type 49/94). Further significant and frequently encountered profiles are elevations on scales 4 and 8 (see 48/84 code type) suggestive of psychotic expressions of antisocial behavior, or elevations on scales 4 and 3 (see 34/43 code type) in which antisocial behavior is expressed through numerous covert and disguised means. Another common corresponding elevation is on scale 2, which suggests anxiety and guilt related to an antisocial person being caught and perhaps facing the consequences of his behavior (see code 24/42).

Low Elevations (T = 20–44). Low scores on scale 4 reflect persons who are conventional, overidentified with social status, cheerful, and good tempered. They are likely to be balanced, modest, and persistent in working towards their goals, although sometimes they have difficulties asserting themselves in heterosexual relationships.

Moderate Elevations (T = 60–69). Moderate elevations are common among adolescents (14–20 years old), and reflect attempts to formulate their separate identity and independence outside the home. Thus, the admission of alienation which the elevation suggests may be the result of an adolescent's search for identity, rather than a permanent and enduring character trait. Therefore, moderately high scores for adolescents should be handled with caution, and separate adolescent norms should always be used. However, extreme scores or other correspondingly high elevations may still reflect significant pathology. Moderate elevations are also found in counterculture groups which reflect their own as well as their peers' disregard of the values and beliefs of the mainstream culture. Graduate students also show high points on this scale, especially those in the humanities and social sciences. More positive characteristics to be found with moderate elevations include frankness, deliberateness, assertion, sociability, and individualism.

High Elevations (T = 70–85). High 4s are characterized by an angry disidentification with their family, society, or both. They have an apparent difficulty in planning ahead as well as a disregard for the consequences of their behavior. Thus, they have an inability to profit from experience, including psychotherapy. Generally, therapy is less effective for high 4 adolescents than it is for high 4 adults. Individuals scoring in this range have a consistent tendency to get into trouble, and can be described as angry, rebellious, impulsive, alienated, and strongly disliking rules and regulations. Usually, their social relationships are shallow, and they rarely develop strong loyalties. It is common to find that in the past, they have been involved in legal problems and heavy drinking, and have had poor work and marital adjustments. Sometimes they leave an initially good impression which is often described as "charming," but longer acquaintance reveals their unreliability, moodiness, and generalized resentment. Their true characteristics are often difficult to identify until a period of stress results in an outbreak of irresponsible, untrustworthy, and antisocial behavior. Usually such individuals are relatively free from conflicts and do not show anxiety until actually in the midst of serious difficulties. Although they seem to demonstrate an apparent lack of concern about potential danger at some future time, they are sensitive to, and even feel remorse when faced with, the actual consequences of their behavior.

Scale 5: Masculinity-Femininity (Mf)

Scale 5 includes 60 items having to do with general interests, vocational choices, and an activity-passivity dimension. Although it was originally designed to measure the relative degree of psychological masculinity or femininity in a male college population, it has turned out to be a far from pure measure. For example, it is definitely correlated with both education and intelligence. More specifically, there are five basic dimensions on which the items seem to be centered. These are personal and emotional stability, sexual identification, altruism, feminine occupational identification, and denial of masculine occupations. When the items are scored for females, the scale is merely inverted. Thus, elevations for either males or females can generally be seen as indicating a nonidentification with traditional masculine or traditional feminine roles.

Since scale 5 is usually not considered a clinical scale and is subject to wide fluctuations related to factors such as education, it is often not interpreted in the same manner as the more "clinically" oriented scales. It is rather used to color or flavor the meanings of other high or low points. A useful approach is to determine single peaks or code types without considering scale 5. Once interpretations have been made without this scale, then the possible implications of 5 can be included. For example, elevations on scales 3, 4, and 5 can be interpreted first by referring to scales 3 and 4 and to the 34/43 code. Later, the meaning of scale 5 can be taken into consideration within the context of scales 3 and 4, but the implications of a person's level of education, occupation, and socioeconomic status also have to be taken into account.

The issue, of course, arises as to whether or not scale elevations are a valid indicator of homosexuality. Although the scale was originally designed with the hope of diagnosing such tendencies, it has become more associated with the previously mentioned characteristics of aesthetic interests, vocational choices, and activity versus passivity. Elevations, especially extremely high ones, may in some cases reflect a homosexual orientation, but this is never sufficient in and of itself to make such a diagnosis. Furthermore, homosexuals who wish to conceal their preference can do so with relative ease since the item contents are relatively transparent with respect to the dimensions they are attempting to measure.

Within normal male populations, elevations reflect imagination, sensitivity, a wide range of cultural interests, and a tendency to be able to apply oneself to work. Furthermore, moderately high scorers are frequently seen as inner directed, clever, curious, and having good judgment and common sense. Males who score low usually typify traditional masculine interests and are seen as adventurous, easygoing, and sometimes coarse.

Females who score high are usually found in traditionally male roles and occupations, particularly the areas of mechanics and science. They are frequently perceived as being adventurous, dominating, aggressive, competitive, and confident. Low female scorers are often described as placing a high value on traditional female interests, and are usually sensitive and modest. However, extreme caution should be used in interpreting low female scores, especially for women of higher intellectual and educational levels.

A frequent pattern with males consists of elevated scales 4 and 5. Such a profile represents a nonconventional individual who is flamboyant in expressing his unconventional beliefs and often is identified with the counterculture. He may, for example, take pleasure in openly defying and challenging conventional modes of appearance and behavior. In contrast, a low 5 accompanied by a high 4 is characteristic of an exaggerated, perhaps even compulsive, display of masculinity. In females, a high 5 and 4 reflects a tendency to rebel against the traditional female role, and as the elevation of scale 4 increases, the specific expression of this rebelliousness becomes correspondingly more deviant. On the other hand, females with a high 5 and a low 4 are also angry and hostile but are unable to express these feelings directly, which thus creates a good deal of inner turmoil and conflict. In males, there is sometimes a pattern of an elevated 5, with accompanying elevations in scales 2, 7, and occasionally 4. Usually such persons have developed a life-style in which they present themselves as weak, inferior, guilty, and submissive. They are typically self-effacing, and shun any outward appearance of strength and pride. The stereotype of the withdrawn "egghead" or the self-critical school clown is representative of this profile. Whereas this pattern is found with an elevated 5 in males, females who demonstrate this style will show a valley on 5.

Males. *Low 5 (T = 26–40).* Males scoring low on scale 5 can be expected to place a high degree of emphasis on traditional expressions of masculinity. They characteristically prefer action to contemplation, and their range of interests tends to be somewhat narrow. Usually they will lack originality and have little insight into their motivations primarily because of a basic lack of interest in self-exploration. They are frequently seen by others as self-indulgent, independent, and narcissistic. In keeping with these traditional expressions of the male role, they place a high degree of emphasis on physical strength and athletic prowess. Their masculine strivings often take on an almost compulsive quality in that these strivings can be overdone and inflexible. However, the overt behaviors may represent attempts to reassure themselves of their strength, power, and control which actually may serve to conceal serious questions regarding their masculinity.

Moderate 5 (T = 41–59). Scores centering around the mean will reflect an average degree of identification with the masculine role and usually represent traditional values with regard to vocational and avocational interests.

Moderate Elevations (T = 60–75). Moderate elevations reflect aesthetic interests and an individual who is sensitive, imaginative, and expresses a variance from the culturally prescribed male role. College or seminary students usually score within this range, particularly if they have literary or artistic interests. They typically are introspective, are psychologically sophisticated, and have a wide range of interests. Their values tend to be idealistic; they are inner directed; and they have the ability to communicate their ideas clearly and effectively. In some men who score particularly high on scale 5, there is a rejection of masculinity combined with a relatively passive, effeminate, and noncompetitive personality.

High Elevations (T = More than 75). Although this may reflect an extremely high degree of artistic interest, there is usually conflict over sexual identity and sometimes homosexual trends may be present. Individuals within this range are basically passive, and there is frequently a history of marital problems due to a difficulty in assertively fulfilling their partners' needs. In some situations, extremely high 5s develop a reaction formation against passivity in which they may display an exaggerated expression of masculinity similar to a low-scoring 5.

Females. *Low 5 (T = 20–45).* This is one of the poorest scale indicators, and research relating to its meaning is generally lacking. Extreme caution should be used when making interpretations, especially for women of higher intellectual and educational levels. Some women scoring within this range are described as passive, submissive, yielding persons and may even have become living caricatures of the female stereotype. They may attempt to assume, or at least appear to assume, an extreme number of burdens which they may later use to create guilt and loyalty in others. In these cases, it is not unusual to find low 5 scores correlated with corresponding elevations in the "neurotic triad" (scales 1, 2, and 3).

Moderate 5 (T = 45–55). It is fairly frequent for women to have this as a relative low point in their overall test profiles. This is reflective of average, middle-class expressions of the culturally endorsed feminine role, which also corresponds to an average avocational interest pattern.

Moderate Elevations (T = 56–65). Women scoring within this range are frequently seen as active, assertive, and competitive in interpersonal relations.

High Elevations (T = More than 65). Women in this range are frequently described as confident, spontaneous, and uninhibited; they usually are found in traditionally masculine occupations and activities. Furthermore, they may be rebelling against the traditional female role and feel uncomfortable in many heterosexual situations. As the scale elevation increases, there is likewise an increase in aggressiveness and a certain "tough-minded" approach to the world. It is relatively rare to find this as a high point in females.

Scale 6: Paranoia (Pa)

Scale 6 includes 40 items which attempt to assess an individual's degree of suspiciousness, interpersonal sensitivity, and self-righteousness. The basic clinical picture of the paranoid personality includes delusional beliefs, ideas of reference, feelings of persecution, pervasive suspiciousness, grandiose self-beliefs, and interpersonal rigidity. In attempting to measure these variables, the scale 6 items range from questions regarding overt psychotic content to milder questions on the perceived ulterior motives of others. More specifically, the item content can be grouped around three basic categories having to do with (1) ideas of external influence, (2) poignancy, and (3) moral virtue.

With normal individuals, moderate elevations on scale 6 suggest that the person is emotional and softhearted, with an excess of personal sensitivity. However, the characteristics of low scorers are not consistent, and there are some differences between males and females. Males are frequently seen as cheerful, balanced, decisive, lacking in a strong sense of conscience, self-centered, and having a narrow range of interests. Females are usually described as balanced, mature, and reasonable. Within more disturbed populations, elevations frequently indicate the presence of delusions of self-reference, an extreme rigidity of attitude, disordered thought processes, and a grandiose self-concept.

Many of the items found in scale 6 are obviously socially undesirable, and therefore some paranoids may decide to answer them in an "unparanoid" direction. For example, the statement "Someone has control over my mind" is fairly transparent as to what it is attempting to assess and thus may not be admitted to. For this reason, the scale is considered one of the weakest, at least with regard to its original intent of detecting paranoid thinking. In fact, many extremely paranoid persons show no elevation at all. Thus, a low score does not necessarily exclude the possibility of a paranoid personality, even if the validity scales are normal. In fact, a low 6 may even be an indicator of paranoid thinking since paranoids typically attempt to hide their suspiciousness out of fear of others' reactions. This is especially true for bright and psychologically sophisticated persons. They could, for example, even mask their paranoid functioning within the context of a more socially approved group such as the Minute-men. However, if the scale is definitely elevated, this tends to be a good indicator of paranoid processes.

If there are pronounced elevations on scales 6 and 8 regardless of implications derived from elevations on other scales, this is highly suggestive of paranoid schizophrenia (see 68/86 code type). Occasionally, an elevated 6 and 3 profile occurs which indicates a repression of hostile and aggressive feelings. Overtly, these people might deny suspiciousness and competitiveness, and even see the world in naively accepting, positive, and almost Polyannaish terms. They can quickly develop comfortable, superficial relationships with relative ease. However, as the relationship's depth and closeness increase, the underlying hostility, egocentricity, and even ruthlessness become more apparent (see 36/63 code type).

Low 6 (T = 27–44). Persons with low scores are difficult to place in a clear-cut category, and there are differences between males and females. Whereas both are perceived as being balanced, males are also cheerful, decisive, lacking in a strong sense of conscience, and self-centered, with a narrow range of interests. Females are more frequently described as mature and reasonable. However, there is likely to be a high degree of variability in the characteristics of low scorers so interpretations should be made with appropriate caution. It is important to differentiate the low scores of normal persons from those of paranoid persons who are attempting to hide their suspiciousness. In these cases, paranoids can have the same features as high 6 scorers in that they are touchy, moody, overly cautious, and extremely sensitive in personal relationships. Furthermore, they are often stubborn, evasive, and wary, and they feel that dire consequences will result from revealing themselves to others. However, they tend to be somewhat better put together than high scorers, and typically find more socially acceptable ways to focus and express their paranoid traits.

Moderate Elevations (T = 60–75).   As the elevation within this range increases, there is also a corresponding increase of undue interpersonal sensitivity. Even moderate criticisms from others can set off a depressive reaction in which the individual will brood over, enlarge, and ruminate on such statements. These people frequently report feelings of being limited and pressed by the social and vocational aspects of their lives. As scale 6 elevations increase, there is a correspondingly higher likelihood of outright suspiciousness, distrust, and resentment which may become focused on either real or imaginary wrongs. Their most frequent defense mechanism is the projection of blame and hostility onto others, and what hostility such individuals do express is done in a covert and indirect manner. Often, for example, they might develop a self-punishing, intropunitive role outwardly, yet arrange social situations in which others will become the victims of their indirectly expressed hostility. They can then fall back on a "what did I do?" position, thus neutralizing criticism directed at them.

High Elevations (T = More than 75).   With elevations in this range, it may be important to consider the content and implications of the individual scale items to differentiate between an overt psychotic delusional system and a more coherent paranoid personality disorder. This distinction can also be aided by referring to the relative elevation of scale 8. It is often helpful to have the person describe why he responded to certain items in a particular way. If the overall profile is valid, an elevation above T = 75 is more likely to suggest a disabling level of pathology. It will certainly indicate a paranoid person who is brooding and suspicious, ruminates on grudges, and feels he has not gotten a fair deal out of life. Frequently, such people have delusions of reference, feelings of persecution, and the likelihood of fixed obsessions, compulsions, and phobias. In treatment, there is a high likelihood that they will be rigid and overly argumentative. They may use either the actual termination of treatment or the implied possibility of termination to protect their system as well as to manipulate and control the therapist.

Scale 7: Psychasthenia (Pt)

Scale 7 consists of 48 items which measure the extent of symptoms related to anxiety, irrational fears, self-devaluation, and excessive doubt. In general, it is the MMPI's best single indicator of anxiety and ruminative self-doubt. However, the items are usually fairly obvious about the information they are requesting, and a defensive orientation can easily reduce the elevation. For this reason, there is a full 1 K addition which is used as a corrective measure to counter the effects of such a defensive position.

Individuals who score high on scale 7 will typically be obsessionally worried, tense, indecisive, and unable to concentrate. They will almost always show extreme obsessional thoughts and utilize the defense mechanisms of intellectualization, rationalization, isolation, and undoing in an attempt to reduce anxiety and tension. However, high scorers on psychasthenia are not the same as individuals who utilize a compulsive defense system. In fact, many rigidly compulsive persons score low precisely because their system effectively wards off such feelings as insecurity, anxiety, and self-doubt. Within a medical context, high scale 7 scorers characteristically overreact and show an extreme amount of concern about relatively minor medical problems. They are usually seen as rigid, anxious, fearful, and agitated, and they typically have cardiac complaints or problems relating to their gastrointestinal or genitourinary systems. Within more normal populations, moderate elevations suggest persons who are dissatisfied, verbal, individualistic, and high strung. They will also tend to have perfectionistic orientations combined with excessively high standards of morality.

As with scale 2, some elevation on scale 7 reflects a favorable prognosis for psychotherapy because there is a sufficient degree of internal discomfort to increase the motivation for self-evaluation and change. These two scales are extremely important clinically since they provide an index of the degree of psychological pain the person is experiencing, and they are often referred to as the "distress scales" (see code type 27/72). However, if the scale elevation is extremely high, this may preclude talking therapy and indicate the need for medication until the individual is sufficiently relaxed to resume more effective communication. Another important consideration is the relative elevation of 7 and 8. If scale 7 is higher, it suggests that the person is continuing to struggle with, and feel anxious about, a psychotic process. However, a scale 7 which is significantly lower than scale 8 can indicate that the person has given up and allowed the psychosis to become more fixed (see code type 78/87).

Low 7 (T = 20–44). In general, an individual who scores within this range has a relaxed, alert attitude, is self confident, and rarely worries over relatively insignificant difficulties. Even if self-referred, it is rare to see low scale 7 scorers in clinical populations. Low male scorers are frequently described as balanced, efficient, independent, relaxed, self-confident, and secure. Women who score low on scale 7 are similarly described as balanced, relaxed, and confident, but also as cheerful, alert, and placid.

Moderate Elevations (T = 60–74). Moderately high scorers tend to be conscientious, orderly, and self-critical, and to worry over minor problems. Typically, they are perfectionistic and have excessively high moral standards. As the scale elevation within this range increases (T = more than 65), there is also the likelihood of strong anxiety, tension, and worry. Rationalization and intellectualization become increasingly more prominent but are likely to be generally inefficient in controlling anxiety.

High Elevations (T = More than 75). With higher elevations, the same general patterns just discussed become even more pronounced. Furthermore, these people are often described as rigid, meticulous, religious, worrisome, and apprehensive. Elevations nearing 80 or more are likely to reflect levels of anxiety sufficiently high to disrupt the individuals' ability to perform daily routine tasks. Furthermore, they may have disabling feelings of guilt, as well as fixed obsessions, compulsions, or phobias, and may be extremely fearful and agitated. The defense mechanisms which are being utilized are unlikely to effectively bring about relief, and the constant rehashing of problems does not create effective solutions because of excessive uncertainty and indecisiveness.

Scale 8: Schizophrenia (Sc)

Scale 8 is the longest one on the MMPI and consists of 78 items which were originally intended to differentiate normals from schizophrenics. However, this differentiation has not been entirely successful primarily because the pattern of schizophrenia is highly varied, and includes complex and sometimes contradictory behavioral features. Thus, great care should be taken when attempting to make a diagnosis of schizophrenia, and other sources of data should be taken into account. Furthermore, the scale should not be interpreted too narrowly since a limited conception of its significance may lead merely to a label rather than to a more full and in-depth understanding of the individual's personality.

Scale 8 items are extremely varied and attempt to assess such factors as unusual thought processes, apathy, feelings of social alienation, poor family relations, and peculiarities of perception. Still other questions are directed towards reduced efficiency, difficulties in concentration, impulse control, a general inability to cope, and general fears and worries. There are basically three wide categories into which the items can be divided: (1) social and emotional alienation, (2) lack of ego mastery, and (3) bizarre sensory experiences.

If the individual has a pronounced elevation on scale 8, he is likely to feel alienated, misunderstood, and apart from social situations. There will be a feeling that somehow he is lacking something significant in his ability to adapt and adjust, and it is unlikely that he will have developed adequate social skills. Furthermore, he may have fundamental questions regarding his personal worth and identity. Many high scorers are painfully withdrawn, have few if any social relationships, and are highly involved in their inner fantasy life. They have a difficult time communicating as well as in maintaining coherent and focused thought processes. Even with moderate elevations, there is likely to be some difficulty thinking and communicating. Even when high scorers are making apparent sense, a person will have the feeling that he is missing the more significant aspects of what they are trying to say. Typically, they avoid making unequivocal statements and will usually not stay on any one idea for an extended length of time.

Clinically, schizophrenic patients usually score between 80 and 90. Thus, with scores below 80, a diagnosis of schizophrenia should be made cautiously. Sometimes, elevations up to 90 are found for extremely anxious patients, adolescent adjustment reactions, prepsychotics, and borderline personalities.

Elevations on scales 4 and 8 frequently occur in individuals who developed an early distrust towards the world. They usually see interpersonal relationships as dangerous and often respond with angry rebelliousness (see 48/84 code type). A rather infrequent but significant pattern which needs to be understood contains elevations on scales 8 and 9 (see 89/98 code type). Individuals with this pattern usually have an extremely difficult time dealing with others, not only because they feel alienated but also because they continually deflect any coherent attempt to focus on a situation. This pattern is extremely difficult to work with therapeutically because these people have a difficult time focusing their attention, and not only have a distorted view of the world but also have the energy to act on these distorted perceptions. Other frequently occurring profiles are the prognostic considerations related to scales 7 and 8 (see scale 7 and the 78/87 code type) and the schizoid configuration of elevated F, 2, 4, 8, and low 0 (see scale 2).

Low 8 (T = 21–44). Low scorers on scale 8 are often compliant, overly accepting of authority, concrete, and practically oriented. In addition, they are usually controlled, restrained, friendly, and adaptable.

Moderate Elevations (T = 60–74). Since scale 8 has 78 highly varied items, the personality descriptions resulting from moderate elevations likewise tend to be highly varied. Thus it is important to look at the overall scale configurations and to include other relevant data. At the lower end of this range, it is not uncommon to find benign or "neurotic" profiles. Often these individuals tend to have abstract interests, are not interested in practical matters, and are not highly involved with people. They frequently have philosophical interests and approach tasks from an innovative perspective, and others may see them as aloof and uninvolved. These latter characteristics are especially likely if there is an additional elevation on scale 0. Adolescents who are seen for evaluation frequently score in this range.

Within the upper ranges of moderate elevations, it is sometimes difficult to distinguish between a sense of general alienation or blatant psychotic content. In assessing the presence of psychotic processes, it is helpful to note whether scales F and 6 are elevated and to look at individual scale items, particularly the critical items (see Appendix I).

High Elevations (T = 75–90). If scale 8 scores are near 75, the individual typically appears unusual, unconventional, and eccentric, but can often maintain an adequate social and vocational adjustment. This is particularly true if the other clinical scales are relatively low. With higher elevations, however, these individuals become progressively more socially withdrawn and have a difficult time relating to others effectively. They often withdraw and tend to be highly invested in autistic, wish-fulfilling fantasies. In even the most basic interpersonal situations, they have a difficult time knowing what is expected of them. As the elevation reaches above 80, and if the overall profile appears valid, there is an increasing likelihood of a significant thought disorder complete with confusion and strange thoughts, beliefs, and actions.

Scale 9: Hypomania (Ma)

Scale 9 includes 46 fairly heterogeneous items which assess the relative degree of an individual's energy level, expansiveness, egotism, and irritability. The scale was originally developed using a group of psychiatric patients who had diagnoses of hypomania and mild acute mania. Their clinical syndrome involved cyclical periods of euphoria, increased irritability, and unproductive activity, much of which could be seen as distractive maneuvers designed to stave off an impending depression. The test items themselves can be broken down into general categories having to do with psychomotor retardation, amorality, imperturbability, and ego inflation.

Among normal males, high scorers are characteristically warm, enthusiastic, outgoing, and uninhibited. Furthermore, they can often be easily offended, are hyperactive and tense, and have an unusual capacity for sustained effort. Other characteristics are that they are frequently generous, affectionate, adventurous, expressive, and individualistic; they enjoy alcohol; and they are interested in national and political matters. Female normals who score relatively high tend to be frank, courageous, idealistic, and often seen by others as talkative, enthusiastic, and versatile.

A general consideration, however, is that the scale can reflect the level of energy at the time of testing and is therefore somewhat subject to fluctuations depending on the individual's mood. Of particular importance is the fact that manic patients, at the time of their initial hospitalization, are often too flighty and incoherent to take the test. When they finally calm down, there can be a strong deflation which may result in a low score on scale 9. Thus, a low score on 9 does not necessarily exclude the possibility of a manic diagnosis. However, as the scale score increases there is increasing likelihood of distractibility, narcissism, poor control, and superficiality. There may also be difficulties in interpersonal relations, aggressive impulses, and amoral behavior.

Low scorers often lack a normal degree of optimism, are listless and apathetic, have low self-esteem, and lack initiative and drive. If their scores are extremely low, this usually reflects a significant depression, even if scale 2 is not significantly elevated.

Two important profile patterns are the relation of scale 9 to scale 2 and its relation to K. Although scales 2 and 9 are usually negatively correlated, in some cases they may both be high (see code type 29/92). This may reflect several possible conditions but, in particular, suggests an agitated state in which the person is acutely aware of pressure from hostile impulses. A combined 2 and 9 elevation may also occur with certain types of organic brain lesions or in individuals with an introspective preoccupation and heightened narcissistic absorption, for example, disturbed adolescents who are experiencing "identity" problems. If scale 9 is moderately elevated and scales 2 and 7 are low, the individual may have an almost compulsive need to seek security through interpersonal power and narcissistic competitiveness. If an elevated K scale is found with an elevated 9, the individual additionally tends to be managerial, autocratic, and power hungry, but also has a high degree of compulsive energy directed towards organizing others. If, on the other hand, K is low, the individual is usually not overly defensive, but may be extremely competitive, narcissistic, and threatened by situations in which he must be submissive or dependent. His self-esteem is based on eliciting weakness and submission from others, but what he actually receives is usually a grudging deference and respect. In females, this profile is often accompanied by an exhibitionistic self-display of physical attractiveness. In therapy, there typically occur a wide range of self-display, power struggles, and a poor likelihood of success due to control issues, flightiness, and an unwillingness to look at one's inner pain and weakness.

Low 9 (T = 21–44). Low 9 scorers usually have an extremely low level of energy and are listless, apathetic, pessimistic regarding the future, and lacking in self-confidence. They may, for example, find it difficult to get out of bed in the morning as well as to maintain enough energy to function effectively throughout the day. If 9 is extremely low, this may reflect a serious depression, even though scale 2 might be within normal limits. However, a significant demographic variable is that it is more frequent to find low scores in older individuals than in younger ones. Thus, if a low score is found in a younger person, it carries greater significance since it is relatively unusual.

Moderate Elevations (T = 60–74). Moderately high scores on 9 are typical from individuals who are pleasant, energetic, enthusiastic, and sociable and who have a wide range of interests. They are usually optimistic, independent, and self-confident, particularly if there are correspondingly low scores on scales 2 and 0. Within higher elevations (65–75), it becomes somewhat difficult to distinguish a normal, energetic, active and ambitious person with a productive life, from a hypomanic who is ineffective, nonfocused, and hyperactive. Thus, the clinical interview and historical data may become particularly useful at this point.

High Elevations (T = More than 75). With higher elevations, there is an increasing probability that individuals are maladaptively hyperactive and agitated, have low impulse control, and become irritable even over relatively small obstacles and delays. They are likely to quickly develop relationships, but since they are restless and unable to remain focused for any length of time, these relationships are usually lacking in any real depth. Their enthusiasm tends to be intense but short-lived, and the expression of their energy is scattered and generally unproductive. In elevations exceeding 80, there is an increasing likelihood of characteristically manic behaviors including a flight of ideas, inflated feelings of self-importance, and hyperactive expressions such as pacing and nervous twitches.

Scale 0: Social Introversion (Si)

Scale 0 is comprised of 70 items which were selected from the responses of college students on an introversion-extroversion continuum. The scale is a fairly stable measure of the extent to which an individual participates in social events and his degree of comfort in interpersonal relations. The social introvert, as suggested by an elevation on scale 0, often has limited social skills, withdraws from many interpersonal situations, and feels uncomfortable in social interactions.

Normal males who score high on scale 0 are typically modest, inhibited, lacking in self-confidence, conforming, sensitive, submissive, and generally deficient in poise and social presence. Normal high-scoring females are modest, shy, self-effacing, sensitive, and prone to worry. Low male scorers, on the other hand, are typically sociable, expressive, exhibitionistic, socially competitive, and verbally fluent. Furthermore, they are somewhat dominant, persuasive, manipulative, and opportunistic. Females are similarly sociable, enthusiastic, talkative, assertive, and adventurous. Although low scores may suggest interpersonal warmth and a relatively high degree of comfort in social relationships, extremely low scores may reflect a person with a wide range of well-developed social techniques who has many social contacts. However, his interactions can often be characterized as flighty and superficial.

In general, scale 0 serves to color many of the other scales in terms of how comfortable and involved the individual is with interpersonal relationships. Typically a low score on 0 reduces the degree of pathology that may be suggested by other scale elevations and indicates that the person has most likely developed socially acceptable outlets for difficulties he may be experiencing. Higher scores, on the other hand, reflect a relatively low level of social adeptness and competence. This is of particular importance if scale 0 elevations are accompanied by a high 2 or 8, in which case the individual is unlikely to have developed an adequate social support system and will typically have a low level of social skills accompanied by strong feelings of social alienation.

Low 0 (T = 25–44). Low scorers are often warm, sociable, outgoing, gregarious, and involved with groups. However, extremely low scores may suggest that these people have very well-developed social techniques but perhaps have few close and meaningful relationships. Behind their somewhat well-developed external image, they may have underlying feelings of insecurity, a high need for social approval, extreme sensitivity, and unresolved conflicts regarding fears of dependency.

Moderate Elevations (T = 60–69). Moderate scorers tend to be reserved, aloof, shy, timid, retiring, and often experienced by others as difficult to know.

High Elevations (T = 70–85). Individuals who score high on scale 9 are usually acutely aware of the discomfort they feel in most social situations. They are perceived by others as shy, introverted, and anxious while around people. Typically, they have feelings of inferiority, lack self-confidence, are moody, and do not have a social support group to help them through difficulties.

TWO-POINT CODES

In this section, we will consider the meaning of the two highest scales. This approach can often assess the relationship between test patterns and indicate how these patterns relate to various classes of nontest behavior. The selection of which two-point codes to include has been based on their frequency of occurrence, the thoroughness of the research performed on them, and their relative clinical importance. Thus, some two-point codes will not be discussed.

An important consideration is that this approach is most appropriate for disturbed populations in which T score elevations are at least 70 and preferably higher. The descriptions are clearly oriented around the pathological dimensions of an individual. The two-point code descriptions, then, do not have the same divisions into low, moderate, and high elevations as the individual scores but are directed primarily towards discussions of high elevations. When considering two-point codes which are in the moderate range (T = 65–70), interpretations should be made with caution and the more extreme descriptions should be considerably modified or even excluded.

Usually, the relative elevation of one of the scales in relation to the other does not make much difference as long as the elevations are still somewhat similar in magnitude. A general approach is that if one scale is 10 points or more higher than the other, then the higher one gives more color to, or provides more emphasis for, the interpretation. Specific elaborations are made for scales in which a significant difference between their relative elevations is especially important. If the scales have an equal magnitude, then they should be given equal emphasis.

In some cases, three or more scales might be equally elevated, thereby making it difficult to clearly establish which scales represent the two-point code. In these cases, clinicians should look at the descriptions provided for other possible combinations. For example, if a particular profile had scales 2, 7, and 8 elevated, then the clinician should look up the 27/72 code as well as codes 78/87 and 28/82. The descriptions of all three of these codes can then be integrated into a more meaningful and accurate interpretation. When there are third or fourth scales that are frequently elevated along with the two-point code, they too will be discussed.

In developing meaningful interpretations it is important to continually consider the underlying significance of the elevated scales. This means taking into account such factors as the manner in which the scales interact, the particular category of psychopathology they suggest, and the recurring patterns or themes indicated. Whenever possible, DSM III classifications have been used, but the term "neurosis" is used occasionally because of its ability to summarize a wide variety of disorders and/or ability to refer to a cluster of related scales ("neurotic triad"). In describing a specific individual, there will always be some characteristics described in the code types which are highly accurate for that person and others which are not particularly relevant or accurate. Clinicians, then, will need to continually reflect on their data so as to develop descriptions that are both accurate and relevant.

12/21

Difficulties experienced by patients with the 12/21 code type revolve around physical symptoms and complaints which can be either organic or functional. Common complaints relate to pain, irritability, anxiety, physical tension, fatigue, and overconcern with physical functions. In addition to these symptoms is the presence of a significant level of depression. Their characteristic style of handling psychological conflict is through repression and attending to real, exaggerated, or imagined physical difficulties. Regardless of whether or not these physical difficulties are organically based, these individuals will exaggerate their symptoms and use them to manipulate others. In other words, they elaborate their complaints beyond what can be physically confirmed, often doing so by misinterpreting normal bodily functions. Typically they have learned to live with their complaints and use them to achieve their own needs. They lack insight, are not psychologically sophisticated, and resent any implications that their difficulties may be even partially psychological. This code pattern is more frequently encountered in males and older persons.

The three varieties of patients which this code is likely to suggest are the generalized hypochondriac, the chronic pain patient, and persons having recent and severe accidents. General hypochondriacs are likely to have significant depressive features and to be self-critical, indirect, and manipulative. If their difficulties are solely functional, they are more likely to be shy and withdrawn, whereas persons with a significant organic component are likely to be loud complainers. Furthermore, complaints are usually focused around the trunk of the body and involve the viscera, in contrast to the 13/31 code in which complaints refer more frequently to the central nervous system and peripheral limbs. When the 12/21 code is produced by chronic pain patients with an organic basis, they are likely to have given in to their pain and learned to live with it. Their experience and/or expression of this pain is likely to be exaggerated, they use it to manipulate others, and they may have a past history of drug or alcohol abuse which represents attempts at "self-medication." The most common profile associated with heavy drinkers consists of elevations in scales 1, 2, 3, and 4. Such persons will experience considerable physical discomfort, digestive difficulties, tension, depression, and hostility, and will usually have poor work and relationship histories. The third category of patient associated with 12/21 codes involves persons who are responding to recent, severe accidents. Their elevations on scales 1 and 2 reflect an acute reactive depression which occurs as a result of their response to the limiting effects of their condition.

The most frequent diagnosis with this code is hypochondriasis, and the somatic overconcern can be further supported if there is a corresponding elevation on scale 3. With a 127 profile, the likelihood of anxiety neurosis is increased. Such people will be fearful, anxious, nonassertive, dependent, and weak, and through the use of their helplessness, they will manipulate others into taking care of them. If scales 1 and 2 are elevated along with 8 and/or F, the person might be diagnosed as having a schizophrenic disorder with somatic delusions. With only moderate elevations in scale 8, the individual may still be hypochondriacal but with the presence of some mild somatic delusions, interpersonal alienation, and mild mental confusion. Less frequent patterns are 124, 126, and 126 4 which may reflect a personality disorder, especially a passive-aggressive personality experiencing depression.

13/31

The 13/31 code type is associated with the classic "conversion V" which occurs when scale 2 is significantly lower (10 points or more) than scales 1 or 3. As 2 becomes lower in relation to 1 and 3, the likelihood of a conversion disorder increases. This pattern is further suggested in males with correspondingly high scales 4 and 5, and in females with a correspondingly high 4 but lowered 5. There is typically very little anxiety experienced by persons with these profiles since they are converting psychological conflict into physical complaints. However, this can be checked by looking at the corresponding elevations of scales 2 and 7. If these are also high, it indicates that persons are experiencing anxiety and depression perhaps because their conversions are currently unable to effectively avoid their conflicts.

Persons with "conversion V's" will typically engage in extensive complaining about physical difficulties. Complaints may involve problems related to eating such as nausea, anorexia, or bulimia, and there may be the presence of vague "neurological" difficulties such as dizziness, numbness, weakness, and fatigue. However, there is often a sense of indifference and a marked lack of concern regarding these symptoms. These individuals have a strong need to appear rational and socially acceptable, yet nonetheless control others through histrionic and symptom-related means. They defensively attempt to appear as hypernormal, which is particularly pronounced if the K scale is also elevated. Usually they are extremely threatened by any hint that they are unconventional and tend to organize themselves around ideals of service to others. Regardless of the actual original cause of the complaints, there is a strong need to exaggerate them. Even if their complaints were originally caused by an organic impairment, there will be a strong functional basis to their problems. Interpersonal relationships will be superficial, with extensive repression of hostility, and oftentimes there will be an exhibitionistic flavor to their interactions. If scale 3 is higher than scale 1, this allows for the expression of a certain degree of optimism and, interestingly enough, any conversion will most likely be to the trunk of the body. Thus, patients might complain of such difficulties as gastrointestinal disorders, or diseases of the lungs or heart. Furthermore, this suggests the strong use of denial and repression. These people are passive, sociable, and dependent; they manipulate others through complaints about their "medical" problems. Conversely, if scale 3 is lower than scale 1, the person tends to be significantly more negative, and any conversion is likely to be to the body extremities such as the hands or legs. If scores are very high on scale 8, a corresponding peak on scale 1 is associated with somatic delusions.

When the "conversion V" is within the normal range (less than 70), persons will be optimistic but somewhat immature and tangential. Under stress, there will usually be an increase in their symptom-related complaints. They can be described as responsible, helpful, normal, and sympathetic.

The most frequent diagnoses with 13 codes are hypochondriasis, conversion disorder, and histrionic personality. Anxiety may be present if either scale 7 or 8 is elevated, but it is usually absent. The 13/31 profile is also found in pain patients with an organic injury whose symptoms typically worsen under stress.

14/41

The 14/41 code is encountered somewhat rarely, but it is important since persons with these elevations will be severely hypochondriacal. Their interpersonal interactions will be extremely manipulative but rarely antisocial. They will be able to maintain control over their impulses but will do so in a way which is bitter, self-pitying, and resentful of any rules and limits that are imposed on them. Furthermore, they will be egocentric, will demand attention, and will express continuous concern with their physical complaints. There will be some similarities to other high-scoring 4s in that they may have a history of alcohol abuse, drug addiction, and poor work and personal relationships. Usually, they will be resistant to therapy, although they may have a satisfactory response to short-term, symptom-oriented treatment. However, long-term therapy will be difficult and characterized by sporadic participation.

The two most frequently encountered diagnoses will be hypochondriasis and a personality disorder, especially antisocial personality. Differentiation between these two can be helped by noting the relative strength of either scale 1 or 4, as well as other related scales. Profiles involving "neurotic" features (anxiety, somatoform, dissociative, and dysthymic disorders) are characterized by a relatively higher scale 1 with 2 and/or 3 also elevated, whereas personality disorders are more strongly suggested when scale 4 is the primary high point.

18/81

Peaks on scales 1 and 8 are found with persons who present a variety of vague and unusual complaints. They may also experience confusion, disorientation, and difficulty concentrating. Focusing on their physical symptoms represents a means of organizing their thoughts, although the beliefs related to these symptoms may represent delusions. Their ability to deal effectively with stress and anxiety is extremely limited. They will experience interpersonal relationships with a considerable degree of distance and alienation. Others will perceive them as eccentric or even bizarre. They will distrust others and may disrupt their relationships because of difficulty in controlling their hostility. There may even be paranoid ideation which will probably, but not necessarily, be reflected in an elevated scale 6. For the most part, their level of insight will be poor, which will make them difficult candidates for psychotherapy.

Common scales which are elevated along with 1 and 8 are 2, 3, and/or 7. These serve to color or give additional meaning to 18/81. Thus, an elevated scale 2 will emphasize self-critical, pessimistic dimensions; 7, the presence of fears and anxiety; and 3, the likelihood of conversions and/or somatic delusions.

The 18/81 code is frequently diagnosed as schizophrenia, especially if the F scale is also high. With a normal F, hypochondriasis is an important possibility, but if scale 7 is elevated an anxiety disorder is also strongly suggested.

19/91

The 19/91 code is rarely encountered but is important in that it may suggest organic difficulties relating to endocrine dysfunction or to the central nervous system. There will be extensive complaining and overconcern with difficulties, but these patients may paradoxically attempt to deny and conceal their complaints at the same time. In other words, they may be significantly invested in avoiding confrontations relating to their complaints, yet will make a display of these techniques of avoidance. They will typically be extroverted, talkative, and outgoing, but also tense and restless. The expectations they have of themselves will be extremely high, yet their goals will be poorly defined and often unobtainable. If there is not an organic basis to their complaints, then their behavior may be an attempt to stave off an impending depression. Often this depression will be related to strong but unacceptable dependency needs.

Both hypochondriasis and manic states are frequent diagnoses and may occur simultaneously. These may be in response to, and exacerbated by, an underlying organic condition, an impending depression, or both. Corresponding elevations on scales 4 and 6 make the possibility of a passive-aggressive personality an important diagnostic consideration.

23/32

Persons with elevations on scales 2 and 3 are lacking in energy, weak, apathetic, listless, depressed, and anxious. They feel inadequate and have difficulty accomplishing their daily activities. Much of their energy is invested in excessively controlling their feelings and behavior. Although situational stress may act to increase their depression, usually this depression is long-standing, and they have learned to live with their unhappiness and general lack of satisfaction. Their level of insight is poor, they will rarely volunteer for psychotherapy, and they usually do not show significant improvement during psychotherapy. This is primarily because their main dynamic is denial and situations such as therapy represent a threat to their style of avoidance. By keeping their relationships superficial, they achieve a certain level of security. Interpersonally, they appear immature, childish, and socially inadequate.

There are some important male-female differences in the expression of this code type. Males are more ambitious, industrious, serious, and competitive, but also immature and dependent. They strive for increased responsibilities, yet also fear them. They want to appear normal and receive recognition for their accomplishments, yet they often feel ignored and their level of work adjustment is often inadequate. In contrast, females are more apathetic and weak, and experience significant levels of depression. They have usually resigned themselves to long-term unhappiness and a lack of satisfaction. Although there is often significant marital strife, they rarely seek divorce. They also rarely seek treatment and seem resigned to living with their unhappiness.

Dysthymic disorder is the most frequent diagnosis given to this code. Corresponding elevations on scales 4, 6, and 0 may provide additional information relating to the personality of these persons. With a high scale 4, there is more likely to be an angry, brooding component to their depression, with underlying antisocial thoughts, yet their external behavior is usually overcontrolled. An elevated scale 6 suggests that their depression relates to extreme interpersonal sensitivity and distrust, whereas a high 0 indicates that they are socially withdrawn and introspective. An additional diagnosis which should be considered is a major depression with psychotic features, especially if scales F and/or 8 are also elevated.

24/42

The most significant aspect of the 24/42 code is that these persons have an underlying antisocial trend to their personality with difficulty maintaining control over their impulses. However, once they act on their impulses, they experience guilt and anxiety regarding the consequences of their actions. This anxiety usually occurs too late to serve as an effective deterrent, and these individuals are unable to plan ahead effectively. The depression they experience then is probably situational, and the distress they do feel may reflect a fear of external consequences rather than an actual internalized moral code. Once the situation has subsided, there is usually further acting out. For this reason, the 24/42 code is sometimes referred to as reflecting an antisocial personality who has been caught. Although such people may promise to change and their guilt is generally authentic, their acting out is usually resistant to change. Effective therapy must include clear limits, a change in their environment, warm supports, and continual contact.

The history of persons with high scales 2 and 4 is often characterized by heavy drinking and/or drug abuse which serves as a form of self-medication for their depression. Their interpersonal relationships are poor, which is reflected in numerous family difficulties and sporadic employment. Their prospects for long-term employment are rarely favorable. These problems have often resulted in numerous legal complications. Such persons respond to their failures with self-criticism and self-doubt. The initial impression that they give may be friendly or even charming, and in a hospital setting they may attempt to manipulate the staff.

The hostility which is present with the 24/42 code may be expressed either directly or indirectly. A more direct expression is suggested if scale 6 is high, since these individuals may feel justified in externalizing their anger due to real or imagined wrongs which have been committed against them. In contrast, a low 6 may reflect a suppression or unconscious denial of hostility. If there are high energy levels suggested by a high scale 9, the persons may be extremely dangerous and volatile, and they may have committed violent behaviors.

The 24/42 code is associated with personality disorders, especially passive-aggressive or antisocial personalities. This is further strengthened if scale 6 is also high. However, this code may also reflect an adjustment disorder with a depressed mood. An important distinction to make is whether the depression is reactive or chronic. If chronic, then difficulties related to anxiety, conversions, and depression (neurotic features) will be more likely to be predominant, especially if scales 1 and 3 are also high. A reactive depression is more likely to represent an antisocial personality who has been apprehended for his impulsive acting out. If scale 4 is extremely elevated (above 90), there may be a psychotic or prepsychotic process, especially if F and 8 are also high.

26/62

The most significant feature of the 26/62 code is extreme sensitivity to real or imagined criticism. These individuals will sometimes read between the lines of what others say in such a way as to create rejection, yet their conclusions will be based on insufficient data. Even minor criticism is brooded over and elaborated upon. Usually, they have long histories of difficulties with interpersonal relationships. Others describe them as resentful, aggressive, and hostile. In order to protect themselves from the impending rejection of others, they will often reject others first which results in other people avoiding them. When they are avoided, they then have evidence that they are being rejected which gives them a justification for feeling and expressing anger. They can then blame others for their difficulties. This cycle is thus self-fulfilling and self-perpetuating, yet such people have difficulty understanding the part they play in creating the interpersonal responses which are directed towards them.

If scales 7, 8, and possibly 9 are also high, there is a greater likelihood of a psychotic or prepsychotic condition, especially paranoid schizophrenia. A more controlled, well-defined paranoid system with a generally adequate level of adjustment may be suggested when scales 2, 6, and F are only moderately elevated. Further possible diagnoses with the 26/62 code are a dysthymic disorder and, if scale 4 is also elevated, a passive-aggressive personality.

27/72

The 27/72 code is extremely common in psychiatric populations and reflects persons who are depressed, agitated, restless, and nervous. This may be accompanied by slowed speech and movements, as well as by insomnia and feelings of social and sexual inadequacy. Scales 2 and 7 reflect the relative degree of subjective turmoil the person is experiencing and therefore are often referred to as the "distress scales." Even though 27/72 persons usually express a great deal of pessimism regarding treatment and the future in general, their psychological distress is ordinarily reactive, and with time, they can be expected to improve. With most patients, the disorder took between one month and one year to develop, and if they report for treatment, it will be their first need for such intervention. The majority are married and their courtships were fairly brief, many marrying within one month of their initial dating. They can be characterized as being perfectionistic, meticulous, and having a high need for recognition. Their thinking is often obsessive, and they experience a wide variety of phobias and fears. Interpersonally they have difficulty asserting themselves, and will be self-blaming and self-punishing. They will rarely be argumentative or provocative. Their consciences are strong and inflexible, and they will often be extremely religious in a rigidly fundamental manner. Physical complaints may include weakness, fatigue, chest pain, constipation, and dizziness.

Moderate elevations on scales 2 and 7 can indicate a good prognosis for therapy, since this suggests that the person is introspective and is experiencing a sufficient amount of distress to be motivated towards change. However, if these scales are extremely high, then the person may be too agitated to be able to focus and concentrate. In such cases, medication may be necessary to relax him sufficiently enough to be able to function in a psychotherapeutic context. The presence of suicidal thoughts is a definite possibility, especially if scales 6 and 8 are also elevated, and the suicidal potential of these patients must be carefully evaluated.

The diagnoses of psychotic and "neurotic" conditions occur with equal frequency with the 27/72 code. The most likely diagnosis in the psychotic direction is either a psychotic depression or a mixed bipolar disorder, and the most important differentiating data come from the client's history. "Neurotic" patients can be either anxious or obsessive-compulsive. However, with only moderate elevations, they may be normals who are fatigued and exhausted, with a high degree of rigidity and excessive worry. This code occurs more frequently with males 27 years or older from higher educational backgrounds.

28/82

Persons with the 28/82 code complain of depression, anxiety, insomnia, fatigue, and weakness, as well as mental confusion, memory impairments, and difficulties in concentrating. They may also feel withdrawn, alienated, agitated, tense, and jumpy. Their motivation to achieve is characteristically low as is their overall level of efficiency. Often they will have fears relating to an inability to control their impulses including suicide. There may also be the presence of delusions and hallucinations, especially if scale 8 is greater than 85. This list of complaints presents a highly diverse description of attributes, only some of which may be present in any specific case. The presence or absence of these complaints must be determined by means other than mere scale elevations. These may include investigating critical items, the use of additional scales such as those developed by Harris and Lingoes, clinical interview data, and personal history. Of particular importance is the determination of the degree to which suicide is a possibility.

Most persons with the 28/82 code are diagnosed as either psychotically depressed or schizophrenic, especially if scale 8 is higher than scale 2. However, a certain percentage can be "neurotic," especially when scales 2 and 8 are only moderately elevated.

29/92

Although anxiety and depression are present with the 29/92 code, there is also a high level of energy which predominates. This energy may be associated with a loss of control, or it may also serve to defend against experiencing underlying depressive feelings. By speeding up their level of activity, these individuals can distract themselves from unpleasant depressive experiences. At times this will be successful, but they may also use alcohol in order either to relax or to decrease their depression. With moderate elevations, this code will at least reflect tension and restlessness.

If both scales are in the higher elevations, it suggests a mixed bipolar depression. However, both scales can change according to the particular phase the patient is in. This code can also reflect certain types of brain-injured patients or a cyclothymic disorder.

34/43

Persons having peaks on scales 3 and 4 are immature and self-centered with a high level of anger which they have difficulty expressing. Thus, it will often be expressed in an indirect, passive-aggressive style. Outwardly, such individuals are continually trying to conform and please other people, but they still experience a considerable degree of anger and need to find ways of controlling or discharging it. They might at times participate in vicariously acting out their aggression through developing a relationship with an individual who directly and spontaneously expresses his hostility. Such a relationship might be characterized by the 34/43 individuals' covertly encouraging and fueling the other person's angry expressions, yet on a more superficial social level, disapproving of them. Typically, these individuals will have poor insight regarding their own behavior. If scale 6 is also high, their lack of insight will be even more pronounced since their hostility will be projected onto others. Usually, past interpersonal relationships have been difficult. There may be a history of acting out, marital discord, and alcohol abuse. Conflicts relating to dependence versus independence are significant since both of these needs are intense. Females are more likely than males to have vague physical complaints. Furthermore, their relationships will be superficial, and will be characterized by naive expectations and a perfectionistic view of the world which is maintained by glossing over and denying conflicts.

The 34/43 code most clearly fits the pattern of a passive-aggressive personality. If both scales are extremely elevated (T greater than 85), then there may be fugue states in which aggressive and/or sexual impulses will be acted out.

36/63

A 36/63 code type indicates that persons are extremely sensitive to criticism, and repress their hostile and aggressive feelings. They are fearful, tense, and anxious, and may complain of physical difficulties such as headaches or stomach problems. Overtly, these people might deny suspiciousness and competitiveness, even seeing the world in naively accepting, positive, and perfectionistic terms. They can quickly and easily develop comfortable, superficial relationships. However, as the relationship's depth and closeness increase, their underlying hostility, egocentricity, and even ruthlessness become more apparent. If scale 6 is higher than scale 3 (by more than 5 points), these individuals will attempt to develop some sense of security in their lives by seeking power and prestige. Their ability to acquire personal insight is limited since they are psychologically unsophisticated and resent suggestions that their difficulties may be even partially psychological. They will usually blame their personal problems on others, which creates one of their major difficulties in relationships. In therapy, they will typically terminate abruptly and unexpectedly, and they can be ruthless, defensive, and uncooperative. If scale 3 is higher than scale 6 (by more than 5 points), their tendency to blame will be reduced, and such people will be more likely to deny any conflicts or problems. This will be consistent with a tendency to idealize both themselves and their world. They will be more likely to develop somatic complaints rather than paranoid ideation, and the chance of a psychotic process is significantly reduced.

38/83

The somewhat rare 38/83 code involves symptoms of anxiety, depression, and complaints such as headaches, gastrointestinal disturbances, and numbness. If scale 8 is significantly higher than scale 3, these individuals may also have thought disturbances including mental confusion, disorientation, difficulties with memory, and at times, delusional thinking. Although they have unusual experiences related to their thought processes and feel socially alienated, they also have strong needs to appear normal and strong needs for affection. However, they feel that if others knew how unusual their experiences were, they would be rejected. Thus, they are extremely afraid of dependent relationships. In order to protect themselves, they use extensive denial which makes their capacity for insight poor.

An important variation from the 38/83 code is when scale 3 is accompanied by an elevation on K, with low F and 8. Persons with this profile are likely to be affiliative, inhibited, and overconventional, and to have an exaggerated need to be liked and approved of by others. Frequently, they maintain an unrealistic, yet unassailable, optimism. They emphasize harmony, perhaps even at the cost of sacrificing their own needs, attitudes, and beliefs. Furthermore, high 3s with low F scores are extremely uncomfortable with anger and will avoid it at all costs. Typically they will also avoid independent decision making and many other situations in which they must exert their power. Since they have an exaggerated sense of optimism and are usually unaware of their personal conflicts, these individuals rarely appear in mental health clinics. It is almost as if any feelings of anger, tension, or defeat are intolerable. Such feelings seem to represent both a personal failure and, perhaps more importantly, a failure in their attempts at controlling their world by developing an overconventional, exaggeratedly optimistic, and inhibited stance.

A frequent diagnosis is schizophrenia, especially if 8 and F are highly elevated. When scale 3 is relatively higher than scale 8, and 8 and/or F is less than 70, somatoform or dissociative disorders (hysterical neurosis) are important considerations.

45/54

High scores on scales 4 and 5 reflect persons who are self-centered, inner directed, and not only nonconformist but likely to openly express this nonconformity in a challenging, confrontive manner. They may also have significant problems with sexual identity and experience sexual dysfunction. A further area of conflict revolves around ambivalence relating to strong but unrecognized dependency needs. Overt homosexuals who make obvious displays of their orientation may have this code, especially if scales 4 and 5 are the only peaks in an otherwise normal profile. However, the 45/54 code should in no way be considered diagnostic of homosexuality but simply, at times, consistent with such an orientation. To obtain further information associated with this or any profile in which scale 5 is a high point, it is extremely helpful to interpret the third highest scale and give it the degree of importance usually associated with the second highest point. Thus, a 456 profile might be interpreted as if it were a 46 code type.

There are some important differences between males and females having this code. Males will be openly nonconformist, but if they are from higher educational levels, they will be more likely to direct their dissatisfaction into social causes and express organized dissent towards the mainstream culture. In these cases, especially if scale 9 is moderately elevated, their pattern of elevation is sometimes referred to as the "peace corps profile." They are dissatisfied with their culture, sensitive, and aware, but they also have the energy to attempt to create change. They are often psychologically sophisticated, and can communicate clearly and openly. In contrast, elevated scales 4 and 9 accompanied by a low scale 5 suggest a high probability of sexual acting out and the probable development of a "Don Juan" type personality. These men are self-centered and have difficulty delaying their gratification, and behind their overt displays of affection is an underlying current of hostility.

Females with the 45/54 code will be openly rebelling against the traditional feminine role. Often motivating this rebellion is an intense fear related to developing dependent relationships. A further alternative interpretation is that these women are merely involved in a subculture or occupation which emphasizes traditionally male-oriented activities.

46/64

Persons with the 46/64 code type are hostile, brooding, distrustful, irritable, self-centered, and usually unable to form close relationships. They have significant levels of social maladjustment often related to continually blaming others for their personal faults. This style of blaming prevents them from developing insight into their own feelings and behavior, since they are constantly focusing on others' behavior rather than their own. They lack self-criticism, and are highly defensive and argumentative especially if L and K are also high. Although they lack self-criticism, they are highly sensitive to real or imagined criticism from others, often inferring hostility or rejection when this was not actually intended. In order to avoid rejection and maintain a certain level of security, they become extremely adept at manipulating others. Often they will have a history of drug addiction or alcohol abuse.

Frequent corresponding high points are on scales 2, 3, and/or 8. Males with high 8s are often psychotic, especially paranoid schizophrenic or prepsychotic, but with 2 and/or 3 also elevated, the chances of a borderline condition are significantly increased. These men are likely to be angry and have significant conflicts relating to their own denied, but strong, needs for dependency. They are likely to rebel against authority figures and may use suicidal threats as a means of manipulating others. Females with a 46/64 code type may be psychotic or prepsychotic, but they are more often passive-aggressive personalities. If scale 3 is also elevated, they will have intense needs for affection and will be egocentric and demanding.

47/74

Persons with high scores on scales 4 and 7 experience guilt over their behavior, and are brooding and resentful. Although they are frequently insensitive to the feelings of others, they are intensely concerned with their own responses and feelings. They justify this insensitivity because they feel rejected or restricted by others. Their behavioral and interpersonal difficulties follow a predictable cycle in which they will alternately express anger and then feel guilty over their behavior. While they feel angry they may have little control over their behavior, which results in impulsive acting out. This is then followed by a phase of excessive overcontrol accompanied by guilt, brooding, and self-pity. Frustrated by these feelings, they may then attempt to selfishly meet their needs through such means as alcohol abuse, promiscuity, or aggressive acting out. Thus the cycle continues and is usually fairly resistant to change. These persons respond to limit setting with anxiety and resentfulness, often either testing the limits or completely ignoring them. This frequently leads to legal problems and to difficulties in their work and home relationships. Although they do feel genuine and even excessive guilt and remorse for their behavior, their self-control is still inadequate and their acting out continues. This is a chronic pattern, and therapeutic attempts to decrease the anxiety of these individuals may actually result in an increase in their acting out because the control created by their guilt and remorse is diminished. Diagnostically, the 47/74 type is most likely to be either an antisocial personality or experiencing an anxiety disorder.

48/84

Persons with the 48/84 code are strange, eccentric, and emotionally distant, and have severe problems with adjustment. Their behavior is unpredictable and erratic, and may involve strange sexual responses. Usually there will be antisocial behavior resulting in legal complications, and these individuals are nonconforming, lack empathy, and are impulsive. Sometimes they will be members of strange religious cults or unusual political organizations. In their early family histories, they learned that relationships were dangerous because of constant confrontation with intense family conflicts. They were rejected and, as a result, felt alienated and hostile, sometimes attempting to compensate with counterrejection and other forms of retaliation. Their academic and later work performance has usually been erratic and characterized by underachievement. In interpersonal relationships, their judgment is generally poor and their style of communication is likely to be inadequate. Often others feel as if they are missing important elements or significant connotations of what the 48/84 is saying, but they can't figure out exactly what or why.

If F is elevated with a low scale 2, these individuals are typically aggressive, cold, and punitive, and have a knack for inspiring guilt and anxiety in others. Often they take on roles in which such behavior is socially sanctioned, for example, a rigid law enforcement officer, an overzealous clergyman, or a school disciplinarian. Their behavior may range all the way from being merely stern, punitive, and disapproving to encompassing actual clinical sadism. Underneath these overt behaviors, they usually have a deep sense of alienation, vulnerability, and loneliness, which may give rise to feelings of anxiety and discomfort.

Criminal behavior occurs frequently in males with a 48/84 code type, especially with an elevated scale 9. The crimes are likely to be bizarre, and often extremely violent, involving homicide and/or sexual assault. These behaviors are usually impulsive, poorly planned, without apparent reason, and generally self-defeating, eventually resulting in self-punishment. Females are less likely to act criminally, but their relationships will usually be primarily sexual and they will rarely become emotionally close. Often they will form relationships with men who are significantly inferior to themselves and who could be described as losers.

The most likely diagnosis is a schizoid or paranoid personality. However, a psychotic reaction — often paranoid schizophrenia — is also common, especially with elevations on scale 6.

49/94

Persons with 49/94 codes not only feel alienated and have antisocial tendencies, but also have the energy to act on them. They can be described as self-indulgent, sensation seeking, impulsive, oriented towards pleasure, irritable, extroverted, violent, manipulative, and energetic. They have poorly developed consciences, with a marked lack of concern for rules and conventions. Since they are free from anxiety, talkative, and charming, they can often make a good initial impression. However, their relationships are usually shallow because any sort of deeper contact with them brings out the more problematic sides of their personality. An investigation of their past history typically reveals extensive legal, family, and work-related difficulties. The 49/94 code, when found in persons over age 30, suggests that this pattern is highly resistant to change. In adolescent males, it is associated with delinquency.

There are numerous difficulties encountered in therapy with these persons. They are unable to focus for any length of time and are constantly embarking on often irrelevant tangents. Furthermore, they have difficulty delaying their gratification and usually do not learn from experience. They will often be irritable, and if confronted by a therapist, their fairly extensive hostility will be expressed. Thus, therapy is likely to be slow, frustrating, and often unproductive.

With a correspondingly low 0, this code is likely to reflect a person with highly developed social techniques who will use these skills to manipulate others. Thus, he may be involved in elaborate, antisocial "con" games. If scale 3 is correspondingly high, it decreases the chance of acting out. In these cases, the expression of hostility is likely to be similar to that of the 34/43 code in that it will be indirect and often passive-aggressive. When scale 6 is elevated along with scales 4 and 9, extreme caution should be taken since these individuals will be very dangerous and have poor judgment. Their acting out will often be violent and bizarre, and will appear justified to themselves because of strong feelings of resentment towards others.

The most likely diagnosis is an antisocial personality, although caution should be made especially when categorizing adolescents since these scales are more commonly elevated for both normal and abnormal adolescents. If scale 8 is also high, it may reflect either a manic state or schizophrenia.

68/86

The key feature of people with the 68/86 code type is that they are suspicious and distrustful, often perceiving the intentions of others as suspect and question-able. They will be extremely distant from others with few or no friends. They can be described as inhibited, shy, resentful, anxious, and unable to accept or appropriately respond to the demands that are made of them. This is because they are highly involved in their fantasy world, uncooperative, and apathetic, and because they have poor judgment and experience difficulty concentrating. Their sense of reality is poor, and they often experience guilt, inferiority, and mental confusion although sometimes their affect will be flat. The content of their thoughts can be expected to be unusual if not bizarre, frequently containing delusions of grandeur and/or self-reference. Surprisingly, their past work history is often adequate, but an intensification of their symptoms brought on by stress will usually disrupt their ability to work. Persons with this code are more often single and younger than 26 years of age. If they are married, their spouses are frequently also emotionally disturbed.

The most frequent diagnosis is paranoid schizophrenia, especially if scale 4 is also elevated. These persons will experience depression, inappropriate affect, phobias, and paranoid delusions. If scale 7 is 10 points or more lower than scales 6 and 8, this pattern is referred to as the "paranoid valley" and emphasizes the presence of paranoid ideation. If F is highly elevated while scales 6 and 8 are above 80, this does not necessarily indicate an invalid profile. A paranoid state is also a frequent diagnosis with the 68/86 code; less frequently, organic brain disorders or severe anxiety disorders may be diagnosed.

78/87

The 78/87 code often occurs among psychiatric patients and reflects a level of agitation sufficiently intense to disrupt their daily activities. Usually this profile represents a reaction to a specific crisis. They may have been previously functioning at a fairly adequate level until some event or series of events triggered off a collapse in their defenses. Their style of relating to others is passive, and they have difficulty developing and sustaining mature heterosexual relationships. They are lacking in self-confidence, often experience insomnia, and may have hallucinations and delusions. Common feelings include guilt, inferiority, confusion, worry, and fear, and they may have difficulties related to sexual performance. There may be significant suicidal risk, which can be further evaluated by looking at the relative elevation of scale 2, checking relevant critical items, taking a careful history, and asking relevant questions related to their thought processes.

The extent of elevations on scales 7 and 8, and the relative heights between them, have important implications both diagnostically and prognostically. If scale 7 is higher than scale 8, the person's psychological condition is more susceptible to improvement and tends to be more benign. This has a tendency to be true regardless of the elevation of 8, so long as 7 maintains its relatively higher position. The higher scale 7 suggests that the person is still actively fighting his problem and has some of his defenses still working. Thus, engrained bizarre thought patterns and withdrawn behavior have not yet become established. A relatively higher scale 8, on the other hand, reflects more fixed patterns and is therefore more difficult to treat. This is particularly true if scale 8 is over 75. If scales 7 and 8 are both greater than 75 (with scale 8 relatively higher), this suggests an established schizophrenic pattern, especially if the "neurotic triad" is low. Even if schizophrenia can be ruled out, the condition tends to be extremely resistant to change, as for example, with a severe, alienated personality disorder. If scale 2 is also elevated, this raises the possibility of either a dysthymic or obsessive-compulsive disorder.

89/98

The 89/98 code suggests persons who are highly energetic, perhaps to the point of hyperactivity. They will be emotionally labile, tense, and disorganized, with the possibility of delusions of grandeur sometimes with a religious flavor, especially if scale 6 is also elevated. Their goals and expectations will be unrealistic; they often make extensive plans which are far beyond their means to accomplish. Thus, their aspirations will be significantly higher than their actual achievements. Usually, they will have significant complaints related to insomnia. Their interpersonal relationships are childish and immature, and they will usually be fearful, distrustful, irritable, and distractible. This likewise makes psychotherapeutic approaches to them extremely difficult. Furthermore, their level of insight is poor, they resist psychological interpretations of their behavior, and they cannot focus on any one area for any length of time.

The most frequent diagnosis is schizophrenia, possibly a schizoaffective disorder with manic states. If there are extensive delusions and hallucinations, antipsychotic medication may be indicated. Sometimes the relative elevation of F can be used as an index of the relative severity of the disorder.

RECOMMENDED READING

Butcher, J.N. (Ed.). *New Developments in the Use of the MMPI.* Minneapolis: University of Minnesota Press, 1979.

Dahlstrom, W.G., Welsh, G.S., and Dahlstrom, L.E. *An MMPI Handbook,* Vol. 1: Clinical Interpretation. Minneapolis: University of Minnesota Press, 1972.

Graham, J.R. *The MMPI: A Practical Guide.* New York: Oxford University Press, 1977.

Hathaway, S.R. and McKinley, J.C. *Minnesota Multiphasic Personality Inventory: Manual for Administration and Scoring.* Minneapolis, Mn: University of Minnesota Press, 1983.

Marks, P.A., Seeman, W., and Haller, D.L. *The Actuarial Use of the MMPI with Adolescents and Adults.* Baltimore: Williams and Wilkins, 1974.

Webb, J.T., McNamara, K.M., and Rodgers, D.A. *Configural Interpretation of the MMPI and CPI.* Columbus: Ohio Psychology Publishing, 1981.

8
The California Psychological Inventory

The California Psychological Inventory (CPI) is a self-administered, paper and pencil test comprised of 468 true-false statements. The test is designed for group administration although it can also be given individually. Even though the test has been used to evaluate individuals between the ages of 12 and 70, it was mainly constructed for use with young adults having a minimum of a fourth grade reading ability. The CPI items request information concerning an individual's typical behavior patterns, usual feelings, opinions, and attitudes relating to social, ethical, and family matters. The results are plotted on 18 scales focusing on aspects of interpersonal relationships that are presented in everyday, commonsense descriptions.

The philosophical orientation of the CPI is based on an appreciation of enduring, commonly discussed, personality variables that are relevant throughout different cultures. Thus, it uses familiar commonsense terms such as dominance, tolerance, and self-control which are often referred to as "folk concepts." The value of using such common, everyday constructs is that they already have "functional validity." In other words, they have immediate cross-cultural relevance, are readily understood by a wide range of people, and have a high degree of power in predicting behavior. This is not to say that just anybody should be allowed to interpret the CPI, but rather that the test's roots and original constructs are based on conceptions of human behavior held by most people within most cultures. It is up to the skilled clinician to go beyond these common constructs and into a more subtle, broad, and integrated description of the person. Thus, the test does not have as its primary goal psychometric elegance, nor is it derived from any specific personality theory. The main focus and concern of the CPI involve practical usefulness and the development of descriptions that strive to be relevant, understandable, and accurate in terms of behavioral predictions.

The CPI was originally developed by Harrison Gough and published in its original form in 1957. Although reviews of the test have been mixed, most reviewers generally describe it in favorable terms. For example, Anastasi (1982, p. 508) has stated that the "CPI is one of the best inventories currently available.

Its technical development is of a high order and it has been subjected to extensive research and continuous improvement." The criticisms that have been directed at it have stimulated extensive efforts to refine and improve the CPI, including numerous studies on predictive validity, the development of alternate scales, and expanded normative data. It is for these reasons that the CPI has become a respected and frequently used device in personality assessment.

HISTORY AND DEVELOPMENT

The CPI was developed as an inventory to assess enduring interpersonal personality characteristics within a normal population. Gough published his original scales in 1948, but the first copyrighted edition of the initial 15 scales appeared in 1951. However, it was not until 1957 that the full 18 scales were published by Consulting Psychologists Press. These 18 scales measure such areas as social ascendancy, social image, intellectual stance, and conceptual interests. Three of these are validity scales which assess test taking attitudes including "fake bad" (Wb), "fake good" (Gi), and the extent to which highly popular responses are given (Cm).

The current CPI questions were derived from an original item pool of 3500 questions. Of the 468 items that were eventually selected, 178 were identical to MMPI items, 35 were very similar, and the remaining 215 were developed specifically for the CPI. The items were selected on the basis of both empirical criterion keying and what Megargee (1972) has referred to as the "rational approach." The rational approach means that a series of questions was generated which, from a rational point of view, seemed to assess the characteristics that the scale was trying to measure. These questions were then given to a sample group and accepted or rejected based on the extent of inter-item correlation. However, the majority of the scales were not developed through the rational approach but rather through empirical criterion keying. Thus, series of questions, which had initially been developed rationally, were administered to different groups having specific, previously assessed characteristics that the scales were eventually intended to measure independently of these groups. Each group might have been selected by use of a number of different criteria. For example, ratings by friends and family on an individual's degree of responsibility were used to select a person for inclusion in the sample group for the development of the scale on responsibility. The achievement via independence scale was based on college students' grade point averages; the socialization scale used delinquents and nondelinquents; and sociability involved the number of extracurricular activities that a student participated in. Items which were found to discriminate between the criterion group (responsibility, sociability, etc.) and a "normal" population were selected for initial inclusion in the scale. It is important to emphasize that, similar to the MMPI items, the empirical relationships are more important than the "truth" of the content. For example, if a person in the group rated for responsibility answers "true" to the statement "I have never done anything dangerous just for the thrill of it," it does not matter whether or not he has actually performed dangerous behaviors for the thrill of it or not. The main consideration from a psychometric point of view is that he answers "true" to that question, which then indicates that the item can be used to differentiate responsible from nonresponsible persons. The final step was having the items cross-validated on other populations to determine the extent to which they could accurately assess the variable the scale was attempting to measure. Of the 18 scales, 13 of them used empirical criterion keying, 4 used the rational approach, and the final one (communality) cannot be easily categorized, although it primarily utilized a combination of the two techniques.

Like the MMPI, the CPI scores are given a standard score (T score) with a mean of 50 and a standard deviation of 10. The scales were standardized on an original normative sample of 6000 males and 7000 females having a fairly wide range in age, socioeconomic status, and geographic area. Means and standard deviations are also given for many special population groups. The scales form four groupings or classes which are based more on conceptual convenience than on any psychometrically pure rationale. The first class containing six scales (Do, Cs, Sy, Sp, Sa, Wb) is centered on poise, social ascendancy, and self-assurance. The second class relates more to a person's social image, including socialization, maturity, and responsibility, and it also contains a total of six scales (Re, So, Sc, To, Gi, Cm). Class 3 has only three scales (Ac, Ai, Ie) and assesses the variables of a person's intellectual stance. The final class, consisting of three scales (Py, Fx, Fe), measures conceptual abilities such as intellectual and interest modes.

Since the initial development of the CPI in 1957, it has been put to numerous uses. Megargee (1972) reported that when the test was first printed, researchers and practitioners used it for many of the more obvious purposes of a psychological test such as the prediction of scholastic achievement, graduation from high school or college, and performance in specific areas such as math and English. Later, its uses became much more diversified to the extent that work has now been done on managerial effectiveness, air traffic controllers, stock market speculators, the degree of creativity in fields such as architecture and mathematics, contraceptive practices, and performance in psychiatric residency programs. Furthermore, cross-cultural studies on validity have been performed in France, Israel, Italy, Japan, Poland, Switzerland, and Taiwan. Within the field of counseling, it has been used to predict response to therapy, to aid in the selection of a college major, and to predict the degree of success in graduate education programs such as medicine, dentistry, nursing, and education. Megargee (1972), in his extensive handbook for use with the CPI, gives evidence of the test's popularity by pointing out that approximately 250,000 answer sheets are filled out each year. Also, it has been translated into numerous languages, and the *Eighth Mental*

Measurements Yearbook (Buros, 1978) listed nearly 1400 references. There are currently available computerized scoring and interpretation services, and several alternate scales have been developed. Although the manual accompanying the CPI was first published in 1957, it was updated in 1969 and again in 1975 (Gough, 1957, 1975). All of this attests to the CPI's extensive diversity, popularity, and success.

COMPARISON WITH THE MMPI

Since there is a similarity in both format and item content, comparisons between the CPI and the MMPI are inevitable. For example, Thorndike (1959) has referred to the CPI as "the sane man's MMPI," and there are indeed a number of surface similarities. The CPI uses approximately half of the MMPI's questions; a conversion is made from raw to standard scale scores with a mean of 50 and a standard deviation of 10; and the final values are charted on a graph with peaks and valleys. However, it is essential that any clinician using the CPI should also appreciate the significant conceptual and psychometric differences between the two tests.

The general intent of the MMPI was to assess a person's intrapsychic processes and emotional distress as these relate to specific psychodiagnostic categories. Each of these categories has a group of internal dynamics surrounding it, such as depression which also includes apathy, lowered capacity for pleasure, and feelings of hopelessness and helplessness. The primary task of the MMPI is to assess either the presence or the absence of these internal dynamics and to place the examinee in either a normal or one or more psychopathological categories. In contrast, the CPI focuses more on a normal population and is highly interpersonal in nature. In fact, there is a marked absence of symptom-oriented questions. Thus, the CPI is concerned with the presence or absence of specific interpersonal skills. In addition, the CPI avoids complex diagnostic nomenclature and emphasizes practical, everyday descriptions that are commonly used in most cultures.

From a psychometric perspective, the MMPI was developed from a bimodal distribution in which the main focus of the test was to be able to classify a specific client in either a pathological group or a normal one. The contrast groups were not high or low on a specific trait but rather were high in pathology when compared with normals. For example, a group that was high in hysterical traits was contrasted not with a group of persons having superior health, but with individuals having only an average number of hysterical traits. In clinical assessment, the pathological group is considered to be anyone scoring greater than 2 standard deviations above the norm. As a result of this emphasis on differentiating pathological groups from "average" or normal groups, the interpretation of profiles within "normal" ranges (i.e., T = 35–64) is uncertain and should be approached with extreme caution. In contrast, the CPI used a normal distribution within a standardized population. Furthermore, Gough used groups whose behavior was extreme on both high and low dimensions of the characteristic being measured. Thus, normal range scores of less than 2 standard deviations from the mean can be interpreted with a fairly high level of confidence. For example, a CPI score on Ac (achievement via conformance) of T = 60 indicates a fairly high level of this particular attribute and a T = 40 score indicates a fairly low level. However, an MMPI T score of 60 on scale 8 (schizophrenia) does not indicate a relatively high degree of schizophrenia, nor does a T score of 40 indicate a low level. Thus, relatively normal profiles on the CPI not only are to be expected but can also be interpreted successfully.

RELIABILITY AND VALIDITY

In general, the reliability and validity studies on the CPI compare favorably with those done on other personality inventories. Short-term test-retest reliability has ranged between .71 and .90, with an average of .83 (Hase and Goldberg, 1967). Long-term reliability, in which the retest was performed one year after the first measurements, was somewhat lower but still showed a moderate level of stability in which correlations ranged from .60 to .70 (Hase and Goldberg, 1967). Measures of internal consistency indicate that there is considerable variability among the test items but overall the scale constructions are adequate. Internal consistency is lowest for the scales of psychological mindedness, flexibility, and femininity, but the average correlation for all 18 scales is .63 (Megargee, 1972). However, correlations between scales are relatively high. All but four of the scales correlate with at least one other scale at a level of .50 or more which suggests a certain degree of redundancy among the 18 scales.

In line with Gough's practical orientation, the main work on validation has been predictive. Thus, Gough is less concerned with areas of psychometric elegance, such as whether or not the scales avoid overlap, than with the practical usefulness of the scales in providing accurate predictions. Extensive studies have been performed to develop patterns that predict specific areas such as the outcome of persons on parole, problems of high school dropouts, profiles reflecting delinquency, and high school and college grades. When the scales were first developed, they were cross-validated with large samples of high school and college students with generally favorable results. Cross-cultural studies have also shown that many of the scales (socialization, femininity) of the CPI are valid indicators even among different cultural groups; however, if they are available, norms for different subgroups should always be consulted (Cross and Burger, 1982). Many studies which have found useful levels of predictive validity are summarized later in "Configurational Interpretation."

ASSETS AND LIMITATIONS

The CPI focuses on diagnosing and understanding interpersonal behavior within normal populations. Instead of focusing on pathology, it assesses areas such as self-control, dominance, and achievement. However, even though its emphasis is on assessing normal variations, extreme scores can also give important information relating to the specifics of a person's expression of maladjustment, particularly with regard to interpersonal relationships. Whereas the MMPI is limited to use with primarily pathologically oriented populations, the CPI is appropriate for normal persons. Thus, it has the significant advantage of addressing issues which interest a great many people.

The main thrust of the research and construction of the CPI has been towards developing accurate, long- and short-term behavioral predictions. The focus is not so much on evaluating and predicting a specific, internal, unidimensional trait, but more on interpersonal behaviors and orientations. Gough (1968, p. 56) clarifies this by stressing that "... a high score on a scale for social status does not mean that the individual has a 'trait' of high status, but rather that in viewpoint or outlook, he tends to resemble people of high status; presumably, therefore, he may be already of high status, or possessed of those talents and dispositions that will lead him toward such attainment." Gough also stresses that certain interpersonal behaviors occur within specific contexts. For example, a person who scores high on "dominance" would be expected to assume control of a group requiring leadership. Thus, the longitudinal studies on the inventory have studied predictions relating to such areas as graduating from high school (Gough, 1966), choice of major field in college (Goldschmid, 1967), assertive behavior (Harris and Brown, 1979), and police performance (Horstman, 1977). The test has generally proved to be a useful tool in the area of prediction and, as a result, has been particularly helpful in counseling high school and college students.

Since the CPI's basic concepts were derived from everyday social interaction, it has the further advantage of being relatively easily understood by a wide range of persons. Descriptions such as dominant, achievement oriented, and self-controlled are generally straightforward and are therefore not easily misinterpreted by untrained professionals. Since they relate to ongoing aspects of behavior, they are also likely to have more immediacy, relevancy, and impact on persons receiving feedback from their test results. These "folk concepts" have the added advantage of being generally found in all cultures and societies. Thus, Gough hoped that the inventory would have cross-cultural relevance and validity. Although some research has been conducted to test this hypothesis, far more work still needs to be performed. This is especially true regarding the relationship of race, socioeconomic status, and other demographic variables. Gynther (1978b), in reviewing the literature on the CPI, stated that some of the research performed raises questions about Gough's assumption that the inventory has cross-cultural equivalence. He further questioned whether or not minorities produce valid results on the inventory. Although this issue is currently not resolved, there are sufficient studies which question the cross-cultural equivalence of the CPI so that scores from persons of differing cultural backgrounds should be treated cautiously.

A number of predictive studies have been conducted from a research perspective, and several useful regression equations have been developed as aids in predicting behavior. However, extremely few studies have been performed which test the validity of predictions made by clinicians in actual practice (Gynther, 1978b). It may be that clinical judgments are generally accurate, but at this point further empirical studies are needed to verify this. It is something of a contradiction that a test which was developed with emphasis on practical usefulness has not been sufficiently evaluated within the clinical context. A further difficulty related to developing accurate predictions is that few studies have been conducted assessing predictions of actual job performance. Most of the predictive studies have attempted to estimate such areas as future college attendance or grade point average in graduate programs. However, college attendance and grade point average do not necessarily correlate with later successful performance. For example, high medical school grades have not been found to correlate with later success as a physician (Loughmiller et al., 1970). This problem is certainly not unique to the CPI but is a general issue with many similar tests, and it relates to a difficulty in adequately establishing appropriate criterion measures. These issues suggest that test users should develop predictions based on test scores within limited and well-researched contexts. For example, if the CPI is being used to evaluate prospective medical students, it should be made clear that predictions are useful only with regard to their academic performance and not their overall clinical skills or later success as physicians.

A further limitation of the CPI is that few studies have investigated the meaning of pairs or triads of scales. In contrast, extensive fruitful research has been conducted on two- and three-point codes for the MMPI. What work has been conducted is summarized later in "Contigural Interpretation." However, it should be stressed that research is largely lacking regarding the 153 possible two-point codes that could potentially be derived from the CPI.

In developing accurate clinical interpretations from the CPI, it is essential to consider the implications of factors such as the overall life situation of the examinee. For example, the profile of a 15 year old on the CPI scale for psychological mindedness (Py) has a different meaning from that of a person of 55. A further caution is that even though subsequent norms have been developed, the inventory was initially standardized on Caucasian adults, 18 years or older, who had I.Q.'s of greater than 80 and a minimum of seven years of education. Although interpretations can be made for persons not falling within this group, they should be made with an appropriate degree of tentativeness and the examiner should obtain additional outside confirmation whenever possible. Another important consideration is the purpose for which the person believes he is being examined. A person who is taking the test in a conscious effort to receive a discharge from the military will be likely to bias his responses in a different direction from a person seeking employment. It is also essential to look at the overall patterns of scores rather than "single sign" indicators, since corresponding elevations on other scales can elaborate or modify the meaning they have for one another. Thus, clinicians should always keep in mind the implications of an examinee's overall life situation, age, education, perceived reason for assessment, and pattern of scores.

The CPI, then, is an extremely useful test in the assessment of the interpersonal characteristics of relatively normal persons. It has the advantages of measuring variables that interest a great number of people, providing helpful behavioral predictions, and using everyday interactional concepts. Significant limitations and cautions relate to limited validity studies in clinical settings, few descriptions of the meaning of two- and/or three-point elevations, and the limitations resulting from a standardization sample derived mainly from Caucasian adults, 18 years of age or over, having I.Q.'s greater than 80 and a minimum of seven years of education.

INTERPRETATION PROCEDURES

Timing

The examiner should note the length of time it took the person to complete the test. A person with an I.Q. within the normal range would be expected to complete the test in approximately one hour. If he takes 1 1/2 hours or more, it suggests (1) a major psychological disturbance such as a severe depression or functional psychosis, (2) a low I.Q. combined with a poor reading ability, or (3) cerebral impairment. Tests which are completed in 20 minutes or less suggest (1) an invalid profile, (2) an impulsive personality, or (3) both. The examiner may prefer to use an oral or tape-recorded administration for persons with unusually low reading skills.

Scoring

In scoring the profile, examiners should check to make sure that the correct sex scoring norms have been used. They may also wish to extend the traditional scale information by using regression equations for such areas as high school achievement, parole success, or medical school performance (see Table 8-2). Alternate scales are also available and may be important in certain contexts.

Determining the Profile Validity

One of the initial considerations in evaluating the profile validity is to note the number of items that have been left blank. If there are 30 or more blank spaces, the test results may not be valid. The examiner should also make sure that the subject has not marked a high number (30 or more) of questions with both "true" and "false" on the same item. Yet another area which should be checked is the possibility of random answering. The subject may have answered randomly as a result of being out of step between the numbers questions in the answer sheet and test booklet or as a result of a poor reading ability which he is attempting to hide. A good indicator of random answering is the communality (Cm) scale which would be expected to be T = 30 or less.

"Faking bad" can usually be detected based on the presence of extremely low scores (T = 35 or less) on well being (Wb) and communality (Cm). A low score on good impression (Gi) is also frequently associated with "faking bad," especially in the profiles of males. It should be stressed that just because a subject "fakes bad" does not mean that he isn't maladjusted. Rather, it indicates that the specifics of his disorder cannot be evaluated because of the distorting effects of the person's need to create an impression of the seriousness of his problem. An important consideration is to assess why the person is "faking bad." It might, for example, represent a "cry for help" in which suicide is a serious possibility, or the person might be malingering because of numerous secondary gains.

To evaluate whether or not a subject is "faking good," the most important scale to evaluate is good impression (Gi). "Fake good" profiles will usually have T scores of 65 or more on this scale, and it will most likely be a relative peak in comparison to the other scales. Usually when a person is asked to "fake good," all the scales with positive social connotations will be elevated but Gi will still be relatively higher than the others. Sometimes it may be difficult to differentiate between someone who has a superior level of adjustment and a person who is "faking good." The most significant consideration here is the person's past history. An individual with a history of poor adjustment combined with an unusually high Gi will probably be "faking good," whereas a person with a history of good adjustment and a moderately high Gi will probably be expressing his superior level of adjustment.

Profile Interpretation

Once clinicians have determined that the test is valid, they should look at the different heights of the scales. Scores of T = 50 or more usually suggest a positive area of adjustment. If scales are significantly below T = 50, this indicates specific problem areas. However, the clinician must also interpret these scores within the overall context, taking into account such variables as the person's age,

Table 8-1. Cluster Analysis.

Cluster	Scales	Interpretation
1	Do, Cs, Sy, Sp, Sa, Wb	Interpersonal effectiveness, style, and adequacy
2	Re, So, Sc, To, Gi, Cm	Intrapersonal controls, values, styles, and beliefs
3	Ac, Ai, Ie	Intellectual stance, achievement, and academic ability
4	Py, Fx, Fe	Conceptual interests

occupational level, cultural background, and educational level. For example, a high school student with an intellectual efficiency (Ie) scale score of 60 represents a fairly high level of this characteristic, whereas the same score for a medical student represents a relatively low level when compared with his fellow students.

After looking at possible areas of adjustment and maladjustment, the clinician can then further evaluate the profile by examining the average elevations on the different clusters (Table 8-1) as organized by Gough (1969). For convenience, the clusters are separated on profile sheets by gray vertical lines. However, these clusters are organized according to conceptual similarity rather than statistically derived parallels. Megargee (1972) recommends examining the scales based on five factors which have been statistically derived from more empirical relations. Factor 1 (Wb, Re, So, Sc, To, Gi, Ac) provides a general index of mental health, adjustment, and social conformity. Factor 2 (Do, Cs, Sy, Sp, Sa) indicates a person's level of social poise and interpersonal effectiveness, and is the same as Gough's first cluster except that Wb is not included. The third factor (Ai, Fx, To, Ie, Py) includes scales that are characterized by assessing to what extent a person can think and behave independently. The fourth and fifth factors comprised of scales Cm, So, and Fe are miscellaneous, and each scale should be carefully examined individually. Clinicians can gain useful information by using either Gough's clusters or the more empirically derived factors developed by Megargee.

Whereas the different factors or cluster analyses give general impressions regarding certain areas of functioning, the clinician can obtain more specific information by evaluating each scale individually. This involves both looking at the relatively highest and lowest scales and developing a description of the dynamics involved with these scales. This is where scale descriptions and the meanings associated with specific high or low scores (which will be provided in the following section) are particularly helpful. The general personality descriptions and discussions of the scales are primarily derived from college students, and have been adapted and modified from the publications of Gough (1968, 1975) and Megargee (1972). The lists of adjectives for males and females are based on peer ratings and are reported in Gough (1968) and Gregory and Morris (1978).

Initial hypotheses can be further evaluated by consulting the section in this chapter dealing with typical scale configurations for different areas including intellectual level, achievement, leadership, adjustment, and specific syndromes. This evaluation may also involve calculating and interpreting the regression equations, which are included in the section on configural interpretations and summarized in Table 8-2.

The final step in interpretation is to integrate all these data into a profile description. An essential here is the clinician's ability to assess the interactions between two scales or more. This suggests that once a specific trend has been established, the clinician should elaborate on it by evaluating how the other scales change their meaning for the individual (cf. Heilbrun, Daniel, Goodstein, Stephenson, and Crites, 1962). For example, dominance may be expressed in numerous ways including rebellion, high achievement, leadership, or delinquency. Once these elaborations have been made within the test data, the clinician can then seek outside confirmation through personal history, behavioral observations, and additional test data.

THE INDIVIDUAL SCALES

1. Dominance (Do)

The Do scale measures areas of leadership ability and has become one of the best validated scales on the CPI. It includes verbal fluency, persuasiveness, and the extent to which a person is likely to take charge of a situation. Thus, high scorers are persistent in approaching a task and will usually take the initiative in interpersonal relationships. Whereas this description is more characteristic of the style in which high-scoring males express their dominance, high-scoring females express their dominance either by initiating attempts to choose a leader or by being somewhat coercive, aggressive, or impatient. The contents of the items deal with social poise, confidence, verbal fluency, persuasiveness, and a sense of duty. Persons with high scores typically endorse items such as No. 53: "I think I would enjoy having authority over other people" (true) and No. 403: "I have a natural talent for influencing people" (true).*

It should be stressed that the conditions in which leadership occurs are at least as important as the actual trait. This means that when the social conditions are conducive to leadership, high scorers will usually become leaders rather than followers and will also set limits, be more assertive, more goal oriented, and more clear and direct regarding their requests. This will be a relatively comfortable

*CPI items reproduced by special permission of the Publisher, Consulting Psychologists Press, Inc., Palo Alto, CA 94306, from *The California Psychological Inventory* by Harrison Gough, Ph.D. Copyright 1958. Further reproduction is prohibited without the Publisher's consent.

and natural role for them to adopt. In contrast, low scorers experience discomfort when requested to take charge. They may be either more submissive, in which case they prefer others to control and direct them, or merely socially isolated and introverted, in which case they don't want to control others but also don't want others to control them and will even actively resist efforts which are made to control them.

High Do (T = 65 or More). High scorers on Do are strong in expressing their opinions and in reaching their goals. This may range from being highly assertive, in which they are clear and direct in expressing their needs, to being aggressive, in which they are more forceful. They would rather take charge of a situation and can effectively do so since they have excellent abilities to plan and are self-confident when directing others. Persons high in dominance can use and develop the resources available to them and often express a sense of optimism. They are generally able to define their goals and work persistently to attain them. Neither males nor females would be particularly compromising, and they would not be the types of person to whom others would feel comfortable admitting their weaknesses. The following is a listing of the adjectives which their peers have used to describe them.

Males: ambitious, dominant, forceful, optimistic, planful, resourceful, responsible, self-confident, stable, stern.
Females: aggressive, bossy, conceited, confident, demanding, dominant, forceful, quick, strong, talkative.

From this list it appears that high-scoring females are more likely to express their dominance in a forceful and coercive manner than males, even though both males and females are equally strong. Thus, females would more likely be impatient towards others who attempt to delay or obstruct their goals.

Moderate Do (T = 50–65). Moderate Do scale scorers have the capacity for leadership but do not, under ordinary circumstances, seek opportunities to use this ability.

Moderately Low Do (T = 40–50). With moderately low Do, people usually feel uncomfortable when leadership is required and much prefer being in the follower role. They are participants rather than organizers. Although some persons who are low in dominance are effective in relatively high leadership positions, they are uncomfortable with this aspect of their job, and usually have a democratic and participative style of decision making. However, most persons scoring low on Do experience a difficult time planning and, as a result, may sometimes appear reckless and impulsive. They are likely to believe, and adhere to the beliefs of, others and can be easily influenced. Often they have a difficult time making direct requests, and they are usually seen as nonassertive. Low scorers, particularly females, are seen as submissive, shy, timid, and inhibited.

Low Do (T = 40 or Less). Persons who score extremely low in Do are socially withdrawn, insecure, and shy. They see themselves as having little or no leadership ability and dislike being directly responsible for either their own actions or the actions of others.

Males: apathetic, having narrow interests, indifferent, irresponsible, pessimistic, reckless, restless, rigid, submissive, suggestible.
Females: cautious, gentle, inhibited, peaceable, quiet, reserved, shy, submissive, trusting, unassuming.

These adjectives suggest that low-scoring females are more comfortable with, and better adjusted to, low dominance than males. In contrast, low-scoring males are more apathetic and indifferent and, at times, act in a reckless and impulsive manner. They are more likely than females to be pessimistic, distrusting, and uninvolved.

2. Capacity for Status (Cs)

An individual's capacity for status has been defined by Gough (1968, p. 61) as being equal to the "relative level of income, education, prestige, and power attained in [his] social-cultural milieu." This definition focuses on status as it has been achieved, but the Cs scale looks at status more as a trait associated with features such as ambition and self-assurance. The specific trait of capacity for status suggests that eventually a person will achieve and maintain a position of status. Thus, in creating the scale, Gough looked at the specific trait variables which would eventually lead to a higher status position. These traits include perseverance, self-direction, ambition, and self-confidence. Persons seeking status are usually willing to go through a fairly high degree of discomfort and personal change in order to achieve their goals. In the scale construction, there is some overlap of test items with social presence (Sp), intellectual efficiency (Ie), and self-acceptance (Sa), indicating that capacity for status also includes dimensions of social poise, efficiency, and self-confidence. Thus, the scale includes such items as No. 186: "I usually don't like to talk much unless I am with people I know very well" (false) and No. 40: "I get very nervous if I think that someone is watching me" (false). The item content also reflects an absence of fears or anxieties, a high degree of social conscience, an interest in belonging to various groups, and an interest in literary and aesthetic activities.

High Cs (T = 60 or More). Individuals with high Cs scales are characterized as independent, imaginative, and taking advantage of opportunities that are presented to them.

> *Males:* discreet, forgiving, imaginative, independent, mature, opportunistic, pleasant, praising, progressive, reasonable.
> *Females:* alert, clear thinking, forceful, having wide interests, individualistic, ingenious, insightful, intelligent, logical, versatile.

Summarizing these adjectives, we can see that males scoring in this range are progressive in their views and are usually seen by others as being reasonable, pleasant, and likely to give praise. They also tend towards a relatively high level of maturity. Females have these characteristics and, in addition, are seen as being insightful, versatile, forceful, individualistic, and clear thinking. Both males and females are highly self-directed, achievement oriented, and able to respond to their environment in such a way as to further their own goals.

Moderate Cs (T = 45–60). As might be expected, moderate scorers are somewhat goal oriented and relatively highly motivated to achieve. They are willing to change and adapt their lives to a certain extent in their attempts to achieve status. They are also moderately ambitious and self-assured.

Moderately Low Cs (T = 35–45). These individuals are minimally goal oriented, but their general lack of self-direction is not sufficiently low to impair their level of functioning. They are unwilling to make very many personal sacrifices in order to achieve power, prestige, or a higher income.

Low Cs (T = 35 or Less). Persons who score extremely low on Cs usually have a low level of energy, and are relatively rigid and inflexible. Their interests are extremely narrow, and they are likely to have little curiosity regarding their environment. They are usually resentful of their current position which results in tension, restlessness, and depression.

> *Males:* bitter, gloomy, greedy, having narrow interests, nagging, resentful, restless, touchy, unkind.
> *Females:* absentminded, cautious, meek, mild, retiring, shy, simple, submissive, timid, weak.

Whereas descriptions for males and females are both unfavorable, the males are characterized more as bitter and dispirited, whereas the females are more resigned and submissive.

3. Sociability (Sy)

The sociability scale was originally designed to measure the extent to which a person participates in social activities. It was later generalized to differentiate between a person who is outgoing, extroverted, and sociable and one who is more introverted, withdrawn, and prone to avoiding social visibility. There is a great deal of item overlap with intellectual efficiency (Ie), social presence (Sp), self-acceptance (Sa), and to a much lesser extent, achievement via independence (Ai), dominance (Do), capacity for status (Cs), and achievement via conformance (Ac). The questions deal with enjoyment of social interactions, a sense of poise, self-assurance in dealing with others, and an interest in cultural and intellectual activities. Thus, items such as No. 242: "I am a good mixer" (true) and No. 102: "I like to be the center of attention" (true) are included in Sy.

High Sy (T = 60 or More). High scorers on Sy have some of the same traits as persons scoring high on capacity for status (Cs), such as a greater sense of maturity and a wide range of interests. They are also described as outgoing, sociable, and confident. In general, they feel comfortable in social settings and can easily mix with others.

Males: clever, confident, having wide interests, logical, mature, outgoing, reasonable, resourceful, self-confident, sociable.
Females: aggressive, confident, dominant, energetic, flirtatious, having wide interests, intelligent, outgoing, sociable, talkative.

Whereas both males and females are seen as being outgoing, sociable, and confident, there are some significant differences. The male descriptions more frequently include reasonable, resourceful, logical, and clever, and the females are characterized as more flirtatious, aggressive, dominant, and intelligent.

Moderate Sy (T = 50–60). Persons in this range have an average level of extroversion and are relatively comfortable in most social situations. Although they prefer to be around others, they do not, by any means, exclusively orient their lives in this direction.

Moderately Low Sy (T = 35–50). Such persons are able to interact with groups of people without experiencing an excessive amount of discomfort, but they prefer to be alone. They feel somewhat anxious around strangers and strongly prefer to be with persons with whom they are already acquainted. Usually they dislike being the center of attention.

Low Sy (T = 35 or Less). Persons who score this low have a definite sense of awkwardness in social situations and frequently have bitter complaints about their lives. They have a marked lack of confidence in their social skills and, as a result, avoid most social encounters, especially in unfamiliar settings or with those they don't know.

> *Males:* awkward, bitter, cold, complaining, confused, hardhearted, having narrow interests, quitting, shallow, unkind.
> *Females:* cautious, inhibited, meek, modest, quiet, retiring, shy, timid, unassuming, withdrawn.

Males scoring in this range deal with their feelings of insecurity by narrowing their range of interests, giving up easily, and attempting to keep their relationships superficial. They often seem cold and hardhearted. Thus, their general method of trying to make their world appear safer and more predictable is by restricting their perceptual focus and keeping their behaviors within a narrow range. Females are similar but, in addition, are more unassuming, quiet, shy, inhibited, and generally less bitter.

4. Social Presence (Sp)

The social presence scale was intended to serve as a measure of a person's degree of poise, self-confidence, verve, and spontaneity in social interactions. It especially assesses the extent to which the person is self-assured and assertive. Sp is very similar to sociability in that an individual scoring high on Sp is outgoing and extroverted, and enjoys being around other people. However, a person who is sociable does not necessarily also have social presence even though this is often the case. Social presence implies not only that the person is sociable but also that he has more of a need to have impact on others and is thus likely to be more verbally aggressive, irritable, and sarcastic. A person exerting social presence might manipulate and control others, especially by working on another person's defenses and self-deceptions. There is some overlap of items with sociability (Sy), self-acceptance (Sa), and to a lesser extent, capacity for status (Cs) and intellectual efficiency (Ie). The primary content of the questions relates to a person's poise and the degree to which he enjoys social interactions. Typical statements include No. 208: "I like to go to parties and other affairs where there's lots of loud fun" (true) and No. 150: "Criticism or scolding makes me very uncomfortable" (false).

High Sp (T = 60 or More). High scorers are often described as being unconventional, spontaneous, witty, and perceptive. They are usually concerned with their own pleasure in interpersonal relationships and will often manipulate interactions in order to feel a sense of personal power. Thus, they not only like to be with other people but also want to be in control.

Males: adventurous, having wide interests, pleasure seeking, relaxed, self confident, sharp witted, unconventional, uninhibited, versatile, witty.
Females: adventurous, daring flirtatious, ingenious, mischievous, outgoing, pleasure seeking, spontaneous, versatile, witty.

Both males and females with high Sp are like those with high Sy in that they have a wide range of interests and like to be with other people. However, they are also extremely perceptive regarding the unique features of others and often use this perceptiveness to make an impact on or to manipulate them. Whereas males are often described as sharp witted and unconventional, females are more likely to be perceived as flirtatious and mischievous.

Moderate Sp (T = 40–60). Persons with moderate scores on Sp are reasonably witty, perceptive, spontaneous, and somewhat socially poised. They are able to accept and even enjoy or at least appreciate human differences and idiosyncrasies.

Low Sp (T = 40 or Less). Whereas high scorers are unconventional and uninhibited, low scorers are extremely cautious and concerned with proper etiquette. They feel that others should conform to set, predefined standards and are disapproving of nonconforming behavior. Their view of what is correct and incorrect falls within relatively narrow limits. In their relationships with others, they emphasize cooperation rather than manipulation and are likely to be kind, appreciative, patient, and serious. However, this kindness and appreciation are expressed only when others' behavior falls within their definition of conventional.

Males: appreciative, cautious, cooperative, having narrow interests, kind, mannerly, patient, prudish, serious, shy.
Females: cautious, conventional, fearful, gentle, reserved, retiring, sensitive, submissive, timid, withdrawn.

Both males and females are perceived as kind, reserved, submissive, and retiring, and their withdrawal from social relationships is primarily the result of a fairly high level of sensitivity to criticism which results in a general fearfulness in relating to others.

5. Self-acceptance (Sa)

The self-acceptance scale is intended to "assess factors such as a sense of personal worth, self-acceptance, and capacity for independent thinking and action." Furthermore, it was hoped that Sa could "identify individuals who would manifest a comfortable and imperturbable sense of personal worth, and who would be seen as secure and sure of themselves whether active or inactive in social behavior"

(Gough, 1969, p. 10). Even though persons high on self-acceptance would be less likely to become upset, the Sa scale should not be used as an index of adjustment and is not related to the absence or presence of pathology. For example, a person might be high in self-acceptance, yet still be rebellious, impulsive, and generally indulge in antisocial behavior. In fact, persons scoring extremely high on Sa are quite likely to be egocentric and indifferent, sometimes even to the point of narcissism. The scale questions have some overlap with sociability (Sy), social presence (Sp), and to a lesser extent, capacity for status (Cs). There is some negative overlap in which answers are scored in the opposite direction from capacity for status (Cs). Thus, there are a number of statements dealing with social poise and self-confidence, such as No. 150: "I am certainly lacking in self-confidence" (false). Additional areas of item content relate to an accepting attitude towards social prohibitions, attention to duty, consideration of others, and an acceptance of human frailties.

High Sa (T = 65 or More). Individuals scoring high on Sa are comfortable with themselves, self-reliant, and independent, and are usually polished, sophisticated, enterprising, and self-seeking in social relations. They also have a clear sense of self-definition, and are characterized as being self-confident and outgoing. However, Sa should not necessarily be tied with sociability since self-acceptance can be high regardless of the quantity of interaction with others. The scale is slightly correlated with hypomania which has often been formulated as a defense against depression. Thus, extremely high scores may suggest an inflated sense of self-acceptance with underlying, but unacknowledged, feelings of self-criticism, pessimism, and hopelessness.

> *Males:* confident, egotistical, enterprising, imaginative, opportunistic, outgoing, polished, self-confident.
> *Females:* adventurous, argumentative, bossy, demanding, determined, dominant, outgoing, sarcastic, talkative, witty.

These descriptions suggest that high-scoring females are more likely than high-scoring males to be outgoing, talkative, and witty, as well as sarcastic, dominant, and prone to arguments.

Moderate Sa (T = 50–65). These persons have an average or somewhat above average level of confidence with a generally good sense of harmony and internal balance. They are somewhat adventurous and outgoing.

Moderately Low Sa (T = 35–50). Moderately low scorers are somewhat low in self-confidence and have some significant doubts about themselves. For the most part, they can adequately cope with their lives, but they are prone to periods of insecurity and depression. One way in which they often attempt to adapt is through conformity and conventionality which frequently has the desired effect of making their world more safe and predictable.

Low Sa (T = 35 or Less). Such individuals have a pronounced lack of self-confidence. They are usually described as being ordinary and have "flat" or unidimensional personalities. They achieve a moderate degree of safety in their world by withdrawing, quitting, and maintaining a relatively narrow range of interests. Although usually submissive and conventional, they may at times impulsively act out in a reckless manner almost as a form of rebellion against their largely self-imposed conventionality.

Males: bitter, commonplace, having narrow interests, quitting, reckless, self-denying, submissive, tense, unintelligent, withdrawn.
Females: cautious, conventional, gentle, mild, modest, patient, peaceable, shy, trusting, unassuming.

Low-scoring males are described as shy, timid, bitter, and tense, and are often involved in emotional turmoil. They have a difficult time making decisions for themselves, experience self-doubts, and are generally lacking in self-direction. Females are likewise cautious, withdrawing, and conventional but are also more patient, gentle, unassuming, and peaceable.

6. Sense of Well Being (Wb)

The scale for well being was originally developed to help recognize profiles in which the person was "faking bad." Thus, it was initially referred to as the dissimulation (Ds) scale, and "fake bad" profiles can usually be detected because they are significantly lower than even valid profiles from psychiatric patients. In contrast, persons who score high do not have a need to emphasize psychological or physical complaints. In fact, high scorers play down their worries and rather emphasize that they are enterprising, energetic, and experience a sense of security. They are also likely to have effective interpersonal relations, a high level of mental health, and a sense of psychological and physical well being. Low scorers usually have diminished health and difficulty meeting the everyday demands of their environment. In general, the Wb scale has come to represent a rough estimate of a person's level of adjustment. However, it is more of a "state" scale than the others and is, therefore, somewhat changeable depending on an individual's mood fluctuations.

The Wb scale has a low degree of item overlap with other scales since most of the questions were designed for exclusive use with this scale. The item content usually reflects a denial of various physical and psychological complaints, as reflected by answering "false" to No. 301: "I am afraid to be alone in the dark." The second main content area reflects the extent to which a person is self-sufficient and independent. For example, persons scoring high on Wb usually respond "true" to No. 312: "Any man who is able and willing to work has a good chance of success."

High Wb (T = 50 or More). Generally, high scorers on Wb have relaxed and satisfying interpersonal relationships, are able to trust others, and come from family backgrounds that were stable and supportive.

Males: conservative, dependable, dependent, good-natured, inhibited, logical, pleasant, poised, praising, relaxed, sincere.
Females: calm, capable, clear thinking, fair-minded, informal, mature, obliging, poised, rational, wise.

These adjectives indicate that males are likely to be pleasant, relaxed, and appreciative, but also more inhibited and dependent than most people. Females tend to be calm, capable, and informal as well as obliging, rational, and wise.

Moderately Low Wb (T = 35–50). Although persons scoring in this range generally feel that life isn't going well, they continue to meet this perceived adversity with a sense of apathy and listlessness. They are often passive, awkward, and defensive. Males are more likely to respond to difficult situations by quitting and being forgetful, and have a sense of overriding dissatisfaction and restlessness. Females are prone to self-pity and sarcasm, and often find fault with others.

Low Wb (T = 35 or Less). With a decrease in Wb, there is a corresponding exaggeration of the trends just discussed. These individuals are usually highly alienated and dissatisfied, and experience a significant level of maladjustment. Characteristically, there is an extreme distrust in interpersonal relationships, with a tendency to dwell on real or imagined wrongs. Such people are seen by others as being pessimistic, tense, and restless. Individuals who use the test situation as a means of complaining and attempt to exaggerate their difficulties will often score in this range.

Males: anxious, blustery, distractible, forgetful, hurried, impulsive, mischievous, quitting, restless, shallow.
Females: awkward, defensive, fault finding, hardheaded, opinionated, sarcastic, self-pitying, tactless, unconventional, unstable.

In interpreting extremely low Wb scores, there are two considerations that should be evaluated. First of all, the scale lowering may in part reflect a downward but temporary mood shift of a person who is only somewhat maladjusted or even normal most of the time. More important, an extremely low score suggests an invalid profile in which the examinee is faking bad.

7. Responsibility (Re)

The intent of the Re scale was to assess to what degree persons are "conscientious, responsible, dependable, [and] articulate regarding rules and order, and who believe life should be governed by reason" (Gough, 1968, p. 65). Although responsibility is somewhat related to sociability and self-control, it also stresses that values and controls are well-defined and significant factors in a person's life. The person who is highly responsible will sacrifice his own needs for the benefit of the group. Such people accept the consequences of their behavior, are dependable and trustworthy, and have a sense of obligation to the larger social structure. However, they are not necessarily leaders, but they do have a high sense of integrity and are committed to carrying through agreements which they have made with others. In general, persons who express antisocial behavior score low on Re, whereas average scores are obtained by occupational groups in which responsible behavior and "attention to duty" are required. The Re scale is scored positively for items which reflect a high degree of commitment to social, civic, or moral values. Two representative items are No. 278: "If I get too much change in a store, I will always give it back" (true) and No. 286: "I have never done anything dangerous just for the thrill of it" (true).

High Re (T = 60 or More). High scorers respond well to tasks in which they are required to be conscientious, dependable, and reasonable. They will give up their own personal satisfactions for the sake of the group and honor any commitments they have made. Their approach to problem solving is extremely rational and clear.

> *Males:* capable, conscientious, dependable, reasonable, reliable, responsible, serious, stable, steady, thorough.
> *Females:* conscientious, cooperative, discreet, foresighted, insightful, planful, reasonable, reliable, responsible, tactful.

The general difference between male and female descriptions is that males are perceived as capable, reasonable, serious, steady, and thorough, whereas females are more discreet, cooperative, and tactful.

Moderate Re (T = 40-60). Such persons respond well to tasks in which they are required to be conscientious, dependable, and reasonable. Generally, they are not comfortable taking responsibility for the behavior of others, but they are seen by others as being reasonably conscientious and straightforward.

Low Re (T = 40 or Less). Individuals with scores this low show a lack of discipline, and are usually rebellious and impulsive. They have difficulty budgeting their finances and are seen by others as restless and careless. Their perceptions are tied to their own personal biases and are mainly concerned with their own needs; they often behave in exploitive and immature ways.

> *Males:* careless, disorderly, forgetful, irresponsible, lazy, mischievous, pleasure seeking, reckless, show-off, spendthrift.
> *Females:* arrogant, awkward, bitter, careless, hardheaded, lazy, obnoxious, rebellious, restless, sarcastic.

8. Socialization (So)

The socialization scale was originally called the "delinquency scale," and its intent was to assess the likelihood of antisocial behavior. The scoring was later reversed, its name changed, and it gradually became a measure of an individual's social maturity, integrity, and rectitude. It is probably Gough's favorite scale and is based on his theory that antisocial behavior is the result of a role that certain individuals assume. There has been an extensive accumulation of literature on this scale at least in part because of Gough's personal interest in it. The research indicates that the So scale has excellent concurrent, predictive, and cross-cultural validity, and is probably the best validated and most powerful scale on the CPI.

The socialization scale was designed to measure the degree to which social norms are accepted and adhered to. An individual, then, can score on a continuum from extremely well socialized to highly antisocial. The scale also estimates the probability of persons' committing behavior which is considered incorrect within their culture. For example, So has been able with relative accuracy to differentiate cheaters from noncheaters in a college population (Kipnis, 1968). It has also differentiated high school dropouts from graduates (Gough, 1966; Hase and Goldberg, 1967). In a further study, Wernick (1955) demonstrated that 50% of the low scorers who were hired as temporary Christmas help stole from the store and none proved to be satisfactory workers. Several researchers have found a negative correlation between So scores and a past lack of family cohesiveness (Glueck and Glueck, 1950; Rosenquist and Megargee, 1969). Thus, many items included in the scale are directed towards whether or not the examinees experienced warmth and satisfaction within their family relationships, for example, No. 444: "My parents never really understood me" (false). Some of the items also reflect the presence or absence of pessimism regarding one's life and environment, as represented by No. 94: "With things going as they are, it is pretty hard to keep up hope of amounting to something" (false). There are several other questions whose content centers on whether or not examinees can properly evaluate the effects of their behavior as well as the extent to which they can be empathetic and sensitive to the feelings of others.

High So (T = 60 or More). Persons scoring high on So are organized, adaptable, and efficient. They are highly dependable, but in order to maintain this level of dependability they are also cautious, self-controlled, and inhibited. In general, they are willing to trust others and express a fairly high level of optimism. They are often described as kind, honest, and practical, and they typically come from a stable, cohesive family environment where warmth and concern were freely expressed. Often they were overprotected, and their current behavior is usually relatively conventional.

> *Males:* adaptable, efficient, honest, inhibited, kind, organized, reasonable, sincere, thorough, wholesome.
> *Females:* cautious, clear thinking, conservative, organized, practical, reasonable, reliable, self-controlled, unassuming, wise.

Moderate So (T = 45–60). Individuals who score in this range are able to trust others and are generally accepting of the mores and rules established by society. They also tend to be inhibited and conventional, sometimes to the point of being overadapted but not as much as those with high So scores.

Moderately Low So (T = 30–45). Individuals scoring in the lower ranges of So are somewhat impulsive and unreliable, and often have a difficult time trusting others. They are not usually followers; rather, they frequently question the rules given to them and, in general, do not have a high degree of respect for society's prescribed forms of behavior. They will often express a moderate level of rebelliousness.

Low So (T = 30 or Less). Such persons have a far greater likelihood of antisocial behavior and are usually unreliable, unconventional, rude, defensive, and impulsive. They reject past family ties primarily because their past family life was filled with chaos and unsatisfying. There is a deep sense of alienation, and they have an extremely difficult time trusting people. Others see them as headstrong, deceitful, rebellious, and pleasure seeking.

> *Males:* deceitful, defensive, headstrong, irresponsible, mischievious, outspoken, quarrelsome, rude, sarcastic, unconventional.
> *Females:* careless, defensive, fickle, foolish, outspoken, peculiar, pleasure seeking, reckless, uninhibited.

9. Self-control (Sc)

The original intent of the Sc scale was to measure the degree to which a person can self-direct his own behavior. More specifically, high scores suggest that a person can delay his behavior and redirect it in a clear, goal-oriented manner. Thus, there is a certain degree of similarity between self-control and both responsibility and socialization. Gough (in Megargee, 1972) clarifies these concepts by stating that responsibility reflects the "degree to which controls are understood," socialization measures the "extent to which they influence a person's behavior," and self-control assesses the "degree to which the individual approves of and espouses such regulatory dispositions" (pp. 65–66). Persons scoring high are self-directed, inhibited persons who withhold their expressions of emotions and behavior. Some types of persons who score extremely high on Sc are often overcontrolled to the extent that for short periods of time, they lose control and become explosive. Individuals with low scores are impulsive and pleasure seeking, have difficulty delaying their impulses, and are not good at evaluating the consequences of their behavior. Thus, both extremely high and extremely low scorers are similar in that they have significant issues dealing with the management of impulses, but they use opposite strategies in coping with these impulses.

The primary overlap of items for Sc is with Gi, and there are several items which are also scored in the opposite direction from Sp and Sa. Some of the most important items are those that emphasize that thought and rationality are the primary determinants of behavior, for example, No. 149: "I consider a matter from every standpoint before I make a decision" (true). Furthermore, high scorers usually endorse items which indicate that they take precautions to avoid irrational behavior and are generally socially inhibited. For example, they usually answer "true" to No. 223: "I keep out of trouble at all costs" and "false" to No. 208: "I like to go to parties where there is lots of loud fun."

High Sc (T = 60 or More). Persons who score high on Sc are considerate, self-denying, and dependable. They have a high need for precision and make every attempt to be reasonable. Other people perceive them as considerate, wholesome, and dependable, but also as stubborn, rigid, and overconforming. They avoid situations in which they might be tempted into acting impulsively, and are generally inhibited and lacking in spontaneity.

> *Males:* considerate, dependable, hardheaded, logical, painstaking, precise, reasonable, reliable, self-controlled, self-denying.
> *Females:* calm, conservative, gentle, moderate, modest, patient, peaceable, quiet, reserved, self-controlled.

Moderate Sc (T = 45–60). Such persons are fairly conventional and somewhat inhibited. They carefully consider the consequences of their behavior before acting. Others usually see them as being reasonable and dependable, although somewhat lacking in spontaneity.

Moderately Low Sc (T = 30–45). Persons scoring in this range sometimes act in a spontaneous, impulsive manner but can usually delay their behavior. Thus, their impulsiveness is not sufficient to impair their interpersonal and work relationships.

Low Sc (T = 30 or Less). Low scorers have a marked difficulty delaying their behavior, are hasty in making decisions, and are usually individualistic and self-seeking. Their impulsiveness may sometimes cause tension in group activities, and they often regret having acted in inappropriate ways. At times they can seem extremely unrealistic and headstrong in regard to their beliefs. They are prone to developing quick relationships which often readily become chaotic and confused.

Males: conceited, faultfinding, hasty, headstrong, impulsive, individualistic, self-seeking, spunky, temperamental, unrealistic.
Females: adventurous, aggressive, arrogant, excitable, impulsive, rebellious, restless, sarcastic, temperamental, uninhibited.

10. Tolerance (To)

The tolerance scale was designed to measure the degree to which persons are socially intolerant versus the extent to which they have accepting, permissive, and nonjudgmental social beliefs and attitudes. The content of most of the items focuses on openness and flexibility versus rigidity and dogmatism. A representative item is a "false" response to No. 67: "I feel sure that there is only one true religion." Other content areas relate to an interest in intellectual and aesthetic activities, one's level of trust, and a lack of hostility or resentment towards others. A person scoring high on tolerance is also indicating that he is not alienated, does not feel isolated, rarely feels anxious, and is relatively poised and self-assured. There is a wide variety of questions on this scale, but there is also a general lack of adequate validity studies. In fact, tolerance is one of the poorer scales on the CPI, and its validity has even been questioned. Thus, interpretations based on this scale should be made cautiously and tentatively.

High To (T = 60 or More). High scorers are likely to be intelligent, have a wide range of interests, and be socially tolerant. They are also able to trust others, and may have a high degree of confidence and social poise. Furthermore, they are nonjudgmental, can easily accept divergent beliefs and values, and are forgiving, generous, and pleasant.

Males: forgiving, generous, good-natured, independent, informal, pleasant, reasonable, softhearted, thoughtful, unselfish.
Females: calm, efficient, insightful, leisurely, logical, mature, responsible, self-controlled, tactful, understanding.

Moderate To (T = 45–60). Moderate scorers are likewise somewhat nonjudgmental and open to the beliefs of others. They usually have a wide range of interests, and are informal and independent.

Low To (T = 40 or Less). Persons scoring in this range are likely to be judgmental and nonaccepting of the beliefs and values of others. This judgmental attitude tends to generalize into other areas of their lives so that, overall, they seem cold, smug, and stern. They are authoritarian and center their lives around a fixed and dogmatic set of beliefs. Furthermore, they are mannerly, fearful, arrogant, and sarcastic. If criticized, they will usually become extremely defensive, bitter, and rejecting.

Males: affected, cold, egotistical, faultfinding, fussy, hardhearted, self-centered, shallow, thankless, whiny.
Females: arrogant, autocratic, bitter, defensive, distrustful, hardhearted, infantile, resentful, restless, sarcastic.

11. Good Impression (Gi)

Although Gi is mainly a validity scale designed to detect persons who are "faking good," it also reflects the degree to which a person with a valid profile is concerned with creating a favorable impression on others. There is a fairly high degree of item overlap with self-control (Sc), which suggests that an important component of creating a favorable impression is a good ability to delay impulses. There are also a number of items that make fairly obvious statements concerning the person's level of functioning, amount of antisocial behavior, the extent to which he is goal oriented, and whether or not he has complaints regarding personal failings. High scorers are prone to exaggerate their positive points and minimize their negative qualities. For example, they deny any aggression, which is reflected in items such as No. 44: "Sometimes I feel like smashing things" (false). Furthermore, they state that they have a high level of confidence and self-assurance, and minimize anxieties or insecurities. They emphasize that they can adapt well to stress and that they have a stable personality, which is reflected by several statements such as No. 150: "Criticism makes me very uncomfortable" (false). Finally, there are several items related to the extent to which they behave in a socially approved manner and experience harmonious relationships with others.

The Gi scale has generally been successful in detecting invalid profiles. For example, in one study, Dicken (1960), by using a cutoff score of T = 60, was able to detect in 79% of the cases the profiles of persons attempting to make a favorable impression. With somewhat different criteria, only 3% of a total sample of profiles of mixed "normal" and "fake good" were incorrectly classified. In the same study, Dicken also demonstrated that even though persons were, in some of the cases, attempting to "fake good" on other scales, Gi still showed the greatest increase. The practical importance of this is that even though a person might be attempting, for example, to exaggerate his level of responsibility, Gi would still be expected to increase. Thus, the use of Gi as a validity scale is not just restricted to persons attempting to create a favorable impression in a global manner; it can be used to detect persons attempting to "fake good" along other specific dimensions as well.

High Gi (T = 60 or More). An examinee's personal history is the best guide for determining whether a score in this range reflects a "fake good" profile or is more likely to indicate a person with an excellent level of adjustment. For example, an alcoholic with a high Gi is probably either consciously attempting to create a favorable impression or demonstrating the use of denial which is often associated with that disorder. A further possibility with an extremely high Gi is that the person may be unaware of the impression he creates on others and has an inflated self-image based on rigidly selective perceptions. His self-image would then be likely to be maintained by ignoring the feedback he receives from others and manipulating others to agree with the perceptions he has of himself.

If the profile is only moderately high and has been determined to be valid, then the person is likely to be conventional, adaptable, self-denying, and capable of a high degree of empathy. These people are often overly sensitive to the criticism of others, and usually respond by attempting to change and adapt in order to gain approval. They feel that it is important to please and to be seen in a favorable light. Others usually see them as kind, warm, considerate, and patient.

Males: adaptable, changeable, considerate, friendly, kind, self-denying, softhearted, tactful, unselfish, warm.
Females: calm, conservative, mild, moderate, modest, patient, peaceable, trusting, understanding, worrying.

Moderate Gi (T = 45–60). Persons with a moderate score on Gi are usually unselfish and concerned with making a favorable impression. They are able to take feedback from others and use it in a constructive way. Others perceive them as peaceable, trusting, understanding, and highly concerned with living up to their social responsibilities.

Moderately Low Gi (T = 30–45). Moderately low scorers are only minimally concerned with the impression they have on others to the extent that they are sometimes seen as insensitive. They alone are the judges of their behavior, and they rarely listen to the evaluations of others. They are often described as independent, witty, and occasionally temperamental and sarcastic.

Low Gi (T = 30 or Less). Persons scoring in this range are typically arrogant and actively reject the judgments of others. They are even prone to exaggerate their negative behavior in a rebellious way, and then expect this behavior to be tolerated and even accepted. Others describe them as temperamental, cynical, sarcastic, and overly frank to the point of being disagreeable, which usually has the effect of disrupting their interpersonal relationships.

Males: complaining, dissatisfied, faultfinding, hasty, headstrong, indifferent, nagging, pessimistic, temperamental, unkind.
Females: changeable, cynical, frank, moody, pessimistic, sarcastic, shrewd, stubborn, temperamental, witty.

12. Communality (Cm)

The Cm scale is a validity scale which was originally designed to detect random answering. The questions are keyed in such a way that normal populations answer 95% of the questions in the keyed direction. For example, almost everyone answers "true" to statement No. 334: "I would fight if someone tried to take away my rights." Although the scale was not designed to measure personality variables, there are some personality indicators which can tentatively be derived from this scale. These are mainly based on the observation that the content of the items reflects the following areas: good socialization, conformity, optimism, denial of neurotic characteristics, and conventionality of behavior and attitudes. Gough points out that this is comparable to the "popular" response on the Rorschach in that it reflects the degree to which examinees see their surroundings in ways that are similar to others.

High Cm (T = 60 or More). High scores suggest that the examinee adheres to highly conventional attitudes and is overly socialized, tending to see his world in a stereotyped manner.

Males: cautious, conscientious, deliberate, efficient, formal, organized, practical, responsible, thorough, thrifty.
Females: clear thinking, confident, energetic, humorous, practical, rational, realistic, rigid, stern, strong.

Low Cm (T = 30 or Less). A low score sometimes suggests that persons have chaotic, conflict-ridden family backgrounds. Their attitudes towards the world would typically be unusual and idiosyncratic.

> *Males:* attractive, careless, courageous, daring, distractible, forgetful, leisurely, pleasure seeking, reckless, spendthrift.
> *Females:* appreciative, artistic, awkward, feminine, forgetful, forgiving, indifferent, irresponsible, unconventional, undependable.

However, scores in this range primarily increase the likelihood that the test is of questionable validity, and scores below 20 almost always confirm that the profile is invalid.

13. Achievement via Conformance (Ac)

The Ac scale involves not only an orientation towards achievement but also a need for structure and organization as a means of channeling that achievement. This scale specifically relates to settings in which conformity is an asset and reflects the degree to which persons prefer to have their criteria of performance clearly specified by some outside source. The content of the items relates to how effectively they can perform within an academic setting and how high their relative levels of energy and efficiency are. For example, a person scoring high on Ac often gives a "true" response to No. 135: "I wake up fresh and rested most mornings." High scorers also see themselves as being productive workers, as reflected by statements such as No. 260: "I always try to do at least a little better than what is expected of me" (true). Additional content areas relate to the extent to which the examinee is even tempered, accepts the rules of socially approved standards of behavior, and dislikes frivolous, unconventional behavior.

The Ac scale has been one of the more thoroughly researched scales on the CPI primarily because of its practical relevance for academic personnel. In a review of the literature, Megargee (1972) reports that it has good criterion validity and has been found to correlate significantly (.36–.44) with grade point average (G.P.A.) and general achievement in high school settings and, to a lesser extent, in college environments.

High Ac (T = 50 or More). Persons scoring above 50 are typically persistent and industrious, especially when conforming to some external standard. They strongly prefer specificity and structure, and may even have a difficult time when structure is lacking, especially if a high Ac is accompanied by a low Ai. Such persons are usually responsible, capable, and ambitious, but they express these behaviors in a conservative, reserved, and obliging manner. Furthermore, they place a high degree of value on intellectual effort.

Males: ambitious, capable, conscientious, considerate, intelligent, logical, mature, reasonable, resourceful, responsible.
Females: conservative, efficient, enterprising, idealistic, logical, obliging, planful, reliable, reserved, responsible.

High-scoring males are mainly described as ambitious, considerate, mature, and resourceful, whereas females are somewhat differently described as efficient, reliable, reserved, and responsible.

Moderate Ac (T = 35–50). Moderate scorers may question the need for structure and organization. Although they prefer not to have structure, they can adequately function in a structured situation when required to do so.

Low Ac (T = 35 or Less). Persons in this range are rejecting of authority and regulations. This rebellion may result in their achieving far below their potential since their energy often goes more towards rejecting external organization and rules rather than to producing within the limits imposed on them. Such persons are often characterized as intellectual rebels, especially if their achievement via independence (Ai) scale is relatively high.

Males: apathetic, distrustful, hardhearted, irresponsible, pleasure seeking, reckless, rude, shallow, shiftless, show-off.
Females: adventurous, careless, easygoing, irresponsible, lazy, rebellious, sarcastic, unconventional, uninhibited, zany.

While males are often described as being distrustful, irresponsible, reckless, shallow, and pleasure seeking, females are somewhat differently perceived as adventurous, rebellious, sarcastic, unconventional, and uninhibited.

14. Achievement via Independence (Ai)

Whereas Ac can be used to predict achievement in high school, Ai was designed to predict achievement in a college environment. Persons who are high in Ai succeed in settings that require creativity, self-actualization, and independence of thought. Gough (1968) has clarified this distinction by describing achievement via conformance (Ac) as being "form enhancing" whereas Ai is "form creating." Ai correlates significantly with college students' G.P.A., yet there is only a low correlation with intelligence. Thus, students who have elevated Ai scales and who also achieve a high G.P.A. do so mainly on the basis of a high need for achievement and only secondarily on the basis of intelligence. They are able to tolerate a high level of ambiguity and usually reject authoritarian or overly stringent regulations. In some cases, high Ai scores can predict achievement in situations in which originality and independence are rewarded. Persons with high scores are not willing to unquestioningly accept conventional advice but rather prefer to think for themselves. For example, high scorers usually answer "false" to the statement No. 255: "Only a fool would try to change the American way of life." There are also questions relating to the degree to which individuals appreciate activities involving the intellect, such as No. 122: "I like poetry" (true). Other content areas attempt to assess their degree of adjustment and the extent to which they are concerned with the deeper aspects of interpersonal relationships.

High Ai (T = 50 or More). Such persons prefer to work without rules and structures, and usually feel dampened within a highly organized environment. They value creativity and originality, and are self-motivated and rejecting of conventional standards of productivity. Their ability to produce and function is significantly impaired if a great deal of structure is required. They produce best and are most efficient when left to regulate their own behavior.

Males: foresighted, independent, informal, intelligent, lazy, pleasant, rational, sarcastic, touchy, versatile.
Females: calm, capable, clear thinking, discreet, intelligent, logical, mature, original, rational, reflective.

Although both sets of descriptions emphasize originality, the male description focuses somewhat more on independence and individuality.

Moderate Ai (T = 35–50). Persons scoring in this range are able to achieve based on their own self-direction but feel somewhat insecure when doing things completely on their own. Thus, they can work either with or without structure, but they prefer a moderate degree of external organization. At times, they can be creative, but when they come to conclusions on their own, they still need external verification in order to feel comfortable.

Low Ai (T = 40 or Less). Low scorers have difficulty trusting their own abilities, and this characteristic becomes more exaggerated as the scale score becomes lower. They require external definition in order to define themselves and need others to specify their proper course of action. Because of this uncertainty and dependence on outside structure, these individuals are moderately anxious, depressed, and self-doubting. They are not intellectually inclined and tend to feel out of place in the world of abstract thinking.

Males: affected, bossy, cautious, cool, egotistical, fearful, frivolous, mannerly, smug, stern.
Females: awkward, excitable, foolish, immature, infantile, rattlebrained, restless, simple, unrealistic, unstable.

In the descriptions of both males and females, there is an element of immaturity, a lack of insight, and a tendency to engage in self-defeating behaviors.

15. Intellectual Efficiency (Ie)

The Ie scale was originally called a "nonintellectual intelligence test" and was designed to measure personality traits which coincided with a high level of intellectual ability. High scorers on Ie tend to be competent, to be clear thinking, and to make efficient use of the potential they possess. Thus, it is not so much an intelligence test but rather a measure of the degree to which a person makes efficient use of the intelligence he does possess. There is a moderate amount of item overlap with sociability (Sy), achievement via independence (Ai), and social presence (Sp). One important content area of the items relates to the degree to which a person enjoys and is interested in wide-ranging intellectual activities, for example, statement No. 228: "I like to read about history" (true). There are also a number of questions relating to self-confidence and assurance as exemplified by item No. 50: "I seem to be as capable and smart as most others around me" (true). Other questions relate to good physiological functioning, positive relationships with others, and an absence of irritability and suspiciousness.

There are a number of representative and noteworthy validity studies which have been performed on Ie. It is positively correlated with measures of intelligence (Gough, 1969), and members of MENSA scored significantly higher on Ie than the national norms (Southern and Plant, 1968). The scale has also been able to successfully discriminate high school dropouts from students who later graduated (Gough, 1966). The autobiographies of high scorers reveal that they see themselves as being well organized, efficient, and committed to pursuing intellectual and cultural activities (Hill, 1967).

High Ie (T = 50 or More). Persons scoring high on Ie indicate that they have a wide range of interests with an excellent ability to utilize their resources. They are capable and confident with good planning abilities, independent, informal, and clear thinking.

> *Males:* capable, confident, efficient, foresighted, independent, intelligent, reasonable, self-controlled, sophisticated, unaffected.
> *Females:* capable, clear thinking, confident, efficient, informal, intelligent, leisurely, logical, rational, relaxed.

Moderate Ie (T = 40–50). Moderate scorers may still be highly competent persons, but they are also likely to have some self-doubts regarding their intellectual capabilities.

Low Ie (T = 40 or Less). Persons in this range may be insecure about their intellectual abilities, and are likely to experience enough self-doubt to create a mild degree of depression and anxiety. They typically appear awkward, shallow, and suggestible. As an alternative interpretation, low scorers may merely be disinterested in intellectual activities which is also likely to be reflected in their choice of occupation. The latter interpretation would not imply the presence of self-doubt and insecurity suggested in the first, but rather merely a lack of interest.

Males: awkward, cold, forgetful, hardhearted, having narrow interests, queer, restless, sensitive, shallow, suggestible.
Females: absentminded, awkward, having narrow interests, nervous, pessimistic, simple, slow, stubborn, tense, withdrawn.

16. Psychological Mindedness (Py)

The original intent of the Py scale was to identify persons who are insightful into the behavior of others in that they can accurately perceive their inner needs and are aware of their inner motivations. This focuses on the ability to figure other people out, and does not necessarily imply that these people are empathic and nurturing. In order to assess their degree of empathy, it would be necessary to consult additional scales such as sociability (Sy) and well being (Wb), or to use the scoring for the "empathy scale" devised by Hogan (1969). However, as further research was done on Py, it came to be more an indicator of persons who were interested in pursuing psychology from an academic perspective. In fact, Megargee (1972) concludes his literature review by stating that the Py scale has limited usefulness as an indicator of a person's ability to accurately perceive the inner needs and motivations of others.

The content of the items relates to the ability to concentrate, one's effectiveness in dealing with ambiguity, and one's degree of enjoyment with regard to his chosen occupation. Representative statements are No. 12: "I often feel I made a wrong choice of occupation" (false) and No. 145: "I have a tendency to give up easily when I meet with difficult problems" (false). Other content areas deal with an ability to stick with long-term goals and an acceptance of unconventional opinions.

High Py (T = 60 or More). High scorers are interested in academic pursuits, especially in the area of research. They place a high level of importance on obtaining recognition for their efforts, and they demonstrate perseverance, the ability to concentrate for long periods of time, and a high degree of satisfaction from their chosen profession. Other people often see them as independent, individualistic, preoccupied, and reserved.

Males: aloof, evasive, foresighted, independent, individualistic, persevering, preoccupied, reserved, unfriendly, wary.
Females: capable, cool, independent, ingenious, leisurely, logical, mischievous, self-confident, sharp witted, undependable.

Low Py (T = 35 or Less). Persons who score low on Py are generally not inclined towards research or scholarly activities. However, they are likely to be sociable, talkative, unassuming, and conventional.

Males: active, cheerful, energetic, flirtatious, humorous, kind, opportunistic, outgoing, sociable, talkative.
Females: conventional, generous, honest, kind, praising, tense, trusting, unassuming, warm, worrying.

17. Flexibility (Fx)

The Fx scale was designed to assess the degree to which an individual is flexible, adaptable, and changeable in his thinking, behavior, and temperament. It was originally based on questions relating to rigidity, but as the scale construction evolved, the scoring was reversed and the name changed from the "rigidity" scale to the "flexibility" scale. A representative statement is a "false" response to No. 340: "Our thinking would be a lot better off if we would just forget about words like probably, approximately, and perhaps." Other content areas relate to an ability to tolerate ambiguity, uncertainty, and impulsiveness, and to a nonjudgmental, tolerant attitude towards moral and ethical formulas of right and wrong. For example, high scorers often give a "false" answer to No. 451: "I set high standards for myself and I feel that others should do the same."

The validity studies in part agree with the intent of the scale in that they do support the hypothesis that low-scoring individuals are somewhat rigid. However, there is little evidence to indicate that extremely high scores reflect a high degree of flexibility (Megargee, 1972). Gough (1975) suggests that scores in the higher ranges are curvilinear in that a moderately high score suggests that the person is relatively flexible, but with increasing elevation, a person becomes progressively more unstable and unpredictable. Megargee (1972) states that given the weak evidence for this scale, especially for high Fx, it is one of the least valid scales on the CPI. Thus, any interpretations derived from it should be made with caution.

High Fx (T = 65 or More). Persons having extremely high scores may feel rootless and are often emotionally unstable. Everything in their lives is open to question, including their sense of values and moral beliefs. Thus, it is difficult for them to internalize clear-cut standards. They can easily approach situations from a number of varying perspectives, which gives them the advantage of having many alternatives but creates the disadvantage of not having a clearly defined direction. The adjectives used to describe them include not only flexibility but also instability and inconsistency.

Males: easygoing, fickle, independent, lazy, optimistic, pleasure seeking, quick, sharp witted, spendthrift, spontaneous.
Females: careless, clever, daring, imaginative, individualistic, ingenious, mischievous, original, pleasure seeking, sociable.

Moderate Fx (T = 50–65). Moderate scorers are open to considering and experiencing alternative perspectives. They are nonjudgmental, intellectually flexible, independent, optimistic, and able to come up with innovative ideas.

Moderately Low Fx (T = 35–50). Persons scoring in this range prefer structure and like to have things clearly defined and specified. Although they can handle a certain degree of uncertainty, it usually creates discomfort. They are usually cautious and practical, and can be described as being relatively rigid.

Low Fx (T = 35 or Less). Low scorers generally dislike new ideas and experiences, and are continually seeking security. They have a strong need to control their thoughts and generally have a difficult time changing their decisions once they have been made. They are usually rigid, stubborn, and defensive.

Males: determined, efficient, organized, planful, practical, stern, stolid, stubborn, thorough.
Females: cautious, conscientious, conservative, defensive, prudish, rigid, self-punishing, simple, sincere, slow.

These adjectives suggest that males express their rigidity by a high degree of pragmatism and seriousness, whereas females are more likely to be defensive, prudish, and conscientious, and usually internalize their anger.

18. Femininity (Fe)

The Fe scale was developed to assess the degree to which examinees were psychologically feminine or masculine regardless of their actual sex. Its original intent was to detect significant conflicts over sexual identity, but this aspect of the scale has become progressively more deemphasized. The scale is currently used to assess the extent to which individuals endorse beliefs, values, and occupations that are traditionally held either by males or by females. The intent of some items is fairly obvious, whereas others are more subtle. Many items relate to traditional masculine or feminine roles, such as No. 240: "I would like to be a nurse" (true). Additional content areas refer to a person's degree of restraint and impulsiveness, as well as the extent to which one is emotional during inter-personal relationships. For example, persons scoring high on Fe often give a "true" response to item No. 58: "I get very tense and anxious when I think other people are disapproving of me." They also answer items in such a way as to reflect a low interest in politics and current affairs, and they place minimal emphasis on achieving. This is one of the scales which has been well researched, and studies indicate that it has a fairly high level of validity.

High Fe (T = 70 or More). Males' scoring within this range suggests the possibility of difficulties related to sexual identity. Females are likely to have extremely high needs for affiliation and are usually highly dependent.

> *Males:* appreciative, complaining, feminine, formal, meek, nervous, self-denying, sensitive, weak, worrying.
> *Females:* conscientious, discreet, generous, gentle, helpful, mature, self-controlled, sympathetic, tactful, warm.

Males are usually described as complaining, sensitive, self-denying, nervous, and weak. In contrast, females are perceived by others as warm, conscientious, self-controlled, and sympathetic. The self-descriptions of females are likewise favorable in that they refer to themselves as self-controlled, ethical, highly socialized, and emotionally sensitive. In contrast, high-scoring males are more likely to perceive themselves as unhappy, somewhat withdrawn, and distrustful. It has also been found that high-scoring females tend to be early terminators in psychotherapy, especially if they also have high scores on self-acceptance (Sa) and good impression (Gi).

Moderately High Fe (T = 60 or More). Both males and females scoring within this range have significant needs for affiliation and dependency. They usually have a difficult time dealing with a high degree of autonomy and feel uncomfortable when independent action is required of them.

Moderate Fe (T = 40–50). Persons scoring within this range can deal effectively with autonomy and have an average level of needs for dependency and affiliation. They are generally practical and self-sufficient but not to an exaggerated extent.

Moderately Low Fe (T = 40 or Less). Such persons are typically task oriented, practical, and emotionally self-sufficient with few dependency needs. They are often perceived as masculine, robust, tough, and even coarse.

Males: adventurous, aggressive, clear thinking, daring, impulsive, masculine, outgoing, pleasure seeking, show-off, strong.
Females: coarse, dissatisfied, lazy, masculine, pleasure seeking, restless, robust, self-centered, touchy, tough.

Females are typically described by others in a somewhat negative fashion as dissatisfied, touchy, masculine, restless, and self-centered. Self-descriptions are likewise unfavorable, whereas males scoring low on Fe perceive themselves in more favorable terms as self-confident, mentally alert, assertive, and possessing social poise and leadership abilities. It has been found that males with low Fe scores are more likely to terminate therapy prematurely especially if they also have high scores on self-acceptance (Sa) and good impression (Gi).

Low Fe (T = 30 or Less). An Fe score this low suggests an exaggeration of the above trends and, in females, the likelihood of difficulties related to sexual identity.

CONFIGURAL INTERPRETATION

Intellectual Level

Megargee (1972) has reported that To, Ac, Ai, Ie, Py, and Fx are all related to an individual's intellectual level. If all or most of these are elevated (T = 55 or more), it is a strong indication that the person has a high interest in intellectual activities and good overall intelligence. If all or most of the above scales are consistently low, it reflects limited intellectual ability and is a strong indication that the person has a narrow range of interests. This narrowing of interests may, in part, be a response to an emotionally upsetting event either in the recent past or at a significant time during the person's earlier development.

Achievement

Predicting and Assessing High School Achievement. The CPI is generally effective at detecting bright high school achievers. They typically have elevated scores on Ie and Ai, whereas underachievers are generally low on these scales. Bright achievers also have relatively high scores on Re, So, To, Ac, and Py. Persons who are high achievers but have average I.Q.'s have relatively high scores (T = 55 or more) on Re and So and, to a lesser extent, on Wb, Ac, and Ie.
   A number of equations have been developed for use in predicting achievement of high school students (see Megargee, 1972). These equations are comprised of the weighted combinations of scales and, when computed, provide the best possible prediction of specific abilities. For predicting the achievement of

both males and females with combined low, medium, and high I.Q.'s, the following equation is recommended:

$$\text{Achievement} = 20.116 + .317 \text{ Re} + .192 \text{ So} - .309 \text{ Gi} + .227 \text{ Ac} + .280 \text{ Ai} + .244 \text{ Ie} \tag{1}$$

This equation correlates from .53 to .56 with overall G.P.A. (Gough, 1964). If a student's I.Q. scores are available, the following equation is recommended:

$$\text{Achievement} = .786 + .195 \text{ Re} + .244 \text{ So} - .130 \text{ Gi} + .19 \text{ Ac} + .179 \text{ Ai} + .279 \text{ I.Q.} \tag{2}$$

Since Ie is a relatively inefficient measure of I.Q., it has been excluded in this equation and the exact I.Q. derived from intelligence testing is included instead. This equation raises the correlation with overall G.P.A. to .68, which is significantly better than the .60 correlation found when using only I.Q. scores.

To evaluate whether students will either drop out of high school or graduate and continue on to college, social factors as measured by the CPI are at least as important as their intellectual ability. The primary scales to predict high school graduation are Re, Ac, and to a lesser extent, Wb, To, and Ie, all of which are usually significantly higher for students who graduate from high school than for students who are high school dropouts (Gough, 1964). High school students who later go on to college score significantly higher on Re, Ac, and Ie (Gough, 1968). The following formula correlates at a level of .52 with later college attendance for high school students (Gough, 1968):

$$\text{College Attendance} = 17.822 + .333 \text{ Do} + .539 \text{ Cs} - .189 \text{ Gi} + .740 \text{ Ac} \tag{3}$$

Predicting and Assessing College Achievement. Several studies have been conducted on the relative importance of single scale and combinations of scale scores in assessing college achievement. Significant correlations have been found between Re, So, Ai, and overall G.P.A. (Hase and Goldberg, 1967). Further studies (Flaherty and Reutzel, 1965; Griffin and Flaherty, 1964) likewise stress the importance of Re, So, and Ai but also include Ie and Cs, and in female samples (Flaherty and Reutzel, 1965), Do was significantly correlated with G.P.A. as well. These scales are somewhat similar to those used to predict achievement in high school students except that whereas Ai becomes more significant, Ac decreases in importance. Also the likelihood of later upward social mobility is correlated with Cs and college G.P.A.

Although positive correlations were found between the above single scales, the magnitude of these correlations was not extremely high, which is represented by the highest correlation only reaching .36 for males on Ai. Most other significant correlations ranged between .20 and .26. However, weighted combinations of scores produced higher correlations ranging from .35 to .54 depending on the type of population that was being assessed. Gough (1964) has found a .41 correlation between the following formula and grades for both males and females in introduction to psychology classes:

$$\text{Achievement (Introduction to Psychology)} = 35.958 - .294 \text{ Sy}$$
$$- .180 \text{ Sp} + .185 \text{ Re} - .189 \text{ Sc} - .152 \text{ Gi} - .210 \text{ Cm} + .275 \text{ Ac}$$
$$+ .523 \text{ Ai} + .241 \text{ Ie} + .657 \text{ Py} \qquad (4)$$

Weighted combinations of scales using SAT scores for males and females who were National Merit scholars were found to have a .32 and .23 correlation with college G.P.A., respectively:

$$\text{Male G.P.A.} = .16 \text{ SAT (Math)} + .11 \text{ So} - .19 \text{ Sp} + .17 \text{ Fe} \qquad (5)$$
$$\text{Female G.P.A.} = .25 \text{ SAT (Verbal)} - .14 \text{ Sp} + .06 \text{ Re} + .20 \text{ Ac} + .08 \text{ Fe} \qquad (6)$$

Although the correlations derived from these formulas are somewhat low, they are an improvement on the use of SAT scores alone for this group.

It can be seen from these rather modest correlations that it is more difficult to predict the performance of college students than it is for those attending high school. This can be traced to the far greater number and complexity of variables involved in a college setting. Both the selection of curricula and the student's motivation for attending college can result from a variety of reasons. Furthermore, there have been significant changes in the curricula and admissions policies of colleges since this research was first done. Finally, a student's life-style can be extremely varied. For example, some students may be attempting to struggle through college with a part- or even full-time job, whereas others may be taking relatively few classes and be supported exclusively by their parents. All of these variables are beyond the scope of what can be measured on a test such as the CPI. The practical implication for clinicians predicting college G.P.A. is that they should consider not only test scores but also as many of the other variables as possible.

Achievement in Vocational Training Programs. *Student Teaching.* Several studies have been performed to assess the effectiveness of teachers in student teaching programs. Veldman and Kelly (1965) found that student teachers who were rated highly by their supervisors scored significantly higher on Ac, Cs, Do, Gi, and Py than those that were rated as less effective. Hill (1960) also emphasized the importance of Ac but did not find Do and Py to be important. A further study with a female population again stressed the importance of Ac but also included Re and Ie as significant factors (Gough, Durflinger, and Hill, 1968). Although these studies consistently emphasize the importance of Ac, none of the individual scales was found to have either consistent or large correlations with teaching effectiveness. However, Gough, Durflinger, and Hill (1968) found a moderate correlation of .44 between CPI scores and teacher effectiveness using the following equation based on weighted scales:

$$\text{Teaching Effectiveness} = 14.743 + .334 \text{ So} - .670 \text{ Gi} + .997 \text{ Ac} + .909 \text{ Py} - .446 \text{ Fx} \tag{7}$$

Using this equation, they were able to correctly categorize 65% of a sample of student teachers.

Medical School. Several scales have been found to correlate positively with overall medical school G.P.A. including Sy (.35), To (.34), and Ie (.40; Gough and Hall, 1964). An equation based on weighted combinations of scores was found to correlate at a magnitude of .43 with both faculty ratings of students and G.P.A. (Gough and Hall, 1964):

$$\text{Medical Promise} = .794 \text{ Sy} + .602 \text{ To} + 1.114 \text{ Cm} - .696 \text{ Cs} \tag{8}$$

Dental School. Most studies using single scale correlations with achievement in dental school have not produced significant correlations, although Kirk, Cumming, and Hackett (1963) do report a correlation of .28 between Ac and dental school G.P.A. However, Gough and Kirk (1970) found a .38 correlation with G.P.A. using the following equation based on weighted combinations of scales:

$$\text{Dental Performance} = 29.938 - .110 \text{ Sp} + .148 \text{ Re} - .262 \text{ Gi} + .727 \text{ Ac} + .230 \text{ Py} \tag{9}$$

Although this correlation is somewhat modest, it is higher than the Dental Aptitude Test's correlation of .29.

Seminary. Query (1966) performed a study on seminary students who were advised to discontinue versus those who successfully completed the program. Although he did not develop any equations based on weighted scores, he did find that those who were unsuccessful tended to score higher on Sy and Sa.

Police and Military Training. Generally, Ie has been found to be most closely correlated with police effectiveness both during training (in which instructor ratings showed a correlation of .40; Hogan, 1973) and after one year in the field (in which the trooper's field commanders gave ratings showing a correlation of .43 with Ie; Mills and Bohannon, 1980). During training Ac, Ai, and Sy were also found to correlate with instructor ratings at a magnitude of .31, .33, and

.45, respectively (Hogan, 1973). However, the high correlation for Sy was found to exist only for cadets in training and not for officers once they were in the field. Field commander ratings for officers who had been in the field for a year were found for Ai, Ie, and Fy to be .32, .43, and .39, respectively (Mills and Bohannon, 1980).

A study by Collins (1967) rated drill sergeants in a training program on the following four criteria of success: academic grades, an assessment of leadership ability, final class standing, and a field test of combat skills. The only scale to correlate significantly was Ie, and it is interesting to note that the scales stressing conformity (Ac) and dominance (Do) did not have any correlation. It has also been found that women who were successful in air force basic training scored higher in all scales except Sc, Cm, Py, and Fe than those who were unsuccessful (Elliott, 1960). A different study found that successful students graduating from an army language training program scored significantly higher on Ai and Ie but not Ac than those who were unsuccessful (Datel, Hall, and Rufe, 1965).

Achievement through Conformance versus Independence. A comparison between Ac and Ai can provide useful information regarding an individual's typical style or preference towards working. This can have important implications for helping a person make a career choice or understanding existing job difficulties. If Ai is high (T = 50 or more) and significantly higher than Ac (10 or more), such persons usually place a high level of trust in their own judgments and conclusions, and are likely to reject conventional formulas. Their acceptance of decisions or ideas depends more on inward verification rather than a respect for, or adherence to, external standards. When left on their own, they are highly motivated to achieve, but they may feel dampened if placed in a structured environment. If Ai is exceptionally high (T = 65 or more), they may spend much of their time rejecting authority. This trend would be further exaggerated with high scores on Do and low scores on Sy. The result might be an almost obsessional quality in their thinking characterized by strong themes of rebelliousness. In general, a significantly higher Ai than Ac is an excellent profile for authors, researchers, and persons in positions of independent leadership.

If Ac is high (T = 50 or more) and is significantly greater than Ai (10 or more), the opposite trend would be apparent. These persons would strongly prefer specificity and external structure. They would be more effective and feel more comfortable when "second in command" such as in a business middle-management position. An overall and generally effective combination occurs with high but evenly balanced scores on Ai and Ac. This suggests that these individuals have the necessary flexibility both to work within a structured environment and to do effective work independently. The following is a listing of the descriptions given to persons scoring with different high and low combinations of Ac and Ai (Gough, 1968):

Ac high

		intelligent	logical
idealistic	mannerly	intelligent	logical
cautious	shy	rational	interests wide
praising	conscientious	realistic	inventive
nervous	inhibited	independent	active
helpful	dull	reasonable	stable

Ai low ——— Ai high

irresponsible	show-off	spunky	tolerant
careless	touchy	reckless	reliable
distrustful	undependable	unexcitable	courageous
disorderly	unstable	foresighted	distractible
indifferent	restless	frank	pleasure seeking

Ac low

Leadership

The Do scale has been consistently shown to be able to accurately differentiate leaders from nonleaders. In discussing leadership, it is helpful to describe the difference between an executive leader who has been appointed and a social leader who has been elected. For both types of leaders, the Do scale is high. However, for the executive leader, there is considerably more variability among the other scales; the style of expressing leadership is more dependent on the conditions that the person is in, and the achievement scales are relatively more important than the other measurements (summarized in Megargee, 1972). This stands to reason since the success of an executive leader is based more on his administrative and supervisory abilities than on his popularity. Social leadership is more likely to have a general elevation in factor 2 scales as well as an elevated Do. Using a combination of weighted scales derived from social leaders in a high school environment, Gough (1969) was able to obtain a modest correlation of .34 between social leadership and weighted CPI scales.

$$\text{Leadership (Social)} = 14.130 + .372 \text{ Do} + .696 \text{ Sa} + .345 \text{ Wb}$$
$$- .133 \text{ Gi} + .274 \text{ Ai} \qquad (10)$$

Gough (1968) has studied the relation between Do and Re and found that the meaning of Do will be altered by the relative elevation of Re. If Do and Re are both high, a leader will be generally progressive, conscientious, and ambitious. In contrast, adjectives describing high Do persons with low Re indicate that they will be dominant in a more aggressive, rigid, and destructive way. The following is a list of adjectives used to describe various combinations of Do and Re:

Do high

touchy	dominant	dominant	ambitious
robust	strong	responsible	foresighted
cynical	tough	progressive	conscientious
hardheaded	aggressive	wise	formal
temperamental	opinionated	stern	alert

Re low ——————————————————————————————— Re high

irresponsible	suggestible	quiet	calm
careless	foolish	peaceable	mild
unstable	pleasure seeking	modest	gentle
apathetic	changeable	reserved	thoughtful
confused	lazy	cooperative	honest

Do low

Executive Success. Success and effectiveness as an executive are frequently found in a profile in which T = 60 on Do, Cs, and Sp; T = 40–50 on Sa, Re, So, Sc; T = 55 or more on Sy; T = 40 or more on Wb; and T = 50 or less on Gi (in Webb et al., 1981). The most important variables are the indicated T scores on Do, Cs, Sp, Sa, Re, So, and Sc. This profile is common among business executives and foremen who prefer managerial types of responsibility. They are usually able to have others adapt to their plans, yet at the same time are flexible enough to adapt to the demands that are placed on them. Although they are generally excellent leaders, they may create a certain degree of family discord by attempting to be too demanding and autocratic in the home. If this combination of scores is present for a person under 25 years of age, it can suggest a naive sense of overconfidence in which the person cannot effectively assess his personal limitations. However, this profile is generally a good predictor of later success in leadership positions.

Leadership and Empathy. If an individual has elevations on both Do (T = 65 or more) and Gi (T = 60 or more), he is likely not only to possess excellent leadership abilities but also to demonstrate a concern with, and empathy for, others (Heilbrun et al., 1962). If Gi is low in relation to Do, then the leadership style will usually be more critical, domineering, egotistical, and autocratic, with a decreased concern for creating and maintaining harmonious interpersonal relationships in the group. A low score on both Gi and Do will reflect a somewhat passive and withdrawn person who is socially inept and resentful, and whose passivity may be expressed in a shy seeking of approval from others.

Decision Making. The interaction between Sa and Wb reflects the degree to which the examinee turns to himself for decision making or depends on others.

If Wb is low and Sa is moderate to high, the person will usually rely on his own self-evaluations, and feel that others are inferior and cannot be trusted. This may be because he is self-assured and independent as reflected by a Wb that is only moderate to slightly low, or he may only listen to his own judgments because of a deep sense of alienation and distrust of others as reflected in a markedly low Wb and high Sa.

If Wb is moderate to high and Sa is low, such individuals will tend to believe that other peoples' judgments are superior and that theirs are poor and inferior by comparison. This may be because they are still fairly accepting of themselves (only slightly low Sa) but think even more highly of others. Thus, they may have a high level of loyalty to people who are in superior positions such as an employer or parent. Such persons may also have a poorly developed ability to accurately perceive the faults and limitations of others, and may have developed this loyalty in response to having had overprotective parents. Yet, a further possibility could be that they do not respect their own judgments and perceptions because they are lacking in their own resources.

With both Sa and Wb low, there are likely to be significant doubts regarding oneself. There may be an excessive level of dependency, fearfulness regarding one's own competence, and a corresponding resentment because of one's continual dependency on others.

Clinical Assessment

The CPI has generally not proved to be as effective in the assessment of psychopathology as it has in the educational and vocational areas. This can be traced to several reasons, the primary one being that it was not designed for clinical assessment and thus there has been relatively little research in this area. The organization and the nature of the scales do not differentiate among the various syndromes of pathology, nor do they give information relating to a person's intrapsychic areas of functioning. Furthermore, there are devices such as the MMPI which are clearly superior for the evaluation of pathology.

Despite these limitations, there are some general as well as specific contributions that the CPI can make. Even though it does not distinguish between the different patterns of pathology, general maladjustment is usually indicated by lowered profiles. The CPI has also been effectively used to detect and assess criminal and delinquent individuals, which involves a more interpersonal, or actually an individual versus societal, type of conflict. Furthermore, the CPI is a good adjunct to more clinically oriented tests in that it can assess the relative strengths in an otherwise pathological individual, and answer questions relating to the type of educational and vocational programs this person might benefit from.

General Maladjustment. An individual's level of maladjustment is indicated by generally lowered profiles which are often accompanied by an elevation on Fe

(Gough, 1969; Webb, 1963). A lowering of factor 1 scales (especially Re, So, and Sc) is often a good indicator of poor adjustment, and men with low Ac and Ie are especially likely to be maladjusted (Stewart, 1962).

Vulnerability to Stress. Persons with a "V" formation in which So is low (T = 35 or less), with Re and Sc significantly higher (T = 40 or more), are likely to be defensive and susceptible to the effects of situational stress (in Webb et al., 1981). They usually come from chaotic, stress-filled families, in which there were episodes of irrational parental abuse. Thus, they have learned that the world is a dangerous place and have developed a precarious balance in which they feel constantly on guard. They keep their emotions carefully controlled, continually attempt to avoid conflict, and feel that they need to be constantly prepared to diffuse potentially stress-filled interactions. Their conformity to their environment is based not on an expectation of achieving positive rewards, but more on fear and an avoidance of negative consequences. These people may have occasional explosive outbursts in which they have an almost dissociative loss of control. This explosiveness is especially likely if their spouse is manipulative, insensitive, and exploitive. As the discrepancy between So and Sc increases, these dynamics become more pronounced.

Depression. The social ascendancy scales are generally lowered by depression, and a T score of 40 or less would be expected on all or most of Do, Cs, Sy, Sp, Sa, and Wb. When the depression begins to lift and the person starts to have more optimism and a greater orientation to his environment, these scales generally increase. The mental and behavioral apathy often associated with depression can also be reflected by a lowering (T = 40 or less) in Ac, Ai, and Ie.

Psychosomatic Disorders. Although the CPI was not designed to diagnose psychosomatic disorders, there are certain personality characteristics that can be assessed on the CPI which are consistent with individuals who are more susceptible to this type of disturbance. Both male and female psychosomatics usually have lowered scores (T = 40 or less) on Wb and Sc and an elevation on Cm (Stewart, 1962). In addition, males often have a lowering on Ie. When the scores from male and female psychosomatics are compared with persons having behavior disorders, psychosomatics have a relatively higher So and Cm, with females also having a higher Re (Stewart, 1962). All of these scores suggest that psychosomatic patients have a significantly higher level of superego control and socialization. This agrees with most formulations of psychosomatic disorders which emphasize the suppression and repression of hostility and antisocial behavior as important predisposing factors. A pattern of psychosomatic disorders is especially likely if Wb has a T score of 35 or less, accompanied by an Fe of 60 or more. This pattern is associated with headaches, gastrointestinal upsets, or functional skin conditions. Such persons are likely to have moderately high needs for dependency which are not being fulfilled, but they also tend to feel distrustful and alienated in their relationships with others.

Defense Mechanisms. Byrne (1964) has theorized that the two basic approaches to defense are either through repression or through sensitization. Whereas repressors attempt to avoid anxiety arousing stimuli, sensitizers approach and attempt to control situations. Byrne, Golightly, and Sheffield (1965) found that high scorers on Sy, Wb, Sc, To, Gi, Ac, and Ie were more likely to use repression.

It has also been found that certain types of assaultive offenders can be characterized as usually being overcontrolled, but occasionally they drop all their inhibitions and impulsively strike out (Megargee, 1964, 1965, 1966d). These persons score high on the "overcontrolled hostility" scale (OH) of the MMPI, and also have higher scores on Sc and Gi with a lowering on Sa. This gives further support to the view that Sc and Gi are associated with the use of repressive defenses.

Juvenile Delinquency and Criminal Behavior. The area of assessing antisocial behavior with the CPI has been well researched with generally useful findings. Both delinquents and criminals tend to have lower overall subscale scores, particularly on Re and So (Laufer et al., 1982). Scores are also somewhat lower on Wb, To, and Ac, and factors 3 and 4 are likewise decreased (Gough, 1969). This pattern suggests that the social poise of delinquents is usually about the same as that of other persons their age, but in most other respects their behavior is definitely unconventional and they usually do not channel these differences into creative or intellectual areas. Mizushima and DeVos (1967) have found significant differences on the CPI between solitary delinquents who have lower scores on Ie and Fe and more socially oriented delinquents who have significantly higher scores on Sy, Sp, and Sa. They also found violent offenders to be higher on Sp and Sa but low on Fe. However, delinquents who committed extremely violent offenses were especially high on Sc which supports Gough's theory that excessive overcontrol in certain individuals periodically breaks down leading to assaultive behavior (Megargee, 1966d). In summarizing these data on delinquency, the most important scales to consider are lowerings in Re and So. Further information regarding the style of delinquency can be derived by the lowered Ie and Fe for solitary delinquents; higher Sy, Sp, and Sa for social delinquents; higher Sp, Sa, and low Fe for violent social delinquents; and outstandingly high Sc for extremely violent offenders who have periodic excessive losses of control.

The likelihood of successful parole for delinquents can, in part, be predicted in that more successful parolees have higher scores on Sp and Sa, and less successful parolees have lower scores on So and Sc (Gough, Wenk, and Rozynko, 1965). Gough and his colleagues have developed the following regression equation to predict successful from unsuccessful parolees.

$$\text{Parole Success} = 45.078 - .353 \text{ Sp} - 182 \text{ Sa} + 532 \text{ So} + .224 \text{ Sc} \qquad (11)$$

Using this equation, Gough was able to predict with 60% accuracy which of a population of California Youth Authority parolees would be successful versus those who were later recidivists.

Social Maturity

The concept of social maturity includes So but is more extensive and also includes areas other than that assessed by the So scale alone. Specifically, the person who is considered to be socially mature is not merely directed by blind conformance but also has a high level of ethical standards which can even vary from the values held by the majority of people. He may, at times, feel a need to resist social pressure. Also, he can accurately perceive the faults in a social system and attempt to deal with them in a mature way. Thus, the socially mature person is clearly different from someone who is merely oversocialized or hypernormal. Gough (1966) developed the following multiple regression equation to assess social maturity using combined weighted scores:

$$\text{Social Maturity} = 25.701 + .408 \text{ Re} + .478 \text{ So} - .296 \text{ Gi} \qquad (12)$$

Table 8-2. Summary of CPI Equations Used for Making Predictions.

1. Achievement (High School) = 20.116 + .317 Re + .192 So − .309 Gi + .227 Ac + .280 Ai + .244 Ie
2. Achievement (High School − Using I.Q.) = .786 + .195 Re + .244 So − .130 Gi + .19 Ac + .179 Ai + .279 I.Q.
3. College Attendance = 17.822 + .333 Do + .539 Cs − .189 Gi + .740 Ac
4. Achievement (Introduction to Psychology) = 35.958 − .294 Sy − .180 Sp + .185 Re − .189 Sc − .152 Gi − .210 Cm + .275 Ac + .523 Ai + .241 Ie + .657 Py
5. Male G.P.A. = .16 SAT (Math) + .11 So − .19 Sp + .17 Fe
6. Female G.P.A. = .25 SAT (Verbal) − .14 Sp + .06 Re + .20 Ac + .08 Fe
7. Teaching Effectiveness = 14.743 + .334 So − .670 Gi + .997 Ac + .909 Py − .446 Fx
8. Medical Promise = .794 Sy + .602 To + 1.114 Cm − .696 Cs
9. Dental Performance = 29.938 − .110 Sp + .148 Re − .262 Gi + .727 Ac + .230 Py
10. Leadership (Social) = 14.130 + .372 Do + .696 Sa + .345 Wb − .133 Gi + .274 Ai
11. Parole Success = 45.078 − .353 Sp − .182 Sa + .532 So + .224 Sc
12. Social Maturity = 25.701 + .408 Re + .478 So − .296 Gi

RECOMMENDED READING

Gough, H.G. An interpreter's syllabus for the California Psychological Inventory. In McReynolds, P. (Ed.) *Advances in Psychological Assessment,* Vol. 1. Palo Alto, Calif.: Science and Behavior Books, 1968.

Gough, H.G. *Manual for the California Psychological Inventory.* Palo Alto, Calif.: Consulting Psychologists Press, 1975.

Megargee, E.I. *The California Psychological Inventory Handbook.* San Francisco: Jossey-Bass, 1972.

9
The Psychological Report

The psychological report is the end product of the assessment procedure. It represents the clinician's efforts to integrate the assessment data into a functional whole so that the information can be of service to the client in solving problems and making decisions. Even the best tests will be useless unless the data from them are written up in a manner which is relevant and clear, and which meets the needs of the client. This requires that clinicians not merely give test results but that they interact with their data in such a way as to make their conclusions useful in meeting the client's needs and helping to solve his problems.

There is no one correct way to write up an evaluation. The manner of presentation will depend on the purpose for which it is intended, as well as the individual style and orientation of the clinician. The format provided in this chapter is merely a suggested outline which follows common and traditional guidelines. It includes sections for elaborating on such essential areas as the referral question, behavioral observations, relevant history, impressions and interpretation, and recommendations. This format is especially appropriate for evaluations which are problem oriented and offer specific prescriptions for change. Additional alternatives for organizing the report are using a letter format, giving only the summary and recommendations, focusing around a specific problem, summarizing the results test by test, or providing client descriptions around a specific theory of personality. The sample evaluations vary somewhat from the suggested format although they usually still include the essential categories of information that will be discussed in this chapter.

One general style which should be avoided is sometimes referred to as a "shotgun" report. This provides a wide variety of often fragmented descriptions in the hopes that there will be useful information somewhere. It is usually vague, stereotyped, and overinclusive. The recommendations for treatment are often neither specific nor practical. The most frequent reason for a "shotgun" report is a referral question that is too general, vague, and therefore, poorly understood. In contrast to this is the "case-focused" report which centers on the specific problems of the referring person. This reveals the unique aspects of the client and describes him accurately, rather than providing stereotyped descriptions which may also be overly "theory linked" or overly "test linked." Furthermore, the recommendations for treatment are both specific and practical.

Vernon (1955) has emphasized that the general approach of the "case-focused" report is not so much *what* is to be known but rather *why* different types of information are important for the purposes of the report.

The case-focused report involves understanding and applying several basic principles. The first of these is that it should be action oriented. The recommendations need to directly relate to what specifically can be done for this client within his particular environment. They may apply to such areas as occupational choice, psychotherapy, institutional programs, or additional testing. However, in certain types of referrals, especially clients self-referred for psychotherapy, an important goal may be to help them increase their level of personal insight. In these cases, a wider description of the client that includes a number of different topics might be more appropriate than the narrower, action-oriented approach. Secondly, there should be a focus on that which differentiates one person from another. This means avoiding discussions of what is average about the client, and emphasizing what stands out and is unique to this individual. Thirdly, there is a current trend, consistent with the case-focused approach, towards de-emphasizing diagnosis and etiology. There is rather an emphasis on current descriptions of the person which are tied to specific behaviors. In certain cases, especially within a medical setting, the clinician may still need to provide diagnoses in addition to behaviorally oriented descriptions. The final consideration is that a case-focused report should be written with an awareness of the reader's point of view. This includes taking into consideration his level of professional expertise, his theoretical or professional orientation, the decisions he is facing, and the possible interpretations he is likely to make of the information.

GENERAL GUIDELINES

Style

The style or "flavor" of a report will be influenced primarily by the training and orientation of the examiner. The literary, clinical, and scientific approaches to report writing are the three general categories which a clinician can choose from (Tallent, 1976). Each of these styles has different strengths, and all have a number of liabilities associated with them. The literary approach uses everyday language, is creative, and is often dramatic. Whereas it is capable of effectively capturing a reader's attention and providing colorful descriptions, it is often imprecise and prone to exaggeration.

The clinical approach focuses on the pathological dimensions of a person. It describes the client's abnormal features, defenses, dynamics involved in maladjustment, and typical reactions to stress. The strength of the clinical approach is that it provides information relating to areas in need of change and alerts a potential counselor to difficulties which are likely to be encountered during the course of treatment. However, such a report tends to be one sided in that it may omit important strengths of the person. The result is likely to be more a description of a "case" rather than a person. Such a "maladjustment bias" is a frequent difficulty in clinical psychology and results in a distorted, unrealistic view of the client. Although a report will, and typically should, describe a person's problem areas, these problem areas should be given appropriate emphasis within the context of the client's relevant strengths and resources.

The scientific approach to report writing emphasizes normative comparisons, tends to be more academic, and to a lesser extent, relates to the nature and extent of a client's pathology. What primarily differentiates the scientific style from other approaches is its reference to concepts, theories, and data. It looks at and describes test findings in an objective, factual manner. Thus there might be frequent references to test data, normative comparisons, probability statements, and cutoff scores to be used for decision making. A scientific approach is likely to discuss the person by addressing different, often isolated segments of personality. Thus, such areas as a client's cognitive, perceptual, and motivational abilities may be described as discrete and often unrelated functions. The scientific approach has the strong advantage of being objective and factual, but it has been criticized as violating the concept of the unity of personality. Many readers, particularly those from other disciplines (Tallent and Reiss, 1959b), do not respect or empathize with scientific evaluations and perceive them as cold, distant, and overly objective. Purely data-oriented evaluations can potentially do the profession a disservice by reinforcing the view that an assessment is like a laboratory test rather than a professional consultation with a clinician. Furthermore, a focus on factual data may not address the practical decisions the client and referral source are facing.

In actual clinical practice, it is unusual to find a pure example of a literary, clinical, or scientific report. Clinicians will generally draw from all three of these but, typically, will emphasize one of them more extensively than the others. An important part of effective report writing is the ability to evaluate the assets and liabilities of each style, and maintain a flexible orientation towards appropriately combining them. In any one report, there may be a need to use creative literary descriptions, elaborate on different pathological dimensions, or provide necessary scientific information. The key is to avoid the pitfalls associated with specializing in any one of these styles and to emphasize their relative strengths.

Topics

There are an extremely wide variety of topics that clinicians may decide to discuss in their reports. These topics serve as conceptual tools which enable report writers to give form and direction to what they are trying to communicate. Possible topics include intellectual functioning, conflicts, interpersonal relationships, suicidal

Table 9-1. Examples of General Personality Topics around Which a Case Presentation May Be Conceptualized.

Achievement	Intellectual controls
Aggresiveness	Intellectual level
Antisocial tendencies	Interests
Anxieties	Interpersonal relations
Aptitudes	Interpersonal skills
Attitudes	Life-style
Aversions	Molar surface behavior
Awareness	Needs
Background factors	Outlook
Behavioral problems	Perception of environment
Biological factors	Perception of self
Cognitive functioning	Personal consequences of behavior
Cognitive skills	Placement prospects
Cognitive style	Psychopathology
Competency	Rehabilitation needs
Cognitive factors	Rehabilitation prospects
Conflicts	Sentiments
Content of consciousness	Sex
Defenses	Sex identity
Deficits	Sex role
Developmental factors	Significant others
Diagnostic considerations	Situational factors
Drives, dynamics	Social consequences of behavior
Emotional cathexes	Social role
Emotional controls	Social stimulus value
Emotivity	Social structure
Fixations	Special assets
Flexibility	Subjective feeling states
Frustrations	Symptoms
Goals	Treatment prospects
Hostility	Value system
Identity	Vocational topics

NOTE: From Norman Tallent, *Psychological Report Writing,* © 1976, p. 114. Reprinted by permission of Prentice-Hall, Inc. Englewood Cliffs, N.J.

potential, defenses, behavior under stress, impulsiveness, or sexuality. Often an adequate description of the person can be developed by describing just a few of these topics. For example, a case-focused report may elaborate on one or two significant areas of functioning, whereas a more general evaluation may discuss seven or eight topics. Table 9-1 is a representative list of possible topics which may be considered for inclusion in an evaluation. This list is by no means complete, but it can provide a general guideline or present a wide variety of possible topics from which a report writer can choose.

Deciding What to Include

The general purpose of a psychological evaluation is to provide that information which will be most helpful in meeting the needs of the client. Within this context, the clinician must balance providing too much information against providing too little, and being too cold against being too dramatic. As a general rule, information should only be included if it serves to increase the understanding of the client. For example, descriptions of a client's appearance should be oriented towards adding to knowledge relating to such areas as his level of self-esteem or anxiety. Likewise an elaboration of family dynamics should be helpful in understanding such areas as a child's current behavioral problems or lack of academic motivation.

A further general rule is that information should focus on the client's unique method of psychological functioning. A reader is concerned not so much with how the client is similar to the average person as in what ways he is different. A common error in psychological reports is the inclusion of generalized statements which are so vague they could apply to the majority of the population. Several researchers (Carrier, 1963; Snyder, 1974; Snyder and Larson, 1972; Sundberg, 1955; Ulrich, Stachnik, and Stainton, 1963) have studied the frequency, manner, and types of vague, generalized statements which individuals are likely to unconditionally accept as applying to themselves even though these statements were randomnly selected. For example, Sundberg (1955) administered a "personality test" to a group of students and gave them all identical "interpretations" based on personality descriptions comprised of 13 statements such as

1. You have a great need for other people to like and admire you.
2. You have a tendency to be critical of yourself.
3. You have a great deal of unused capacity which you have not turned to your advantage.
4. While you have some personality weaknesses, you are generally able to compensate for them.
5. At times you have serious doubts as to whether you have made the right decision or done the right thing.

Virtually all the students used in the study reported that the evaluation statements were accurate descriptions of themselves. Klopfer (1960) has referred to this uncritical acceptance of universally valid statements as the "Barnum effect" because of Phineas Barnum's famous saying that "there is a fool born every minute." Although, "universal statements" may add to the "subjective" validity of the report when read by the client, such statements should be avoided in favor of stressing the person's essential uniqueness.

The general guidelines for deciding what to include in a report relate to considering the referral setting, the background of the readers, the purpose of

Table 9-2.

Tests Administered / Topics	WAIS	Bender	House-Tree-Person	MMPI	TAT
Intellectual aspects					
Interpersonal relations					
Emotional controls					
Basic conflict areas					
Defenses					
Hostility					
Personal resources					

Modified from Klopfer, W.G. *The Psychological Report: Use and Communication of Psychological Findings.* New York: Grune & Stratton, 1960, p. 36. Reprinted by permission.

testing, the relative usefulness of the information, and whether or not the information describes unique characteristics of the person. Once these general guidelines have been understood, the next step is to focus on and organize the information derived from the tests. For example, if the area of interpersonal relationships is one of the general topics that a clinician has decided to elaborate on, then he can look at each test to determine what information it can provide regarding this dimension. Klopfer (1960) recommends using a grid with the topics for consideration in the left column and the tests administered in the top row. This enables the clinician to list the essential findings in the appropriate box where the topic and the test intersect. When actually writing the report, he can then review all the findings within a particular topic and summarize them on the report. An example of such a grid is given in Table 9-2. The list of tests is dependent on which tests the examiner has administered, but the topics can be chosen and arranged according to which areas the clinician would like to focus on.

Once the conclusions have been summarized on the grid, the next step is deciding on the manner in which to present them. This involves clear communication regarding the relative degree of emphasis of the results, proper use of terminology, and the extent to which the raw data will be discussed.

Emphasis

Conclusions should be given careful consideration with regard to their appropriate emphasis. This is particularly important when indicating the relative intensity of a client's behavior. General summaries may be given, such as "this client's level of depression is characteristic of inpatient populations," or the relative intensity of certain aspects of a client's disorders may be more specifically discussed. To continue with the example of depression, a clinician may discuss the client's cognitive self-criticisms, degree of slowed behavior, or suicidal potential. In addition to discussing and giving the appropriate degree of emphasis to a client's pathology, his psychological strengths also need to be compared with his relative weaknesses. Furthermore, the report should not bring up areas of minor relevance unless they somehow relate to the purpose of the evaluation. These issues relating to proper emphasis again stress the need for the examiner and the referral source to clarify and agree on the purpose of the evaluation. Only after this has been accomplished can the examiner decide whether certain information should be elaborated in depth, briefly mentioned, or deleted.

When clinicians present their conclusions, it is essential that they indicate their relative degree of certainty. Is a specific conclusion based on an objective fact, or is the clinician merely presenting a speculation? For example, the statement "John scored in the dull normal range of intelligence" is an objective fact. However, even in this case examiners may still want to give the standard error of measurement in order to provide an estimate of the probable range of the scores. If there are only mild supporting data or if clinicians are presenting a speculation, then phrases such as "it appears ...," "tends to ...," or "probably ..." may be used. This is especially important when clinicians are attempting to predict a person's behavior because the predicted behavior has not yet been observed. It may be useful for the clinician to indicate that his predictions cannot be found directly in the tests themselves but rather represent inferences which have been made based on test data. There should be a clear distinction between what the client did as opposed to what he might do. If a statement made in a report is a speculation, then it should be clearly indicated that there is only a moderate or small degree of certainty about the statement. Whenever a speculation is included, it should also be relevant to the referral question.

Improper emphasis either can reflect an incorrect interpretation by the examiner or may result in an incorrect interpretation by the reader. Clinicians sometimes arrive at incorrect conclusions because their personal bias results in selective perception of the data. Thus they can develop an overly narrow focus in which potentially relevant data are overlooked. Personal bias may result from such factors as restrictive theoretical orientations, subjective feelings towards the client, or an overemphasis on pathology. Inaccurate conclusions can also result from attempts to please the referral source or from interpretations based on insufficient data. The reader may also be likely to misinterpret the conclusions if the report is generally overspeculative or if speculations are not specified as such but, rather, are disguised as assertions. If speculations are overly assertive, not only can this lead the reader into developing incorrect conclusions, but the report may also become overly authoritative and dogmatic, and result in the reader's becoming irritated and feeling skeptical.

Misinterpretations can also result in vague and ambiguously worded sentences which give incorrect or misleading emphasis to a client's behavior. A statement such as "the client lacks social skills" is technically incorrect in that the client must have some social skills but they may not be adequate. A more correct description would be to state that the client's skills are "poorly developed" or "below average." Likewise, a statement such as "the client uses socially inappropriate behavior" is subject to a myriad of interpretations. This could be rephrased to include more behaviorally oriented descriptions such as "frequently interrupts" or "would often take off on irrelevant tangents."

The responsibility for the report's conclusions clearly rests on the examiner. This responsibility should not and cannot be transferred to the tests themselves. To take this a step further, decisions made about a person should never be in the hands of tests which may even have questionable validity in certain contexts. Rather, conclusions and decisions regarding people should always be in the hands of responsible persons. Thus, the style of emphasizing results should reflect this. Phrases such as "test results indicate . . . " may give the impression that the examiner is trying to hide behind and transfer responsibility for his statements onto the tests. Not only is this *not* where the responsibility should be, but the reader may develop a lack of confidence in the clinician. If a clinician feels uncertain about a particular conclusion, then either he should be clear about his uncertainty or, if he cannot personally stand by the results, he should exclude them from the report.

Use of Raw Data

In general, a report writer should avoid adhering closely to the raw data in the impressions and interpretation section. However, for certain purposes it may be useful to include raw data or even to describe the tests themselves. Describing the tests allows untrained persons to know specific behaviors the client engaged in rather than merely the final inferences. For example, a report may include a description such as "Mr. A had an average level of recall for short-term visual information, as indicated by his being able to accurately recall and reproduce five out of a possible nine geometric designs which he had previously worked with for 5 minutes." This sentence gives a more behaviorally referenced description than one like "Mr. A had an average level of recall as measured on the Bender memory." Thus, it is apt to give the reader a more in-depth, precise, and familiar reference regarding the subject's abilities. In addition to describing the tests themselves, the test responses can sometimes be included for illustrative purposes. Test responses can also serve to make the description behavior specific and to balance high-level abstractions with concrete responses. For example, a clinician might discuss a client's impulsiveness and include illustrative items on the MMPI, such as

38. During one period when I was a child I engaged in petty thievery. (true)
205. At times it has been impossible for me to keep from stealing or shop-lifting something. (true)

Discussing the same issue, a clinician could also include a portion of a TAT story which illustrates a similar point:

... so he took the violin and, without even thinking about it, threw it into the fire and ran outside.

However, it is crucial to stress that the purpose of providing raw data and behavioral descriptions is to enrich and illustrate the topic and not to enable the reader to follow the clinician's line of reasoning or document the inferences which have been made. In developing inferences, clinicians must draw upon a wide variety of data. They cannot possibly give all the patterns, configurations, and relationships that they used to come to their conclusions. Any attempt to do so would necessarily be overly detailed, cumbersome, and incomplete. Statements such as "in considering the pattern of elevated scales 4 and 9 on the MMPI, it is safe to conclude . . ." are unnecessary and rarely contribute to a report's overall usefulness. In certain types of reports, such as those for legal purposes, it might be helpful to include some of the raw data. However, the purpose of doing this is not to "prove" that the conclusions are valid or to repeat the thinking process of the clinician, but more to provide a point of reference for discussing the results and indicating what assessment procedures were used.

Terminology

There are varying arguments regarding the use of technical as opposed to non-technical language in psychological reports. Hammond and Allen (1953) argue that technical terminology is precise and economical, and can communicate concepts which it is impossible to convey through other means. However, there are a number of potential difficulties that are often encountered with the use of technical language. One of the more frequent ones involves the varying back-grounds and levels of sophistication of the persons' reading the report. The most frequent readers of reports include teachers, administrators, judges, attor-neys, psychiatrists, and social workers, most of whom do not have the necessary background to interpret technical terminology accurately. Even psychologists with different theoretical persuasions may be apt to misinterpret some of the terms. Take, for example, the differing uses of "ego" by Freud, Jung, and Erikson. Likewise the term "anxiety" has been found to have seven different categories of use (Grayson and Tolman, 1950). Although technical words can undoubtedly be precise, their precision is only helpful within a particular context and with a reader who has the proper background. Even amongst readers who have the proper background to understand technical terms, many prefer a more straightforward presentation (Tallent and Reiss, 1959c). Technical terms also run the danger of becoming nominalisms in which, by merely naming the phenomenon, we develop an illusory sense of having a greater degree of understanding than is actually the case. For example, terms such as "immature" or "sadistic" cover a great deal of information because they are so general, but they say nothing about what the person is like when he is behaving in these maladaptive ways. They do not adequately differentiate one person from the next and are frequently ambiguous. Furthermore, technical terms are often used inappropriately, for example, when a person who is sensitive and cautious in interpersonal relationships is labeled "paranoid," or when "compulsive" is used to describe someone who is merely careful, conscientious, and effective in dealing with details.

Klopfer (1960) provides the following excellent rationale for using basic English rather than technical terminology. First, and perhaps most important, basic English means that the examiner, through his report, can communicate with and effect a wide audience. Furthermore, basic English is more specific and descriptive of an individual's uniqueness, whereas technical terms tend to deal with generalities. Terms such as "sadomasochistic" and "hostile" do not provide essential information about whether the person is assaultive or suicidal. Finally, the use of basic English generally indicates that the examiner has a more in-depth comprehension of the information he is working with and can communicate this comprehension in a precise, concrete manner. Klopfer stresses that any description found in a psychological report can be made comprehensible to any literate person who possesses at least average intelligence. He provides the following examples of translating technical concepts into basic English (Klopfer, 1960 pp. 58-60).

"Hostility towards the father figure" becomes "the patient is so fearful and suspicious of people in positions of authority that he automatically assumes an aggressive attitude towards them, being sure that swift retaliation will follow. He doesn't give such people an opportunity to demonstrate their real characteristics since he assumes that they are all alike."

"The patient projects extensively" becomes "the patient has a tendency to attribute to other people feelings and ideas originating within himself regardless of how these other people might feel."

"The defenses the patient uses are . . ." becomes "the methods characteristically employed by the patient for reducing anxiety are . . .".

"Empathy" becomes "the patient can understand and sympathize with the feelings of others, since she finds it relatively easy to put herself in their place."

"The client is hostile and resistant" may be changed to include a behavioral description; "when the client entered the room she stated, 'My Dad said I had to come and that's the only reason I'm here' " or "later on in the testing she made several comments such as 'This is a stupid question.' "

The general principle involved here is to translate high-level abstract terms into basic English that provides concrete behavioral descriptions. The resulting descriptions will be less subject to misinterpretation, less ambiguous, and more likely to accurately convey the unique personality of the client. Although abstract technical terms can be important components of a psychological report, they should be used sparingly and only when appropriate. This particularly means a careful consideration of the background of the persons who will be reading the report. When technical terms are used, they should also be tied to concrete behavioral descriptions.

Content Overload

There are no exact rules about how much information to include in a report. A general guideline is to estimate how much information a reader can realistically be expected to assimilate. If there are too many details, the information may begin to become poorly defined and vague and, therefore, lack impact or usefulness. When clinicians are confronted with a wide variety of data from which to choose, they should not necessarily attempt to include it all. A statement such as "the client's relative strengths are in abstract reasoning, general fund of knowledge, short-term memory, attention span, and mathematical computation" is likely to overload the reader with too many details. The clinician should instead only focus on and discuss those areas which are most relevant to the purpose of the report.

FORMAT FOR A PSYCHOLOGICAL EVALUATION

Name:
Date of Birth:
Date of Examination:
Examiner:
    I. Referral Question
    II. Evaluation Procedures
    III. Behavioral Observations
    IV. Relevant History
    V. Test Results
    VI. Impressions and Interpretation
    VII. Recommendations

Referral Question

The purpose of a discussion of the referral question is to give a brief description of the client and a statement of the general reason for conducting the evaluation. This should also include a brief description of the nature of the problem. If this section is adequately completed, it should give an initial focus to the report by orienting the reader to what will follow and to the types of issues that will be addressed. A necessary prerequisite is that the clinician has developed an adequate clarification of the referral question. The purpose of testing should be stated in a precise and problem-oriented manner. Thus, phrases such as "the client was referred for a psychological evaluation" or "to aid in a class project" are inadequate in that they lack focus and precision. It is helpful to include both the specific purpose of the evaluation and the decisions facing the referral source. Whenever possible, the referral should be discussed directly with the referring person, and it may sometimes be necessary or useful to discuss the rationale for testing with the client. Examples of general reasons for referrals include:

1. Intellectual evaluation: routine, retarded, gifted
2. Differential diagnosis, such as the relative presence of psychological versus organic impairment
3. Assessment of the nature and extent of brain damage
4. Evaluation as a component of vocational counseling
5. Evaluation of appropriateness for, and possible difficulties encountered in, psychotherapy
6. Personal insight regarding difficulties with interpersonal relationships

These represent general referral questions which, in actual situations, would still require further clarification especially regarding the decisions facing the referral source. The key to writing an effective referral question is that it should accurately describe the client's and the referral source's current problems. In the report itself, the question(s) should then be answered in the summary of the report, and the recommendations should be relevant to the client's problem.

Evaluation Procedures

The section dealing with evaluation procedures simply lists the tests used and does not include the test results. Usually, full test names are included along with their abbreviations. Later in the report the abbreviations can be used, but the initial inclusion of the entire name provides a reference for readers who may not be familiar with test abbreviations. For legal evaluations or other occasions in which precise details of administration are important, it may be helpful to include the date on which different tests were administered and the length of time required to complete each one. It may also be important to include whether or not a clinical interview or mental status examination was given and, if so, the amount of time required for the examination.

Behavioral Observations

A description of the client's behaviors can provide insight into his problem and may be a significant source of data to confirm, modify, or question the test-related interpretations. Descriptions should be tied to specific behaviors and should not represent a clinician's inferences. For example, instead of making the inference that the client was "depressed," it is preferable to state that "her speech was slow and she frequently made self-critical statements such as 'I knew I couldn't get that one right anyway.'"

Important areas for discussion include the client's physical appearance, behavior towards the task and examiner, and degree of cooperativeness. A description of the client's physical appearance should focus on any unusual features relating to facial expressions, clothes, body types, mannerisms, and movements. It is especially important to note any contradictions, for example a 14-year-old boy who acts more like a 25 year old or a person who appears dirty and disheveled but has an excellent vocabulary and a high level of verbal fluency. The behaviors the client expresses towards the test material and the examiner often provide a significant source of information. These may include behaviors which reflect the level of affect, manifest anxiety, presence of depression, or degree of hostility. The client's role may be as an active participant or generally passive and submissive; he may be very much concerned with his performance or relatively indifferent. The client's method of problem solving is often a crucial area to note, and may range from careful and methodical to impulsive and disorganized. Any unusual verbalizations that the client makes about the test material are also important to note. One factor involved in assessing the validity of the tests is the level of cooperativeness expressed by the client. This is especially important for intelligence and ability tests, since a necessary prerequisite is that the client be alert and attentive, and put forth his best effort. It may also be important to note events prior to testing, such as situational crises, previous night's sleep, or use of medication. If there are situational factors that may modify or bring into question the test's validity, they should be noted with phrases like "the test results should be viewed with caution since . . ." or "the degree of maladjustment indicated on the test scores may represent an exaggeration of the client's usual level of functioning because of conditions surrounding the test administration." Often the most important way of determining test validity is through a careful look at the client's behaviors relating to the tests and his life situation prior to testing.

Sattler (1982) has developed a "behavior and attitude checklist" comprised of ten major categories which can be rated on a seven-point scale (see Table

Table 9 3. Behavior and Attitude Checklist.

Name: Examiner:
Age: Date of Report:
Test(s) Administered: Date of Examination:
I.Q.:   Grade:

Instructions: Place an "X" on the appropriate line for each scale.

I.   Attitude toward examiner and test situation:
 1. cooperative   ___:___:___:___:___:___: uncooperative
 2. passive   ___:___:___:___:___:___: aggressive
 3. tense   ___:___:___:___:___:___: relaxed
 4. gives up easily   ___:___:___:___:___:___: does not give up easily

II. Attitude toward self:
 5. confident   ___:___:___:___:___:___: not confident
 6. critical of own work ___:___:___:___:___:___: accepting of own work

III. Work habits:
 7. fast   ___:___:___:___:___:___: slow
 8. deliberate   ___:___:___:___:___:___: impulsive
 9. thinks aloud   ___:___:___:___:___:___: thinks silently
10. careless   ___:___:___:___:___:___: neat

IV. Behavior:
11. calm   ___:___:___:___:___:___: hyperactive

V.   Reaction to failure:
12. aware of failure   ___:___:___:___:___:___: unaware of failure
13. works harder after failure ___:___:___:___:___:___: gives up easily after failure
14. calm after failure   ___:___:___:___:___:___: agitated after failure
15. apologetic after failure ___:___:___:___:___:___: not apologetic after failure

VI. Reaction to praise:
16. accepts praise gracefully ___:___:___:___:___:___: accepts praise awkwardly
17. works harder after praise ___:___:___:___:___:___: retreats after praise

VII. Speech and language:
18. speech poor   ___:___:___:___:___:___: speech good
19. articulate language ___:___:___:___:___:___: inarticulate language
20. responses direct   ___:___:___:___:___:___: responses vague
21. converses spontaneously ___:___:___:___:___:___: only speaks when spoken to
22. bizarre language   ___:___:___:___:___:___: reality-oriented language

VIII. Visual-motor:
23. reaction time slow   ___:___:___:___:___:___: reaction time fast
24. trial and error   ___:___:___:___:___:___: careful and planned
25. skillful movements   ___:___:___:___:___:___: awkward movements

IX. Motor:
26. defective motor coordi-
    nation   ___:___:___:___:___:___: good motor coordination

X.   Overall test results:
27. reliable   ___:___:___:___:___:___: unreliable
28. valid   ___:___:___:___:___:___: invalid

XI. Other:

NOTE: From Jerome Sattler, *Assessment of Children's Intelligence and Special Abilities,* Second Edition. Copyright © 1982 by Allyn and Bacon, Inc. Reprinted with permission.

9-3). The examiner may wish to use this checklist as a tool to help focus on areas which it might be significant to mention or discuss. It is important to emphasize that other crucial behaviors may occur which are not covered in the checklist and which will still require discussion.

Behavioral observations should usually be kept concise, specific, and relevant. If a description does not serve to develop some insight about the person or demonstrate his uniqueness, then it should not be included. Thus, if a behavior is normal or average, it will usually not be important to discuss it other than to mention briefly that the person had, for example, an average level of cooperativeness, alertness, or anxiety. The focus, then, should be on those client behaviors which created a unique impression. The relative length of this section will vary from a few brief sentences to considerably longer depending on the amount of relevant information the clinician has noticed. The relative importance of this section in relationship to the overall report will likewise be extremely varied. Sometimes it can be almost as important as the test results, whereas at other times it might consist of a few minor observations.

Relevant History

The write-up of a client's history should include aspects of his background which are relevant to the problem he is confronting and to the interpretation of the test results. The history, along with the referral question, should also serve to place the problem and the test results in a proper context. In accomplishing these goals, the clinician does not need to include a long, involved chronology with a large number of details, but rather should be as succinct as possible. In selecting which areas to include and which to exclude, a clinician must continually evaluate these areas in relation to the overall purpose of the report. It is difficult to specify exact rules since each individual will be different from the next. Furthermore, each clinician may have his own personal and theoretical orientation which will alter the types of information he feels are significant. Whereas one clinician may primarily describe interpersonal relationships, another may focus on intrapsychic variables, birth order, early childhood events, or details about the client's present situation and environment. The key is to maintain a flexible orientation so that the interviewer will be aware of the most significant elements in the client's life. In general, the end product should include a good history of the problem along with areas such as important life events, family dynamics, work history, personal interests, daily activities, and past and present interpersonal relationships.

Usually a history will begin with a brief summary of the client's general background, including age, sex, family constellation, education, health, and a restatement of the problem. The first sentence might read something like "Mary Smith is a 48-year-old, white, divorced female, with a high school education, who presents complaints of nervous tension, insomnia, and depression." This can be followed by sections describing family background, personal history, history of the problem, and current life situation.

The extent to which a clinician decides to pursue and discuss a client's family background is subject to a wide degree of variability. Often a brief description of the client's parents is warranted; this may include whether they are separated/divorced, and alive/deceased, their socioeconomic level, occupation, cultural background, and health status. Sometimes it is important to include information relating to the emotional and medical backgrounds of parents and close relatives, since certain disorders occur with greater frequency in some families than in the overall population. A description of the general atmosphere of the family is often helpful, including the client's characteristic feelings towards family members and his perceptions of their relationships with each other. Additional areas to include might be common family activities and whether the family was from an urban or a rural environment. If one or both of the parents died while the client was young, the clinician can still look at issues such as what sort of speculations the client had regarding his parent(s) and who were significant persons for the client as he was growing up.

The client's personal history can include information from infancy, early childhood, adolescence, and adulthood. Each of these stages has typical areas to investigate and problem areas to be aware of. The information from infancy will usually either represent vague recollections or be secondhand information derived from parents or relatives. Thus, it may be subject to a great deal of exaggeration or fabrication. If possible, it may be helpful to have details verified by additional sources, such as through direct questioning of parents or consulting medical records. The degree of contact with parents, toilet training, family atmosphere, and developmental milestones can all be important areas to discuss. Since physical and psychological difficulties often are related and occur simultaneously, a medical history is sometimes helpful. The most significant tasks during childhood are the development of peer relationships and adjustment to school. What was the quality of clients' early friendships, how much time did they spend with others, and were there any fights or rebellious acting out? Were they basically loners or did they have a large number of friends? Did they join clubs and have group activities, hobbies, or extracurricular interests? In the academic area, it may be of interest to note their usual grades, best or worst subjects, and whether they skipped or repeated any grades. Furthermore, what was their relationship with their parents, and did their parents restrict their activities or were they relatively free? During the adolescent years, clients faced further academic, psychological, and social adjustments to high school. Of particular importance are their reaction to puberty and their early heterosexual relationships. Did they have difficulties with sex role identity, abuse drugs or alcohol, or rebel against authority figures? The adult years center around occupational adjustment and establishing marital and family relationships. During early adulthood, what were their feelings and plans regarding marriage? What were their early career goals? Did they effectively establishing independence from their parents? As adulthood progressed, were there any significant changes in the quality of their close relationships, employment, or expression of sexuality? What activities did they engage in during their leisure time? With advancing age, clients face problems relating to their declining abilities, limitations, and developing a meaningful view of their lives.

Whereas the personal history can help to place the problem in its proper context and explain certain causative factors, it is usually essential to spend some time focusing directly on the problem itself. Of particular importance are the initial onset and the nature of the symptoms. From the time when the client first noticed these symptoms, have there been any changes in their frequency, intensity, or nature? Furthermore, were there any previous attempts at treatment, and if so, what was the outcome? In some reports, the history of the problem will be the longest and most important aspect of the relevant history.

The family and personal histories usually reveal information relating to the predisposing cause of the client's difficulties, whereas the history of the problem often provides an elaboration of the precipitating causes. To complete this picture, the clinician also has to develop a sense of the factors which are currently reinforcing the problem. This requires information relating to the client's current life situation. Significant areas may be the client's life stresses, including changes that he is confronting. Also what are the nature of, and resources provided by, his family and work relationships? Finally, it is important to understand the alternatives and decisions which the client is facing.

The quantity of such information may seem immense. However, this history format is intended only as a general guideline. At times it may be appropriate to ignore many of the areas mentioned and focus on others. In condensing the client's history into the report, it is important to avoid superfluous material and continually question whether the information obtained is relevant to the general purpose of the report.

Test Results

For certain reports, it may not be necessary to list test scores. However, they should be included in legal reports or when professionals who are knowledgeable about testing will be reading the report. Intelligence test scores are traditionally listed first and, for the Weschler scales, should include Verbal I.Q., Performance I.Q., and Full Scale I.Q., along with the subtests and their scaled scores. This is often followed by the Bender results which may simply be summarized as "empirically not in the organic range, although there were difficulties organizing the designs and frequent erasures." There are several alternatives for listing

MMPI results, one of the more frequent of which is to give them in Welsh code. MMPI results are also often listed with the validity scales given first, followed by scales ordered from highest to lowest. They can also be listed in the order in which they appear on the profile sheet. Any MMPI results should always be referred to by their T scores and not the raw scores. Whereas it is fairly straightforward to list the objective and intelligence test scores, it is considerably more difficult to adequately describe the scores on projective tests. The Rorschach summary sheet can be included, but the results from projective drawings and the TAT are usually omitted. Should a clinician wish to summarize projective drawings, a quick statement such as "projective drawings were miniaturized and immature, with the inclusion of two transparencies" is usually sufficient. Likewise, TAT "scores" can be summarized by a brief statement of the strongest needs and press, and a mention of the most common themes encountered in the stories.

Impressions and Interpretation

The main findings of the tests must be presented in the form of integrated hypotheses. This section can be considered the main body of the report. The areas discussed and the style of presentation will vary according to the personal orientation of the clinician, the purpose of testing, the individual being tested, and the types of tests administered. All inferences made in this section should be based on an integration of the test data, behavioral observations, relevant history, and additional available data. The conclusions and discussion may relate to areas such as the client's overt behavior, self-concept, family background, intellectual abilities, emotional difficulties, medical disorders, school problems, or interpersonal conflicts.

A client's intellectual abilities often provide a general frame of reference for a variety of personality variables. For this reason, a discussion of the client's intellectual strengths and weaknesses usually occurs first. Although this should include a general estimate of his intelligence as indicated by I.Q. scores, it is also important to provide a discussion of more specific abilities. This may include an analysis of areas such as memory, problem solving, abstract reasoning, concentration, and fund of information. If the report is to be read by persons who are familiar with test theory, it may be sufficient to include I.Q. scores without an explanation of their normative significance. In most reports, it is helpful to include the I.Q. scores as well as the percentile ranking and general intellectual classification (high average, superior, etc.). Some examiners may even prefer to omit the actual I.Q. scores in favor of including only percentile rank and general classification. This can be useful in cases where persons reading the report might be likely to misunderstand or misinterpret unexplained I.Q. scores. Once a general estimate of intelligence has been made, it should whenever possible be followed by a discussion of the client's relative intellectual strengths and weaknesses. This may involve elaborating on the meaning of the difference between Verbal I.Q. and Performance I.Q. or a discussion of subtest scatter. In addition, it can be useful to elaborate on the client's potential level of functioning as opposed to his actual performance. If there is a wide discrepancy between these two, then offering reasons for this discrepancy is warranted. The client may be underachieving because of factors such as anxiety, low motivation, emotional interference, or perceptual processing difficulties.

Whereas a discussion of intellectual abilities is relatively clear and straightforward, the next sections are frequently more difficult to select. There is an extremely wide number of possibilities to choose from, many of which have been listed in Table 9-1. If the referral question is clearly focused on a specific problem, then it may only be necessary to elaborate on two or three topics. A referral question that is general may require a wider approach in which six or more areas are discussed.

Some of the more common and important topics are the client's level of psychopathology, dependency, hostility, sexuality, interpersonal relationships, diagnosis, and behavioral predictions. A client's level of psychopathology refers to the relative severity of the disturbances he is experiencing. It is important to distinguish whether the results are characteristic of normals, outpatients, or inpatients, and whether the difficulties are long term or a reaction to current life stresses. Does the client use behaviors which are adaptive or those which are maladaptive and self-defeating? Within the area of ideation, are there persistent thoughts, delusions, hallucinations, loose associations, blocking of ideas, perseveration, or illogical thoughts? It may also be important to assess the adequacy of the client's judgments and relative degree of insight. Can he effectively make plans, understand the impact he has on others, and judge the appropriateness of his behavior? In order to assess the likelihood of successful therapy, it is especially important to assess the client's level of insight. This includes assessing his ability to think psychologically, awareness of his own changing feelings, understanding of others' behaviors, and ability to clearly conceptualize and discuss his insights.

Usually a client's greatest conflicts will center on difficulties with dependency, hostility, and sexuality. In discussing a client's dependency, it is important to discuss the strength of these needs, the typical roles played with others, and present or past significant relationships. In what ways does the client defend himself against, or cope with, feelings of dependency? This may include a discussion of defense mechanisms, thoughts, behaviors, feelings, or somatic responses as they relate to dependency. The relative intensity of a client's hostility is also important. Is the expression of hostility indirect, or is it direct in the form of either verbal criticisms or actual assaultive behavior? If the expression of hostility is covert, it may be the result of factors such as fear of loss of love, retaliation, or guilt. When the client does feel anger, what are his characteristic defenses against these feelings? For example, some clients might express opposite behaviors, with overly exaggerated concern for others, or they might direct the anger inward by developing physical aches and pains which serve as self-punishment for having aggressive impulses. They may also adapt through such means as extreme suspiciousness of others, created by denying their hostility and attributing it to others, as through becoming highly submissive towards authority figures. A discussion of clients' sexuality usually involves noting the relative intensity of their urges and the degree of anxiety associated with the expression of these urges. Do they inhibit their sexuality because of a belief that it is dirty, anxiety over possible consequences, or associating it with aggressiveness? Defenses against sexual urges may be handled in ways similar to hostility, such as by performing the opposite behaviors through extreme religiosity and celibacy or by denying the feelings in themselves and attributing them to others. On the other hand, clients may impulsively act out their sexual urges and become promiscuous at least in part out of a need to obtain self-affirmation through sexual contact. Clinicians may also want to discuss the dynamics involved in any unusual sexual practices.

Discussing the clients' characteristic pattern and roles in interpersonal relationships can also be extremely useful. This can often be discussed in relation to the dimensions of submissiveness/dominance and love/hositlity (Leary, 1957), or the extent to which they orient themselves around inclusion, control, or affection (Schutz, 1958). Is their style of communicating typically guarded, or is it open and self-closing to the extent that they can discuss such areas as painful feelings and fears? Can they deal with the specifics of a situation or are they usually vague and general? Do they usually appear assertive and direct, or passive and indirect? Finally, it is often important to determine the extent to which they are perceptive about interpersonal relationships and their typical approaches towards resolving conflict.

Whether or not to include a diagnosis has been an area of some controversy. Some clinicians feel that it is important to avoid labels since they may create self-fulfilling prophecies, be overly reductionistic, and allow clients to avoid responsibility for their own behavior. Other objections to diagnosis stem from researchers who feel that many of the terms are not scientifically valid or from psychiatrists who feel that it should be their role to provide diagnoses (Tallent and Reiss, 1959c). If a clinician does decide to give a diagnosis, he must first have a clear operational knowledge of the diagnostic terms. He should also include the client's premorbid level of adjustment, and the severity and frequency of the disturbance. Along with the diagnosis, it is usually important to include possible causes of the disorder. A discussion of causes should not be simplistic and one dimensional but should rather appreciate the complexity of causative factors. Thus, causes may be described from the perspective of primary, predisposing, precipitating, and reinforcing factors. The clinician may also discuss the relative significance of biological, psychosocial, and sociocultural variables.

A frequently asked question is whether or not the client's difficulties will continue or, if currently absent, recur. If the client's future prospects are poor, then a statement of the rationale for this conclusion should be given. For example, if a clinician predicts that the response to treatment will be poor, then he should elaborate that this is because of such factors as a strong need to appear hypernormal, poor insight, and a high level of defensiveness. Likewise, favorable predictions should include a summary of the client's assets and resources such as psychological mindedness, motivation to change, and social supports. If difficulties are likely to be encountered during the course of treatment, then the nature and intensity of these difficulties should be discussed. The prediction of suicidal potential, assaultive behavior, child abuse, or continued criminal behavior is essential in certain types of reports. Often the test results themselves are not useful in predicting behavior. For example, one of the best ways of predicting suicidal potential is to evaluate the client's past history, and current environmental and personal resources.

A summary paragraph should follow after the main impressions and interpretations have been discussed. The purpose of the summary is to restate succinctly the primary findings and conclusions. This requires that the clinician select only the most important issues and that he be careful not to overwhelm the reader with needless details. If the summary is included at the end of the section on impressions and interpretation, there is no need to summarize the entire report but only the major interpretations. However, some clinicians prefer to include a separate summary and recommendations section at the end of the entire report. In this case, the section must summarize the entire report and include the recommendations. Either location is acceptable; the choice can be based on the clinician's personal preference and the needs of the report as suggested by the referral question and background of the readers.

Recommendations

The ultimate practical purpose of the report is contained in the recommendations since they suggest what steps clients can take in order to solve their problems. Such recommendations should be clear, practical, and obtainable, and should relate directly to the general purpose of the report. This requires that the clinician clearly understand the nature of the problem, the best alternatives for remediation, and the resources within the community. Once these factors have been carefully considered, recommendations can be developed. These recommendations should be as specific as possible. Thus, a recommendation which states that the client should begin psychotherapy is not as useful as a statement of the need for "individual therapy focusing on the following issues: increased assertiveness, techniques for reducing anxiety, and increased awareness of the self-defeating patterns he creates in relationships." Likewise, a recommendation for "special education" can be improved by expanding it to "special education two hours a day, emphasizing exercises in auditory sequencing and increasing immediate recall for verbally meaningful information." Once the report with its recommendations has been submitted, this should be followed by continued contact to make sure that it has not been filed and forgotten. Even the best report will not be functional unless the recommendations are practical, obtainable, and actually put into action.

SAMPLE REPORTS

The psychological reports in this section are from the more common settings in which clinicians work and consult. The dimensions in which they vary are format, the extent to which history rather than test data is emphasized, the types of tests used, and the degree to which they include a variety of descriptions as opposed to being case focused with a relatively limited range of topics. Within each of the settings, there are specific questions which have been presented and decisions which must be made relating to the client. The different reports illustrate how the clinician has integrated the test data, client's history, and behavioral observations in order to handle these questions.

The first report was developed for a psychiatric setting and was intended to be read by professional mental health personnel. For this reason, there is some use of technical language, with a focus on developing a detailed, traditional DSM III diagnosis. What is noteworthy in the handling of the test data is that the bulk of the discussion relating to test interpretation revolves around projective test findings (Rorschach, TAT, projective drawings). Furthermore, much of the projective data are used in a qualitative, content-oriented manner. This was achieved by providing actual verbatim responses which give a more colorful and rich portrayal of the client's thought processes than could be achieved through quantitative scores. For example, Rorschach responses are written out to illustrate such personality dimensions as regressive themes, castration anxiety, aggressiveness, and paranoia.

The evaluation conducted in a legal context approaches the client from a variety of angles including his relationship with his family, his early background, descriptions of the client's behavior, his current work relationships, his reaction to the charges, and psychological test interpretations. This illustrates the importance of diversity in describing a client since each of these areas provides important but different types of information. The test data and interpretations based on this data constitute only one of several angles of approach. Not only are the various ways of approaching the client emphasized in this report, but also the importance of understanding the client within the context of his interpersonal relationships is stressed. The structure of the report has some additional noteworthy features. Initially, there is a personal letter format directed to the referral source. When a report is being directed to one primary referral person, this is often extremely helpful. It makes the report more immediate, thereby potentially enhancing the rapport between the clinician and the referring person. The section summarizing the report is placed at the end and is given considerable emphasis. This section ties together the information not only from the psychological tests but also from other sources. Furthermore, the recommendations are included in, and closely tied to, the summary findings.

The third report from an educational context is the most case focused of all the reports. It mainly discusses the intellectual strengths and weaknesses of the client, and connects these in a general way with her social development. For the most part, the report avoids a discussion of personality dynamics because these were not requested by the referral source. Furthermore, her history indicated that the client's level of interpersonal adjustment was good. The most important part of the report is the recommendations. These are given the most discussion, and are as specific and concrete as possible. Once the client's cognitive weaknesses are documented in the section on interpretation and impressions, the main thing her parents and teachers need to know is what specific measures can be taken to work with these weaknesses.

The final evaluation emphasizes a more global personality description of the client derived primarily from test data. In contrast to the previous educational evaluation, the decisions and issues facing the client are not as specific and concrete. Instead, an understanding of the client's general dynamics, including intellectual abilities, interpersonal relationships, impulse control, specific presenting problem, and potential for benefiting from psychotherapy, is the major concern. The evaluation, then, is more globally oriented towards insight into the client. Thus, the client may benefit from a knowledge of the information included in the report perhaps even more than his probation officer or attorney. It is intended to be used as an aid in the psychotherapeutic process as much as it is a tool in decision making. As such, the recommendations are de-emphasized in favor of a more qualitative understanding of the client's personality.

THE PSYCHIATRIC SETTING*

NAME: J.M.
DATE OF BIRTH: 15 August 1974
DATES OF EVALUATION: 25 and 30 September 1982

Identifying Information

J.M. is an 8-year-old third grader who was admitted to Monte Hospital for the fourth time on September 5, 1982. He was referred for an interview and psychological

---

*Submitted by Thomas MacSpeiden, Ph.D.

testing by Dr. S. to assist in estimating his intelligence, differential diagnosis, behavioral dynamics, and potential for treatment. There was also some question as to whether or not J. could adequately function outside a 24-hour inpatient facility.

Presenting Problem

After an extended visit with his grandparents in Detroit, which resulted in his beginning school a year late, J. became increasingly aggressive and hyperactive. His scholastic performance decreased, and on the day prior to his hospital admission, he told his therapist he felt he should kill himself. Past evaluations indicate a learning disability. At the time of this interview, when asked why he was in the hospital, J. said, "Because I never mind."

Background Information

The following information was obtained from J.'s hospital chart and from J. himself who was an extremely limited historian. Reportedly, J. has been hyperactive since birth and has suffered both abandonment and abuse from his parents. His mother, age 32, has suffered a series of emotional regressions and was hospitalized at Monte in 1979 when floridly psychotic. She has openly rejected J. and his four siblings. J.'s father told Dr. S. that he was very interested in J., but in the past he had little involvement with his son. Clinically, the father appears distant and withdrawn, and manages his anxiety by being an active air force pilot. J. reported having four brothers and no sisters, although his hospital record makes mention of only one sister and no brothers. The sister lives in New Mexico and has been abused by the maternal grandparents.

This examiner knows very little about J.'s early years. The record indicates that his biological father left the home early in J.'s life, after J. had undergone episodes of beating by either the mother or the father. There was a second marriage, apparently by the father, which was also unstable and led to what appears to be J.'s first psychiatric admission at age 5 for hyperactivity and destructive behavior. Following a long stay at Southcrest Hospital with little improvement, he was transferred to Monte Hospital with improvement thereafter. He was then placed in a foster home where his course of adjustment was erratic. Apparently he was hospitalized twice more at Monte and then, last July, went to Detroit to visit his paternal grandparents. Reportedly, he engaged in considerable testing behavior to see if the people there cared for him. The grandparents kept him two weeks past the time he was to return to San Francisco, and the family there obtained the services of an attorney in an attempt to keep him against professional advice. After his return, he displayed marked ambivalence between wanting to return to Detroit to live with family members and wanting to remain in his current familiar surroundings in San Francisco. J.'s medical history is significant for several allergies and he is currently receiving allergy shots.

Previous testing at Monte Hospital in November and December 1980 at age 6 years and 3 months yielded a WISC-R Verbal I.Q. of 105, a Performance I.Q. of 114, and a Full Scale I.Q. score of 109. Projective testing results indicated disorganization, aggression, rage, and a perception of nurturance as distasteful. Although J. failed to see popular responses on the Rorschach, his form levels were positive. He received a diagnosis of borderline personality disorder with paranoid features. An evaluation one year earlier by Dr. Y. indicated he suffered from a learning disability.

Test Results

WISC-R: Full Scale I.Q. = 105
Verbal I.Q. = 106
Performance I.Q. = 104

	Subscale Scores		Subscale Scores
Information	11	Picture Completion	11
Similarities	9	Picture Arrangement	14
Arithmetic	10	Block Design	14
Vocabulary	13	Object Assembly	10
Comprehension	12	Coding	4

Rorschach:

Location	Determinants	Contents
$R = 14$	$F = 9$	$A = 11$
$W = 12$	$FM = 1$	$Na = 1$
$D = 1$	$m = 1$	$Objects = 2$
$S = 1$	$CF = 2$	$P = 4$
	$FC = 1$	

Ratios, Percentages, and Derivations

$EB = 0:2.5$	$W:M = 12:0$
$EA = 2.5$	$W:D = 12:1$
$eb = 2/0$	$L = 3.6$
$ep = 2$	$A\% = 79\%$
$FC/(CF + C) = 1/2$	$F+\% = 70\%$

Bender: Overlapping, collisions, inability to make dots, poor angulation, difficulty connecting figures (see Figure 9-1).

Draw-A-Person: Lack of details, immature (see Figure 9-2).

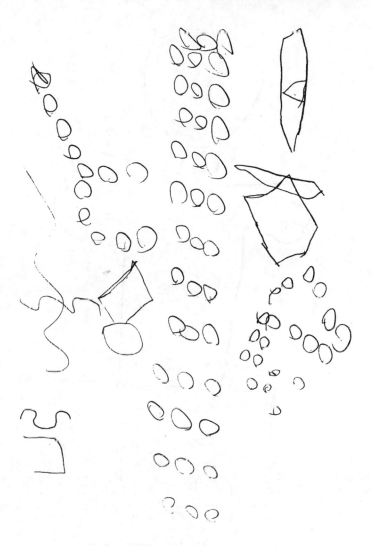

Figure 9-1. CASE: J.M. Age: 8 years, 1 month.

Figure 9-2. CASE: J.M. Age: 8 years, 1 month.

Psychological Impressions

J.M. was seen on the Delta Unit at Monte Hospital on September 15, 1982. At that time he seemingly suffered from a drug reaction, was extremely hyperactive, was hallucinating feelings of bugs crawling on himself, and as a result, was experiencing strong panic. After a brief interview, testing was postponed. When seen on September 30, 1982 he was more composed, and there were no indications of hallucinations. He presented himself with conventionally cut blond hair and wearing a red, white, and blue striped T-shirt and blue jeans. His lips and the area around his mouth appeared chapped, and he was moderately hyperactive although less so when actively engaged in conversation with the examiner or when involved in a task. He demonstrated mixed dominance, being left eyed, right handed and right footed. Despite his hyperactivity, he emanated a moderate charm.

J. was administered the Wechsler Intelligence Scale for Children — Revised (WISC-R), Rorschach, Children's Apperception Test (CAT), Bender Visual Motor Gestalt Test (Bender), and the Draw-A-Person Test (D-A-P).

On the WISC-R, J. obtained a Verbal I.Q. of 106, a Performance I.Q. of 104, and a Full Scale I.Q. of 105. Overall, he functions intellectually in the average to high average range and at the 63rd percentile rank. His verbal subtests showed very little subtest scatter, with a relative strength in Vocabulary (13) and a relative weakness in ability to perceive the similarity between one object or event and another (Similarities = 9). In contrast, his performance subtests showed an extremely high degree of scatter with a significant lowering in Coding (4). This score was profoundly influenced by his current level of hyperactivity and can account for the majority of the ten-point discrepancy between his present Performance I.Q. score and that obtained last year. It suggests that currently he has difficulty concentrating on and learning tasks requiring rote memorization and sequencing.

The structure of J.'s personality as estimated from his 14 responses to the Rorschach is difficult to determine because of his restlessness during the inquiry portion of the test. He appears to be anxious, and to use repression and denial as his primary defenses. When these defenses fail he attempts to suspend his affect (L = 3.6).

Unlike the testing of one year ago, he is currently able to see those things in the environment seen by most persons (populars = 4). He also appears capable of perceiving the external world without profound pathological distortions (F+% = 70%). His archaic impulses are minimally sublimated and dispose him to impulsivity [FC/(CF+C) = 1/2]. Because of his limited sublimation, he is without the capacity to attain goals requiring persistence (W:M = 12:0), and may respond in a disorganized manner which he experiences as being beyond his ability to control (eb = Z/o). To maintain a semblance of affective control, he attempts to deny emotional stimuli in the environment (sum C = 1.5) but when he does respond he has limited affective control [FC/(CF + C) = 1/2].

The content of J.'s personality as estimated from his responses to the Rorschach is characterized by a preoccupation with excretory bodily functions, a preoccupation generally found among persons four or five years his junior. Typical of this content was his single response to Card IV:

This one looks like Big Foot. Head and big feet, and he's going pee-pee. You can tell. Look at all that stuff. And then he's going BM, bowel movement.

J. is not totally fixated in an anal phase of development and gave several responses indicating his phallic preoccupation and concern about castration. Typical were his first and second responses to Card II:

1. This looks like a monster. That's all it looks like. (*Question:* What else do you see on the card?)
2. There's a rocket ship on top of him. He got shot with the rocket all right here. (J. rubs his groin and looks at the examiner.)

His phallic aggressiveness was almost perseverative and was directed in a testing manner toward this examiner in his response to Card VI, the "phallic" card:

This one is like a key, a monster key. You stick it in there, and then it runs out of key and bites people — not the monster though. And it eats people like you.

Several responses depicted eyes in unusual places, a characteristic performance of paranoid individuals. Similarly, his aggression was projected in frequently seen "sharp, sharp teeth." For the last three cards, which are highly chromatic, he linked his three single responses together to reflect his need to express anger arbitrarily and his desire to grow strong in order to be less fearful of the environment. However, he views his acting out behavior as evil, which creates an internal struggle vividly portrayed in his single response to Card X:

This one looks like they (lions from Cards VIII and IX) came down from the mountain, and they turned into crabs, crabs who eat people. See like those teeth and they have pincers and pincers shoot out pellets and kill people. This is the good side and this is the bad side. And the good side fights the bad side.

The content of J.'s personality as estimated from his responses to the CAT cards is characterized by an admiration for his father, despite whatever rejection he may have felt from him in the past. This admiration stems from a need for identification so that he might better control threatening internal and external forces. He feels rejected by his grandparents as well as by his mother, and in fantasy says in effect, "If you don't love me, I have many friends who will." This latter content was typified in his response to card 8: .

Once upon a time there was a grandma and a grandpa — were talking and the mother said to the kid, "You go out and play. We have some work to do here." Then the kid goes and plays with all his friends which he has three hundred trillion.

Despite what he experiences as rejection from his grandparents, possibly because he did not understand why he was returned to San Francisco this September, he nonetheless feels attracted to them as depicted in his response to card 9:

> Once upon a time this kid was trying to get out of bed and opened the door and run away from home. He came back, picked up all his clothes, and went back to his grandma who lived 2000 miles away in a car. He's only around 6 years old, and he knows how to drive a car.

Besides the grandiosity noted above, this story reflects only one pole of an ambivalence. Subconsciously, J. associates the grandmother with the mother and the grandmother suffers as a result. His anger was reflected in his response to card 10:

> Once upon a time the grandmother was going to speak to the kid. The kid killed the mother, I mean the grandmother. Then he killed everybody but not his friend. His whole family except one, me.

On his Bender results, there were clear indications of his minimal brain dysfunction apparently associated with a learning disability. Some of his reproductions were almost unrecognizable compared to the figures on the stimulus cards. He was virtually incapable of drawing dots which he replaced with large circles. Most 45° angles were impossible for him to complete, and he was frequently unable to join the component parts of the Gestalt.

When asked to draw a picture of a person, J. drew the frontal view of a figure approximately 6 inches tall which he described as "this is my friend's baby girl, Jean." The picture consisted of a round circle for a head, a rectangular body with two very short arms (each with three fingers), and legs with round feet. The head and body were devoid of detail. The drawing reflects his inability to form empathic or sympathetic relationships with people, whom he views largely as animated objects. He feels much like an infant without the capacity to change his environment significantly.

When asked to draw a picture of his family, he drew a series of eight stick figures. The father was drawn along the right margin of the pages, and moving from right to left he depicted his mother, "Jim, Sam, Bill, 'my friend,' Sue" (his sister), and J. He depicted himself most distant from his parents and indeed separated from his siblings by a nonrelative. The drawing clearly reflects his feelings of isolation and his belief that friends care more for him than his family.

Summary

J.M. functions intellectually in the average to high average range, and appears to suffer from a minimal brain dysfunction associated with a learning disability and hyperkensis. His personality structure is nonpsychotic and characterized by a high level of anxiety, ideas of reference, impulsivity, and difficulty relating empathically or sympathetically, high aspirations which he attempts to accomplish in fantasy, a denial of emotional stimuli, and excessive lability. He is preoccupied with bodily excretions and anal expulsive behaviors as well as with concern over castration as he attempts to compensate for his impotent posture in life. He seeks to identify with a strong masculine image to better control threatening impulses and reduce threats to his existence, threats that are both internal and external. His potential for violence is real and he maintains a capacity for suicide. He feels rejected by his grandmother, possibly because he does not understand why he was returned to San Francisco in September, but he seems to prefer the grandmother to his mother. He feels like an impotent child who is more loved by his friends than by his relatives.

Diagnostic Impression

AXIS I	312.00	Conduct disorder, undersocialized, aggressive.
	314.01	Attention deficit disorder with hyperactivity.
AXIS II	315.50	Mixed specific developmental disorder.
	301.83	Borderline personality disorder.
AXIS III		Multiple allergies previously diagnosed.
AXIS IV		Psychosocial stressors: disagreement with maternal grandparents and authorities, and his late start in the school year. Severity: 4 — moderate.
AXIS V		Highest level of adaptive functioning past year: 5 — poor.

Recommendations

Currently J. is too disturbed to function in other than a 24-hour facility. Although he maintains the capacity to adjust at a higher level, he will require an extended hospitalization, with treatment and a structured environment to shore up his flagging ego functions. It is highly probable that thereafter he could return to a well-structured foster home. The adequacy of the paternal grandparents home and whether or not it is a viable possibility for future placement should be determined.

THE LEGAL CONTEXT*

Dear Mr. Blake:

Thank you for referring your very interesting client S.T. to me. I first saw Mr. T. in my office on November 5, 1982. He was dressed neatly, but casually,

---

*Submitted by George Sargent, Ph.D.

in slacks, a knit shirt, and a light canvas jacket. Mr. T. is of Mexican extraction, dark skinned, with graying hair. He is of average build, and smiles easily and engagingly.

My understanding is that Mr. T. was referred to me for psychological testing and evaluation in connection with his originally being charged with two separate acts of misdemeanor child molest. I understand that in his 23 years of teaching in the Monterey Union High School District, Mr. T. has received good teaching evaluations. There have been other complaints of his touching students in the past, but this is the first time a criminal charge has been lodged. I further understand that as of November 10, when we last talked, several more complaints have been lodged with the District Attorney's office.

Current Situation

Mr. T. lives with Lisa, his wife of 29 years, and their youngest child of five children (and only boy) Robert, 15 years of age. All four daughters are out of the home. The oldest, Susan, age 29, is married. She and her husband have a 7-year-old son, Frank, and live together in Texas. The youngest daughter, Sarah, age 22, is in Yale Law School after graduating from Harvard. She and a friend are doing a legal synopsis project on child molestation cases in California, in response to Mr. T's being charged. All the family members are supportive of Mr. T., and are angry and dismayed at the way in which the school district handled the complaints. Robert attends the high school where his father teaches. The charges are public, and he has received some harrassment by fellow students.

Mr. T. is 53 years of age and has average health. He takes two medications for medical conditions: Dilantin for epilepsy, which was diagnosed in 1964 after a grand mal seizure, and cimetidine for a (duodenal) ulcer for which he was hospitalized in the mid-1960s. The ulcer condition still causes him occasional problems. There has been no recurrence of the seizures. He could remember several severe head injuries that occurred in the past which might have led to the epilepsy. He did receive a full neurological evaluation in 1964, including an EEG. The findings were unremarkable.

Mrs. T. is on the Board of the Monterey Community College District. She, like the rest of the family, has reacted with anger at the handling of her husband's case. She has been supportive of him and, in his attorney's opinion, does not believe the charges against him. It sounds, however, as if she has handled all of their recent problems almost too well, i.e., she has adapted to the situation almost too swiftly and competently.

Background

Mr. and Mrs. T. have lived in Monterey for 23 years and at their present address since 1968. He was born in Arizona, the second youngest in a family of 13 children. His mother and father fled from Mexico (and Pancho Villa) around the turn of the century, to settle in Arizona. His father was a laborer. His mother raised their large and very cohesive family. Mr. T. remembers working in the fields with his father as early as 10 years of age. Every summer he would work as a laborer.

When he graduated from high school, Mr. T. entered the air force. He was 19 years old. He rose to the rank of staff sergeant in his four years with the military and left with an honorable discharge in 1953. From 1953 to 1960, before he became a teacher, he engaged in a variety of jobs, including a runner for Convair and a janitor. He also attended Monterey Peninsula College from 1952 to 1954, and San Jose State from 1954 to 1960. He graduated with teachers' credentials and went to work for the Monterey Union High School in 1959. He has been on the faculty since that time.

Mr. T. said that his sexual education was relatively traditional for a Mexican-American family. His father was strict, not only with the girls but also with the boys, about no sex before marriage. In general, sex was not discussed in the family. He began masturbation when he was about 11 years old, and claims no homosexual involvements as a youth or adult and no sexual problems. He described his current sexual relationship with his wife as "satisfactory" and felt his wife would have "no complaints" if asked about this area. He stated that he had no history of getting in trouble because of sexual behavior at any time in his life. He admitted to having had several extramarital affairs with adult women. One was 20 years ago; the other was several years ago and his wife was made aware of it. Apparently he and she cried together, fought over it, and brought the situation to a mutually satisfactory conclusion. When I asked if he was drawn to the girls at the high school, he denied any sexual attraction to them. He stated that once his own girls had reached high school age, he saw the other high school girls as more like daughters.

One of the most stressful periods of Mr. T.'s life was when he was coaching at the high school. During the year his basketball team went undefeated, he experienced the most pressure. In describing how he experienced this pressure he stated, "Even when you win a game there are people who tell you how it should have been coached, and I was my own worst critic. I always felt I hadn't done enough. There was one man who ran for the school board one year on the platform of getting me out of the head coaching position. It made me feel not appreciated. I think bigotry was operating here. Even now I believe there are some who are happy I'm in trouble today." It was during this year that Mr. T.'s grand mal seizure took place and that he was also first hospitalized for bleeding ulcers.

Reaction to the Charges

Mr. T. has taught Spanish since 1960, and my understanding is that he has received generally good evaluations during this period. The several complaints

concerning his past behavior with students never developed into legal complications. They were settled at the school level. He cited one example where his old
friend and principal at the time once came into observe his classroom. Mr. T.
quoted him as saying after an hour of observation: "You dumbell!" (said in a
friendly manner). "Now I know what's wrong. When you put your foot on
that basket under the students' chairs, your leg is touching *their* legs. Keep your
feet on the floor and your hands clasped behind your back like I do."

While I as examiner have not discussed these incidents in any greater detail
with school personnel or the victims, I feel they are minimizations of what
actually occurred, i.e., selective recollections. For example, when I confronted
Mr. T. regarding the information in the police report on the first legal complaint,
he finally admitted to having pulled the female student closer to him by putting
his hand in her pants, the back of his fingers toward her body, and simultaneously
saying, "You're not fat, what do you mean?" As he said this to me, his tone of
voice, eye contact, and general affect, however, suggested less than total belief in
this explanation himself. When I confronted him about not being truthful with
me, he was neither righteously angry nor frightened, but said that I had to call
them as I saw them. "You're the professional," he said.

Test Results

WAIS: Full Scale I.Q. = 142
Verbal I.Q. = 153
Performance I.Q. = 122

Subscale Scores		Subscale Scores	
Arithmetic	12	Picture Completion	10
Digit Span	15	Block Design	15
Vocabulary	19	Picture Arrangement	9
		Object Assembly	12

MMPI:

L	42	5	58
F	50	6	59
K	70	7	73
1	76	8	58
2	56	9	53
3	69	0	35
4	60		

Bender: Not in organic range (see Figure 9-3).

House-Tree-Person: (See tree, Figure 9-4).

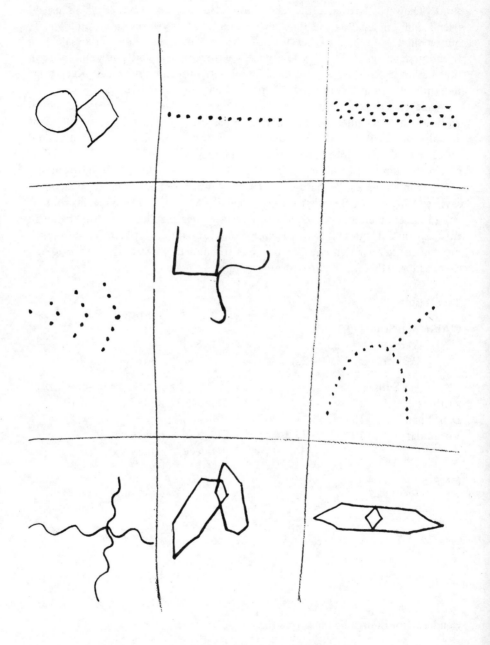

Figure 9-3. CASE: S.T. Age: 53 years.

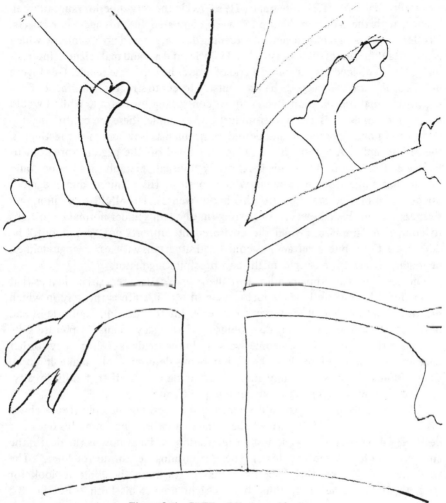

Figure 9-4. CASE: S.T. Age: 53 years.

Interpretation and Impressions

Mr. T. was administered the Bender Visual Motor Gestalt Test (Bender), portions of the Wechsler Adult Intelligence Scale (WAIS), the Thematic Apperception Test (TAT), the Minnesota Multiphasic Personality Inventory (MMPI), the House-Tree-Person Text (H-T-P), and the Draw-A-Family Test (D-A-F). The test instruments tended to support each other in their view of the psychological makeup of Mr. T. and appear to be accurate assessments of his current level of functioning.

Intellectually, Mr. T. is quite smart. He scored in the very superior range of intelligence, with the scores in the top 2% when compared with his age-related peers. His Bender, although only a general screening device, showed no organicity, which is important in light of his history of head injuries and a grand mal seizure. Interestingly, Mr. T. divided his paper into a grid of nine as he began the Bender (see Figure 9-3), a procedure that suggests he uses outside forces to structure his life, not finding his internal organization always up to controlling his output. While I would not overemphasize this as a trait from just one example, there are continuing suggestions of impulse problems and boundary problems elsewhere in the testing. In the H-T-P and D-A-F tests, his drawings extended off the page in three out of five cases (see Figure 9-4). This is relatively unusual. Metaphorically one could say he has some trouble knowing where to stop. His planning and judgment might sometimes be preempted by his impulsiveness. His MMPI score in impulsiveness was not high, however, suggesting that he tends under normal conditions to control his impulses. When the environment supports not "acting out," he does not act out, but in certain less controlled situations with less clear guidelines, he might. Stress, for example, might be a precipitating factor.

On the Thematic Apperception Test there were certain repetitive themes that came through powerfully. One major issue in Mr. T.'s life is the way in which his father and mother labored to make a better life for their children. He is, and has been, concerned with not disappointing that legacy. Thus, in picture 2 he sees the girl overlooking the people working in the fields as feeling sorry for her parents for having to work so hard, but being determined to make it up to them. Similar themes of family members helping one another, family loyalty, and the older man helping the younger one proliferate.

His comments on the last card seemed to be speaking metaphorically about his current situation. He described the scene as a father who found his daughter dead of a drug overdose. (The loss in reputation he faces now is the death; the charge of molest is the overdose.) There is nothing he can do for "her." The way the man resolves this dilemma is that he turns to the Bible to look for strength, because the "only thing he has right now is his faith." For Mr. T., religion is likewise very important. He told me he never missed church on Sunday. "You just don't," he said. "There's no good excuse."

Lastly, the MMPI profile, though it should be interpreted carefully in light of a certain degree of guardedness, is of interest. It suggests that he may use physical complaints to manipulate others. His T score of 69 on the Hy scale suggests that his optimism is maintained at the cost of somatic complaints. It also supports a view of him as possibly acting out sexually or aggressively, accompanied by a convenient lack of insight into his own motives or into the impact his actions have on others. People with some of the same personality traits as Mr. T. tend to perceive life events globally, not in detail, making it easier to use personality defenses of denial and repression.

Mr. T. lacks self-confidence. He is often worried and tense, and struggles with a poor self-image. He covers all of this with a veneer of optimism and some verbal bravado, but he is quite sensitive to hurt and criticism from others.

Summary of Findings and Recommendations

Mr. T. is a very bright, 53-year-old Chicano male from a first generation Mexican-American family of 13 children. He is married to a high-achieving Caucasian woman whose family never accepted Mr. T. because of his background. Though he denies the current charges of sexually touching several of his female high school students, his personality is that of a person who has difficulty controlling strong impulses unless he is in situations where the rules are evident and the consequences clear. He is a worrier who is likely to use his real and imagined somatic complaints to manipulate others indirectly, and his major defenses are those of denial and repression. He is a family man, both worrying most about his family and liking most to be with them. He is likable and gregarious. He has had no previous legal problems because of his sexual behavior, but there have been earlier complaints that point to other alleged instances of what might, psychologically, best be termed very poor judgment. He stands to lose a great deal because of the current accusations against him.

Mr. T. does not have a criminal mentality; that is, he has a conscience, feels guilt, and has an overall record in the school and the community of being responsible and principled. He does have a problem with feeling worthwhile about himself, however. I believe that he has never felt fully worthy of his wife or his career position, and the current criticisms of him reinforce a deep suspicion within himself that his own self-criticisms are correct. In this light, the alleged molestations are self-destructive behaviors designed by his subconscious to strip him of much that he feels he does not deserve.

If one accepts this psychological explanation for the roots of his motivation, it seems clear that incarceration would serve to deepen this unconscious belief in his own unworthiness. Incarceration might serve the purpose of punishment, but it should not be seen as aiding his rehabilitation. Rather, it seems more humane and sensible to structure Mr. T.'s environment so as to help him monitor his own behavior appropriately, a job he seems to have done will most of the time.

First and foremost, if he is found guilty, Mr. T. must be able to admit his culpability. This would be the first step in rehabilitation, and his family must be able to let him admit the guilt, not support an ongoing denial of it. He should no longer be a teacher of minors. He should enter psychotherapy of a type which focuses on building up his self-esteem and deepening the connections with his community. Mr. T. is bright enough and anxiety ridden enough to make use of psychotherapy. Some long-term legal leverage over his future behavior should be maintained for supervision and monitoring of progress.

THE EDUCATIONAL SETTING

NAME: M.K.
DATE OF BIRTH: February 8, 1972
DATE OF EXAMINATION: May 12, 1981
EXAMINED BY: G.G.-M.

Referral Question

M. was referred by her mother for a psychological evaluation to assess her current level of functioning. An evaluation had become of particular importance since a decision was imminent regarding continued placement in her special education class as opposed to mainstreaming. Furthermore, the last psychological evaluation which had been performed on M. was over two years ago, and Mrs. K. requested a follow-up evaluation to assess possible improvement, stability, or deterioration in M.'s cognitive abilities.

Evaluation Procedures

M. was administered the Wechsler Intelligence Scale for Children — Revised (WISC-R), the Bender Visual Motor Gestast Test (Bender), and the House-Tree-Person Test (H-T-P).

Behavioral Observations

M. appeared neatly dressed, and was cooperative and friendly throughout the testing procedure. When confronted with more difficult tasks, she would at times discontinue trying to perform as best as she could. However, for the most part, she gave the tasks her best efforts, and the test results appear to be an accurate assessment of her current level of functioning.

Relevant History

M. is a right-handed female, 9 years and 3 months of age, with a history of delayed development resulting from a hypothyroid condition that was diagnosed and treated when she was 5 years old. She is currently living with her natural parents, and her older sister Susan (17) also lives with the family.

Mrs. K. reported that during her pregnancy with M., she was consistently under a doctor's care. There were no unusual features at birth, and she stated that M.'s early developmental milestones were normal. Between the ages of 2 and 4, Mr. and Mrs. K. noticed a gradual but progressive slowness in M.'s behavior. During the end of her fourth year, this pattern became more pronounced, and she was referred to a physician who diagnosed and treated her.

Her parents have responded to her condition with conscientiousness and support. She was assessed at the Speech, Hearing, and Neurosensory Center and treated for a period of six months. She has been enrolled in a special education class in school following a psychological evaluation performed by Dr. Lewis of the Los Angeles Union School District on August 15, 1979. He diagnosed her as being educable mentally retarded and summarized his report by stating that M. is "functioning with apparent developmental delays in many areas. She has significant cognitive difficulties along with severe academic deficiencies. Her ability to participate in a regular education program is extremely limited at this time" (p. 3). She was placed in a learning handicapped program including speech therapy and a special education class. An important aspect of her overall program with regard to her interpersonal development was that all her social activities took place with a regular first grade class. Her interpersonal adjustment in these activities has been described by her mother as good. Her mother reported that in most areas she has seen a great deal of improvement over the past year. M.'s parents are currently concerned with the most suitable academic and social placement for her, as well as what assets and limitations she may have for the future.

Test Results

WISC-R: Full Scale I.Q. = 70
Verbal I.Q. = 73
Performance I.Q. = 71

	Subscale Scores		Subscale Scores
Information	5	Picture Arrangement	1
Comprehension	7	Picture Completion	10
Digit Span	3	Block Design	5
Arithmetic	3	Object Assembly	7
Similarities	8		
Vocabulary	8		

Bender: Impaired; lack of closure, distortions, difficulty making dots, rotations, perseverations (see Figure 9-5).

Bender Memory: Two designs recalled.

House-Tree-Person: Disorganized, immature (see house, Figure 9-6).

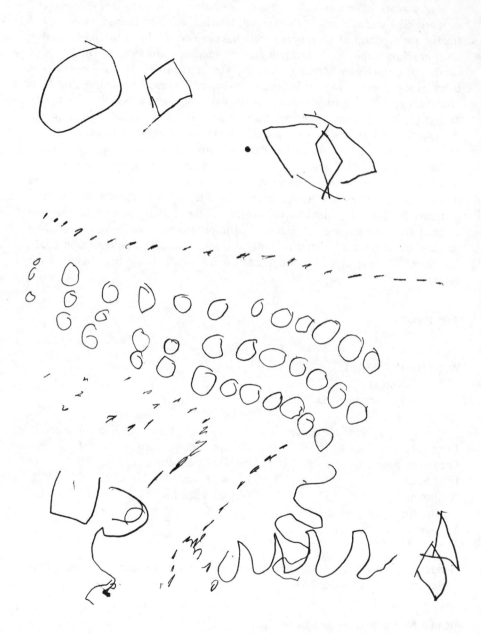

Figure 9-5. CASE: M.K. Age: 9 years, 3 months.

Figure 9-6. CASE: M.K. Age: 9 years, 3 months.

Interpretation and Impressions

M. scored in the borderline range of intelligence on the WISC-R with a Full Scale I.Q. of 70, a Performance I.Q. of 71, and a Verbal I.Q. of 73, which places her in the second percentile when compared to her age-related peers. These scores are roughly equivalent to those taken by Dr. Lewis on August 9, 1979. Relative strengths were in the areas of ability to distinguish relevant from irrelevant details in her environment (10, within normal range), ability to conceptualize the similarity between one object or event and another (8), and vocabulary (8). Relative but pronounced weaknesses were in tasks requiring sequencing and a sustained attention span. This suggests that her overall social and verbal skills are nearly within normal limits, whereas her academic abilities, particularly in reading, writing, and arithmetic, are moderately impaired.

M.'s performance on the Bender was clearly in the impaired range and characterized by difficulties with closure, distortions of the designs, producing dashes instead of dots, rotations, and perseverations. This suggests that she is definitely lagging in her visual-motor abilities when compared with her age-related peers and may have a difficult time organizing the spatial information in her environment. Drawings of her house, tree, and person, although of appropriate size and good line pressure, were likewise disorganized and generally more like someone 6 years of age rather than 9.

In summary, M.'s performance is consistent with generalized impairment to both cerebral hemispheres. Her relative strengths are that she has normal abilities in noticing the relevant details in her environment, as well as good comprehension and vocabulary. In other words, she has made a good adjustment in learning how to deal with her environment, which reflects the impact that speech therapy and her special education program have had on her. Weaknesses, on the other hand, are in the academic areas, particularly attention, mathematical computation, sequencing, and visual organization. In these areas her abilities have stayed the same during the past two years. Although she has progressed academically, she has done so at a rate consistent with a child having an I.Q. of 70.

Recommendations

1. Continued placement in special education classes emphasizing sequencing, math, memory training, visual organization, and sustained attention.
2. Social activities should be designed to increase or maintain social contacts with age-related peers in the normal school program. This is particularly important since M.'s social-verbal skills are close to normal, and contact with children in the normal school program would provide her with normal role models. On the other hand, her academic abilities are

certainly well below most children, and placement in a normal program would be likely to create turmoil and a sense of inferiority.

3. Home tutoring emphasizing drill and repetition is recommended, in addition to what the school provides.

4. M. should have follow-up psychological assessment every 12–24 months since, as she gets older, the precision of measurements increases, and continual evaluations of her level of progress or stability can be made to aid in further academic or interpersonal recommendations.

THE PSYCHOLOGICAL CLINIC

NAME: B.C.
DATE OF BIRTH: March 12, 1948
DATE OF EXAMINATION: November 10, 1982
EXAMINER: G.G.-M.

Referral Question

Mr. C. was referred for a psychological evaluation in connection with his being arrested on two counts of exhibitionism. The specific questions which it was hoped the evaluation would answer related to whether or not the client could benefit from psychotherapy, important personality dynamics relevant to therapy, and possible difficulties likely to be encountered between the client and the therapist.

Evaluation Procedures

On November 10, 1982, I interviewed Mr. C. and administered the following tests: Wechsler Adult Intelligence Scale — Revised (WAIS-R), Bender Visual Motor Gestalt Test (Bender), Draw-A-Person Test (D-A-P), Thematic Appercep- tion Test (TAT), and the Minnesota Multiphasic Personality Inventory (MMPI).

Behavioral Observations

Mr. C. appeared for both interviews casually dressed in jeans and a T-shirt. He had a mustache and long hair tied back in a ponytail. His eye contact was good, and his speech, although sometimes hesitant, was clear and soft. He was articulate and friendly; he expressed concern over his past behavior; and his overall style of speaking was engaging. There were no indications of delusions or hallucinations, and he was oriented in all three spheres. When approaching the tasks presented to him, he was cooperative and his problem solving style was usually adequate although sometimes slightly disorganized. Based on the above observations and the MMPI validity scales, the test results appear to be an accurate assessment of his current level of functioning.

Relevant History

Mr. C. is a 34-year-old, white, unmarried male with a university education who was apprehended on two counts of exhibitionism. He was born and raised in Riverside, California, where his father was a plumber. An important incident relating to his birth and early childhood was that he was raised by his grandparents but, until the age of 15, was led to believe that his grandparents were his parents. To this day, he still refers to, and thinks of, his grandmother as his mother. He is the youngest of three children, having two older sisters — Carol (50, actually his biological mother) and Susan (47).

Mr. C.'s "parents" (actually grandparents) were somewhat distant from each other, and he describes his "mother" as extremely "introverted and passive." He states that she "tried to stamp out every expression of assertiveness in me" and usually "controlled me by making me feel guilty." There was also a great deal of closeness between the two of them, in contrast to his "father" whom he describes as somewhat distant. He states that in school he was a loner, but the few friends he did have were fairly close. His grades were good, and his performance in English and art was excellent. He did not date until his last year of high school and, throughout his early school years, felt shy and awkward around females.

Upon graduating from high school, he identified with counter-culture groups and used drugs to a moderate extent. His college attendance was inconsistent, although he did complete a master's degree in drama and has credit towards a master's in fine arts. Despite his university education he is currently working, and has in the past worked, in construction, never actually utilizing his educational background. His relationships with females have usually been short; the longest lasted for two years, and he lived with this woman for 1 1/2 years. As he describes it, his main difficulty is that he can be with a woman for a while, but several times a month he will have a feeling of being "extremely distant and I can't come out of my shell." He describes this as an intense sense of helplessness, passivity, and feeling "jagged." This is also accompanied by sexual impotence which he indicated had become an increasing problem for him over the past four years.

Mr. C. reports that his first episode of exhibitionism occurred approximately eight years ago, but the episodes have been increasing in frequency over the past three years. He stated that prior to three years ago, he would exhibit himself only three or four times per year. During the past two to three years, this has increased to four to five times per month. His usual procedure is to pick up a female who is hitchhiking and, after a few minutes, open up his pants. Although most of the time he reports having an erection, he stated that he does not masturbate. He correlates an increase in his exhibitionism with a corresponding increase in feelings of helplessness and passivity, both in regard to his life and in terms of any relationship he is involved in at the time. After these episodes, he does feel guilt over his behavior and his need to exhibit temporarily subsides. However, he compares the excitement or "rush" he experiences to the feeling a drug addict must have. Eventually, his need for the "rush" increases to the extent that "I find myself doing it again."

During the past four months, Mr. C. has been arrested on two counts of exhibitionism. As a result, he is spending weekends in jail so as not to jeopardize his job as a construction worker. His case will be reevaluated in three weeks, and his probation officer is considering making counseling a requirement.

Test Results

WAIS-R: Full Scale I.Q. = 132
Verbal I.Q. = 142
Performance I.Q. = 114

Subscale Scores		Subscale Scores	
Information	15	Picture Completion	11
Digit Span	15	Picture Arrangement	9
Vocabulary	15	Block Design	13
Arithmetic	17	Object Assembly	17
Comprehension	16	Digit Symbol	10
Similarities	17		

MMPI:

L	46	5	78
F	55	6	60
K	63	7	34
1	68	8	64
2	72	9	78
3	71	0	64
4	76		

Bender: See Figure 9-7.

Draw-A-Person: See Figure 9-8 and 9-9.

Interpretation and Impressions

Mr. C. obtained a Full Scale I.Q. of 132, a Verbal I.Q. of 142, and a Performance I.Q. of 114, thereby placing him in the 98th percentile when compared with his

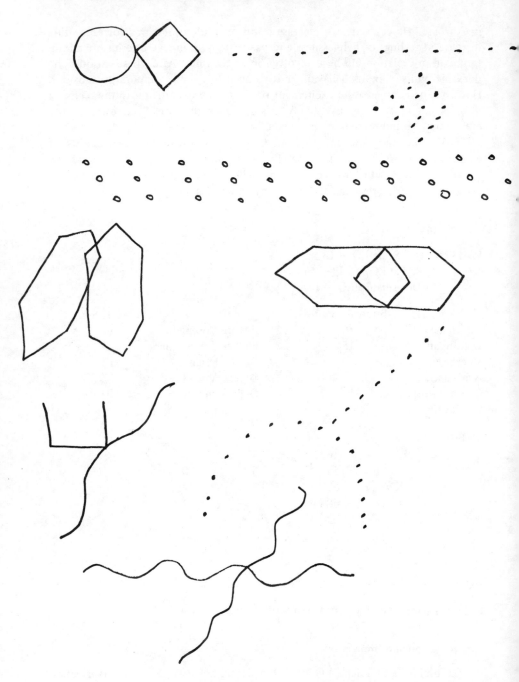

Figure 9-7. CASE: B.C. Age: 34 years.

Figure 9-8. CASE: B.C. Age: 34 years. "Fu Manchu Man" (1st drawing).

Figure 9-9. CASE: B.C. Age 34 years. "Dairy Queen Mama" (2nd drawing).

age-related peers. Relative cognitive strengths were in his overall verbal abilities, especially in mathematical computation and the ability to perceive the similarity between one event or object and another. Although his verbal ability to comprehend social interactions is excellent, a noteworthy weakness is his relatively poor ability to understand nonverbal social interactions. This is combined with a second relative weakness: learning rote tasks requiring visual-motor sequencing. In fact, overall, he appears to have some mild difficulties in organizing and sequencing his perceptions.

Within interpersonal relationships, Mr. C. is likely to experience a moderate level of distance and alienation. However, he also has a sufficient degree of verbal skills and psychological sophistication to begin to work with these feelings. Perhaps his major concern in relationships is the manner in which he deals with anger and dependency. What anger he does experience is likely to be both denied and turned inward in the form of self-criticism. In order to defend himself from the depression which would, and sometimes does, result from this self-criticism, he speeds up his level of activity in an attempt to distract himself from any unpleasant feelings. Another important area in relationships involves significant conflicts regarding strong dependency needs and a sense of being controlled and dominated by females. For example, after a long pause on card 2 of the TAT, he gave the following story fragment:

"Big Mama's looking around. Mother looks like she's overseeing [long pause]. It's a family. The kids are going to school and mother's supervising. No, she's seeing the husband off to work.

The way he resolves this sense of dominance by females is through distracting himself by speeding up his level of activity, by impulsive acting out, or by emotional and/or physical withdrawal.

A significant area of concern is his difficulty in adequately controlling his impulses. In some ways he is overcontrolled in that he is prone to self-criticism and prefers to deny or withdraw from conflict. However, in other ways he is undercontrolled. He experiences a sense of underlying anger and alienation, and also has the energy to act on these feelings. Many of his thoughts and feelings are characterized by antisocial themes. For example, when asked what he would do if he found an addressed envelope with a stamp on it, he initially said, "I would probably soak the stamp off." The following MMPI critical items indicated authority conflicts and family discord:

59: I have often had to take orders from someone who did not know as much as I did. (true)
294: I have never been in trouble with the law. (false)
212: My people treat me more like a child than a grownup. (true)

Furthermore, he has a need for excitement which, given his usually somewhat passive personality, is not likely to be met in overt ways but rather in indirect, impulsive ones. There are some indications that he can adequately control his impulses by being self-critical, withdrawing from conflict, and denying anger. In contrast, his underlying sense of anger, occasionally high energy level, antisocial thoughts, and need for excitement suggest that his pattern of acting out may be somewhat resistant to change.

Mr. C.'s exhibitionism can be perceived as serving the following important functions:

1. It serves as a means of exerting control over his environment. It is significant in this respect that as he feels progressively more passive, distant, and helpless in relationships, his need to exhibit himself increases. The increase in control he achieves through exhibiting, although temporary, reduces his feeling that he is being dominated and controlled by females.
2. Since most direct feelings of anger are denied, exhibitionism serves as an indirect expression of anger. He will then be likely to rationalize his exhibitionism and perceive it as not in fact hostile through ignoring the effects it has on others.
3. Finally, it provides a feeling of excitement.

Mr. C. definitely has the intellectual capability to benefit from therapy and to develop significant insights into his behavior. However, there are numerous difficulties which would be likely to be encountered when working with him. First of all, he would have difficulty focusing on any one topic for any length of time and would tend to go off on irrelevant tangents. Secondly, his anger either would be denied or, in contrast, might be directed indiscriminately at the therapist. Third, his approach to therapy might be manipulative in that he would superficially comply with the rules and make it look "as if" he were attempting to change. He might also attempt to bend the rules and push the limits to see how much he could get away with. Finally, he would be likely to continually rationalize his behavior, denying the effects that it has on others. Even though he might say the "right thing" in therapy to make it look as if he was clearly seeing the consequences, on a deeper, more permanent level, this might still be denied. This is not intended to indicate that he should not enter therapy, but rather that any person working with him would need to confront and deal with these problems.

In summary, Mr. C. is a bright, articulate man who appears, at the present time, to be genuinely remorseful regarding his episodes of exhibitionism. Interpersonally he experiences moderate levels of alienation and has significant conflicts relating to dependency, a sense of being dominated by females, and denied anger. Although his verbal social judgment is good, his ability to control his impulses is sometimes deficient. He does maintain a usually adequate level of control through self-criticism, withdrawal from conflict, and denial of anger. His episodes of exhibitionism serve to increase his experience of control, provide an indirect expression of his underlying anger, and create a sense of excitement. Mr. C. would be likely to benefit from therapy if clear limits were set regarding attendance and payment of fees, and if the therapist was willing to actively work with his distractive maneuvers, underlying anger, testing of limits, and denial of the negative effects he has on others.

Recommendations

1. Individual therapy once a week is recommended, emphasizing a confrontive approach and behavioral techniques, directed towards changing Mr. C.'s episodes of exhibitionism. Therapy should also focus on his relationships with females and creating skills for developing a sense of more overt assertive control.
2. After three months, group therapy should be considered, to enable Mr. C. to more accurately understand the impact he has on others.
3. There should be close monitoring by, and follow-up contact between, his probation officer and his therapist.

RECOMMENDED READING

Hollis, J.W. and Donna, P.A. *Psychological Report Writings: Theory and Practice.* Muncie, In.: Accelerated Development, Inc., 1979.

Sattler, J.M. Report writing. In *Assessment of Children's Intelligence and Special Abilities* (rev. ed.). Boston: Allyn and Bacon, 1982, pp. 491–512.

Appendix A

Distribution of Bender Test Mean Scores
and Standard Deviations.

Age Group	1964 Normative Sample†			1974 Normative Sample‡		
	N	Mean	SD	N	Mean	SD
5–0 to 5–5	81	13.2	3.8	47	13.1	3.3
5–6 to 5–11	128	10.2	3.8	130	9.7	3.4
6–0 to 6–5	155	8.0	3.8	175	8.6	3.3
6–6 to 6–11	180	6.4	3.8	60	7.2	3.5
7–0 to 7–5	156	5.1	3.6	61	5.8	3.3
7–6 to 7–11	110	4.2	3.4	47	4.6	2.8
8–0 to 8–5	62	3.4	3.1	53	4.2	2.5
8–6 to 8–11	60	2.7	2.8	60	3.0	2.5
9–0 to 9–5	65	2.2	2.5	78	2.8	2.2
9–6 to 9–11	49	1.8	2.2	47	2.3	2.1
10–0 to 10–5	27	1.5	1.8	76	1.9	1.9
10–6 to 10–11	31	1.2	1.5	68	1.8	1.8
11–0 to 11–11				73	1.4	1.4

†N = 1104; socioeconomic cross section: 98% white, 2% nonwhite.
‡N = 975; socioeconomic cross section: 86% white, 8.5% black, 1% Oriental, 4.5% Mexican-American and Puerto Rican.

*Reprinted, by permission, from *The Bender Gestalt Test for Young Children, Vol. 2: Research and Applications 1963 1973,* by E.M. Koppitz, Grune & Stratton, 1975.

Appendix B

	Figure A	Figure 1	Figure 2	Figure 3	Figure 4	Figure 5	Figure 6	Figure 7	Figure 8
Adult	100%	25%	100%	100%	100%	100%	100%	100%	100%
11 yr	95%	95%	65%	60%	95%	90%	70%	75%	90%
10 yr	90%	90%	60%	60%	80%	80%	60%	60%	90%
9 yr	80%	75%	60%	70%	80%	70%	80%	65%	70%
8 yr	75%	75%	75%	60%	80%	65%	70%	65%	65%
7 yr	75%	75%	70%	60%	75%	65%	60%	65%	60%
6 yr	75%	75%	60%	80%	75%	60%	60%	60%	75%
5 yr	85%	85%	60%	80%	70%	60%	60%	60%	75%
4 yr	90%	85%	75%	80%	70%	60%	65%	60%	60%
3 yr		← Scribbling →							

Appendix C
Scoring System for the
Bender Gestalt Test
Jack D. Hain, Ph.D.

INSTRUCTIONS

The instructions used here in presenting the Bender Gestalt test are somewhat different from Bender's original instructions. Unless the instructions given here are used in administering this test, this scoring system should not be utilized.

The cards are presented one at a time and are aligned at the top of the sheet of paper. The paper is placed in front of the subject in a vertical position. The subject is told, "Here are some figures (designs) for you to copy. Make your copy as much like the drawing on the card as you can." If the subject asks questions such as, "Should I count the dots," or "Does it have to be exactly like the card," answer, "Just make your drawing as much like this one (indicating the design on the card) as you can."

The subject is allowed to pick up the card, *but* he is not allowed to rotate the card or paper. If he does, the examiner should put the card or paper or both back into the correct orientation and say, "It must be copied this way." The paper may be temporarily turned by the patient to complete one part of a design; but if it seems as if the subject intends to execute the entire design with the paper turned, the examiner should reorient or direct the subject to reorient the paper into its original position.

A. Scoring Directions

Each sign is scored once per record. The Score Sheet [see Appendix D] is designed to facilitate scoring. The easiest and most accurate procedure for scoring is to follow the order of the signs on the record sheet. Consider one sign at a time and review the entire protocol one design at a time by looking for the sign under consideration. When a sign is noted, its weight as given on the Score Sheet is recorded on the Score Sheet in the appropriate place. The procedure is repeated for the next sign and so on until the protocol has been reviewed for all fifteen signs. The total score is the sum of the weights (points) recorded on the Score Sheet.

*From Hain, J.D. ADI 7785, 1964. Courtesy of the Library of Congress. Reprinted by permission of the author.

B. Scoring Criteria

Signs score only on designs indicated in parentheses.

1. Perseveration. Two types of perseveration are scored. If both occur, the sign is scored only once.

(a) Type 1 — Intra-design perseveration (designs 1, 2, 3, 5, and 6)

Design 1: More than 14 dots

Design 2: More than 12 (13) rows where the stimulus figure has 10 (11) rows

Design 3: More than 1 dot in 1st element

4 dots in 2nd

7 dots in 3rd

9 dots in 4th

More than 5 elements

Design 5: More than 27 dots in the arc or more than 10 dots in the diagonal

Design 6: More than 6 crests of sinusoidal waves in either horizontal or vertical waves

(b) Type 2 — Repeated design perseveration (all designs)

Scored when the subject makes and fails to erase or cross out more than two reproductions of any design. If the subject asks if he may repeat the design, the sign is not scored.

2. Rotations and Reversals (all designs). This item is scored if a design is rotated more than 45 degrees from its axis. Reversals (90 degree–270 degree rotations) are scored as rotations. The axes are illustrated below by dotted lines.

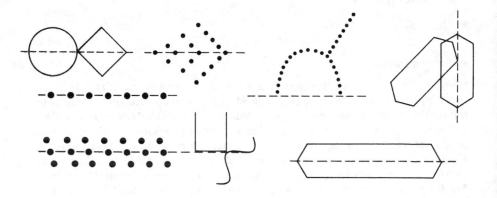

Do not score if only one subpart of a design is rotated. For example, the following do not score for this sign. They score for sign #9 (partial rotation) instead.

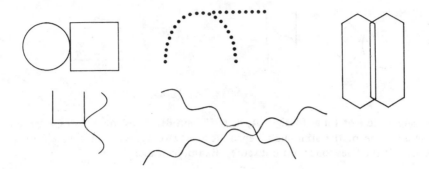

3. Concretism (all designs). This design is rarely encountered. To score, a design must be reproduced as a concrete object other than the stimulus object. Examples are one long unbroken line to represent the line of dots in Figure 1; diagonal lines to represent the rows of circles in Figure 2; a formation of bird-like elements for Figure 3 or Figure 3 drawn to resemble a tree; Figure 6 drawn to resemble snakes. Substitution of a written word such as "dot," "circle," or "angle" for the drawn representation of such elements also scores. Where objects such as birds, trees, or snakes are drawn, the subject will usually verbalize the object he is attempting to draw or often will label the drawing as such. The sign is not scored if a subject only comments that a design resembles some object and does not distort the reproduction in an attempt to make it look like the object.

4. Added Angles (designs A, 4, 7, and 8). This item scores when an extra angle is added. The lines forming the extra angle must be approximately straight and must form a definite angle. Ears score. Curves or arcs resulting in change of direction of a line do not score. Gross tremor resulting in a jagged line does not score. Examples which score:

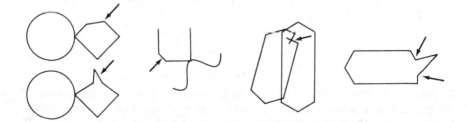

Examples which do not score:

5. Separation of Lines (designs A, 4, 6, 7, and 8). This item scores when any one-unit line of the stimulus is reproduced as two separate lines which do not touch. If the lines touch, do not score. Examples which score:

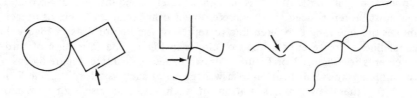

6. Overlap (all designs). This item scores when the elements of one design overlap or run into the "space" of another design. Examples which score:

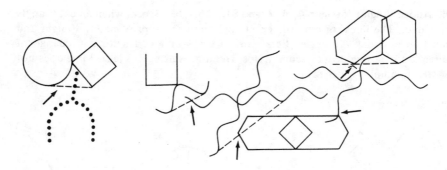

7. Distortion (all designs). This item is scored when there is a destruction of the gestalt of any design so that there is an extreme departure from the stimulus. If the shape of the original stimulus is not recognizable, this item is scored. If the figure has lost its form because of concretism (item 3), this item does not score. Examples which score:

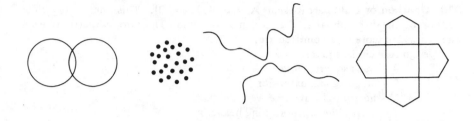

8. Embellishments (designs A, 4, 6, 7, and 8). This deviation occurs rarely; but when it does, it usually is found on curved designs. To score, an extra meaningless line must be included in the design. Extra lines that are not integrated into a design are scored. Such lines are usually in an entirely opposite direction from the line to which they are near or attached. They are easily overlooked in scoring, for they are often small and drawn lightly. Examples which score:

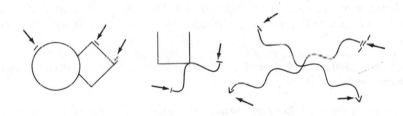

9. Partial Rotations. Two types of partial rotation score:
  Type 1 (all designs) — When a design is rotated more than 20 degrees but less than 45 degrees from its axis (see axis illustrated in Sign 2 above).
  Type 2 (designs A, 4, 5, 6, 7, and 8) — When one, and only one, subpart is rotated more than 20 degrees, this item scores.

Examples that score:

10. Omission of a Subpart (designs A, 4, 5, 6, 7, and 8). This item scores when either of the two subparts of a design is omitted. The two subparts of each design which score when omitted are:

Design A — circle, square
      4 — open square, curve
      5 — arc, diagonal extension
      6 — horizontal wavy line, vertical wavy line
      7 — vertical hexagon, leaning hexagon
      8 — hexagon, center diamond

11. Abbreviation (designs 1 and 2).
    Design 1: Scores when the design is reproduced with less than 11 dots
    Design 2: Scores where the design is reproduced with less than 9 (10) rows
            of circles where the stimulus figure has 10 (11) rows

12. Separation (designs A, 4, 5, 6, 7, and 8). This sign scores when there is a separation between subparts of a design. If the subparts touch at all, the sign does not score. The designs and subparts involved in this score are the same as those outlined in Omission of Subpart item above.

13. Absence of Erasures. This item scores if there is a failure to attempt to erase blatant errors. If there is any erasure on any design, this item does not score.

14. Closure (designs A, 4, 7, and 8). This item scores when on any one design more than one angle is not closed.

15. Design A Point of Contact (design A). This item scores when the square and circle touch so that either (a) the point of the square penetrates the circle with space seen within the overlap or (b) the square is imperfectly formed so that two of its sides do not join each other but touch the circle.
    Example: (a)

      (b)

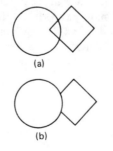

(a)

(b)

Appendix D
Bender Adult Scoring Sheet*

Name: _____

Date: _____

BENDER GESTALT TEST SCORE SHEET

4 Points
Perseveration   _____
Rotation or Reversal   _____
Concretism   _____

3 Points
Added Angles   _____
Separation of Lines   _____
Overlap   _____
Distortion   _____

2 Points
Embellishments   _____
Partial Rotation   _____

1 Point
Omission   _____
Abbreviation #1 or #2   _____
Separation   _____
Absence of Erasure   _____
Closure   _____
Point of Contact on Figure A   _____

         TOTAL   _____

Appendix E
Questions for the
House-Tree-Person Test

HOUSE

1. Is there anybody who lives in the house?
2. Does the person you drew live in the house?
3. How do the other people who live in the house feel about this person?
4. How does the person you drew feel about the house?
5. Do you think the house is strong or weak?
6. Do you think it would be difficult to get into the house?
7. What sort of activities occur in the house?
8. If the house were a person, how would it feel?
9. If there was a fire in the house, what do you think the person you drew would do?
10. What are the strongest and what are the weakest parts of the house?

TREE

1. What type of tree is this?
2. How does the person you drew feel about the tree?
3. What would the person like to use the tree for?
4. What are the weakest and strongest parts of the tree?
5. Is the tree flexible or rather rigid?
6. Would it be easy to climb the tree?
7. Are there any birds or other animals which live in the tree?
8. If the person you drew were to hurt the tree, how would he/she feel?
9. What do the people in the house think of the tree?
10. Do you think the tree is attractive or unattractive?

PERSON

1. Is the person you drew a male or a female?
2. How does he/she usually feel?
3. What things does this person most like to do?
4. What does he/she least like to do?
5. What are the best and worst qualities of the person?
6. What sort of things make this person angry?
7. What does he/she do when angry?
8. What sort of an animal does this person most remind you of?
9. What part of this person is the strongest and what is the weakest?
10. What do other people usually think of this person?

Appendix F
Percentages for Roschach
Form Quality

**Mean Percentages (%) of +, *o, w,* and – Scorings
in the Protocols of Four Reference Groups.**

Scoring	Nonpsychiatric (N = 200)	Outpatient (N = 100)	Inpatient Nonschizophrenic (N = 70)	Inpatient Schizophrenic (N = 125)
+	26	31	16	21
o	58	47	65	37
w	12	14	15	24
–	4	8	4	19

*Reprinted, by permission, from Exner, J.E. *The Rorschach: A Comprehensive System,* New York: John Wiley & Sons, 1974, p. 248. Copyright 1974 by John Wiley & Sons, Inc.

Appendix G

Group Means for Rorschach Location, Determinant, and Some Content Scores, and Various Summary Scores for Adult Nonpatients plus Four Psychiatric Groups.

Category	Nonpatient (N = 325) M	SD	Outpatient Nonpsychotic (N = 185) M	SD	Inpatient Character Problems (N = 90) M	SD	Inpatient Depressive (N = 155) M	SD	Inpatient Schizophrenic (N = 210) M	SD
R	21.75	5.1	25.20	6.3	22.35	4.8	16.50	4.3	24.20	7.2
LOCATION FEATURES										
W	7.04	2.8	6.47	3.1	8.23	3.7	5.29	2.4	7.38	3.2
D	13.50	4.7	15.92	5.6	13.22	5.2	9.42	3.2	11.49	4.1
Dd	1.21	1.1	2.81	1.1	0.91	0.6	1.79	0.8	5.33	2.7
S	1.05	0.7	2.64	1.3	3.48	1.3	1.26	0.9	1.74	1.2
DETERMINANTS										
F	9.83	3.2	7.87	3.6	7.13	2.8	5.61	2.4	7.29	3.8
M	3.48	1.8	3.77	2.2	1.85	0.9	2.13	1.1	3.92	1.9
FM	2.36	1.4	4.12	1.6	3.95	1.2	2.07	1.3	2.96	1.2
m	0.73	0.6	1.21	0.8	1.23	1.1	1.35	0.9	1.18	0.8
FM + m	3.09	1.5	5.33	1.9	5.18	2.2	3.42	1.6	4.14	1.9
FC	3.56	1.2	1.72	1.3	1.41	1.2	0.87	1.1	1.87	1.3
CF	1.23	0.9	2.81	1.4	3.22	1.8	1.93	1.2	3.31	1.6
C + Cn	0.48	0.6	1.13	1.1	1.30	1.3	0.56	0.8	1.56	0.9
Sum C	5.27	2.3	5.66	2.7	6.13	4.3	3.36	1.4	6.74	2.9
Sum weighted C	3.73	1.8	5.37	3.1	6.18	3.9	3.21	1.8	6.58	3.7
FC' + C'F + C'	0.63	0.8	1.41	0.9	0.94	0.7	1.91	1.1	1.18	1.2
FT + TF + T	1.18	0.9	2.57	1.3	1.05	0.8	1.78	1.0	2.36	1.4
FY + YF + Y	1.11	0.6	2.34	1.2	0.82	0.9	2.16	1.1	0.94	0.8
FV + VF + V	0.36	0.3	1.13	0.9	0.21	0.4	1.89	0.8	0.64	0.9
RATIOS AND DERIVATIONS										
P	6.45	2.7	7.41	3.1	6.83	3.1	4.94	2.3	2.48	1.8
Lambda	0.82	0.3	0.45	0.4	0.47	0.4	0.52	0.3	0.43	0.2
X + %	0.81	0.12	0.78	0.13	0.75	0.14	0.73	0.09	0.57	0.14
F + %	0.89	0.08	0.83	0.13	0.85	0.11	0.77	0.10	0.62	0.08
A%	0.39	0.08	0.42	0.07	0.51	0.08	0.46	0.07	0.31	0.10
Afr	0.69	0.06	0.82	0.09	0.96	0.13	0.61	0.08	0.95	0.12
EA > ep (frequency)	229	–	87	–	19	–	68	–	72	–
H + Hd	4.74	1.4	3.93	1.6	3.77	1.4	2.96	0.92	3.14	1.1

*Reprinted, by permission, from Exner, J.E. *The Rorschach: A Comprehensive System,* Vol. 2, New York: John Wiley & Sons, 1978, pp. 4–5. Copyright 1978 by John Wiley & Sons, Inc..

Appendix H

Group Means for Rorschach Location, Determinant, and Some Content Scores, plus Various Summary Scores for Nonpatients and Two Psychiatric Groups, for Ages 5 through 16.

	5 Year Olds						6 Year Olds					
	Non-patients N = 70		Behavior Problems N = 45		With-drawn N = 30		Non-patients N = 80		Behavior Problems N = 55		With-drawn N = 40	
Category	M	SD	M	SD	M	SD	M	SD	M	SD	M	SD
R	15.6	4.1	13.7	3.5	13.9	3.4	16.7	4.4	14.8	3.9	15.9	4.6
LOCATION												
W	9.4	3.6	8.6	2.8	7.4	2.6	8.8	3.2	8.2	3.6	7.2	2.9
D	5.8	2.1	4.9	1.8	5.3	1.9	6.3	2.4	5.7	2.5	6.4	3.1
Dd	0.4	0.3	0.2	0.4	2.2	1.3	1.6	1.0	0.9	0.6	2.3	1.8
S	1.1	0.7	1.9	0.6	0.7	0.6	1.3	0.6	1.8	0.7	1.5	0.8
DETERMINANTS												
F	7.7	2.6	5.6	2.3	5.8	2.6	7.9	2.8	5.4	3.1	5.9	2.7
M	0.9	0.6	0.5	0.4	1.4	0.8	1.2	0.7	0.8	0.6	1.5	0.7
FM + m	2.7	1.3	2.6	1.4	2.2	1.3	3.0	1.3	3.3	1.4	2.1	0.9
FC	0.4	0.6	0.3	0.3	1.4	0.8	0.7	0.5	0.4	0.4	1.3	0.8
CF + C + Cn	1.9	1.2	2.7	1.4	1.8	1.1	2.3	1.2	2.9	1.2	2.0	0.7
Weighted sum C	3.1	1.6	4.2	1.9	2.7	1.5	3.7	1.8	4.2	1.7	2.9	1.4
Sum C'	0.2	0.3	0.8	0.5	1.0	0.7	0.3	0.2	0.7	0.4	1.2	0.8
Sum T	0.8	0.4	1.2	0.8	1.3	0.6	0.9	0.4	1.1	0.6	1.1	0.5
Sum Y	0.5	0.4	0.7	0.4	0.6	0.4	0.7	0.4	0.3	0.2	1.0	0.6
Sum V	0	–	0	–	0	–	0	–	0.2	0.2	0.7	0.5
Sum all shading	1.5	0.7	2.7	1.1	2.9	1.2	1.9	1.1	2.3	1.1	4.0	2.3

| | 5 Year Olds | | | | | | 6 Year Olds | | | | | |
| | Non-patients N = 70 | | Behavior Problems N = 45 | | With-drawn N = 30 | | Non-patients N = 80 | | Behavior Problems N = 55 | | With-drawn N = 40 | |
Category	M	SD	M	SD	M	SD	M	SD	M	SD	M	SD
RATIOS AND DERIVATIONS												
P	3.1	2.2	3.5	1.9	3.7	2.1	3.8	1.7	3.4	1.8	4.2	2.4
Lambda	.97	.38	.69	.26	.72	.29	.90	.31	.57	.27	.59	.24
X + %	.79	.11	.72	.19	.74	.13	.85	.13	.74	.09	.77	.12
F + %	.82	.10	.76	.17	.78	.08	.88	.07	.73	.11	.79	.09
A%	.54	.14	.63	.21	.58	.13	.55	.08	.61	.13	.51	.10
Afr	1.06	.27	1.36	.34	0.91	.21	0.98	.29	1.04	.19	0.86	.13
H + Hd	2.7	1.2	1.6	1.0	1.4	.08	3.6	1.4	3.8	1.8	2.9	1.1
RATIO DIRECTIONALITY (FREQUENCIES)												
EA > ep	9(13%)		1(2%)		5(16%)		14(17%)		5(9%)		9(23%)	
M > sum C	4(5%)		0		7(23%)		13(16%)		1(2%)		10(25%)	

*Reprinted, by permission, from Exner, J.E. *The Rorschach: A Comprehensive System,* Vol. 2, New York: John Wiley & Sons, 1978, pp. 7–12. Copyright 1978 by John Wiley & Sons, Inc.

	7 Year Olds						8 Year Olds					
	Non-patients N = 95		Behavior Problems N = 60		Withdrawn N = 35		Non-patients N = 100		Behavior Problems N = 85		Withdrawn N = 45	
Category	M	SD	M	SD	M	SD	M	SD	M	SD	M	SD
R	18.7	4.6	17.1	3.7	16.7	3.8	20.3	4.4	18.1	3.8	17.2	3.6
LOCATION												
W	9.1	2.9	9.8	3.0	8.2	2.6	9.5	2.8	9.4	3.1	8.7	2.7
D	8.2	1.8	6.4	2.5	6.1	1.7	9.1	3.2	7.6	2.8	7.3	2.1
Dd	1.4	0.8	0.9	0.7	2.4	1.1	1.7	0.6	1.1	0.6	1.2	0.7
S	2.3	0.9	2.4	1.1	0.9	0.6	1.6	0.8	2.2	1.2	0.9	0.5
DETERMINANTS												
F	8.3	2.6	6.4	2.1	5.1	1.9	8.5	2.6	7.2	2.8	4.9	1.8
M	1.5	0.8	1.1	0.6	2.3	0.8	1.9	0.9	1.3	0.7	2.8	1.4
FM + m	3.1	1.2	3.4	1.6	2.5	1.1	2.8	0.7	3.6	1.3	2.3	1.1
FC	1.2	0.6	0.4	0.3	1.6	0.8	1.1	0.7	0.6	0.4	1.2	0.8
CF + C + Cn	2.7	1.1	2.9	1.1	2.0	0.9	2.6	0.9	3.1	1.4	1.6	0.7
Weighted sum C	3.8	1.4	4.9	1.8	2.8	1.2	3.1	1.2	4.2	1.7	2.4	0.9
Sum C'	0.5	0.3	0.4	0.3	1.2	0.6	0.3	0.2	0.6	0.4	1.2	0.7
Sum T	0.8	0.5	1.2	0.8	1.4	0.9	0.9	0.6	1.3	0.7	1.9	1.1
Sum Y	0.4	0.3	0.6	0.2	1.0	0.6	0.2	0.2	0.5	0.3	0.9	0.4
Sum V	0	—	0	—	0.3	0.2	0.2	0.2	0	—	0.6	0.3
Sum all shading	1.7	0.9	2.2	0.8	3.9	1.4	1.6	0.7	2.4	1.1	3.6	1.5
RATIOS AND DERIVATIONS												
P	4.1	1.3	3.7	1.8	5.2	1.9	4.4	1.8	3.5	1.3	5.1	2.1
Lambda	.81	.24	.60	.16	.44	.21	.72	.19	.66	.14	.40	.26
X + %	.85	.11	.73	.15	.79	.13	.87	.13	.71	.16	.74	.13
F + %	.82	.10	.76	.12	.80	.09	.79	.12	.74	.08	.81	.11
A%	.52	.12	.58	.15	.62	.14	.51	.09	.56	.12	.59	.10
Afr	0.89	.19	0.96	.16	0.72	.13	0.82	.13	0.92	.14	0.74	.14
H + Hd	3.9	1.1	3.1	1.3	3.0	1.2	4.3	1.6	3.7	1.4	3.2	1.1
RATIO DIRECTIONALITY (FREQUENCIES)												
EA > ep	18(19%)		8(13%)		10(28%)		24(24%)		14(16%)		13(29%)	
M > sum C	21(22%)		5(8%)		14(40%)		26(26%)		11(13%)		16(36%)	

| | 9 Year Olds | | | | | | 10 Year Olds | | | | | |
| | Non-patients N = 100 | | Behavior Problems N = 90 | | Withdrawn N = 35 | | Non-patients N = 100 | | Behavior Problems N = 100 | | Withdrawn N = 40 | |
Category	M	SD	M	SD	M	SD	M	SD	M	SD	M	SD
R	20.6	4.7	18.2	4.3	17.1	3.8	20.1	4.5	18.9	4.1	16.9	4.1
LOCATION												
W	9.9	3.1	7.8	2.9	7.4	3.0	9.4	2.8	7.0	2.7	7.3	2.9
D	9.2	2.6	9.7	2.6	7.3	2.5	9.1	2.6	10.4	3.1	7.8	2.3
Dd	1.5	0.6	0.7	0.4	2.4	1.1	1.6	0.8	1.5	0.6	1.8	1.2
S	1.2	0.5	2.7	1.1	2.3	0.9	1.4	0.6	2.5	0.8	2.6	0.9
DETERMINANTS												
F	8.9	3.2	9.1	3.1	6.1	2.2	9.1	2.4	9.8	2.5	5.8	1.6
M	1.8	0.8	1.1	0.7	2.8	1.1	1.9	0.9	1.3	0.7	2.6	0.8
FM + m	3.2	1.2	3.6	1.1	2.7	0.9	3.1	0.7	3.0	1.8	2.8	1.1
FC	1.2	0.7	0.7	0.4	2.1	0.8	1.4	0.8	0.6	0.3	2.3	0.9
CF + C + Cn	2.1	0.8	2.6	1.1	1.9	0.9	2.0	0.7	2.8	1.2	1.8	0.7
Weighted sum C	2.9	1.1	3.9	1.4	3.1	1.4	2.8	0.9	4.3	1.3	2.7	0.9
Sum C'	0.5	0.2	0.3	0.1	0.9	0.5	0.4	0.3	0.2	0.2	0.8	0.4
Sum T	0.9	0.6	1.1	0.7	1.4	0.6	0.8	0.4	0.9	0.5	1.1	0.6
Sum Y	0.3	0.1	0.2	0.2	0.7	0.4	0.4	0.2	0.3	0.2	0.7	0.5
Sum V	0	–	0	–	0.4	0.2	0.2	0.1	0.5	0.3	0.4	0.2
Sum all shading	1.7	0.8	1.6	1.0	3.4	1.3	1.8	0.8	1.9	0.7	3.0	1.1
RATIOS AND DERIVATIONS												
P	4.8	1.3	4.1	1.6	6.4	2.1	5.7	1.4	4.8	1.4	6.7	2.1
Lambda	.76	.13	1.00	.23	.57	.16	.82	.14	1.07	.27	.52	.16
X + %	.86	.09	.74	.08	.78	.10	.84	.08	.75	.11	.72	.13
F + %	.89	.11	.76	.09	.71	.08	.82	.08	.73	.14	.72	.09
A%	.47	.09	.57	.13	.58	.11	.48	.09	.55	.08	.61	.11
Afr	0.88	.14	1.04	.19	0.69	.12	0.91	.12	1.16	.17	0.71	.16
H + Hd	3.8	1.2	2.9	0.8	3.3	1.1	4.1	1.3	2.7	0.9	3.9	1.1

RATIO DIRECTIONALITY (FREQUENCIES)

EA > ep	29(29%)	17(19%)	10(29%)	33(33%)	26(26%)	16(40%)
M > sum C	26(26%)	16(18%)	19(54%)	27(27%)	18(18%)	17(43%)

| Category | 11 Year Olds | | | | | | 12 Year Olds | | | | | |
| | Non-patients N = 100 | | Behavior Problems N = 75 | | With-drawn N = 50 | | Non-patients N = 100 | | Behavior Problems N = 85 | | With-drawn N = 45 | |
	M	SD	M	SD	M	SD	M	SD	M	SD	M	SD
R	19.7	4.2	19.6	4.8	17.7	3.8	20.4	4.6	19.8	3.9	18.1	3.9
LOCATION												
W	8.4	3.1	7.0	1.9	7.4	2.6	7.9	3.7	7.3	3.6	6.8	3.1
D	11.0	3.3	10.4	3.1	9.2	1.4	12.3	2.7	11.4	3.2	8.8	2.9
Dd	1.3	0.7	2.2	0.9	1.1	0.4	1.1	0.7	1.1	0.8	2.5	1.1
S	1.4	0.4	2.6	1.1	2.4	0.9	1.2	0.6	2.2	0.7	2.6	0.9
DETERMINANTS												
F	9.3	3.2	9.6	3.2	5.9	2.1	8.9	2.7	10.1	3.6	6.4	1.9
M	2.5	1.2	1.9	0.8	2.3	0.8	2.7	1.0	1.7	0.8	3.1	1.2
FM + m	3.1	0.9	3.7	1.5	2.4	1.3	3.3	1.2	3.8	1.1	2.8	1.1
FC	2.0	0.8	1.8	0.9	2.2	1.0	2.7	1.3	2.1	0.8	2.1	1.1
CF + C + Cn	2.2	1.0	2.9	1.4	1.7	.07	2.1	0.9	3.1	1.1	2.0	0.7
Weighted sum C	3.3	1.2	4.6	1.2	3.1	.09	3.4	1.2	4.9	1.6	3.1	0.8
Sum C'	0.3	0.1	0.4	0.1	0.9	0.7	0.5	0.3	0.2	0.2	1.1	0.6
Sum T	0.7	0.4	0.5	0.3	1.1	0.4	1.0	0.4	0.1	0.1	0.9	0.4
Sum Y	0.2	0.1	0.1	0.1	0.7	0.4	0.5	0.3	0.2	0.1	0.6	0.3
Sum V	0	—	0.2	0.1	0.4	0.3	0.2	0.1	0.4	0.2	0.6	0.4
Sum all shading	1.2	0.6	1.2	0.9	3.1	1.2	2.2	0.8	0.9	0.5	3.2	1.3
RATIOS AND DERIVATIONS												
P	6.1	2.1	4.7	1.5	6.8	2.2	6.3	2.1	4.9	1.8	6.2	2.3
Lambda	.89	.17	.96	.13	.50	.14	.77	.12	1.04	.23	.55	.10
X + %	.83	.09	.72	.11	.75	.14	.81	.10	.70	.09	.77	.08
F + %	.81	.11	.74	.13	.72	.08	.86	.09	.76	.07	.78	.10
A%	.48	.08	.55	.09	.53	.11	.49	.11	.56	.09	.59	.09
Afr	0.81	.11	0.96	.12	0.69	.16	0.83	.09	0.97	.13	0.64	.14
H + Hd	4.2	1.2	3.1	1.4	3.7	1.2	4.4	1.3	2.9	1.1	3.9	1.8

RATIO DIRECTIONALITY (FREQUENCIES)

EA > ep	49(49%)		26(35%)	17(38%)	52(52%)	27(32%)	20(44%)
M > sum C	31(31%)		20(24%)	26(52%)	34(34%)	19(22%)	22(49%)

| | 13 Year Olds | | | | | | 14 Year Olds | | | | | |
| | Non-patients N = 80 | | Behavior Problems N = 65 | | With-drawn N = 35 | | Non-patients N = 100 | | Behavior Problems N = 75 | | With-drawn N = 40 | |
Category	M	SD	M	SD	M	SD	M	SD	M	SD	M	SD
R	20.7	4.9	19.4	5.1	17.6	4.6	21.8	5.3	19.6	4.5	17.2	4.8
LOCATION												
W	7.4	2.1	6.8	2.4	5.7	2.5	7.9	2.4	7.3	2.2	5.9	2.1
D	11.8	3.6	11.4	2.9	9.8	2.1	12.1	3.3	11.2	2.7	9.1	2.3
Dd	1.5	0.7	1.2	0.9	2.1	0.9	1.8	1.1	1.1	0.6	2.2	1.2
S	0.7	0.4	2.4	1.2	1.6	0.7	0.8	0.5	2.6	1.3	1.9	0.8
DETERMINANTS												
F	8.9	2.7	9.3	3.1	5.4	1.6	9.3	2.6	10.3	3.9	6.1	1.9
M	2.7	1.1	1.4	0.8	3.6	1.4	2.8	1.2	1.6	0.9	3.3	1.2
FM + m	3.4	1.6	3.6	1.5	3.9	1.8	3.1	1.1	3.8	1.4	3.5	1.7
FC	1.8	0.8	0.9	0.7	2.7	1.2	2.0	1.3	1.1	0.8	2.9	1.2
CF + C + Cn	2.1	0.9	2.7	1.3	1.6	0.9	2.4	1.1	2.5	1.3	1.4	0.7
Weighted sum C	3.8	1.6	4.4	1.8	3.1	1.2	3.6	1.4	4.3	1.5	3.3	1.3
Sum C'	0.3	0.2	1.3	0.8	0.9	0.7	0.2	0.2	1.1	0.8	1.1	0.6
Sum T	0.7	0.5	1.6	0.9	1.2	0.6	0.6	0.4	1.3	0.7	1.0	0.4
Sum Y	0.4	0.2	0.6	0.3	0.9	0.6	0.3	0.2	0.5	0.3	0.8	0.5
Sum V	0.3	0.2	0.2	0.2	0.8	0.5	0.2	0.1	0.3	0.2	0.7	0.4
Sum all shading	1.7	0.8	3.7	1.4	3.8	1.2	1.3	0.7	3.2	1.6	3.6	1.4
RATIOS AND DERIVATIONS												
P	6.4	2.1	5.4	1.8	6.7	2.3	6.1	2.3	5.5	2.4	6.8	2.2
Lambda	.75	.13	.92	.23	.44	.18	.74	.16	1.10	.26	.55	.17
X + %	.82	.09	.74	.11	.78	.13	.84	.10	.72	.09	.79	.11
F + %	.80	.08	.76	.12	.81	.09	.79	.08	.74	.11	.83	.09
A%	.44	.08	.57	.10	.38	.12	.46	.07	.54	.09	.36	.12
Afr	0.72	.14	0.89	.15	0.63	.16	0.74	.11	0.91	.14	0.61	.19
H + Hd	4.2	1.3	3.7	1.6	3.3	1.1	4.6	1.8	3.6	1.2	3.9	1.7
RATIO DIRECTIONALITY (FREQUENCIES)												
EA > ep	36(45%)		22(34%)		23(66%)		54(54%)		29(39%)		22(55%)	
M > sum C	23(29%)		9(14%)		24(69%)		31(31%)		11(15%)		26(65%)	

Category	15 Year Olds						16 Year Olds					
	Non-patients N = 100		Behavior Problems N = 80		With-drawn N = 45		Non-patients N = 100		Behavior Problems N = 100		With-drawn N = 65	
	M	SD	M	SD	M	SD	M	SD	M	SD	M	SD
R	21.4	5.2	19.9	4.8	17.9	4.6	22.7	5.1	19.4	4.5	18.1	4.7
LOCATION												
W	8.4	3.1	7.6	2.8	6.2	2.1	9.4	3.2	7.3	2.8	6.6	2.9
D	11.7	3.2	11.8	3.6	9.5	1.4	12.1	2.9	11.3	3.1	9.4	2.6
Dd	1.3	0.8	0.5	0.3	2.7	1.1	1.2	0.6	0.8	0.6	2.1	0.8
S	0.5	0.3	2.3	0.9	1.7	1.1	0.6	0.4	2.7	1.2	1.9	0.8
DETERMINANTS												
F	9.7	2.6	9.1	2.4	5.4	1.3	9.9	2.8	9.5	2.8	6.2	1.4
M	2.6	1.1	2.0	0.8	3.6	1.3	2.8	0.9	1.9	1.1	3.4	1.2
FM + m	3.3	1.3	4.3	1.2	3.1	1.2	3.0	1.2	3.8	1.4	2.8	1.4
FC	2.1	0.8	1.3	0.7	3.2	1.1	1.9	0.9	1.6	0.8	3.1	1.3
CF + C + Cn	2.0	0.9	3.2	1.1	1.6	0.7	2.1	1.1	3.4	1.3	1.8	0.9
Weighted sum C	3.1	1.2	4.7	1.5	3.0	1.4	3.3	0.9	4.9	1.7	3.3	1.1
Sum C'	0.4	0.2	1.1	0.7	1.4	0.9	0.5	0.3	0.9	0.6	1.2	0.8
Sum T	0.9	0.5	1.3	0.8	1.7	0.8	0.8	0.4	1.0	0.4	1.4	0.9
Sum Y	0.2	0.1	0.6	0.4	1.1	0.7	0.3	0.2	0.4	0.3	0.9	0.6
Sum V	0.4	0.2	0.2	0.2	0.8	0.3	0.3	0.1	0.2	0.1	0.7	0.4
Sum all shading	1.9	0.8	3.2	1.4	5.0	1.6	1.9	1.1	2.5	1.2	4.2	1.3
RATIOS AND DERIVATIONS												
P	6.7	1.1	5.5	1.2	6.8	1.6	6.4	1.5	5.2	1.8	6.2	1.3
Lambda	.83	.08	.84	.16	.44	.13	.77	.11	.96	.18	.52	.14
X + %	.80	.08	.73	.13	.78	.09	.84	.08	.71	.09	.81	.10
F + %	.83	.11	.77	.08	.79	.12	.85	.10	.78	.08	.76	.09
A%	.43	.08	.53	.11	.42	.09	.46	.13	.51	.09	.39	.12
Afr	0.79	.17	0.89	.15	0.61	.19	0.73	.10	0.85	.11	0.58	.17
H + Hd	4.6	1.3	3.6	1.2	4.0	1.2	4.8	1.4	3.2	1.6	4.2	1.2
RATIO DIRECTIONALITY (FREQUENCIES)												
EA > ep	64(64%)		29(36%)		22(49%)		63(63%)		31(31%)		30(46%)	
M > sum C	39(39%)		14(18%)		31(68%)		37(37%)		22(22%)		44(68%)	

Appendix I
MMPI Critical Terms*

Distress and Depression

    5. I am easily awakened by noise. (true)

  27. Evil spirits possess me at times. (true)

  86. I am certainly lacking in self-confidence. (true)

142. I certainly feel useless at times. (true)

152. Most nights I go to sleep without thoughts or ideas bothering me. (false)

158. I cry easily. (true)

168. There is something wrong with my mind. (true)

178. My memory seems to be all right. (false)

182. I am afraid of losing my mind. (true)

259. I have difficulty in starting to do things. (true)

337. I feel anxiety about something or someone almost all the time. (true)

Guilt and Suicide

  88. I usually feel that life is worthwhile. (false)

139. Sometimes I feel as if I must injure either myself or someone else. (true)

202. I believe I am a condemned person. (true)

209. I believe my sins are unpardonable. (true)

339. Most of the time I wish I were dead. (false)

Ideas of Reference, Persecution, and Delusions

33 and/or 331. If people had not had it in for me I would have been much more successful. (true)

110. Someone has it in for me. (true)

121. I believe I am being plotted against. (true)

123. I believe I am being followed. (true)

151. Someone has been trying to poison me. (true)

200. There are persons who are trying to steal my thoughts and ideas. (true)

275. Someone has control over my mind. (true)

284. I am sure I am being talked about. (true)

---

*Listing of critical items reprinted by permission of Alex B. Caldwell, Ph.D., Caldwell Report, 3122 Santa Monica Blvd., Santa Monica, CA 90404. Items from the MMPI reproduced by permission of the University of Minnesota; © 1943, renewed 1970.

293. Someone has been trying to influence my mind. (true)
347. I have no enemies who really wish to harm me. (false)
364. People say insulting and vulgar things about me. (true)

Peculiar Experiences and Hallucinations

33 and/or 323. I have had very peculiar and strange experiences. (true)
48. When I am with people I am bothered by hearing very queer things. (true)
66. I see things or animals or people around me that others do not see. (true)
184. I commonly hear voices without knowing where they come from. (true)
291. At one or more times in my life I felt that someone was making me do things by hypnotizing me. (true)
334. Peculiar odors come to me at times. (true)
345. I often feel as if things were not real. (true)
349. I have strange and peculiar thoughts. (true)
350. I hear strange things when I am alone. (true)

Sexual Difficulties

20. My sex life is satisfactory. (false)
37 and/or 302. I have never been in trouble because of my sex behavior. (false)
69. I am very strongly attracted by members of my own sex. (true)
74. I have often wished I were a girl. (Or if you are a girl) I have never been sorry that I am a girl. (male: true; female: false)
133. I have never indulged in any unusual sex practices. (false)
179. I am worried about sex matters. (true)
297. I wish I were not bothered by thoughts about sex. (true)

Authority Problems

38 and/or 311. During one period when I was a youngster I engaged in petty thievery. (true)
59. I have often had to take orders from someone who did not know as much as I did. (true)
118. In school I was sometimes sent to the principal for cutting up. (true)
205. At times it has been impossible for me to keep from stealing or shoplifting something. (true)
294. I have never been in trouble with the law. (false)

Alcohol and Drugs

156. I have had periods in which I carried on activities without knowing later what I had been doing. (true)
215. I have used alcohol excessively. (true)

251. I have had blank spells in which my activities were interrupted and I did not know what was going on around me. (true)
460. I have used alcohol moderately (or not at all). (false)

Family Disorder

21 and/or 308. At times I have very much wanted to leave home. (true)
96. I have very few quarrels with members of my family. (false)
137. I believe that my home life is as pleasant as that of most people I know. (false)
212. My people treat me more like a child than a grown-up. (true)
216. There is very little love and companionship in my family as compared to other homes. (true)
237. My relatives are nearly all in sympathy with me. (false)
245. My parents and family find more fault with me than they should. (true)

Somatic Concerns

2. I have a good appetite. (false)
9. I am about as able to work as I ever was. (false)
23. I am troubled by attacks of nausea and vomiting. (true)
55. I am almost never bothered by pains over the heart or in my chest. (false)
114. Often I feel as if there were a tight band about my head. (true)
125. I have a great deal of stomach trouble. (true)
153. During the past few years I have been well most of the time. (false)
175. I seldom or never have dizzy spells. (false)
189. I feel weak all over much of the time. (true)
243. I have few or no pains. (false)

Appendix J
MMPI Scoring Directions

1. Place score keys, one at a time, over the answer sheet and count the number of blackened holes. Be careful to use the keys for the front on the front side of the answer sheet, and the keys for the back on the back side. Record the totals for each score key on the place indicated at the side of the answer sheet.
2. Transfer the totals for each scale (be sure to add totals for front and back in each scale) onto the profile sheet beneath the graph.
3. "?" is determined by counting the number of responses left blank on the answer sheet. "L" is determined by counting the number of FALSE responses on items #15, 45, 75, 105, 135, 165, 195, 225, 255, 285, 30, 60, 90, 120, 150.
4. On the small table at the right of the profile, locate the "K" total in the "K" column, and draw a line under the other numbers to the right. Now add the required amount of "K" beneath the scale totals. You can get these amounts quickly on the table just consulted. For example, if "K" is 10, draw a line in the table at 10 on the "K" column. You then have K = 10; .5K = 5; .4K = 4; .2K = 2. Add these numbers to the following scales, as indicated: Hs + .5K; Pd + .4K; Sc + 1K; Ma + .2K.
5. Plot all the raw scores (with "K" added when indicated) by marking the raw score for each scale on the profile with the raw scores which have been determined in the columns below in steps 2 or 4. T scores can be noted by looking either to the right or left side of the profile sheet. For example, a raw score of 25 on scale 2 for males converts to a T score of 70.

References

Abrams, E. Prediction of intelligence from certain Rorschach factors. *Journal of Clinical Psychology,* 1955, *11,* 81–83.

Ackerman, P.T., Peters, J.R., and Dykman, R.A. Children with specific learning disabilities: Bender Gestalt Test findings and other signs. *Journal of Learning Disabilities,* 1971, *4,* 437–446.

Adams, H., Cooper, G., and Carrera, R. The Rorschach and the MMPI: a concurrent validity study. *Journal of Projective Techniques,* 1963, *27,* 23–24.

Adcock, C.J. Thematic Apperception Test. A review. In Buros, O.K. (Ed.) *The Sixth Mental Measurements Yearbook,* Vol. I. Highland Park, N.J.: Gryphon Press, 1965, pp. 533–535.

Affleck, D.C. and Mednick, S.A. The use of the Rorschach test in the prediction of the abrupt terminator in individual psychotherapy. *Journal of Consulting Psychology,* 1959, *23,* 125–128.

Alcock, T. *The Rorschach in Practice.* Philadelphia: J.B. Lippincott, 1963.

Alden and Benton, A.L. Relationship of sex of examiner to incidence of Rorschach responses with sexual context. *Journal of Projective Techniques,* 1951, *15,* 231–234.

Alker, H.A. Minnesota Multiphasic Personality Inventory: a review. In Buros, O.K. (Ed.) *The Eighth Mental Measurements Yearbook,* Vol. I. Highland Park, N.J.: Gryphon Press, 1978, pp. 931–935.

Allen, R.M. *Introduction to the Rorschach Technique.* New York: International Universities Press, 1953.

Allen, R.M. *Elements of Rorschach Interpretation.* New York: Harper & Row, 1954.

Allison, J. and Blatt, S.J. The relationship of Rorschach whole responses to intelligence. *Journal of Projective Techniques,* 1964, *28,* 255–260.

Allison, J., Blatt, S.J., and Zimet, C.N. *The Interpretation of Psychological Tests.* New York: Harper & Row, 1968.

American Psychiatric Association. *Diagnostic and Statistical Manual of Mental Disorders* (3rd ed.). Washington, D.C.: 1980.

American Psychological Association. *Casebook on Ethical Standards of Psychologists.* Washington, D.C.: 1967.

American Psychological Association. *Standards for Educational and Psychological Tests.* Washington, D.C.: 1974.

American Psychological Association. *Ethical Principals of Psychologists.* Washington, D.C.: 1981.

Ames, L.B. Further check on the diagnostic validity of the Ames danger signals. *Journal of Projective Techniques,* 1959, *23,* 291–298.

Ames, L.B. and Gillespie, C. Significance of Rorschach modified by responses to other projective tests. *Journal of Personality Assessment,* 1973, *37,* 316–327.

Ames, L.B., Learned, J., Metraux, R., and Walker, R.N. *Child Rorschach Responses.* New York: Hoeber, 1952.

Ames, L.B., Metraux, R.W., Rodell, I.L., and Walker, R.N. *Rorschach Responses in Old Age* (rev. ed.). New York: Brunner/Mazel, 1973.

Ames, L.B., Metraux, R.W., Rodell, J.L., and Walker, R.N. *Child Rorschach Responses: Developmental Trends from Two to Ten Years* (rev. ed.). New York: Brunner/Mazel, 1974.

Ames, L.B., Metraux, R.W., and Walker, R.N. *Adolescent Rorschach Responses: Developmental Trends from Ten to Sixteen Years* (2nd ed.). New York: Brunner/Mazel, 1971.

Amolsch, T. and Henrichs, T. Behavioral correlates of WAIS profile patterns: an exploratory study. *Journal of Personality Assessment, 1975, 39,* 55–63.

Anastasi, A. Psychologists and psychological testing. *American Psychologist, 1967, 22,* 297–306.

Anastasi, A. *Psychological Testing* (5th ed.). New York: Macmillan, 1982.

Anderson, S. and Messick, S. Social competency in young children. *Developmental Psychology, 1974, 10,* 282–293.

Andert, J.N., Hustak, T., and Dinning, W.D. Bender-Gestalt reproduction times for retarded adults. *Journal of Clinical Psychology, 1978, 34,* 927–929.

Armstrong, R.G. and Hauck, P.A. Correlates of the Bender-Gestalt scores in children. *Journal of Psychological Studies, 1960, 11,* 153–158.

Arnaud, S. A system for deriving quantitative Rorschach measures of certain psychological variables for group comparisons. *Journal of Projective Techniques, 1959, 23,* 400–311.

Arnoff, J. Sex differences in the orientation of body image. *Journal of Projective Techniques, 1960, 24,* 292–309.

Arnold, M.B. *Story Sequence Analysis: A New Method of Measuring and Predicting Achievement.* New York: Columbia University Press, 1962.

Atkinson, J.W. and Feather, N.T., (Eds.) *A Theory of Achievement Motivation.* New York: John Wiley & Sons, 1966.

Baldwin, M.V. A note regarding the suggested use of the Bender-Gestalt Test as a measure of school readiness. *Journal of Clinical Psychology, 1950, 6,* 412.

Bannatyne, A. Diagnosis – a note on recategorization of the WISC scaled scores. *Journal of Learning Disabilities, 1974, 7,* 272–273.

Barber, T.X. and Silver, M.J. Fact, fiction and the experimenter bias effect. *Psychological Bulletin Monograph Supplement, 1968, 70,* 1–29.

Barnouw, V. Cross-cultural research with the House-Tree-Person Test. In Buck, J.N. and Hammer, E.F. (Eds.) *Advances in the House-Tree-Person Technique: Variations and Applications.* Los Angeles: Western Psychological Services, 1969.

Barron, F. An ego-strength scale which predicts response to psychotherapy. *Journal of Consulting Psychology, 1953, 17,* 327–333.

Baucom, D.H. Independent CPI masculinity and femininity scales: psychological correlates and a sex role typology. *Journal of Personality Assessment, 1980, 44,* 262–271.

Baughman, E.E. The role of the stimulus in Rorschach responses. *Psychological Bulletin, 1958, 55,* 121–147.

Beck, H.S. A study of the applicability of the H-T-P to children with respect to the drawn house. *Journal of Clinical Psychology, 1955, 11,* 60–63.

Beck, H.S. A comparison of convulsive organics, non-convulsive organics, and non-organic public school children. *American Journal of Mental Deficiency, 1959, 63,* 866–875.

Beck, S.J. *Rorschach's Test: A Variety of Personality Pictures,* Vol. II. New York: Grune & Stratton, 1945.

Beck, S.J. The Rorschach test: a multi-dimensional test of personality. In Anderson, H.H. and Anderson, G. (Eds.) *An Introduction to Projective Techniques.* Englewood Cliffs, N.J.: Prentice-Hall, 1951, pp. 101–122.

Beck, S.J. *The Rorschach Experiment.* New York: Grune & Stratton, 1960.

Beck, S.J. *Rorschach's Test,* Vol. I: Basic Processes. New York: Grune & Stratton, 1961.

Beck, S.J. Reality, Rorschach and perceptual theory. In Rabin, A.I. (Ed.) *Projective Tech niques in Personality Assessment*. New York: Springer, 1968.

Beck, S.J. and Molish, H.B. *Rorschach's Test*. Vol. II: A Variety of Personality Pictures (2nd ed.). New York: Grune & Stratton, 1967.

Beck, S.J., Rabin, A.I., Thieson, W.C., Molish, H.B., and Thetford, W.N. The normal personality as projected in the Rorschach test. *Journal of Psychology*, 1950, *30*, 241–298.

Bellak, L. *The TAT, CAT, SAT in Clinical Use* (3rd ed.). New York: Grune & Stratton, 1975.

Bellak, L. and Bellak, S.S. *Manual: Senior Apperception Test*. Larchmont, N.Y.: C.P.S., 1973.

Bellak, L. and Hurvich, M.S. A human modification of the Children's Apperception Test (CAT-H). *Journal of Projective Techniques and Personality Assessment*, 1966, *30*, 228–242.

Bender, L. *A Visual Motor Gestalt Test and Its Clinical Uses*, Research Monograms No. 3. New York: American Orthopsychiatric Association, 1938.

Bender, L. Use of the visual motor Gestalt test in the diagnosis of learning disabilities. *Journal of Special Education*, 1970, *4*, 29–39.

Bennett, F. and Schubert, D. Use of local norms to improve configural reproducibility of an MMPI short form. *Journal of Personality Assessment*, 1981, *45*, 33–39.

Bergin, A.E. The evaluation of therapeutic outcomes. In Bergin, A.E. and Garfield, S.L. (Eds.) *Handbook of Psychotherapy and Behavior Change*. New York: John Wiley & Sons, 1971.

Bernstein, L. The examiner as an inhibiting factor in clinical testing. *Journal of Consulting Psychology*, 1956, *20*, 287–290.

Beutler, L.E., Karacan, I., Anch, A.M., Salis, P., Scott, F.B., and Williams, R. MMPI and MIT discriminators of biogenic and psychogenic impotence. *Journal of Consulting and Clinical Psychology*, 1975, *43*, 899–903.

Billingslea, F.Y. The Bender-Gestalt: an objective scoring method and validating data. *Journal of Clinical Psychology*, 1948, *4*, 1–27.

Billingslea, F.Y. The Bender-Gestalt: a review and a perspective. *Psychological Bulletin*, 1963, *60*, 233–251.

Binet, A. and Simon, T. Le developpement de l'intelligence chez les enfants. *L'Anee Psychologique*, 1908, *14*, 1–94.

Blain, G.H., Bergner, R.M., Lewis, M.L., and Goodstein, M.A. The use of objectively scorable House-Tree-Person indicators to establish child abuse. *Journal of Clinical Psychology*, 1981, *37*, 667–673.

Blashfield, R.K. and Draguns, I.G. Evaluative criteria for psychiatric classification. *Journal of Abnormal Psychology*, 1975, *85*, 140–148.

Blatt, S.J. and Allison, J. The intelligence test in personality assessment. In Rabin, A.I. (Ed.) *Projective Techniques in Personality Assessment*. New York: Springer, 1968.

Block, J. *The Challenge of Response Sets: Unconfounding Meaning, Acquiescence, and Social Desirability in the MMPI*. New York: Appleton-Century-Crofts, 1965.

Blum, L.H., Davidson, H.H., and Fieldsteel, N.D. *A Rorschach Workbook*. New York: International Universities Press, 1975.

Boerger, A.R. *The utility of some alternative approaches to MMPI scale construction*. Doctoral dissertation, Kent State University, 1975.

Bolander, K. *Assessing Personality Through Tree Drawings*. New York: Basic Books, 1977

Boll, T.J. The Halstead-Reitan neuropsychological battery. In Filskov, S.B. and Boll, T.J. (Eds.) *Handbook of Clinical Neuropsychology*. New York: John Wiley & Sons, 1981.

Bradway, K., Lion, E., and Corrigan, H. The use of the Rorschach in a psychiatric study of promiscuous girls. *Rorschach Research Exchange,* 1946, *9,* 105–110.

Brandt, D. Comparison of various WISC-R summary scores for a psychiatric sample. *Journal of Clinical Psychology,* 1982, *38,* 830–837.

Brar, H.S. Rorschach content responses of East Indian psychiatric patients. *Journal of Projective Techniques and Personality Assessment,* 1970, *34,* 88–94.

Bravo, L. The conservation, stimulation, and development of superior mental ability. Paper presented to the California Association of School Psychologists, 1972.

Brayfield, A.H. (Ed.). Testing and public policy. *American Psychologist,* 1965, *20,* 857–1005.

Brennan, M. and Reichard, S. Use of the Rorschach test in predicting hypnotizability. *Bulletin of the Menninger Clinic,* 1943, *7,* 183–187.

Brown, F. Adult case study: clinical validation of the House-Tree-Person drawings of an adult case (chronic ulcerative colitis with cleostomy). In Hammer, E.F. (Ed.) *The Clinical Application of Projective Drawings.* Springfield, Ill: Charles C. Thomas, 1958, pp. 261–275.

Brown, F. The Bender-Gestalt and acting out. In Abt, L.E. and Weissman, S.L. (Eds.) *Acting Out: Theoretical and Clinical Aspects.* New York: Grune & Stratton, 1965.

Brown, F.G. The SOMPA: a system of measuring potential abilities. *School Psychology Digest,* 1979, *8*(1), 37–46.

Brown, W.R. and McGuire, J.M. Current assessment practices. *Professional Psychology,* 1976, *7,* 475–484.

Buck, J.N. The H-T-P technique, a qualitative and quantitative scoring manual. *Journal of Clinical Psychology,* 1948, *4,* 317–396.

Buck, J.N. *The House-Tree-Person Technique: Revised Manual.* Beverly Hills, Calif.: Western Psychological Services, 1966.

Buck, J.N. The use of the H-T-P in the investigation of intrafamilial conflict. In Buck, J.N. and Hammer, E.F. (Eds.) *Advances in the House-Tree-Person Technique: Variations and Applications.* Los Angeles: Western Psychological Services, 1969.

Buhler, C. and Le Fever, D. A Rorschach study on the psychological characteristics of alcoholics. *Quarterly Journal of Studies on Alcoholism,* 1947, *8,* 197–260.

Burgemeister, B. *Psychological Techniques in Neurological Diagnosis.* New York: Hoeber-Harper, 1962.

Burke, H. and Marcus, R. MacAndrew MMPI Alcoholism Scale: alcoholism and drug addiction. *Journal of Psychology,* 1977, *96,* 141–148.

Burns, R.C. *Self-growth in Families: Kinetic Family Drawings (K-F-D) Research and Application.* New York: Brunner/Mazel, 1983.

Burns, R.C. and Kaufman, S.H. *Action, Styles, and Symbols in Kinetic Family Drawings (K-F-D).* New York: Brunner/Mazel, 1972.

Buros, O.K. (Ed.). *Personality Tests and Reviews.* Highland Park, N.J.: Gryphon Press, 1972. (a)

Buros, O.K. (Ed.). *Seventh Mental Measurements Yearbook.* Highland Park, N.J.: Gryphon Press, 1972. (b)

Buros, O.K. (Ed.). *Tests in Print II.* Highland Park, N.J.: Gryphon Press, 1974.

Buros, O.K. (Ed.). *Eighth Mental Measurements Yearbook.* Highland Park, N.J.: Gryphon Press, 1978.

Butcher, H.J. *Human Intelligence: Its Nature and Assessment.* London: Methuen, 1968.

Butcher, J.N. Use of the MMPI in personnel selection. In Butcher, J.N. (Ed.) *New Developments in the Use of the MMPI.* Minneapolis: University of Minnesota Press, 1979.

Butcher, J.N., Ball, B., and Ray, E. Effects of socioeconomic level on MMPI differences in Negro-white college students. *Journal of Consulting Psychology,* 1964, *11,* 83–87.

Butcher, J.N. and Clark, L.A. Recent trends and application. In Butcher, J.N. (Ed.) *New Developments in the Use of the MMPI*. Minneapolis: University of Minnesota Press, 1979.

Butcher, J.N. and Owen, P.L. Objective personality inventories: recent research and some contemporary issues. In Wolman, B.B. (Ed.) *Clinical Diagnosis of Mental Disorders: A Handbook*. New York: Plenum, 1978.

Butcher, J.N. and Pancheri, P. *A Handbook of Cross-national MMPI Research*. Minneapolis: University of Minnesota Press, 1976.

Byrne, D. Repression-sensitization as a dimension of personality. In Mohrer, B.A. (Ed.) *Progress in Experimental Personality Research*, Vol. 1. New York: Academic Press, 1964, pp. 69–220.

Byrne, D., Golightly, C., and Sheffield, J. The repression-sensitization scale as a measure of adjustment: relationship with the CPI. *Journal of Consulting Psychology*, 1965, *29*, 585–589.

Caldwell, A.B. *MMPI Critical Items*. Available from Caldwell Report, 3122 Santa Monica Blvd., Penthouse West, Los Angeles, Calif., 1969 (mimeograph).

Calvin, J. *A replicated study of the concurrent validity of the Harris-Lingoes Subscales of the MMPI*. Doctoral dissertation, Kent State University, 1975.

Canter, A. A background interference procedure for graphomotor tests in the study of deficit. *Perceptual and Motor Skills*, 1963, *16*, 914.

Canter, A. A background interference procedure to increase sensitivity of the Bender-Gestalt Test to organic brain disorder. *Journal of Consulting Psychology*, 1966, *30*, 91–97.

Canter, A. A comparison of the background interference procedure effect in schizophrenic, non-schizophrenic, and organic patients. *Journal of Clinical Psychology*, 1971, *27*, 473–474.

Canter, A. *The Canter Background Interference Procedure for the Bender-Gestalt Test. Manual for Administration, Scoring, and Interpretation*. Nashville, Tenn.: Counselor Recordings and Tests, 1976.

Carnes, G.D. and Bates, R. Rorschach anatomy response correlates in rehabilitation of failure subjects. *Journal of Personality Assessments*, 1971, *35*, 527–537.

Carrier, N.A. Need correlates of "gullibility." *Journal of Projective Techniques*, 1963, *66*, 84–86.

Cass, W.A. and McReynolds, P.A. A contribution to Rorschach norms. *Journal of Consulting Psychology*, 1951, *15*, 178–183.

Cassel, R.H., Johnson, A.P., and Burns, W.H. Examiner, ego defense, and the HTP test. *Journal of Clinical Psychology*, 1958, *14*, 157–160.

Cattell, R.B. Theory of fluid and crystallized intelligence: a critical experiment. *Journal of Educational Psychology*, 1963, *54*, 1–22.

Cattell, R.B., Eber, H.W., and Tatsuoka, M.M. *Handbook for the Sixteen Personality Factor Questionnaire*. Champaign, Ill.: Institute for Personality and Abilities Testing, 1970.

Chapman, L.J. and Chapman, J.P. Genesis of popular but erroneous psychodiagnostic observations. *Journal of Abnormal Psychology*, 1967, *72*, 193–204.

Clark, J.H. The interpretation of the MMPI profiles of college students; mean scores for male and female groups. *Journal of Social Psychology*, 1954, *40*, 319–321.

Clawson, A. The Bender Visual Motor Gestalt Test as an index of emotional disturbance in children. *Journal of Projective Techniques*, 1959, *23*, 198–206.

Clawson, A. *The Bender Visual Motor Gestalt for Children. A Manual*. Beverly Hills, Calif.: Western Psychological Services, 1962.

Cleary, T.A. Test bias: prediction of grades of Negro and white students in integrated colleges. *Journal of Educational Measurement*, 1968, *5*, 115–124.

Clopton, J.R. A note on the MMPI as a suicide predictor. *Journal of Consulting and Clinical Psychology.* 1978, *46,* 335–336(a).

Clopton, J.R. Alcoholism and the MMPI: a review. *Journal of Studies on Alcohol,* 1978, *39,* 1540–1558. (b)

Clopton, J.R., Weiner, R.H., and Davis, H.G. Use of the MMPI in identification of alcoholic psychiatric patients. *Journal of Consulting and Clinical Psychology,* 1980, *48*(3), 416–417.

Coan, R. A factor analysis of Rorschach determinants. *Journal of Projective Techniques,* 1956, *20,* 280–287.

Cohen, J. A factor-analytically based rationale for the Wechsler Adult Intelligence Scale. *Journal of Consulting Psychology,* 1957, *21,* 351–457. (a)

Cohen, J. The factorial structure of the WAIS between early adulthood and old age. *Journal of Consulting Psychology,* 1957, *21,* 283–290. (b)

Cohen, J. The factorial structure of the WISC at ages 7–6, 10–6, and 13–6. *Journal of Consulting Psychology,* 1959, *23,* 285–299.

Cole, S. and Hunter, M. Pattern analysis of WISC scores achieved by culturally disadvantaged children. *Psychological Reports,* 1971, *29,* 191–294.

Coleman, J.C. *Abnormal Psychology and Modern Life,* (6th ed.). Glenview: Scott, Foresman and Co., 1980, pp. 127–128.

Collins, D.J. Psychological selection of drill sergeants: an exploratory attempt in a new program. *Military Medicine,* 1967, *132*(a), 713–715.

Conley, J.J. An MMPI typology of male alcoholics. *Journal of Personality Assessment,* 1981, *45,* 40–43.

Cooper, H.M. and Rosenthal, R. Statistical versus traditional procedures for summarizing research findings. *Psychological Bulletin,* 1980, *87,* 442–449.

Costello, C.G. The Rorschach records of suicidal patients. *Journal of Projective Techniques,* 1958, *22,* 272–275.

Cowan, T.A. Decision theory in law, science, and technology. *Science,* 1963, *140,* 1065–1075.

Cox, F.N. and Sarason, S.B. Test anxiety and Rorschach performance. *Journal of Abnormal and Social Psychology,* 1954, *49,* 371–377.

Crenshaw, D.A., Bohn, S., Hoffman, M., Matheus, J.M., and Offenbach, S.G. The use of projective methods in research: 1947–1965. *Journal of Projective Techniques and Personality Assessment,* 1968, *32,* 2–9.

Cronbach, L.J. *Essentials of Psychological Testing* (3rd ed.). New York: Harper & Row, 1970.

Cronbach, L.J. Black intelligence test of cultural homogeneity: a review. In Buros, O.K. (Ed.) *The Eighth Mental Measurements Yearbook,* Vol. 1. Highland Park, N.J.: Gryphon Press, 1978.

Cross, D.T. and Burger, G. Ethnicity as a variable in responses to California Psychological Inventory items. *Journal of Personality Assessment,* 1982, *46*(2), 155–158.

Crowne, D.P. and Marlowe, D. *The Approval Motive: Studies in Evaluative Dependence.* New York: John Wiley & Sons, 1964.

Crumpton, E. The influence of color on the Rorschach test. *Journal of Projective Techniques,* 1956, *20,* 150–158.

Dahlstrom, W.G. Recurrent issues in the development of the MMPI. In Butcher, J.N. (Ed.) *MMPI: Research Developments and Clinical Applications.* New York: McGraw-Hill, 1969.

Dahlstrom, W.G. and Welsh, G.S. *An MMPI Handbook: A Guide to Use in Clinical Practice and Research.* Minneapolis: University of Minnesota Press, 1960.

Dahlstrom, W.G., Welsh, G.S., and Dahlstrom, L.E. *An MMPI Handbook,* Vol. 1: Clinical Interpretation. Minneapolis: University of Minnesota Press, 1972.

Dahlstrom, W.G., Welsh, G.S., and Dahlstrom, L.E. *An MMPI Handbook*, Vol. 2: Research Developments and Applications. Minneapolis: University of Minnesota Press, 1975.

Dana, R.H. Clinical diagnosis and objective TAT scoring. *Journal of Abnormal and Social Psychology*, 1955, *50*, 19–24.

Dana, R.H. Six constructs to define Rorschach M. *Journal of Projective Techniques and Personality Assessment*, 1968, *32*, 138–145.

Dana, R.H. and Cocking, R.R. Cue parameters, cue probabilities, and clinical judgment. *Journal of Clinical Psychology*, 1968, *24*, 475–480.

Dana, R.H., Field, W., and Bolton, B. Variations of the Bender Gestalt Test: implications for training and practice. *Journal of Personality Assessment*, 1983, *47*(1), 76–84.

Datel, W.E., Hall, F.D., and Rufe, C.P. Measurement of achievement motivation in army security agency foreign language candidates. *Educational and Psychological Measurement*, 1965, *25*, 539–545.

Deabler, H.L. The H-T-P in group testing and as a screening device. In Buck, J.N. and Hammer, E.F. (Eds.) *Advances in the House-Tree-Person Technique: Variations and Applications*. Los Angeles: Western Psychological Services, 1969.

Dean, E.F. A lengthened Mini: the Midi-Mult. *Journal of Clinical Psychology*, 1972, *28*, 68–71.

Delatte, J.G. and Hendrickson, N.J. Human figure drawing size as a measure of self-esteem. *Journal of Personality Assessment*, 1982, *46*, 603–606.

Dicken, C.F. Simulated patterns on the California Psychological Inventory. *Journal of Counseling Psychology*, 1960, *7*, 24–31.

DiLeo, J.H. *Young Children and Their Drawings*. New York: Brunner/Mazel, 1970.

DiLeo, J.H. *Children's Drawings as Diagnostic Aids*. New York: Brunner/Mazel, 1973.

Diller, L., Ben-Yishay, Y., Gertsman, L.J., Goodkin, R., Gordon, W., and Weinberg, J. *Studies in Cognition and Rehabilitation in Hemiplegia* (Rehabilitation Monograph, No. 50). New York: New York University Medical Center, Institute of Rehabilitation Medicine, 1976.

Donahue, D. and Sattler, J.M. Personality variables affecting WAIS scores. *Journal of Consulting Psychology*, 1971, *36*, 441.

Donnelly, E.F. and Murphy, D.L. Primary affective disorder: Bender-Gestalt sequence of placement as an indicator of impulse control. *Perceptual and Motor Skills*, 1974, *38*, 1079–1082.

Dopplet, J.E. Estimating the full scale score of the Wechsler Adult Intelligence Scale from scores on four subtests. *Journal of Consulting Psychology*, 1956, *20*, 63–66.

Dopplet, J.E. and Wallace, W.L. Standardization of the Wechsler Intelligence Scale for older persons. *Journal of Abnormal and Social Psychology*, 1955, *51*, 312–330.

Dorken, H.A. A psychometric evaluation of 68 medical interns. *Journal of the Canadian Medical Association*, 1954, *70*, 41–45.

Dove, A. Taking the Chitling Test. *Newsweek*, 1968, *72*, 51–52.

Draguns, J.G., Haley, E.M., and Phillips, L. Studies of the Rorschach content: a review of the research literature. Part 1: Traditional content categories. *Journal of Projective Techniques and Personality Assessment*, 1967, *31*, 3-32.

Drake, L.E. A social I.E. scale for the MMPI. *Journal of Applied Psychology*, 1946, *30*, 51–54.

Drake, L.E. and Oettings, E.R. *An MMPI Codebook for Counselors*. Minneapolis: University of Minnesota Press, 1959.

DuBois, P.H. *A History of Psychological Testing*. Boston: Allyn and Bacon, 1970.

DuBois, P.H. Increase in educational opportunity through measurement. *Proceedings of the 1971 Invitational Conference on Testing Problems*. Princeton, N.J.: Educational Testing Service, 1972.

Dudek, S.Z. *M* and active energy system correlating Rorschach *M* with ease of creative expression. *Journal of Projective Techniques and Personality Assessment*, 1968, *32*, 453–461.

Duran, P., Pechoux, R., Escafit, M., and Davidow, P. Le contenu des reponses dans le test de Rorschach chez les schizophrenes. *Annual of Medical Psychologie*, 1949, *107*, 198–200.

Ebel, R.L. Must all tests be valid? *American Psychologist*, 1961, *16*, 640–647.

Eber, M. A Bender Gestalt validity study: the performance of mentally retarded children. *Dissertation Abstracts*, 1958, *18*, 296.

Edwards, A.L. The Social Desirability Variables in Personality Assessment and Research. New York: Dryden Press, 1957.

Edwards, A.L. Social desirability and performance on the MMPI. *Psychometrika*, 1964, *29*, 295–308.

Egeland, B.R. Examiner expectancy: effects on the scoring of the WISC. *Psychology in the Schools*, 1969, *6*, 313-315.

Eichler, R.M. Experimental stress and alleged Rorschach indices of anxiety. *Journal of Abnormal and Social Psychology*, 1951, *46*, 169–177.

Eisdorfer, C. The WAIS performance of the aged: a retest evaluation. *Journal of Gerontology*, 1963, *18*, 169–172.

Elashoff, J. and Snow, R.E. (Eds.). *Pygmalion Revisited*. Worthington, Ohio: C.A. Jones, 1971.

Elliot, L.L. WAF performance on the California Psychological Inventory. *Wright Air Development Division Technical Note 60-218*, Lackland AFB, Air Research and Development Command, 1960.

Elstein, A.A. Behavioral correlates of the Rorschach shading determinant. *Journal of Consulting Psychology*, 1965, *29*, 231–236.

Equal Employment Opportunity Commission (EEOC). Guidelines on employee selection procedures. *Federal Register*, 1970, *35*(140), 12333–12336.

Erginel, A. On the test-retest reliability of the Rorschach. *Journal of Personality Assessment*, 1972, *36*, 203–212.

Eron, L.D. A normative study of the Thematic Apperception Test. *Psychological Monographs*, 1950, *64*(315).

Exner, J.E. The influence of achromatic color in Cards IV and VI of the Rorschach. *Journal of Projective Techniques*, 1961, *25*, 38–41.

Exner, J.E. *The Rorschach Systems.* New York: Grune & Stratton, 1969.

Exner, J.E. *The Rorschach: A Comprehensive System*, Vol. 1. New York: John Wiley & Sons, 1974.

Exner, J.E. *The Rorschach: A Comprehensive System*, Vol. 2: Current Research and Advanced Interpretations. New York: Wiley-Interscience, 1978.

Exner, J.E., Armbruster, G.L., and Viglione, D. The temporal stability of some Rorschach features. *Journal of Personality Assessment*, 1978, *42*, 474–482.

Exner, J.E. and Exner, D.E. How clinicians use the Rorschach. *Journal of Personality Assessment*, 1972, *36*, 403–408.

Exner, J.E. and Weiner, I.B. *The Rorschach: A Comprehensive System*, Vol. 3: Assessment of Children and Adolescents. New York: John Wiley & Sons, 1982.

Exner, J.E. and Murillo, L.G. Effectiveness of regressive ECT with process schizophrenics. *Diseases of the Nervous System*, 1973, *34*, 44–48.

Fauschingbauer, T.R. A 166-item short form of the group MMPI: the FAM. *Journal of Consulting and Clinical Psychology*, 1974, *42*, 645–655.

Fauschingbauer, T.R. and Newmark, C.S. *Short Forms of the MMPI*. Lexington, Mass: Heath, 1978.

Feldman, S.E. and Sullivan, D.S. Factors mediating the efforts of enhanced rapport on children's performance. *Journal of Consulting and Clinical Psychology*, 1971, *36*, 302.

Fieldler, F.E. and Spiegal, S.M. The Free Drawing Test as a predictor of non-improvement in psychotherapy. *Journal of Clinical Psychology*, 1949, *5*, 386–389.

Filskov, S.B. The prediction of impairment from figure copying. Paper presented at the Southeastern Psychological Association Convention, Atlanta, 1978.

Finney, B.C. Rorschach test correlates of assaultive behavior. *Journal of Projective Techniques*, 1951, *15*, 250–254.

Finney, J.C., Smith, D.F., Skeeters, D.E., and Auvenshine, C.D. MMPI alcoholism scales: factor structure and content analysis. *Quarterly Journal of Studies on Alcohol*, 1971, *32*, 1055–1060.

Fisher, S. The value of the Rorschach for detecting suicidal trends. *Journal of Projective Techniques*, 1951, *15*, 250–254.

Fisher, S. Relationship of Rorschach human percepts to projective descriptions with self reference. *Journal of Projective Techniques*, 1962, *26*, 231-233.

Fiske, D.W. and Baughman, E.E. Relationships between Rorschach scoring categories and the total number of responses. *Journal of Abnormal and Social Psychology*, 1953, *48*, 25–32.

Fitzhugh, L.C. and Fitzhugh, K. Relationship between Wechsler-Bellevue Form I and WAIS performances of subjects with longstanding cerebral dysfunction. *Perceptual and Motor Skills*, 1964, *19*, 539–543.

Flaherty, M.R. and Reutzel, G. Personality traits of high and low achievers in college. *Journal of Educational Research*, 1965, *58*, 409–411.

Flaugher, R.L. The many definitions of test bias. *American Psychologist*, 1978, *33*, 671–679.

Flaugher, R.L. and Schrader, W.B. *Eliminating Differentially Difficult Items as an Approach to Test Bias* (RB-78-4). Princeton, N.J.: Educational Testing Service, 1978.

Foster, A. Writing psychological reports. *Journal of Clinical Psychology*, 1951, *7*, 195.

Fowler, R.D. and Coyle, F.A. Collegiate normative data on MMPI content scales. *Journal of Clinical Psychology*, 1969, *25*, 62–68.

Friedman, H. Perceptual regression in schizophrenia: an hypothesis suggested by the use of the Rorschach test. *Journal of Genetic Psychology*, 1952, *81*, 63–98.

Fuller, G.B. *The Minnesota Percepto-Diagnostic Test* (rev. ed.). Brandon, Vt.: Clinical Psychology Publishing Co., 1969.

Fuller, G.B. and Chagnon, G. Factors influencing rotation in the Bender Gestalt performance of children. *Journal of Projective Techniques*, 1962, *26*, 36–46.

Garcia, J. The logic and limits of mental aptitude testing. *American Psychologist*, 1981, *36*, 172–1180.

Gardner, R.W. Impulsivity as indicated by Rorschach test factors. *Journal of Consulting Psychology*, 1951, *15*, 464–468.

Garron, D.C. and Chiefetz, D.I. Comment on Bender Gestalt discernment of organic pathology. *Psychological Bulletin*, 1965, *63*, 197–200.

Gavales, D. and Millon T. Comparison of reproduction and recall size deviations on the Bender Gestalt as measures of anxiety. *Journal of Clinical Psychology*, 1960, *16*, 278–280.

Gilberstadt, N. and Duker, J. *A Handbook for Clinical and Actuarial MMPI Interpretation.* Philadelphia: W.B. Saunders, 1965.

Gilbert, J. *Clinical Psychological Tests in Psychiatric and Medical Practice.* Springfield, Ill.: Charles C. Thomas, 1969.

Gill, H.S. Delay of response and reaction to color on the Rorschach. *Journal of Projective Techniques and Personality Assessment*, 1966, *30*, 545–552.

Glasser, A.J. and Zimmerman, I.L. Clinical interpretation of the Wechsler Intelligence Scale for Children. New York: Grune & Stratton, 1967.

Glueck, S. and Glueck, E. *Unravelling Juvenile Delinquency.* New York: Common Wealth Fund, 1950.

Gocka, E. American Lake norms for 200 MMPI scales. Unpublished materials, 1965.

Golden, C.J. *Clinical Interpretation of Objective Psychological Tests.* New York: Grune & Stratton, 1979.

Goldfried, M.R., Stricker, G., and Weiner, I.B. *Rorschach Handbook of Clinical and Research Application.* Englewood Cliffs, N.J.: Prentice-Hall, 1971.

Goldman, R. Changes in Rorschach performance and clinical comparison in schizophrenia. *Journal of Consulting Psychology,* 1960, *24,* 403–407. (a)

Goldman, R. Changes in Rorschach performance and clinical improvement in schizophrenia. *Journal of Consulting Psychology,* 1960, *24,* 403–427. (b)

Goldman, R.D. and Hartig L. The WISC may not be a valid predictor of school performance for primary grade minority children. *American Journal of Mental Deficiency,* 1976, *80,* 583–587.

Goldschmid, M.L. Prediction of college majors by personality tests. *Journal of Counseling Psychology,* 1967, *14*(4), 302–308.

Goldstein, G. and Shelly, C.H. Similarities and differences between psychological deficit in aging and brain damage. *Journal of Gerontology,* 1975, *30,* 448–455.

Goldstein, K. and Sheerer, M. Abstract and concrete behavior. An experimental study with special tests. *Psychological Monographs,* 1941, *53*(239).

Gonen, J.Y. and Brown, L. Role of vocabulary in deterioration and restitution of mental functioning. *Proceedings of the 76th Annual Convention of the American Psychological Association,* 1968, *3,* 469–470 (summary).

Goodenough, F. *Measurement of Intelligence by Drawings.* New York: World Book, 1926.

Gordon, N.G. and Swart, E.C. A comparison of the Harris-Lingoes subscales between the original standardization population and an inpatient Veterans Administration hospital population. *Newsletter for Research in Mental Health and Behavioral Sciences,* 1973, *15,* 28–31.

Gottlieb, A. and Parsons, O. A coaction compass evaluation of Rorschach determinants in brain damaged individuals. *Journal of Consulting Psychology,* 1960, *24,* 54–60.

Gough, H.G. A new dimension of status. I. Development of a personality scale. *American Sociological Review,* 1948, *13,* 401–409.

Gough, H.G. Identifying psychological femininity. *Educational and Psychological Measurement,* 1952, *12*(3), 427–439.

Gough, H.G. *California Psychological Inventory Manual.* Palo Alto, Calif.: Consulting Psychologists Press, 1957.

Gough, H.G. Academic achievement in high school as predicted from the California Psychological Inventory. *Journal of Educational Psychology,* 1964, *65,* 174–180.

Gough, H.G. Cross-cultural validation of a measure of asocial behavior. *Psychological Reports,* 1965, *17,* 379–387.

Gough, H.G. Graduation from high school as predicted from the California Psychological Inventory. *Psychology in the Schools,* 1966, *3*(3), 208–216.

Gough, H.G. An interpreter's syllabus for the California Psychological Inventory. In McReynolds, P. (Ed.) *Advances in Psychological Assessment,* Vol. 1. Palo Alto, Calif.: Science and Behavior Books, 1968.

Gough, H.G. *Manual for the California Psychological Inventory* (rev. ed.). Palo Alto, Calif.: Consulting Psychologists Press, 1969.

Gough, H.G. *Manual for the California Psychological Inventory* (rev. ed.). Palo Alto, Calif.: Consulting Psychologists Press, 1975.

Gough, H.G., Durflinger, G.W., and Hill, R.F., Jr Predicting performance in student teaching from the California Psychological Inventory. *Journal of Educational Psychology,* 1968, *52*(2), 119–127.

Gough, H.G. and Hall, W.B. Prediction of performance in medical school from the California Psychological Inventory. *Journal of Applied Psychology,* 1964, *48,* 218–226.

Gough, H.G. and Kirk, B.A. Achievement in dental school as related to personality and aptitude variables. *Measurement and Evaluation in Guidance,* 1970, *2,* 225–233.

Gough, H.G., Wenk, E.A., and Rozynko, V.V. Parole outcome as predicted from the CPI, the MMPI, and a Base Expectancy Table. *Journal of Abnormal Psychology,* 1965, *70,* 432–441.

Graham, J.R. *The MMPI: A Practical Guide.* New York: Oxford University Press, 1977.

Graham, J.R. A review of some important MMPI special scales. In McReynolds, P. (Ed.) *Advances in Psychological Assessment,* Vol. IV. San Francisco: Jossey-Bass, 1978.

Gravitz, M.A. The height of normal adult figure drawings. *Journal of Clinical Psychology,* 1968, *24,* 75.

Grayson, H.M. *A Psychological Admissions Testing Program and Manual.* Los Angeles: Veterans Administration Center, 1951.

Grayson, H.M. and Tolman, R.S. A semantic study of concepts of clinical psychologists and psychiatrists. *Journal of Abnormal and Social Psychology,* 1950, *45,* 216–231.

Green, B.F. In defense of measurement. *American Psychologist,* 1978, *33,* 664–670.

Greenbaum, R.S. A note on the use of the Word Association Test as an aid to interpreting the Bender-Gestalt. *Journal of Projective Techniques,* 1955, *19,* 27–29.

Greene, R.L. Some reflections on "MMPI short forms: a literature review." *Journal of Personality Assessment,* 1983, *46*(5), 486–487.

Gregory, R. and Morris, L. Adjective correlates for women on the CPI scales: a replication. *Journal of Personality Assessment,* 1978, *42*(3), 258–264.

Griffin, M.L. and Flaherty, M.R. Correlation of CPI traits with academic achievement. *Educational and Psychological Measurement,* 1964, *24,* 369–372.

Griffith, R.M. Rorschach water percepts: a study in conflicting results. *American Psychologist,* 1961, *16,* 307–311.

Guertin, W.H., Ladd, C.E., Frank, G.H., and Rabin, A.I. Research with the Wechsler intelligence scales for adults: 1955–1960. *Psychological Bulletin,* 1962, *59,* 1–26.

Guertin, W.H., Ladd, C.E., Frank, G.H., and Rabin, A.I. Research with the Wechsler intelligence scales for adults: 1965–1970. *Psychological Bulletin,* 1971, *66,* 289–339.

Guertin, W.H., Ladd, C.E., Frank, G.H., Rabin, A.I., and Hiester, D.S. Research with the Wechsler intelligence scales for adults: 1960–1965. *Psychological Bulletin,* 1966, *66,* 385–409.

Guilford, J.P. The structure of intellect. *Psychological Bulletin,* 1956, *53,* 267–293.

Guilford, J.P. *The Nature of Human Intelligence.* New York: McGraw-Hill, 1967.

Gynther, M.D. White norms and black MMPI's: a prescription for discrimination? *Psychological Bulletin,* 1972, *78,* 386–402.

Gynther, M.D. Item response differences and their implications. In Graham, J.R. (Chair) *Minority Status and MMPI Scales: Empirical Findings on Normal Blacks.* Symposium presented at the meeting of the American Psychological Association, Toronto, 1978. (a)

Gynther, M.D. The California Psychological Inventory: a review. In Buros, O.K. (Ed.) *The Eighth Mental Measurements Yearbook,* Vol. I. Highland Park, N.J.: Gryphon Press, 1978. (b)

Gynther, M.D. Aging and personality. In Butcher, J.N. (Ed.) *New Developments in the Use of the MMPI.* Minneapolis: University of Minnesota Press, 1979. (a)

Gynther, M.D. Ethnicity and personality: an update. In Butcher, J.N. (Ed.) *New Developments in the Use of the MMPI.* Minneapolis: University of Minnesota Press, 1979. (b)

Gynther, M.D. and Shimkuras, A.M. Age and MMPI performance. *Journal of Consulting Psychology*, 1966, *30*, 08–112.

Haan, N. An investigation of the relationships of Rorschach scores, patterns and behaviors to coping and defense mechanisms. *Journal of Projective Techniques and Personality Assessment*, 1964, *28*, 429–441.

Hain, J.D. The Bender Gestalt Test: a scoring method for identifying brain damage. *Journal of Consulting Psychology*, 1964, *28*, 34–40.

Halpern, F. Rorschach interpretation of the personality structure of schizophrenics who benefit from insulin therapy. *Psychiatric Quarterly*, 1940, *14*, 826–833.

Halpern, F. The Bender Visual Motor Gestalt Test. In Anderson, H.H. and Anderson, G.L. (Eds.) *An Introduction to Projective Techniques.* New York: Prentice-Hall, 1951.

Halpern, F. Rotation errors made by brain-injured and familial children on two visual motor tests. *American Journal of Mental Deficiency*, 1955, *59*, 485–489.

Halstead, W.C. Biological intelligence. In Jenkins, J.J. and Paterson, D.G. (Eds.) *Studies in Individual Differences.* New York: Appleton-Century-Crofts, 1961, pp. 661–668.

Hammer, E.F. A comparison of H-T-P's of rapists and pedophiles. *Journal of Projective Techniques*, 1954, *18*, 346–354.

Hammer, E.F. *The Clinical Application of Projective Drawings.* Springfield, Ill.: Charles C. Thomas, 1958.

Hammer, E.F. The House-Tree-Person (H-T-P) drawings as a projective technique with children. In Rabin, A.I. and Haworth, R. (Eds.) *Projective Techniques with Children.* New York: Grune & Stratton, 1960.

Hammer, E.F. Acting out and its predictor by projective drawing assessment. In Abt, L. and Weissman, S. (Eds.) *Acting Out.* New York: Grune & Stratton, 1965, pp. 288–319.

Hammer, E.F. Projective drawings. In Rabin, A.I. (Ed.) *Projective Techniques in Personality Assessment.* New York: Springer, 1968, pp. 366–393.

Hammer, E.F. Hierarchical organization of personality and the H-T-P, achromatic and chromatic. In Buck, J.N. and Hammer, E.F. (Eds.) *Advances in the House-Tree-Person Technique: Variations and Applications.* Los Angeles: Western Psychological Services, 1969. (a)

Hammer, E.F. The use of the H-T-P in a criminal court: predicting acting out. In Buck, J.N. and Hammer, E.F. (Eds.) *Advances in the House-Tree-Person Technique: Variations and Applications.* Los Angeles: Western Psychological Services, 1969. (b)

Hammond, K.R. and Allen, J.M. *Writing Clinical Reports.* New York: Prentice-Hall, 1953.

Handler, L. and McIntosh, J. Predicting aggression and withdrawal in children with the Draw-A-Person and Bender-Gestalt. *Journal of Personality Assessment*, 1971, *35*, 331–337.

Handler, L. and Reyher, J. The effects of stress on the Draw-A-Person Test. *Journal of Consulting Psychology*, 1964, *28*, 259–264.

Harriman, M. and Harriman, P. The Bender-Gestalt as a measure of school readiness. *Journal of Clinical Psychology*, 1950, *6*, 175–177.

Harris, D.B. *Children's Drawings as Measures of Intellectual Maturity.* New York: Harcourt, Brace and World, 1963.

Harris, J.G. Validity: the search for a constant in a universe of variables. In Rickers-Ovsiankina, M. (Ed.) *Rorschach Psychology.* New York: John Wiley & Sons, 1960.

Harris R. and Lingoes, J. *Subscales for the Minnesota Multiphasic Personality Inventory* (mimeographed materials). Department of Psychology, University of Michigan, 1968.

Harris, T.L. and Brown, N.W. Concurrent validity of the Rathus Assertiveness Schedule. *Educational and Psychological Measurement*, 1979, *39*(1), 181–186.

Hase, H.D. and Goldberg, L.R. Comparative validity of different strategies of constructing personality inventory scales. *Psychological Bulletin,* 1967, *67,* 231–248.

Haynes, J.P. and Bensch, M. The PV sign on the WISC-R and recidivision in delinquents. *Journal of Consulting and Clinical Psychology,* 1981, *49*(3), 480–481.

Hebb, D.O. *Textbook of Psychology* (3rd ed.). Philadelphia: W.B. Saunders, 1972.

Heilbrun, A.B., Jr. Male and female personality correlates of early termination in counseling. *Journal of Counseling Psychology,* 1961, *8,* 31–36.

Heilbrun, A.B., Jr., Daniel, J.L., Goodstein, L.D., Stephenson, R.R., and Crites, J.O. The validity of two-scale pattern interpretation on the California Psychological Inventory. *Journal of Applied Psychology,* 1962, *46,* 409–416.

Heinicke, C.M. Learning disturbance in childhood. In Wolman, B.B. (Ed.) *Manual of Child Psychopathology.* New York: McGraw-Hill, 1972, pp. 662–705.

Henrichs, T., Krauskapf, C.J., and Amolsch, T.J. Personality description from the WAIS: a comparison of systems. *Journal of Personality Assessment,* 1982, *46,* 544–549.

Henry, E.M. and Rotter, J.B. Situational influences on Rorschach responses. *Journal of Consulting Psychology,* 1956, *20,* 457–462.

Henry, W.E. *The Analysis of Fantasy: The Thematic Apperception Test in the Study of Personality.* New York: John Wiley & Sons, 1956.

Hersen, M. and Greaves, S.T. Rorschach productivity as related to verbal performance. *Journal of Personality Assessment,* 1971, *35,* 436–441.

Hersh, C. The cognitive functioning of the creative person: a developmental analysis. *Journal of Projective Techniques,* 1962, *26,* 193–200.

Hertz, M.R. Personality patterns in adolescence as portrayed by the Rorschach ink blot method: IV. The "Erlebnistypus." *Journal of General Psychology,* 1943, *29,* 3 45.

Hertz, M.R. The organization activity. In Rickers-Ovsiankina, Mr. (Ed.) *Rorschach Psychology.* New York: John Wiley & Sons, 1960, pp. 25–57.

Hertz, M.R. and Paolino, A. Rorschach indices of perceptual and conceptual disorganization. *Journal of Projective Techniques,* 1960, *24,* 310–388.

Hetherington, R. The effects of E.C.T. on the drawings of depressed patients. *Journal of Mental Science,* 1952, *98,* 450–453.

Hill, A.H. Use of a structured autobiography in the construct validation of personality scales. *Journal of Consulting Psychology,* 1967, *31,* 551–556.

Hill, R.E., Jr. Dichotomous prediction of student teaching excellence employing selected CPI scales. *Journal of Educational Research,* 1960, *53,* 349–351.

Hirschenfang, S.A. A comparison of Bender-Gestalt reproductions of right and left hemiplegic patients. *Journal of Clinical Psychology,* 1960, *16,* 439. (a)

Hirschenfang, S.A. A comparison of WAIS scores of hemiplegic patients with and without aphasia. *Journal of Clinical Psychology,* 1960, *16,* 351. (b)

Hoey, H.P. Lethality of suicidal behavior and the MMPI. *Psychological Reports,* 1974, *35*(2), 942.

Hoffman, H., Loper, R.G., and Kammeier, M.L. Identifying future alcoholics with MMPI alcoholism scales. *Quarterly Journal of Studies on Alcohol,* 1974, *35,* 490–498.

Hogan, R. Development of an Empathy Scale. *Journal of Consulting and Clinical Psychology,* 1969, *33*(3), 307–316.

Hogan, R. Personality characteristics of highly rated policemen. *Personnel Psychology,* 1971, *24*(4), 679–686.

Holland, T., Lowenfeld, J., and Wadsworth, H. MMPI indices in the discrimination of brain damaged and schizophrenic groups. *Journal of Consulting and Clinical Psychology,* 1975, *43,* 426–434.

Hollis, J.W. and Donna, P.A. *Psychological Report Writing: Theory and Practice.* Muncie, In. Accelerated Development Inc., 1979.

Holt, R.R. Yet another look at clinical and statistical prediction: or is clinical psychology worthwhile? *American Psychologist,* 1970, *25,* 337–349.

Holzberg, J.D. and Belmont, L. The relationship between factors on the Wechsler-Bellevue and Rorschach having common psychological rationale. *Journal of Consulting Psychology,* 1952, *16,* 23–29.

Horstman, P. Assessing the California Psychological Inventory for predicting police performance. *Dissertation Abstracts International,* 1977, *37,* 6387.

Huesmann, L.R., Lefkowitz, M.M., and Eron, L.D. Sum of MMPI scales F, 4 and 9 as a measure of aggression. *Journal of Consulting and Clinical Psychology,* 1978, *46,* 1071–1078.

Hutt, M.L. Revised Bender Visual-Motor Gestalt Test. In Weider, A. (Ed.) *Continuations toward Medical Psychology,* Vol. 2. New York: Ronald Press, 1953.

Hutt, M.L. *The Hutt Adaptation of the Bender-Gestalt Test* (3rd ed.). New York: Grune & Stratton, 1971.

Hutt, M.L. and Briskin, G.J. *The Clinical Use of the Revised Bender-Gestalt Test.* New York: Grune & Stratton, 1960.

Hutt, M.L. and Gibby, R.G. *An Atlas for the Hutt Adaptation of the Bender-Gestalt Test.* New York: Grune & Stratton, 1970.

Jacks, I. The clinical application of the H-T-P in criminological settings. In Buck, J.N. and Hammer, E.F. (Eds.) *Advances in the House-Tree-Person Technique: Variations and Applications.* Los Angeles: Western Psychological Services, 1969.

Jansky, J. and de Hirsch, K. *Preventing Reading Failure.* New York: Harper & Row, 1972.

Jensen, A.R. How much can we boost I.Q. and scholastic achievement? *Harvard Educational Review,* 1969, *39,* 1–23.

Jensen, A.R. *Genetics and Education.* New York: Harper & Row, 1972.

Johnson, J.H. Bender-Gestalt constriction as an indicator of depression in psychiatric patients. *Journal of Personality Assessment,* 1973, *37,* 53–55.

Jolles, I.A. *A Catalogue for the Qualitative Interpretation of the H-T-P.* Beverly Hills, Calif.: Western Psychological Services, 1952.

Jolles, I.A. The use of the H-T-P in a school setting. In Buck, J.N. and Hammer, E.F. (Eds.) *Advances in the House-Tree-Person Technique: Variations and Applications.* Beverly Hills, Calif.: Western Psychological Services, 1969, pp. 223–241.

Jolles, I.A. *A Catalogue for the Qualitative Interpretation of the H-T-P.* Beverly Hills, Calif.: Western Psychological Services, 1971.

Jolles, I.A. and Beck, H.S. A study of validity of some hypotheses for the quantitative interpretation of the H-T-P for children of elementary school age: II. Horizontal placement. *Journal of Clinical Psychology,* 1953, *9,* 161–169. (b)

Jolles, I.A. and Beck, H.S. A study of validity of some hypotheses for the qualitative interpretation of the H-T-P for children of elementary school age: III. Horizontal placement. *Journal of Clinical Psychology,* 1953, *9,* 164–167(a).

Judson, A.J. and McCasland, B. A note on the influence of the season on tree drawings. *Journal of Clinical Psychology,* 1960, *16,* 171–173.

Kagan, J. *Understanding Children.* New York: Harcourt, Brace, Jovanovich, 1971.

Kagan, J., Moss, H.A., and Siegel, I.E. Psychological significance of styles of conceptualization. *Monographs of the Society for Research in Child Development,* 1963, *28*(2), 73–124.

Kahn, T.C. and Giffen, M.B. *Psychological Techniques in Diagnosis and Evaluation.* New York: Pergamon, 1960.

Kaldegg, A. Psychological observations in a group of alcoholic patients with analysis of Rorschach, Wechsler-Bellevue and Bender-Gestalt test results. *Quarterly Journal of Studies of Alcohol,* 1956, *17,* 608–628.

Kallstedt, F.E. A Rorschach study of sixty-six adolescents. *Journal of Clinical Psychology,* 1952, *8,* 129–132.

Kamin, L.J. *The Science and Politics of I.Q.* Hillsdale, N.J.: Erlbaum, 1974.

Kaplan, R.M. and Sacuzzo, D.P. *Psychological Testing: Principles, Applications, and Issues.* Belmont: Wadsworth, 1982.

Karon, B.P. Projective tests are valid. *American Psychologist*, 1978, *33*, 764–765.

Kaufman, A.S. Factor analysis of the WISC-R at eleven ages between 6 1/2 and 16 1/2 years. *Journal of Consulting and Clinical Psychology*, 1975, *43*, 135–147.

Kaufman, A.S. *Intelligent Testing with the WISC-R.* New York: John Wiley & Sons, 1979.

Keller, J. The use of a Bender-Gestalt maturation level scoring system with mentally handicapped children. *American Journal of Orthopsychiatry*, 1955, *25*, 563–573.

Keogh, B. and Smith, C. Group techniques and a proposed scoring system for the Bender-Gestalt Test with children. *Journal of Clinical Psychology*, 1961, *17*, 172–175.

Khan, R.Z. *Visual Apperception Test '60.* Minneapolis: Midwest Psychological Services, 1960.

Kincannon, J.C. Prediction of the standard MMPI scale scores from 71 items: the Mini-Mult. *Journal of Consulting and Clinical Psychology*, 1968, *32*, 319–325.

Kipnis, D. Social immaturity, intellectual ability, and adjustive behavior in college. *Journal of Applied Psychology*, 1968, *52*, 71–80.

Kirk, B.A., Cumming, R.W., and Hackett, H.H. Personal and vocational characteristics of dental students. *Personnel and Guidance Journal*, 1963, *41*, 522–527.

Klopfer, B. The shading response. *Rorschach Research Exchange*, 1938, *2*, 76–79.

Klopfer, B., Ainsworth, M.D., Klopfer, W.G., and Holt, R.R. *Developments in the Rorschach Technique:* Vol. I. Yonkers, N.Y.: World Book Company, 1954.

Klopfer, B., Ainsworth, M.D., Klopfer, W.G., and Holt, R.R. *Developments in the Rorschach Technique:* Vol. II. Yonkers, N.Y.: World Book Company, 1956.

Klopfer, B. and Davidson, H. *The Rorschach Technique: An Introductory Manual.* New York: Harcourt, 1962.

Klopfer, B. and Kelly, D. The Rorschach Technique. Yonkers, N.Y.: World Book Company, 1942.

Klopfer, W.G. *The Psychological Report.* New York: Grune & Stratton, 1960.

Kobler, F.J. and Stiel, A. The use of the Rorschach in involutional melancholia. *Journal of Consulting Psychology*, 1953, *17*, 365–370.

Koch, C. *The Tree Test.* New York: Grune & Stratton, 1952.

Kohlberg, L. and Zigler, E. The impact of cognitive maturity on the development of sex-role attitudes in the years 4 to 8. *Genetic Psychology Monographs*, 1967, *75*, 89–165.

Kokonis, N.D. Body image disturbance in schizophrenics: a study of arms and feet. *Journal of Personality Assessment*, 1972, *36*, 573–575.

Kolb, L.C. *Modern Clinical Psychiatry* (9th ed.). Philadelphia: W.B. Saunders, 1977.

Koppitz, E.M. Relationships between the Bender-Gestalt Test and the Wechsler Intelligence Scale for Children. *Journal of Clinical Psychology*, 1958, *14*, 413–416. (a)

Koppitz, E.M. The Bender-Gestalt Test and learning disturbance in young children. *Journal of Clinical Psychology*, 1958, *14*, 292–295.

Koppitz, E.M. Teacher's attitude and children's performance on the Bender-Gestalt Test and human figure drawings. *Journal of Clinical Psychology*, 1960, *16*, 204–208.

Koppitz, E.M. The Bender-Gestalt Test for children: a normative study. *Journal of Clinical Psychology*, 1960, *16*, 432–435. (b)

Koppitz, E.M. Diagnosing brain damage in young children with the Bender-Gestalt Test. *Journal of Consulting Psychology*, 1962, *26*, 541–546. (a)

Koppitz, E.M. The Bender-Gestalt Test with the Human Figure Drawing Test for young school children. Columbus, Ohio: Department of Education, 1962. (b)

Koppitz, E.M. *The Bender Gestalt Test for Young Children.* New York: Grune & Stratton, 1963.

Koppitz, E.M. Use of the Bender Gestalt Test in elementary school. *Skolepsykologi*, 1965, *2*, 193–200.

Koppitz, E.M. *Psychological Evaluation of Children's Human Figure Drawings.* New York: Grune & Stratton, 1968.

Koppitz, E.M. The Bender Gestalt Test and Visual Aural Digit Span Test and reading achievement. *Journal of Learning Disabilities*, 1975, *8*, 154–157. (a)

Koppitz, E.M. *The Bender Gestalt Test for Young Children:* Vol. II: Research and Applications 1963-1973. New York: Grune & Stratton, 1975. (b)

Koppitz, E.M., Mardis, V., and Stephens, T. A note on screening school beginners with the Bender Gestalt Test. *Journal of Educational Psychology*, 1961, *52*, 80–81.

Koss, M.P. MMPI item content: "recurring issues." In Butcher, J.N. (Ed.) *New Developments in the Use of the MMPI.* Minneapolis: University of Minnesota Press, 1979.

Koss, M.P., Butcher, J.N., and Hoffman, N. The MMPI critical items: how well do they work? *Journal of Consulting and Clinical Psychology*, 1976, *44*, 921-928.

Kuhn, R. Uber die kritische Rorschach-Forschung and einige ihrer Ergebnisse. *Rorschachiana*, 1963, *8*, 105–114.

Kurz, R.B. Relationship between time imagery and Rorschach human movement responses. *Journal of Consulting Psychology*, 1963, *29*, 379–382.

Lachar, D. *The MMPI: Clinical Assessment and Automated Interpretation.* Los Angeles: Western Psychological Services, 1974.

Lachar, D. and Alexander, R.S. Veridicality of self-report: replicated correlates of the Wiggins MMPI content scales. *Journal of Consulting and Clinical Psychology*, 1978, *46*, 1346-1356.

Lachar, D. and Wrobel, T.A. Validation of clinician's hunches: construction of a new MMPI critical item set. *Journal of Consulting and Clinical Psychology*, 1979, *47*(2), 277–284.

Lachman, F.M. Perceptual-motor development in children retarded in reading ability. *Journal of Consulting Psychology*, 1960, *24*, 427–431.

Lakin, M. Certain formal characteristics of human figure drawings by institutionalized aged and by normal children. *Journal of Consulting Psychology*, 1956, *20*, 471–474.

Landisberg, S. The use of the H-T-P in a mental hygiene clinic for children. In Buck, J.N. and Hammer, E.F. (Eds.) *Advances in the House-Tree-Person Technique: Variations and Applications.* Los Angeles: Western Psychological Services, 1969.

Leary, T. *Interpersonal Diagnosis of Personality.* New York: The Ronald Press Co., 1957.

Leon, G.R., Gillum, B., Gillum, R., and Gouze, M. Personality stability and change over a 30-year period – middle age to old age. *Journal of Consulting and Clinical Psychology*, 1980.

Leonard, C.V. Bender-Gestalt as an indicator of suicidal potential. *Psychological Reports*, 1973, *32*, 665–666.

Lerner, E.A. *The Projective Use of the Bender-Gestalt Test.* Springfield, Ill.: Charles C. Thomas, 1972.

Lesser, G.S., Fifer, G., and Clark, D.H. Mental abilities of children from different social-class and cultural groups. *Monographs of the Society for Research in Child Development,* 1965, *30*(4), Serial No. 102.

Levi, J. Rorschach patterns predicting success or failure in rehabilitation of the physically handicapped. *Journal of Abnormal and Social Psychology*, 1951, *46*, 240–244.

Levi, J. Acting out indicators on the Rorschach. In Abt, L. and Weissman, S. (Eds.) *Acting Out.* (2nd Ed.) New York: Aronson, 1976, pp. 252–256.

Levine, A. and Sapolsky, A. The use of the H-T-P as an aid in the screening of hospitalized patients. In Buck, J.N. and Hammer, E.F. (Eds.) *Advances in the House-Tree-Person Technique: Variations and Applications.* Los Angeles: Western Psychological Services, 1969.

Levine, D. Why and when to test: the social context of psychological testing. In Rabin, A.I. (Ed.) *Assessment with Projective Techniques.* New York: Springer Publishing Co., 1981.

Levitt, E.E. Results of psychotherapy with children: an evaluation. *Journal of Consulting Psychology*, 1957, *21*, 189-196.

Levitt, E.E. Psychotherapy with children: a further evaluation. *Behavioral Research and Therapy*, 1963, *1*, 45-51.

Levitt, E.E. *Primer on the Rorschach Technique.* Springfield, Ill.: Charles C. Thomas, 1980.

Levitt, E.E. and Truumaa, A. *The Rorschach Technique with Children and Adolescents: Applications and Norms.* New York: Grune & Stratton, 1972.

Levy, S. Figure drawing as a projective test. In Abt, L.E. and Bellak, L. (Eds.) *Projective Psychology.* New York: Knopf, 1950, pp. 257-297.

Levy, S. Projective figure drawing. In Hammer, E.F. (Ed.) *The Clinical Application of Projective Drawings,* Springfield, Ill.: Charles C. Thomas, 1958, pp. 83-112; 135-161.

Light, B.H. and Amick, J. Rorschach responses of normal aged. *Journal of Projective Techniques,* 1956, *20*, 185-195.

Lindzey, G. and Herman, P.S. Thematic Apperception Test: a note on reliability and situational validity. *Journal of Projective Techniques,* 1955, *19*, 36-42.

Linton, H.B. Rorschach correlates of response to suggestion. *Journal of Abnormal and Social Psychology,* 1954, *49*, 75-83.

Lison, S., and Van der Spuy, H.I.J. *Cross-national MMPI research: group personality in South Africa.* Unpublished manuscript, University of Capetown, 1977 (mimeograph ed.).

Loosli-Usteri, M. Le test de Rorschach applique a differents groupes d'enfants de 10-13 ans. *Archives de Psychologie,* 1929, *22*, 51-106.

Lotsoff, E.J. Intelligence, verbal fluency, and the Rorschach test. *Journal of Consulting Psychology,* 1953, *17*, 21-24.

Loughmiller, G.C., Ellison, R.L., Taylor, C.W., and Price, P.B. Predicting career performances of physicians using the autobiographical inventory approach. *Proceedings of the American Psychological Association,* 1970, *5*, 153-154.

Lovell, V.R. The human use of personality tests: a dissenting view. *American Psychologist,* 1967, *22*, 383-393.

Lowenfeld, M. *The Lowenfeld Mosaic Test.* London: Newman Neame, 1954.

Luscher, M. *The Luscher Color Test* (translated and edited by I.A. Scott). London: Cape, 1970.

MacAndrews, C. The differentiation of male alcoholic outpatients from nonalcoholic psychiatric patients by means of the MMPI. *Quarterly Journal of Studies on Alcohol,* 1965, *26*, 238-246.

Machover, K. *Personality Projection in the Drawings of the Human Figure.* Springfield, Ill.: Charles C. Thomas, 1949.

Machover, K. Drawings of the human figure. A method of personality investigation. In Anderson, H.H. and Anderson, G. (Eds.) *An Introduction to Projective Techniques.* Englewood Cliffs, N.J.: Prentice-Hall, 1951, pp. 341-369.

Machover, K. Adolescent-case study: a disturbed adolescent girl. In Hammer, E.F. (ed.) *The Clinical Application of Projective Drawings.* Springfield, Ill.: Charles C. Thomas, 1958, pp. 130-134.

Machover, K. Sex differences in the developmental pattern of children seen in human figure drawings. In Rabin, A.I. and Haworth, E. (Eds.) *Projective Techniques with Children.* New York: Grune & Stratton, 1960.

Majumber, A.K. and Roy, A.B. Latent personality content of juvenile delinquents. *Journal of Psychological Research*, 1962, *1*, 4–8.

Maloney, M.P. and Ward, M.P. *Psychological Assessment: A Conceptual Approach*. New York: Oxford University Press, 1976.

Marks, P.A., Seeman, W., and Haller, D.L. *The Actuarial Use of the MMPI with Adolescents and Adults*. Baltimore: Williams and Wilkins, 1974.

Marley, M.L. *Organic Brain Pathology and the Bender Gestalt Test: A Differential Diagnostic Scoring System*. New York: Grune & Stratton, 1982.

Marzoff, S.S. and Kirchner, J.H. Characteristics of House-Tree-Person drawings by college men and women. *Journal of Projective Techniques and Personality Assessment*, 1972, *36*, 148–165.

Masland, R.L., Sarason, R.B., and Gladwin, T. *Mental Subnormality*. New York: Basic Books, 1958.

Matarazzo, J.D. *Wechsler's Measurement and Appraisal of Adult Intelligence* (5th ed.). Baltimore: Williams and Wilkins, 1972.

Mayman, M. Style, focus, language, and content of an ideal psychological test report. *Journal of Projective Techniques*, 1959, *23*, 453–458.

McCarthy, D.A. *Manual for the McCarthy Scales for Children's Abilities*. New York: Psychological Corporation, 1972.

McClelland, D.C. *The Achieving Society*. New York: The Free Press, 1961.

McCreary, C.P. Trait and type differences among male and female assaultive and nonassaultive offenders. *Journal of Personality Assessment*, 1976, *40*, 617–621.

McElhaney, M. *Clinical Psychological Assessment of the Human Figure Drawing*. Springfield, Ill.: Charles C. Thomas, 1969.

Meer, B. The relative difficulty of the Rorschach cards. *Journal of Projective Techniques*, 1955, *9*, 43–59.

Megargee, E.I. *Undercontrol and overcontrol in assaultive and homicidal adolescents* (doctoral dissertation, University of California, Berkely). *University Microfilms*, 1964, No. 64-9923.

Megargee, E.I. Assault with intent to kill. *Trans-Action*, 1965, *2*(6), 27–31.

Megargee, E.I. Estimation of CPI scores from MMPI protocols. *Journal of Clinical Psychology*, 1966, *22*, 456–458. (a)

Megargee, E.I. (Ed.). *Research in Clinical Assessment*. New York: Harper & Row, 1966. (b)

Megargee, E.I. The Edwards SD Scale: a measure of dissimulation or adjustment? *Journal of Consulting Psychology*, 1966, *30*, 566. (c)

Megargee, E.I. Undercontrolled and overcontrolled personality types in extreme anti-social aggression. *Psychological Monographs*, 1966, *80*(3) No. 611. (d)

Megargee, E.I. *The California Psychological Inventory Handbook*. San Francisco: Jossey-Bass, 1972.

Megargee, E.I. and Parker, G.V. An exploration of the equivalence of Murrayan needs as assessed by the Adjective Check List, the TAT, and the Edwards Personal Preference Schedule. *Journal of Clinical Psychology*, 1968, *24*, 47–51.

Merbaum, M. and Hefetz, A. Some personality characteristics of soldiers exposed to extreme war stress. *Journal of Consulting and Clinical Psychology*, 1976, *44*, 1–6.

Mercer, J.R. In defense of racially and culturally non-discriminatory assessment. *School Psychology Digest*, 1979, *8*(1), 89–115.

Messick, S. and Jackson, D.N. Acquiescence and the factorial interpretation of the MMPI. *Psychological Bulletin*, 1961, *58*, 299–304.

Meyer, M.M. and Caruth, E. Rorschach indices of ego processes. In Klopfer, B. et al. (Eds.) *Developments in the Rorschach Technique*, Vol. III, Ch. 2. New York: Harcourt, Brace, Jovanovich, 1970.

Meyers, H. *Frohliche Kinderkunst un der Schule*. Munich: Barth, 1953.

Miller, C., Knapp, S.C., and Daniels, C.W. MMPI study of Negro mental hygiene clinic patients. *Journal of Abnormal Psychology*, 1968, *73*, 168-173.

Mirza, L. Multiple administration of the MMPI with schizophrenics. Unpublished manuscript, Fountain House, Pakistan, 1977.

Mizushima, K. and De Vos, G. An application of the California Psychological Inventory in a study of Japanese delinquency. *Journal of Clinical Psychology*, 1967, *71*, 45-51.

Modell, A.H. and Potter, H.W. Human figure drawing of patients with arterial hypertension, peptic ulcer, and bronchial asthma. *Psychosomatic Medicine*, 1949, *11*, 282-292.

Molish, H.B. Critique and problems of the Rorschach. A survey. In Beck, S.J. and Molish, H.B. (Eds.) *Rorschach's Test*, Vol. II: A Variety of Personality Pictures (2nd ed.). New York: Grune & Stratton, 1967.

Mukerji, M. Rorschach indices of love, aggression, and happiness. *Journal of Projective Techniques and Personality Assessment*, 1969, *33*, 526-529.

Muhle, G. *Entwicklungs-psychologie des zeichnerischen Gestaltens* (2nd ed.). Munich: Barth, 1967.

Mundy, J. The use of projective techniques with children. In Wolman, B.B. (Ed.) *Manual of Child Psychopathology*. New York: McGraw-Hill, 1972, pp. 791-819.

Munsinger, H. The adopted child's I.Q.: a critical review. *Psychological Bulletin*, 1975, *82*, 623-659.

Murillo, L.G. and Exner, J.E. The effects of regressive ECT with process schizophrenics. *American Journal of Psychiatry*, 1973, *130*, 269-273.

Murray, H.A. *Explorations in Personality*. New York: Oxford University Press, 1938.

Murray, H.A. *Thematic Apperception Test Manual*. Cambridge, Mass.: Harvard University Press, 1943.

Mursell, G.R. The use of the H-T-P with the mentally deficient. In Buck, J.N. and Hammer, E.F. (Eds.) *Advances in the House-Tree-Person Technique: Variations and Applications*. Los Angeles: Western Psychological Services, 1969.

Murstein, B.I. Factor analysis of the Rorschach. *Journal of Consulting Psychology*, 1960, *24*, 262-275.

Murstein, B.I. *Theory and Research in Projective Techniques (Emphasizing the TAT)*. New York: John Wiley & Sons, 1963.

Nahas, A.D. The prediction of perceptual motor abnormalities in paranoid schizophrenia. *Research Communications in Psychology, Psychiatry and Behavior*, 1976, *1*, 167-181.

Neal, E. Moderating effects of age and sex on the association of medical diagnoses and 1-3/3-1 MMPI profiles. *Journal of Consulting and Clinical Psychology*, 1972, *28*, 502-510.

Newmark, C.S., Owen, M., Newark, L., and Fauschingbauer, T.R. Comparison of three abbreviated MMPI's for psychiatric patients and normals. *Journal of Personality Assessment*, 1975, *39*, 261-270.

Newmark, C.S. and Thibodeau, J.R. Interpretive accuracy and empirical validity of abbreviated forms of the MMPI with hospitalized adolescents. In Newmark, C.S. (Eds.) *MMPI: Clinical and Research Trends*. New York: Praeger, 1979.

Norman, R.D. A revised deterioration formula for the Wechsler Adult Intelligence Scale. *Journal of Clinical Psychology*, 1966, *22*, 287-294.

Norton, J.C. The Trail Making Test and Bender Background Interference Procedure as screening devices. *Journal of Clinical Psychology*, 1978, *34*, 916-922.

Nunez, R. *Aplicacion del Inventario Multifasico de la Personalidad (MMPI) a la Psicopatologia* (Application of the MMPI to Psychotherapy). Mexico: El Manual Moderno, 1968.

Nunez, R. *Aplicacion del Inventario Multifasico de la Personalidad (MMPI) a la Psicopatologia* (2nd ed.). Mexico: El Manual Moderro, 1980.

Office of Science and Technology. *Privacy and Behavioral Research.* Washington, D.C.: U.S. Government Printing Office, 1967.

Overall, J.E. and Gomez-Mont, F. The MMPI-168 for psychiatric screening. *Educational and Psychological Measurement,* 1974, *34*, 315–319.

Padilla, A.M. and Ruiz, R.A. Personality assessment and test interpretation of Mexican Americans: a critique. *Journal of Personality Assessment,* 1975, *39*, 103–109.

Palmer, J.O. *The Psychological Assessment of Children.* New York: John Wiley & Sons, 1970.

Pascal, G.R. and Suttell, B.J. *The Bender Gestalt Test: Quantification and Validity for Adults.* New York: Grune & Stratton, 1951.

Paulker, J.D. Relationship of Rorschach content categories to intelligence. *Journal of Projective Techniques and Personality Assessment,* 1963, *27*, 220–221.

Paulker, J.D. A quick-scoring system for the Bender-Gestalt: interrater reliability and scoring validity. *Journal of Clinical Psychology,* 1976, *32*, 86–89.

Payne, F.D. and Wiggins, J.S. MMPI profile types and the self-reports of psychiatric patients. *Journal of Abnormal Psychology,* 1972, *79*, 1–8.

Pfeifer, C. and Sedlacek, W. The validity of academic predictors for black and white students at a predominantly white university. *Journal of Educational Measurement,* 1971, *8*, 253–261.

Phares, E.J., Stewart, L.M., and Foster, J.M. Instruction variation and Rorschach performance. *Journal of Projective Techniques,* 1960, *24*, 28–31.

Phillips, L. and Smith, J. *Rorschach Interpretation: Advanced Technique.* New York: Grune & Stratton, 1953.

Piaget, J. *The Psychology of Intelligence.* New York: Harcourt, Brace & World, 1950.

Piotrowski, Z.A. The Rorschach ink-blot method in organic disturbances of the central nervous system. *Journal of Nervous and Mental Disorders,* 1937, *86*, 525–537.

Piotrowski, Z.A. *Perceptanalysis.* New York: Macmillan, 1957.

Piotrowski, Z.A. The movement score. In Rickers-Ovsiankina, M. (Ed.) *Rorschach Psychology.* New York: John Wiley & Sons, 1960.

Piotrowski, Z.A. A Piotrowski interpretation. In Exner, J.E. (Ed.) *The Rorschach Systems.* New York: Grune & Stratton, 1969. (a)

Piotrowski, Z.A. Long-term prognosis in schizophrenia based on Rorschach findings: the LTPTI. In Sira Sankar, D.V. (Ed.) *Schizophrenia, Current Concepts and Research.* Hicksville, N.Y.: PJD Publications, 1969, pp. 84–103. (b)

Piotrowski, Z.A. and Berg, D.A. Verification of the Rorschach alpha diagnostic formula for underactive schizophrenics. *American Journal of Psychiatry,* 1955, *112*, 443–450.

Piotrowski, Z.A. and Bricklin, B.A. A second validation of a long-term prognostic index for schizophrenic patients. *Journal of Consulting Psychology,* 1961, *25*, 123–128.

Piotrowski, Z.A. and Schreiber, M. Rorschach perceptanalytic measurement of personality changes during and after intensive psychoanalytically oriented psychotherapy. In Bychowski, G. and Despert, J.L. (Eds.) *Specialized Techniques in Psychotherapy.* New York: Basic Books, 1952.

Plenk, A.M. and Jones, J. An examination of the Bender-Gestalt performance of three and four year olds and its relationship to Koppitz scoring system. *Journal of Clinical Psychology,* 1967, *23*, 367–370.

Pope, B. and Scott, W.H. *Psychological Diagnosis in Clinical Practice.* New York: Oxford University Press, 1967.

Quast, W. The Bender Gestalt: a clinical study of children's records. *Journal of Consulting Psychology,* 1961, *25*, 405–408.

Query, W.T. CPI factors and success of seminary students. *Psychological Reports,* 1966, *18,* 665–660.

Quiroga, I.R. and Besner, V.F. Cross-cultural comparison of HMA profile differences between Anglo and Mexican-American psychiatric patients. Unpublished manuscript, Department of Youth and Family Development, Miami, Fla., undated.

Rabin, A.I. *Projective Techniques in Personality Assessment: A Modern Introduction.* New York: Springer, 1968.

Rabin, A.I. and Beck, S.J. Genetic aspects of some Rorschach factors. *American Journal of Orthopsychiatry,* 1950, *20,* 595–599.

Rabin, A.I., Nelson, W., and Clark, M. Rorschach content as a function of perceptual experience and sex of examiner. *Journal of Clinical Psychology,* 1954, *10,* 188–190.

Rapaport, C., Gill, M., an Schafer, J. *Diagnostic Psychological Testing,* Vol. II. Chicago: Year Book Publishers, 1946.

Rapaport, C., Gill, M., and Schaeffer, J. *Diagnostic Psychological Testing,* Vol. I. Chicago: Year Book Publishers, 1968.

Rawls, J.R. and Slack, G.K. Artists versus non-artists: Rorschach determinants and artistic creativity. *Journal of Projective Techniques and Personality Assessment,* 1968, *32,* 233–237.

Raychaudhuri, M. Relation of creativity and sex to Rorschach *M* responses. *Journal of Personality Assessment,* 1971, *35,* 27–36.

Redfering, D.L. and Collings, J. A comparison of the Koppitz and Hutt techniques of Bender Gestalt administration correlated with WISC-R performance scores. *Educational and Psychological Measurement,* 1982, *42,* 41–47.

Reed, H.B.C., Jr. and Reitan, R.M. Intelligence test performances of brain damaged subjects with lateralized motor deficits. *Journal of Consulting Psychology,* 1963, *27,* 102–106.

Reichter, R.H. and Winter, W.D. Holtzman ink-blot correlates of creative potential. *Journal of Projective Techniques and Personality Assessment,* 1966, *30,* 62–67.

Reilly, R.R. and Knight, C.G. MMPI scores of Mexican-American college students. *Journal of College Student Personnel,* 1970, *11,* 419–422.

Reitan, R.M. Validity of the Rorschach test as a measure of the psychological effects of brain damage. *Archives of Neurology and Psychiatry,* 1955, *73,* 445–451.

Reitan, R.M. Methodological problems in clinical neuropsychology. In Reitan, R.M. and Davison, L.A. (Eds.) *Clinical Neuropsychology: Current Status and Applications.* New York: John Wiley & Sons, 1974. (a)

Reitan, R.M. Psychological effects of cerebral lesions in children of early school age. In Reitan, R.M. and Davison, L.A. (Eds.) *Clinical Neuropsychology: Current Status and Applications.* Washington, D.C.: V.H. Winston and Sons, 1974, pp. 53–90.

Reynolds, C.R., Gutkin, T.B., Dappen, L., and Wright, D. Differential validity of the WISC-R for boys and girls referred for psychological services. *Perceptual and Motor Skills,* 1979, *48,* 868–870.

Reynolds, C.R. and Hartlage, L. Comparison of WISC and WISC-R regression lines for academic prediction with black and white referred children. *Journal of Consulting and Clinical Psychology,* 1979, *47,* 589–591.

Reznikoff, M. and Nicholas, A. An evaluation of human-figure drawing indicators of paranoid pathology. *Journal of Consulting Psychology,* 1958, *20,* 395–397.

Rickers-Ovsiankina, M.A. *Rorschach Psychology.* New York: Robert E. Krieger, 1977.

Riessman, F. and Miller, S.M. Social class and projective tests. *Journal of Projective Techniques,* 1958, *22,* 432–439.

Risetti, F., Butcher, J.N., Agostini, J., Elgueta, M., Gaete, S., Margulies, T., Morians, I., and Ruiz, R. Translation and adaptation of the MMPI in Chile: use in a university student health service. Papers given at the 14th Annual Symposium on the Recent Developments in the Use of the MMPI, St. Petersburg, 1979.

Ritzler, B.A., Sharkey, K.J., and Chudy, J.F. A comprehensive projective alternative to the TAT. *Journal of Personality Assessment*, 1980, *44*, 358–362.

Roback, H.B. Human figure drawings: their utility in the clinical psychologist's armamentarium for personality assessment. *Psychological Bulletin*, 1968, *70*, 1–19.

Rodgers, D.A. The MMPI: a review. In Buros, O.K. (Ed.) *Seventh Mental Measurements Yearbook*, Vol. 1. Highland Park, N.J.: Gryphon Press, 1972, pp. 243–250.

Roe, A. Analysis of group Rorschachs of psychologists and anthropologists. *Journal of Projective Techniques*, 1952, *16*, 212–242.

Rorschach, H. *Psychodiagnostics*. Bern: Bircher, 1921 (transl. Hans Huber Verlag, 1942).

Rosenquist, C.M. and Megargee, E.I. *Delinquency in Three Cultures*. Austin: University of Texas Press, 1969.

Rosenthal, M. Some behavior correlated to the Rorschach experience-balance. *Journal of Projective Techniques*, 1962, *26*, 442–446.

Rosenthal, R. *Experimenter Effects in Behavioral Research*. New York: Appleton-Century-Crofts, 1966.

Rosenthal, R. and Fode, K.L. The effects of experimenter bias on the performance of the albino rat. *Behavioral Science*, 1963, *8*, 183–189.

Rosenthal, R. and Jacobson, L. *Pygmalion in the Classroom*. New York: Holt, Rinehart and Winston, 1968.

Rosenzweig, S. *Manual for the Rosenzweig Picture-Frustration Study, Adolescent Form*. St. Lewis: 1976.

Rosenzweig, S. *Manual for the Children's Form of the Rosenzweig Picture-Frustration (P-F) Study*. St. Louis: Roma House, 1977.

Rosenzweig, S. *Adult Form Supplement to the Basic Manual of the Rosenzweig Picture Frustration (P-F) Study*. St. Louis: Roma House, 1978.

Rossi, A. and Neuman, G. A comparative study of Rorschach norms: medical students. *Journal of Projective Techniques*, 1961, *25*, 334–338.

Rourke, B.P. and Telegdy, G.A. Lateralizing significance of WISC verbal-performance discrepancies for older children with learning disabilities. *Perceptual and Motor Skills*, 1971, *33*, 875–883.

Royer, F.L. and Holland, T.R. Rotations of visual designs in psychopathological groups. *Journal of Consulting and Clinical Psychology*, 1975, *43*, 346–356.

Rugel, R.P. WISC subtest scores of disabled readers: a review with respect to Bannatyne's recategorization. *Journal of Learning Disabilities*, 1974, 7(1), 48–55.

Russell, E.W. Effect of acute lateralized brain damage on a factor analysis of the Wechsler-Bellevue intelligence test. *Proceedings of the 80th Annual Convention of the American Psychological Association*, 1972, *7*, 421–422.

Russell, E.W. Three patterns of brain damage on the WAIS. *Journal of Clinical Psychology*, 1979, *35*, 611–620.

Ryan, J.J. Clinical utility of a WISC-R short form. *Journal of Clinical Psychology*, 1981, *37*, 389–391.

Saarni, C. and Azara, V. Developmental analyses of human figure drawings in adolescence, young adulthood, and middle age. *Journal of Personality Assessment*, 1977, *41*, 31–38.

Sachman, H. *An investigation of certain aspects of the validity of the formal Rorschach scoring systems in relation to age, education, and vocabulary score*. Doctoral dissertation, Fordham University, 1952.

Sacuzzo, D.P. and Lewardowski, D.G. The WISC as a diagnostic tool. *Journal of Clinical Psychology*, 1976, *32*, 115–124.

Salmon, R., Arnold, J.M., and Collyer, Y.M. What do the determinants determine: the internal validity of the Rorschach. *Journal of Personality Assessment*, 1972, *36*, 33–38.

Sanders, R. and Cleveland, S.E. The relationship between certain examiner personality variables and subjects' Rorschach scores. In Murstein, B.I. (Ed.) *Handbook of Projective Techniques*. New York: Basic Books, 1965, pp. 333–335.

Sanford, R.N. *Thematic Apperception Test – Directions for Administration and Scoring*. Cambridge, Mass.: Harvard Psychological Clinic, 1939 (mimeographed).

Sattler, J.M. Examiners scoring style, accuracy, ability, and culturally disadvantaged children. In Mann, L. and Sabatino, D. (Eds.) *The First Review of Special Education*, Vol. 2. Philadelphia: J.S.E. Press, 1973. (a)

Sattler, J.M. Racial experimenter effects. In Miller, K.S. and Dreger, R.M. (Eds.) *Comparative Studies of Blacks and Whites in the United States*. New York: Seminar Press, 1973. (b)

Sattler, J.M. Learning disabled children do not have a perceptual organization deficit: comments on Dean's WISC-R analysis. *Journal of Consulting and Clinical Psychology*, 1980, *48*(2), 254–255.

Sattler, J.M. *Assessment of Children's Intelligence and Special Abilities*. Boston: Allyn and Bacon, 1982.

Sattler, J.M. and Gwynne, J. White examiners generally do not impede the intelligence test performance of black children: to debunk a myth. *Journal of Consulting and Clinical Psychology*, 1982, *50*(2), 196–208.

Sattler, J.M., Hillix, W.A., and Neher, L.A. Halo effect in examiner scoring of intelligence test responses. *Journal of Consulting and Clinical Psychology*, 1970, *34*, 172–176.

Sattler, J.M. and Winget, B.M. Intelligence testing procedures as affected by expectancy and I.Q. *Journal of Clinical Psychology*, 1970, *26*, 446–448.

Schachtel, E.G. *Experimental Foundations of Rorschach's Test*. New York: Basic Books, 1966.

Schachtel, M. Virgt medecins etudies au test de Rorschach. *Acta Neurologia de Belgium*, 1948, *48*, 22–36.

Schaefer, W. The relationship between self-concept and the Draw-A-Person test. *Journal of Clinical Psychology*, 1975, *31*, 135–136.

Schafer, R. *The Clinical Application of Psychological Tests*. New York: International University Press, 1948.

Schafer, R. *Psychoanalytic Interpretation in Rorschach Testing*. New York: Grune & Stratton, 1954.

Schaie, K.W. and Hess, R. *Colour and Personality*. Bern and Shettgar: Huber, 1964.

Schildkrout, M.S., Shenker, I.R., and Sonnenblick, M. *Human Figure Drawings in Adolescence*. New York: Brunner/Mazel, 1972.

Schmidt, H.O. and Fonda, C.P. Rorschach scores in the manic state. *Journal of Psychology*, 1954, *38*, 427–437.

Schneidman, E.S. Some relationships between thematic and drawing materials. In Hammer, E.F. (Ed.) *The Clinical Application of Projective Drawings*. Springfield, Ill.: Charles C. Thomas, 1958, pp. 620–627.

Schoor, D., Bower, G.H., and Kiernan, R. Stimulus variables in the block design task. *Journal of Consulting and Clinical Psychology*, 1982, *50*, 479–487.

Schulman, I. *The relation between perception of movement on the Rorschach test and levels of conceptualization*. Doctoral dissertation, New York University, 1953.

Schultz, C.B. and Sherman, R.H. Social class, development, and differences in reinforcer effectiveness. *Review of Educational Research*, 1976, *46*, 25–59.

Schutz, W.C. *FIRO Awareness Scales Manual.* Palo Alto, Calif.: Consulting Psychologists Press, 1958.

Seamons, D.T., Howell, R.J., Carlisle, A.L., and Roe, A.V. Rorschach simulation of mental illness and normality by psychotic and nonpsychotic legal offenders. *Journal of Personality Assessment,* 1981, *45,* 130–135.

Semeonoff, B. *Projective Techniques.* New York: John Wiley & Sons, 1976.

Serkownek, K. Subscales for scales 5 and 0 of the Minnesota Multiphasic Personality Inventory. Unpublished materials, 3134 Whitehorn Road, Cleveland Heights, Ohio 44118, 1975.

Shalit, B. Effects of environmental stimulation on the *M, FM,* and in response to the Rorschach. *Journal of Projective Techniques and Personality Assessment,* 1965, *29,* 228–231.

Shapiro, D. Color-response and perceptual passivity. *Journal of Projective Techniques,* 1956, *20,* 52–69.

Shapiro, D.A. Perceptual understanding of color response. In Rickers-Ovsiankina, M. (Ed.) *Rorschach Psychology.* New York: John Wiley & Sons, 1960, pp. 154–199.

Shapiro, M.B., Field, J., and Post, F. An inquiry into the determinants of a differentiation between elderly "organic" and "non-organic" psychiatric patients on the Bender-Gestalt Test. *Journal of Mental Science,* 1981, *103,* 364–374.

Shatin, L. Psychoneurosis and psychosomatic reactions: a Rorschach contrast. *Journal of Consulting Psychology,* 1952, *16,* 220–223.

Sherman, M.A. A comparison of formal and content factors in the diagnostic testing of schizophrenia. *Genetic Psychology Monographs,* 1952, *46,* 183–234.

Sigel, I.E. How intelligence tests limit understanding of intelligence. *Merril-Palmer Quarterly,* 1963, *9,* 39–56.

Silverstein, A.B. Validity of WISC short forms at three age levels. *California Mental Health Research Digest,* 1967, *5*(4), 253–254.

Silverstein, A.B. Cluster analysis of the Wechsler Intelligence Scale for Children – Revised. *Educational and Psychological Measurement,* 1980, *40,* 51–54.

Silverstein, A.B. and Mohan, P.J. Bender-Gestalt figure rotations in the mentally retarded. *Journal of Consulting Psychology,* 1962, *26,* 386–388.

Simon, W.E. Expectancy effects in the scoring of vocabulary items: a study of scorer bias. *Journal of Educational Measurement,* 1969, *6,* 159–164.

Singer, J.L. The experience type: some behavioral correlates and theoretical implications. In Rickers-Ovsiankina, M. (Ed.) *Rorschach Psychology.* New York: John Wiley & Sons, 1960.

Small, L. *Neuropsychodiagnosis in Psychotherapy.* New York: Brunner/Mazel, 1973.

Smith, C.E. and Keogh, B.K. The group Bender-Gestalt as a reading readiness screening instrument. *Perceptual and Motor Skills,* 1962, *15,* 639–645.

Smith, C.P. and Graham, J.R. Behavioral correlates for the MMPI standard F scale and the modified F scale for black and white psychiatric patients. *Journal of Consulting and Clinical Psychology,* 1981, *49*(3), 455–459.

Smith, D.C. and Martin, R.A. Use of learning cues with the Bender Visual Motor Gestalt Test in screening children for neurological impairment. *Journal of Consulting Psychology,* 1967, *31,* 205–209.

Smith, M.D., Coleman, M.J., Dokecki, P.R., and Davis, EW.E. Recategorized WISC-R scores of learning disabled children. *Journal of Learning Disabilities,* 1977, *10,* 437–443.

Snyder, C.R. Acceptance of personality interpretations as a function of assessment procedures. *Journal of Consulting and Clinical Psychology,* 1974, *42*(1), 150.

Sommer, R. and Sommer, D. Assaultiveness and two types of Rorschach color responses. *Journal of Consulting Psychology,* 1958, *22,* 57–62.

Southern, M.I. and Plant, W.T. Personality characteristics of very bright adults. *Journal of Social Psychology*, 1968, *75*, 119–126.

Spearman, C. *The Abilities of Man: Their Nature and Measurement*. New York: Macmillan, 1927.

Spera, J. and Robertson, M. A 104-item MMPI: the Maxi-Mult. Paper presented at the meeting of the American Psychological Association, New Orleans, 1974.

Staats, A.W. Intelligence, biology, or learning? Competing conceptions with social consequences. In Haywood, H.C. (Ed.) *Social-Cultural Aspects of Mental Retardation: Proceedings of the Peabody-NIMH Conference*. New York: Appleton-Century-Crofts, 1970, pp. 246–277.

Stein, M. *The Thematic Apperception Test: An Introductory Manual for Its Clinical Use with Adults* (2nd ed.). Springfield, Ill.: Charles C. Thomas, 1981.

Steisel, I.M. The Rorschach test and suggestibility. *Journal of Abnormal and Social Psychology*, 1952, *47*, 607–614.

Sternberg, D. and Levine, A. An indicator of suicidal ideation on the Bender Visual-Motor Gestalt Test. *Journal of Projective Techniques and Personality Assessment*, 1965, *29*, 377–379.

Stewart, L.H. Social and emotional adjustment during adolescence as related to the development of psychosomatic illness in adulthood. *Genetic Psychology Monographs*, 1962, *65*, 175–215.

Stotsky, B.A. A comparison of remitting and non-remitting schizophrenics on psychological tests. *Journal of Abnormal and Social Psychology*, 1952, *47*, 489–496.

Stroup, A. and Manderscheid, R. CPI and 16PF second-order factor congruence. *Journal of Clinical Psychology*, 1977, *33*(4), 023–1026.

Sundberg, N.D. The acceptability of "fake" versus "bona fide" personality test interpretations. *Journal of Abnormal and Social Psychology*, 1955, *50*, 145–147.

Sundberg, N.D. The practice of psychological testing in clinical services in the United States. *American Psychologist*, 1961, *16*, 79–83.

Swenson, C.H. Empirical evaluation of human figure drawings. *Psychological Bulletin*, 1957, *54*, 431–466.

Swenson, W.M., Pearson, J.S., and Osborne, D. *An MMPI Source Book: Basic Item, Scale, and Pattern Data on 50,000 Medical Patients*. Minneapolis: University of Minnesota Press, 1973.

Symmes, J. and Rapaport, J. Unexpected reading failure. *American Journal of Orthopsychiatry*, 1972, *42*, 82–91.

Szasz, T.S. *The Myth of Mental Illness*. New York: Harper & Row, 1961.

Tallent, N. *Psychological Report Writing*. Englewood Cliffs, N.J.: Prentice-Hall, 1976.

Tallent, N. and Reiss, W.J. Multidisciplinary views on the preparation of written psychological reports: I. Spontaneous suggestions for content. *Journal of Clinical Psychology*, 1959, *15*, 218–221. (a)

Tallent, N. and Reiss, W.J. Multidisciplinary views on the preparation of written psychological reports: II. Acceptability of certain common content variables and styles of expression. *Journal of Clinical Psychology*, 1959, *15*, 273–274. (b)

Tallent, N. and Reiss, W.J. Multidisciplinary views on the preparation of written psychological reports: II. The trouble with psychological reports. *Journal of Clinical Psychology*, 1959, *15*, 444–446. (c)

Temp, G. Test bias: validity of the SAT for blacks and whites in thirteen integrated institutions. *Journal of Educational Measurement*, 1971, *8*, 245–251.

Terman, L.M. *The Measurement of Intelligence*. Boston: Houghton Mifflin, 1916.

Terman, L.M. and Merril, M.A. *Stanford-Binet Intelligence Scale*. Boston: Houghton Mifflin, 1960.

Terrell, F., Taylor, J., and Terrell, S.L. Effects of types of social reinforcement on the intelligence test performance of lower-class black children. *Journal of Consulting and Clinical Psychology*, 1978, *46*, 1538–1539.

Thiesen, J.W. A pattern analysis of structural characteristics of the Rorschach test in schizophrenia. *Journal of Consulting Psychology*, 1952, *16*, 365–370.

Thompson, G.M. MMPI correlates of movement responses on the Rorschach. *American Psychologist*, 1948, *3*, 348–349.

Thorndike, R.L. The California Psychological Inventory: a review. In Buros, O.K. (Ed.) *Fifth Mental Measurements Yearbook*. Highland Park, N.J.: Gryphon Press, 1959, pp. 99.

Thorndike, R.L. Review of Pygmalion in the classroom by R. Rosenthal and L. Jacobson. *American Educational Research Journal*, 1968, *5*, 708–711.

Thweatt, R.C., Obrzut, J.F., and Taylor, H.D. The development and validation of a soft-sign scoring system for the Bender Gestalt. *Psychology in the Schools*, 1972, *9*, 170–174.

Tolor, A. and Brannigan, G.C. *Research and Clinical Applications of the Bender Gestalt Test*. Springfield, Ill.: Charles C. Thomas, 1980.

Tolor, A. and Schulberg, H.C. *An Evaluation of the Bender-Gestalt Test*. Springfield, Ill.: Charles C. Thomas, 1963.

Towbin, A.P. When are cookbooks useful? *American Psychologist*, 1960, *15*, 119–123.

Townsend, J.K. The relation between Rorschach signs of aggression and behavioral aggression in emotionally disturbed boys. *Journal of Projective Techniques and Personality Assessment*, 1967, *31*, 13–21.

Ulrich, R.E., Stachnik, T.J., and Stainton, N.R. Student acceptance of generalized personality interpretations. *Psychological Reports*, 1963, *13*, 831–834.

Urban, W.H. *The Draw-A-Person Catalogue for Interpretive Analysis*. Los Angeles: Western Psychological Services, 1963.

Veldman, D.J. and Kelly, S.J. Personality correlates of a composite criterion of teaching effectiveness. *Alberta Journal of Educational Research*, 1965, *11*, 702–707.

Verma, S.K., Wig, N.N., and Shah, D.K. Validity of Bender Gestalt Test in Indian psychiatric patients. *Indian Journal of Applied Psychology*, 1962, *9*, 65–67.

Vernon, P.E. *The Structure of Human Abilities*. London: Methuen, 1950; (2nd ed.) 1961.

Vernon, W.H.D. Diagnostic testing and some problems of communication between psychiatrists and clinical psychologists. *Bulletin of the Maritime Psychological Association*, 1955, Spring, 12–29.

Wagner, E.E. The interaction of aggressive movement responses and anatomy responses on the Rorschach in producing anxiety. *Journal of Projective Techniques*, 1961, *25*, 212–215.

Wagner, E.E. Structural analysis: a theory of personality based on projective techniques. *Journal of Personality Assessment*, 1971, *37*, 5–15.

Wallbrown, J.D., Wallbrown, F.H., and Engin, A.W. The validity of two clinical tests of visual-motor perception. *Journal of Clinical Psychology*, 1977, *33*, 491–495.

Webb, A.P. Sex-role preferences and adjustment in early adolescents. *Child Development*, 1965, *34*, 609–618.

Webb, J.T., McNamara, K.M., and Rodgers, D.A. *Configural Interpretation of the MMPI and CPI*. Columbus: Ohio Psychology Publishing, 1981.

Wechsler, D. *Manual for the Wechsler Intelligence Scale for Children*. New York: Psychological Corporation, 1949.

Wechsler, D. *Manual for the Wechsler Adult Intelligence Scale.* New York: Psychological Corporation, 1955.

Wechsler, D. *The Measurement and Appraisal of Adult Intelligence* (4th ed.) Baltimore: Williams and Wilkins, 1958.

Wechsler, D. *Manual for the Wechsler Preschool and Primary School of Intelligence.* New York: Psychological Corporation, 1967.

Wechsler, D. *Manual for the Wechsler Adult Intelligence Scale − Revised.* New York: Psychological Corporation, 1981.

Wedemeyer, B. Rorschach statistics on a group of 136 normal men. *Journal of Psychology,* 1954, *37,* 51–58.

Weider, A. and Noller, P. Objective studies of children's drawings of human figures. II. Sex, age, intelligence. *Journal of Clinical Psychology,* 1953, *9,* 20–23.

Weiner, J.B. *Psychodiagnosis in Schizophrenia.* New York: John Wiley & Sons, 1966.

Wells, F.L. and Reusch, J. *Mental Examiner's Handbook.* New York: Psychological Corporation, 1969.

Welsh, G.S. Factor dimensions A and R. In Welsh, G.S. and Dahlstrom, W.G. (Eds.) *Basic Readings on the MMPI in Psychology and Medicine.* Minneapolis: University of Minnesota Press, 1956, pp. 264–281.

Wernick, R. The modern-style mind reader. *Life,* September 12, 1955, 95–108.

Wertheimer, M. Studies in the theory of Gestalt psychology. *Psychological Forsch.* 1923, *41,* 301–350.

White, R.B., Jr. and McCraw, R.K. Note on the relationship between downward slant of Bender figures 1 and 2 and depression in adult psychiatric patients. *Perceptual and Motor Skills,* 1975, *40,* 152.

White, R.W. An analysis of motivation in hypnosis. *Journal of General Psychology,* 1941, *24,* 145–162.

White, W.G. A psychometric approach for adjusting selected MMPI scale scores obtained by blacks (doctoral dissertation, University of Missouri, 1974). *Dissertation Abstracts International,* 1975, *35,* 4669-B.

Wiener-Levy, D. and Exner, J.E. The Rorschach Comprehensive System: an overview. In McReynolds, P. (Ed.) *Advances in Psychological Assessment,* Vol. 5. San Francisco: Jossey-Bass, 1981.

Wiggins, J.S. Substantive dimensions of self-report in the MMPI item pool. *Psychological Monographs,* 1966, *80*(22), No. 630.

Wiggins, J.S. Content scales: basic data for scoring and interpretation. Unpublished materials, 1971.

Wiggins, N. and Kohen, E.S. Man versus model of man revisited: the forecasting of graduate school success. *Journal of Personality and Social Psychology,* 1971, *19,* 100-106.

Williams, A., Heaton, R.K., and Lehman, R.A. An attempt to cross-validate two actuarial systems for neuropsychological test interpretation. *Journal of Consulting and Clinical Psychology,* 1980, *48,* 317–326.

Williams, A.F., McCourt, W.F., and Schneider, L. Personality self-descriptions of alcoholics and heavy drinkers. *Quarterly Journal of Studies on Alcohol,* 1971, *32,* 310–317.

Williams, M.H. The influence of variations in instructions on Rorschach reaction time. *Dissertation Abstracts,* 1954, *14,* 2131.

Williams, R.L. Scientific racism, and I.Q.: the silent mugging of the black community. *Psychology Today,* 1974, *7,* 32–41.

Witmer, J.M., Bornstein, A.V., and Dunham, R.M. The effects of verbal approval and disapproval upon the performance of third and fourth grade children of four subtests of the Wechsler Intelligence Scale for Children. *Journal of School Psychology*, 1971, *9*, 347–356.

Wolff, W. *Personality of the Pre-school Child.* New York: Grune & Stratton, 1946.

Wolman, B.B. *Children without Childhood: A Study in Childhood Schizophrenia.* New York: Grune & Stratton, 1970.

Zeeuw, J. de. *Colour Preference in Psychodiagnostics.* The Hague: Hague University Press, 1957.

Zolik, E.S. A comparison of the Bender-Gestalt reproduction of delinquents and non-delinquents. *Journal of Clinical Psychology*, 1958, *14*, 24–24.

Zolliker, A. Schwangerschaftsdepression and Rorschach'scher formdeutversuch. *Schweiz Archeives Neurologie und Psychiatrie*, 1943, *53*, 62–78.

SUPPLEMENTARY REFERENCES

Bellak, L. *The Thematic Apperception Test and the Children's Apperception Test in clinical use.* New York: Grune & Stratton, 1954.

Boll, T.J. Behavioral correlates of cerebral damage in children age 9–14. In R.M. Reitan and L.A. Davison (Eds.) *Clinical neuropsychology: Current status and application.* Washington, D.C.: V.H. Winston & Sons, 1974.

Brown, F. An exploratory study of dynamic factors in the content of the Rorschach protocal. *Journal of Projective Techniques*, 1953, *17*, 251–279.

Buck, J.N. *House-Tree-Person (HTP) Manual supplement.* Los Angeles: Western Psychological Services, 1950.

Dean, R.S. Reliability of the WISC-R with Mexican-American children. *Journal of School Psychology*, 1977, *15*, 267–268.

Freed, E. Susceptibility of individual Bender-Gestalt test designs by psychiatric patients. *Journal of Clinical Psychology*, 1966, *22*, 98–99.

Greene, R. Fuller, M. Rutley, B. It-Scale for children and the Draw-A-Person Test: 30 feminine vs. 25 masculine boys. *Journal of Personality Assessment*, 1972, *36*, 349–352.

Gurvitz, M. *The dynamics of psychological testing.* Grune & Stratton, 1951.

Hafner, A.J. Response time and Rorschach behavior. *Journal of Clinical Psychology*, 1958, *14*, 154–155.

Harmon, M.H. The Barron Ego Strength Scale: A study of personality correlates among normals. *Journal of Clinical Psychology*, 1980, *36*, 433–436.

Hathaway, S.R. and Mckinley, J.C. *Manual for the Minnesota Multiphasic Personality Inventory.* New York: Psychological Corporation, 1943.

Hathaway, S.R. and Mckinley, J.C. *Manual for the Minnesota Multiphasic Personality Inventory.* Minneapolis: University of Minnesota Press, 1982.

Hertz, M. Detection of suicidal risks with the Rorschach. In Abt, L. and Weissman, S.L. *Acting Out: theoretical and clinical aspects.* Second Edition. New York: Aronson, 1976.

Hogan, R. and Kurtines, W. Personological correlates of police effectiveness. *Journal of Psychology*, 1975, *92*, 289–295.

Howes, R.J.   The Rorschach: does it have a future?   *Journal of Personality Assessment,*   1981, *45,* 339-351.

Hutt, M.L.   The projective use of the Bender-Gestalt test.   In A.I. Rabin (Ed.), *Projective techniques in personality assessment.*   New York: Springer, 1968.

Hutt, M.L.   *The Hutt adaptation of the Bender-Gestalt test.*   (2nd Ed.) New York: Grune & Stratton, 1969.

Ireland-Galman, M. Padilla, G. Michael, W.   The relationship between performance on the Mazes subtest of the Wechsler Intelligence Scale for Children—Revised (WISC-R) and speed of solving anagrams with simple and difficult arrangements of letter and order.   *Educational and Psychological Measurement,* 1980, *40,* 513-524.

Imre, P.D.   A correlation study of verbal I.Q. and grade achievement, *Journal of Clinical Psychology,* 1963, *19,* 218-219.

Kagan, J.   The long term stability of selected Rorschach responses.   *Journal of Consulting Psychology,* 1960, *24,* 67-73.

Kallingal, A.   The prediction of grades for Black and White students at Michigan State University, *Journal of Educational Measurement,* 1971, *8,* 263-265.

Keogh, B.K.   The copying ability of young children.   *New Research in Education,* 1968, *11,* 43-47.

Kelly, D. Marguilies, H. and Barrera, S.   The stability of the Rorschach method as demonstrated in electroconvulsive therapy cases.   *Rorschach Research Exchange,* 1941, *5,* 44-48

Klinger, E.   Fantasy need achievement as a motivational construct.   *Psychological Bulletin,* 1966, *66,* 291-308.

Kunce, J.T. and Tamkin, A.S.   Rorschach movement and color responses and MMPI social extraversion and thinking introversion personality types.   *Journal of Personality Assessment,* 1981, *45,* 5-10.

Kurtzberg, R. Cavior, N., and Lipton, D.   Sex drawn first and sex drawn larger by opiate addict and non opiate addict inmates on the Draw-A-Person test.   *Journal of Projective Techniques and Personality Assessment,* 1966, *30,* 55-58.

Lacks, P. and Newport, K.   A comparison of scoring systems and level of scorer experience on the Bender Gestalt test.   *Journal of Personality Assessment,* 1980, *44,* 351-357.

Laufer, W.S., Skoog, D.K., and Day, J.M.   Personality and criminality: A review of the California Psychological Inventory.   *Journal of Clinical Psychology,* 1982, *38,* 562-573.

Lansdell, H.C. and Smith, F.J.   Effect of focus of cerebral injury on WAIS factors and the course of their recovery.   Paper presented at the American Psychological Association Convention, Honolulu, 1972.

Leavitt, F. and Garron, G.C.   Rorschach and pain characteristics of patients with low back pain and "conversion V" MMPI profiles.   *Journal of Personality Assessment,* 1982, *46,* 18-25.

Lerner, J. and Shanon, J.   Coping style of psychiatric patients with psychiatric complaints.   *Journal of Personality Assessment,* 1972, *36,* 28-32.

Maley, R.   The relationships of premorbid social activity level of psychiatric patients to test performance on the WAIS and the MMPI.   *Journal of Clinical Psychology,* 1970, *26,* 75-76.

McClelland, D.C.   *The achieving society.*   Princeton, N.J.: Van Nostrand, 1961.

McClelland, D.C.   Longitudinal trends in the relation of thought to action.   *Journal of Consulting Psychology,* 1966, *30,* 479-483.

McClelland, D.C.   *Assessing Human Motivation.*   New York: General Learning Press, 1971.

Mills, C.J. and Bohannon, W.E.   Personality characteristics of effective state police officers.   *Journal of Applied Psychology,* 1980, *65,* 680-684.

Murray, E. and Roberts, F. The Bender-Gestalt Test in a patient passing through a brief manic-depressive cycle. *U.S. Armed Forces Medical Journal*, 1956, *7*, 1206-1208.

Naches, A.M. The Bender-Gestalt Test and acting out behavior in children. *Dissertation Abstracts*, 1967, *28*, 2146.

Naglieri, J.A. A comparison of McCarthy General Cognitive Index and WISC-R I.Q. for educable mentally retarded, learning disabled, and normal children. *Psychological Reports*, 1980, *47*, 591-596.

Newmark, C.S. Brief synopsis of the utility of MMPI short forms. *Journal of Clinical Psychology*, 1981, *37*, 135-137.

Page, H.A. Studies in fantasy-daydreaming frequency and Rorschach scoring categories. *Journal of Consulting Psychology*, 1957, *21*, 111-114.

Pardue, A.M. Bender-Gestalt test and background interference procedure in discernment of organic brain damage. *Perceptual and Motor Skills*, 1975, *40*, 103-109.

Parsons, O.A., Vega, A. Jr., and Burn, J. Different psychological effects of lateralized brain damage. *Journal of Consulting and Clinical Psychology*, 1969, *33*, 551-557.

Peteroy, E.T., Pirrello, P.E. and Adams, N. The relationship between two Wiggins content scales and length of hospitalization. *Journal of Clinical Psychology*, 1982, *38*, 344-346.

Pickford, R.W. *Pickford Projective Pictures.* London: Tavistock, 1963.

Pritchard, D.A. and Rosenblatt, A. Reply to Gynther and Green. *Journal of Consulting and Clinical Psychology*, 1980, *48*, 273-274.

Prytola, R.E., Phelps, M.R., Morrisey, E.F. and Davis, S.F. Figure drawing size as a reflection of self concept or self esteem. *Journal of Clinical Psychology*, 1978, *34*, 207-214.

Reschley, D.J. Psychological testing in educational classification and placement. *American Psychologist*, 1981, *36*, 1094-1102.

Richter, R.H. and Winter, W.D. Holtzman ink-blot correlates of creative potential. *Journal of Projective Techniques and Personality Assessment*, 1966, *30*, 62-67.

Rockland, L.H. and Pollin, W. Quantification of psychiatric mental status. *Archives of General Psychiatry*, 1965, *12*, 23-28.

Schafer, R. *Psychoanalytic interpretation in Rorschach testing.* New York: Grune & Stratton, 1954.

Schilder, P. *Medical Psychology.* New York: International Universities Press, 1953.

Skolnick, A. Motivational imagery and behavior over twenty years. *Journal of Consulting Psychology*, 1966, *30*, 463-478.

Smith, N.M. The relationship between the Rorschach whole response and level of cognitive functioning. *Journal of Personality Assessment*, 1981, *45*, 13-19.

Snyder, C.R. and Larson, G.R. A further look at student acceptance of general personality interpretations. *Journal of Consulting and Clinical Psychology*, 1972, *38*, 384-388.

Steichen, E. *Family of man.* New York: Simon & Schuster, 1955.

Stormant, C.T. and Finney, B.C. Projection and behavior: A Rorschach study of assaultive mental hospital patients. *Journal of Projective Techniques*, 1953, *17*, 349-360.

Svanum, S., Levitt, E. and McAdoo, W.G. Differentiating male and female alcoholics from psychiatric outpatients: The MacAndrew and Rosenberg alcoholism scales. *Journal of Personality Assessment*, 1982, *46*, 81-84.

Swenson, C.H. Empirical evaluations of human figure drawings: 1957-1966. *Psychological Bulletin*, 1968, *70*, 20-44.

Terman, L.M. and Miles, C.C. Sex and personality: Studies in masculinity and femininity. New York: McGraw-Hill, 1936.

Thurstone, L.L. Primary mental abilities. *Psychometric Monographs*, 1938, No. 1.

Tucker, E.W., Campion, P.A., Kellehor, J. and Silberfarb, P.M. The relationship of subtle neurologic impairments to disturbances of thinking. *Psychotherapy Psychosomatics.* 1974, *24,* 165.

Van Dyne, W.T. and Carskadon, T.G. Relationships among three components of self concept and same sex and opposite sex human figure drawings. *Journal of Clinical Psychology,* 1978, *34,* 537–538.

Wade, T.C. and Baker, T.B. Opinions and use of psychological tests: A survey of clinical psychologists. *American Psychologist,* 1977, *32,* 874–882.

Wagner, E. and Daubner, J. Test-retest reliability of the Rorschach on neurologically impaired subjects. *Journal of Personality Assessment.* 1976, *40,* 579–581.

Waugh, K.W. and Bush, W.J. *Diagnosing learning disorders.* Columbus, Ohio.: Merril, 1971.

Weiner, I.B. Cross-validation of a Rorschach checklist associated with suicidal tendencies. *Journal of Consulting Psychology,* 1961, *25,* 312–315.

Wickham, T. WISC patterns in acting-out delinquents, poor readers, and normal controls. Unpublished doctoral dissertation. United States International University, 1978.

Windle, C. Psychological tests in psychopathological prognosis. *Psychological Bulletin,* 1952, *49,* 451–482.

Wolk, R.L. and Wolk, R.B. *Manual: Gerontological Apperception Test.* New York: Human Sciences Press, 1971.

Woody, R.W. (Ed.) *Encyclopedia of Clinical Assessment,* Vol. 1, San Francisco: Jossey-Bass Publishers, 1980.

Wyatt, F. The scoring and analysis of the Thematic Apperception Test. *Journal of Psychology,* 1947, *24,* 319–330.

Wysocki, B.A. and Wysocki, A.C. The body image of normal and retarded children. *Journal of Clinical Psychology,* 1973, *29,* 7–10.

Author Index

Subject Index